Cognitive Psychology
Mind and Brain

EDWARD E. SMITH   and   **STEPHEN M. KOSSLYN**

Department of Psychology   *Department of Psychology*
Columbia University   *Harvard University*

With the contributions of:
Lawrence W. Barsalou
Marlene Behrmann and Joy Geng
Todd S. Braver
Jean Decety and Jessica Sommerville
Kevin Dunbar and Jonathan Fugelsang
Reid Hastie and Alan Sanfey
Maryellen C. MacDonald
Elizabeth Phelps
Adriane E. Seiffert, Jeremy M. Wolfe, and Frank Tong
Anthony D. Wagner

PEARSON
Prentice
Hall

Upper Saddle River, New Jersey, 07458

Library of Congress Cataloging-in-Publication Data

Smith, Edward E.,
   Cognitive psychology : mind and brain / Edward E. Smith, Stephen M. Kosslyn.—1st ed.
   p. cm.
   ISBN 0-13-182508-9
   1. Cognition—Textbooks.   2. Cognitive psychology—Textbooks.   3. Cognitive
neuroscience—Textbooks.   I. Kosslyn, Stephen Michael.   II. Title.
   BF311.S584 2007
   153—dc22

                                                                    2006005432

Executive Editor: Jessica Mosher
Editorial Director: Leah Jewell
Editorial Assistant: William Grieco
Marketing Manager: Jeanette Moyer
Assistant Managing Editor: Maureen
   Richardson
Production Liaison: Fran Russello
Permissions Coordinator: Kathleen
   Karcher
Manufacturing Buyer: Sherry Lewis
Cover Design: Kiwi Design
Cover Illustration/Photo: Manfred/Phontica/
   Getty Images, Inc.

Director, Image Resource Center:
   Melinda Reo
Manager, Rights and Permissions:
   Zina Arabia
Interior Image Specialist: Beth Brenzel
Cover Image Specialist: Karen Sanatar
Image Permission Coordinator: Fran Toepfer
Photo Researcher: Kathy Ringrose
Composition/Full-Service Project
   Management: Techbooks/Shelley L. Creager
Printer/Binder: Courier Companies, Inc.
Cover Printer: Lehigh Press
Color Insert Printer: Lehigh Press

Credits and acknowledgments borrowed from other sources and reproduced, with
permission, in this textbook appear on appropriate page within text.

Pearson Education LTD. London
Pearson Education Singapore, Pte. Ltd
Pearson Education, Canada, Ltd
Pearson Education—Japan
Pearson Education Australia PTY, Limited

Pearson Education North Asia Ltd
Pearson Educación de Mexico, S.A. de C.V.
Pearson Education Malaysia, Pte. Ltd
Pearson Education, Upper Saddle River,
   New Jersey

10 9 8 7 6 5 4 3 2 1
ISBN: 0-13-182508-9

Contents

■ Preface

The study of cognition has progressed enormously during the past decade, but no currently available book summarizes and makes accessible the new key findings and theories. We take a fresh look at the field, and present it as it actually is practiced today. In so doing, our book has two major, distinctive features.

First, much of the recent progress in cognitive studies has come from the advent of cognitive neuroscience, which uses neuroscientific methods and data to address psychological issues. This is the first textbook to incorporate neuroscience seamlessly into the study of cognition. Rather than simply present facts and findings in neuroscience for their own sake, or list contributions from cognitive psychology alongside contributions from neuroscience, we use findings in neuroscience to illuminate and motivate key distinctions in cognitive psychology.

Specifically, we survey findings about the neural bases of cognition from neuroimaging, studies of patients with brain damage, single-cell recordings, studies of electrical and magnetic signals, and selective pharmacological effects on cognition. We use such data to argue that processes or representations used in two tasks (e.g., imagery and perception) are the same or different, and that certain explanations for phenomena are plausible (e.g., the role of implicit emotions in "hunches"). In addition, in some cases we use neuroscientific findings simply to make concrete what otherwise would seem a very abstract process (e.g., "encoding"), discussing its neural implementation and workings within the system as a whole. In still other cases, we use neuroscientific results as a new way of looking at an old problem (e.g., separate memory systems for visual-spatial and visual-object information). But the focus of this book is not neuroscience. We have written a *cognitive psychology* book that is informed by neuroscience.

Second, there has been a gradual shift in the "paradigm" way of viewing cognition, including the order in which cognitive processes come into play, as well as what constitutes a cognitive process. In this book we use this emerging consensus as an organizational device. Specifically, virtually all previous texts rely on the organizational framework created by Donald Broadbent in the late 1950s. According to this view, information is first processed perceptually, then enters short-term memory, and then enters long-term memory; information subsequently can be retrieved from long-term memory back into short-term memory if necessary. However, this view has long since been replaced by researchers active in the field. For example, we know that information must enter long-term memory before one can identify a stimulus, before the stimulus can become "meaningful." And we also know that information in short-term memory is indeed "meaningful." Hence the contents of short-term memory typically must arrive from long-term memory—not the other way around. Indeed, the very concept of "short-term memory" has been replaced by the concept of "working memory," which is now seen to be essential to thought itself (and not just another memory system). In addition, we now recognize the key roles of attention and emotion in modulating the operation of information processing (and hence treat emotion as part of the field); and we finally acknowledge the importance not just of input, but also output (and hence treat motor control as part of the field).

When we began to conceive of the appropriate outline for this book, we developed a heuristic that further showed the need for a new way of viewing cognition. We deconstructed in detail "two minutes in a student's life." In particular, we discussed what happens when a student opens the door to a room to a party and sees an attractive person. In so discussing "cognition in the real world," we realized that we needed chapters on perception, attention, and then—a relatively unique feature of the book—a chapter on representation in long-term memory (essential for ascribing meaning to input). We also realized that some pieces of activated information are delivered up to consciousness, for deliberate consideration. These observations led us to decide that we should first present a chapter on encoding/retrieval from long-term memory and then one on working memory. Next, what about the emotional reactions to people, food, and the din of party music? In another break with tradition, we decided that a chapter on emotion would be central to a book that summarizes the study of cognition as it is done today.

Moreover, the panoply of activated information—based on retrieving into working memory information previously encoded into long-term memory—leads one to need to make decisions. If there are obstacles to making decisions, one must engage in planning and problem solving. Perhaps one decides to talk to a particular friend, but other people are blocking the way; how does one get around them without bumping into someone, getting sidetracked in unwanted conversation or offending somebody? Thus, we included chapters on executive control (another unique feature for a cognitive psychology textbook), decision making, problem solving, and motor cognition and simulation (another novel feature of this book). Finally, after reaching the friend, the student will engage in conversation. Thus, we needed to consider language.

We initially conceived the idea of using this "two-minute" snapshot as an organizing thread for the entire book. But on reflection, it seemed strained. What worked well in our discussions really wouldn't work well in the book. Instead, each chapter opens with a different activity or event that illustrates the subject matter of the chapter.

The goal of this book is to help students master classic studies mixed with exciting new work, both of which illustrate the key concepts of the field. The goal is not to review each area in *total* detail. To help the students learn, the book is replete with everyday examples, contemporary illustrations, and vivid analogies. In each chapter we also include a *Debate* feature to stress that the field is a living entity, continually evolving, and we include *A Closer Look* feature that allows us to zero in on a study in detail. We also include learning objectives and a summary and critical thinking questions (Revisit and Reflect).

This book has an unusual history. Early on, we confronted the fact that we were not experts in all of the areas of the new cognitive psychology, and so decided to enlist the help of distinguished researchers in the different areas. However, we were also mindful of the need to write a book, not edit a collection of independent chapters. Thus, we engaged in an intricate dance with our contributors. First, we met with all of them simultaneously in New York in 2002, giving them our ideas of what their chapters should try to do and getting their feedback on how our ideas needed to be changed. Next, we asked the contributors to submit an outline for a chapter, and we revised these outlines (eliminating redundancy, ensuring that key topics were covered, adding pedagogical features). Then, the contributors wrote a first draft (other than Chapters 1 and 7, which were written by SMK and EES, respectively). We next revised and edited the chapters, and sent them to editor and wordsmith Nancy Brooks. Nancy then read the chapters closely and asked us to clarify anything that was not crystal clear to her. She substantially edited and rewrote to ensure that the book has a single voice. This process inevitably raised a host of questions, some of which we answered and some of which were posed to the contributors. We then revised again, based on the responses, and Nancy put the final touches on making the prose flow. Lastly, we both independently read and revised the entire manuscript, striving for consistency and coherence.

We thus must thank our teams of contributors, who drafted the chapters as follows.

Chapter 2: Adriane E. Seiffert, Jeremy M. Wolfe, and Frank Tong
Chapter 3: Marlene Behrmann and Joy Geng
Chapter 4: Lawrence W. Barsalou
Chapter 5: Anthony D. Wagner
Chapter 6: Todd S. Braver
Chapter 8: Elizabeth Phelps
Chapter 9: Reid Hastie and Alan Sanfey
Chapter 10: Kevin Dunbar and Jonathan Fugelsang
Chapter 11: Jean Decety and Jessica Sommerville
Chapter 12: Maryellen C. MacDonald

Next, we would like to thank our editors, Jayme Hefler, Susanna Lesan, Jessica Mosher, and especially editor extraordinaire Nancy Brooks. Nancy made what could have been an awkward collection of styles into a coherent book. We also thank Lera Boroditsky for her input to our treatment of language and thought, Amy Blum Cole, Jennifer Shephard, Julia LeSage and William Thompson for helping with all the myriad details, and Shelley Creager for her able management of the project. Last, we thank the people at Prentice Hall for their patience in allowing this complex project to run to fruition. We feel that it was worth the wait, and can only hope that you—the reader—feel the same way!

Edward E. Smith
Stephen M. Kosslyn

How the Brain Gives Rise to the Mind

Learning Objectives

You've just taken your seat and are about to begin your first job interview. You are sitting on one side of an immaculately clean desk, facing a well-dressed woman on the other side. You're asking yourself: Why am I doing this? Do I really want to go through all this stress when I may not get the job—and even if I do get it, I might not even like it?

Well, why are you? Perhaps it was the only opportunity available, and you don't have the luxury of waiting for a better opportunity. But why this type of job, rather than some other type of job? Because you've heard other people talk about it, and it sounded interesting? Or perhaps you saw an article in a newspaper or magazine, picked it up, and read about someone who has this job. Whatever the impetus for your looking into it, the job had to pay enough for you to live and had to have a future. Nobody likes being evaluated, but that's just part of the process. So, there you are, at the interview, wondering what else you could have done, where else you could be instead.

Resolving a life-altering question such as whether or not to try to get a particular job is an enormously complicated activity. If you want to understand all the cogitation that led up to your deciding to apply for the job and that is used during the interview—and, should you be offered the job, that allows you to decide whether or not to take it—you will need to understand the following:

- *perception,* the processing of information from the senses, which you require in order to hear and read about the job and, of course, to listen to the interviewer and watch her face for telltale signs as to how you are doing;

- *emotion,* such as the anxiety surrounding the interview and your enjoyment of the work in question; emotion can arise when you perceive something (like the warm smile of the interviewer at the end of your discussion), and—perhaps paradoxically— is a central aspect of much of cognition;

- *representation in long-term memory,* your actual memories of previous summer jobs and relevant classroom experiences, as well as your memories of your leadership roles in clubs and your memories of your skills;

- *encoding,* which occurs when you enter new information into memory, such as when you describe to yourself what you see in the workplace (which you later can reflect on when thinking about whether you would really want the job), and *retrieving information from long-term memory* (critical if you are going to answer the interview questions, and also when you later want to think about the pros and cons of what you learned during the interview);

- *working memory,* which allows you to hold information in awareness and think about it (important if you try to scope out any themes that are emerging from the questions);

- *attention,* which allows you to focus on specific information, including both the interviewer's words and her nonverbal signals, and which allows you to filter out irrelevant information (such as the sounds of cars outside);

- *executive processes,* which manage your other mental events, allowing you to pause before you speak and to inhibit yourself from saying the wrong thing, and which enable you to act on your decisions;

- *decision making, problem solving,* and *reasoning,* which allow you to figure out which jobs you might like and how best to apply for them, as well as what to say during the interview;

- *motor cognition* and *mental simulation,* which involve setting up your responses, mentally rehearsing them, and anticipating the consequences of your behaviors (useful for preparing for the interview in advance and anticipating the interviewer's likely response to points you make);

■ and—of course—*language*, which is what you use to understand the questions and reply to them; what you say ultimately will make or break your interview.

This book is about all these mental activities—for that is in fact what they are—and more.

Mental activity, also known as cognition, is the internal interpretation or transformation of stored information. You acquire information through your senses and you store it in memory. Cognition occurs when you derive implications or associations from an observation, fact, or event. For example, you might realize that you would have to move to a new city for one job but not another and then consider the pros and cons of the night life of that new city. Similarly, when you consider whether or not to apply for a particular job, you weigh facts and considerations about the salary, cost of living, possible promotions, skills you can learn that might help you move onto a better job, and so on. Mental activity, in one form or another, is what allows you to play out in your head the various ramifications of such facts and considerations.

How can we study mental activity? We seem to think effortlessly, and often can easily talk about our beliefs and desires. Perhaps you know that you want a certain type of job because you've majored in that subject and focused like a laser beam on such employment ever since high school—end of story. But how can you come to realize whether a particular job situation is a good fit for your own personal circumstances? In fact, how is it that you, and not your pet dog or cat, has the concept of a "job"? And what do you mean by the "mind"? Do you mean "consciousness," that is, what you are aware of? If so, then what is responsible for the presence of some thoughts in consciousness but not others? Neither you, the authors, nor any other human beings are aware of most mental activities. So how can we come to understand them?

This chapter sets the stage for our investigation, first describing the nature of theories of mental activities and then looking at ways in which scientists have come to develop and evaluate such theories in detail. We specifically address four questions:

1. How did the field of cognitive psychology arise?
2. What is a scientific theory of cognition, and what roles does knowledge about the brain play in such theories?
3. What are the major structures of the brain, and what roles do they play in our skills and abilities?
4. What methods are used to study cognition?

1. A BRIEF HISTORY: HOW WE GOT HERE

Most of the topics in this book, in one guise or another, are old hat for philosophers, who have picked over numerous and varied theories of the mind for well over two thousand years. For example, the Greek philosopher Plato (427–347 B.C.) believed that memories are like etchings on a wax tablet—and that people differ in the hardness and purity of the "wax," which would explain why some people have better memories than others. This notion is interesting in part because there is no clear-cut distinction between the physical substance (the wax) and its function (to retain memories). The French philosopher and mathematician René Descartes (1596–1650) gave us the famous distinction between mind and body, asserting that mind is qualitatively distinct from body, as different as heat is from light. This distinction has permeated our culture and now seems obvious to many, but in fact research is now revealing that it is not as clear-cut as it may seem (as we shall see when we consider the effects of mind on body—and vice versa—when we discuss emotion). John Locke (1632–1704), writing in England, considered what the contents of the mind might be like and argued that thought is a series of mental images. Bishop George Berkeley (1685–1753) begged to disagree, arguing in part that abstract concepts—such as "justice" and "truth"—could not be conveyed effectively by images. Such discussions set the stage for many contemporary research programs, such as those aimed at discovering the various ways in which we can store information, which—as Berkeley argued—cannot be limited to mental images.

Although philosophers raised many fascinating ideas and often identified key issues that are still with us today, their methods simply were not up to the task of resolving many questions about mental activity. Philosophy rests on argument (that's why logic is taught in philosophy departments), but sometimes the available facts are not sufficient to allow argument alone to answer a question. Science, unlike philosophy, relies on a method that produces new facts, and by so doing allows all participants to agree on the answer to a question. The scientific study of the mind began in the late nineteenth century, which by the standards of science means that it is still in its infancy.

1.1. In the Beginning: The Contents of Consciousness

We can mark the birth of the scientific study of mental activity with the establishment of the first modern psychology laboratory in 1879, in Leipzig, Germany. The head of that laboratory was Wilhelm Wundt (1832–1920), who focused on understanding the nature of consciousness (Figure 1–1). Wundt's guiding idea was that the contents of consciousness—the things we are aware of—can be approached by analogy to the way chemists approach the structure of molecules: (1) by characterizing basic sensations (such as feeling heat or cold, or seeing red or blue) and feelings (such as fear and love), and (2) by finding the rules whereby such elements are combined (such as the ways simple sensations are combined to form the perception of seeing an entire object, with its shape, texture, and color). An American student of Wundt, Edward Titchener (1867–1927), extended this approach to cover not only sensations and feelings but all mental activity.

The early psychologists of Wundt's school made at least two major contributions. First, they showed that mental activity can be broken down into more basic operations (such as the perception of color, shape, and location); this strategy of "divide and conquer" has withstood the test of time. Second, they developed objective methods for assessing mental activity, such as measuring the amount of time people need to make certain decisions.

However, these scientists also relied heavily on introspection, the process of internal perception, that is, looking within oneself to assess one's mental activity. To

FIGURE 1–1 Wilhelm Wundt (standing, with gray beard) and colleagues
The first psychology laboratories focused on understanding the nature of mental activity, but used introspection in ways that later proved unreliable.
(Archives of the History of American Psychology—The University of Akron.)

experience introspection, try to answer this question: What shape are a cat's ears? Most people report that they visualize the animal's head and "look" at its ears. Did you have this experience? Not everyone does. What can we conclude when people disagree about their introspections? And now consider, what color were the ears, what texture? Were these characteristics present in your mental image? Are you sure? What do we do when people who report on their own mental activity aren't certain?

Wundt trained observers to be sensitive to their reactions to stimuli, noticing subtle changes in the duration, quality, or intensity when stimuli were changed slightly (for example, having a different shade of color or tone). Nevertheless, this reliance on introspective reports turned out to be their Achilles' heel; no amount of training could solve another difficulty. Oswald Kulpe (1862–1915), another German philosopher-scientist, demonstrated that mental images do not always accompany mental activity. A mental image is signaled by the experience of perceiving when the appropriate sensory input is absent; a mental image creates the experience of "seeing with the mind's eye" (or "hearing with the mind's ear," and so on). Some types of mental activity, such as those occurring in your head as you understand these words, are unconscious—they are not accompanied by mental images. Kulpe and his colleagues found, for example, that when participants were asked to heft two weights and decide which was the heavier, they could do this, but they had no idea how they reached their decisions. Participants reported that they had kinesthetic images of the weights (that is, they had the "feeling" of lifting them), but the decision process itself left no trail in consciousness. Similarly, you will be aware of your decision to apply for a particular job and not to apply for others, but you may not be aware of just *how* you made that decision.

1.2. Psychology in the World

At about the same time that Wundt's laboratory was up and running, another approach to scientific psychology was developed, primarily in America, by William James (1842–1910). These "functionalist" psychologists, as they became known, focused not on the *nature* of mental activity, but rather on the *functions* of specific mental activities in the world. The idea was that certain practices or approaches are better suited than others to accomplishing certain tasks, and that we should change our thoughts and behavior as we discover those that are increasingly "better adapted" to our environment. For example, if you discover that you learn better by listening to lectures than by reading the text, you should be sure to attend all the lectures. But more than that, you should note what it is about lectures (the chance to ask questions? the visual aids?) that engages you and try to select courses in which the lectures have those characteristics.

The functionalist approach produced firm foundations for future studies. In particular, in proposing theories of the functions of behaviors and mental activities, it relied in large part on ideas about evolution proposed by Charles Darwin—and this evolutionary perspective has flourished (e.g., Pinker, 1997, 2002). Conceiving of mental activities and behavior in an evolutionary context has led researchers to study animal behavior, which has continued to be a valuable source of insights into some mental functions, especially with regard to their relationship to the brain (Hauser, 1996).

1.3. Behaviorism: Reaction against the Unobservable

The early psychologists sensibly tried to model their new science on the success stories of the day, the methods of physics, chemistry, and biology. But different psychologists took different lessons from the successes of other sciences, and some declared that psychology should not attempt to understand hidden mental events but rather should focus purely on the immediately observable: stimuli, responses, and the consequences of those responses (Figure 1–2). This was the central doctrine of the behaviorists, who avoided discussion of mental activity. Behaviorist theories specify ways in which stimuli lead to responses, and ways in which the consequences of responses set up associations between stimuli and responses. Some of the behaviorists, among them Clark L. Hull (1884–1952), were willing to propose internal events that are inferred directly from behavior, such as motivation, even though these events were not themselves immediately observable. However, many later behaviorists, notably B. F. Skinner (1904–1990) and his followers, went so far as to

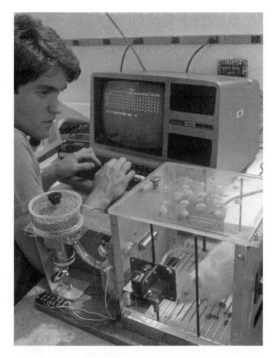

FIGURE 1–2   Observing rat behavior

Behavioral methods, if not the theory that initially led to their pursuit, have proved important to the study of cognition.

(Photograph by Richard Wood. Courtesy of Index Stock Imagery, Inc. Royalty Free.)

reject absolutely all discussion of internal events. In all cases, however, the approach of the behaviorists had severe limits; in fact, it simply could not explain the most interesting human behaviors, notably language (Chomsky, 1957, 1959). Behaviorism also failed to provide insights into the nature of perception, memory, decision making—in fact, virtually every topic discussed in this book.

Nevertheless, the behaviorists contributed a host of rigorous experimental techniques that have since been put to good use in the study of cognition. In addition, the behaviorists made many discoveries, particularly about the nature of learning, that now must be explained by all theories in psychology. Moreover, behaviorist approaches led to sophisticated views of how animals use information to make choices, which in turn have inspired much contemporary work (e.g., Grafen, 2002; Herrnstein, 1990).

1.4. The Cognitive Revolution

Today the study of mental activity is again respectable. As the limitations of behaviorism became widely appreciated, researchers became open to other approaches—but this backlash against behaviorism would have had much less of an effect if not for key technological changes, which led to a new way to envision mental activity.

This new approach, developed in the late 1950s and early 1960s, was directly tied to the development of the computer (Gardner, 1985) and so dominated the field that this period of transition is now known as the *cognitive revolution*. The behaviorists had simply described stimulus–response–consequences relations. Now researchers seized on the computer as a model for the way in which human mental activity takes place; the computer was a tool that allowed researchers to specify the internal *mechanisms* that produce behavior. Psychologist/computer scientists Herbert A. Simon and Alan Newell and linguist Noam Chomsky played a central role in this revolution, providing examples of how progress could be achieved by comparing the mind to a computing machine (Figure 1–3).

The cognitive revolution blossomed when researchers developed new methods to test predictions from computational models, which often specified the order in which specific mental activities purportedly take place. These methods were an important part of the cognitive revolution because they allowed mental activity to be studied more objectively than did introspection, thereby allowing many researchers

FIGURE 1–3   **BINAC, the Binary Automatic Computer, developed in 1949**

Computer technology has evolved so quickly that complex models of mental activity can now be programmed into an ordinary desktop machine.

(Courtesy of Corbis/Bettmann.)

to move beyond behaviorism without giving up a desire for empiricism, the discovery of new facts via systematic observation.

One reason why the computer was so important as a model is that it demonstrated, once and for all, why researchers need to think about internal events, not just observable stimuli, responses, and consequences of responses. For example, imagine that your word-processing program has started printing EVERYTHING YOU TYPE IN UPPERCASE. What do you do? First, you would probably look to see if the shift key is stuck. Any good behaviorist would approve of this: you are looking at stimuli and responses. But say it isn't stuck. Now what? Now you suspect that something has gone wrong inside. For some reason, the key presses aren't being *interpreted* correctly. To fix the problem, you must examine the program itself to see exactly what it is doing. Studying stimuli and responses is only the beginning; a true understanding of what's going on, in people and in computers, requires going inside, looking at the mechanism that underlies what you can observe directly.

Finally, in recent years biology has come to be a major part of the mix. To see why, we need to consider the nature of mental activity in more detail, to which we turn in the following section.

Comprehension Check:

1. What are the differences between behaviorism and the cognitive approach?
2. Why did the "cognitive revolution" occur?

2. UNDERSTANDING THE MIND: THE FORM OF THEORIES OF COGNITION

The cognitive revolution led to a detailed conception of the form of a theory of mental activity, but to say that mental activities are like computer programs is a leap. Consider the machines that run computer programs versus the "machine" that produces mental activity—that is, the brain. Certainly, computers and brains look very different and are composed of different materials. Moreover, computer programs are separate from the computers that run them; the same program can run on many different machines. But the mental activities taking place in your head right now are yours and yours alone. Why should we assume that programs for computers have anything to do with mental activities produced by brains? Clearly the analogy is restricted to only certain aspects of computer programs. But which ones?

2.1. Mind and Brain

The distinction between a computer's software—its programs—and its hardware is a good first step because it focuses us on how computers operate, not simply on their physical natures. But the idea that mental activity is like software and the brain itself is like hardware isn't quite right. If a computer program is useful, it sometimes is converted into a chip and thus "becomes" a piece of hardware. Once converted, what used to be a program (that is, the instructions to the computer) is now etched as physical pathways in the chip; the program as such no longer exists—you cannot identify parts of the chip with the different instructions in the computer program. For example, in a program we could write one instruction to make the computer add 10 numbers, and then another to have it divide the sum by 10 to find the average. In a chip, such instructions would not exist; instead circuits would accomplish the same goals. Even so, the chip can be described as doing what the program does: adding the numbers and dividing by the number of digits to find the average. Here's the important point: in spite of the fact that software—a program—does not exist, we can still describe what the hardware is doing using the same vocabulary we used to describe the program.

The crucial distinction is not between software and hardware per se, but rather between levels of analysis, the various degrees of abstraction we can use to describe an object. Different levels of analysis typically rely on different vocabularies. Let's start with the computer: on one level, we can describe the computer in terms of its physics, noting how electricity changes magnetic fields, observing how heat is produced and dissipated, and the like. On another level, we can describe the computer in terms of its function, that is, in terms of *what the computer is doing:* it receives input in the form of symbols, converts the symbols into a special code, stores this information, and operates on this information (adding, sorting lists, comparing input to stored information, and so on). At this level, instead of relying on the language of physics, we depend for accurate description on the language of information processing, that is, the storage, manipulation, and transformation of information. In cognitive psychology, mental activity is often described in terms of information processing. When you are sitting there, smiling and trying to look relaxed as a job interview is progressing, your brain is working hard to allow you to come up with the most effective responses. To understand all of what goes into each of your responses and questions, we need to understand information processing.

A critical aspect of the idea of levels of analysis is that a description at one level cannot be replaced by one at another level; the levels may provide equally valid analyses, and even reinforce one another, but they are not interchangeable. In particular, the analysis of mental activity—the level of information processing—cannot be replaced by the level of a physical description of the brain. Why not? Consider some analogies. Can you replace a description of a building's architecture with a description of its bricks, boards, and other building materials? No. Can you replace a description of the function of a pair of scissors with a description of the arrays of atoms in its blades? Clearly not. How about the human hand: would a description of bones, tendons, and muscles replace descriptions of grasping, stroking, and poking? No. The computer—and the brain—are no different from these examples: for a full understanding we must distinguish between a functional level of analysis (what the architectural features of a building must achieve, the actions a pair of scissors and a hand perform) and a physical level of analysis (in which we characterize the physical properties of the parts that make up all these objects).

Descriptions at the different levels of analysis cannot be replaced by one another because they specify qualitatively different kinds of things. And that is why we cannot dispense with a description of the information processing that accomplishes mental activity and instead simply discuss the physical brain that gives rise to it.

Does this mean that studying the brain has no place in the study of cognition? Not at all! Although we cannot replace one level of analysis with another, we can gain insights into characteristics of one level from the others. You probably couldn't make a working pair of scissors out of wet cardboard: it's important to know about the physics of materials to understand how a blade can hold an edge (and why some materials do so better than others). Similarly, the physical structure of the hand is what allows it to do all those marvelous things: no palm, no fingers, and no thumb mean no grasping, no stroking, and no poking. As we shall see throughout this book, researchers have realized that conceiving of mental activity by analogy to the computer was a good start, but to understand mental activity fully we need to consider the neural mechanisms that give rise to them, which ultimately requires understanding how the brain gives rise to mental activity. Knowledge about the brain, that most complex of organs, helps us understand cognition, feelings, and behavior. To see how, we first must consider in more detail the nature of the information processing that underlies mental activity.

2.2. Mental Representation

All our mental activity is *about* something—a possible job you could choose, a friend's face you see across the way, fond thoughts of last night's date. Cognitive psychologists try to specify how information is internally represented. A representation is a physical state (such as marks on a page, magnetic fields in a computer, or neural connections in a brain) that conveys information, specifying an object, event, or category or its characteristics. Representations have two distinct facets. On the one hand, there's the *form* of a representation, the means by which it conveys information—in other words, its format. For example, a drawing (that is, a depiction) and a verbal description (of the sort found in a text) are different formats (Figure 1–4). Drawings represent something by means of a graphic resemblance between the lines in the drawing and the corresponding portions of the depicted object or scene; descriptions (such as these words) represent something by means of conventions that allow symbols (letters and punctuation marks) to be combined in certain ways but not others (*word* is an acceptable order of symbols for written English, but "odwr" is not; Kosslyn, 1980, 1994). On the other hand, there's the *content,* the meaning, conveyed by a particular representation. The same content can usually be conveyed in more than one format: spoken words and Morse code are different formats that can convey the same content. (Your decision to apply for a particular job often may depend on information you acquired in at least two formats, written and spoken words.)

2.3. Mental Processing

Does a tree falling in the forest make a sound if nobody is there to hear it? The answer, at least for psychologists, is clear: no. "Sound" is a psychological quality, which is not the same thing as compressed air waves. A brain must be present in order to *register* the pattern of compression in the waves, and it is the neural impulses in the brain that give rise to our experience of sound. No brain, no sound. Similarly,

"A BALL IS ON A BOX"

Description (Propositional Representation)	Depiction (Quasi-Pictorial Representation)

ON (BALL, BOX)

1. Relation (e.g., ON)	1. No distinct relation
2. Argument(s) (e.g., BALL, BOX)	2. No distinct arguments
3. Syntax (rules for combining symbols)	3. No clear syntax
4. Abstract	4. Concrete
5. Does not occur in spatial medium	5. Occurs in spatial medium
6. Arbitrarily related to represented object	6. Resemblance used to convey Information

FIGURE 1–4   Examples of different formats

The same content can be represented either by descriptions (abstract, language-like propositional representations) or depictions (picture-like representations). Some of the differences between the two types of formats are listed. A "relation" specifies how entities are combined, and an "argument" is an entity that is affected by a relation.

(Adapted and reprinted with permission of the publisher from *Image and Mind* by Stephen M. Kosslyn, p. 31, Cambridge, Mass: Harvard University Press, Copyright © 1980 by the President and Fellows of Harvard College.)

to understand how representations work we need to consider something else, namely, the processes that operate on them. French words convey information to speakers of French, and smoke signals convey information to combustion-literate Americans, because they know how to interpret them; to others, they are meaningless. Similarly, these black swiggles on the page in front of you have meaning only because you've learned how to *process* them appropriately. A process is a transformation of information that obeys well-defined principles to produce a specific output when given a specific input. For a computer, you can provide an input by pressing the key labeled "4" and a process produces an output, the pattern "4" on the screen. The process connects an input to an output.

Think about your computer's word-processing program. If there were no way to keyboard text, no way to cut-and-paste or delete, no way to save and retrieve what you've written, what good would it be? The representations of the words in random access memory (RAM) and on the hard disk are useful only because they can be processed. Similarly, a *mental representation* is a representation that conveys meaning within a processing system—a system that includes various processes that intepret and operate on representations, doing various things to them. Mental representations would not represent anything if they did not occur within a processing system. For example, if representations were never accessed and operated on by processes that use them in specific ways (such as by interpreting their meaning or finding other representations that are associated with them), for all intents and purposes they would not exist. To be more specific, a processing system is a set of processes that work together to accomplish a type of task, using and producing representations as appropriate. A processing system is like a factory that takes metal, plastics, and paint as input and produces cars as output. Many separate operations are performed in the factory, but they all work together to achieve a common goal.

A key idea is that a complex activity cannot be accomplished by a single process, but rather needs to be carried out by a set of processes, each of which accomplishes a different aspect of the overall job (think again about the analogy to an automobile factory). No large computer program is a single uninterrupted list of code. Rather, programs are written in modules, which interact in different ways depending on the nature of the input and the required output. Such is also true of the information processing that underlies mental activity (Marr, 1982; Simon, 1981).

An **algorithm** is a step-by-step procedure that guarantees that a certain input will produce a certain output. A good recipe is an algorithm: follow a list of procedural steps involving certain amounts of flour, eggs, milk, sugar, and butter, the actions of stirring, kneading, and baking, and you'll have a nice cake. *Serial algorithms* specify sequences of steps, with each step's sequence depending on the one before. In contrast, *parallel algorithms* specify operations that are performed at the same time, just as you can make the frosting for a cake at the same time the pan of batter is cooking in the oven. Some algorithms involve both serial and parallel processing. An algorithm that accomplishes a mental process combines specific operations, using and creating representations as needed. By analogy, when you stir the eggs, milk, sugar, and butter into the flour, you create something new: dough. This is like creating a new representation, which is a prerequisite to performing particular processing, such as kneading, and then, after such processing, baking.

2.4. Why the Brain?

At its inception, cognitive psychology was concerned only with function, only with characterizing mental activity (Neisser, 1967). More recently, cognitive psychology has come to rely on facts about the brain. This development has occurred for two main reasons, which concern the concepts of identifiability and adequacy. *Identifiability* refers to the ability to specify the correct combination of representations and processes used to accomplish a task. The problem is that, in principle, different sorts of information processing can produce the same result; thus, additional sorts of evidence—such as knowledge of specific brain activity—are necessary to discover how mental processing in fact takes place. The goal of any theory in science is to discover the facts of the matter, to understand the principles and causes that underlie phenomena. Just as you can correctly or incorrectly describe the way a particular computer program operates, you can correctly or incorrectly describe mental representations, processes, and the ways they are used during a specific mental activity. You can get it right or get it wrong.

It is difficult to disagree with the idea that some theories (or aspects of theories) are correct and some are incorrect, but identifiability is much easier said than achieved. One reason this black-and-white approach has proven difficult to realize is that theories in cognitive psychology can be undermined by *structure–process trade-offs*. This is a key idea, so let's pause to consider an example.

Saul Sternberg (1969b) developed a method to examine how information is accessed in memory. He gave people sets of digits, each set containing one to six items.

He then presented single items and asked the participants to decide as quickly as they could whether those items had been in the set. For example, the participants first would memorize "1, 8, 3, 4" and would later be asked to decide whether "3" was in the set, whether "5" was in the set, and so on. A key result was that the time to respond increased linearly for increasingly large memorized sets; that is, an equal increment of time was added for each additional item included in the set. This led Sternberg to hypothesize that people hold *lists* of items in memory and *serially scan* these lists (when asked whether "3" was in the set, they go through and check each item in the list of numbers they are holding in their memory). The theory thus specified a representation (a list) and an accompanying process (serial scanning). However, it wasn't long before others (e.g., Monsell, 1978; Townsend, 1990; Townsend & Ashby, 1983) formulated alternative theories that varied the representation and compensated for this change by varying the accompanying process. For example, instead of a list, the items could be stored as an *unordered collection*, like pool balls sitting in a bowl. Instead of searching them one at a time, they could be searched *in parallel,* all at the same time (Figure 1–5). But how would this theory explain the increase in time for larger sets? The essential idea is that—as in everything else in nature—there is variation in the time to examine each item, whether it's examining them one at a time in a list or in parallel as a group. Think about the amount of time people spend in a job interview: some interviews finish up very quickly (for better or worse!), some end up dragging on at length. Just as in interviews, some comparisons of remembered information are faster than others. And here's the trick that makes this alternative theory work: the larger the number of items to be considered, the more likely it is that one of the comparisons will be particularly slow, just as it is more likely that there will be a particularly long interview as the number of people interviewed increases. Thus, if all items must be checked before a decision is made, then the more items, the more time in general will be required until all comparisons are complete.

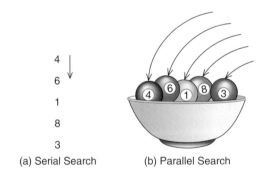

(a) Serial Search   (b) Parallel Search

FIGURE 1–5   Two theories of memory scanning

(a) A set of digits can be ordered into a list and scanned serially, one digit at a time. (b) Alternatively, the representation can be changed, creating an unordered collection, and the process can then be changed to compensate for the change in representation—with all digits examined in parallel. This structure–process trade-off can produce models that can mimic each other, both predicting increased times when larger sets of digits must be searched.

In short, the two theories, list-with-serial-scan and collection-with-parallel comparison, can mimic each other. The point: we can change the theory of the representation, and compensate for that change by altering the theory of the process. The representation and process trade off against each other, with change in one compensating for change in the other.

Anderson (1978) proved mathematically that information-processing theorists can always use this sort of structure–process trade-off to create a theory that mimics another theory. The problem is that all the characteristics of both the representations and the processes are up for grabs; a theorist can change one aspect and then can adjust the other aspects of the theory arbitrarily—nothing is nailed down in advance. Anderson also pointed out, however, that the brain can serve to limit this arbitrariness. A theorist *cannot* make up properties of the brain willy-nilly to account for data. Cognitive theories are limited by facts about the brain; the facts don't dictate the theories, but they limit the range of what can be proposed. Facts about the brain anchor theories so that theorists cannot always use structure–process trade-offs to invent alternative accounts for sets of data; the accompanying *Debate* box illustrates an example of the way such facts can help us understand mental activity.

Turning to the brain helps us to grapple with the challenge of identifiability. But this is not all that can be gained by considering the brain when formulating theories of mental activity. Facts about the brain can help us test the *adequacy* of a theory, which lets us know whether a theory is—to that point—valid.

How do we know when a theory, taken on its own terms (and not compared to another, competing theory), is worth its salt? At first glance, this seems obvious: a theory should be taken seriously if it explains all relevant phenomena and makes correct predictions. That standard holds to evaluate a final, complete theory—but it is not clear that such theories ever really exist! What about theories that are just being worked out now, as is true in almost all of cognitive psychology? How do we know whether we are on the right track? Clearly, the theory must be testable, and it must be capable of being disproved; if a theory can explain any result *and* its opposite, it explains nothing at all.

In addition, in psychology we can use facts about the structure and function of the brain to help us evaluate theories; such facts can provide strong justification and support for a theory (what Chomsky, 1967, called *explanatory adequacy*). For example, a cognitive theory might claim that nouns and verbs are stored separately, and this theory might perhaps be based on differences in how easily the two categories can be learned. If researchers can then show that the brain "respects" this distinction, perhaps by showing that different parts of the brain are active when people produce or comprehend the two types of words, the theory is supported. And it is supported more strongly than it would be if you simply collected more data on learning, of the sort that were used to formulate the theory in the first place. In this book, we use facts about the brain in this way, as a separate source of justification and support for cognitive theories. If a theory incorporates two distinct processes, this theory gains support when researchers show that different parts of the brain carry out each process.

What Is the Nature of Visual Mental Imagery?   DEBATE

Perception occurs after our sense organs (e.g., our eyes and ears) register a stimulus that is physically present and our brain allows us to organize the sensory input; mental imagery occurs when you have a similar experience of perception, but is based on information you previously stored in memory. For example, can you recall how many windows there are in your bedroom? To answer, most people visualize their room, which is an example of using mental imagery. Although mental imagery may seem similar to perception, it clearly is not the same thing; we can change our images at will (for instance, by adding or deleting windows), and the images fade very quickly.

The "imagery debate" concerns the nature of the representations used during mental imagery, and has focused on visual mental imagery (although the issues apply equally well to other forms of imagery, such as the auditory images you have when you "hear" a song in your mind). This debate began when Zenon Pylyshyn (1973) claimed that mental imagery relies entirely on the same sorts of descriptive representations that are used in language. Kosslyn and Pomerantz (1977) marshaled both theoretical arguments and empirical results in an attempt to counter Pylyshyn's assertion and to support the idea that imagery relies in part on depictive representations. In depictive representations, each point in the representation corresponds to a point on the object being depicted such that the distances between points in the representation correspond to the distances between the corresponding points on the object. Pictures are an example of a depictive representation. Many exchanges followed, without conclusion. Every finding produced by the depictive camp was quickly undermined by the descriptive camp. Structure–process trade-offs ran rampant (Anderson, 1978; Kosslyn, Thompson & Ganis, 2006).

Today, the debate finally appears to be going somewhere, thanks to new knowledge of key facts about the brain mechanisms used in vision. In the monkey brain, some areas involved in visual processing are *topographically organized,* and new methods have shown that the human brain also has such visual areas (e.g., Sereno et al., 1995). These brain areas (such as areas 17 and 18, as the regions are known) literally use space on the surface of the brain to represent space in the world. When you see an object, the pattern of activity on your retinas is projected back into the brain, where it is reproduced (although with some distortions) on the surface of the brain. There literally is a "picture in your head"; brain areas support genuinely depictive representations. And at least two of these topographically organized areas (the largest ones) are also activated when participants close their eyes and visualize objects clearly enough that they could "see" fine details (Kosslyn & Thompson, 2003). Moreover, the size and orientation of the image affects activation in these areas in very much the same way as when people actually see objects at different sizes or orientations (Klein et al., 2003; Kosslyn et al., 1995). In fact, temporarily disrupting neural functioning in these areas temporarily disrupts both visual perception and visual mental imagery—and does so to the same extent (Kosslyn et al., 1999).

However, some patients with brain damage in these areas apparently still retain at least some forms of imagery (e.g., Behrmann, 2000; Goldenberg et al., 1995), and thus the precise role of these brain areas in imagery has yet to be established. If future research conclusively shows that at least some forms of imagery rely on depictive representations in topographically organized brain areas, the debate will either end or be forced to change direction.

Comprehension Check:

1. What is the relationship between mental activity and brain activity?
2. Why is information about the brain important for theorizing about mental activity?

3. THE COGNITIVE BRAIN

Volumes and volumes have been written about the brain, but fortunately we need not concern ourselves here with most of this avalanche of information. Rather, we need focus only on those aspects that can be brought to bear on theories of mental activity. This section is a brief overview, which will be supplemented in later chapters as the need arises. Although we note the major functions of different brain structures, we must emphasize from the outset that virtually all cognitive functions are *not* carried out by a single brain area; rather, as we will see in later chapters, systems of brain areas working together allow us to perform specific tasks. Nevertheless, each brain area plays a role in some functions and not others—and knowing these roles will help in understanding later discussions.

3.1. Neurons: The Building Blocks of the Brain

What do neurons have to do with mental processes? That's a bit like wondering what the properties of bricks, boards, and steel have to do with architecture. It is true that architecture cannot be reduced to these components, but they nevertheless influence architecture. For example, London, England, is relatively flat and spread out because most of it was built before steel was readily available—and you cannot build skyscrapers with just brick because the weight of upper stories becomes so great that the walls at street level cannot support them. Although the building materials do not *dictate* the way they are used, they place limitations—*constraints*—on the types of possible architectures. So too with the components of nervous systems. As we will see in this book, the nature of our neurons and the ways they interact feed into theories of how large groups of neurons can function in mental activity.

Brain activity arises primarily from the activities of neurons. *Sensory neurons* are activated by input from sensory organs such as the eyes and ears; *motor neurons* stimulate muscles, causing movements. *Interneurons,* the vast majority of the neurons in the brain, stand between sensory and motor neurons or between other interneurons; often interneurons are connected to other interneurons, forming vast networks. In addition to 100 billion neurons or so, the brain also contains *glial cells*. Glial cells initially were thought to be involved solely in the care and feeding of neurons, but now are recognized to play a critical role in the way connections among neurons are set up (Ullian et al., 2001). They also modulate chemical interactions among neurons (Newman & Zahs, 1998). There are about 10 times as many glial cells as neurons in the brain.

The crucial parts of a neuron (Figure 1–6) are its dendrites, axon, and cell body. The *dendrites* receive input from other neurons, as does the *cell body,* and the *axon* transmits output to other neurons. The axon is usually covered with myelin, a fatty insulator that improves transmission. Typical neurons have thousands of dendrites, and the axon branches at the end so that each neuron can in turn affect thousands of other neurons. The connection between neurons is called a *synapse,* and the gap in the synapse is called the *synaptic cleft.* Most neurons affect others by releasing specific *neurotransmitters* at the tip of the axon via small structures known as *terminal*

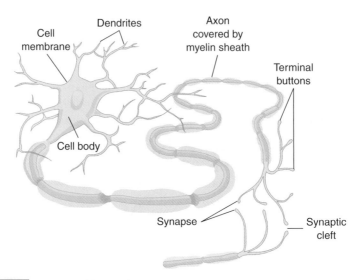

FIGURE 1–6   Structure of a neuron

Neurons have distinct parts that perform distinct roles in information processing.

buttons. Neurotransmitters cross the synaptic cleft, moving from the axon of one neuron to the dendrites (or, sometimes, directly on the cell membrane, the outer covering of the cell body itself) of another.

The effects of a neurotransmitter depend on the *receptors* present on the receiving end. The standard analogy is to a lock and key: the chemical corresponds to a key, and the receptor to a lock. When the appropriate "messenger molecule," the neurotransmitter, binds to a receptor, it can excite the neuron (making it more active) or inhibit it (damping down its activity). The same neurotransmitter can have different effects depending on the nature of the receptor. If the excitatory input reaching a neuron is sufficiently greater than the inhibitory input, the neuron will produce an *action potential;* that is, it will "fire." Neurons obey an all-or-none law: either they fire or they don't.

3.2. Structure of the Nervous System

The nervous system is traditionally considered to have two major parts, the *central nervous system* (CNS) and the *peripheral nervous system* (PNS). The CNS consists of the brain and spinal cord; the PNS consists of the skeletal nervous system and the *autonomic nervous system* (ANS). We start with the more basic, and (in evolutionary terms) older, PNS and then turn to the brain itself.

3.2.1. The Peripheral Nervous System

The skeletal system governs *striated* (that is, very finely "striped") muscles, which are under voluntary control. The skeletal system plays a major role in motor cognition and mental simulation (Chapter 11). In contrast, most of the functions of the

ANS are carried out by smooth muscles, but the ANS also controls some glands. Smooth muscles, found in the heart, blood vessels, stomach lining, and intestines, are usually not under voluntary control. The ANS plays a key role in emotion and it also affects how memory works.

The ANS is traditionally divided into two major parts, the sympathetic and parasympathetic nervous systems. The *sympathetic nervous system* prepares an animal to respond more vigorously and accurately during an emergency. Among other things, it:

- increases the heart rate (so more oxygen and nutrients are delivered to organs),
- increases the breathing rate (thus providing more oxygen),
- dilates the pupils (resulting in greater sensitivity to light),
- causes the palms of the hands to become moist (thus providing better grip),
- reduces digestive functions, including salivation (putting them "on hold"), and
- relaxes the bladder (suspending another function that isn't crucial in an emergency).

These changes prepare an organism for successful challenge or successful escape, and are often called the *fight-or-flight response*. Why should we care about this response in a book on cognition? For one thing, the events surrounding this response can actually improve memory (Chapter 5), while at the same time they can disrupt reasoning (Chapter 10).

We modern human beings have the same sympathetic nervous system that served our ancestors well, but now its responses can be activated by stimuli very different from those encountered in previous eras. If during a job interview you are asked to explain some weak spot on your résumé, you may not find the features of the fight-or-flight responses so adaptive—it is not easy making your explanation when your heart is pounding and you have a dry mouth!

The *parasympathetic nervous system* in many ways counters the sympathetic nervous system. Whereas the sympathetic system tends to rev things up, the parasympathetic system dampens them down. Moreover, whereas the sympathetic system causes a whole constellation of effects (producing arousal in general), the parasympathetic system targets single organs or small sets of organs. In a job interview, you are grateful when the interviewer moves onto another part of your résumé where you are on rock-solid ground—and the parasympathetic system then dampens down the fight-or-flight response you were struggling to contain.

3.2.2. The Cerebral Cortex

Now let's consider the central nervous system, specifically the brain—the seat of mental activity. Imagine that you are in a neuroanatomy lab, dissecting a human brain. The first thing you see, covering the surface of the brain, is the topmost of three membranes, called the *meninges*. Putting on surgical gloves (an absolute necessity to guard yourself against viruses), you peel back the meninges to uncover a rich network of blood vessels clinging to the surface of the brain, like ivy clinging to a wall. The surface of the brain contains most of the cell bodies of neurons, which are a gray color, hence the term "gray matter." These cells are in a layer about 2 millimeters deep, which is called the *cerebral cortex*. The cortex of the brain is noticeably wrinkled; the wrinkles allow more cortex to be crammed into the skull. Each up-bulging fold is called a *gyrus,* and each crease a *sulcus.* The various gyri and sulci have individual names, and as we shall see throughout this book, many have been identified as playing a role in particular mental activities.

In your neuroanatomy lab you are equipped with a scalpel as well as surgical gloves. Now slice into the brain and examine its interior. The interior is packed with white fibers (the color giving rise to the term "white matter"), which connect the neurons. Keep exploring deeper to find the *subcortical structures* (so called because they lie beneath the cortex), which contain gray matter, and—at the very center of the brain—a series of connected cavities, the *ventricles.* The ventricles are filled with the same fluid that runs inside the spinal cord.

The brain is best considered not as a single entity but rather as a collection of components that work together, in the same way that the hand is a collection of separate bones, tendons, and muscles, all of which depend on one another to carry out the functions of the hand. One of the first things you have noticed in the neuroanatomy lab is that the brain is divided into two halves, the left and right *cerebral hemispheres.* Although the same physical structures are duplicated in the two cerebral hemispheres, they can differ both in their size and their functions (as will be discussed later in the book). The hemispheres are connected in the interior of the brain by a massive collection of nerve fibers (some 250 to 300 million of them), called the *corpus callosum,* as well as several smaller, less important connections.

Modern neuroanatomy divides each hemisphere into four major parts, or *lobes:* the *occipital,* at the posterior (rear) of the brain; the *temporal,* directly under the temples; the *parietal,* at the superior (upper) posterior part of the brain; and the *frontal,* at the anterior (front) part of the brain, right behind the forehead (Figure 1–7). The lobes are named after the bones of the skull that cover them, and hence this organization of the brain is somewhat arbitrary—so you won't be surprised to find that mental activities are not neatly assigned to one or another lobe. Nevertheless, at least some mental representations and processes occur mainly in a specific lobe, and we can make some generalizations about the different functions of the various lobes. But always keep in mind that the lobes work together, like the bones, tendons, and muscles of the hand.

The occipital lobes process only visual input, both from the eyes and from memory (at least in some cases, in mental imagery). If you were to slip while roller skating and fall on the back of your head, you would probably "see stars." This visual effect (which is not worth the pain of inducing it) occurs because the impact causes compression of the neurons in the occipital lobes. Curiously, if you stare straight ahead, the left occipital lobe receives inputs from the right side of space, and the right occipital lobe receives inputs from the left side of space. Why? The back of the eye, the retina, is actually part of the brain that's been pushed forward during development (Dowling, 1992); hence the left side of each eye (not just the left eye) is connected to the left part of the brain, and the right side of each eye (not just the right eye) is connected to the right side of the brain. When you stare straight ahead, light

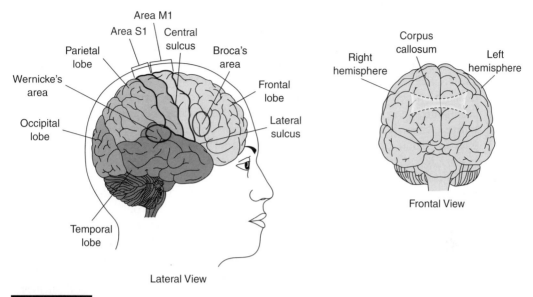

FIGURE 1-7   The major lobes and landmarks of the brain

The anatomical landmarks of the brain only imperfectly correspond to distinct functions, but these landmarks nevertheless are useful ways to describe brain location. Specific terms are used to describe locations in the brain: *Medial* means closer to the midline; thus, the medial views show the inside of the brain. *Lateral* means toward the side, farther away from the midline; thus the lateral views show the outside surface of the cerebral cortex. The terms *dorsal* (the "back" side) and *ventral* (the "stomach" side) are also used. Because we stand fully upright, these terms have no literal meaning with reference to the human brain, but by convention *dorsal,* like *superior,* describes "above," and *ventral,* like *inferior,* describes "below."

from your left strikes the right sides of each eye, and light from your right strikes the left sides of each eye. Vision, like all cognitive functions, is itself carried out by a set of distinct representations and processes. In fact, the occipital lobes contain numerous different areas, each of which plays a key role in a different aspect of vision: for example, some areas primarily process motion, others color, and others shape. If the occipital lobes are damaged, partial or complete blindness results.

The temporal lobes are involved in many different sorts of functions. One of them is the retention of visual memories. In addition, they receive input from the occipital lobes and match visual input to visual memories. When you've already stored an image of what you currently are seeing, this matching process makes the stimulus seem familiar. The temporal lobes also process input from the ears, and the posterior portion of the left temporal lobe contains *Wernicke's area,* which is crucial for comprehending language. At the anterior (i.e., front) portion of the temporal lobes are a number of areas that are critical for storing new information in memory, and areas involved in deriving meaning and in emotion.

The parietal lobes are crucially involved in representing space and your relationship to it. The most anterior gyrus of the parietal lobes, the *somatosensory cortex* (area S1), represents sensations on different parts of the body; S1 is organized so that the different parts of the body are registered by different portions of cortex. In addition, the left-hemisphere S1 registers sensations on the right side of the body, and vice versa for the right hemisphere. The parietal lobes also are important for consciousness and attention. Moreover, they are also involved in mathematical thinking. Albert Einstein (1945) reported that he relied on mental imagery when reasoning, and often imagined "what would happen if. . . ." This is interesting: after his death researchers discovered that his parietal lobes were about 15 percent larger than normal (Witelson et al., 1999).

The frontal lobes are generally involved in managing sequences of behaviors or mental activities. They play a major role in producing speech; *Broca's area* is usually identified with the third frontal gyrus in the left hemisphere, and this area is crucial for programming speech sounds. Several other areas in the frontal lobes are involved in controlling movements. The most posterior gyrus in the frontal lobes is called the *primary motor cortex* (area M1; also called the *motor strip*); this area controls fine motor movements, such as those necessary to type up your résumé. Like S1, M1 is organized so that different parts of the cortex correspond to different parts of the body. The left-hemisphere M1 controls the right part of the body, and vice versa. The frontal lobes are also involved in looking up specific information stored in memory, in planning and reasoning, in storing information briefly in memory so that it can be used in reasoning, in some emotions, and even in personality (Davidson, 1998, 2002). The frontal lobes obviously are crucial in helping you decide what sort of job to pursue, and will play crucial roles in allowing you to do well in your chosen career.

Although many functions are duplicated in the corresponding lobes in the two hemispheres (just as they are in our two lungs and two kidneys), in some cases the lobes function differently on the left and right sides. For example, the left-hemisphere parietal lobe produces representations that describe spatial relations (such as, "one object is *above* another"), whereas the right produces representations of continuous distances (Laeng et al., 2002). However, even when the hemispheres are specialized differently, in most cases the difference is a matter of degree, not of kind. Other than for some language functions, both hemispheres generally can carry out most functions, but perhaps not equally well (Hellige, 1993).

3.2.3. Subcortical Areas

The subcortical areas of the human brain (Figure 1–8) often appear very similar to those of other animals, and research suggests that these areas perform similar functions in various species. This is not to say that these areas perform simple functions: they typically carry out complex functions that either are essential for life or fundamental to the survival of the organism.

The *thalamus* is usually regarded as a kind of switching station. The sensory organs, such as the eye and the ear, as well as parts of the brain involved in controlling voluntary movements, send fibers to the thalamus, and the thalamus in turn sends fibers widely throughout the brain. The thalamus is ideally situated to regulate the flow of information in the brain, and it does: *attention* is the selective aspect of information processing, and parts of the thalamus play a crucial role in attention. The *pulvinar nucleus* (a nucleus, in neuroanatomy, is a cluster of cells) is involved in focusing attention. The thalamus is also important in regulating sleep.

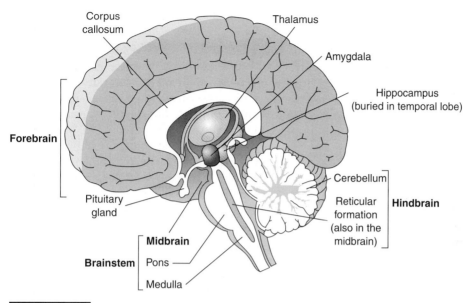

FIGURE 1–8   **The major subcortical areas of the brain**

The mammalian brain is divided into the *forebrain, midbrain,* and *hindbrain.* In nonhuman mammals, these are essentially in front-to-back order. In humans, *hindbrain* seems a misnomer, both because of human posture and the evolutionary expansion of the forebrain over the midbrain and the hindbrain.

Directly under the thalamus lies the *hypothalamus,* which controls many bodily functions, including maintaining a constant body temperature and blood pressure, eating and drinking, keeping the heart rate within appropriate limits, and regulating sexual behavior. Some of these functions are accomplished by various hormones (which are chemicals that affect various organs, and can even modulate the activity of neurons) regulated by the hypothalamus.

The *hippocampus* is located at the anterior of the temporal lobes, tucked inside. Its internal structure and connections to other areas allow it to play a central role in entering new information into memory. The hippocampus itself is not the repository of new memories; rather, it governs processes that allow memories to be stored elsewhere in the brain (such as in other regions of the temporal lobe).

The *amygdala* (named, based on its shape, for the Greek word for "almond") nestles next to the hippocampus, and for good reason. The amygdala is central both in the appreciation of emotion in others and in the production of behaviors that express our own emotions, especially fear. The amygdala can modulate the functioning of the hippocampus, a relationship that helps you store vivid memories of highly emotional information. The amygdala and hypothalamus serve to connect the CNS to the PNS. Both structures are central to triggering fight-or-flight responses.

The amygdala and hippocampus, along with several other subcortical structures, are part of the *limbic system.* At one time researchers believed that the limbic system regulated emotion, but this turned out to be incorrect. Not only are some parts of the limbic system used in other ways (such as in encoding new memories), but also other structures (such as the frontal lobes) are involved in emotion (Davidson, 2002; LeDoux, 1996).

The *basal ganglia* are absolutely critical for day-to-day life, allowing us to plan movements and to develop habits. Can you imagine what life would be like if you had to think through everything you do every time you do it? Think about the difference between the second time you went to a particular classroom in a basement of an unfamiliar building (which you now remember from the previous visit) and the tenth time you sauntered in: without the basal ganglia, every visit would be like that effortful, alert, second time. The basal ganglia lie at the outer sides of the thalami. The *nucleus accumbens,* a structure that is near the basal ganglia and sometimes considered to be part of it, plays an important role in learning. As the behaviorists emphasized, animals will learn a behavior when it produces a pleasant consequence. (If you make eye contact with the interviewer and receive a warm smile in return, you are likely to make eye contact again later in the interview.) This happy consequence is called a *reward.* The nucleus accumbens signals other brain areas when reward occurs (Tzschentke & Schmidt, 2000), both when it is actually received and when an animal only anticipates receiving it (Hall et al., 2001; Knutson et al., 2001; Pagnoni et al., 2002). By studying the brain, then, researchers have discovered that a mental state—anticipation—can affect the brain in a way that in turn enhances learning.

The *brainstem* is located at the base of the brain, and contains many structures that receive information from and send information to the spinal cord. A set of small structures, collectively known as the *reticular formation,* is involved in sleep and alertness. Some of the neurons in this structure produce *neuromodulators,* which are chemicals that affect far-flung portions of the brain. (These chemicals do just what their name suggests: they alter, or modulate, the functions of neurons.) The *pons* ("bridge" in Latin) connects the brainstem to the cerebellum, and contributes to functions that both structures perform, such as controlling sleep and forming facial expressions.

Finally, the *cerebellum* is concerned with physical coordination. It is also involved in some aspects of attention and in the estimation of time. The surface area of the cerebellum is about the same as the surface area of the cerebral cortex, which implies that this structure is engaged in many complex processes; researchers have only begun to comprehend its functions.

✓ Comprehension Check:

1. What are the four lobes of each hemisphere of the brain?
2. What roles are played by the major subcortical structures?

4. STUDYING COGNITION

Cognition is investigated in several fields, each of which uses a different approach. When first conceived, *cognitive psychology* focused exclusively on the level of information processing (e.g., Lindsay & Norman, 1977; Neisser, 1967). *Artificial intelligence* (AI), concentrating at the same level of analysis, is the field in which researchers attempt to program computers to perform cognitive tasks. Many AI researchers believe that cognition is so complicated that figuring out how to build a processing system that performs comparably to humans will lend insight into human cognition (Minsky, 1986). Neither early cognitive psychology nor AI pays much attention to the way such information processing takes place in the brain. But even computer buffs have noted that it isn't quite right to assume that information processing is independent of the machine itself: some programs rely on specific features of the hardware, such as the presence of a certain amount of RAM or a particular graphics or sound card. Studying the hardware can lead to insights about what the machine does and how it functions.

In fact, taking this view further, other researchers argue that understanding the hardware in sufficient detail allows you to understand its function. *Neuroscience* aims to understand the "wetware," the brain itself, which also must be understood at different levels of analysis. At one extreme, we must understand the nature of the genetic and molecular events that regulate cells in order to know how individual neurons work; at the other extreme, we must understand the functions of lobes and interactions among the different brain regions in order to know how the brain as a whole operates. Theories of such large-scale interactions among brain areas meld into theories of information processing (cf. Dowling, 1992).

Cognitive neuroscience stands at the intersection of neuroscience and cognitive psychology. The guiding idea is "the mind is what the brain does." Cognition is information processing, but information processing carried out by a brain with specific characteristics. Thus, cognitive neuroscience uses knowledge of the brain, such as the existence of brain areas that are specialized for different processes, in theories of processing systems. However, as indicated by the name of the approach, in which *neuroscience* is the noun that's modified by *cognitive,* cognitive neuroscience is focused on understanding the brain itself—what different parts of it do and how they interact.

In this book we focus on the subject matter of cognitive psychology—the study of mental activity—and draw on related fields to further the investigation. Our goal is twofold: to integrate what has been learned about cognition from the various approaches and to integrate the brain into the traditional laboratory approaches of cognitive psychology. As we conceive it, the goal of the new cognitive psychology is to understand mental activity so well that you could program a computer to mimic the way the brain functions when we perform tasks.

4.1. Converging Evidence for Dissociations and Associations

The first thing you will notice as we continue is that there are a lot of different methods. No one method is ideal; they all have limitations and potential problems. But— and this is a critical point—they have *different* limitations and potential problems. Using several different methods has two desirable outcomes. First, a more complete picture can be painted. For example, some sorts of neuroimaging (also called brain scanning) require a relatively long time to obtain an image, but can detect changes in relatively small parts of the brain, and the opposite is true of other neuroimaging methods. By using both types of methods, researchers can learn about different aspects of the same phenomenon. Second, the results from any one study are rarely conclusive; findings from any method are typically open to more than one interpretation. But if the results from different methodologies all point in the same direction, the weaknesses of any one method are compensated by the strengths of another. Thus, converging evidence, different types of results that imply the same conclusion, lies at the heart of successful investigations in cognitive psychology.

Many of the methods in cognitive psychology are used to accomplish two general types of goals. The first is to establish a dissociation, that is, to establish that an activity or a variable affects the performance of one task (or aspect of one task) but not of another. A dissociation, therefore, is evidence for the existence of a specific process. For example, Alan Baddley (1986) has argued that people can use at least two distinct types of "working memory" structures, one that briefly holds visual-spatial information and one that briefly holds articulatory-verbal information. If you look up a phone number and keep it in mind as you cross the room to the telephone, you are holding that information in the articulatory-verbal working memory. In contrast, if you are given a map of how to find the office where a job interview will take place, you might hold that map in visual-spatial working memory after you enter the building and begin to walk down the halls. The primary evidence for the existence of these two types of memory structures is a dissociation between the two kinds of memories in the effects of different sorts of interference. Having to count backward disrupts the ability to retain articulatory-verbal information, but not visual-spatial information; in contrast, having to trace a route through a maze has the opposite effect. In this example, we have a double dissociation: in this case, an activity or variable affects one process but not another and a second activity or variable has the reverse properties (e.g., Sternberg, 2003). Double dissociations are powerful evidence for the existence of two distinct processes, and they can be obtained with virtually any of the methods used in cognitive psychology.

In addition to dissociations, cognitive psychologists try to document associations. An association, in this sense, occurs when the effects of an activity or variable on one task are accompanied by effects on another task. Such shared effects indicate that common representations or processes are being affected. For example, if someone suffered brain damage that led to the inability to recognize faces (which actually does happen, and is discussed in Chapter 2), you might want to test whether that patient also had difficulty forming mental images of faces. In fact, if patients have one problem, they often have the other. This association suggests that a common representation or process is shared by perception and mental imagery.

So much for goals and general approaches. How do we actually get on with it? How do we actually collect observations—data—and formulate theories? Researchers in cognitive psychology ask a wide variety of questions about information processing, and many different methods can be used to answer them. In this book you will see how different methods complement one another, and how researchers have used methods in clever ways to discover some of the secrets of one of Nature's most intricate and intriguing creations—the human mind. So to get oriented, let's open the toolbox and see what's inside.

4.2. Behavioral Methods

A **behavioral method** measures directly observable behavior, such as the time to respond or the accuracy of a response. Researchers attempt to draw inferences about internal representation and processing from such directly observable responses. Table 1–1 summarizes the main behavioral measures and methods used in cognitive psychology and their primary advantages and disadvantages. We pause briefly here to consider some observations about the most important behavioral methods.

First, the accuracy with which participants perform a task is used to address a wide variety of types of processing, ranging from those that require making a discrimination (either perceptually or from memory) to those that require recall. With all accuracy measures, however, researchers must be on guard against two possible hazards:

1. If the task is too easy, participants may exhibit *ceiling effects*, where no differences are seen in the responses because the participants all score the highest

TABLE 1–1   Major Behavioral Measures and Methods Used in Cognitive Psychology

Measure or Method	Example	Advantages	Limitations
Accuracy (percent correct or percent error)	Memory recall, such as trying to remember the main job requirements during an interview	Objective measure of processing effectiveness	Ceiling effects (no differences because the task is too easy); floor effects (no differences because the task is too hard); speed–accuracy trade-off ("jumping the gun")
Response time	Time to answer a specific question, such as whether you know the requirements of a certain job	Objective and subtle measure of processing, including unconscious processing	Sensitive to experimental expectancy effects and to effects of task demands; speed-accuracy trade-off
Judgments	Rating on a seven-point scale how successful you felt an interview was	Can assess subjective reactions; easy and inexpensive to collect	Participant may not know how to use the scale; may not have conscious access to the information; may not be honest
Protocol collection (speaking aloud one's thoughts about a problem)	Talking through the pros and cons of various job possibilities	Can reveal a sequence of processing steps	Cannot be used for most cognitive processes, which occur unconsciously and in a fraction of a second

possible score. For example, if you want to know whether emotion boosts memory and you test only two highly emotional items and two neutral ones, the participants will recall all the items so well that no difference will emerge. But that result does not mean that no difference exists, merely that your test was too easy to demonstrate it. Similarly, if the task is too difficult, participants may exhibit *floor effects,* where no differences are seen among responses because the participants are doing terribly on all the conditions.

2. Participants can make errors because they are jumping the gun, that is, responding before they are ready. This pattern of responses produces a *speed–accuracy trade-off* in which errors go up as response times go down. Such a trade-off can be detected only if response times are assessed at the same time as accuracy. Therefore, as a rule, the two measures should be taken together. Incidentally, this problem is not limited to the laboratory: such speed–accuracy trade-offs can occur in real life, which is why you should be sure to reflect on your decisions: there's truth in "haste makes waste."

Second, a large amount of research in cognitive psychology rests on measures of the amount of time participants take to respond when making a judgment. In general, participants should require more time to respond when a task requires more cognitive processing.

Finally, some researchers also collect judgments of various sorts (such as ratings of confidence that a participant recalls information correctly) and others collect protocols (such as records of what participants say they are doing as they work through a problem).

In general, purely behavioral methods are prone to a number of problems:

1. Participants sometimes change their speed of responding after figuring out what the investigator expects, trying, perhaps unconsciously, to cooperate. The influence of the investigator on the participant's responses is known as *experimental expectancy effects.*

2. Participants may respond to *task demands,* aspects of the task itself that participants believe require them to respond in a particular way. For example, results of mental imagery scanning experiments might reflect such task demands (Pylyshyn, 1981, 2002, 2003). In these experiments, participants are asked to scan an object in their visual mental image, with their eyes closed, until they have focused on a specific target (at which point they press a button). Response times typically increase with the distance scanned (for a review, Denis & Kosslyn, 1999). This result could be explained if participants *interpret the task* as requiring them to mimic what would happen in the corresponding perceptual situation, and thus take more time when they think they should be scanning longer distances. Task demands can be ruled out, but this requires clever experimentation. For example, the scanning results have been obtained even when no instructions to scan, or even to use imagery, are employed (Finke & Pinker, 1982, 1983).

3. Behavioral methods are necessarily incomplete. They cannot give us a rich picture of underlying processing, in part because of structure–process trade-offs. These methods are probably most useful when employed to test a specific theory that makes specific predictions about the specific measures being collected.

4.3. Correlational Neural Methods: The Importance of Localization

Cognitive psychology has become extraordinarily exciting during the past decade because researchers have developed relatively inexpensive, high-quality methods for assessing how the human brain functions. These methods are *correlational*: although they reveal the pattern of brain activity that accompanies information processing, they do not show that activation in specific brain areas actually results in the task's being carried out. Correlation does not necessarily imply causation. Some of the activated brain areas could be just along for the ride—activated because they are connected to other areas that do play a functional role in processing. One of the main virtues of these methods is that they allow researchers to begin to *localize* mental activity, to show that particular parts of the brain either give rise to specific representations or carry out specific processes.

Such data can establish both dissociations and associations, thereby giving insight into the nature of representations and processes used during mental activity. On the one hand, if two tasks activate different brain areas (a dissociation), this is evidence that they are accomplished at least in part by separate representations or processes. For example, the parts of the brain used when one holds verbal information in working memory (sometimes refered to as "short-term memory") are different from those used when one recalls previously stored information (Nyberg et al., 1996; Smith, 2000), showing that working memory is not just an activated portion of the information previously stored in memory. On the other hand, if the same brain area is activated in two tasks (an association), this is evidence that at least some of the same representations or processes may be used in the two tasks. For example, once part of the parietal lobe was shown to be involved in representing space, Dehaene and colleagues (1999) could interpret activation in this region when participants compare relative magnitudes of numbers. They argued that people use a "mental number line" in this task. Their interpretation was then supported with a variety of additional forms of evidence. However, this sort of inference must be made with great caution: what appears to be activation of the same area in two different tasks may in fact be activation in two different, nearby areas, but the technique is too insensitive to register the difference. As usual, we must be very careful in affirming the null hypothesis; that is, in claiming that a failure to *find* a difference means that there is in fact no difference.

We can evaluate the various correlational neural methods on four dimensions: (1) *spatial resolution,* how precisely they localize the brain area that produces a signal; (2) *temporal resolution,* how precisely they track changes in brain activity over time; (3) *invasiveness,* the degree to which they require introduction of foreign substances into the brain; and (4) *cost,* both for the equipment (and any special facilities) and for its use in each participant test. The three most important neuroimaging

TABLE 1–2 Correlational Neuroimaging Methods

Method	Example	Spatial Resolution	Temporal Resolution	Invasiveness	Cost (Initial; Use)
Electrical (electroencephalography, EEG; event-related potentials, ERP)	Track stages of sleep (EEG), brain response to novelty (ERP)	Poor (perhaps 1 inch)	Excellent (milliseconds)	Low	Low purchase cost; low use cost
Magnetoencephalography (MEG)	Detect activity in auditory cortex to tones of different pitches	Good (under 1 centimeter), but only in sulci, not in gyri (because of the way dendrites line up)	Excellent (milliseconds)	Low	High purchase cost (and needs a special magnetically shielded room); medium use cost (needs servicing so superconductors remain extremely cold)
Positron emission tomography (PET)	Detect activity in language areas as participants speak	Good (about 1 centimeter, but in theory higher)	Poor (an image every 40 seconds)	High (must introduce radiation)	High purchase cost (needs a cyclotron plus the PET camera); high use cost (about $2,000 per participant)
Magnetic resonance imaging (MRI) and functional magnetic resonance imaging (fMRI)	Show structure of the brain (for MRI), show activity in brain areas, same as PET (for fMRI)	Superb (millimeter range); fMRI often about 0.5 centimeter	Depends on level of resolution; typically several seconds	Low	High purchase cost (needs a specially shielded room); medium use cost (needs servicing)
Optical imaging	Show activity in brain areas, same as PET	Poor at present (about 2 centimeters)	Depends on level of resolution; typically several minutes	Medium/low (light is shined through the skull)	Low purchase cost; low use cost

methods for cognitive psychology currently are event-related potentials (ERP), positron emission tomography (PET), and functional magnetic resonance imaging (fMRI), and so it is worth considering them briefly in more detail. Table 1–2 summarizes these methods.

The oldest correlational methods record brain activity from the scalp. *Electroencephalography* (EEG) uses electrodes placed on the scalp to record fluctuations in electrical activity over time (Figure 1–9a). These "brain waves" are analyzed to reveal how much activity is present in different "bands," which are sets of frequencies. For example, the "alpha rhythm" is 8 to 12 Hz (that is, 8 to 12 cycles per second), and the amplitude of waves in this range increases when a participant becomes relaxed. Recording *event-related potentials* also relies on scalp electrodes, but here they are used to observe fluctuations in activity in response to a specific stimulus. Investigators note changes in electrical activity, positive or negative, that occur specific amounts of time after a stimulus has been presented. For example, the "P-300" is a positive fluctuation that occurs about 300 milliseconds after a stimulus; this fluctuation is thought to reflect detection of novelty. These methods have several drawbacks:

1. Both EEG and ERP are disrupted by slight movements because muscles produce electric activity when they twitch.

2. Both techniques have relatively poor spatial resolution, in part because electrical waves travel over the surface of the brain and the scalp, and in part because the electrical activity at any point on the scalp is a composite of activity that has originated from various places in the brain. It is as if you were measuring the amount of water falling into paper cups during a rainstorm, and trying to figure out how much water the cloud immediately overhead held; the water you collect came from multiple parts of the cloud (the wind affects where raindrops land) as well as from multiple altitudes. Researchers are working on techniques to use recordings at multiple electrodes to try to zero in on the source of electric activity, but these techniques are still being developed. At present, the spatial resolution of electric techniques is probably about 1 inch, but this is a rough estimate. In spite of their poor spatial resolution, these techniques have several virtues: they have excellent temporal resolution, they are not invasive, and both purchase and use of the equipment are relatively inexpensive.

A relatively recent variant of ERP, *magnetoencephalography* (MEG), records magnetic rather than electric fields (Figure 1–9b). Unlike electrical fields, magnetic fields are not distorted as they pass through bone and they do not travel over the surface of the brain or the scalp. MEG has relatively good spatial resolution (probably under a centimeter), but because of the way dendrites are arranged in cortex it primarily detects activity in sulci, not on gyri. It has superb temporal resolution (detecting fluctuations of a few milliseconds) and is not invasive. However, MEG is expensive; the machine must be housed in a special magnetically shielded room, and the detectors must be serviced regularly. (They need to be extremely cold, so that superconductors can detect the faint magnetic fields in the brain.)

(a)

FIGURE 1–9   Recording the brain

(a) An EEG machine, which records electrical activity.

(Photograph by Deep Light Production. Courtesy of Photo Researchers, Inc.)

PET provides a different type of information than what we can learn from ERP and thus is very useful as a complementary technique (Figure 1–10a). The most common use of PET in cognitive psychology relies on a radioactive isotope of oxygen, ^{15}O. Water in which some of the oxygen is in the form of this isotope is injected into a participant who is performing a task. When a part of the brain becomes active, it draws more blood to it (rather like the way a washing machine draws more water from the main when the machine is turned on). As more blood flows to an area, more of the radioactively tagged water goes along with it. Detectors surrounding the head record the amount of radioactivity, and computers later reconstruct a three-dimensional image from this information. This technique can detect activity in structures smaller than 1 centimeter across (in theory as small as 2 millimeters, but in practice perhaps three times larger than that). Among the drawbacks are the following:

1. Although the levels of radiation are very low (10 scans deliver about the same amount of radiation as what an airline pilot typically receives in a year and a half), the technique is still invasive.

2. The temporal resolution is relatively poor; it takes at least 40 seconds to obtain an image.

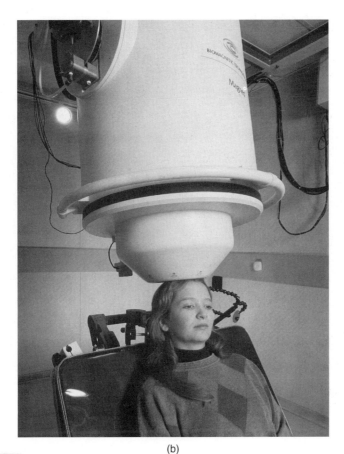

(b)

FIGURE 1–9 *(continued)*

(b) A MEG machine, which records magnetic activity, in use.

3. PET is expensive, requiring radioactive material that is manufactured immediately before use (because the radiation decays quickly) and special machines to perform the scans.

Another technique has recently come to replace most of the research that used to be done with PET. This technique grew out of magnetic resonance imaging (MRI). So, let's first look at MRI, and then consider the newer functional magnetic resonance imaging methods that assess brain activity. The American Paul C. Lauterbur and the Englishman Peter Mansfield won the 2003 Nobel Prize in Physiology or Medicine for their roles in developing MRI. Their discoveries not only changed the face of medicine for all time but also dramatically improved our ability to understand the brain. The original use of MRI was to assess brain structure, not function. For example, this technique has revealed that musicians who play string instruments (such as violins) have a larger area M1 in their right hemispheres (controlling their left hands) than is present for other members of an orchestra (Münte et al., 2002). MRI uses magnetic fields to

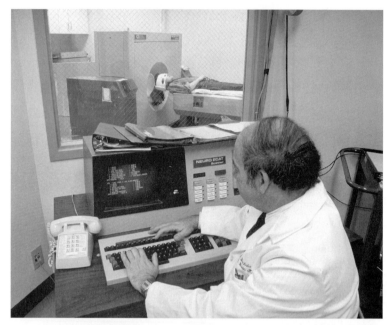

(a)

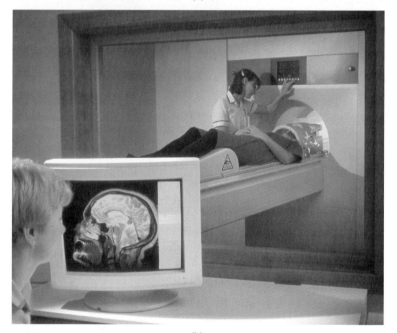

(b)

FIGURE 1–10 Neuroimaging methods

PET and fMRI are probably the most common neuroimaging methods used today. (a) A PET scan in progress.

(Photograph by Spencer Grant. Courtesy of PhotoEdit Inc.)

(b) An MRI machine.

(Photograph by Geoff Tompkinson. Courtesy of Photo Researchers, Inc.)

alter the orientations of specific atoms in a substance. A strong reference magnet is turned on, causing all the atoms to line up with it (atoms have a north and south pole, and line up accordingly with a large magnet). A quick pulse of radio waves is then used to disorient the atoms, which give off detectable signals when they return to normal. (This pulse is created by magnets that are so strong that they flex when they are turned on, and they displace air, which creates a sound, just as a loudspeaker pushes air to create sound. But in the case of MRI, the sound is a loud knocking noise.) The MRI records a signal as the atoms return to their original alignment; the recorded current is then amplified and used to create an image. Gray matter and white matter can be identified by the way their component atoms resonate to different frequencies of radio waves. MRI has extraordinarily good spatial resolution (less than 1 millimeter, in principle), good temporal resolution (an image can be created in a few seconds), and it is noninvasive. But the machines are very expensive and require special facilities (Figure 1–10b).

Functional magnetic resonance imaging is based on the same principles as structural MRI. However, instead of charting the structure of the brain, fMRI tracks activity in different parts of the brain. The most common fMRI technique is called BOLD, for *blood oxygenation level dependent*. Red blood cells contain iron (in the hemoglobin), which can have oxygen bound to it or can have oxygen stripped off when it is used up in metabolism. When a brain area begins to function, it draws more oxygenated red blood cells than it actually needs, and thus oxygenated red blood cells pile up. The iron-with-oxygen and the iron-without-oxygen affect the nearby hydrogen atoms in water (the major constituent of blood) differently. And that's the key: the magnetic pulse sequence is designed to reveal where oxygenated red blood cells have piled up, which is an indirect measure of activity in that brain area. fMRI has about the same spatial resolution as structural MRI (at least 1 millimeter) and is noninvasive. Nevertheless, this technique does have drawbacks, including these:

1. fMRI can detect changes that occur over the course of about 6 seconds, which is much less precise than ERP or MEG.
2. The machines (and the necessary specially shielded rooms) are expensive.
3. The machines are very noisy (which can make participants uncomfortable and therefore make certain studies hard to do).
4. The tube in which participants lie is very narrow, which some people find disturbing.

Finally, it is worth mentioning a very new member of the neuroimaging toolbox, which holds promise of becoming increasingly popular in the near future. *Optical imaging* takes advantage of two facts about light: first, the skull is transparent to near-infrared light; second, some frequencies of such light are absorbed more by oxygenated hemoglobin than by hemoglobin stripped of its oxygen (Obrig & Villringer, 2003). The *diffuse optical tomography* (DOT) method positions a collection of very weak lasers at different locations on the skull and shines light onto the cortex; the reflected light is measured by detectors placed on the scalp. Each laser flickers at a distinct rate, and thus it is possible to calculate where the reflected light originated. This technique allows researchers to track blood flow in the cortex. It is relatively inexpensive to build the machines and costs almost nothing to use them.

Although the technique is in a sense invasive, it is very safe; the level of light reaching the cortex is less than what an uncovered bald head receives outdoors on a sunny day (the technique has been approved for use with very young infants). The major drawbacks are as follows:

1. Light penetrates only 2 or 3 centimeters before it becomes too diffuse to be recorded accurately, and thus no subcortical areas can be assessed and only about 80 percent of the cortex can be reached.
2. This technique has about the same temporal resolution as BOLD fMRI, and the spatial resolution depends on the number and placement of the lasers and detectors.

In general, neuroimaging techniques suffer from a number of weaknesses, which should make you cautious when interpreting their results:

- First, we cannot tell the difference between results caused by excitatory or inhibitory activity.
- Second, more activation does not necessarily mean more processing. A champion runner can run a mile faster than a couch potato and use less energy in the process; similarly, if you are an expert at specific processes, you may be able to accomplish them with less brain processing.
- Third, the same functional area can lie in slightly different anatomical regions in different brains, which makes averaging over participants difficult.
- Fourth, the brain is always "on," even during sleep. Thus, researchers always must compare two conditions and observe how activation changes from one to the other. The problem is that we do not know exactly what processing takes place during either a "test" or "baseline" comparison condition, and so the difference between the two conditions can be difficult to interpret.
- Fifth, if no difference in activation between two tasks is found in a brain area, this can mean that the process was active in both tasks, not active in either task, or the difference was too subtle to detect. This last possibility is particularly worrisome because blood vessels can expand only so much, and therefore increases in blood flow with neural activity cannot be linear—they cannot increase by the same increment for each additional increment of processing. If an area is relatively active in two conditions, the difference in blood flow between them may not reflect the difference in processing.
- Finally, processes need not be implemented in distinct neural tissue. For example, area 17 contains neurons that process color, and these neurons are interspersed among those that process shape (Livingstone & Hubel, 1984). If we average over a centimeter or so (the resolution used in most PET and fMRI studies), we cannot distinguish these two classes of neurons. In short, "converging evidence" must be our watchword!

4.4. Causal Neural Methods

Researchers have depended on other types of studies to establish causal connections between brain activation and performance. Such methods, summarized in Table 1–3,

TABLE 1–3   **Causal Neural Methods Used in Cognitive Psychology**

Method	Example	Advantages	Limitations
Neuropsychological studies (of patients with localized or diffuse brain damage)	Examine deficit in understanding nouns but not verbs	Tests theories of causal role of specific brain areas; tests theories of shared and distinct processing used in different tasks; relatively easy and inexpensive to collect	Damage is often not limited to one area; patients may have many deficits
Transcranial magnetic stimulation (TMS)	Temporarily disrupt occipital lobe and show that this has the same effects on visual perception and on visual mental imagery	Same as for neuropsychological studies, but the transient "lesion" is more restricted, and the participant can be tested before and after TMS	Can be used only for brain areas near the surface (TMS affects only tissue about 1 inch down)
Drugs that affect specific brain systems	Disrupt the action of noradrenaline, which is crucial for the operation of the hippocampus	Can alter the processing of specific brain systems; typically is reversible; can be tested in advance with animals	Many drugs affect many different brain systems; the temporal resolution may be very poor

show that activity in a particular brain area actually gives rise to specific representations or carries out specific processes.

If a part of the brain plays a key role in performing a specific task, then a patient should have difficulty performing that task if that part of the brain has been damaged. Following this logic, researchers have tried to use deficits in performance of particular tasks (such as reading, writing, or arithmetic) following brain damage to infer the causal role of specific parts of the brain. People suffer brain damage primarily for one or the other of five reasons:

- They have a stroke, an event that occurs when blood flow—with its life-sustaining oxygen and nutrients—to the brain is disrupted. When this happens, neurons in part of the brain may die.
- Surgery to remove a tumor may also have removed specific parts of the brain.
- They have suffered various sorts of head injuries that can damage the brain. (In a car, use the seat belt! On a bike, wear a helmet!)
- They have a brain-damaging disease. Alzheimer's disease, for example, initially selectively impairs parts of the brain involved in memory.
- They have ingested brain-damaging toxins. Drinking too much alcohol for too long, for example, can lead to bad dietary habits, which in turn damage specific parts of the brain involved in memory. (The problem is not the alcohol per se, but rather how drinking too much affects nutrition.)

Researchers have studied patients with brain damage in order to discover which cognitive abilities are disrupted and which are left intact. Their goal is to document dissociations and associations (Caramazza, 1984, 1986; Shallice, 1988). In these studies, a dissociation is said to occur when one ability is impaired while another is spared, and an association is said to occur when two tasks are always disrupted together (suggesting that the two tasks rely on at least one common underlying representation or process). However, associations can also occur because nearby brain areas are damaged together (or neurons that have different functions are present in the same area).

In general, it can be difficult to relate changes in performance after brain damage to the normal function of damaged areas. Why?

1. Brain damage typically affects a large area of neural tissue, and also affects connections among brain areas.

2. Such damage does not leave the rest of the brain as it was before the injury; rather, the brain compensates in various ways. Gregory (1961) offers a useful metaphor: if you remove a resistor from a radio and it begins to howl, this does not mean that the resistor was a howl suppressor. Removing the part changes the way the entire system works.

Nevertheless, if one has a theory of what a specific brain area does, then damage to that area provides a strong test of the role of that area: if an area does play a causal role in a particular type of performance, then damage to that part of the brain should disrupt such tasks (Fellows et al., 2005).

A new technique sidesteps many of the difficulties encountered when studying people with brain damage. *Transcranial magnetic stimulation* (TMS) temporarily disrupts normal brain activity in a relatively small area, perhaps 1 cubic centimeter (Walsh & Pascual-Leone, 2003). TMS involves placing a coil on the participant's skull and briefly running a large current through the coil (Figure 1–11). The current produces a magnetic field, which in turn temporarily disrupts neural activity of brain areas beneath the coil. There are two main variants of this technique. In the single-pulse version, a pulse is delivered a specific amount of time after a stimulus is presented. This method can be used to discover the duration of particular processes, as well as their causal roles in a specific task. In the other version, known as repetitive TMS (rTMS), a series of magnetic pulses is delivered to a brain area before a task is performed. If enough pulses are delivered, the neurons eventually become less responsive and continue to be sluggish for a period thereafter. Thus, researchers can deliver rTMS to a particular part of the cortex and then observe performance in specific tasks. This technique in some ways induces a temporary lesion, but does not disrupt connections. For example, if TMS is delivered to Broca's area, the result is difficulty in producing speech immediately afterward. It is not always clear, however, exactly which areas are affected by the pulses, nor is it clear whether affecting one area also affects another to which it is connected. The method has drawbacks:

1. The effects of stimulating one area can be transmitted to other areas, which can make it difficult to infer which area is in fact responsible for observed effects.

2. If not used according to safety guidelines, rTMS can produce seizures.

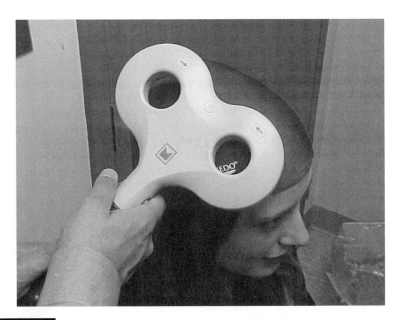

FIGURE 1–11 Investigation by transcranial magnetic stimulation

A TMS test, as shown here, can be administered easily in a laboratory; it can temporarily impair very specific cognitive processing.

(Courtesy of Julian Paul Keenan, PhD.)

3. The technique affects only the cortex, and only the portions of it that lie directly beneath the skull.

4. Muscles at the sides of the forehead twitch when TMS is applied to that area, which can be uncomfortable.

Finally, another method involves administering drugs that affect the workings of specific brain systems. This technique provides another way to demonstrate that particular brain systems play a causal role in particular types of performance. For example, Cahill and colleagues (1994) showed participants pictures that either illustrated neutral events (such as walking past a junk yard) or aversive events (such as being in a horrible accident). One hour after seeing the pictures, they gave the participants one of two pills: half the participants took a drug that interferes with noradrenaline, a neurotransmitter that is crucial for the operation of the hippocampus; this drug thus impaired the operation of that brain structure, which is crucial for entering new information into memory. The other half of the participants received a placebo, a medically inert substance. (The participants did not know whether they received the active drug or a placebo.) A week later, the participants were tested—without being warned in advance that such a test was in the works—on their memory for the pictures. The group that received the placebo recalled more pictures of emotional events than pictures of neural events. Why? The answer may be that the group that received the drug that blocks noradrenaline did not show the typical memory advantage for emotional events, which is evidence that the hippocampus (along with the amygdala) plays a role in our enhanced memory for emotional material. However, this method also has drawbacks:

1. Drugs often affect many different brain systems.
2. Drugs may take a relatively long time to operate and their effects may linger for a relatively long time.

In general, the causal methods are most effective when used in combination with neuroimaging techniques, which can establish that certain areas are active during a task; those areas then can be specifically examined (in patients with brain damage or by TMS or specific drugs). Advances in localizing activation in individual participants are allowing researchers to use TMS with increasing precision, and this technique is likely to play an increasingly large role in research.

4.5. Modeling

Mental activity also can be studied by constructing models. Models can not only tell you whether a set of principles or mechanisms can in fact explain data, but they can also make new predictions. What's the difference between a theory and a model? A theory proposes a set of abstract principles that can account for a range of phenomena; a model is a specific, concrete version of a theory. Models have three types of characteristics (Hesse, 1963):

1. those that are relevant to a theory, such as the shape of a model airplane's wings or the order in which processes are carried out in a computer program;
2. those that are clearly not relevant to a theory, such as the color of a model airplane or the actual time a computer program requires to perform a process; and
3. those that are not clearly in either category, such as the shape of the belly of a model airplane and the role of the central processing unit in executing routines in a computer model. Sometimes research is focused on the third category, attempting to assign these characteristics to one of the first two categories.

In psychology, models are often implemented as computer programs. Such **computer simulation models** are intended to mimic the underlying mental representations and processes that produce specific types of human performance. Computer simulations must be distinguished from programs in artificial intelligence, which are intended to produce "intelligent" behavior but may incorporate underlying processes far different from those used by humans. In addition, we must note that models of mental activity are not always implemented in computer programs; they can also be realized as a set of equations or simply formulated verbally or with diagrams.

At its inception, cognitive psychology relied primarily on **process** models, which specify a sequence of processes that convert an input to an output. Such models can be illustrated with a flowchart, and are sometimes called "box and arrow" models. Figure 1–12 presents an example of a model to explain how people decide whether

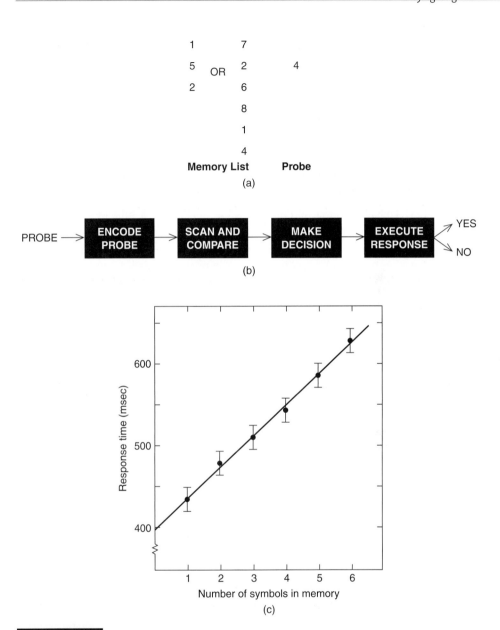

FIGURE 1–12   Sternberg's process model

(a) The first task is to memorize a short list of items—here, numbers. Then a probe item, say, "4," is presented that may or may not have been on the list. The task is to decide whether it was or was not. (b) The probe item is encoded and thus entered into memory. The list stored in memory is scanned and the probe compared to each item on the list; if the list is scanned an item at a time, then the longer the list, the more time should be required to scan it. Next, a decision is made about how to respond. Finally, the actual response is executed, leading the participant to press either the YES or the NO key. (c) The prediction was confirmed: more time was required to scan longer lists.

a stimulus was on a list they just studied. (We earlier considered this task when discussing structure–process trade-offs.) Most of these models specify each process in terms of its input and output, but the internal workings of each process are not specified in detail—they remain in a metaphoric "black box." Process models are often used to explain and predict response times on the basis of the relative number of operations the model would perform to accomplish a task. In addition, because such models specify distinct processes, they are also used to explain and predict patterns of deficits following brain damage (Caramazza, 1984, 1986); the central idea here is that some processes can be impaired selectively by damage. But process models also have drawbacks as investigative tools:

1. They typically assume serial processing, one step at a time in sequence, and rarely model parallel processing, in which processes occur simultaneously.

2. *Feedback,* the effect of a process later in the sequence on one earlier in the sequence, typically occurs only after the processes leading up to it are complete. The brain is not like this; later areas send output to earlier ones well before earlier processing is complete.

3. They typically do not learn, and learning clearly shapes mental activity from the earliest ages.

4.6. Neural-Network Models

Neural-network models, also called connectionist models, were created in part in response to the weaknesses of process models. As their name implies, these models take into account key properties of how the brain works (Plaut et al., 1996; Rumelhart et al., 1986; Vogels et al., 2005). **Neural-network** models rely on sets of interconnected units, each of which is intended to correspond to a neuron or a small group of neurons. Units are not the same thing as neurons, but rather they specify the input–output process a neuron or group of neurons performs. The simplest models include three layers of units, as illustrated in Figure 1–13. The *input layer* is a set of units that receives stimulation from the external environment. The units in the input layer are connected to units in a *hidden layer,* so named because these units have no direct contact with the environment. The units in the hidden layer in turn are connected to those in the *output layer.* In the simplest models, each unit can be "on" or "off," as designated by 1 or 0. The heart of these networks is their connections (hence the alternative name "connectionist"). Each connection from an input unit either excites or inhibits a hidden unit. Furthermore, each connection has a *weight,* a measure of the strength of its influence on the receiving unit. Some networks include feedback loops, for example, with connections from hidden units to input units. Here is a crucial point: the pattern of weights in the entire network serves to represent associations between input and output. Neural networks not only use parallel processing, they rely on *distributed* parallel processing, in which a representation is a pattern of weights, not a single weight, node, or connection.

Neural nets have several interesting properties. For one, they learn. The weights typically are set randomly at first, and various training techniques are used to allow

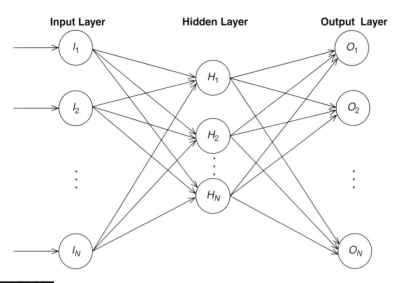

Input Layer   **Hidden Layer**   **Output Layer**

FIGURE 1–13 A simple feed-forward neural network

Three inputs are shown; there may be many more between the second (I_2) and the Nth (I_N). More complex networks not only can have feedback loops, but the connections between units can be organized in specific ways.

(Reprinted with permission from the Commonwealth Scientific & Industrial Research Organisation, Australia.)

the network to set the weights automatically so that input produces appropriate output. For another, they generalize: when a neural network is given a set of inputs that is similar, but not identical, to one on which the net was trained, it still can respond appropriately. Moreover, when damaged they degrade gradually. In a standard computer program, by contrast, if even one command is wrong, the entire program crashes. In a neural net, units or connections can be removed and—up to a point— the net will still function, although not as well. And sometimes it will function well in some ways but not in others. This is similar to what happens in a brain.

Finally, neural networks are useful because they help us understand the difference between a neural code and a mental representation. The neural code consists of a specific level of activity for each neuron (or, in these models, for each node) and a specific strength for each of the connections among neurons (or among nodes, in the models). But simply knowing the state of each individual node and connection won't tell you how and why particular inputs produce particular outputs; you need to consider the system as a whole in order to understand how it represents and processes information. Neural codes are like the bricks in a building, and the mental representations are like the architectural features that emerge from arranging bricks in certain ways.

We have just considered the basic methods, but researchers have cleverly extended and developed these methods as needed to address specific issues. Thus, in later chapters you will see additional methods, built on the basic ones we've just reviewed.

✔ **Comprehension Check:**

1. What are the major methods used to study mental activity?
2. What roles do studies of the brain play in revealing facts about mental activity?

5. OVERVIEW OF THE BOOK

Recall how we opened this chapter; the questions remain: how will you decide to apply for certain jobs, and how will you cope with the interviews? In what follows, we will look at the wide variety of mental activities you will need to land a job and perform it effectively.

You probably read or heard about the opportunity to apply for a job: perception is a necessary first step for many mental activities that are concerned with objects and situations in your environment. Chapter 2 focuses on perception; perceptual processing provides foundations for much of what comes thereafter by providing grist for the cognitive mill.

One result of processing information from the senses is that attention is shifted, allowing you to take in additional information of particular interest. Once you started the interview, you were probably alert for even the smallest evidence of heightened interest in the interviewer's face. And you probably chose to ignore any grumbling in your stomach or uncomfortable tugging of your clothing. Attention, discussed in Chapter 3, is the activity whereby some information processing is facilitated and other information processing is inhibited.

However, much mental activity does not focus on stimuli that are currently being perceived, but rather relies on previously stored representations of such stimuli. When you learned about the job, you interpreted that information in terms of what you already knew and what you remembered about similar jobs or related activities. Chapter 4 picks up where Chapter 3 leaves off, addressing how information is represented in long-term memory, the relatively permanent store of information in our brains. We store not only what we actually perceive, but also our interpretations and responses to stimuli.

How did relevant information come to be stored in long-term memory? Chapter 5 addresses how new information is stored in long-term memory and how information is later retrieved. If information could not be accessed, for all practical purposes it would not exist; information retrieval is a crucial component of virtually all forms of reasoning, language, and other mental activities.

Once retrieved, information is often stored and operated on in working memory, the contents of which are presumably in consciousness. If you had the experience of "turning over in your mind" the various pros and cons of taking a job, you were using working memory. Chapter 6 discusses working memory and addresses the question of how information stored there can be operated on, allowing you to draw inferences and solve problems.

What determines how you use working memory? Chapter 7 focuses on "executive processes," which not only control the course of activity in working memory but also direct the flow of information processing more generally. But this "CEO of the mind" isn't a little corporate boss nestled in your brain; rather, the brain has a system of processes that operates on input in an effort to produce output that will help you achieve your goals.

Goals—where do they come from? Emotional reactions are one source of our goals. You probably had a reaction of liking (or in some cases not liking) activities like those required in particular jobs (for example, you might enjoy writing and finding out what's going on, which makes you suspect that working for a newspaper might be for you). Chapter 8 addresses the most basic way in which we react to objects and events, namely, by experiencing emotion. Human beings are not cold, calculating computers; we have emotional reactions to most stimuli, and these emotional reactions affect much of how we subsequently process information.

How will you finally decide to accept a particular job? Why will you choose it over possible alternative jobs? Part of what executive processes must do is organize other processes that make decisions. Chapter 9 focuses on these mechanisms.

Often obstacles prevent the immediate achievement of a goal; perhaps in order to apply for a particular job you needed to take specific courses as a student—but taking these courses presented a conflict with some other activity, so you had to shift your schedule around. Your decision making ("I'm going to take this course") may have been to some extent based on problem solving ("If I take this course, how can I persuade my roommate to switch our weekly review sessions?"). The obstacle poses a problem to be solved; Chapter 10 reviews what researchers have learned about problem solving.

After (or accompanying) all this mental activity, you actually did something. In Chapter 11 we consider how you plan and anticipate the consequences of acting on a plan, such as what you did when you thought about how best to interact with the interviewer while you were waiting out in the hallway. More than that, we consider how you learn new ways to behave, through imitation, and how you use knowledge about movements to organize what you see and how you think.

When you actually have an interview, you of course must listen and speak—which are arguably the most complex of all human mental activities. Chapter 12 reviews the key theories and findings about language, a phenomenon that draws on virtually all other aspects of cognition.

Let's begin.

Revisit and Reflect

1. *How did the field of cognitive psychology arise?*

   Cognitive psychology began as a science in 1879, in the laboratory of Wilhelm Wundt in Germany. The early methodologies were flawed, however (in part because of an overemphasis on the use of introspection), which eventually led the behaviorists to reject the study of the mind altogether. The behaviorists focused solely on immediately observable events, but this approach proved too limiting. It failed to lend insight into many important phenomena, such as language and perception, and could not characterize the mechanisms that actually produce behavior. The cognitive revolution occurred when the computer provided new ways to conceptualize mental activity, and new methodologies provided new ways to test theories of mental activity. These advances allowed scientists to go beyond stimuli, responses and consequences of responses, and led them to begin to understand the mechanisms responsible not only for behavior, but for perception, language, and cognition in general.

Think Critically

- What knowledge about mental activity could help you do better in this course?
- Would it be useful to know how to improve your memory? What about your decision-making abilities?
- In what ways does integrating the study of the brain into the study of the mind affect what you might be able to do with knowledge about the mind?
- In what ways could you use such information to test the efficacy of new drugs that are supposed to improve cognitive processing?

2. *What is a scientific theory of cognition, and what roles does knowledge about the brain play in such theories?*

Theories of cognition have often been likened to descriptions of software, as opposed to the hardware of the computer itself. This is an oversimplification. Theories of cognition are cast at a specific level of analysis, namely, in terms of how the brain functions to process information. You cannot replace a theory of cognition with a theory of neural activity any more than you can replace a description of a building's architecture with one of its constituent bricks and boards.

A processing system can be understood in terms of its representations and processes; representations serve to store information, and processes interpret or transform stored information. The traditional cognitive psychology was grounded entirely in inferences drawn from studies of behavior. These methods could not distinguish between many alternative theories, in part because of structure–process trade-offs. Considering facts about the brain not only provides additional constraints, which facilitates theorizing, but also provides additional reasons to develop theories in specific ways. Moreover, by grounding theories in the brain, a set of new and powerful methods becomes appropriate for evaluating such theories.

Think Critically

- Do you think a computer could ever be programmed to have a "mind"? Why or why not? If your answer is no, what do you think would be missing?
- Say we could program a computer to mimic your thinking processes. Would you have any use for such a computer? Could it be more than a fancy telephone answering machine?
- Would you be comfortable allowing such a computer program to choose your job interviews for you? Which sorts of things would you be most reluctant to delegate to that program? Why?

3. *What are the major structures of the brain, and what roles do they play in our skills and abilities?*

The central nervous system (CNS) consists of the brain and spinal cord, and the peripheral nervous system (PNS) consists of the skeletal nervous system and the autonomic nervous system (ANS). The ANS is involved in the fight-or-flight-response, preparing an animal to cope with an emergency and then allowing it to recover from that special emergency-readiness state when the emergency has passed. The cerebral cortex is the outer covering of the brain, which contains most of the cell bodies of neurons in the brain; most mental activity relies on the cerebral cortex. The brain is divided into two cerebral hemispheres, and each of those is divided into four major parts, or lobes: the occipital, the temporal, the parietal, and the frontal lobes. Numerous subcortical structures work together with the cortex. For example, some of these structures (such as the hippocampus) are involved in storing new memories, others (such as the thalamus) are involved in attention, and others (such as the amygdala) are involved in emotion, and yet others are involved in motor control (such as the cerebellum and basal ganglia). These structures have rich and varied roles, as we shall see in later chapters.

Think Critically

- The ancient Greeks believed that the heart—not the head—was the site of mental processes. What difference does it make that they were wrong?
- Say there is a new drug that will protect one part of your brain from stroke, but only a single part. Which part would you choose to preserve above all the others?
- What role, if any, would that part of your brain play in helping you in job interviews? Why?

4. *What methods are used to study cognition?*

The strongest evidence for a theory arises when numerous different methods provide support for it; such converging evidence covers potential pitfalls with any one method. A main goal of research on the nature of mental activity is to document distinctions proposed by theories. The method of dissociation is often used to support the claim that different representations or processes exist, whereas the method of association is used to implicate a specific representation or process in two or more tasks. Correlational neural methods, such as the event-related potential (ERP), positron emission tomography (PET), and functional magnetic resonance imaging (fMRI), assess the brain activity that accompanies the performance of specific tasks. Causal neural methods—such as studying the deficits of patients with brain damage and impairments following transcranial magnetic stimulation (TMS)—establish that a specific brain area is at least partially responsible for a particular cognitive function. Finally, modeling can not only document that a set of principles or mechanisms can in fact explain data, but also can make new predictions. Neural-network models appear to capture some key characteristics of how the brain operates and are proving a promising way to explain research findings and generate new predictions. However, such models are only approximations, and they do not accurately reflect exactly how the brain works.

Think Critically

- Say that neuroimaging machines drop way, way down in price so that you can afford one. And say that they become small, portable, and very easy to use, so you can put on a helmet and watch the activity in your own brain as it occurs. Would this be useful for you? For example, what if you could use it to determine when you've memorized material so well you will know it for the exam in two days?
- Would you want such a machine?
- Are there any drawbacks you can think of to having small, portable, inexpensive, easily obtainable brain-scanning machines?

Perception

Learning Objectives

Take a dream. You are walking through the woods. In a clearing you come upon a marble statue of a human figure. There is an inscription on the pedestal: "Behold one possessed of mind without idea, form without sensation." You continue walking. Evening comes on, and the woods are full of sounds and shadows. Suddenly, to your right, you see a hulking form. You leap back, ready to run—is this a bear? No, there is no danger; the "bear" is only a bush. The night grows darker. The path is rising now, and at the top of a dimly outlined hill, you can see the lights of a château. By the time you reach it and take shelter, all is dark outside, and from your curtained room inside you have no idea what lies outside the walls. Morning comes, the curtains are thrown back, you see. . . .

These imaginary experiences, and their resolution, illustrate the essential problems of perception and its relation to cognition. This chapter is a discussion of what perception is and how it works. We specifically address six questions:

1. What is perception and why is it a difficult ability to understand?
2. What general principles help us to understand perception?
3. How do we put together parts to recognize objects and events?
4. How do we recognize objects and events?
5. How does our knowledge affect our perception?
6. Finally, how do our brains put together the many and varied cues we use to perceive?

1. WHAT IT MEANS TO PERCEIVE

The "sculptor" of the mysterious statue was the French philosopher Etienne Bonnot de Condillac (1715–1780), who created it in his *Treatise on Sensations* (1754a). The statue, he imagined, had in working order what we would call the "mental hardware" and "software" of a normal human being, but no senses. Condillac believed that such a being would have no mental life, that no ideas were possible in the absence of sensation.

Pursuing his thought experiment, he imagined opening up the nose of the statue so that it could now smell. "If we offer the statue a rose," wrote Condillac, "it will be, in its relation to us, a statue which smells a rose; but, in relationship to itself, it will be merely the scent of the flower." That is, Condillac thought that if the statue had only a single sensation, then that sensation would be the whole content of its mind.

Even if we adopt a position less absolute than Condillac's, we can agree that the mental life of an organism without senses would be unimaginably different from the mental life we experience. Sensation and perception provide the raw material for cognition, certainly, but this assessment underplays their role. Our perceptions are not a simple registration of sensory stimuli. Sophisticated cognitive processes begin to work on this material almost immediately, producing the brain's interpretation of the external world as incoming stimuli are analyzed, and existing knowledge guides these dynamic processes.

The second and third parts of your dream are illustrations that make clear why perception is much more than the straightforward registration of sensory stimuli. In your second dream experience, the menacing shape in the forest seems familiar but only faintly so. This is because the images appear outside their original context of Shakespeare's *A Midsummer Night's Dream*: "In the night," says Theseus, Duke of Athens, "imagining some fear, how easy is a bush supposed a bear." Shakespeare understood that sensory stimuli typically are *ambiguous*, open to multiple interpretations; this is the first problem of perception.

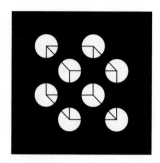

FIGURE 2–1   Illusion: what do you see?

The figure has eight white circles, and in each circle there are three black lines. There are no lines between the circles; there is no cube. Most people, however, see a cube, either floating in front of a black sheet with white circles, or behind a black sheet with eight holes. What you perceive is more than just what you sense of the image properties.

What do you see in Figure 2–1? Probably a cube. Does it seem to be floating in front of a black background with white dots on it? Or, rather, to be lying behind a black sheet with holes punched into it? As to the cube itself, is the surface that seems closest to you angled up and to the left or angled down and to the right? *Why see a cube at all?* The image, of course, is actually flat on the page. You might swear that you can see the lines of the cube crossing the black region, but they are not present in the image. There are only eight carefully positioned white dots, each containing a carefully positioned set of three line segments. Nonetheless we see the cube, even though the image doesn't have all the properties of a real cube, even one drawn on a two-dimensional surface, but only a sparse subset of those properties. We fill in the missing pieces and perceive more than is actually there. So the first problem is that *sensory input does not contain enough information to explain our perception.* When you looked at and interpreted Figure 2–1, for example, you had to infer an object from mere hints.

In the last part of your dream, you get out of bed, walk to the window, and throw open the heavy curtains. In an instant, you are exposed to a panorama of mountains, fields, houses, towns. What do you *perceive*? Condillac thought you would see only a patchwork of colored regions, an experience full of sensations but without the organization that makes perception (1754b). In fact, we know that you could understand the gist of the scene after it had been exposed to your visual sense for only a small fraction of a second: studies have shown that you can look at pictures on a computer screen at a rate of eight per second, monitor that stream, and find, for example, the picnic scene in the series (Potter & Levy, 1969) or even the scene in a series that does not contain an animal (Intraub, 1980). Still, Condillac was right in noting a problem: this second problem is that the world presents us with *too much sensory input to include into our coherent perceptions at any single given moment.*

Figure 2–2 is a scene of a beautiful summer afternoon in a park with lots going on. The image is not difficult, but it has many elements: although you can see and understand it, you cannot fully process it in one rapid step. Quick—is there a dog in it? Because it is impossible to process everything in the image at one go, you may not

FIGURE 2–2   What's in the picture?

Is there more than one dog present? How do you know? You probably moved your eyes to fixate on the different objects in the scene until you spotted the dogs.

(Georges Seurat, "A Sunday Afternoon on the Island of La Grande Jatte". 1884–86. Oil on Canvas. 6'9½" × 10'1¼" (2.07 × 3.08 m). Helen Birch Bartlett Memorial Collection. Photograph © 2005, The Art Institute of Chicago. All rights reserved.)

know whether there is a dog until you have searched for it. Moving your eyes over the image, you pause at different parts of it and fixate your gaze, bringing the center of the retina, the region with sharpest vision, over the area you wish to examine. There's a dog! Even though we can see over a large region at one time, we can see relatively fine detail only in a small region—at the point of fixation. Searching is one way to deal with the excess of input.

Much information, for example information about the precise differences in the intensity of light at each point in space, is thrown away at the very start of the journey from sensation to understanding. One of the dogs on Grand Jatte, however, is not small. You certainly can see it without moving your eyes from the center of the image. But it is very likely that you could not determine whether there is a dog in the painting until you selected that portion of it for further consideration. Our ability to engage in *selective attention* allows us to choose part of the current sensory input for further processing at the expense of other aspects of that input; we will consider the nature of attention in detail in Chapter 3.

The two problems of perception in relation to the sensory world, then, are "not enough" and "too much." In both cases, cognitive mechanisms are necessary to provide the means to interpret and understand the material our senses bring to us.

Comprehension Check:

1. Why is perception important for cognition?
2. What are the two main problems that make perception difficult?

2. HOW IT WORKS: THE CASE OF VISUAL PERCEPTION

The goal of perception is to take in information about the world and make sense of it. Condillac's statue tells us that our mental life depends on meeting this goal. Theseus's bear reminds us that the information available to us may be ambiguous and therefore insufficient for the determinative interpretation that only cognitive processes and background knowledge can make. The view from Condillac's château reveals that there is too much information for us to process and we need to select.

An analogous action of selection needs to be made right now: all our senses are vitally important and no sense acts in isolation from the others. For example, consider the interplay of vision, hearing, taste, smell, and touch in your most recent dining experience. Sadly, all that richness cannot be adequately captured in a single chapter, so, sacrificing breadth for a modicum of depth, we will select vision to discuss and we will further select a restricted set of examples within the visual domain.

Vision, like hearing, is a distance sense, evolved to sense objects without direct contact. It can tell us *what* is out there and *where* it is. If we think of humans and other creatures as organisms that must interact with the world, we see that our senses also provide something further: a nudge toward *action*. What is out there, where is it, what can I do about it? (Oh, look, a lovely low-hanging apple—I'll pick it!) Visual perception takes in information about the properties and locations of objects so that we can make sense of and interact with our surroundings.

2.1. The Structure of the Visual System

The main visual pathways in the brain can be thought of as an intricate wiring pattern that links a hierarchy of brain areas (Figure 2–3). Starting at the bottom, the pattern of light intensity, edges, and other features in the visual scene forms an image on the *retina*, the layer of cells that respond to light, called *photoreceptors*, and nerve cells at the back of each eye. There light is converted into electrochemical signals, which are transmitted to the brain via the *optic nerves* (one from each eye); each optic nerve is a bundle of the long axon fibers of the *ganglion cells* in the retina. The axons make contact with the neurons of the *lateral geniculate nucleus* (LGN) in the thalamus, a structure lying under the surface of the brain. From there, axons of LGN neurons send signals up to the primary visual cortex (which is also called *V1* for "visual area 1," or "striate cortex" because when stained it has the appearance of a stripe across it that can be seen with a microscope). Output from the striate cortex feeds a host of visual areas (V2, V3, V4, and others) as well as areas that are not exclusively visual in function.

Beyond the primary visual cortex, two main pathways can be identified. A dorsal pathway reaches up into the parietal lobes and is important in processing information about where items are located and how they might be acted on, guiding

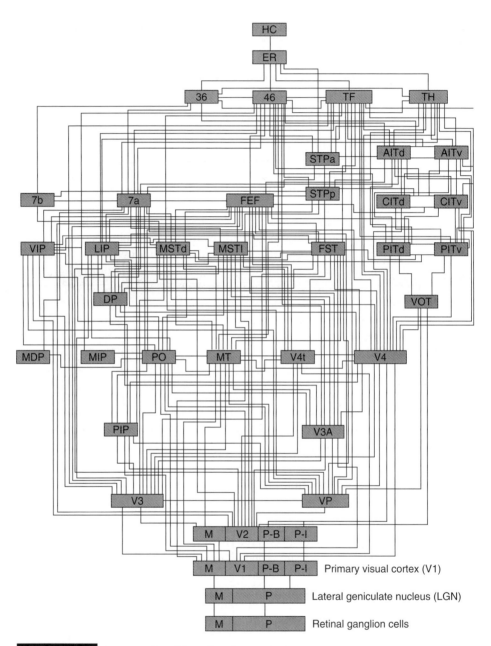

FIGURE 2–3 Structural and functional complexity

A "wiring diagram" of the visual system, showing connections among brain areas. Note that there are two types of retinal ganglion cells (magnocellular, abbreviated *M*, and parvocellular, abbreviated *P*); these cells project axons to different portions of areas V1 and V2.)

(Felleman, D. J. & Van Essen, D. C. (1991). Distributed hierarchical processing in the primate cerebral cortex. *Cerebral Cortex, 1,* 1—47 (Fig. 4 on p. 30). Reprinted with permission of Oxford University Press.)

movements such as grasping. A ventral pathway reaches down into the temporal lobes; this pathway processes information that leads to the recognition and identification of objects. This two-pathways story is valid, but as Figure 2–3 shows, it is a great simplification of an extremely complicated network.

2.2. Top-Down and Bottom-Up Processing

The daunting complexity of the visual system is functional as well as structural, as is shown in Figure 2–3. The pathways and their many ramifications are not one-way streets. Most visual areas that send output to another area also receive input from that area; that is, they have *reciprocal connections*—for example, LGN provides input to V1 and V1 provides other input to LGN. This dynamic arrangement reflects an important principle of visual perception: visual perception—in fact, all perception—is the product of bottom-up and top-down processes. *Bottom-up processes* are driven by sensory information from the physical world. *Top-down processes* actively seek and extract sensory information and are driven by our knowledge, beliefs, expectations, and goals. Almost every act of perception involves both bottom-up and top-down processing.

One way to experience the distinction consciously is to slow part of the top-down contribution. Look at Figure 2–4. There is certainly something there to be seen: bottom-up processes show you lines and define regions. But if you play with the image mentally and consider what the regions might signify, you can feel a top-down contribution at work. The image could be . . . a bear climbing up the other side of a tree! Whether or not you came up with this solution yourself, your appreciation of it depends on top-down knowledge: your knowledge of what a tree and a bear's paws look like, your knowledge of how bears climb trees. This kind of knowledge not only organizes what you see, but also can even modulate the processes that created the representations of the lines and regions.

Another example that points to the distinction between bottom-up and top-down processing and the relationship between them can be seen in visual search tasks. If you're told to find the target in Figure 2–5a, you have no problem. Bottom-

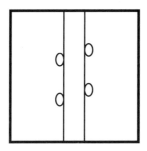

FIGURE 2–4 **What's this?**

The picture has two vertical lines and four ovals—yet you can see more. See the text for details.

(From Droodles—The Classic Collection by Roger Price. Copyright © 2000 by Tallfellow Press, Inc. Reprinted with permission. www.tallfellow.com.)

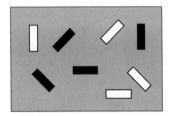

(a) Bottom-up processing is sufficient.   (b) Top-down processing is needed.

FIGURE 2–5 **Displays for visual search tasks**

Each display has one item that is the target. In (a), the target is obvious: bottom-up processing of the attributes of each object tells you that one is very different from the rest. In (b), bottom-up processing doesn't help, because all the items differ. Top-down guidance of your attention to the target occurs after you are told that the target is a black, horizontal line.

up processing quickly identifies the white star as the stand-out. But bottom-up processing isn't enough to guide you to the target in Figure 2–5b. There you see a number of items that differ in various ways—in shape, color, orientation. To find the target you need information—"the target is the horizontal black bar"—and thus top-down processing. Now you have the means to search for the target.

Both of these examples demonstrate that perceptions (this is a bear, this is a target) are *interpretations* of what we see, representations produced by the interaction of bottom-up and top-down processing.

2.3. Learning to See

Our interpretations of the world around us are determined by the interaction of two things: (1) the biological structure of our brains and (2) experience, which modifies that structure. The visual system in newborn infants is nearly fully developed at birth, and most of the major structural changes are complete in the first year of life (Huttenlocher, 1993, 2002). Babies open their eyes almost immediately after birth and soon they begin to look around, moving their eyes to investigate their surroundings and to fixate on objects of interest. Typically fixations last about half a second, so babies have on the order of 10 million glimpses of the world in their first year of life. That's an enormous amount of information. A baby may see a parent's face, the surrounding crib, a nursing bottle many thousand times, often from different viewpoints, at different times of day, and in different contexts. As the lingering memory of each occurrence combines with each new instance, the cascade of information somehow accumulates to form lasting mental representations of the people, places, and things in the environment. These representations form the basis for the subsequent recognition of objects.

Research on the development of visual perception in newborn animals has shown that the characteristics of the infant's environment at particular times strongly influence some of the capabilities of the adult. The early stages of life include biologically determined critical periods, periods during which the animal must develop particular responses. If exposure to the natural environment is limited during the critical period for a particular response, the animal will fail to develop that ability properly, even with normal exposure during adulthood. For example, a kitten reared with a patch over one eye for 6 months may grow into a cat with two normal eyes, but with impairments in the perception of depth that depends on integrating information from both eyes (Wiesel & Hubel, 1963). In such a cat, a greater area of visual cortex is devoted to analyzing input from the unpatched eye than the patched eye. Interestingly, a kitten with patches over both eyes during the same period will not have deficits in the perception of depth as an adult and will have more balanced cortical organization (Wiesel & Hubel, 1965). Different aspects of sensory processing have different critical periods.

In addition, different sources and different modalities of sensory input seem to compete for representation in cortex (Le Vay et al., 1980). If one channel, such as input from one eye, is more active than another, cortical resources are redeployed in that direction and, once assigned in infancy, such resources are not easily modified in adulthood. Competition for neural representation has been demonstrated throughout the brain and for many different abilities: there is competition between auditory and visual perception (Cynader, 1979; Gyllensten et al., 1966); competition to register sensation from different fingers (Jenkins et al., 1990; Merzenich & Kaas, 1982); and competition between different languages in bilingual people (Neville & Bavelier, 1998).

Because it is known that experience alters the course of visual development, programs have been developed for stimulating the fetus with lights and sounds not normally present in the womb in an attempt to speed or enhance development. Normal prenatal stimulation, such as the sound of the mother's voice, can lead to better perception in infants. However, our knowledge in this area is far from complete, and it is possible that abnormal stimulation can lead to impoverished rather than superior development. Indeed, some studies have shown that some prenatal stimulation can impair normal perceptual development later in life (Lickliter, 2000). Although we know that our environment shapes the brain structures that support our capacity for normal cognition, we do not yet know how to control that process.

Comprehension Check:

1. In what ways is the brain structured like a hierarchy? In what ways is it not?
2. What is the difference between bottom-up and top-down processing?
3. How does visual experience influence what we see?

3. BUILDING FROM THE BOTTOM UP: FROM FEATURES TO OBJECTS

Condillac's statue had all the machinery for cognition but no sensory input, so its brain never used its tremendous capability for representation and processing of the physical world. The brain's ingenious techniques for combining perceived features, so that we can understand the complexity surrounding us by resolving it into objects familiar and unfamiliar, lay idle and useless. If the statue's eyes were open to the world, they would let in a flood of information through neural pathways, and a re-markable amount of sophisticated analysis would be performed to detect important aspects of the environment. And we, who have access to the world through our senses, have very busy brains. In the modality of vision, starting from the bottom up, let's discuss what happens.

3.1. Processing Features, the Building Blocks of Perception

Visual features include spots and edges, colors and shapes, movements and textures. These are all attributes that are not in themselves objects, but in combination they can define the objects we see. They are the building blocks of perception.

In the eyes, photoreceptor cells in the retina convert light energy (*photons*) reflected from the various objects in the physical world into an electrochemical sig-nal that can travel through the nervous system. The more light, the more signal. Varying intensities of light fall on the array of photoreceptors, so the input at any given moment might be conceived of as a set of numbers, each number equivalent to an intensity of light, one number per photoreceptor, such as the array of numbers shown in Figure 2–6. The task of the bottom-up processes in the visual system is to extract from the physical equivalent of this mass of numbers the features that will permit the subsequent processes to figure out what is out there in the world.

3.1.1. Spots and Edges

We can see progress toward this goal of feature extraction if we look at a *ganglion cell,* one of those neurons in the retina whose axon fibers form the optic nerve. Each ganglion cell is connected, through a series of other cells, to a collection of photore-ceptors that are neighbors to each other. This means that the ganglion cell will re-spond only to light that lands on those receptors and, thus, to light in one specific region in the visual field, the portion of the world that is visible at the present mo-ment. Look at Figure 2–7. There is a spot of light out in the world, the stimulus. The receptors, in this example, respond with 100 units of signal where the light is bright and just 10 where the light is dimmer. Our ganglion cell gets input from the recep-tors that lie in its receptive field, the region shown in color at the bottom of the fig-ure. In vision, the receptive field of a cell is the area of the visual field in which a stimulus will affect the activity of the cell. If we were talking about a cell that responds to touch, the receptive field would be a patch of skin.

Most important, the connections from photoreceptors to ganglion cell are not all the same. Light in some portions of the receptive field *excites* the cell, that is, makes it more active. Light elsewhere *inhibits* the cell, making it less active. Specif-ically, the wiring is arranged so that input in the central zone (white) excites the ganglion cell, whereas input in the surrounding region (gray) inhibits the cell. Since we have arranged for the spot of light to fall on that excitatory central portion, this ganglion cell will be quite strongly excited. If the center region was stimulated by a gray area, the cell would not be very excited. And if the whole field were 100 units bright, *the cell would not be very excited either,* because the strong excitation of the

732	579	587	72	781	89	582	732	579	587	72	781	89	582
513	472	456	554	469	137	354	513	472	456	554	469	137	354
380	922	848	806	18	210	559	380	922	848	806	18	210	559
964	423	278	549	10	122	867	964	423	278	549	10	122	867
336	338	438	576	419	698	786	336	338	438	576	419	698	786
578	937	649	585	97	210	561	578	937	649	585	97	210	561
433	959	124	949	563	204	26	433	959	124	949	563	204	26
979	333	813	643	872	547	762	979	333	813	643	872	547	762
256	712	203	56	185	86	667	256	712	203	56	185	86	667
313	499	254	82	307	763	285	313	499	254	82	307	763	285
142	521	377	22	16	970	383	142	521	377	22	16	970	383
93	875	232	346	509	852	423	93	875	232	346	509	852	423
311	435	477	319	243	55	205	311	435	477	319	243	55	205
251	544	790	650	888	280	342	251	544	790	650	888	280	342
140	805	494	549	5	487	756	140	805	494	549	5	487	756
984	31	55	525	655	394	929	984	31	55	525	655	394	929
489	785	801	860	429	941	935	489	785	801	860	429	941	935
555	999	108	445	301	429	379	555	999	108	445	301	429	379
861	123	887	760	473	919	41	861	123	887	760	473	919	41
869	418	277	546	33	920	373	869	418	277	546	33	920	373
305	20	497	848	531	638	497	305	20	497	848	531	638	497
730	626	541	885	509	768	647	730	626	541	885	509	768	647
180	212	913	867	747	559	848	180	212	913	867	747	559	848
557	191	92	549	638	757	525	557	191	92	549	638	757	525
616	162	664	954	330	139	327	616	162	664	954	330	139	327

FIGURE 2–6 Luminance levels for each point in space in a particular scene

Values like these might be generated by measuring the activity of an array of photoreceptors in the eye. But what is the eye seeing? Much more analysis is necessary.

center would be offset by strong inhibition from the surround. So this cell is maximally excited when a bright spot of the size of that central region falls on the central region.

Something interesting happens if a collection of photoreceptors organized into these *center–surround* receptive fields receives input across an edge in the image in the visual scene, such as the border between light and dark rectangles in Figure 2–8. Assume that maximum stimulation of the center of each receptive field produces 10 units of excitation and stimulation of the surround produces 5 units of inhibition. A spot falling just on the center would produce 10 units of response. A

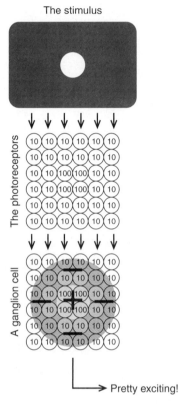

The stimulus

The photoreceptors

A ganglion cell

Pretty exciting!

FIGURE 2–7   **Stages of analysis to the retinal ganglion cell**

Top: A simple visual scene has a white dot on a dark background, the stimulus. *Middle:* An array of photoreceptors detects light at each portion of the scene and reports the amount; 10 for the dark and 100 for the light parts (arbitrary units). *Bottom:* A ganglion cell takes inputs from the photoreceptors in its receptive field, according to the center–surround rule shown by the "–" and "+" areas. Signals in the inhibitory area ("–") are subtracted from signals in the facilitatory area ("+"). For this particular example, facilitation adds up to 400 units and inhibition subtracts only about 200 units, so the ganglion cell finds this stimulus pretty exciting.

bright field, filling the whole receptive field (as is happening on the left in Figure 2–8) produces only 5 units; this is the light rectangle. The area on the right is dark; say that absolutely no light is falling here, and the value is 0. Now look what happens at the edge between the light and dark areas. Here one receptive field is mostly on the light side, another mostly on the dark side. When the center is on the bright side and a bit of the surround is in darkness, the response goes up, perhaps to 7 units. When the center is on the dark side and only a bit of the surround is on the bright side, the response could go down to a "darker-than-dark" level, quantified here as −2. In this way, the structure and arrangement of photoreceptors can serve to enhance the contrast at edges.

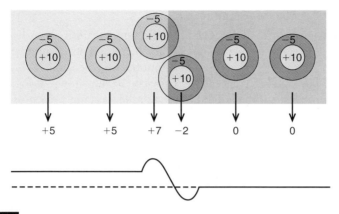

How we detect edges

Ganglion cell receptive fields (large, outer circles) with +10 excitatory regions and −5 inhibitory regions are shown over a visual display of a light rectangle next to a dark rectangle. Interesting responses happen at the edge between the two rectangles. The graph at the bottom of the figure plots the amount of response over the different regions of the display.

Figure 2–8 analyzes the effect; Figure 2–9 demonstrates it. The gray areas (the bars, or rectangles) are in fact each uniform, but each lighter bar *appears* a bit lighter on the right side, where it abuts a darker bar, and each darker bar *appears* a bit darker on the corresponding left side. This phenomenon was described by the Austrian physicist Ernst Mach in the mid-nineteenth century (Mach, 1865; Ratliff, 1965), and bars like those in Figure 2–9 are called *Mach bands*. This perceptual phenomenon is predicted by responses of ganglion cell neurons. The center–surround organization of ganglion cells is well designed to pick out edges in the visual environment.

A demonstration of Mach bands

Six uniform rectangles are shown abutting one another, ordered from lightest to darkest. Even though the level of gray in each rectangle is uniform, it looks as if each one is a bit lighter on its right edge than its left edge and darker on its left edge. These edge effects come from the neighboring rectangle, and are predicted from the responses of ganglion cell neurons shown in Figure 2–8.

3.1.2. Throwing Away Information

The visual system seems to be designed to collect information about features, such as spots and edges, and not to spend unnecessary energy on nearly uniform areas where nothing much is happening. This bias is demonstrated by the Craik–O'Brien–Cornsweet illusion (Cornsweet, 1970; Craik, 1940; O'Brien, 1958), shown in Figure 2–10. Part (a) of the figure appears to be a lighter and a darker rectangle, each of them shading from darker to lighter. But if we cover the edge at the center between the two rectangles, as in part (b), we see that most of the areas of the two rectangles is the same gray level. The visual system found the light–dark edge at the center and, in effect, made the not unreasonable assumption that the image was lighter on the light side of the edge than on the darker side. Because edge information is important for defining the shape of objects and providing cues for where to direct action, it makes sense that the visual system is tuned to pick out edges. Throwing away information about the intensity of lightness at every point in space—information that would have enabled you to see that the extreme left and right parts of the figure are the same shade of gray—demonstrates that visual perception efficiently extracts visual features by ignoring some data.

The human visual system processes its input in great detail, but not in every part of the visual field. Here again information is thrown away. For example, when you read you point your eyes at word after word, fixating at a succession of points on the page. When you do that, the image of the word falls on the *fovea*, a part of the retina that is served by many ganglion cells with tiny receptive fields, each sometimes so small that its entire center region takes input from only a single photoreceptor. The result is that this area is capable of high resolution, and fine details (like the distinguishing squiggles of letters and numbers) can be perceived. Farther out from the point of fixation, the receptive fields get bigger and bigger, so that hundreds of

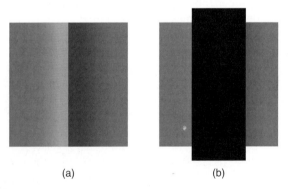

(a)   (b)

FIGURE 2–10   The Craik-Cornsweet-O'Brien illusion

(a) A gray rectangle is shown with a special edge in the middle. The rectangle seems to be divided with a lighter region on the left and darker region on the right. If you look closely, you will see that actually the two regions are not uniform. There is a gradual transition in each side, producing a sharp change from light to dark in the middle. (b) This is the same figure as in (a), but with the middle region covered by a black rectangle. Now you can see that the gray regions are actually the same. Try putting your finger over the middle of (a) to reveal the illusion.

receptors may be lumped together into a single receptive-field center. These big receptive fields cannot process fine detail and, as a result, neither can you in those portions of the field. Look at the letter "A" in the display below:

A   B   C   D   E   F   G   H   I   J

How far up the alphabet can you read without moving your gaze from the "A"? If you say you can get beyond "E" or "F," you're probably cheating. Why throw away all this information? Because it would be wasted: your brain simply could not process the whole image at the detailed resolution available at the fovea.

3.1.3. Neural Processing of Features

The route to the brain from the ganglion cells is via the optic nerves, which meet just before entering the brain to form the *optic chiasm,* so called from the shape of the Greek letter "χ," or chi. Here some of the fibers from each optic nerve cross to the opposite hemisphere of the brain, sending information from the left side of each eye's visual field to the right hemisphere and information from the right sides to the left hemisphere. Various pathways carry the information to the lateral geniculate nucleus and thence to the primary visual cortex.

In the primary visual cortex, the extent of the whole visual field is laid out across the surface of the cortex. Cells in primary visual cortex (V1), striate cortex, respond to variations in basic features such as orientation, motion, and color. Output from V1 via the dorsal or ventral pathway feeds a collection of visual areas known collectively as extrastriate cortex (and individually as V2, V3, V4, and so on). Extrastriate cortex contains areas whose cells appear to be specialized for the further processing of these basic features and of more elaborate representations, such as of faces.

Neurons are organized functionally in depth as well as along the surface of cortex. The visual cortex is divided up into *hypercolumns,* chunks of brain with a surface area about 1 millimeter by 2 millimeters and a thickness of about 4 millimeters. All the cells in a hypercolumn will be activated by stimuli in one small part of the visual field. Cells in the next hypercolumn will respond to input from a neighboring portion of visual space. Many more hypercolumns are devoted to the detailed processing of input to the fovea than to the cruder processing of more peripheral parts of the visual field. Within a hypercolumn there is further organization. Here cells are ordered by their sensitivity to specific aspects of the visual feature, such as edges at a specific orientation. Thus, if one cell within a hypercolumn sensitive to edge orientation responds the most to vertical lines, the next cell over will respond most to lines tilted a bit off vertical, and the next to those even a bit more tilted.

It is worth examining the response to orientation a little more closely to appreciate the fine discrimination of neural processing. We are very sensitive to variation in orientation. Under good viewing conditions (with good lighting and nothing blocking the view), we can easily tell the difference between a vertical line and a line tilted 1 degree off the vertical. Does this mean that each hypercolumn needs 180 or more precisely tuned, orientation-detecting neurons, at least one for each degree of tilt from vertical through horizontal (at 90 degrees) and continuing the tilt further to vertical again at 180 degrees? (Think of the tilt of the second hand on a clock dial as it sweeps from 0 to 30 seconds.) No, the system appears to work differently. Individual neurons respond to a fairly broad range of orientation. A neuron might respond best to lines tilted 15 degrees to the left of vertical *and also* respond to vertical lines and lines tilted 30 degrees. Precise assessments of orientation are made by comparing activity across a *population* of neurons. Thus, simplifying for the sake of argument, if some neurons are optimally tuned for tilt 15 degrees to the left and others for the same amount of tilt to the right, a line perceived as vertical would be one that stimulates both these populations of neurons equally.

How do we know this is how it works? One way to demonstrate the differential orientation tuning of neurons is to fixate your gaze on a pattern of lines that have the same tilt, which soon will tire out some of the neurons. Suppose that "vertical" is defined as equal output from neurons sensitive to left and to right tilt; further, suppose we tire out the right-tilt neurons. Now a line that is actually vertical appears to be tilted to the left. The line, which would normally produce equal activity in the left- and the right-sensing neurons, produces more activity in the left-sensing neurons because the right-sensing ones have been fatigued. The comparison of left and right will be biased to the left, resulting in the perception of a tilted line. This bias in perceiving orientation is known as the **tilt aftereffect** (Figure 2–11)—try it yourself. Similar effects occur in color, size, and (most dramatically) direction of motion. In all cases, the principle is the same: the value of a particular feature is determined by comparison between two or more sets of neurons—with different sensitivities—

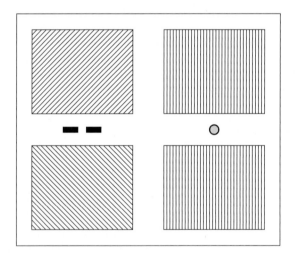

FIGURE 2–11   The tilt aftereffect

First, notice that the patterns on the right are both identical and vertical. Now, adapt your visual neurons to the patterns at the left by fixating on each of the black bars between the two patterns. Slowly go back and forth between these two bars 20 times. Immediately thereafter, move your eyes to the circle between the two patterns on the right. Notice that the patterns no longer look perfectly vertical, but seem to tilt. The illusory tilt you see is in the opposite direction of the tilt that you adapted to, so the top will look tilted to the left and the bottom will look tilted to the right.

responding to that stimulus. If you change the relative responsiveness of the sets of neurons that are being compared, you change the perception of the feature.

Motion is detected in area V5 (also known as MT, for "middle temporal" visual area), an area on the lateral sides of the extrastriate cortex (Dubner & Zeki, 1971). Cells in this area respond to an object moving in a particular direction, such as up or down, or perhaps moving toward or away from the observer. How is it known that this particular brain area is crucial for representing and processing motion in the human brain? Transcranial magnetic stimulation (TMS, see Chapter 1) of this area can temporarily prevent people from seeing motion or induce them to see motion that does not occur (Beckers & Homberg, 1992; Beckers & Zeki, 1995; Cowey & Walsh, 2000). In addition, damage to this area results in akinetopsia, or motion blindness—the loss of the ability to see objects move (Zihl et al., 1983). Those affected report that they perceive a collection of still images. They have difficulty making judgments about moving things: When will that moving car pass me? When do I stop pouring water into the glass?

Other TMS studies have found a specialized region for color perception. Moreover, brain damage to this specific part of the extrastriate cortex, in V4, cause achromatopsia, or cortical color blindness (Zeki, 1990). All color vision is lost and the world appears in shades of gray. And in achromatopsia, unlike as in blindness caused by damage to the eyes or optic nerve, even memory of color is gone.

The existence of these specialized areas suggests that perception starts by breaking down the visual scene into features that are processed separately.

3.2. Putting It Together: What Counts, What Doesn't

Earlier, we noted that the world does not look like a collection of brightness values (as in Figure 2–6). Nor does it look like a collection of visual properties such as orientation, motion, and so forth. We see a world of objects and surfaces. Those perceived objects and surfaces represent our best guesses about the meaning of the particular visual properties that we are seeing right now. A large set of rules governs the complex process by which we infer the contents of the visual world. In the next sections we will offer a few illustrative examples.

3.2.1. Grouping Principles

To begin, the system must determine which features go together (Gerlach et al., 2005). What features are part of the same object or surface? In Germany in the early twentieth century, researchers known collectively as the Gestalt psychologists (*Gestalt* is the German for "form" or "shape") began to uncover some of the grouping principles that guide the visual system and produce our perception of what goes with what. Some of these are shown in Figure 2–12. Figure 2–12a is a 4 × 4 set of identical, evenly spaced dots. In Figure 2–12b, the effect of *proximity*, one of the most basic of the grouping principles, groups those dots into rows because, all else being equal, things that are closer to one another are more likely to grouped together —that is, perceived as a whole—than things that are farther apart (Chen & Wang, 2002; Kubovy & Wagemans, 1995; Kubovy et al., 1998). Figure 2–12c shows what happens when all is not equal. Here, the principle of *uniform connectedness* forms a

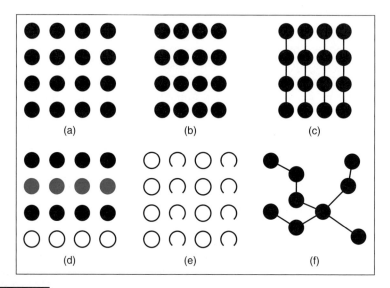

FIGURE 2–12 **Grouping by proximity and similarity**

(a) A 4 × 4 array of identical, evenly spaced dots. (b) The dots are closer together horizontally than vertically, so they group into rows by *proximity.* (c) The linked dots group as columns by *uniform connectedness,* which overrides proximity. (d) The dots may group by *similarity* of color or other attribute, such as a hole, here making rows. (e) *Closure* or *line termination* groups these dots into columns. (f) *Good continuation* groups the dots into two intersecting lines like stops on a subway map.

vertical organization that overrules proximity. Other principles, shown in Figures 2–12d–f, include properties drawn from topology (for example, does an element have a "hole" in it? Chen et al., 2002).

In the center of Figure 2–13a, you can see a potato-shaped ring of line segments grouping together. Why do these lines group whereas others do not? Here the principle is *colinearity:* lines group when their orientations are close to that of a neighbor's. Colinearity is a particular case of *relatability* (Kellman & Shipley, 1991). The basic idea of relatability is embodied in Figure 2–13b. If line 1 is part of an extended contour in the world, which of the other lines in the neighborhood is likely to be part of the same contour? Line 3 is a good bet. Lines 2 and 4 are plausible. Line 5 is unlikely. Neurons that detect each oriented edge in the image also play a role in computing the extension of that edge into neighboring portions of the image. The potato in Figure 2–13a is the result of a computation performed by a set of those feature detectors. Grouping that occurs between line segments links parts that likely belong to the same contour, helping us move from information about a local edge to information about the shapes of objects.

3.2.2. Filling in the Gaps

The grouping principles hold even when only parts of objects are visible, which is very useful when making sense of the confusion of stimuli in the real world. With the proper cues, something not there at all can be interpreted as something that's there but

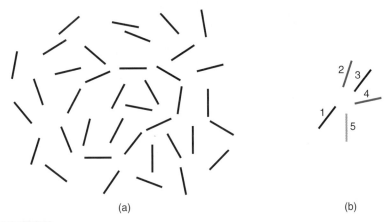

(a)   (b)

FIGURE 2–13   Grouping by colinearity and relatability

(a) Some of the lines within this scattered array form a potato-shaped figure. Lines group if their orientation is close to that of a neighbor's *(colinearity)*, and if it is easy to connect one line to the next *(relatability)*. (b) If line 1 is part of an extended contour in the world, which of the other lines is likely to be part of the same contour?

hidden—a big difference to our perception, and recognition, of objects. Figure 2–14a shows a mixture of apparently unconnected shapes. When the horizontal bars are drawn between them, as in Figure 2–14b, the shapes cohere into recognizable forms (Bregman, 1981). The edges of the shapes alone have insufficient relatability to suggest how they should connect, but when the bars are added, a new interpretation is possible. The bars reveal that the white areas in Figure 2–14a can be perceived not as voids but as hidden, or *occluded*, elements of the display. With that additional information

(a)   (b)

FIGURE 2–14   Putting parts together

(a) Shapes and parts with no apparent meaning. (b) The same parts shown with "occluding" black bars. Now the shapes ("B"s) are visible because you can connect the pieces.

(Adapted from Bregman, A. S. (1981). Asking the "what for" question in auditory perception. In Michael Kubovy, James R. Pomerantz (eds). *Perceptual Organization*. Mahwah, NJ: Lawrence Erlbaum Associates, pp. 99–118. Reprinted with permission.)

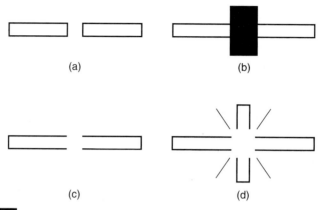

(a)   (b)

(c)   (d)

FIGURE 2–15 Illusory contours

(a) Two white rectangles. (b) A black rectangle is added. The interpretation changes so that now the figure looks like one long white rectangle instead of two short ones. The black rectangle is seen as occluding part of a single white one. (c) The two white rectangles have open ends. One interpretation is, again, one long white rectangle partly occluded by an invisible shape. (d) With more lines added, the invisible rectangle is visible: you see a "subjective" or "illusory" contour.

the visible edges are relatable and the shapes can be inferred as the visible parts of larger forms. This demonstration shows that perceptual processes can help us fill in the gaps to infer a coherent visual world even when not all the information is given.

Such processing can also lead us to see things that are not in fact there. If a black rectangle is placed across the two white rectangles in Figure 2–15a, we infer that there is just one white bar, continuing under an occluding rectangle (Figure 2–15b). Why do our brains engage in this sort of processing? Because it is unlikely that two white rectangles and a black one would line up just so to produce Figure 2–15b, but it is likely that one surface (the black rectangle) might occlude another (the proposed long white one) (Shimojo et al., 1988).

Things get a bit more interesting in Figure 2–15c. Here the open ends of the two white rectangles hint at the occlusion of that figure by an invisible white surface. If a bit more evidence for that surface is provided, as in Figure 2–15d, we see it, although there is no physical contour present. The border of this invisible surface is known as a subjective or illusory contour, one that is not physically present in the stimulus but is filled in by the visual system (Kanizsa, 1979). It is very unlikely that all four rectangles and the four lines should end in perfect alignment at the same spot; it is much more likely that they are all occluded by a form that lies in front of them. Perceptual processes settle on the more likely interpretation. The illusory contours that you see are the product of your perceptual processes at work. Filling in the missing pieces provides relevant information that is not present in the sensory stimulus.

Neuroscientific research has discovered the mechanisms that fill in missing contours. Neurons in the primary visual cortex respond to the location and orientation of edges in the sensory world. Connections among the different neurons that respond to edges in different orientations allow them to compare their inputs. Using

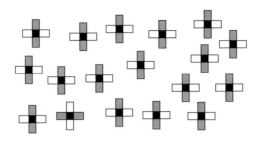

FIGURE 2–16 A demonstration of the binding problem

Look for the white vertical bar (or the gray horizontal one). All the pluses are made from vertical and horizontal bars that are *either* gray or white. You need to deploy attention to each particular one in turn to determine whether the gray color goes with the vertical or the horizontal line.

some simple circuitry, neurons that respond to actual edges induce responses in neighboring neurons (Francis & Grossberg, 1996). The end result is that neurons respond to illusory edges in a way similar to the way they respond to a real line in the same space (Bakin et al., 2000; Grosof et al., 1993; Sugita, 1999). The perception of the illusory line is supported by the interaction among neighboring neurons in the primary visual cortex. Construction of perception from sparse cues in the environment is built into the earliest stages of information processing.

3.2.3. The Binding Problem

The examples considered so far have all dealt with the grouping of the same sort of feature—does line 1 go with line 2? What happens when we need to determine whether line 1 goes with color A? This question illustrates the binding problem; that is, how do we associate different features, say, shape, color, and orientation, so that we perceive a single object? The binding problem arises in part because of the way that information processing is carried out by the brain, where one system analyzes color, another shape, and another motion. How do we combine this information so that we see a red ball flying through the air? Part of the answer is that spatial location can serve as the required "glue." If the roundness, the redness, and the particular motion all occupy the same point in space at the same time, then it seems reasonable that they would be bound together. However, there are limits to the utility of simple spatial co-occurrence. Look for the white vertical bar (or the gray horizontal one) in Figure 2–16; you won't find it easily. Until you deploy attention to a specific "plus" in the pattern, you cannot tell whether or not grayness goes with verticalness (Wolfe et al., 1990). Although many grouping processes can occur at the same time across the visual field, some—notably binding of different sorts of features to the same object—require attention (Treisman, 1996).

Comprehension Check:

1. What are some of the building blocks of visual perception?
2. What principles are followed when the brain puts it all together?

4. ACHIEVING VISUAL RECOGNITION: HAVE I SEEN YOU BEFORE?

To understand the world, visual information is not enough. Theseus's bear is the emblem of the problem of recognition, which is to compare current visual information (large, round, dark, rough edged) with knowledge of the world. (A previously seen object has a certain shape and color, a bush has another shape, another color.) **Recognition** is the process of matching representations of organized sensory input to stored representations in memory. Determining what is out there in the world—and reacting to it safely and efficiently if it turns out to be a bear—depends on our ability to find a correspondence between input from our eyes at the moment and earlier input that we organized and stored in memory.

4.1. A Brain That Cannot Recognize

Most of the time we don't even think about what it means to recognize objects. Sighted people look into a room, see the chairs, tables, books, and ornaments that may be there and know essentially what these things are, quickly and effortlessly. Blind people recognize objects by touch or by sound. Recognition is not dependent on a particular sensory modality. But there are people who have no sensory deficit at all who nonetheless cannot readily recognize the objects around them. This condition, which is called **agnosia** (literally, "without knowledge"), results from damage to the brain, not to the sensory organs. When sight is unimpaired and yet recognition fails, the deficit is known as *visual agnosia*. The experience of a patient known as John illustrates the cause and effects of visual agnosia (Humphreys & Riddoch, 1987).

John, who grew up in England, was a pilot in World War II. After the war, he married and then worked for a company that manufactured windows for houses, in time becoming head of marketing for Europe. Following an emergency operation for a perforated appendix, he suffered a stroke: a small blood clot traveled to his brain and blocked the arteries that sustained tissue in the occipital lobes. After his stroke, although he was perfectly able to make out the forms of objects about him and navigate through his room, John was unable to recognize objects. He didn't know their names or purposes. He was unable to read. Even after recovering from surgery and returning home, his ability to recognize objects did not fully return. He even had difficulty recognizing his wife.

When shown a line drawing of a carrot (Figure 2–17a), John remarked, "I have not even the glimmerings of an idea. The bottom point seems solid and the other bits are feathery. It does not seem logical unless it is some sort of brush." When shown the drawing of an onion (Figure 2–17b), he said, "I'm completely lost at the moment. . . . It has sharp bits at the bottom like a fork. It could be a necklace of sorts." Shown a set of line drawings like these, John recognized fewer than half. He was better at naming real objects than drawings, but nonetheless correctly named only two-thirds of the objects shown to him, even though they were very common objects such as a book and an apple. Asked to name the same objects by touch, John's recognition was much better, establishing that he did not have a general difficulty

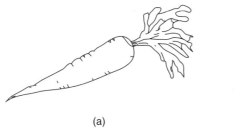
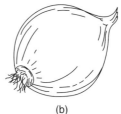

(a)　　　　　　　　　　　　　　　　　(b)

FIGURE 2–17 **Do you know what these are?**

A visual agnosic patient had difficulty identifying these drawings.

(From Huttenlocher, P. R. (1993). Morphometric study of human cerebral cortex development. Chapter in M. H. Johnson (ed.). *Brain Development and Cognition*. Basil Blackwell Ltd., Oxford, UK, pp. 112–124. Reprinted with permission.)

understanding or speaking the name of the objects, but instead a selective difficulty with visual recognition.

One remarkable aspect of John's experience is that his impairment did not include failure to detect features or groups. As evident from his descriptions above, he could accurately see features such as pointy edges and shapes. Further, he was fairly good at copying pictures and even drawing objects from memory (although he didn't recognize what he drew). What he is missing since his stroke is the ability to take the organized visual information he has access to and match it to his visual memories of objects. The selective impairment produced by visual agnosia demonstrates that there are at least some processes used for visual recognition that are not used to extract or organize visual features.

4.2. Models of Recognition

Recognition seems simple for us as we go about the world. But even with an intact brain, recognition is not a trivial act. It remains extremely difficult for even the most sophisticated computer programs. Work in developing computer recognition systems and models by which recognition is achieved has led to remarkable advances during the last 20 years in our understanding of human recognition systems.

Powerful challenges face both computer and brain in the effort to recognize objects. One is **viewpoint dependence**: an object can be viewed from an infinite combination of possible angles and possible distances, each of which projects a slightly different two-dimensional image on a plane (and on the retina), varying in size or orientation or both. Recognition of an object viewed from different angles presents a particular challenge: the projected two-dimensional image of *each three-dimensional part* (for example, the seat and the various legs of a chair) changes in size, appearance, and position as a function of rotation (Figure 2–18), yet we have little difficulty recognizing the object as a chair. This challenge is very similar to one of the fundamental problems in perception we discussed earlier, namely, that the sensory input does not contain enough information. All that is

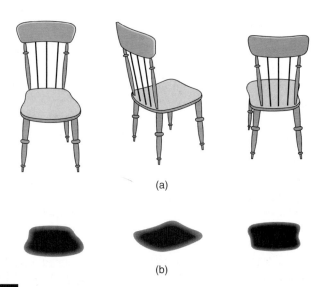

(a)

(b)

FIGURE 2–18 Different viewpoints

(a) An ordinary chair seen from different views projects an image in which the parts vary in size and shape. (b) The three black blobs may not look like the same shape, but they are the same as the seats of the chairs in (a). The chair seat projects a very different shape in the image with each viewpoint. To recognize that the chair is the same chair seen from different viewpoints, we must discount these changes in the image and extract the three-dimensional shape of the object.

available from any one viewpoint is the two-dimensional projection, so how do we determine the object's three-dimensional structure?

Then there is the challenge of exemplar variation: there are many different instances of each object category. (The chair in Figure 2–18 is not the only chair in the world.) Any object category consists of many possible examples, yet we readily recognize dining chairs, beach chairs, office chairs, and rocking chairs as all being chairs. This challenge is very similar to the other fundamental problem discussed earlier, namely, that the sensory input contains too much information. How does a computer (and how do we) manage this abundance? One solution would be to store each of these views and each of these examples of chairs as independent representations, but this would make it difficult to generalize our perception of objects to new views or examples. Another way would be to capitalize on the regularities and redundancies of the world by identifying salient features or their underlying structure—in other words, the discriminating features of "chair"—to be able efficiently to match sensory input with stored representations of objects. Understanding how computer systems are designed to overcome these challenges of recognition can help us understand how the human brain might be performing the same feat.

Four types of models have been proposed, each with a different approach to overcoming the challenges of recognition. *Template-matching models* match the whole image to a stored representation of the whole object. *Feature-matching models* extract important or discriminating features from the image and match these with known features of objects. The *recognition-by-components model* represents the three-dimensional structure of objects by specifying their parts and the spatial relations among those parts. *Configural models* distinguish among objects that share the same basic parts and overall structure by coding each exemplar according to how it deviates from the average or prototypical object. Each model has advantages and disadvantages that make it suitable for recognition of some objects and not others. It is entirely possible that the human recognition system uses multiple sets of representations and processes, which may be more or less effective for different types of objects.

4.2.1. Template-Matching Models

A template is a pattern, like a cookie cutter or a stencil. It can be used to compare individual items to a standard. A batch of cookies can be compared to a cookie cutter; a broken cookie is rejected (or immediately eaten) because it does not match the specifications of the template cookie cutter. The template-matching method as initially conceived is straightforward and useful as long as the item to be recognized and the template to which the system compares it are almost identical and different from others. However, models based on the traditional idea of a template cannot accommodate variations in object size and orientation—variation that, as we've seen, occurs in our sensory life. A template that's doing its job would reject such apparently different versions.

However, the template-matching models used in modern computer programs are more sophisticated and flexible. These models adjust a scanned image by transformations of size and rotation, stretching it and warping it, to provide a view that is the best possible fit to the templates. Template matching is the method used to recognize bar codes and fingerprints. When the object to be identified is well specified and unique, template matching is a quick and reliable method.

That's how computers typically do it. Similarly, for humans and other animals representations of objects in memory could be used as templates to match with the sensory input for the recognition of objects. In theory, you could recognize letters of the alphabet by comparing the shape you see with your memory of the shape of each letter of the alphabet until you come up with a match (Figure 2–19a). This method would work reasonably well for printed text because, although type fonts differ, each letter style has a characteristic design that is identical every time that letter appears. But the main disadvantage of the template-matching method is that recognition often demands great flexibility; think of the variety in handwritten letters from one person to another and in different circumstances. No rigid template would reliably match everybody's "A," sometimes scrawled in a hasty note, sometimes carefully drawn (Figure 2–19b). Some computer programs designed to recognize handwriting use flexible templates with algorithms that take into consideration factors such as the direction of strokes of the pen and the context of the word. Flexibility is further provided by templates that are constructed from a hierarchy of component templates that each detect a part of the pattern of interest. Computers use flexible hierarchical templates to recognize people from the unique pattern in the iris of the eye (Daugman, 1993). It is still unclear whether or in what circumstances the human brain uses stored representations as templates to recognize objects.

(a) Template for "A"

Letters to recognize

Overlap of template and typed letters

(b) Overlap of template for "A" and written letter "A"s

FIGURE 2-19 **A template-matching model of recognition**

(a) A possible template for recognizing the letter "A" is shown at the top. The next line shows printed letters for recognition. The third line shows the overlap of the template with each printed letter. Notice that the overlap with the "A" is perfect, but the other letters do not fit well. (b) When the same template is used to recognize written letters, the fit is poor even though all are the letter "A."

4.2.2. Feature-Matching Models

In some circumstances, accurate recognition does not require that the whole object be fully specified, only some discriminating "features." Note that we are using the term *features* here in a more general sense than in the discussion of, for example, edges and colors, so it can mean any attribute that distinguishes one object from others. How do you know that's a tree you're looking at? You don't know the exact locations of the branches or the measurements of the trunk, but that doesn't matter: if you can determine that the thing has those two features—branches and a trunk—it's a tree.

Feature-matching models search for simple but characteristic features of an object; their presence signals a match. What constitutes a feature in these models? That varies with the type of object. The first stage of visual analysis detects edges and colors, and some models use these simple attributes as features: a feature-matching model could recognize printed letters with a limited set of features that are line segments of different orientations and degrees of curvature. The letter "A" has three such features: a right-slanted line, a left-slanted line, and a horizontal line. No other letter of the roman alphabet has this combination of features. The model would detect these line segments (and only these), and the letter "A" would be accurately recognized (Selfridge, 1955, 1959). Other models require more complex features: models designed for face recognition use eyes, nose, and mouth as features, and models for animal recognition use head, body, legs, and tail. This type of model is more flexible than template-matching models because as long as the features are present it will work, even if the object has parts that may be rearranged. Feature-matching models may also require less storage space than template models because relatively few features would render recognizable many objects of the same category that are not identical.

The feature-matching approach also lends itself well to the idea that processing of information in the brain is parallel (that is, happening at the same time) and distributed (that is, happening in different neural areas). The brain is a network of interconnected neurons with largely interactive components arranged in a loose hierarchy. Such an architecture, diagrammed in the neural-network model discussed in Chapter 1 (see Figure 1–13), has been used to model letter and word recognition as a feature-matching model such as the one shown in Figure 2–20. Recognition is mimicked by a set of simple processing elements, the units of a neural-net model, that interact with one another through excitatory and inhibitory connections. Excitatory connections increase the activity of a unit, inhibitory connections decrease it. In a letter-recognition model, units representing different line segments are connected to units in the next level that represent letters. A connection is excitatory if the letter has the feature specified by that line segment, inhibitory if it does not. When the letter "A" is presented to the network, the right-slant, left-slant, and horizontal line segments become active and excite the units in the letter level that have those features. Some letter units have no additional features beyond what an "A" has but lack some feature of an "A" (for example, neither "V" nor "X" has a horizontal line), so these letter units will become only partially active. Other letter units share some of those features and also have another feature (both "K" and "Y" have slanted lines and also a vertical line); these too will become only partially active. Only the representation of the letter that matches all the features will be maximally active, and go on to influence recognition at the next level of the net, where units representing individual letters excite or inhibit units representing words. By representing those features in an interactive, distributed network, models such as this can recognize any object that has the right features.

For a feature-matching model to be a plausible explanation of how we recognize objects, neurons or populations of neurons should show selectivity to parts of the input similar to the features in the model. Whereas there is much evidence (see the

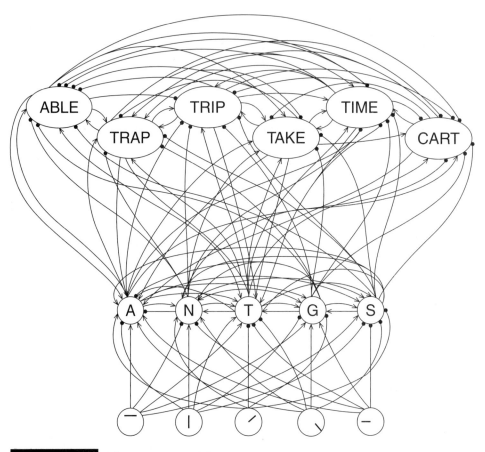

FIGURE 2–20 A feature net model

Each circle is a unit of the model that may correspond to groups of neurons in the brain. Lines between units show the connections between units. Connections are excitatory *(arrowheads)* or inhibitory *(dots)*. Presentation of a stimulus to the network excites the feature-level units in the bottom
row. These influence activity in the letter units (middle row), which in turn influence the word units
(top row).

(Revised from Rumelhart, D. E., McClelland, J. L. (1987). *Parallel Distributed Processing: Explorations in the
Microstructure of Cognition, Vol. 1: Foundations.* The MIT Press; Cambridge, MA. Reprinted with permission.)

accompanying *A Closer Look*) to show that neurons in the visual cortex are tuned
to lines of specific orientation and degree of curvature (Ferster & Miller, 2000;
Hubel & Wiesel, 1959), we do not know whether there are neurons tuned to specific letters or words. Selectivity has been found for other features, such as color,
size, texture, and shape (Desimone et al., 1984; Tanaka et al., 1991). Neurons have
even shown selectivity to features that are specific parts of objects, such as the eyes
of a face (Perrett et al., 1982), and they can become more selective for specific features of objects through experience. Animals that are trained to classify objects as

A CLOSER LOOK
Visual Feature Detectors in the Brain

Space limitations prevent us from describing each experiment in detail, but to get an idea of the logic of experimentation it is useful to look at the details of at least one study cited in the text. For this purpose, we consider a ground-breaking experiment done by David Hubel and Torsten Wiesel (reported in 1959 in "Receptive Fields of Single Neurons in the Cat's Striate Cortex," *Journal of Physiology, 148,* 574–591), which was part of the work that won these researchers a Nobel Prize in Physiology or Medicine in 1981.

Introduction

The investigators were interested in how the neurons in the occipital cortex may be responsible for visual perception. What types of things make neurons respond, and how are the neurons organized?

Method

To test responses of individual neurons, the investigators implanted an electrode into neurons in the occipital lobes of anesthetized cats. By recording the change in voltage on the electrode, they recorded the activity of each neuron and could determine when the neuron was responding. To test what types of things the neurons would respond to, they set the cats up to look at a large projection screen and shined spots of light on the screen. Previous research had successfully used this method to elicit specific responses from photoreceptors and ganglion cells in the eye and map out their receptive fields. The investigators used the same method, but they were recording responses from the primary visual cortex in the occipital lobe.

Results

Unlike the responses of photoreceptors and ganglion cells, most neurons in the primary visual cortex did not respond very much when spots of light were shown to the cat. Diffuse light was also not effective. Instead, the investigators discovered that responses were much stronger to bars of light of a specific orientation. For example, one neuron might respond best when a horizontal bar of light was shown, whereas another neuron would respond best when a vertical bar of light was shown. Testing many neurons adjacent to one another in the occipital lobe, they discovered a regular organization of the responses of neurons. The orientation that elicited the strongest response in one neuron, also called the "preferred" orientation, was only slightly different from that of a neighboring neuron. Across a row of adjacent neurons, the preferred orientation varied systematically to map out all orientations.

Discussion

The finding that neurons in the primary visual cortex respond to bars of different orientation demonstrates that these neurons perform a much more sophisticated analysis of the visual world than the photoreceptors or ganglion cells. These cortical neurons can detect lines and may be responsible for detecting the boundaries or edges of objects.

members of different categories (for example, deciding whether an object is—using human terms—a dog or a cat) have neural populations that increase in selectivity for the features that best distinguish the categories (in this case, long neck and short tail) (Freedman et al., 2001, 2002).

The fact that neurons are selective for an array of different features may suggest that the particular features that are important for recognition may vary with the level of detail required at the moment. In the state of high emotional alert described by Theseus—"In the dark, imagining some fear"—a rough outline and round shape can be enough to "recognize" a bear. Our use of feature matching rather than template matching may depend also on how difficult it is to see, and how closely the object matches the "canonical," or traditional, picture of it. For example, a robin is a canonical bird shape and might be recognized by a template, whereas an emu is not a typical bird and might be recognized by feature matching (Kosslyn & Chabris, 1990; Laeng et al., 1990). Feature matching seems to be a mechanism for recognition that can be used by the brain to recognize categories of objects rather than individual entities.

A major difficulty with early feature models was that they could not distinguish objects with the same component features but arranged in a different spatial relationship, for example, the letters "V" and "X." Modern computer models, however, encode not only the features in the object but also the spatial relations among them. Thus the representation of "V" might include termination of the lines after meeting at the vertex at the base, and the representation of "X" would include the property of intersection. These more flexible models are fairly successful at recognizing objects in a specific category such as two-dimensional handwritten letters and words, and some models can even recognize exemplars from a particular category of three-dimensional objects such as faces seen across a limited range of views (Penev & Atick, 1996).

4.2.3. Recognition-by-Components Model

Although templates and simple features might work in building models for recognition of two-dimensional objects, it is not easy to see how they can solve the problems inherent in recognition of three-dimensional objects across different views, or in recognition of some objects as being different exemplars of the same type of object. Perhaps one clue to how the brain solves these problems is that we may describe objects according to their parts and the spatial relations among those parts (Cave & Kosslyn, 1993; Laeng et al., 1999). The utility of many objects is contingent on the correct arrangement of parts (Figure 2–21). To explain our ability to recognize objects in the varying circumstances presented by the real world, we require a model built on something more flexible than a template and that matches structural information beyond features.

The recognition-by-components (RBC) model provides a possible method for recognizing three-dimensional objects across variations in viewpoint or exemplars (Biederman, 1987). The model assumes that any three-dimensional object can be generally described according to its parts and the spatial relations among those parts. The current model proposes that a set of 24 geometrical three-dimensional

FIGURE 2–21 Recognition, arrangement, and utility

Three practical objects shown next to three other objects made of the same parts scrambled into a different arrangement. The utility of many objects is contingent on the correct arrangement of parts.

shapes, such as cylinders and cones, can be used to represent just about any object; in the language of the model, these shapes are called **geons** (Figure 2–22a) (Biederman, 1995). In addition, the spatial relations among geons must be defined: a cone might be "on top of" or "attached to the side of" a cylinder. Almost any object can be specified by its *structural description,* that is, its components and their spatial relations. A bucket, for example, is a cylinder with a curved rod on the top; a mug is a cylinder with a curved rod on the side (Figure 2–22b). The RBC model detects the geons and their spatial relations and attempts to match the assembled parts to a stored three-dimensional representation of a known object (Hummel & Biederman, 1992).

Geons are useful units for describing objects because their properties are viewpoint invariant (the opposite of viewpoint dependent); that is, they are in the image regardless of the direction from which the object is viewed. Viewpoint-invariant properties include straight lines, corners, and vertices. A straight line, such as the edge of a rectangle, will project to a straight line on any two-dimensional image plane, regardless of the viewpoint (as do the chair legs in Figure 2–18). Each geon is associated with a set of viewpoint-invariant properties that uniquely specify it from the other geons. Thus,

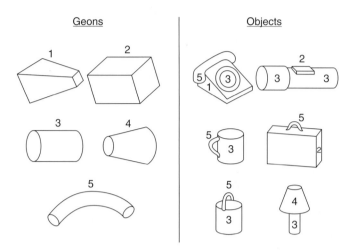

Geons

Objects

FIGURE 2-22 Geons and objects

(a) Five of the 24 geons and (b) objects showing their geon parts.

(From Biederman, I. (1995). Visual Object Recognition. In S. M. Kosslyn & D. N. Osherson, *An Invitation to Cognitive Science, Vol. 2: Visual Cognition.* The MIT Press; Cambridge, MA. Reprinted with permission.)

the structural description of an object is viewpoint invariant even when the perceived shape of the object as a whole changes dramatically with viewing conditions.

There is some evidence in support of the RBC model. Participants in behavioral studies can easily recognize geon renditions of man-made objects, suggesting that these simplified representations may have some validity. Evidence also comes from studies making use of visual priming, which produces faster recognition observed when an object is seen for the second time. In general, the effect of priming occurs when a stimulus or task facilitates processing a subsequent stimulus or task—priming "greases the wheels," so to speak. Using this technique, Irving Biederman (1995) created complementary pairs of images of a given object (say, a flashlight) with some contours deleted (Figure 2-23). Each image in a pair had half the contours of the entire object, and the two images had no contours in common. A second pair of contour-deleted images presented the same object, but one of a different design and, therefore, described by different geons. Participants were shown one member of a pair, then either its partner (built with the same geons) or a member of the other pair (the same object, but described by different geons). Recognition was faster when the second image presented had the same geons as the first.

There is some evidence that neurons in inferior (i.e., bottom) temporal cortex are sensitive to properties that are viewpoint invariant (Vogels et al., 2001), but many neurons respond to an object from only a limited set of views, such as the front view but not the side view of a head (Logothetis et al., 1995; Perrett et al., 1991). The observation that many neurons fail to generalize across all possible views seems to contradict what the RBC model would seem to predict. In addition, although the

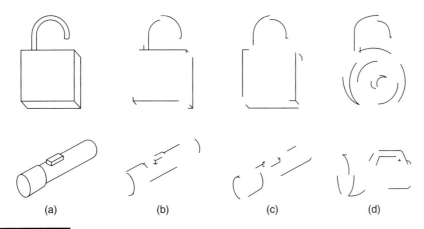

(a)   (b)   (c)   (d)

FIGURE 2–23   Visual priming and recognition

Two objects as (a) intact, (b) with half their contours removed, and (c) with the other half of the contours removed. (d) A different example of the same type of object but with different geons (again, half the contours are removed). It was easier for participants to recognize the objects when they saw (b) followed by (c) than when they saw (b) and (d).

(From Biederman, I. (1995). Visual Object Recognition. In S. M. Kosslyn & D. N. Osherson, *An Invitation to Cognitive Science, Vol. 2: Visual Cognition.* The MIT Press; Cambridge, MA. Reprinted with permission.)

RBC theory may account for our recognition of man-made objects, it is less clear how it can be applied to our recognition of natural objects such as animals or plants. Faces are a good illustration of the problem. Faces generally include two eyes, a nose, and a mouth in the same arrangement. The RBC model would construct the same arrangement of geons for *every* face, and so would not detect individual differences between one face and another—the very way we often, and easily, recognize people. RBC-style models can be good at finding the most commonly used category name of an object (mug, dog), but they have more trouble identifying the specific exemplar (my special coffee mug, my neighbor's standard poodle).

4.2.4. Configural Models

Configural models often can deal with the limitations of RBC models. They propose that objects that share the same parts and a common structure are recognized according to the spatial relations among those parts *and the extent to which those spatial relations deviate from the prototype, or "average," object.* Configural models of recognition help explain how we recognize different individual examples of a category; they have been especially successful in the domain of face recognition (Diamond & Carey, 1986; Rhodes et al., 1987).

In a configural model, specific faces are described by their deviations from the prototypical face, as defined by quantified average proportions in a population. All faces would have the same component parts in the same spatial arrangement, but their relative sizes and distances make each unique.

FIGURE 2–24 Face perception adaptation

First, notice that the face in the middle looks normal. The face on the far left has features too close together and the face on the far right has features too far apart. Note that the distance between features of the face, such as the space between the eyes, has a strong impact on our perception of the face. Now, stare at the face on the far left for 60 seconds. Then switch your gaze back to the middle picture. If you have adapted for long enough, the face in the middle will now look distorted in that it will appear as if the features are too far apart.

(Courtesy Michael A. Webster and Paul Ekman Ph.D.)

Several lines of evidence support the configural theory of face recognition. For one thing, we are somewhat better at recognizing caricatures of famous faces, which accentuate the differences from the average face, than more veridical line drawings; this finding suggests that we code faces according to such deviations (Rhodes et al., 1987). Studies have also shown that participants instructed to stare at a particular face and then look at an average face may briefly experience a visual aftereffect in which they perceive the "opposite" or "anticaricature" of the original face (Leopold et al., 2001; Webster & MacLin, 1999; Webster et al., 2004; Zhao and Chubb, 2001). Try it yourself with Figure 2–24.

Several lines of evidence also suggest that only upright faces are processed in this special way. If participants are shown a set of pictures of faces and objects, they are better at recognizing upright faces than a variety of different upright objects, but poorer at recognizing upside-down faces than inverted objects (Yin, 1969). Other studies have shown that inverted faces, like objects that are not faces, are processed in a piecemeal manner, whereas upright faces—the view usually seen in life—elicit more configural or holistic processing (Young et al., 1987). Participants are better at learning the difference between two upright faces that differ only by the shape of a single element, such as the nose, than at learning the difference between two noses shown in isolation (Tanaka & Farah, 1993; Tanaka & Sengco, 1997). Moreover, even though the facial context provides no additional information about the shape of the nose, participants do better at encoding and remembering the nose shape in the context of an upright face. However, no such benefit of holistic processing was found for inverted faces. We are also apparently better at evaluating the overall configuration or spatial relationships among facial features, such as the distance between the eyes or between the nose and the eyes, for upright than for inverted faces (Searcy & Bartlett, 1996).

Neuroscientific research also provides support for the configural model of face recognition. Single-unit recordings from face-selective neurons in the monkey temporal lobes suggest that many neurons respond to the configuration of multiple features rather than to any single face part (Young & Yamane, 1992). In humans, damage to the fusiform face area, a part of the temporal lobes, produces the disorder known as *prosopagnosia,* the inability to recognize different faces. The deficit is specific; patients have no trouble recognizing that something is a face as opposed to, say, a pumpkin, but have difficulty telling one face from another. The configuration of parts of the face seems to be particularly difficult for them to discern, lending support to the idea that configural processing is important for face recognition. The discovery of a specialized area of the brain for face recognition has ignited debate between scientists who study object recognition, as discussed in the accompanying *Debate* box.

A variant of this view is the *expertise hypothesis,* which proposes that a specialized neural system develops that allows expert visual discrimination, and is required to judge subtle differences within any particular visual category (Gauthier et al., 2000). We probably spend more time looking at faces than at any other object. We are face experts—in a single glance we can quickly process the identity, sex, age, emotional expression, viewpoint, and gaze-direction of a face. It is possible that the specialized neural system in the fusiform gyrus is responsible for any recognition process for which we have expertise. Research shows that, while looking at pictures of birds, bird experts show stronger activity in the fusiform gyrus than do other people (Gauthier et al., 2000).

A contrasting view is that many—if not most—visual representations are spatially distributed throughout the ventral pathway. Perhaps the ventral temporal cortex often serves as an all-purpose recognition area for telling apart all different types of objects. Indeed, typically patients with damage to the inferior temporal cortex have difficulty recognizing all categories of objects. In addition, neuroimaging studies of normal object recognition have found that regions outside the fusiform face area that respond suboptimally to faces still show differential responses to faces and to other types of stimuli (Haxby et al., 2001). This means that sufficient visual information is analyzed outside the fusiform face area to distinguish faces from other objects. However, neuropsychological evidence of double dissociations between face recognition and object recognition are difficult to explain if representations are completely distributed. One possible reconciliation is that all ventral areas are involved in object recognition and provide useful information for categorization, but certain distinct systems are necessary for performing fine-tuned discriminations within a category. This is an active area of ongoing research, and no doubt more will be learned about the organization of visual recognition in time.

Comprehension Check: ✓

1. What is visual agnosia?
2. What are the four types of models of object recognition?

A Set of Blocks or Cat's Cradle:
Modular or Distributed Representations?

DEBATE

There are two possible designs for the organization of the visual recognition system in the human brain. The organization could be *modular*, with specialized systems that process different types of objects, or *distributed*, with a single general-purpose recognition system that represents all types of objects. Proponents of the modular view believe that perception of any given type of object relies on a specialized neural module, that is, a specific area of the brain that specializes in the recognition of that particular object category. They cite research that suggests that there are specialized modules in the ventral temporal cortex, such as a face area specialized for recognizing upright faces (Kanwisher et al., 1997a), and a place area specialized for recognizing spatial layout and landmarks (Epstein & Kanwisher, 1998). However, other research argues against the idea that there are specialized areas for recognizing objects (Haxby et al., 2001), and other investigators propose that our representations of objects are distributed over a number of areas of the ventral temporal cortex.

Human neuroimaging studies have revealed a discrete region in the fusiform gyrus, the fusiform face area, that responds preferentially to upright human faces as compared to a variety of other stimuli (Kanwisher et al., 1997a; McCarthy et al., 1997). However, this region responds not only to human faces but also to faces of animals and faces in cartoons. By contrast, this region responds weakly to common objects, scrambled faces, back views of heads, and to other parts of the body (Tong et al., 2000). Brain damage to this area is associated with prosopagnosia, the selective impairment in the ability to recognize faces (Farah et al., 1995; Meadows, 1974). Is it possible that face recognition is simply harder than object recognition and so is more easily impaired by brain injury? Unlikely, since some patients exhibit the opposite pattern of impairment: they are capable of recognizing faces but very poor at recognizing objects (Moscovitch et al., 1997). This double dissociation between face and object recognition supports the argument that face and object recognition processes are separate in the brain. However, other accounts are still being tested—such as the idea that the "face area" is actually involved in processing highly familiar types of stimuli (e.g., Gauthier et al., 2000).

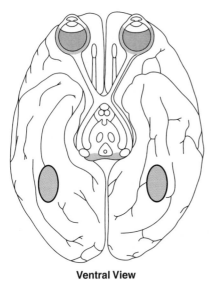

Ventral View

Looking at the brain from below, we see the location of the fusiform face area (marked with blue ovals) on the inferior side of the cortex. Cortex that is responsive to faces can be found in both hemispheres, as depicted, but for most people the area in the right hemisphere is larger and more responsive.

5. INTERPRETING FROM THE TOP DOWN: WHAT YOU KNOW GUIDES WHAT YOU SEE

Perception is not a one-way flow of information; we are predisposed to understand new information in relation to what we already know. As bottom-up information comes in from sensory organs and is passed up the hierarchy of analysis, concurrent information moves top down (in accordance with your knowledge, beliefs, goals and expectations) and affects earlier processes. Theseus's bear is more likely to be perceived as the bush it is if you are in the middle of a well-tended garden, not "imagining some fear" in a dark forest where the appearance of a bear is more likely. We use knowledge to make perception more efficient, accurate, and relevant to the current situation, filling in the missing parts of sensory input on the basis of information previously stored in memory. Context counts.

5.1. Using Context

The things we see are not perfect reflections of the world—how can they be? What is the "real" color of a brick wall, the part in sunlight or the part in shadow? Our perception of the basic components of the world, such as colors and objects, is simply inaccurate, as has been demonstrated by psychological experiments and observations during the past hundreds of years (Wade, 1998). So how do we manage in a world so rich with sensory stimuli? We manage because information is interpreted relative to context across all levels of perceptual representation and processing. Our perceptual system has heuristics—problem-solving short-cuts, as opposed to exhaustive algorithms—for making sense of the world by making inferences from the information it receives. Perception is the result of these inferences.

5.1.1. Context Effects for Feature and Group Processing

Visual illusions demonstrate how perception can infer properties that do not exist in the image; a good example is the illusory white rectangle in Figure 2–15. The readily perceived edges of the rectangle are in fact not present in the image; our perceptual systems supply them from the context of black edges and lines. The phenomenon of illusory contours is one way in which perception fills in the missing pieces to make an understandable interpretation of the world.

Studies of visual illusions have revealed that context—including our knowledge, beliefs, goals and expectations—leads to a number of different assumptions about visual features. We expect the brick wall to be "in reality" the same color throughout, so despite the evidence before us caused by changes in illumination across its surface, we believe it to be all the same color; this effect is known as the *brightness illusion* (Figure 2–25). Similarly, *size illusions* demonstrate that we assume objects maintain their "true" size across changes in apparent distance from the observer (Figure 2–26). If we did not make these assumptions, and saw "literally" rather than perceived inferentially, the world would be very confusing indeed.

FIGURE 2–25 A brightness illusion

We tend to see the sheep as the same color, even though in the picture the lightness of their coats varies dramatically.

Grouping is an automatic process, and a context of many items can make it difficult to perceive a single item independently. In the design by M. C. Escher shown in Figure 2–27, grouping creates an interestingly ambiguous figure. On the periphery of the image we have clearly defined birds (top) and fish (bottom). As we move toward the center from top and bottom, the objects become respectively less like birds and less like fish. The bird context strives to maintain the avian identity while the fish context supports a piscine interpretation. The result is a region in the middle where you can see either the birds or the fish, but it is hard to see both simultaneously. Grouping makes it difficult to see each item independently, but it allows us to see common attributes of many items at once—here we see the birds as one flock, the fish as one school. We can then perform operations on the group as a whole. It will be less demanding, for instance, to follow the motion of the group than to track each bird independently.

We assimilate all the birds in the Escher design into a single flock because they all look similar. What if one were different? The context effects produced by a group can also be contrasting, making one odd item in a group look even more unusual than in

OUR WASHINGTON CAPITOL SERIES.   CORRIDOR LEADING TO THE HALL OF REPRESENTATIVES.

FIGURE 2–26   A size illusion

Most of these people in a corridor of the U.S. Capitol appear to be similarly sized in life. The anomaly is the tiny foreground couple (arrow), who are in fact duplicates of, and therefore the same actual size as, the couple in the background. Moving the background couple out of their context reveals the illusion.

fact it is. A classic example, the Ebbinghaus illusion (named for its discoverer, the German psychologist Hermann Ebbinghaus, 1850–1913), is shown in Figure 2–28. The central circles in each group are the same size, but the one in the context of the smaller circles looks larger. This illusion is strongest when all the shapes are similar and are perceived as belonging together (Coren & Enns, 1993; Shulman, 1992).

FIGURE 2–27 Grouping in art

M. C. Escher creatively embedded figures among each other in his works of art. In this design, where does the sky stop and the water start?

(M. C. Escher's "Sky and Water I" © 2006 The M. C. Escher Company-Holland. All rights reserved. www.mcescher.com.)

Inferring the motion of the flock of birds as a whole may make it easier for us to see a deviation within that common motion.

5.1.2. Context Effects for Object Recognition

Recognition is dependent on our previous experience with the world and the context of that experience. Recognition of an object may be improved if it is seen in an *expected* context (you'd agreed to meet your friend at the diner) or a *customary* one (your friend often eats at that diner), and impaired if the context is *unexpected* (what's my cousin from Australia doing at this U.S. diner?) or *inconsistent with previous experience* (I've never seen *you* here before!). Experiments have shown that the influence of context on recognition of simple objects may be based on allocation of attention (Biederman et al., 1982), or strategies for remembering or responding to objects in scenes (Hollingworth & Hendersen, 1998). Context effects in object recognition reflect the information that is important for and integral to the representation of objects.

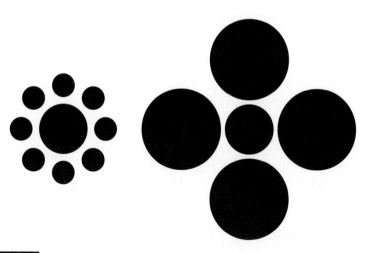

FIGURE 2–28 The Ebbinghaus size illusion

The central circles in the two sets are the same size. However, the central one on the left looks larger than the central one on the right. In the context of the smaller circles, the central one looks bigger—and vice versa.

Research has demonstrated that top-down processing can influence our perception of parts of objects. For example, the context of surrounding letters can manipulate the perception of a target letter in an effect known as word superiority, demonstrated in Figure 2–29 (Selfridge, 1955). The middle letter of each word is actually the identical arrangement of lines, but it is seen as either an "H" or an "A" to fit the context provided. In behavioral studies, participants are better at identifying a briefly flashed letter (for example, "A") if it is shown in the context of a word ("FAT") rather than in isolation ("A") or in a nonword ("XAQ") (Reicher, 1969; Wheeler, 1970). This is surprising because participants are asked only to identify a single letter and do not need to read the word. You might think that the correct identification of the letters of the word is required *before* the word can be recognized,

TAE CAT

FIGURE 2–29 Easy as ABC

You may find it easy to read these words, but a simple feature detector would not. The letters in the middle of each word are actually the identical set of lines. The context of the surrounding letters and their suggestion of a meaningful word let us interpret the central letter as an "H" in the first word and an "A" in the second, so we read "THE CAT."

(After "Pattern Recognition and Modern Computers," by O. Selfridge, in *Proceedings of the Western Joint Computer Conference*, 1955, Los Angeles, CA.)

because words are made up of letters. So how can the word context help, if you already see the letters? Research like this demonstrates that the recognition of objects is not strictly a matter of putting together the pieces via bottom-up processing. The whole word is recognized by the combined influence of all the letters, thus supporting the identification of each letter because of its context. Later on in this chapter, we will see how an interactive model of recognition can explain the influence of words on the perception of letters and the word superiority effect.

Similar results are obtained when participants are asked to make judgments about components of objects. When asked to judge the color of line segments, participants do better if the line is in a recognizable letter or shape than if it appears in an unusual arrangement (Reingold & Jolicoeur, 1993; Weisstein & Harris, 1974; Williams & Weisstein, 1978). The processing of faces also illustrates the power of context: as we have noted, participants are better at distinguishing faces that differ only by the configuration of the nose than they are at distinguishing various noses presented in isolation. However, the context effect on nose identification disappears if the faces are inverted. This effect, known as **face superiority**, demonstrates that the parts of an upright face are not processed independently, but rather are recognized in the context of the whole face. These context effects with words and objects demonstrate that our recognition of one part of an image is often dependent on our processing of other aspects of that image. Figure 2–30 shows a striking example of the effect of face context (after Thompson, 1980). The two pictures are faces, one right-side up and the other upside-down. The upside-down one may look a bit strange, but not extraordinarily so. However, if you look at the picture upside-down, so you see the strange image upright, you'll see that it is actually quite gruesome. The context of the face in its upright position makes it easier for you to see how strange it really is.

5.2. Models of Top-Down Processing

As we have seen, perception is a product of top-down and bottom-up processing. Working from the bottom up, features are combined into some representation of the object and then the object is matched to representations in memory. Working from the other direction, how can we model the effects of context on object recognition?

5.2.1. Network Feedback Models

One of the models proposed for recognition discussed earlier is the network-based feature-matching model, diagrammed in Figure 2–20. In that discussion, our concern was the linking of features to form larger recognizable entities. Because in network models the units at different levels of representation process information at different, and *interacting*, levels of organization, this same architecture can be used to understand how information at the higher levels (for example, words) can influence information at earlier stages (for example, letters or features of letters). This direction of information flow is *feedback* because it

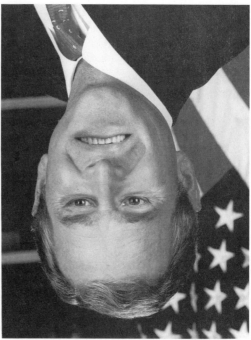

FIGURE 2–30 **The power of face superiority**

The face on the left is normal upright. The face on the right doesn't look quite right, and is in fact distorted: the eyes and mouth of the face are upright while the rest of the picture is upside-down. Still, it doesn't look too strange: not having the appropriate context of the face hides the detail. However, you will get the full impact of the distortion when you see it upright. Rotate the book and look at the image as an upright face.

(Photograph by Eric Draper. Courtesy of The White House Photo Office.)

presumably is a reaction to incoming, bottom-up information that in turn tunes earlier stages of the system for better performance (Mesulam, 1998).

The feature net model of word recognition demonstrates the mechanics of top-down effects such as word superiority. The feature net model can detect a particular letter from its characteristic line features, such as the curves in the letter "O." So far, so good—but our visual environment is much more cluttered, variable, and unpredictable than a perfect white printed page. What if ink spilled over part of a letter, as possibly happened in Figure 2–31? Without top-down knowledge, it might be impossible to identify the letter "O"; the visible portions are compatible with "C," "G," "O," and "Q." However, at the word level of representation, there are only a few three-letter words that begin with the letter "C" and end with the letter "T." The letters "C" and "T" would make each of these words—"CAT," "COT," and "CUT"—partially active. This word unit then feeds information back to the letter representations "A," "O," and "U," while the incoming bottom-up information from the features weakly activates the letters "C," "G," "O," and "Q." When the

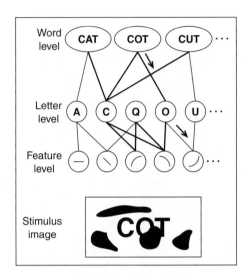

FIGURE 2–31   A feature net showing interactive processing with word superiority

The stimulus image is a word with some "ink" spilled over one of its letters. The bottom-up activity between units at different levels (thick lines) signals what features are present, and what letters these might correspond to. The top-down activity (arrows) facilitates connections that would fill in the missing part with a known word.

(Rumelhart, D. E., McClelland, J. L. (1987). *Parallel Distributed Processing: Explorations in the Microstructure of Cognition: Vol. 1: Foundations.* The MIT Press; Cambridge, MA. Reprinted with permission.)

top-down influence is added to the feature information, the "O" receives the strongest facilitation and the word "COT" emerges as the most active unit in the top layer. Feedback facilitation from the top layer resolves the problem of recognition of imperfect input by using stored information about words to guide processing.

The other models of recognition can also use feedback methods between different types of representations to model top-down influences; for example, the recognition of the configuration of an upright face, influenced by our top-down knowledge of what faces usually "look like," can similarly explain why we perceive parts better in upright faces.

5.2.2. Bayesian Approaches

A different approach to modeling the influence of top-down effects is based on the observation that the influence of stored information is *probabilistic;* that is, it reflects what has often happened in the past and is therefore likely to happen again. Is it possible that our perceptual systems store information about the likelihood of different events in the perceptual world? If so, the problem of identifying objects becomes similar to the mathematical problem of estimating probabilities. Consider this example: There is a high probability that a banana is yellow, curved, and elongated. A summer squash is also likely to be yellow, curved, and elongated. If you are looking at something yellow, curved, and elongated, is the object a banana, a squash, or something else? Well, it's hard to say; a number of things in the world—balloons, for one—could be yellow, curved, and elongated. The probability that a banana has these properties doesn't really help. Recognition would be easier if we knew the *reverse* probability, the odds that something yellow, curved, and elongated *is a banana*. It is possible to estimate reverse probability from the available probabilities by a mathematical rule known as Bayes's theorem (after the eighteenth-century English mathematician, Thomas Bayes). Bayesian methods use information from previous experience to make guesses about the current environment. Thus, by application of Bayes's theorem, if you have seen lots of bananas and only a few summer squash, it is a reasonable guess that the present yellow, curved, and elongated object is a banana.

Researchers use the Bayesian approach to demonstrate that previous experience can determine people's current perceptions. As with context effects, we build up expectations of what we will see based on what we have seen before. During learning of simple tasks, such as detecting black and white patterns, Bayesian models have correctly predicted participants' abilities (Burgess, 1985). Knowing more, from experience, about which pattern is likely to appear improves the accuracy of perception at the rate Bayesian theory predicts. In more demanding tasks, such as judging the shades of gray of boxes under different lighting, Bayesian models capture our ability to judge the shades and our tendency to assume that the brightest box in any display is painted white (Brainard & Freeman, 1997; Land & McCann, 1971). Bayesian probabilities are even successful in describing much more complicated perceptual judgments such as how we see objects move and change shape (Weiss & Adelson, 1998). Recognition of many other attributes and objects also has been modeled with this approach (Knill & Richards, 1996) because it is a powerful and quantifiable method of specifying how previously stored information is included in the interpretation of current experiences.

Comprehension Check:

1. In what ways does context affect perception of objects?
2. How can top-down processing change how features are perceived?

6. IN MODELS AND BRAINS: THE INTERACTIVE NATURE OF PERCEPTION

A broader view of perceptual processes is provided by the view from the window of your room in Condillac's hilltop château. Remember the situation: you arrived in the dark, with no idea of your surroundings. Now it is morning; someone brings you your brioche and café au lait and opens the curtains. What do you see in your first glance out the window? The panoramic view is too much information to perceive all at once. Yet, immediately, your perceptual processes begin to detect the features and put together the parts, and simultaneously your knowledge about the environment—about trees, fields, mountains, whether or not you've seen these particular ones before—gives you some context for shaping the incoming sensory information.

Bottom-up processing is determined by information from the external environment; top-down processing is guided by internal knowledge, beliefs, goals, and expectations. What method do we usually use? That is not a useful question. At any given moment, and for the various interpretations of different stimuli—which in life arrive constantly, and in multitudes—we rely more on one process than the other, but both are essential for perception. Many top-down context effects result from interactions between bottom-up processing and top-down knowledge.

6.1. Refining Recognition

Most of the time, bottom-up and top-down processes work together—*and simultaneously*—to establish the best available solution for object recognition. Information does not percolate upward through the visual system in a strictly serial fashion, followed by a trickling down of information from processes operating on stored representations. The essence of perception is dynamic interaction, with feed-forward and feedback influences going on all the time. Interactive models of recognition, such as the feature net model (McClelland & Rumelhart, 1981), assume that units influence one another between all layers. Line-orientation units and word-level units influence letter-level units *at the same time* to specify the degree of activation of the letter-level units.

Similar interaction is observed in the brain. Some visual areas in the dorsal pathway, including MT and attention-related areas in the parietal and frontal lobes, respond soon after the fastest neurons in V1 fire and well before neurons in the ventral pathway can respond (Schmolesky et al., 1998). These fast-reacting high-level areas may be preparing to guide activity in lower level areas.

Interactions between processes can be implemented in the brain because the connections between visual areas are reciprocal. Visual structures (such as the lateral geniculate nucleus, LGN) that process input at earlier stages feed information forward to areas (such as V1) that process later stages; there is also substantial feedback from later stages to earlier stages. Reciprocal connections between different visual areas generally occur between groups of neurons that represent similar locations in the visual field, so these neurons can rapidly exchange information about what features or objects are in that location (Rockland, 2002; Salin & Bullier, 1995). Some of this information processing involves building from center–surround units in the LGN to orientation detectors in V1. Feedback connections from high-level areas to low-level areas help to guide processing in low-level areas. The visual system invests a lot of biologically expensive wiring in these feedback connections. Area V1 sends more projections back to the LGN that it receives from the LGN, and receives more feedback projections from area V2 than it sends upward to V2. "No man is an island," and no visual area operates independently of its neighbors. These reciprocal connections allow for iterative processing, that is, processing in which information is repeatedly exchanged between visual areas, each time with additional data, to refine the representation of the stimulus and extend the duration of its representation (Di Lollo et al., 2000). The brain appears to be organized in a way that promotes the interaction of top-down and bottom-up processing.

6.2. Resolving Ambiguity

Information from any single vantage point is fundamentally ambiguous. Because we can never be sure what is out there in the real world, the brain must analyze incoming information to provide the most likely result. Usually there is only one best solution, but sometimes there is more than one. Take the Necker cube (Figure 2–32), for example, named after the nineteenth-century Swiss crystallographer Louis Albert Necker, who observed that some of his line drawings of crystal structures seemed spontaneously to reverse their orientation. This famous figure can be perceived as a three-dimensional cube seen either from above or from below (or occasionally as a flat two-dimensional figure). When looking at such ambiguous stimuli, we typically experience bistable perception—that is, we can perceive both interpretations, *but only one at a time*. We can't see both interpretations at once, even though we know that both exist and in fact have seen them. Bistable perception leads to spontaneous alternations between the two interpretations, even when we keep our eyes focused on a fixation point so that the bottom-up input is held constant. The phenomenon is a demonstration that the visual system is highly dynamic and continuously recalculates the best possible solution when two are initially in equilibrium.

Neural networks can model these spontaneous alternations by relying on two principles, *competition* and *adaptation*. If one of two possible interpretations produces a stronger pattern of activation, it will suppress the other, producing a single winning interpretation. However, the ability of the "winner" to suppress the "loser" gradually adapts or weakens over time, until the "loser" can dominate. The process is similar to a contest between two wrestlers. As they roll on the mat trying to pin each other, the one who is on top seems to be succeeding but is vulnerable to attacks from the one below. If their skills are equal, or nearly so, they will do many turns, with each wrestler enjoying a series of momentary, and alternating, successes and failures. Perceptual interpretations compete in similar fashion to be the "winner;" when two possibilities can both fit the incoming information, so there is no clear winner, we see, as it were, the wrestling match in progress (Levelt, 1965).

Bistability can occur at many levels in the visual system, as demonstrated by the different types of ambiguous figures that can vex us. Some, such as the Rubin vase

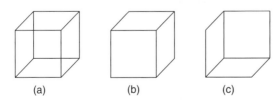

(a)   (b)   (c)

FIGURE 2–32   An ambiguous figure: the Necker cube

The cube (a) has two possible interpretations. You can see either a cube facing down to the left (b) or one facing up to the right (c). This ambiguous figure will appear to flip back and forth between the two interpretations spontaneously.

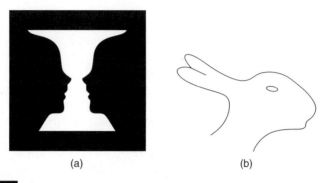

(a)   (b)

FIGURE 2–33 More ambiguous figures

(a) The Rubin face–vase illusion: the image looks either like two facing silhouettes or a white vase on a black background. (b) The duck–rabbit figure: the drawing is either of a duck facing to the left or a rabbit facing to the right.

(Figure 2–33a), named for the Danish psychologist Edgar Rubin (1886–1951), and Escher's birds and fish, present an ambiguity of *figure–ground* relations. In these cases the two interpretations differ according to the part of the image that appears to be the figure, "in front," and the part that appears to be the background. Other ambiguous figures, such as the duck–rabbit figure (Figure 2–33b), show a competition between two representations that correspond to different interpretations. Parts of the ventral extrastriate cortex involved in object recognition become active during the spontaneous reversals of these ambiguous figures (Kleinschmidt et al., 1998), suggesting that these extrastriate object areas are probably linked to our conscious experience of objects.

Further hints regarding the nature and origins of consciousness are provided by a form of bistable perception called binocular rivalry, a state in which individual images to each eye compete (Andrews et at., 2005). If a different monocular image— that is, an image seen by only one eye—is viewed in the fovea of each eye, we spontaneously alternate between the two images, reversing every few seconds and never seeing both at the same time. This is a particularly interesting phenomenon because a clear distinction can be made between what is presented and what is consciously perceived. The images are there, in front of a healthy visual system. When they are presented together but perceived only alternately, what neural activity is taking place in the brain beyond the retina? Neurophysiological studies in monkeys have found neural activity that is correlated with awareness in higher visual areas (Leopold & Logothetis, 1996). Human neuroimaging studies have found corresponding alternation of activation of high-level face- and place-selective brain areas during rivalry between a face image and a house image (Tong et al., 1998). More important, such effects have been found in the primary visual cortex (Polonsky et al., 2000; Tong & Engel, 2001), suggesting that this form of perceptual competition occurs at the earliest stage of cortical processing. Studies of rivalry provide evidence for the locus of the neural correlate of consciousness, and the results suggest that activity even as early as the primary visual cortex may be involved in consciousness.

But these neurophysiological studies and neural-net models do not explain the essential element of bistable perception—mutual exclusivity. Why can't we have multiple perceptual interpretations at once? The full answer is not yet known, but one explanation is that bistability is a by-product of the inhibition that is necessary for the successful functioning of our brains and neural networks. Seeing *both* stimuli in binocular rivalry would not be helpful to the human organism. If you hold your hand in front of one eye so that one eye sees the hand and the other sees a face in front of you, it would be a mistake—that is, very far from the reality of the stimuli—for the visual system to create a fused hand-face. One percept has to win and inhibit the other possibilities. Most of the time, there is one clear winner. The conditions that produce strong rivalry and bistability arise in the lab more often than in our everyday perceptual lives.

6.3. Seeing the "What" and the "Where"

Vision is about finding out what is where. To guide our actions, we need to be able to identify objects and know their precise spatial position. As previously mentioned, the processes for determining what and where are implemented in separate pathways in the brain (Figure 2–34). Spatial processing of location relies on the dorsal "where" pathway, which consists of many visual areas that lead from V1 to the parietal lobes. Object recognition relies on the ventral visual pathway, which projects from V1 to ventral areas such as V4 and the inferior temporal cortex. In a classic study, Ungerleider and Mishkin (1982) demonstrated that these two anatomical

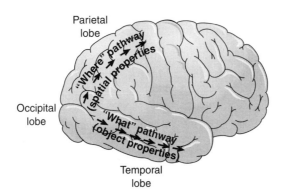

Right Lateral View

FIGURE 2–34   The two visual processing pathways

The "where," or dorsal, pathway includes brain areas in the occipital and parietal lobes that are involved in localizing objects in space and feeding information to the motor systems for visually guided action. The "what," or ventral, pathway includes areas in the occipital and temporal lobes that are involved in object recognition.

(Image of the brain from Martin's *Neuroanatomy*, Fig. 4.13. New York: McGraw-Hill. Reprinted with permission.)

pathways perform these specific functions by lesioning the brains of monkeys that were trained to do both a recognition and a localization task. Monkeys with damage to the inferior temporal cortex, in the ventral pathway, had selective impairments in object recognition. They were no longer able to distinguish between blocks of different shapes, such as a pyramid and cube. Monkeys with damage to the posterior parietal cortex, in the dorsal pathway, had impaired ability for localizing objects. They were no longer able to judge which two of three objects were closer together. Neuroimaging of normal brain function in humans also shows this dissociation: there is more activity in dorsal areas with localization tasks and more activity in ventral areas with recognition tasks.

"What" and "where" may have separable neural substrates, but we experience a visual world in which "what" and "where" are integrated. Information about what an object is must interact with information about where an object is to be combined into our perception of the world. Very little is understood about how the brain accomplishes this feat; so far, research has been able only to describe the responsibilities of the two visual pathways. One proposal is that the dorsal pathway may be involved in planning visually guided actions as well as in localizing objects (Goodale & Milner, 1992). Investigators tested a patient who had diffuse damage throughout the ventral stream as a result of carbon monoxide poisoning. She had severe *apperceptive agnosia*, that is, impairment in judging even basic aspects of the form or shape of objects (Goodale et al., 1990, 1991). She could not even describe a line as vertical, horizontal, or tilted. However, if she was asked to "post" a card through a slot tilted at a particular angle, she could do so accurately (Figure 2–35; A. D. Milner et al., 1991), but could not say

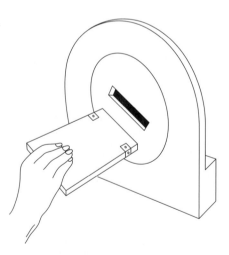

FIGURE 2–35   Investigating the dorsal and ventral pathways

A diagram of the card and the slot used in Goodale and Milner's experiment with an apperceptive agnosic patient *(see text)*. The slot is in a wheel that can be rotated to any orientation.

(Biederman, I. (1995). Visual object recognition. In S. M. Kosslyn & D. N. Osherson, *An Invitation to Cognitive Science, Vol. 2: Visual Cognition.* The MIT Press; Cambridge, MA. Reprinted with permission.)

which way the slot was oriented. Her deficit could not be attributed to impaired language ability or to an inability to understand the task, because when she was asked to rotate the card to the same angle as the slot seen at a distance, she could; but she couldn't report which way (or whether) the slot was oriented. These findings suggest that she had access to the information about orientation of the slot only through action.

By contrast, damage to the dorsal pathway can lead to *apraxia*, the inability to make voluntary movements even though there is no paralysis (for a review, see Goodale et al., 1990; Koski et al., 2002). Patients with apraxia can perform actions from memory and have no difficulty describing what they see; they would not have difficulty reporting the orientation of the card slot. However, they have tremendous difficulty performing new actions on what they see, such as posting the card through the slot. These and other findings support the notion that the dorsal and ventral pathways can be doubly dissociated and therefore support separate functions. Models of recognition and spatial localization suggest that the separation of these functions leads to better performance of each, as long as enough resources (that is, nodes and connections) are available (Rueckl et al., 1989). Just what types of functions each pathway supports and how the two interact are still being explored.

Comprehension Check:

1. Does perception come from bottom-up or top-down processing?
2. What are the "what" and "where" pathways?

Revisit and Reflect

1. *What is perception and why is it a difficult ability to understand?*

   The senses are our window into the world, and they provide the raw material for building an understanding of the environment. The primary goals of perception are to figure out what is out there and where it is. But perception is not a simple registration of sensations: it involves interpretation of often ambiguous, insufficient, or overwhelming information in the light of knowledge, beliefs, goals and expectations. Ambiguous: Is it a bear or a bush, a rabbit or a duck? The context of the night scared you—it's only a bush. And bistability lets you see duck–rabbit–duck–rabbit and protects you from the confusion of duckrabbit. Not enough: Sensory input does not contain enough information to specify objects precisely, so we must make unconscious assumptions and guesses. Too much: Too much sensory input is available at any given moment, so processing must, again unconsciously, capitalize on redundancies and expectations to select the important data for detailed analysis.

   ### Think Critically

   - Do you think it is possible that aliens from another planet might have better perceptual systems than ours? Why or why not?

- Is what constitutes "too much" information always the same, from moment to moment, or does this depend on context? If the latter, how do perceptual systems alter their performance depending on context to take in more or less information?

2. *What general principles help us to understand perception?*

In the brain, bottom-up processes and top-down processes continuously interact, enabling the development and refinement of useful percepts. Bottom-up processes detect the features of sensory stimuli—such as edges, spots, color, and motion. The visual system makes conscious and (as when supplying missing portions of a form) unconscious inferences from these groupings. Occasionally the inferences are "incorrect," as in the case of illusory contours, but often are nonetheless useful, enabling us to navigate the sensory world. Top-down processes rely on knowledge, beliefs, goals and expectations to guide perceptual exploration and interpretation. Perceptual mechanisms in the brain throw away some information that is redundant so they can pare down input to the essential features and fill in missing information from stored information about how things usually look and expectations about what is of interest at the moment.

Think Critically

- When is perception more or less demanding in everyday life? How might actions such as driving a car in traffic or reading in a noisy environment rely more or less on top-down processing?
- How might adults and children be different in their perception of common objects, such as bottles and faces? How about rare objects, such as a wing nut and a platypus?

3. *How do we put together parts to recognize objects and events?*

The building blocks of visual processing are detected at early stages of visual analysis and then combined to bring about object recognition. Feature detectors, such as the neurons that respond to lines and edges, can have local interactions that can promote a global interpretation, such as a long line or edge. Grouping principles are rules that perception uses to put together features that likely belong together, for example because they are close together (grouping by proximity) or alike (grouping by similarity). Various other principles also underlie how we organize features into patterns that are likely to correspond to objects.

Think Critically

- Why do we say that two things are "similar" or "dissimilar"? It has sometimes been said that in order to understand the nature of similarity we would need to understand most of visual perception. Why might this be true?
- Say you were magically transported to the planet Ziggatat in a different dimension and when you looked around you didn't see any object you recognized. How would you describe what you saw? How could you tell where one object ended and another one started?

4. *How do we recognize objects and events?*

   Models of ways in which the brain may recognize objects and events include template-matching models, which match sensory information in its entirety to a mental template; feature-matching models, which match discriminating features of the input to stored feature descriptions of objects; recognition-by-components models, which match parts arranged in a specified structure to stored descriptions of objects; and configural models, which match the degree of deviation from a prototype to a stored representation. Objects may be broken into three-dimensional parts (such as geons) that lead to recognition through their arrangement; configurations of object parts may be the key element that allows recognition of some objects, such as faces. It is likely that the brain recognizes objects by a combination of these representations and processes to maximize reliability of perception and make recognition faster and more economical. Visual perception seems to capitalize on the best method to recognize objects depending on the object to be recognized.

   Think Critically

   - What are the relative advantages and disadvantages of the main methods of recognizing objects?
   - "Recognition" is sometimes distinguished from "identification." When this distinction is made, recognition consists of simply matching the perceptual input to stored perceptual information, so that you know the stimulus is familiar; in contrast, identification consists of activating information that is associated with the object (such as its name and categories to which it belongs). Do you think this distinction is useful? What predictions might it make about possible effects of brain damage on perception?

5. *How does our knowledge affect our perception?*

   Knowledge about objects provides the basis for recognition. Knowledge also guides perception to the most likely interpretation of the current environment; this interpretation allows us to compensate for missing segments of an edge by extending the detected edges to fill in our perception. In addition, the context surrounding a feature, group, or object helps to determine perception; context can facilitate recognition when it is complementary, or impair recognition when it is misleading. Interactions between knowledge and current perceptual input bring about perception.

   Think Critically

   - How might people from different parts of the world perceive things differently? What types of surroundings would improve or impair recognition for different peoples?
   - Back on the planet Ziggatat, say you've figured out what parts belong to what and have come up with names for the objects. What problems will remain as you learn this new environment?

6. *Finally, how do our brains put together the many and varied cues we use to perceive?*

Reciprocal neural connections between brain areas play a key role in integrating cues that are processed in different pathways—no visual area operates independently of its neighbors—ensuring that information can be fed forward and back between levels of representation. The essence of perception is dynamic interaction, with feed-forward and feedback influences going on all the time; interactive models of recognition assume that units influence one another between all layers. Moreover, perceptual systems find a single interpretation of the input in which all of the pieces fit together simultaneously, even if another interpretation is possible. Interpretations are achieved and changed in accordance with the principles of competition and adaptation: if one of two (or more) possible interpretations produces a stronger pattern of activation, this interpretation suppresses the other(s); however, the "winner" gradually adapts and weakens over time, until a "loser" can dominate. Thus, if the stimulus is ambiguous, your perception of it will change over time. Finally, in some cases, distinct systems—such as those used to determine "what" and "where"—operate simultaneously and relatively independently, and are coordinated in part by the precise time when specific representations are produced; this coordination process relies on attention, which is the subject of the following chapter.

Think Critically

- Why does it make sense that processes are always interacting, instead of only after each has "finished" its own individual job?
- Is it better to have one interpretation of an ambiguous stimulus than to try to keep in mind all the ways the stimulus could be interpreted? Why do you think the brain "wants" to find a single interpretation?

Attention

Learning Objectives

A t a very large and very noisy party, you're looking for a friend you've lost in the crowd. You look for her green dress amid the sea of colors. You try to catch the sound of her voice in the general roar. There she is! Somehow, above the loud music and noisy conversation, now you hear her calling your name. But before you can move very far, you are stopped in your tracks by the sound of shattering glass—you turn your head sharply and see that a pitcher has fallen off a nearby table. While others tend to the glass, you set off across the crowded room toward your friend.

The processes by which you were able to spot your friend, hear your name despite the noise of the party, and then quickly turn toward and then away from the sound of the breaking glass involved attention. In the context of human information processing, **attention** is the process that, at a given moment, enhances some information and inhibits other information. The enhancement enables us to select some information for further processing, and the inhibition enables us to set some information aside.

Throughout life—indeed, throughout the day and throughout the minute—we are bombarded by an overwhelming amount of perceptual information; the party is simply a highly dramatic example of what's going on all the time. Our information-processing capacity cannot make sense of the constant input from many sources all at once. How do we cope? How do we manage to keep from being overloaded and thus rendered incapable of action? How do we, moment to moment, choose the information that is meaningful and avoid distraction by irrelevant material? One solution is to focus on some particular piece of information (such as the sound of your own name or a color of interest) and to *select* it for processing in preference to other bits of available information because of its immediate importance in a given situation. Is attention, then, something that we summon up by will that enables concentration on some piece of the incoming stimuli? The answer, briefly, is yes; but this is not the whole story. Even if our intentions and goals are clear and we know exactly what information we are interested in, other aspects of the input, if sufficiently salient, can capture our attention and distract us, as the sudden noise of breaking glass interrupted your search for your friend.

A host of questions immediately arises: while we are attending to one thing, do we actively inhibit and suppress distractions, or do we simply ignore them and let them hover in the background? What happens to the information to which we do not attend? What brain systems and mechanisms underlie these attentional abilities, and what disorders arise when these systems and mechanisms are damaged?

This chapter explores attention as a cognitive ability. We specifically address four issues:

1. What is attention, and how does it operate during cognition?
2. What information-processing models have been devised to understand attention?
3. How have new techniques for studying the brain enhanced our understanding of attention?
4. Attention, according to one contemporary theory, is a competition among different sources of information, all jockeying for further processing. Can such a theory explain both the behavioral and brain perspectives on attention?

1. THE NATURE AND ROLES OF ATTENTION

Although we have an intuitive understanding of what it means to "pay attention" to an object or event, the study of attention has a long and checkered history in cognitive psychology, filled with debate and disagreement. Some have suggested that "everyone knows what attention is;" others have countered that "no one knows what attention is" (Pashler, 1998). For example, Moray (1970) proposed six different meanings of the term *attention*, whereas Posner and Boies (1971) suggested that attention has three components: orienting to sensory events, detecting signals for focused processing, and maintaining a vigilant or alert state. Still others have used terms such as *arousal, effort, capacity, perceptual set, control,* and *consciousness* as synonymous with the process of attention. Adding to the difficulty is the problem of designing and carrying out careful and systematic studies of attention, for the very reason that attentional selection seems to occur so naturally and effortlessly that it is difficult to pin down experimentally.

Nonetheless, there is broad agreement that attention involves selecting some information for further processing and inhibiting other information from receiving further processing. One possible way to understand how this might work is to explore what happens when attention fails. After this, we will examine what happens when attention succeeds. Outlining the failures and successes will allow us to develop a clearer idea of what attention is. Thereafter, we will present some theories of attention and some experiments that look at how attention operates in the brain.

1.1. Failures of Selection

When we fail to attend to information, what kind of information do we miss? One sort of failure occurs when there is a lot of information simultaneously present in front of you, as at a party, and you are simply not capable of noticing all of it at once. These failures are referred to as *failures of selection in space*. Failure can also occur with information that unfolds in time. When new information (even if only a small amount) arrives in a rapid stream, spending time processing it will cause you to miss some other incoming information, resulting in what are called *failures of selection in time*. These failures to attend to information in space or in time are a by-product of a system that prevents us from becoming overloaded with irrelevant information—that is, of a system of selective attention. As such, these failures are an important part of effective cognitive processing and highlight the function of attention. Later, when we come to theories of attention, it will be important to remember that understanding attention is as much about information that is not selected as well as information that is selected. In the following subsections, we provide illustrative examples of failures and successes of attentional selection.

1.1.1. Failures of Selection in Space

Failures of selection in space can be of surprising magnitude. You'd notice, wouldn't you, if someone who stopped you on the street to ask for directions suddenly changed into a different person in the middle of the conversation. Actually, you might not. Demonstrations of the failure to detect changes between flashes of the same scene have now been replicated many times. Perhaps the most dramatic of these was a demonstration by Simons and Levin (1998) in which an experimenter stopped pedestrians on a college campus to ask for directions. During each conversation, two people carrying a door walked between the experimenter and the pedestrian. As they did, the experimenter switched places with a second experimenter who had been concealed behind the door as it was being carried. This second experimenter then continued the conversation with the pedestrian. Only half the pedestrians reported noticing the change of speaker—even when they were explicitly asked, "Did you notice that I am not the same person who first approached you to ask for directions?" This failure to detect changes in the physical aspects of a scene has been referred to as change blindness (Simons & Rensink, 2005). This phenomenon often goes to the movies: errors in continuity, such as the switch from the breakfast croissant to the pancake in *Pretty Woman*, go unnoticed by many in the audience. We can also be insensitive to changes in modalities other than vision. It has been shown that we miss changes between voices in an auditory scene, a phenomenon referred to as *change deafness* (Vitevitch, 2003).

That we miss some perceptual information is interesting. Even more interesting from a cognitive perspective is the implication that this does not occur by chance: we are *selecting* only partial information from the world around us and are not very attentive to the rest. Change blindness indicates that not all available information is attended and subsequently represented. Fortunately for our evolutionary survival, those aspects of the input that are more relevant and meaningful

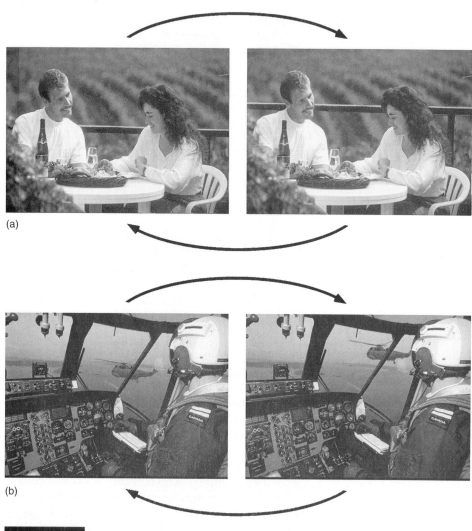

FIGURE 3–1   Changes in the scene

(a) A change of marginal interest (the height of the railing) and (b) a change of central interest (the position of the distant helicopter). Participants required more alternations between the two frames and more time overall to detect a change of marginal interest (average 16.2 alternations, 10.4 seconds) than one of central interest (average 4 alternations, 2.6 seconds).

(Courtesy of Ron A. Rensink, Ph.D.)

may be attended and well noticed, although much other information is not. Rensink and colleagues (1997) showed that changes of "central interest," those relating to the thematic content of a scene, were detected much more quickly than changes of "marginal interest" (Figure 3–1). This finding suggests that although we do extract the most important elements of the visual world, many of the supporting features may be lost.

A further implication is that our attention is driven and controlled via top-down processing, which can change in a flexible and dynamic manner; what is important at one moment may no longer be so at the next, and our goals shift accordingly. If you're hungry, you may notice a basket of luscious-looking fruit on a nearby table—but if you've just eaten, your attention may glide right over it with barely a pause. Knowledge, beliefs, goals and expectations can alter the speed and accuracy of the processes that select meaningful or desired information; that's what is happening when you rapidly scan a book to find a particular reference and are able to skip over large, irrelevant passages of material. The ability to use top-down processing to affect selection and attention is highly adaptive and such processing is an efficient way of extracting critical information from a flood of input.

However, because of the wealth of competing stimuli, top-down attentional selection does not always lead immediately to your goal. For example, in the opening scene at the party, the moment you recognized that the flash of green was your friend's dress was probably not the first moment that patch of green had appeared in your visual field, and the first time you heard your name was probably not the first time your friend had called to you. Further, you were actively diverted from looking for your friend by the sound of the crashing glass—your top-down processing was overridden by a sensory event, that is, by bottom-up attentional processing. The result? Failure in space: attention was captured away from the current goal of seeking your friend.

Failures to select information in space can also occur when far fewer stimuli are present. For instance, if you are presented with only two sources of information simultaneously (say, a drama on television and a story in the newspaper) and are required to process both, you will not be able to do them both full justice. The ability to attend to two sources is impaired compared to the ability to process information from one source alone: there is a cost associated with doing both tasks together. When you try to do both things at once, there are two possibilities: either you will follow the television plot perfectly and lose the news story altogether (or the other way round), or you will lose parts of both show and story.

Concentration on one source of input to the exclusion of any other is known as **focused attention;** in cases of **divided attention,** in which more than one source is attended, the information selected is imperfect (as in the example of following *part* of the newspaper story and *part* of the television story). One explanation for the loss of information when attention is divided is that the two sources of information vie for limited attentional resources, which are sometimes described as "mental effort." An oversimplified but helpful image is that we each have a pool of attentional effort into which each task taps. The harder the tasks, and the more of them there are at any one time, the more of such "mental effort" is drawn from the pool. When the available capacity is less than that required for completion of a task, failures are more frequent. When tasks are easier or fewer, there is less demand on this limited resource.

One clear example of what happens when attention is divided comes from a study conducted by Neisser and Becklen (1975). Participants were shown two

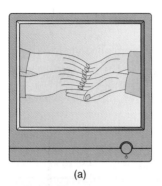  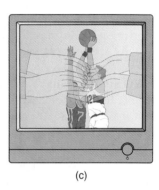

(a)   (b)   (c)

FIGURE 3–2 Divided attention

Drawings of (a) a frame from the video sequence of a hand-slapping game and (b) one from the basketball game. One is superimposed on the other in (c). Participants were shown (c) and asked to track only one of the games. They were successful, although less so than when following either (a) or (b) alone. Tracking both games in (c) proved almost impossible.

(Russell, J. A., & Barrett, L. F. (1999). Core affect, prototypical emotional episodes and other things called emotion: Dissecting the elephant. *Journal of Personality and Social Psychology, 76,* pp. 805–819. Reprinted with permission.)

superimposed video sequences. In one, two people were playing a hand game in which one player tries to slap the opponent's hand; in the other, three men were throwing a basketball and moving about (Figure 3–2). When participants were instructed to track one of the two games, they were successful; but keeping track of both games at once was almost impossible.

A divided-attention task like this one seems, at first blush, artificial. Yet this is exactly what, after much practice with simulations, highly trained air traffic controllers do, with many simultaneous stimuli to monitor (Figure 3–3). Fortunately, those who do this kind of work have sufficient expertise and skill that failures are extremely rare.

1.1.2. Failures of Selection in Time

Just as there are limitations on the quantity of information that can be processed simultaneously in space, there are limitations on the speed with which information can be processed in temporal sequence. These limitations, of differing degree and quality, apply to everyone.

Perhaps the simplest way to determine how fast information can be processed is to ask participants to report the presence of stimuli shown in a rapid sequence. Researchers interested in the question of the temporal constraints of attention have developed experiments that push the attentional processing system to its limit. In such studies (e.g., Shapiro et al., 1984), participants are shown a stream of letters, one of them (denoted by the researchers as the *first target*, or T1, letter) white and the rest

FIGURE 3–3   **Highly divided attention**

Air traffic control personnel are required to track the movements of many planes simultaneously.
(Photograph by Roger Tully. Courtesy of Getty Images Inc—Stone Allstock.)

of them black (Figure 3–4a). In some of the trials, a second target "X" (denoted as T2 and referred to as a *probe*) was included in the stream of letters at various intervals (either immediately afterward or after a number of intervening letters) following the appearance of the white letter. Each letter was on the screen very briefly, for only 15 milliseconds; the interval between letters was 90 milliseconds. The first part of the experiment was a single task: participants were instructed to ignore T1 (the white letter) and simply indicate whether or not T2 (the probe "X") was present in the sequence of letters. The percentage of correct detection of T2 was recorded as a function of how long after T1 it appeared. Next, in a dual-task condition (one in which two tasks must be performed simultaneously), participants were shown the

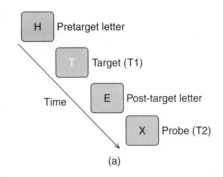

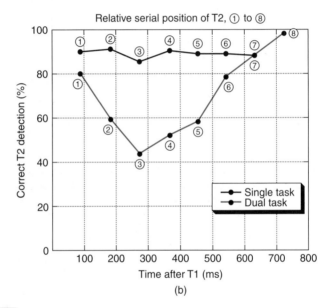

FIGURE 3–4 Investigating attentional blink

(a) Target 1 (T1) is white and is embedded in a stream of letters. The probe, the letter "X" (target 2, or T2), is presented at variable serial positions in the stream after the target. (b) The participants were more accurate in the single task (reporting the presence of the X without having to report the white T1 letter) than in the dual task (reporting the presence of an X after correctly reporting the identity of the white T1 letter). The attentional blink occurs after 100 ms, and is present even after a lag of about a half a second—but it is most severe when T2 is presented about 300 ms after T1.

identical stream of letters but this time they were asked to report the presence of T2, as in the single-task case, *and* to identify T1 whenever it appeared.

The results in both conditions are graphed in Figure 3–4b. In the single-task condition, participants consistently did well at detecting T2 regardless of how long after T1 it appeared; this result is not surprising because, following instructions, they ignored T1. The interesting finding is that, in the dual-report condition, participants failed to report T2 on the occasions when it appeared between about 100 and 500 milliseconds after an appearance of T1 (remember, other letters intervene). After greater delays between an appearance of T1 and an appearance of T2, however, participants were again able to spot the T2. The decrease in performance in reporting a T2 if it appears within a certain temporal window following the appearance of a T1 is an instance of attentional blink. As the term suggests, attentional blink is a short period during which incoming information is not registered, similar in effect to the physical blanking out of visual information during the blink of an eye. The phenomenon of attentional blink also occurs for two objects (not just letters) that are presented in rapid succession (Raymond, 2003). The hallmark of attentional blink is the missed detection of a stimulus that is presented within a particular time frame after an earlier stimulus is presented. When stimuli are presented so quickly, attention to the first seems to preclude attention to the second—showing the failure to select items in time.

A similar effect involves the failure to detect objects presented in a rapid sequence when some of these stimuli are identical, even when the stimuli are shown for a long enough time to avoid the attentional blink. For example, Kanwisher and colleagues (1997b) showed participants a sequence of nine serially presented displays with two or three consecutive pictures sandwiched in between visually "noisy" patterns called *masks* (Figure 3–5). A large masking field was also shown at the beginning and end of each trial. Each image was shown for 100 milliseconds. The important finding is that when the first and third picture in the series were identical, participants were markedly less likely to report seeing the third picture (the repeat). This was also true when the first and third pictures depicted the same object even if the objects were of

(a)

(b)

FIGURE 3–5   A demonstration of repetition blindness

Masks and *(center)* representational pictures were shown to participants. (a) When the first and third pictures were identical, participants failed to report the repetition, even if the objects were different in size or shown from different viewpoints. (b) When the first and third picture differed, participants had no difficulty reporting their identities.

different sizes or were shown from different viewpoints. When the two pictures were of different objects, however, participants had no problem identifying the third picture. The failure to detect the later appearance of a stimulus when the stimuli are presented in a rapid sequence has been termed repetition blindness (Kanwisher, 1987).

Repetition blindness can occur for words as well as for objects. For example, when the sentence "It was work time so work had to get done" was presented rapidly, participants failed to detect the second occurrence of "work" and recalled the sequence as "It was work time so had to get done" (Kanwisher, 1991). Blindness to a repetition can also be observed if several words come between the two instances of the repeated word or even if they are written in different styles ("WORK" and "work"). It is believed that the failure to encode the second stimulus occurs because it is not individuated or selected as a distinct event when it rapidly follows the first. Instead, the second occurrence is assimilated to the first, and only one event is registered. The phenomenon of repetition blindness suggests that when we do not have much time, we do not form a second, separate representation of an object we have just processed and so are not aware of the repetition.

1.1.3. Sources of Limitation

Why do we fail to select information in space or in time? Some have argued that the failure is on the sensory end; that is, the limitation is, literally, in the eye of the beholder (or, if the stimuli are auditory, in the ear of the beholder). Human peripheral vision is not very precise, and, in many studies, the information that participants miss appears at the edges of the screen. But failures to select all the information present cannot be explained solely by the drop-off in visual acuity for information appearing farther from the center of the visual field. In the Neisser and Becklen study (with superimposed video sequences), for example, all the necessary information appeared in the center of the screen. In the attentional blink and repetition blindness studies, the information is also presented in the center of the field. In these circumstances, then, the failure cannot be one of poor vision. Rather, the limitation appears to have to do with the *quantity* of information. Some models propose the notion of a bottleneck, a restriction on the amount of information that can be processed at once; because of the bottleneck, certain critical mental operations have to be carried out sequentially (Pashler & Johnston, 1998).

Divided-attention studies demonstrate that performance is hampered when you have to attend to two separate sources of visual information (like the television screen and the newspaper page) or two separate visual events (the hand-slapping game and the basketball play). There is also an added cost in accuracy or reaction time when you attempt to perform two tasks at once. In all these cases, the decrement in performance is referred to as dual-task interference.

One might wonder whether this decrement occurs because there is too much interference when all the information is similar, because it is all visual (or is all uditory) and we simply cannot cope with the quantity of data presented. There is, in fact, greater interference when the sources are both of the same type of information than when they are different (Brooks, 1968). If you are trying to recall a sentence, performing another verbal task such as counting will impair your performance much more than if you are trying to recall a sentence and examine a picture. By the same token, a spatial task such as visualizing a map of the United States and scanning along its borders, noticing which states are wider than they are tall, would impede recall of a picture but not of a sentence.

But the limitation is more general, and the failure to select information can occur even if the two sources of information are of two different types, or even if the information is presented in two different sensory modalities, say, one auditory and one visual, although the interference is not as great as when the types of information are the same. Some investigators believe that the extent of the interference depends on the extent of the "cross-talk" between the various representations and processes drawn upon by the incoming information: if similar representations and processes are activated in the two tasks, they may be confused. For example, both recalling a sentence and counting engage verbal representations; these representations may infiltrate each other and hinder processing. But recalling a sentence and visualizing a map of the United States have less overlap of representations and, hence, produce less interference with each other. A practical issue in dual tasking is discussed in the accompanying *Debate* box.

The bottlenecks in attention we have looked at so far have all been perceptual: too many competing stimuli, or fewer stimuli but of the same type and therefore competing. A bottleneck in attention can also occur when, even with a single sensory input, the outputs required are too great. In such cases, the bottleneck is motor in nature. Consider this: You've just picked up a ringing phone. The only sensory input is the sound of the caller's voice. The call is not for you. Is your roommate around? You have to check. The caller's in a hurry—can you take a message? Sure—where's the pad . . . and while you're looking you've missed the beginning of the message. OK—but now the pencil's dropped . . . gosh, this is taking a long time. . . . One sensory stimulus is requiring a number of responses. Coordinating them will be difficult, and some information will be missed, unless you take all the required responses a little more slowly or in turn. As with multiple sensory inputs, coordinating two output responses is more difficult than simply making a single response. It is not impossible to do two things at once, and, indeed, we can get better at this with practice, but there is usually some associated cost or failure even when one is skilled.

Just as divided-attention failures, in which sensory information is not attended, do not result from a limitation in vision, the failures in motor output when you try to do a number of things at once or in quick succession do not result from a limitation in the ability to program your muscles to move. Back to the party for a moment: you've found your friend and are comfortably chatting. Someone offers you a sandwich, but you're holding a glass in your right hand, your dominant one. You hesitate: should you put the glass down (where?) and take the sandwich with your right hand, or take the sandwich with your left hand? The interference, in the form of a slowing down of your actions, that arises when you try to select between two possible responses to even a sole sensory stimulus is referred to as a **response bottleneck**. The additional time needed to move through this kind of bottleneck has been measured experimentally. In one study, for example, participants were instructed to press a button with the left hand when a light appeared on the left of the

The use of cellular phones has skyrocketed worldwide in the last
few years. Recent surveys have shown that about 85 percent of cell-phone users in the United
States use a cell phone while driving. Redelmeier and Tibshirani (1997) found that cell-phone use
was associated with a fourfold increase in the likelihood of an accident. (Note that, in many states, it is il-
legal to drive and use a handheld phone, which makes sense given the increased risk of accidents when
cell phones are used.) What we do not know from this early study is whether the accidents occur more often when people are dialing a number, when they are talking, or when they are reaching for the phone; that
is, whether there is more dual-task interference in some conditions than in others.

More recent studies try to sort out these possibilities. For example, Strayer and Johnston (2001) designed an experiment in which participants undertook a simulated driving task requiring them to "follow" a
target car. Participants were assigned randomly to one of three conditions: during the driving task, some
participants listened to a radio program of their choosing (group 1); others conversed on a cell phone about
the presidential election of 2000 or the Olympic games on either a handheld (group 2) or hands-free
(group 3) phone. At irregular intervals, a signal flashed red or green; participants were instructed to press
a "brake" button when they saw a red signal. The experimenters recorded both the number of times the
participants missed the red signal and the time it took for the individual to press the brake button.

The results were straightforward: both cell-phone groups missed the red signal twice as many times
as did the radio group; and when they did spot the signal, their response (measured by the time to press
the brake button) came later. This lag in response time was more pronounced when the participant was
talking rather than listening. The difference in performance between the radio and cell-phone groups could
not be explained by different levels of driving skills in the two groups; all participants performed the driving
task alone (no cell phone) and there was no difference in performance between the groups in this single-
task condition. It was only the addition of the cell-phone task that led to the different results.

In just what way is attention affected? In a follow-up study, Strayer, Drews, and Johnston (2003)
showed that the consequence of adding the task of conducting a phone conversation to the task of driving led the participants to withdraw attention from the visual scene. Participant drivers who held cell-
phone conversations missed or had imperfect recall of billboard signs along the route. It turns out that
these drivers did not really look at the information: the eye movements of drivers who were talking on the
phone were not drawn to information along the route, even when it was presented in the center of the visual field and, consequently, they had poorer memory for that information. These failures to process and
select information are very similar to those reported in other experiments on failures to select information;
in all cases, the participants could not take in all the visual information that is present and, therefore,
focused on only small amounts.

computer screen; if a tone sounded, however, they were also to press a pedal with a
foot. Preliminary experiments determined that it took about 500 milliseconds for
participants to press the foot pedal after the onset of the tone. If the light flashed (requiring the left-hand response) 50 milliseconds before the tone sounded, participants
took even longer than the 500 milliseconds to press the pedal. Response selection for
the tone–pedal could not begin until the response selection for the light had been
completed, accounting for the additional time to press the pedal (Pashler, 1998).

1.1.4. Problems in Interpretation

Although cognitive psychologists have spent a great deal of time and effort examining divided attention and the costs associated with dual tasks, many questions remain. For one thing, researchers can never guarantee that the two sources of input are always being attended simultaneously, or that the two outputs are always being selected simultaneously, or that the two tasks are always performed simultaneously. Even under conditions in which one task apparently demands constant attention (for example, driving), it appears that the same level of attention is not required at every single moment. An effective strategy for multitasking, then, may be simply to switch quickly back and forth between the two tasks (or inputs or responses) rather than try to deal fully with both simultaneously. But how do you pick your moments? Listening to the car radio for a moment, then watching the road, then listening again is not a very practical (or recommended) procedure, no matter how short each alternate period of attention is! We still do not know whether it is possible to perform two tasks at exactly the same time or, if it is, what burden this arrangement places on the cognitive system.

A second problem that has muddied the dual-task waters is that it is not possible to guarantee that when you do two things at the same time, you're doing them in exactly the same way as you would if you were performing each task singly. Several researchers have suggested that the participants learn to restructure the two tasks and combine them into a single task (Schmidtke & Heuer, 1997; Spelke et al., 1976). If this is in fact what happens, and the dual tasks morph into a single task, it is difficult to separate out and quantify performance on each of the tasks. Also, in this morphing, each task has in some way been altered to make the combination possible, and so comparisons of the cost of dual tasks relative to the single task may not be legitimate.

In any event, dual tasking may not be impossible, and one can develop immunity to its adverse effects by becoming more proficient at one or both tasks. Let's look again at the dual task of using a cell phone and driving. Using simulated conditions, researchers asked drivers to drive normally and, while doing so, to perform a secondary task such as changing the radio station or selecting and calling a number on a cell phone (Wikman et al., 1998). To perform the secondary task, novice drivers frequently looked away from the road for more than 3 seconds at a time, a long (and dangerous) amount of time when you are on the highway. Under the same conditions, experienced drivers glanced away from the road only for brief periods. Because they were proficient at driving and this skill had become more automatic for them, the experienced drivers knew how much time they could spend on the secondary task without greatly affecting their driving. With enough practice and experience, a task can become more automatic and, as a result, less interference will be observed when it is performed in conjunction with another task.

In the late 1970s two researchers used just this terminology and described processing as being either *automatic* or *controlled* (Shiffrin & Schneider, 1977). Just as our example of driving experience suggests, they found that people use automatic processing on easy or very familiar tasks but are forced to use controlled processing for difficult or new tasks. However, controlled tasks can also become automatic with practice over time.

1.1.5. When the Brain Fails

The failures of selection described so far are part and parcel of the human experience—we have all experienced them at one time or another. This normal pattern of failures, however, is massively exaggerated in those who suffer from hemispatial neglect, a deficit of attention in which one entire half of a visual scene is simply ignored. The cause of hemispatial neglect is often a stroke that has interrupted the flow of blood to the right parietal lobe, a region of the brain that is thought to be critical in attention and selection (Figure 3–6a on Color Insert A). When these patients are asked to copy or even draw from memory a clock or a daisy (Figure 3–6b on Color Insert A), they do not attend to (that is, they fail to select) information on the side of space opposite the lesion and so do not incorporate this information in their pictures. Similarly, when they are asked to put a mark through all the lines that they see on a page set before them, their results often show gross disregard of information on the left side: they cancel lines far to the right, as if the left part of the image were simply not there (Figure 3–6c on Color Insert A). The reason for failure to select the information on the left (opposite the lesion) is not that they are blind on that side and fail to see the information. Rather, they do not seem to orient toward information on the left side of the scene before them and attend to it. If it is pointed out to them that there is information missing on the left side of their drawing, they may then go back and fill in the missing information; but, left to their own devices, they apparently do not select information from the left side. The neglect is not restricted to visual information (further demonstrating that it is not a visual problem per se)—such patients may also ignore sounds or touch delivered to the left side, or even fail to detect smells delivered to the left nostril.

Hemispatial neglect can make daily life unpleasant and sometimes dangerous. Patients may eat food from only the right side of the dish, ignoring the food on the left, and then complain about being hungry. (If the plate is turned around so the remaining food is on the right side, the problem is rectified.) They may shave or apply makeup to only the right half of the face. They may attend to only the right portion of text, reading a newspaper headline

SPECTACULAR SUNSHINE REPLACES FLOODS IN SOUTHWEST

as

FLOODS IN SOUTHWEST

and may even neglect the left of some words that appear on the right side too, reading the title as

FLOODS IN   WEST

They may neglect a left sleeve or slipper, and leave hanging the left earpiece of their eyeglasses (Bartolomeo & Chokron, 2001).

People with hemispatial neglect suffer deficits in their mental imagery as well as in perception. Even when there is no sensory input, and the image is solely created by their own memory, the side opposite the site of damage to the brain is a blank. Bisiach and Luzzatti (1978) demonstrated this by asking a group of hospitalized patients with hemispatial neglect, all of them residents of Milan, to describe in detail the Piazza del Duomo, a landmark of their city. Because the piazza was not in sight, this instruction required the patients to generate a mental image of it in order to describe it. Even though the information was being read off entirely from an internal representation and not from sensory input, the patients reported few details on the side of space opposite the damage. This was not the result of memory failure or forgetting: the experimenters then asked the patients to imagine walking around the piazza and viewing it from the side of the piazza opposite their point of view in their first mental image. Once again, patients neglected the details on the side of space opposite their lesion, but now described the buildings and shops they had ignored in their first description. The finding that hemispatial neglect patients neglect the left of their mental images suggests that attention can operate not only to select information from real perceptual input but can also select from a scene that is internally generated.

There are some situations in which left-sided information can capture the attention of the patient with neglect. Very strong and salient information that appears on the neglected side of the input may successfully capture the patient's attention in a bottom-up fashion; a bright light or a sudden sound on the left side may do the trick. Top-down guidance may also be helpful: specifically instructing the patient to attend to the left may reduce the extent of the neglect, but such guidance must be frequently reiterated.

Although the most obvious deficit in these patients is a failure to attend to left-sided information in space, there is also evidence that there may be a failure to select information in time. For example, Cate and Behrmann (2002) presented letters (such as an "A" or an "S") briefly (100-millisecond exposures) on the left and right sides of a computer screen and asked a patient with left-sided neglect to report which letters appeared. When a letter was presented alone on the left side, the patient identified 88 percent of the letters correctly; this percentage was comparable to the 83 percent reported correctly when the letters appeared alone on the intact right side. The interesting finding occurred when both letters were presented together. (In some patients, it is under these dual presentation conditions that the deficit for the left emerges most strongly.) If the letter on the left appeared first and remained on the screen for about 300 milliseconds before the appearance of the right letter, it was reported correctly almost as often as when it appeared alone. When the right letter appeared ahead of the left letter by 300 milliseconds however, the left letter was correctly reported only about 25 percent of the time. If, however, the right letter was presented first but enough time, say, 900 milliseconds, elapsed before the left letter appeared, the attraction associated with the right letter apparently decayed and the patient was free to attend to the left letter. In this case, detection went back up to about 80 percent. These results are reminiscent of those in the attentional blink experiment.

This study makes two important points: (1) When the left letter is on its own and has no competitor to its right, it can survive the neglect; (2) when a competitor is present on the right, the probability of the left letter's being detected following a short temporal interval is reduced because the patient is still attending to the more rightward letter. If enough time passes, however, the patient can attend to the left letter once again (Husain et al., 1997). Because the time also affects the outcome, it suggests that spatial (left–right) and temporal attentional mechanisms interact in determining how much information is neglected.

Are there patients who neglect information that appears on the *right* side after a stroke to the *left* side of the brain? Yes, but not many. The explanation usually offered lies in the greater, and asymmetric, specialization of brain areas in humans. In humans, the areas involved in processing language are generally in the left hemisphere, and attentional and spatial processes may therefore have been shifted into the right hemisphere. In humans, then, damage to the right hemisphere gives rise to neglect more often and with greater severity than does damage to the left hemisphere.

1.2. Successes of Selection

Fortunately, the normal attention system is not as dumb as it may appear. Despite the many failures of selection we are prone to—which may come about because too much information is present at any one location, or because too much information streams rapidly in time, or because our attention is divided—there are many conditions under which we can successfully and efficiently select the necessary information from the input presented to us.

1.2.1. Endogenous and Exogenous Effects in Space

When you were looking for your friend at the party, two kinds of information affected your search. One came from within you: your knowledge of the color of her dress. The other came from outside you: the sound of breaking glass. (In this case, knowing the color of dress helped; the glass crash distracted.) These two types of sources of information have been found to be highly effective determiners of what information is attended.

When you came into the room, you searched very broadly and rapidly for all green things in the array of colors that surrounded you and then, within this subset of green things, specifically for your friend's dress. This sort of attentional process, which has a voluntary aspect, is top down; it originates from *within* (from your own knowledge, in this case) and hence is called endogenous attention. But this form of goal-driven or top-down attention, can be overridden: salient and powerful stimuli can capture attention and direct you away from the task at hand. Attention thus captured is described as exogenous attention, because it is driven in a bottom-up fashion by stimuli generated *outside* oneself. (Like the sound of the breaking glass, strong color can provide an exogenous cue, and can be very useful: little children on field trips and prisoners in work-release programs wear brightly colored shirts for the same reason.)

The most systematic studies that examine endogenous and exogenous forms of attention are based on the idea of *covert attention,* which was developed by Hermann von Helmholtz (1821–1894), the German physiologist and physicist. Von Helmholtz demonstrated that although the eyes may be directed at a specific spot, visual attention can be directed elsewhere "covertly," that is, without overt motion of the eyes. (Helmholtz achieved his experimental conditions by flashing a spark of light, which, as a highly salient stimulus, prevented physical motion of his eyes toward the region of space he was attending.)

In modern studies, investigators seek to understand how endogenous and exogenous cues influence information processing (Posner et al., 1980, 1982). In one experiment, two boxes appear on a computer screen, one to the right and one to the left of a central fixation point (Figure 3–7a). An endogenous cue such as an arrow leads the participants to focus attention to that location even while their eyes are kept on the fixation point. The arrow is a symbol; only after its meaning is understood does a participant know how to shift attention—and hence attention is controlled by endogenous processes. On a large proportion of trials (usually around 80 percent), designated as "valid trials," a target such as a small box is subsequently presented at the cued location and participants press a response key as soon as they detect the presence of the target. In "invalid trials" an arrow cue appears pointing in the direction opposite the position of the target. Finally, in other, "neutral," trials, the target appears at the same location but the arrow is not informative—it points both leftward and rightward.

This study produced two main results. First, participants detected the target faster (and more accurately) in the valid condition compared to a neutral condition, suggesting that attending to a location can facilitate processing in that location, even in the absence of eye movements. Second, participants detected the target in the invalidly cued location significantly more slowly than in the neutral condition (and, obviously, more slowly than in the valid condition). What was happening? The participants were deceived or misled by the cue in the "wrong" position, which guided their attention in a top-down, endogenous fashion; the subsequent shifting of attention to the other side of the display cost them time. In normal participants, this pattern of costs and benefits is roughly the same whether the target appears on the left or the right of fixation (Figure 3–7b). Data from patients with hemispheric neglect show a very different pattern (see Figure 3–7b).

Attention is also facilitated by a valid cue and inhibited by an invalid cue when the cue is exogenous. An example: this time two boxes are on the screen and one brightens momentarily, presenting a salient bottom-up cue. The target (e.g., a small white box as in Figure 3–7a) then appears in either the cued or the noncued box; in the neutral condition, both boxes brighten. Attention is automatically drawn to the side of the display with the salient bright box. As with endogenous cuing, the participants detect the target faster when it appears in the location indicated by the cue (the valid condition) and detect it more slowly in the invalid condition.

Although the pattern of findings is very similar in the endogenous and exogenous cases, there is one difference. In the exogenous version, attention can be rapidly and automatically drawn toward the powerfully salient brightening cue and no extra processing time is needed. But exploiting the arrow cue in the endogenous version requires that participants process the cue perceptually, understand its content, and then use this information in a top-down fashion. If the arrow appears and the target follows immediately thereafter, participants show neither the benefit nor the cost of the presence of the cue. Given enough time (perhaps 150 milliseconds) to process and implement the information provided by the cue, the facilitation and inhibition emerge clearly.

These studies amply demonstrate that facilitation and inhibition of detection are influenced by the direction of attention alone, without overt eye movement. More recent results suggest that although it is possible under experimental conditions

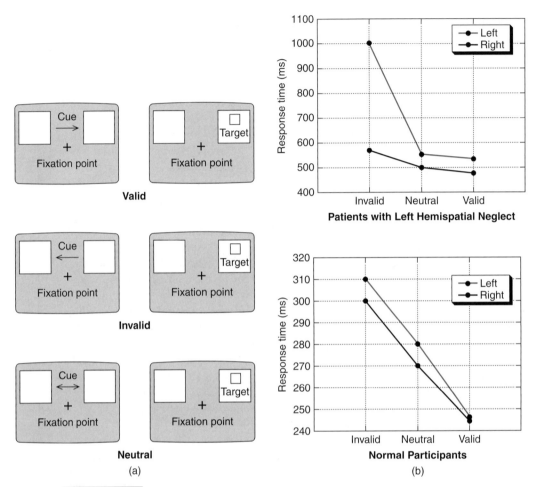

FIGURE 3–7 Endogenous cueing task

(a) In the valid trial, the arrow cue correctly indicates the location of the upcoming target. In the invalid trial, the target appears on the side opposite the cued direction. In the neutral condition, the cue arrow is doubleheaded and therefore not informative about the likely location of the upcoming target. Usually, in such experiments, there are many more valid than invalid trials so participants take advantage of the predictiveness afforded by the cue. (b) Data from normal participants and from patients with hemispatial neglect. Results from normal participants show the advantage—the faster detection time—afforded by the valid cue: target detection in this condition is even better than in the neutral condition. Note that detection time is slowed in the invalid condition, showing the cost when the arrow cue misleads the participant. There is no real difference in detection performance if the target appears on the left or right side. Patients with left hemispatial neglect were substantially slower when the left target was invalidly cued (note the need for a greater range on the y axis). In this case, the arrow cue points to the right and attention is directed to the right. When the target appears on the patient's neglected left side, target detection is very slow.

(such as those described here) to dissociate covert attention and eye movements, under more natural circumstances, the two are tightly linked and may even rely on the same underlying network in the brain (Corbetta & Shulman, 2002). In fact, some researchers have suggested that the coupling of attention and eye movements is particularly advantageous: attention can scout the visual scene first and then the eyes can be moved to regions containing particularly useful or salient information (Hoffman & Subramaniam, 1995).

1.2.2. Components of Attention

What happens when patients with hemispatial neglect perform this attentional cueing task? Patients with lesions to the right parietal lobe, many of whom also suffered hemispatial neglect, detected the valid targets normally on the nonneglected right side and almost normally on the neglected left side (Posner et al., 1984, 1987). That is, they could still take advantage of the cue even though their performance was a little poorer when the target appeared on the neglected side, and this was true whether the cue was endogenous or exogenous. In the invalid trials, when the cue occurred on or pointed to the neglected left side but the target appeared on the nonneglected right side, these patients detected the target more slowly than in the valid trials. The extent of the slowing, however, was in the normal range; neurologically healthy participants, as we have seen, also showed a cost in the reaction time in invalid trials. The important result is that in those invalid trials in which the cue occurred on (or pointed to) the nonneglected right side and the target appeared on the neglected left side, the patients with brain damage needed roughly an additional 500 milliseconds to detect the target.

The findings from patients with brain damage led Posner and colleagues to construct a model for attention that involves three separate mental operations: disengaging of attention from the current location; moving attention to a new location; and engaging attention in a new location to facilitate processing in that location (Posner, 1990; Posner & Cohen, 1984). In the case of the right-hemisphere patients, the model suggests that when the cue directed attention to the nonneglected right side and the target appeared on the neglected left side, the patients had trouble disengaging attention from the good right side, and this deficit produced the dramatically slower target-detection times. No "disengage" problem was apparent for targets on the nonneglected side when the preceding cue indicated the neglected side. In this model then, there are several subcomponents of attention, and results indicate that the parietal lobe (especially on the right) plays a key role in one of them.

Interestingly, Posner and colleagues found other patient groups who appeared to be impaired in either the "move" or "engage" operations posited by their attention model. Patients with damage to the midbrain and suffering from a disorder called *progressive supranuclear palsy* seemed to have no difficulty with "disengage" or "engage" operations (Posner et al., 1985). Rather, they were slow in responding to cued targets in the direction in which they had difficulty orienting, suggesting a problem in *moving attention* to the cued location. On the other hand, patients with lesions to the pulvinar, a part of the thalamus (a subcortical structure), were slow to detect both validly and invalidly cued targets that appeared on the side of space opposite their lesion, but performed well when the targets appeared on the intact side

(Rafal & Posner, 1987). These results led the researchers to suggest that the thalamic patients cannot *engage attention* on the affected side. The different patterns of performance revealed by these three patient groups support the idea that attention can be decomposed into three separate functions (disengage–move–engage) and that each can be selectively affected depending on which brain structures are damaged (for an overview, see Robertson & Rafal, 2000).

1.2.3. Cross-Modal Links

Although many studies have focused on attentional effects in vision, there is also evidence that facilitatory and inhibitory effects can be found within and across different sensory modalities. Once you spotted your friend at the party visually, you suddenly heard her calling your name, but it was likely she'd been calling you for some time. Why did seeing her make her voice more audible?

A series of experiments has demonstrated cross-modal priming under both exogenous and endogenous conditions (Driver & Spence, 1998; Kennett et al., 2002). (As noted in Chapter 2, *priming* occurs when a stimulus or task facilitates processing of a subsequent stimulus or task.) In one experimental design, participants held tactile stimulators that could vibrate at either the thumb or index finger in each hand. Four light-emitting diodes were placed in corresponding locations in space. When participants were asked to report the location of the tactile stimulus, the presence of a noninformative visual flash on the same side of space speeded responses. The reverse condition was also true: a random tactile stimulus primed responses to visual targets on the same side. When participants crossed their hands, the priming was found to be aligned with external space (that is, the left hand crossed to the right side of the body primed detection of a visual stimulus on the right). These effects have also been found between audition and touch, and between audition and vision.

Similar cueing effects have been found when participants expect a stimulus in a location in one modality and an unexpected stimulus appears on the same side of space in a different modality. For example, when expecting a visual stimulus on the right, participants are quicker to detect a random tactile event on that side of space than one on the left. This finding suggests that directing attention to one side of space in one modality automatically results in attention to that location for other modalities as well.

1.2.4. Object-Based Attention

In life, we are surrounded by objects, animate and inanimate, of all sorts, and attention is directed toward them as well as to locations in space and positions in temporal sequence. Recent studies of object-based attention show that when attention is directed toward an object, all the parts of that object are simultaneously selected for processing (e.g., Jarmasz et al., 2005). An immediate example: you think of your friend in green as a single object (and no doubt, because she's a friend, as greater than the sum of her parts). As you focus on her, you would be more likely to notice the watch on her wrist, because it is a part of her, than to notice the watch worn by the person standing next to her, even if that person is standing just as close to you as she is—that watch is a part of a different object.

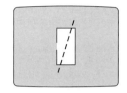 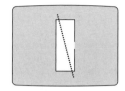

FIGURE 3–8 A behavioral demonstration of object-based attention

These stimuli were used to test whether two features belonging to the same object are processed better than two features from different objects (details in text). Participants performed better when the two features belonged to the same object, evidence for object-based attentional processing, in which selection of one feature of an object automatically results in the selection of the object's other features.

(Duncan (1984). Image taken from Palmer, S. E. (1999). *Vision Science: Photons to Phenomenology*. Cambridge, MA: The MIT Press. Reprinted with permission.)

Many studies of object-based attention demonstrate that an object and its associated parts and features are selected together. In one of the best-known studies (Duncan, 1984), participants saw in the center of a computer screen a rectangular box with a gap in one side and a line through the box (Figure 3–8). When they were instructed to respond with two judgments about a single object—whether the box was big or small in relation to the frame of the screen and whether the gap was on the left or right side—accuracy of report was high. In fact, participants were almost as good at reporting on the two features as when they were required to make only a single judgment, on box size *or* gap side. Similar results were obtained when participants were asked to make the two judgments about the line itself—was it slanted or upright, was it dashed or dotted? In a further condition, the two judgments the participants were asked to make concerned the box *and* the line, for example, the size of the box and the texture of the line. This time, although again no more than two judgments were required, accuracy fell significantly.

The important aspect of this study is that both objects—box and line—were superimposed one on the other in the center of the screen, thus occupying the same spatial location. The results with one object (box *or* line) and two objects (box *and* line) cannot be explained by preferential attention to a particular location in space. Instead, the result is compatible with the idea of object-based attention. Apparently, our perceptual system can handle two judgments quite well when attention is focused on a single object. When attention must be divided across two different objects, however, making two judgments becomes very difficult and performance suffers badly (this is similar to the cost that occurs under dual-task conditions). These findings support the idea that attention can be directed to a single object and all features of the object attended.

Neuroimaging has confirmed these behavioral results: when we attend to one aspect of an object, we perforce select the entire object and all its features (O'Craven et al., 1999). Participants were shown pictures of a semitransparent face superimposed on a semitransparent house and instructed to fixate on the dot in the center of the superimposed images (Figure 3–9). On each trial, the position of either

(a)

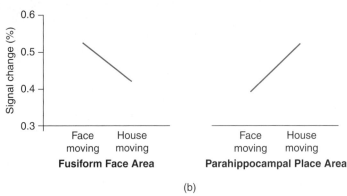

(b)

FIGURE 3–9 fMRI support for object-based attention

(a) Example of overlapping stimuli used in an fMRI experiment investigating the effect of attention to faces and to houses on activation in brain regions thought to specialize in processing of one or the other of those objects. (b) Changing levels of activation in the fusiform face area and the parahippocampal place area when the participants attended to motion and the moving object was a face and when it was a house.

(Downing, P., Liu, J., & Kanwisher, N. Testing cognitive models of visual attention with fMRI and MEG. *Neuropsychologic,* 2001; 39(12): 1329–42.)

the house or the face shifted; participants were instructed to attend only to the house, only to the face, or to the shift in position, and their brain activation was measured by functional magnetic resonance imaging (fMRI). This study exploited the fact that different regions of the brain respond more to houses or buildings (the parahippocampal place area), to faces (the fusiform face area), and to motion (area

MT). If attention were directed toward a spatial location, then we might have expected to see activation in all three brain regions, corresponding to the three stimulus types, given that all three occurred in the same region of space. If, however, selectively attending to one attribute of an object also enhances processing of other attributes of the same object, then we would expect greater activation in the brain area representing co-occurring attributes of the selected object. And, indeed, that was the case. When motion was selectively attended, not only was MT activated, as expected, but the area representing the attended object (face or house) was also activated. Thus, for example, the fusiform gyrus face area was activated when the face was moving compared to when it was static, even though the face itself was not preferentially attended. The same was true for the parahippocampal place area when the house moved. This suggests that in object attention, more than one feature is simultaneously selected (say, house-and-moving or face-and-moving) and the corresponding neural areas reflect this coactivation.

Evidence from brain damage also supports the notion of object-based attention. Although hemispatial neglect is predominantly thought of as a deficit in processing in which attention to the left side of space after a right-hemisphere lesion is demonstrably poor, it has been shown that the left side of individual objects is also neglected. In one study with neglect patients (Behrmann & Tipper, 1994; Tipper & Behrmann, 1996), participants were shown a static schematic image of a barbell, with each end a different color (Figure 3–10). Participants were instructed to press a key when they detected a small white flashing light in either the left or right end of the barbell. As expected of patients with left-sided neglect, detection on the left was poorer than on the right. But was this because the target appeared on the left of *space* (space-based neglect) or because the target appeared on the left of the *object* (object-based neglect)?

In a second condition, while participants watched, the barbell rotated so that the original left end (as identified by its color) appeared on the right of space and the right end of the barbell appeared on the left of space. Surprisingly, when the target—the flashing light—appeared on participants' "good" side, the right of space (but in the end of the barbell that had previously appeared on the left), participants took longer to detect its presence. The poorer detection in the rotating case occurred presumably because the target fell on what had been the left end of the barbell. Similarly, when the target appeared on the left of space, performance was better than in the static condition, because it now fell on the right end of the object. A further, and important, finding was that when the two circles that depicted the ends of the barbell were not joined by a connecting bar, participants' detection of targets on the right of space was always good and detection of targets on the left of space was always poor. In other words, no object-based neglect occurred, presumably because the two circles were not perceived as two ends of a single object; therefore, only space- and not object-based attention operated.

An even more extreme case of object-based selection—or rather its deficit—can be seen in patients with Bálint's syndrome (for more information about this syndrome, see Rafal, 2001). This neurological disorder follows after bilateral (that is, on both sides of the brain) damage to the parietal-occipital region; it is sometimes referred to

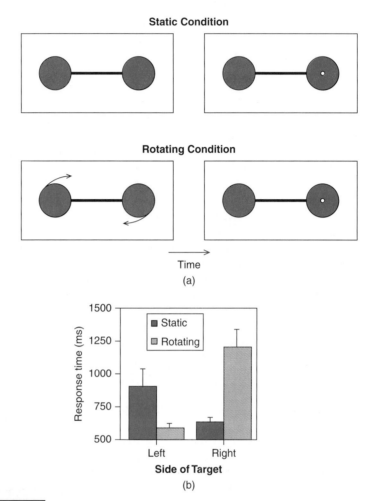

FIGURE 3–10 A demonstration of object-based hemispatial neglect

(a) The barbell display used to assess neglect for the relative left of a single object in people with right-hemisphere lesions and left-sided neglect (see text for details). (b) The crucial result: in comparison with the static condition, performance in the rotating condition is poorer (that is, the time to detect the probe is longer) when the probe appears on the right of space and better when it appears on the left of space. The decrement in performance on the right of space and improvement on the left is attributed to the fact that the probe is appearing on the left and right, respectively, of the *object*.

(Modified from Behrmann, M. & Tipper S. (1994). Object-based attention mechanisms: Evidence from patients with unilateral neglect. In: Imilta, C. & Moscovitch, M. (eds), *Attention and Performance XV: Conscious and Nonconscious Processing and Cognitive Functions*. Cambridge, MA: The MIT Press. Reprinted with permission.)

as simultanagnosia. (*Agnosia* is a defect in recognition; *simultanagnosia* is the inability to recognize two things at the same time.) Bálint's patients neglect entire objects, not just one side of an object as in hemispatial neglect. The disorder affects the selection of entire objects irrespective of where the objects appear in the display, and a whole object (a line drawing) may be neglected even if it occupies the same spatial position as another drawn object. These patients are able to perceive only one object at a time; it is as if one object captures attention and precludes processing of any others.

However, the failure to select more than one object can be reduced if the objects are grouped perceptually. In one such study (Figure 3–11), Humphreys and Riddoch (1993) had two patients with simultanagnosia view a display containing colored circles (each itself an object). On some trials, the circles were all the same color and on other trials half the circles were one color, half another. The patients were to report whether the circles in a display were all the same color or were of two different colors. In some displays, the circles were unconnected (the random condition); in others, circles of the same color were connected by lines, and in still others (the single condition), circles of different colors were connected (the mixed condition). In displays of unconnected circles, the patients found it difficult to judge color, especially when there were two circles of different color—there were just too many different objects. If, however, the two differently colored circles formed a single object by virtue of a connecting line, some of the difficulty of attending to each circle separately was offset, and the patients did better in the mixed condition than in the other two conditions. The cost of dividing attention between differently colored circles was reduced when these circles were joined to make a single object, and this improvement was more dramatic than in either the random or single condition.

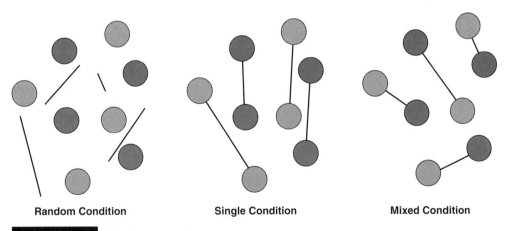

Random Condition	**Single Condition**	**Mixed Condition**

FIGURE 3–11 Simultanagnosia

Patients with simultanagnosia can attend to only a single object at a time; these patients can be helped when information in the visual scene is bound together to make a single object. Patients were shown displays with circles of two different colors, some disconnected (the random condition), some linked according to color (the single condition), and some in which differently colored circles were connected (the mixed condition). Joining the circles (thus making them into single objects) made it easier for these participants to perform the task of judging whether one or two colors were present; joining circles of two different colors (the mixed condition) led to the most improved performance.

✔ **Comprehension Check:**

1. Selection of information can fail when too much information is present at any one time or when information comes in faster than we can process it. What are some examples of failures in space and in time?

2. What are the distinctions between exogenous and endogenous forms of attention?

2. EXPLAINING ATTENTION: INFORMATION-PROCESSING THEORIES

"Paying attention" encompasses dynamic processes that involve the enhancement or selection of particular information and the inhibition of other information. Attention may be thought of as a mechanism that controls processing so that we are not overwhelmed by too much information. Endogenous factors such as one's knowledge and goals and exogenous factors such as the salience of external information can influence the selection. But how does attention work? A number of different information-processing theories have attempted to capture the dynamics of attentional effects. Although none of these theories can explain all the attentional phenomena we have described so far, the theories offer important insights into the principles that underlie attentional effects.

2.1. Early versus Late Attentional Selection

Almost all the experiments described here show that we can attend only to some of the sensory information that surrounds us and not to all of it. In the language of information processing, this selective aspect of attention is often a consequence of inadequate channel capacity or a fundamental limitation in the flow of information. One question is, when does selection occur, early or late in processing? Where is the bottleneck? How much and what kind of information is processed before it, how much and what kind after it? That essentially is the problem of "early versus late attentional selection."

The British psychologist Donald Broadbent (1926–1993) favored the view that selection is made at an early stage of processing. He proposed a model of the attentional system as containing a limited-capacity channel through which only a certain amount of information could pass (Broadbent, 1958). The many sensory inputs capable of entering later phases of processing, he believed, had to be screened to let only the most important information through. In his view, at an early stage of processing, information comes into a very brief sensory store in which physical characteristics of the input are analyzed: in the visual modality, these characteristics are motion, color, shape, spatial location; in the auditory modality, pitch, loudness, and, again, spatial location. Broadbent argued that the bottleneck is immediately after the sensory store, and only a small amount of information, selected on the basis of physical characteristics, passes through for further, semantic processing.

Broadbent's ideas were well received at the time; they successfully accounted for a range of empirical evidence. Some of this evidence had been presented by E. Colin Cherry (1953), another British psychologist, who recruited volunteers to participate in an auditory experiment. Using a technique called *dichotic listening* (the literal meaning is listening with "two ears"), he played competing speech inputs through headphones to the two ears of his participants. For example, the right ear might receive "the steamboat chugged into the harbor" while the left ear simultaneously received "the schoolyard was filled with children." Cherry instructed participants to "shadow," that is, to follow and repeat as rapidly as possible one stream of speech input and to ignore the other. Cherry found that participants had no memory of what was played in the unattended ear; in fact, they did not even notice if the unattended message switched to another language or if the message was played backward. They did, however, notice whether the sex of the speaker was different or whether the speech became a pure tone.

Cherry's results (1953) are consistent with the early-selection bottleneck theory: unattended inputs are filtered out and attended signals are admitted through on the basis of their physical characteristics. Changes in the physical aspects of a stimulus were attended, but if there were no such changes, the stimulus would either be attended or filtered out. Consistent with the claim that unattended stimuli are filtered, when the same word list was played to the unattended ear of participants 35 times (Moray, 1959), the participants never noticed. The failure to detect the repeated word lists indicates that the unattended signals were not processed deeply and the participants did not have a representation of the words or their meaning.

But one important piece of evidence suggests that a theory of early selection cannot be the whole story. Only a theory of late selection—which holds that, before the bottleneck, *all* information is processed perceptually to determine both physical characteristics *and* semantic content—could account for the finding that some information *could* be detected in the unattended channel even when there was no change in its physical features. This was especially true if the information was salient and important to the participant. Hearing your friend call your name above the din of the party is a good example of how unattended but high-priority information can still be detected. Hearing your name at a loud party is such a good example of this phenomenon that it's known as the cocktail party effect. By early-selection views, the cocktail party effect should not be possible; but there it is. Because it now seemed that unattended inputs were able to intrude and capture attention, Broadbent's ideas had to be modified.

Additional evidence to support late selection came from a number of studies using dichotic listening. In one (Treisman, 1960), a different message was played into each ear of participants. The logical content of each, however, was confused: the left ear heard "If you are creaming butter and *piccolos, clarinets, and tubas seldom play solos*"; the right ear heard "Many orchestral instruments, such as *sugar, it's a good idea to use a low mixer speed*." Participants were told to shadow the right ear, but some must have switched channels to follow meaning: they reported a reasonable sentence about an orchestra, and believed they had shadowed the correct ear all along.

The late-selection idea was also tested by presenting a participant's own name on the unattended channel, a controlled equivalent of the cocktail party effect (Wood & Cowan, 1995). About one-third of the participants reported hearing their own name (and none reported hearing a different name). This finding is difficult to accommodate within the early-selection view; it is also difficult to accommodate it entirely within the late-selection view, because only one-third of the participants detected their names on the unattended channel. One possible explanation is that this one-third occasionally switched attention to the unattended channel. This may indeed be what happened: when Wood and Cowan instructed participants ahead of time to be ready for new instructions during the task, 80 percent of the participants now heard their name on the unattended channel. This finding undermines late selection and suggests that participants may, for one reason or another, switch attention to the other channel despite instructions.

How can we reconcile these various results? One suggestion is that some kind of analysis must be done before the bottleneck, or filter, so that one's own name or other salient information can pass through (Moray, 1970). Arguing against this, another suggestion holds that the early-selection view requires only a slight modification (Treisman, 1969): that in each person's "dictionary," or lexical store, some words have lower thresholds of activation than others. Thus, information is still filtered out early, but words that are well known by the listener are more easily detected and require less analysis—and hence the information that does get through the filter is sufficient. Thus, one's own name or a shouted "Fire!" would appear to pass through the bottleneck and capture the listener's attention. Also, words that are highly probable given the semantic context (such as *piccolo* following shortly after *instruments*) may also pass through to our awareness.

2.2. Spotlight Theory

Like a spotlight that highlights information within its beam, in this view, spatial attention selectively brings information within a circumscribed region of space to awareness, and information outside that region is more likely to be ignored. This metaphor works—up to a point.

Consistent with the idea that spatial locations can be enhanced when they fall in and around the spotlight, participants who correctly named letters appearing at multiple locations in the visual field were more likely to succeed at an orientation discrimination task when the forms to be discriminated appeared near the letters. These data (Hoffman & Nelson, 1981) suggest that information is enhanced when it appears near the current position of the spotlight.

But the spotlight metaphor breaks down. For one thing, a number of experiments, discussed earlier, have shown that attention can be directed to a single object, even if superimposed on another object, demolishing the idea that a "spotlight" of attention highlights information in a particular spatial region. If that were true, all objects would be selected together, but we know that one object can be preferentially selected. Another difficulty is the assumption of the spotlight model that the beam of attention sweeps through space. If that's what happens, one would expect that if an obstacle intervened in the course of the sweep, attention would be captured or hampered by this obstacle. But it isn't. In a study that investigated this expectation (Sperling & Weichselgartner, 1995), participants monitored a stream of *digits* appearing at a fixation point. At the same time, they were to attend to a rapidly changing stream of *letters* appearing to the left of the fixation point and to report any appearance of the letter "C." Occasionally another character appeared between the fixation stream and the letters on the left—that is, it interfered with any "spotlight beam." But this "interference" made no difference: whether or not intervening information appeared, the time taken to detect a letter "C" was constant. These results suggest that attention is not influenced by the presence of spatially intervening information, as would be expected from a spotlight model.

Rather than thinking about attention as a spotlight where information outside the selected region is simply ignored, more recent studies have begun to characterize attention as a dynamic process in which information selection is automatically accompanied by active inhibition of other information. Thus, rather than as a spotlight, attention can be understood as a competitive system in which tuning into one thing results in the inhibition of competing information. Attending to green things will result in inhibition of things of other colors (helping you find your friend on our party example), attending to a single object such as a person will result in inhibition of other people or objects, attending closely to music may inhibit to some degree unrelated visual information. Attention, then, is a dynamic push–pull process that involves both increasing and decreasing the likelihood that certain locations or objects will be processed in detail. These ideas are elaborated in greater detail in the final section of this chapter.

2.3. Feature Integration Theory and Guided Search

This theory, which has a very different emphasis from ideas of bottlenecks, filters, and spotlights, is mostly concerned with the role attention plays in selecting and binding complex information. This question has been particularly well investigated in experiments using a visual search task. In this design, a display is presented on a computer screen; participants are instructed to find a target piece of information and press a response key when they do. For example, participants may be instructed to search for the circle in a display such as that shown in Figure 3–12a. In

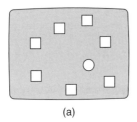
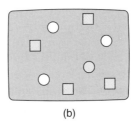

(a)   (b)

FIGURE 3–12   Selecting and binding complex information

Schematic depictions of (a) a disjunctive visual search display and (b) a conjunctive one. In which is it easier to spot the "odd-man-out"?

a separate block of trials, participants may search for the colored circle in a display such as that shown in Figure 3–12b. Try it: the difference between these two types of trials will be immediately apparent. It is absurdly easy to locate the target on the left, but the display on the right poses more difficulty. Displays like that on the left are referred to as disjunctive (or feature) search trials. In these trials the target differs from the other characters or symbols—the distractors—by a single feature, such as shape (circle among squares). A distractor is a nonrelevant stimulus that is supposed to be ignored. Displays such as the one in Figure 3–12b are conjunctive search trials, in which the target is defined by a conjunction of features—here, color (blue versus white) and shape (circle versus square).

Your experience with Figure 3–12 no doubt suggested that disjunctive search is generally easier; you're right. Even increasing the number of elements in the display in disjunctive search does not slow down target detection—the search can be done effortlessly and rapidly. The target seems to pop out at you; this kind of search is described as *preattentive;* that is, it takes place before attention is engaged. Because the target pops out regardless of the number of elements in the display, it is likely that the search is conducted in parallel across the display; that is, all elements are evaluated at the same time. In conjunctive search, however, each element must be attended and evaluated individually to determine whether or not it is the target. Adding more elements to conjunctive search slows you down substantially and, in fact, an additional increment of time is required to detect the target for each additional item included in the display. Because you must examine each item serially to see whether it has the requisite conjunction of attributes, the time to find the target increases dramatically as the number of distractors increases.

The cognitive difference between disjunctive and conjunctive search is well captured by *feature integration theory* (FIT) (Treisman & Gelade, 1980). According to FIT, the perceptual system is divided into separate maps, each of which registers the presence of a different visual feature: color, edges, shapes. Each map contains information about the location of the features it represents. Thus, the shape map of the display in Figure 3–12a would contain information about something of a particular shape at the right of the screen. If you know that you are looking for a target defined by that shape, you need only refer to the shape map, which contains all the shapes present in the display. The shape you are looking for will pop out of this shape map and target detection proceeds apace, irrespective of the number of distractors of another shape. Looking for a conjunctive target, however, requires the joint consultation of two maps, the shape map and the color map. FIT suggests that attention is required to compare the content of the two maps and serves as a kind of glue to bind the unlinked features of, say, "COLORness" [blue] and "circleness" to yield a blue circle.

Feature integration theory has illuminated other aspects of the way attention operates in visual search. One important finding is that you can search faster for the *presence* of a feature than for its *absence;* participants are able to find the "Q" (essentially a circle *with* a tail) among the "O"s in Figure 3–13a much faster than the "O" (essentially a circle *without* a tail) among the "Q"s in Figure 3–13b. In fact,

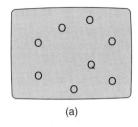 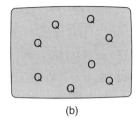

(a)   (b)

FIGURE 3–13   Looking for an absence

Schematic depictions of a visual search display in which the target has the critical feature (a) present or (b) absent. Participants found that spotting the "Q" among the "O"s—the element *with* a feature (a tail)—took less time than seeing the "O" among the "Q"s—the element *without* a feature.

search time for the target "O" increased dramatically as the number of "Q" distractors increased, but it did *not* increase when more "O" distractors were added to the display surrounding the "Q" (Treisman & Souther, 1985).

FIT is also supported by some of the sorts of errors that occur when attention is overloaded or selection fails. For example, participants sometimes make illusory conjunctions, that is, incorrect combinations of features. For instance, if participants report on the elements present in Figure 3–12b, if the display is presented very briefly, they may report the presence of a white square. This response, incorrectly combining features (COLORness and squareness) present in the display, suggests that these features are registered separately but that they are not properly bound together. When attention is overloaded or the features are not selected together, the isolated features remain unbound and may be incorrectly attached to other features (Treisman & Schmidt, 1982).

Do brain studies support the distinction between disjunctive and conjunctive processes? Some neuroimaging studies have indicated that different types of features really are being registered by partially distinct neural mechanisms, as assumed by feature integration theory. But the evidence is not incontrovertible, and some findings from patients with hemispatial neglect present a challenge to FIT. Patients with hemispatial neglect fail to take into account information on the side of space opposite the lesion, and the deficit has been assumed to be one of failing to attend to that side. According to FIT, disjunctive search is preattentive and does not engage attention, whereas conjunctive search does involve attention. If this distinction is correct, then one might predict that neglect patients would be able to perform disjunctive search well, even when the target appears on the neglected side. The findings suggest that this is not true. Behrmann and colleagues (2003) tested the visual search performance of a large group of neglect patients on the "Q"s and "O"s search task, manipulating the number of elements in the display from 1 to 16 items. As expected, these patients took a very long time, compared with control participants, to detect the presence of the "O" among the "Q"s on the right side (remember, this is the more difficult search, for the *absence* of a feature). They were also impaired in their search for the "Q" among the "O"s when the target "Q" was located on the left of the visual display. The "Q" did not pop out for these patients: either they failed to locate the target or took a very long time to do so, suggesting that even disjunctive search may require attention and the preattentive–attentive distinction between these forms of search may not hold.

Additionally, even behavioral studies with neurologically unimpaired participants have found that some conjunctions are easier to detect than a purely serial search model predicts (Nakayama & Silverman, 1986). Consequently, a new theory, *guided search,* was proposed (Wolfe, 2003; Wolfe et al., 1989). As indicated by the name, output from a first stage of information processing guides later serial search mechanisms. Although the first stage is similar to that of FIT in that it is constructed of different feature maps, it differs in that items that cannot possibly be the target are eliminated in parallel in the feature maps. In the example of Figure 3–12, processing within the color feature map would label all the white items as distractors and all the blue items as potential targets. The same sort of labeling would occur for the square versus circle stimuli within a shape feature map. Thus, by the time information reaches the second attentive stage, the number of candidate targets is already much reduced compared to the total number of items possessing one feature of the target. Guided searching accounts for a relatively efficient search of conjunction targets by allowing information from the preattentive feature stage to reduce the number of items over which attentionally demanding serial searches occur.

✔ Comprehension Check:

1. What are the differences between a spotlight view of attention and a feature integration view of attention?
2. Distinguish between "attention operating early" and "attention operating late" and provide examples of studies that support each of these two views.

3. LOOKING TO THE BRAIN

The study of attention has become a very hot topic in the twenty-first century because of a number of very successful studies of the neural basis of attention. These in turn have furthered our knowledge of the mechanisms that give rise to attention. For example, it is now a well established behavioral finding that when attention is directed to a location, perception of that information is enhanced. Until fairly recently, however, we did not know whether this was because the target at the cued location was more efficiently processed in the visual areas of the brain or because the motor system was biased to produce faster responses. Both these explanations are reasonable accounts of the findings of faster target detection. To explore further, researchers have conducted attention studies with animals and humans using various biological methods.

3.1. Electrophysiology and Human Attention

In the late 1960s, technology was developed that allowed researchers to measure with considerable precision the variation in electrical activity generated by the brain. Although it was known that faint waves are emitted by the brain in response to a stimulus, it had not previously been possible to average these tiny signals and relate them specifically to the processing of that stimulus. More sensitive electrodes placed on the scalp and more powerful computers to make the calculations could do the job. With technological advances, it became possible to distinguish between an event-related potential (ERP)—the change in electrical activity in response to a stimulus—and the sorts of brain activity that go on all the time. Investigators were now able to explore the neural mechanisms associated with various cognitive processes, including the phenomenon of selective attention.

The major result from some of these ERP studies was that directing attention toward a stimulus results in an increase in the amplitude of the waveform as early as 70 to 90 milliseconds after the onset of the stimulus. These changes are recorded in the first positive, or P1, wave over lateral occipital regions of the scalp (in the visual system) and suggest that attention enhances the early processing of visual stimuli in the brain, which leads to better perceptual detection of the attended target stimulus. For example, a study that recorded ERPs during tasks involving covert attentional cueing (such as that depicted in Figure 3–7) found a difference in the P1 waveform (and also in the first negative wave, N1) between cued and uncued trials for targets in both the left and right visual fields. Larger sensory ERPs were recorded in early stages of visual processing when the targets were in cued locations (Mangun & Hillyard, 1991). Attending to a location apparently increased the amount of visual processing, giving rise to a larger ERP signal. A similar increase in the sensory ERP occurs when attention is exogenously drawn to a location if the target appears within 300 milliseconds of the exogenous cue. Again, an early occipital wave is enhanced, consistent with enhanced visual processing of the target.

Taken together, these results suggest that exogenous, automatic attention and endogenous, voluntary attention (in other words, bottom-up and top-down forms of attention) have at least some underlying processes in common, an implication consistent with the behavioral findings discussed earlier. Furthermore, the enlargement of early waveforms at the occipital cortex is consistent with the idea that selection occurs early in the processing stream and that incoming sensory signals may be enhanced early as a result of attention. But, as we will see, some attentional processing may also occur later.

Interestingly, just as cross-modal links confer benefits in behavioral tasks, interactions between different primary sensory areas revealed by ERP studies have similar effects. For example, paying attention to either an auditory or a tactile stimulus appearing on one side of space resulted in enhanced ERPs within the first 200 milliseconds at electrodes in primary visual areas. Thus, attending to one side of space in the tactile *or* the auditory domain automatically resulted in enhanced attention to visual information on that side. This result indicates that when a salient event takes place at a given location in one modality, spatial attention is directed to that location in other modalities as well (Eimer & Driver, 2001; Eimer et al., 2002). This seems to be a very efficient way of wiring up the attentional system, and the result at a crowded party is that when you spot your friend visually, you are better able to hear and localize the sound of your own name.

3.2. Functional Neuroimaging and Transcranial Magnetic Stimulation

Data from ERP studies have been very useful in demonstrating that some attentional modulation occurs during the first phases of cortical processing, and in showing similarities across endogenous and exogenous cueing and across visual, auditory, and tactile domains. These data have been able to do this because of the temporal precision of the ERP technique, allowing measurement of changes in brain waves over time even down to a matter of milliseconds. But ERP methods are not that good at indicating exactly which region of the brain is responsible for generating the brain waves. Because the electrodes are placed on the head and the potentials are recorded at the surface of the scalp, we can never be perfectly sure of the location of the brain region producing the potentials. Functional neuroimaging serves as a good complementary approach: its temporal precision is not as good as that achieved by ERP methods, but its spatial precision is far better. The two main functional neuroimaging methods, positron emission tomography (PET) and fMRI, measure blood flow or metabolism in very particular regions of the brain. Their use in attention studies can demonstrate the regional consequences of attending to a stimulus. (For a fuller discussion of methodological issues, see Chapter 1, Section 4.)

In one of the early PET studies, participants were required to shift attention between locations—in this case, boxes aligned horizontally across the visual field—and to press a button when a target appeared in one or the other of the boxes (Corbetta, et al., 1993). The experimenters found that the superior (i.e., upper) parietal lobe in the right hemisphere was consistently activated during attentional shifts compared to periods when fixation was maintained in the middle of the screen (Corbetta et al., 1993; Vandenberghe et al., 2001). The involvement of the superior parietal lobe was also evident in another visual search study, especially when the target contained a conjunction of features. Although other regions of the brain, including the basal ganglia, thalamus, insular cortex, frontal cortex, and the anterior cingulate, also show enhanced activation during attentional switching in visual search tasks, the parietal lobe seems to play the primary role.

Another experimental design used PET to monitor brain activation as participants inspected an image for a change in either its color, motion, or shape (Corbetta et al., 1990). In addition to the parietal cortex, brain areas associated with processing motion were activated when participants attended to motion. Similarly, when participants attended to color, brain areas associated with color were activated. The importance of this correspondence is the demonstration that while the parietal cortex plays an important role, it is intimately linked with other brain areas that reflect the attentional modulation of the relevant features of a display.

The studies of attention have become increasingly sophisticated, and there have been attempts to differentiate the neural processes associated with different forms of attention. For example, Corbetta & Shulman (2002) showed that different neural systems are used when attention is directed to a location before the appearance of a stimulus (an endogenous condition) and when an unexpected salient stimulus appears (an exogenous condition) and redirects a participant's attention. They found that in cases of endogenous attentional orientation, a network of frontal and dorsal parietal areas (including the intraparietal sulcus, IPS; superior parietal lobule, SPL; and the frontal eye fields, FEF) was involved. Searching for your friend in a crowded room involved voluntary reorientation of attention that would activate this frontoparietal network of brain areas. On the other hand, effects involving exogenous mechanisms of attention, such as those arising from the harsh sound of shattering glass, were found to activate a more ventral system that included the temporal parietal junction (TPJ) and ventral frontal cortex. The authors hypothesized that this latter system is involved in the detection of unexpected salient or novel information. The two systems were described as functionally independent but interactive (Figure 3–14). Information from

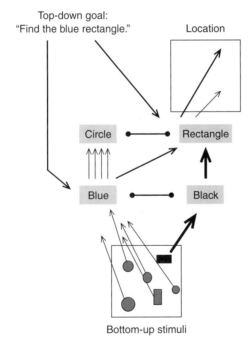

FIGURE 3–14 The interaction of attentional systems

Where is the blue rectangle? Finding it requires the interaction of top-down (endogenous) and bottom-up (exogenous) attentional systems. Arrows indicate activation; lines with dots on their ends indicate inhibition.

the ventral system may interrupt processing in the voluntary frontoparietal system and reorient attention toward the bottom-up, salient stimulus (as you were drawn to the sound of the crashing glass). Conversely, information about the importance of the stimulus from the voluntary system may modulate the sensitivity of the ventral system, providing a top-down way for your intentions or goals to influence how strongly your attentional system will be distracted by exogenous information.

The notion that attention operates over time as well as over space—for which there is behavioral evidence from studies on attentional blink and repetition blindness—is supported by evidence from neuroimaging. You've been looking for your friend for some time without success. Have you missed her? Has she left? Some people are beginning to leave the party. As more and more people start looking for their coats, you become ever more vigilant in looking for a patch of green. Such expectations for the appearance of a stimulus in time have also been reflected in activation of the frontoparietal brain areas, suggesting that the voluntary attentional neural network operates temporally as well as spatially (Coull et al., 2000; Wojciulik & Kanwisher, 1999). It is probably not surprising that after damage to this region, patients not only are impaired in attending to information on the side of space opposite the lesion (as in hemispatial neglect), they are also impaired in attending to information that is presented in a rapid temporal stream.

Evidence from a completely different technique, transcranial magnetic imaging (TMS), has also confirmed the critical role of parietal cortex in attention. This technique, which was also discussed in Chapter 1, allows a magnetic field to be passed through the neurons in a particular region of the brain, putting those neurons into a state in which they are inhibited from being activated by incoming stimuli. This technique, which is used with nonneurological participants, in effect induces a temporary "lesion" in healthy brains lasting a few seconds or minutes (with no demonstrable consequences after the study is completed). TMS studies with normal participants can therefore be thought of as analogous to studies of patients with damage to specific regions of the brain (such as patients with hemispatial neglect). TMS applied to the right parietal cortex of normal participants led them to require more time for conjunctive search but not for searches for simple features (Ashbridge et al., 1997). (Recall from earlier in the chapter that conjunctive search, but not simple-feature search, requires attention.) Interestingly, this increased time to search after TMS can be eliminated by training participants on the conjunctive search task (Walsh et al., 1998), perhaps thus making it more automatic and less demanding of attention. Another TMS study, which disrupted the IPS in one or the other brain hemisphere, resulted in impaired detection of stimuli on the side of space opposite the site of TMS; but this was true only when two stimuli were presented, one on the left and one on the right (Hilgetag et al., 2001). Together these studies appear to support the idea that the superior and posterior parietal lobes are involved in attentional shifts, and that damage to these areas results in a bias for attention to be directed to the side of space that is registered by the "intact" hemisphere, as is true in hemispatial neglect.

The ERP studies provide much support for early selection and enhancement of visual cortex processing during periods of attention; the PET and fMRI studies indicate that many other areas of cortex are activated as well in attention. These include parietal cortex and frontal cortex; imaging studies have also shown activation in occipital cortex, confirming the ERP studies (Gandhi, et al., 1999). The most important message from these studies is that attention does not simply engage one area of the brain. Rather, attention is implemented in a wide, distributed circuit to which different brain regions contribute. "Attention" involves selection that can occur early, late, or at both times, and be driven by our will or by the strength of stimuli in the environment and on the basis of space or objects or time. And so the most fruitful way of thinking about attention is as a dynamic system that flexibly allows for selection in many different ways. These studies of neural systems in the human brain complement the behavioral studies described in previous sections.

Comprehension Check:

1. Describe two different methods that have been used to study the brain basis of attention.
2. Do the ERP studies support an early or a late view of attentional selection? In principle, could ERP results provide support for both views? If so, how? If not, why not?

4. COMPETITION: A SINGLE EXPLANATORY FRAMEWORK FOR ATTENTION?

Conceptualizations of selective attention have undergone many transformations over the history of attention studies. Early theories drew analogies between attention and a filtering mechanism or bottleneck that operated in accordance with a set of early perceptual or later semantic criteria. Later theories recast attention as the selective distribution of a limited amount of cognitive resources. Now attention was seen not as a discrete gateway or bottleneck but as a modulatory influence that could increase or decrease the efficiency with which demanding processing is performed. Considered in this way, attention is a far more flexible mechanism—capable of facilitating or inhibiting processing of the input—than a simple spotlight or filter. Data from many differently designed studies have suggested ways in which attention may be implemented in the brain; many different brain areas, from the posterior occipital lobe, to the anterior frontal lobe, appear to be involved in attentional processing.

Is there a general theory of attention that embraces the findings from neural studies and observed behavior? The answer is yes. This is the theory of *biased competition,* or *integrated competition,* developed by Desimone and Duncan (1995) and Duncan and colleagues (1997).

From the perspective of this theory, attention is seen as a form of competition among different inputs that can take place between different representations at all stages of processing. In a simple competition model, the input receiving the greatest proportion of resources (say, because it possesses salient bottom-up attributes) would be the one that is most completely analyzed. A very strong bottom-up signal (such as a shattering glass at a party) would be rapidly and efficiently processed, even above the ambient noise of the party. Competition (and selection, which is the result of the competition) between noise-of-breaking-glass and general-noise-of-party would occur in auditory cortex. The same sort of competition would occur with inputs in other sensory modalities.

The competition between inputs can be biased by the influence of other cognitive systems. Focusing on visual processing, Desimone and Duncan (1995) argue that attention is "an emergent property of many neural mechanisms working to resolve competition for visual processing and control of behavior" (p. 194). Instead of characterizing attention as a spotlight that highlights particular regions of space for processing, or as a bottleneck or filter, these investigators characterize attention as an integral part of the perceptual or cognitive process itself. Competition occurs because it is impossible to process everything at once; attention acts as a bias that helps resolve competition between inputs. So, for example, if the input contains a gray circle, competition would occur between different color representations (or the neurons that constitute the representations), and gray would win; the neurons of that representation would fire, and gray would be considered the winning input. The source of the bias can come either from the features in the external stimulus (exogenous) or from the relevance of a stimulus to one's goals of the moment (endogenous).

The competition that takes place between possible inputs occurs in multiple different brain regions. For example, competition in earlier areas of the visual system will tend to be influenced by exogenous factors such as color or motion. This competition will, in turn, affect more anterior brain regions to which these lower-level areas send information for further processing. There, however, endogenous factors, such as relevance or goals, will tend to bias the competition in regions of the brain involved in formulating plans for how to pursue specific goals. This later competition can also send information back to the regions of lower-level processing and modulate the influence of exogenous factors at that level. The theory holds that many different brain regions are involved in such competition, and because they are connected, the competition is integrated across them. The ultimate winner of the competition—the item that is ultimately attended—is determined by a consensus among all the different regions working together. Given this perspective, findings that so many different brain areas contribute to attentional selection are not surprising.

One of the original motivations for the idea of competition came from a single-cell recording study in which monkeys were trained to perform a visual search task (Moran & Desimone, 1985). The important result was that when two targets were in the same receptive field, they competed for the cell's responses. However, when one of the objects was the target and the other was a distractor, the neuron responded primarily to the target stimulus and blocked processing of the distractor stimulus. If you imagine these competitive processes occurring all along the processing stream, one way to understand attention is to think of it as a gating mechanism that biases processing according to a combination of external salience and internal goals. The outcome of the competition is a winner that is selected for further, preferential processing.

Several ERP and fMRI studies have shown how the ERP waveform or the activation of various brain regions is enhanced or magnified under conditions of competition. These increases occur when participants perform more difficult discriminations (Lavie, 1995), when distractors compete with targets, and when the demands of a task are increased. When task demands are increased as in dual-task conditions, less activation is observed in areas associated with a simultaneous secondary task, reflecting the decrease in processing of nonselected information.

Competitive effects are also seen when stimuli appear simultaneously rather than sequentially, probably reflecting mutual suppression by simultaneously competing stimuli. When four visual stimuli were present, there was less activation in visual cortical area V4 than when only one was present (Kastner et al., 1998). However, when participants were asked to attend to just one of the four stimuli that were presented simultaneously, activation went up to a level similar to that observed with a single stimulus presented alone (see accompanying, *A Closer Look* box). In the framework of integration competition theory, attending to a single object effectively reduced the amount of competition from other stimuli and biased processing toward that stimulus.

Other demonstrations of attentional modulation, obtained with both fMRI and ERP techniques, have been found in V1 and other early visual cortical areas (Brefczynski & DeYoe, 1999; Gandhi et al., 1999; Luck & Hillyard, 2000; Noesselt et al., 2002; Somers et al., 1999). Some researchers have even found very early attentional effects in the lateral geniculate nucleus of the thalamus, a key informational relay station between the retina and visual cortex in the back of the brain (O'Connor et al., 2002). These results indicate that, as the theory holds, information can be sent back to areas that accomplish earlier processing and thereby bias subsequent processing. Moreover, there is some suggestion that feedback connections to early visual cortex are involved in determining our conscious experience of visual information (Pascual-Leone & Walsh, 2001).

Competition is also evident when a participant is required to divide attention across two perceptual features. Compared with a simple condition in which no stimulus appears on the screen and the participant stares at a fixation point, attending to the color or the shape of a stimulus that appears on the screen leads to greater activation of many visual areas. Moreover, if the participant has to switch between attending to the color and attending to the shape, additional areas of the brain become engaged and—no surprise—regions of parietal cortex are also active (Le et al., 1998; Liu et al., 2003).

Many of the findings that demonstrate failures of selection in space or in time can be explained by the idea of competition between stimuli. For example, in covert attentional cueing (see Figure 3–7) the invalid trials can be thought of as cases in which there is competition between the location indicated by the invalid cue and the location where the target appears; in the valid condition, the location

A CLOSER LOOK
Competition and Selection

Wₑ examine here an investigation that explored mechanisms by which competition by stimuli might be enhanced or decreased. The work, by Sabine Kastner, Peter De Weerd, Robert Desimone, and Leslie Ungerleider, was reported in 1998 in "Mechanisms of Directed Attention in the Human Extrastriate Cortex as Revealed by Functional MRI," *Science, 282,* 108–111.

Introduction

The investigators used fMRI to test ideas about competition and attentional selection. The idea being explored is that the visual system is limited in its capacity to process multiple stimuli at any given time. The hypothesis: in order for objects to be selected, competition must occur between available objects to yield a "winner." The suppression of the eventual winner by the "losing" stimuli would give rise to a reduction in the signal measured by fMRI. In addition, the investigators argue that this suppression can be overcome even when multiple objects are present: if attention is directed to one of the objects specifically, the response would be enhanced and lead to stronger fMRI signals.

Method

Eight participants viewed images appearing on a screen while lying in the fMRI scanner. Two conditions were used in the first experiment. In the *sequential condition,* four complex images were shown in random locations on the screen but only one object was ever present at a single time. In contrast, in the *simultaneous condition,* the same four complex images were present, but in this condition all four were present at the same time. Because competition (and suppression) can take place when all four are simultaneously present, the expectation was that the fMRI signal from visual cortex in the simultaneous condition would be lower than the sum of the four fMRI signals in the sequential condition. The second experiment was the same as the first but now, in some sets of trials, participants were instructed to attend to a particular location in which one stimulus was presented and to count the occurrences of a particular target stimulus at that location.

Results

Markedly weaker signals were observed in many visual areas of the brain in the simultaneous than in the sequential condition, supporting the idea that the stimuli presented together competed with one another and, in so doing, led to the suppression of some of them. When stimuli are presented one at a time, each can activate the brain fully and so the sequential condition leads to stronger fMRI signals. It is interesting and important that in the second experiment, when the participants attended to the location of one of the stimuli, there was an increase in the strength of the fMRI signal, and this signal was even larger than in the sequential condition in some visual areas of the brain.

Discussion

The hypothesis was that competition among multiple stimuli would lead to suppression and that this would be reflected by a reduction in the fMRI signal. This was indeed the case, and this finding provides support for the idea that attention is a dynamic process in which stimuli compete for selection. Competition, then, may be the means by which unwanted stimuli are filtered out (they are suppressed and have little or no activation). The second experiment shows that one can enhance some stimuli by attending to them even if there are many stimuli present; this finding shows that along with suppression, enhancement occurs when one selects a subset of items for further processing.

of the valid cue and the location of the target are one and the same, and hence co-operation rather than competition prevails. Also, the effects of divided attention can be interpreted as the result of competition between different inputs or different tasks, as opposed to the noncompetitive case, in which the focus is exclusively on a single input or a single task. The improvement, in the form of automaticity, that comes with greater practice with dual tasks may be thought of as a reduction in the competition between the two tasks. Moreover, the performance of patients with hemispatial neglect can also be understood within this framework of competition. If the damage to the right side of the brain allows the intact hemisphere to produce a bias away from the left side and toward the right side, that bias increases the competitive strength of right-sided stimuli and reduces that of left-sided stimuli.

Failures of selection in time lend themselves to a similar explanation. The failure to report T2 in the attentional blink task (see Figure 3–4) might arise from competition between T1 and T2. Reporting T2 when it is not preceded by T1 is not problematic—there is no competition. However, the requirement to report T2 when it is preceded by T1 and is very similar to T1 in appearance (say, the letters are "A" and "H") establishes a highly competitive environment and reduces the chances of detection of T2. Competition may also explain the failures of selection in time observed with patients with hemispatial neglect. When visual stimuli are presented on both sides, reporting of the stimulus on the neglected side improves depending on the timing of presentation of the two stimuli and their grouping. One might think of these two factors, time and grouping, as biases that can influence the outcome of the competition between stimuli on the right and on the left.

It seems, then, that almost all the behavioral experiments we have discussed can be interpreted in terms of a competition between "stronger" and "weaker" stimuli, with strength defined by a combination of bottom-up and top-down influences. Although not all the details of biased competition have been worked out yet, this framework allows us to explain a wide range of findings; its direction is promising. The advantage of this theory is that it underscores the idea that attention is a bias in processing, and that processing occurs through cooperative and competitive interactions among brain areas. Because the different brain areas are connected, they will all contribute to the selection of the target. By combining the behavioral results with the inferred involvement of particular brain areas, it is possible to begin to develop an understanding of how attentional effects are manifested in the neural system and how those changes affect cognition and behavior.

Comprehension Check:

1. How might an attentional blink result from competition between two stimuli?
2. Give an example of how a salient bottom-up signal might compete with and win over another stimulus.

Revisit and Reflect

1. *What is attention, and how does it operate during cognition?*

   Attention is the process whereby we can select from among the many competing stimuli present in our environment, facilitating processing of some while inhibiting processing of others. This selection can be driven endogenously by our goals (e.g., to find a particular friend, to follow an instruction, to use an arrow to direct attention), or exogenously by a salient or novel stimulus that captures attention away from the task at hand (e.g., bright light, loud noise). Because there is too much information at any given moment for us to cope with, attention is the mechanism by which the most important information is selected for further processing. The type of information that we miss and the conditions under which we miss it are, therefore, the flip side of the cognitive processes involved in attentional selection. Being unaware of the posters on the wall at a party is a failure of selection that is a property of selectively searching for features of a friend. Although we are capable of processing only a limited quantity of information in both space and time, fortunately selection does not occur randomly. Both our goals and the salience of information around us determine where and to what we attend. This balance between endogenous and exogenous factors not only allows us to accomplish our goals effectively, such as finding an individual in a crowd, but also to be sensitive to important external information, such as a fire alarm or crashing glass.

   Think Critically

   - Describe the differences between endogenous and exogenous attentional processing in space and in time.
   - What would it be like if you were equally aware of all the visual and auditory details of your environment at once? Would this be an advantage or a disadvantage?
   - Does studying in a noisy environment such as a coffee shop help you focus or does it distract you? Do the level of noise and the difficulty of the subject matter or its type (verbal, pictorial) affect the suitability of a study location? How?
   - How do cross-modal processes (e.g., visual-to-auditory) facilitate attentional selection of goal-relevant information such as looking for a friend in a crowd? How can cross-modal processes hinder it?

2. *What information-processing models have been devised to understand attention?*

   Different models of attention have each been successful in capturing particular aspects of attentional processing. The debate over whether attention operates at an early or late stage highlighted two aspects of attention. First, attention can have an effect on the very earliest levels of perceptual processing by reducing the amount of information that enters into our cognitive system. Second, some unattended information reaches very late stages of processing, which shows that not all unattended information is entirely filtered out. Information that is contextually consistent with our goals or likely to be of extreme importance, such as our name, penetrates the attentional filter. The spotlight metaphor for attention reflected the reality that space is a powerful coordinate system for our perceptual systems, and that attention operates on these sensory systems directly. For example, turning toward the sound of crashing glass at a party might result in the incidental selection of other things in that spatial location such as a piece of furniture, which you would have otherwise failed to notice. Later theories, such as feature integration theory and guided search, proposed more complex models of attention that involved early preattentive and later attentive stages of processing. These theories provided a mechanism for how attention integrates information. As theories change over time, they build on ideas from previous theories and increase in the detail of explanation. In this way, our understanding of attention builds over time.

Think Critically

- According to research findings, would it be more effective to search for your friend at a crowded party along a particular dimension (e.g., color of her dress, her height) or in terms of a combination of dimensions? Which and why?

- From knowledge of the different theories of attention, what advice would you give to advertising agencies for creating advertisements that are likely to be noticed and read? What advice would you give to Web masters who want to control the distractability of Web advertisements on their pages?

- In what way is the spotlight an appropriate metaphor for attention, and in what way is it not?

- According to feature integration theory, what is the difference between preattentive and attentive processing?

3. *How have new techniques for studying the brain enhanced our understanding of attention?*

Together, ERP, TMS, PET, and fMRI studies have corroborated and extended information-processing concepts of attention. They have shown that attention modulates processing in early sensory areas such as the primary visual cortex but that the attentional signal may be generated from processing in the parietal and frontal lobes. The parietal and frontal areas associated with attention are separated into two neural systems that are interconnected. The more dorsal system is involved in endogenous attention and tightly connected with the motor systems that produce eye and other body movements. This system underlies the voluntary selection of relevant information and the transformation of it into discrete actions, such as moving one's eyes toward a person in green. The more ventral system is sensitive to the appearance of new exogenous stimuli, such as the sound of breaking glass, and this system can modulate, and be modulated by signals from the dorsal system. The results suggest that the attentional system in the brain involves highly interconnected areas that interact to produce effective selection of relevant information.

Think Critically

- Damage to which areas of the brain would impair the endogenous and exogenous attentional systems, respectively?
- What deficits in searching for a friend in a crowded room would you expect to occur if you had brain damage in each of the two attentional systems?
- What properties of the neural systems involved in attention have TMS, ERP, PET, and fMRI helped us to understand?
- What areas of the brain have been found to be involved in attentional processing, and how are they involved?

4. *Attention, according to one contemporary theory, is a competition among different sources of information, all vying for further processing. Can such a theory explain both the behavioral and brain perspectives on attention?*

The competition framework characterizes attention as a signal that biases processing toward the most relevant or salient features, which are then processed further. Attention as a biasing signal acts within as well as between perceptual and cognitive systems. The outcome of the bias present in one phase of processing is passed on to other phases and acts as a bias there. The effects of competition are dynamic, just as experiments have shown attentional effects to be. According to the competition framework, the reason why it is so difficult to find your friend in a crowded room is because there are too many competing objects that are either too similar, such as other people, or too salient, such as crashing glass and loud voices. Your friend, as an object, does not immediately win the competition for processing. If the party were less crowded or noisy, it would be easier for properties of your friend to be selected and other properties to be inhibited. This example also points out the continuous nature of competition: rather than selection's being binary, biased competition suggests that the selection process is continuous and graded.

Think Critically

- How does biased competition differ from the other theories of attention?
- How can the idea that the information we are aware of is essentially the "winner" of competing information be used to inform laws about using cell phones while driving?
- How can we use the principle of biased processing to produce more effective road signs?

Representation and Knowledge in Long-Term Memory

Learning Objectives

Y ou walk into a room. People are standing around a table covered with objects wrapped in a brightly colored covering. There is an object on a plate with small cylindrical projections coming out of it. Someone sets these sticks on fire. People exclaim things, but what do their words mean? Now the people begin to sing. They seem to be singing at or to you, and they seem to be happy and friendly. But it's hard to understand what they're singing, because while they all seem to know this song—it's quite short, melodically very simple—they are singing raggedly and not very well, although with enthusiasm.

Is this a dream? No. Through an exercise of the imagination, you just attended your own birthday party while being denied access to your knowledge in long-term memory—which meant you had no knowledge of your culture or tribal customs, no knowledge of the significance of the objects in front of you or the words called out or sung to you. This kind of knowledge normally comes to each of us easily, from the times of our earliest experiences in the world, and has an enormous influence on our lives. How is it stored, how is it used, how does it work?

In this chapter we will explore the answers to the following general questions:

1. What roles does knowledge play in cognition, and how is it represented in the brain?

2. What representational formats are most likely to exist in the brain, and how do multiple representational formats work together to represent and simulate an object?

3. How do representations distributed across the brain become integrated to establish category knowledge?

4. What different types of representational structures underlie category knowledge, and how are they accessed on particular occasions?

5. How are different domains of categories represented and organized?

1. ROLES OF KNOWLEDGE IN COGNITION

Knowledge is often thought of as constituting particular bodies of facts, techniques, and procedures that cultures develop, such as "knowledge of baseball statistics," "knowledge of the guitar," "knowledge of how to order a meal in a restaurant." Such knowledge in most cases comes consciously, after long and often difficult practice. But in its larger sense knowledge mostly exists and operates outside awareness: we are typically clueless about the constant and vast impact that knowledge has on us each moment. The formal sort of knowledge—the causes of the American Revolution or the designated-hitter rule in baseball—is a relatively small and uninfluential subset of the totality of what you know and of what affects your life. The bulk of your knowledge—and the knowledge that most influences your daily life—is relatively mundane knowledge about things such as clothing, driving, and love (well, perhaps not so mundane). Thus, knowledge, in its most inclusive sense, and the sense in which the term is used in cognitive psychology, is information about the world that is stored in memory, ranging from the everyday to the formal. Knowledge is often further defined as information about the world that is likely to be true, that you have justification for believing, and that is coherent (for further discussion, see Carruthers, 1992; Lehrer, 1990).

Knowledge so defined makes ordinary life possible in a number of ways. It is essential for the competent functioning of most mental processes, not only in memory, language, and thought, but also in perception and attention. Without knowledge, *any* mental process would stumble into ineffectiveness. Just how would you experience your birthday party if knowledge simply switched off?

For one thing, you'd be unable to get beyond the surface of the objects and sensations that surround you in the world. Each one would be unique, without history or meaning. Specifically, you would be unable to *categorize* things. Categorization is the ability to establish that a perceived entity belongs to a particular group of things that share key characteristics. "Cakes," for example, form a category of entities that people perceive as related in their structure and use. Without knowledge, you can't categorize—so the cake on the table at your birthday party meant nothing to you. Consider a camera that registers on film an image of your birthday bash. Would the camera *know* that the scene contains a cake? No. A camera can show an image of the cake, but it is simply recording a particular arrangement of light on film, no different in quality or significance from any other arrangement of light; the camera lacks knowledge about meaningful entities and events in the world. And in the "thought experiment" of your birthday party, you have become something like a camera, able to register images but unable to grasp what they mean, what commonality they have with other entities present or not present in the scene. So categorization is one thing that would go if you lost your knowledge.

Once you assign a perceived entity to a category, further knowledge about the category becomes available for your use. If you know it is a cake, associations arise: Is this a celebration? Is this a special treat for dessert? Indeed, the whole point of categorization is to allow you to draw *inferences,* namely, to allow you to derive information not explicitly present in a single member of a category but available because of knowledge of the characteristics of the group or groups to which it belongs. Once you categorize a perceived entity, many useful inferences can follow. If you are able to assign an object wrapped in brightly colored paper to the category of "gifts," your knowledge of gifts would produce inferences about the wrapped object that go beyond what you-as-a-camera currently see—the object is a box, which might contain a thoughtful gift that a friend has bought you or a not-so-thoughtful gag. Though you cannot yet see inside the box, your inferential knowledge about gifts suggests these possibilities. Without being able to categorize, could you produce these inferences? Would a camera be able to infer that the wrapped box could contain a gift or a gag? Of course not, and neither would you if you had lost your knowledge.

Standing in the doorway, looking at this scene, you do not know it is your birthday party. You can't know this because you lack knowledge to draw inferences that go beyond what you see. What about *action*? Would you know what to do in this situation? Would you know to blow out the candles, respond to your friends' joshing, open your presents? There's no biological reflex that would help you here. So again, the answer is, no: no knowledge means no appropriate action. Think of the camera—on registering a box in its viewfinder, would it know that the box is a gift to be unwrapped? No, it wouldn't; and neither would you without knowledge about gifts.

Now someone is standing in front of the birthday table, obscuring from your view half your name on the uncut cake. Normally, you would readily infer the whole name. In your present no-knowledge state, however, would you? No; no more than would a camera. Without knowledge, you cannot complete the partial perception,

FIGURE 4–1 Knowledge leads to inferences during perception

Although the letters in the figure most closely approximate l-e-a-r-t, the likely assumption is the word *heart*. This inference comes from knowledge of familiar words and of how it is possible for spills to obscure them. Essentially, the brain reasons unconsciously that the word is more likely to be *heart* than *leart* and that a spill has partly obscured an "h."

but with knowledge you can. Ordinarily you constantly complete partial perceptions in this manner as you encounter occluded objects in the environment. What do you see in Figure 4–1? The letters l-e-a-r-t or the word *heart*? The nonword *leart* is actually closest to what is on the page, but your first categorization of the string of letters was probably *heart*. Why? Because—as we saw in Chapter 2—knowledge of the word *heart* in memory led to the inference that the word was present but partially occluded by some sort of spill on the page; it's doubtful you have *leart* in memory. As we saw in Chapter 2, knowledge affects *perception*.

A party guest yells, "Look out the window! That looks like Madonna starting the truck in the driveway!" If you were in your normal, not your no-knowledge, state, when you look out the window, where would your *attention* go? You'd probably try to see inside the truck's cab, not scan its exterior. But nothing in the guest's exclamation directed your attention inside, so why would you look there? The obvious answer is that knowledge about what starting a vehicle entails guided your attention. Even if you don't drive yourself, you know generally where someone who is driving sits. But if you lacked knowledge—or, again, if you were a camera—you would have no idea where to focus your attention.

A few weeks before the party, you borrowed $50 from a friend, whom you've been avoiding because you haven't yet got the funds together to repay the loan. Now this friend is standing at the front of the crowd in your room, offering you one of the large boxes. Are you embarrassed? Nope. Without knowledge you'd be blissfully unaware that you should feel guilty about not having repaid your friend. Even if you remembered borrowing the money and when you borrowed it, you wouldn't be able to infer that you should have paid it back by now, and that because you haven't, you're a jerk. A specific memory without knowledge doesn't help you very much, because without knowledge you're not able to draw useful inferences from what you remember.

After the song, everyone at the party shouts at you in unison, "We love you!" Pretty nice—but you have no idea what they're saying. Why not? Because the ability to understand *language* requires knowledge. First, you need knowledge to recognize words and to know what they mean. If you didn't have knowledge about English, you would no more know that *love* is a word than that *loze* is not. Similarly, you would no more know that *love* means to hold people dear than to tattoo them. Second, you need knowledge to assemble the meanings of the words in a sentence.

When your friends say, "We love you," how do you know they're saying that they love you, not that you love them? How do you know that "we" refers to the lovers and that "you" refers to the lovee? Why isn't it the other way around? Knowledge about the verb *to love* specifies that the lover comes before the verb in an active sentence, and that the lovee comes after it. In a passive sentence, such as "You are loved by us," your knowledge specifies that these roles are reversed. Instantly on hearing sentences like these, you are able, because of your knowledge, to make accurate interpretations of who is doing what to whom.

Now the party's in high gear, and the karaoke machine comes out. Two of your friends are singing, one of them a real belter. Another song, and now the belter is paired with someone who sings even louder. Now it's your turn, but you're a bit shy. The quieter singer from the first duet and the really loud one from the second both volunteer their services. You need the support of a really strong voice. Whom do you pick? The vocally fortified type from the second pair, of course. But wait—how did you unerringly pick her as the louder of the two volunteers—they haven't sung together, so how could you judge? Well, in a no-knowledge state, you couldn't. But you could with knowledge of the relationship described by the principle of transitivity, which you may or may not ever have heard of, but which nonetheless you have internalized through experience. If X is louder than Y, and Y is louder than Z, then X is louder than Z. So you can pick the singer who will make the duet with you a song to remember—but without knowledge you'd be up a creek, unable to draw the inference that successfully guided your choice. Transitivity is but one example of the many ways in which knowledge enables sophisticated *thought*. Knowledge underlies virtually every form that thought takes, including decision making, planning, problem solving, and reasoning in general.

Without knowledge in its various roles, in categorization and inference, action, perception and attention, memory, language, and thought, you'd be a zombie at the party. You'd simply be registering images of the scene passively like a camera, and that's about it. You'd be frustratingly inept at understanding anything about the situation, or acting suitably in it. Because knowledge is essential for the competent functioning of all mental processes, without it your brain couldn't provide any of the cognitive services it normally performs for you. To understand cognition, it is essential to understand knowledge and its ubiquitous presence in all aspects of mental activity.

Comprehension Check:

1. In what ways do you use knowledge?
2. Why is it useful to categorize what we perceive?

2. REPRESENTATIONS AND THEIR FORMATS

A key aspect of knowledge is that it relies on representations. Representation is a complicated and controversial topic that cognitive scientists from many disciplines have argued about for a long, long time. No definition has been fully accepted, and most of those proposed are very technical. The definition we used here is relatively simplified, but it captures some of the core ideas in many accounts. (For diverse treatments of this important concept, see Dietrich & Markman, 2000; Dretske, 1995; Goodman, 1976; Haugeland, 1991; Palmer, 1978.) As noted in Chapter 1, a representation is a physical state (such as marks on a page, magnetic fields in a computer, or neural connections in a brain) that stands for an object, event, or concept. Representations also carry information about what they stand for. Consider a map of a subway system. The map is a representation because it stands for the various lines, stops, and connections, and it carries information about them, namely, the ordering of stops and the relative directions of the various lines. But representation involves more than this, as we explore in the following section.

2.1. Memories and Representations

Imagine that you're seeing a lava lamp for the first time at your birthday party. The lamp is not lit. You see a cone-shaped jar on a metal stand, the jar containing a mixture of colored liquids and solids. Now, to add to the festivities, the lamp is turned on. The contents of the jar brighten and globules of material inside begin undulating. A basic property of brains is that to some extent, but far from perfectly, they store perceived experiences—that is, they allow memories. When you store your first memory of a lava lamp, are you storing a representation? Well, does this memory meet the following criteria for a representation?

The intentionality criterion: A representation must be constructed intentionally to stand for something else. This may seem a little problematic. People usually don't try intentionally to set up their daily experiences for easy later recall. As you're watching the lava lamp for the first time, you probably aren't saying to yourself, "This is so cool, I have to remember it for the rest of my life." Nonetheless, you do remember it: much research (and a good deal of anecdotal evidence) shows that your brain stores information automatically, even when you're not trying to fix it in your memory (e.g., Hasher & Zacks, 1979; Hyde & Jenkins, 1969). Indeed, trying consciously to preserve information for later recollection often leads to no improvement in memory relative to simply perceiving and processing the information well. This suggests that you have the unconscious goal of storing information about experience, independent of your conscious goals. It is as if the ability to store information is so important that evolution couldn't leave the job to people's conscious intentions (some of us can't even remember to take out the garbage). Instead, evolution entrusted part of the storage of information to unconscious automatic mechanisms in the brain.

So is the intentionality criterion met? Yes, because the brain at an unconscious level has the design feature of storing information about experiences of the world to stand for those experiences. If a camera is set by a photographer to take a picture every second whether the photographer is present or not, the intention to capture information is built into the system, whether or not the originator of the system, the photographer, is there to take each picture. Similarly, the intention to capture information is built into the brain system, whether or not you consciously direct each memory.

The information-carrying criterion: A representation must carry information about what it stands for. Does your first memory of a lava lamp meet this criterion? Imagine that on the next day, someone asks what's new, and you remember having seen a novel object, the lava lamp. Drawing on your memory of the lava lamp, you describe it. How are you able to do this? Because your memory of the lava lamp carries information about it—details of its shape, color, and function. Further evidence that your memory of the lamp carries information is that you are able to categorize from it. If you were to see another, not necessarily identical, lava lamp, you could say that it belongs to the same group of objects as the one in your memory. Because your memory of the first lava lamp carries information about what it looked like, you can use this information to recognize other things like it. Similarly, if the second lava lamp in your experience, the one you're looking at now, is unlit, you can consult your memory of the first one to conjecture that the second one can probably be turned on to make it brighten and cause its contents to undulate. Because your memory carries information about the first lava lamp, it can produce useful inferences about other ones you encounter.

In these ways, representations lay the groundwork for knowledge. Once the brain intentionally establishes memories that carry information about the world, all sorts of sophisticated cognitive abilities become possible.

2.2. Four Possible Formats for Representations

What more can we say about a mental representation? One aspect of a representation is its format. *Format* refers to the type of its code, as discussed in Chapter 1. We can now unpack this idea further. *Format* not only refers to the elements that make up a representation and how these elements are arranged, but also relies on characteristics of the processes that operate on them to extract information. As we will see, representations may be *modality specific*, that is, they may make use of perceptual or motor systems, or they may be *amodal*, residing outside the perceptual and motor modalities. Another aspect of a representation is its *content*—the information it conveys.

2.2.1. Modality-Specific Representations: Images

In talking about the birthday party, the metaphor of a camera was useful. Images such as those that a camera captures are one possible representational format, which depicts information (see p.12); perhaps the brain constructs a similar type of representation. Certainly we often talk as if it does, saying things like "I can't get that picture out of my mind" and "I see it clearly in my mind's eye." Let's look at what is involved in images, and see whether it is likely that the brain contains representations of this form.

Several wrapped boxes and a birthday cake are on a table. Part of the scene has been captured by a digital camera and registered by pixels, or "picture elements," the units of visual information in an image, and thus stored. Specifically, an image has three elements, which taken together determine its content: a *spatiotemporal window, storage units,* and *stored information.*

A photograph taken of the scene in front of the camera does not capture everything in that scene, but only that part of it within a spatiotemporal window (Figure 4–2a).

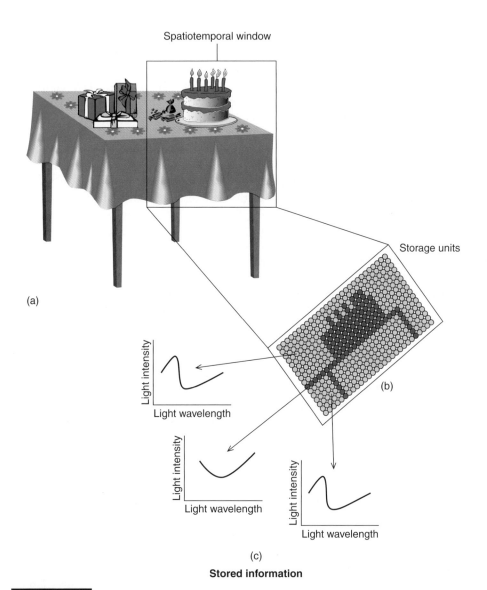

FIGURE 4-2   The components of an image: the birthday scene

(a) A spatiotemporal window of the information captured in the viewed scene. Within the spatiotemporal window, (b) an array of pixels captures the light information present. Each pixel stores (c) information about the intensity of light across the range of light wavelengths to which the pixel is sensitive. Together the stored information across pixels in the spatiotemporal window constitutes one possible image representation of the birthday scene.

Spatially, there are infinitely many pictures that a camera could take of the same scene, depending on its position relative to the scene—here the image has cut off the gifts and the table legs. Temporally, the scene is not captured continuously over time, just in one time slice when the shutter is open. Thus, any image is defined to some extent by its spatiotemporal window.

Next consider the storage units (Figure 4–2b) of the image in the spatiotemporal window. An image contains an array of storage units—pixels if the camera is digital, or light-sensitive grains for a film camera—laid out in a grid. Each storage unit is sensitive to the light impinging on it. Like the complete array of storage units, each individual unit also has a spatiotemporal window. It captures only the information within a bounded spatial and temporal region nested within the larger window of the entire array.

Finally, consider the information in the storage units (Figure 4–2c). In the case of a photograph, this information is the intensity of light at visible wavelengths in each storage unit. Across storage units, the collective information specifies the content of the image.

Much additional—and important—information resides implicitly in the image. For example, a contiguous group of pixels might form a square. And distances between pixels correspond to distances in the world: if the horizontal distance between pixels A and B is shorter than the horizontal distance between pixels C and D, the points in the world that correspond to points A and B are closer horizontally than the points that correspond to points C and D. But extracting these additional types of information requires a processing system, and the camera does not possess such a system (or put another way, the camera's processing system is the brain of the human viewer using it). The essential question now is, do images constructed like the one of the birthday cake on the table in Figure 4–2 exist in the brain?

Many people (but not all) say that they experience mental images that they can "see with the mind's eye" or "hear with the mind's ear." Clearly self-reported experience is important, but scientific evidence is essential for drawing firm conclusions, especially given the illusions our minds are capable of producing. Much scientific evidence supports the presence of images in the human brain (for reviews, see Farah, 2000; Finke, 1989; Kosslyn, 1980, 1994; Kosslyn et al., 2006; Shepard & Cooper, 1982; Thompson & Kosslyn, 2000).

First, consider an example of evidence from brain anatomy research (Tootell et al., 1982). Figure 4–3a is the visual stimulus that a monkey viewed; Figure 4–3b shows activation in Area V1 of that monkey's occipital cortex, as measured by a neural tracer, while the monkey was looking at the stimulus. A striking correspondence is immediately apparent: the pattern of brain activation on the brain's surface roughly depicts the shape of the stimulus. The reason is that the cortex of early visual processing areas is laid out somewhat like the pixels of a digital image and responds similarly. When neurons that are arranged in this manner fire, the pattern of activation forms a topographical map—their spatial layout in the brain is analogous to the layout of space in the environment. The presence of many such topographically organized anatomical structures in the brain suggests the presence of images.

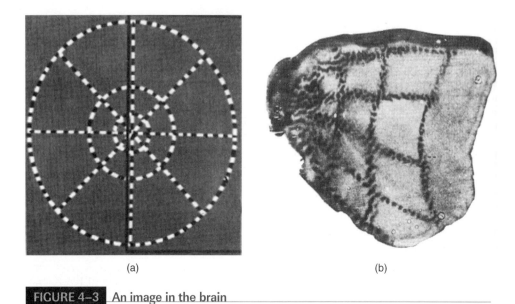

(a)   (b)

FIGURE 4–3 **An image in the brain**

(a) The "spokes of a wheel" stimulus shown to a monkey. (b) The activation that occurred on the surface of Area V1 of the monkey's brain in the left occipital lobe (which processed only the right half of the stimulus) as the monkey viewed the stimulus. The pattern of brain activation is similar to the visual pattern, suggesting that the brain is using some form of image-like representation in early visual processing. (Tootell, R. B. H., Silverman, M. S., Switkes, E., & DeValois, R. L. [1982].)

Another example of neural evidence for images comes from the case of patient M.G.S. (Farah et al., 1992). Clinical diagnosis of M.G.S.'s seizures had localized their source in her right occipital lobe, the region that processes the left half of the visual field. To reduce her seizures, M.G.S. elected to have her right occipital lobe removed. In addition to reduction of seizures, another result was, as expected, blindness in her left visual field.

What would be the effect of this removal on M.G.S.'s ability to process visual images? Much research has shown that visual images are represented partly in the brain's occipital lobes, and that the brain represents these images topographically, at least in some cases (e.g., Kosslyn et al., 1995, 2006). The investigators reasoned that if the occipital lobes do indeed represent visual images, then the loss of M.G.S.'s right occipital lobe should decrease the size of her visual images by one-half (a proportion analogous to her loss in vision). To test this hypothesis, the investigators measured the size of M.G.S.'s visual-imagery field before and after her surgery. As predicted, M.G.S.'s imagery field after the operation was approximately half its original size (Figure 4–4).

The two studies reviewed here, along with many others, have convinced most researchers that the brain uses images as one form of representation. Not only have mental images been found in the visual system, they have also been found in the motor system, as discussed in Chapter 11 (e.g., Grèzes & Decety, 2001; Jeannerod, 1995, 1997), and in the auditory system (e.g., Halpern, 2001).

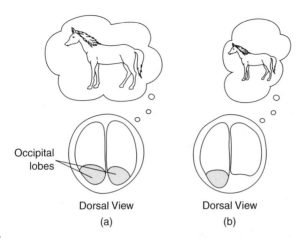

Occipital lobes

Dorsal View   Dorsal View
(a)   (b)

FIGURE 4–4   Brain diminished, image diminished

(a) Diagram of an intact, undamaged brain and a perceived visual image. (b) After surgery. Because visual images are represented in the occipital lobes, removing the right occipital lobe reduced image size by one-half (because the horizontal dimension was now restricted to one half of its previous extent). (Fig. 66.2 from p. 968 of Farah, M. J. (2000). The neural bases of mental imagery. In M. S. Gazzaniga (ed.), *The Cognitive Neurosciences* (2nd ed., pp. 965–974). Cambridge, MA: The MIT Press. Reprinted with permission.)

In addition to all the neural evidence that has accumulated for mental images, much behavioral evidence has accumulated as well. Indeed many clever behavioral experiments provided the first evidence for imagery, preceding the neural evidence by two decades (for reviews, see Finke, 1989; Kosslyn, 1980; Shepard & Cooper, 1982). In these experiments, researchers asked research participants to construct mental images while performing a cognitive task. If the participants actually constructed mental images, then these images should have perceptual qualities, such as color, shape, size, and orientation. Experiment after experiment did indeed find that perceptual variables like these affected task performance, suggesting that participants had constructed mental images having perceptual qualities. See the accompanying *A Closer Look* box for a detailed discussion of such a finding for the perceptual variable of size.

Although the camera has proved a useful metaphor in this discussion, brain images differ significantly from those taken by a camera. In particular, brain images are not as continuous and complete as photographs. For example, work on the phenomenon of change blindness, the failure to be aware of changing stimuli in the visual field (see Chapter 3), indicates that people's perceptual images do not have a uniform level of detail; some areas are not as well represented as others (e.g., Henderson & Hollingworth, 2003; Wolfe, 1999). Figure 4–5 illustrates this contrast. Figure 4–5a captures a relatively even and complete image of a scene, whereas an image in the brain, like the manipulated picture in Figure 4–5b, is much more uneven, with some areas better represented than others. Visual attention appears responsible for this unevenness: the well-represented patches of a scene are often regions where attention is focused (Hochberg, 1998). When attention does not focus on a region of a scene, the content of that region is not encoded as well into the image (e.g., Coltheart, 1999).

(a)

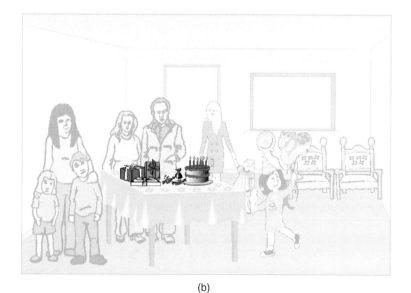

(b)

FIGURE 4–5   Selective attention encodes some aspects of images better than others.

(a) The birthday scene. (b) Rather than representing the scene at the top at equal resolutions across all points, attended parts of the image (in this case, the cake and gifts) are represented at a higher resolution than the unattended parts of the image (in this case, the table and everything in the background). As a result of the unequal distribution of attention, the image represents some parts of the scene better than others.

A CLOSER LOOK
Behavioral Evidence for Mental Imagery

Although there has been considerable anecdotal evidence for mental imagery, scientific behavioral evidence was sought by Kosslyn; he reported his results in 1975 in "Information Representation in Visual Images," *Cognitive Psychology, 7,* 341–370.

Introduction

It is an obvious perceptual fact that when something is close up and large in the visual field, it is easy to recognize, but when it is far away and small, the task is not so easy. You have no trouble recognizing a friend standing just a few feet away, but recognizing your friend would be much harder if the two of you were at opposite ends of a football field. The investigator used this fact about perception to demonstrate that people have mental images.

Method

Participants were asked to visualize a target object (for example, a goose) next to one of two reference objects, a fly or an elephant. Each pair of objects was to fill the frame of a participant's mental image, and in each case the proportional size of the target object relative to that of the reference object was to be maintained. (Thus, the image of the goose would be larger when paired with the fly than when paired with the elephant.) While holding one of these two pairs of images in mind, such as goose-and-fly or goose-and-elephant, participants heard the name of a property (for example, "legs") and had to decide as quickly as possible whether or not the target animal has that property by referring to their image; the participants were told that if the animal has the property, they should be able to find it in the image.

Results

Participants were an average of 211 milliseconds faster to verify properties when they imagined the target objects next to the fly than when next to the elephant. In a control condition, in which participants visualized enormous flies and tiny elephants next to the normal-sized animals, the results were reversed—the participants were faster when the queried animal was visualized next to a tiny elephant. So, it wasn't the fly or elephant per se that produced the results, but rather their size relative to that of the queried animal.

Discussion

The finding parallels the motivating observation, namely, that recognizing a friend is easier up close than across a football field. When a given object was imaged as relatively large (next to a fly), it was easier to process visually than when it was imaged as relatively small (next to an elephant). As the property named became larger in the image, it was easier to identify. From this result, the investigator concluded that the participants used images to answer the questions asked of them and to verify the properties named.

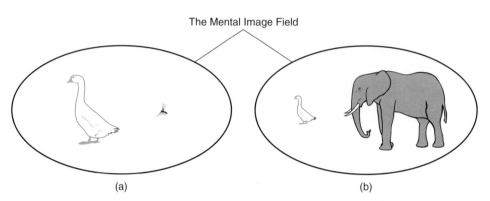

What do we see in the mental image field? (a) On some trials, participants were asked to imagine a target object, such as a goose, next to a fly. They were asked to fill the image field with the two objects, while maintaining their true relative sizes (that is, keeping the goose much larger than the fly). (b) On other trials, they were asked to imagine the same object next to an elephant, again while filling the image field and maintaining relative size. The size of the critical object (the goose, in this case) was larger in absolute terms when imaged next to the fly than when imaged next to the elephant. As a result, parts of the critical object (for example, the goose's legs) were larger next to the fly, and could be "seen" faster. This result provides behavioral evidence that we can use images to verify object properties.

Another important qualification about mental images is that they are interpreted (e.g., Chambers & Reisberg, 1992). If you focus your attention on the left edge of the ambiguous object in Figure 2–33b on page 96, it appears to be a duck, but if you focus your attention on the right edge, it appears to be a rabbit. Depending on where you focus attention, your interpretation of the object varies. A photograph does not contain interpretations of the entities it contains. If you consider the image format in isolation, you can see that nothing in it offers the potential to aid in the interpretation of its contents. A photographic image is simply a record of light energy that impinges on each pixel; it contains no categorizations of larger entities across pixels. But mental images are representations within a processing system that interprets them in specific ways; to understand imagery, we must consider both the representation and the accompanying processes. The importance of interpreting representations will become a central theme in this chapter.

2.2.2. Modality-Specific Representations: Feature Records

From this point on, the representations we consider will be more sophisticated than those taken by image-capturing artifacts such as cameras. It will become clear that natural intelligence is superior to current technology when it comes to representation. Art will imitate nature: the future of sophisticated representational technology lies in implementing the natural representations we will be discussing.

At the heart of sophisticated representation lies the categorization of meaningful entities. A meaningful entity is an object or event that plays an important role in an organism's survival and pursuit of goals. In contrast, a pixel is a relatively meaningless entity. We don't just want to know whether light impinges on a particular point in space; we want to know what the patterns of pixels—or areas of neural activation—represent in the world. This doesn't mean that images are useless. Indeed, more meaningful representations are derived from images.

The visual system of the frog presents a case of more sophisticated representation. If you were a frog, what would be meaningful to you? Bugs. What does a frog need in order to get bugs? Clearly it needs a motor system that can capture a bug flying by, but before it can do that it must be able to detect the bug. Here nature has applied meaningfulness and interpretation to the problem of representation, taking natural representational systems beyond images.

Early and important work (Lettvin et al., 1959) showed that neurons in the frogs visual system respond differentially to small objects moving within the frog's visual field (Figure 4–6). These researchers inserted electrodes into individual neurons of a frog's brain and then varied the stimulus—sometimes a round stationary object, sometimes a moving object—to the frog's eyes. They found that some neurons fire in response to small round objects (largely independent of motion), whereas others fire in response to object movement (largely independent of the object). Different populations of neurons appeared to detect different types of information in the visual field.

The information that these neurons detect is information that is meaningful to frogs: "small, round" and "moving" are features of flying insects. We have discussed

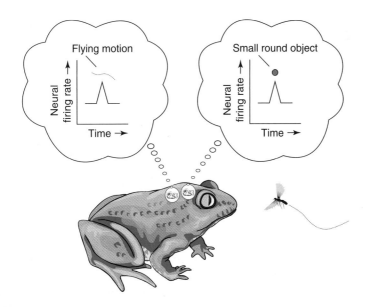

FIGURE 4–6   The frog sees the bug

In the frog's brain, one population of neurons is firing in response to the small round object; a second population is firing in response to the motion of this object. Together these two sets of neurons, along with others, allow the frog to detect the presence of a small, round, flying object.

features in the two previous chapters, but will now look at them from a new point of view: A *feature* is a meaningful sensory aspect of a perceived stimulus. Unlike a pixel, which registers all light that falls on it in a general and undifferentiated accumulation of information, these frog neurons respond only when information meaningful to a frog is present. They could be tricked if a small, round, moving object in the frog's visual field isn't a bug—but in nature it probably *is* a bug, and that's the point. The function of these populations of neurons is to detect entities in the world meaningful to frogs. They don't constitute an image of the visual field, patchy or otherwise. Instead, they *interpret* regions of images as indicating the presence of a particular feature. When these feature-detecting neurons become active, they categorize a region of an image as containing a meaningful feature of an object or event. Feature detection is accomplished not by single neurons, but by populations of neurons. This allows for a graded, rather than an all-or-nothing, response and is therefore more reliable. Furthermore, these neurons are often sensitive to more than a single feature, and the information to which they respond may change both with experience and with the organism's goals at a given time (e.g., Crist et al., 2001).

Do feature-detecting neurons meet the criteria for a representation? Yes. First, intentionality: they have been honed by evolution to stand for things in the world, to wit, bugs. Second, information: the neurons themselves, by their firing, carry information about the world. The evidence? If a frog blinks (closes its eyes), these neurons, once activated, *continue* to fire and carry information about the entity they collectively stand for—a bug.

As we saw in Chapter 2, the discovery of feature-detecting neurons in the brain revolutionized the field of perception. Since then, there have been hundreds if not thousands of follow-up studies, and much has been learned about such populations of neurons in the primate visual system. Examples of the processing stages to which such populations contribute are illustrated in Figure 4–7. As we saw in Chapter 2, as visual signals travel along pathways from the primary visual cortex in the occipital lobe to the temporal and parietal lobes, various types of features are extracted, such as the shape, orientation, color, and movement of objects. Farther along the processing stream, populations of conjunctive neurons, as their name suggests, integrate featural information extracted earlier into object representations. Conjunctive neurons, for example, might integrate information about size, shape, and movement to establish a featural representation of a flying bug, which can be of interest to humans as well as to frogs, especially in summer.

The collection of feature detectors active during the processing of a visual object constitutes a representation of that object. This representational format, unlike an image, is not depictive; its elements do not correspond to spatial points of contrast, or to edges of the object. Instead, it draws on different meaningful features of the object, that is, aspects of meaningful entities found in an organism's environment. Such a representation built up of features complements an image of the same object that might reside in early topographically organized areas.

Researchers have found populations of feature-detecting neurons for all modalities, not just vision. Feature-detection systems also reside in audition, touch, taste, and smell (e.g., Bear et al., 2002).

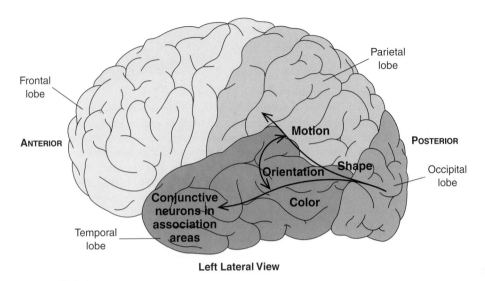

Left Lateral View

FIGURE 4–7   Visual processing systems in the human brain

From visual input, populations of neurons extract shape, color, orientation, and motion, along with other features, along pathways in the occipital, temporal, and parietal lobes. At later stages of processing, conjunctive neurons in various brain regions, such as the temporal lobes, combine these features to form integrated featural representations of perceived entities.

2.2.3. Amodal Symbols

Modality-specific representations reside in the perceptual and motor systems of the brain, and are thus perceptually related to the objects they represent. Is it possible that *amodal* representations exist that are built from arbitrary, abstract symbols? The dominant view is "yes," but the question is still open; see the accompanying *Debate* box.

How would amodal symbols work? Imagine the birthday scene, as in Figure 4–8a. An image of that scene resides early in the visual system. Farther along the ventral stream, feature detectors that represent aspects of meaningful entities have become active. Finally, amodal symbols—abstract and arbitrary—describe the properties of and relations among meaningful entities in the scene (see p. 12). Figures 4–8a–c present some examples of what these symbols might stand for.

Amodal symbols, lying outside the modalities and with no modality-specific characteristics, are usually assumed to reside in a knowledge system that constructs and manipulates descriptions of perceptual and motor states. Thus, the amodal representations in Figure 4–8 describe the contents of a visual state but lie outside the visual system, and are part of a more general system that is used in language and other tasks that do not involve vision per se.

The content of the amodal representations in Figure 4–8 are symbols such as *ABOVE, LEFT-OF, candles*. So are amodal representations words? Certainly there's nothing in the line forms that constitute the word *candles* (or *velas* in Spanish, or *bougies* in French) that relates to a visually (or tactilely) perceived candle. So the answer is, close—but no cigar. Researchers exploring the idea of amodal symbols

Do Amodal Representations Exist?

DEBATE

As useful as they are in building theory, a strong empirical case has never been established for amodal symbols in the brain (Barsalou, 1999). Nonetheless, the idea of amodal symbols has dominated theories of representation for decades. The intellectual reasons are attractive to many. First, amodal symbols provide powerful ways of expressing the meaningful content of images by representing objects (and their properties) and the relations between them. Second, the important functions of knowledge such as categorization, inference, memory, comprehension, and thought arise readily from the theory of amodal symbols (e.g., J. R. Anderson, 1976, 1983; Newell, 1990; Newell & Simon, 1972). Third, the idea of amodal symbols has allowed computers to implement knowledge; amodal descriptive representations can be easily implemented on computers.

There is in fact a theoretical gap as well as a deficiency of empirical support for amodal symbols. What are the mechanisms? What process links regions of visual images to the relevant amodal symbols? Conversely, when the amodal symbol for an object becomes active in memory, how does the symbol activate visual representations of the object's appearance? No one has yet figured out a compelling theory of how amodal symbols become linked to perceptual and motor states. Theorists are increasingly finding fault with the notion of amodal symbols (e.g., Barsalou, 1999; Glenberg, 1997; Lakoff, 1987; Newton, 1996). Some researchers are turning away from amodal symbols, arguing that other formats underlie knowledge representation in the brain.

(a)   (b)   (c)

FIGURE 4–8 Three amodal representations of elements in the birthday scene at left

(a) A frame, (b) a semantic network, and (c) a property list. Although words are used here for clarity, amodal representations are assumed to be constructed of nonlinguistic symbols.

believe that amodal symbols and words *are two different things*, that words *stand for* the amodal symbols that underlie them. According to this view, underlying the word *candles,* for example, is an amodal symbol in the brain that stands for *candles.* To make this distinction clear, researchers could use a symbol like @ to stand for the things that are *candles.* They use the word *candles,* though, so that it is easier to see what the symbol stands for.

The amodal symbols named in Figure 4–8 build three types of amodal representations: *frames, semantic networks,* and *property lists.* A **frame** is a structure, rather like an algebraic expression, that specifies a set of relations that links objects in the environment. For example, the frame in Figure 4–8a specifies that the gifts are to the left of the cake, and that this LEFT-OF configuration is ABOVE the table. A semantic network (Figure 4–8b) represents essentially the same relations and objects in diagram form. A property list names the characteristics of the entities belonging to a category; for instance, the property list in Figure 4–8c names some of the properties of a cake, such as frosting and candles. Unlike frames and semantic networks, property lists omit the relations between properties. How do the properties in a property list differ from the features in modality-specific records? First, the symbols that represent properties in a property list are amodal, lying outside perceptual and motor systems, whereas the features in modality-specific records are modal, lying in a perceptual or motor system (for example, vision). Second, the properties in a property list capture relatively abstract aspects of an object, such as the presence of frosting, whereas the features in modality-specific records tend to capture fundamental perceptual details such as edges and colors.

Amodal symbols complement images in that they categorize the regions of an image meaningfully—they don't just record points of light or other sensory data. Amodal symbols continue the interpretive process begun when feature detectors categorize elementary properties of images, in the service of identifying meaningful entities. In the semantic network in Figure 4–8c, the amodal symbol for *cake* categorizes the respective region of the image as being a particular kind of thing. The same region could be categorized differently if different amodal symbols were assigned to it that categorize the same entity in different ways: *dessert, pastry, fattening food.* Furthermore, a symbol could categorize an entity inaccurately: you might dimly see the cake in the dark and categorize it as a hat—and meet with disaster when you put it on your head.

2.2.4. Statistical Patterns in Neural Nets

Although amodal symbols work well in computers, it's not clear how well they would work in biological systems. Another possible means of representation is the neural net (see pp. 42–43), a construct in which the cake in the birthday scene is represented by a statistical pattern such as 1100101000101 (Figure 4–9), which offers greater scope than the amodal system for two reasons (Smolensky, 1988).

First, the elements of a statistical pattern can be viewed as neurons or as populations of neurons that are on or off—that fire or do not fire. Each 1 in the pattern represents a neuron (or neuron population) that fires, and each 0 represents one that does not. Thus the statistical approach has a natural neural interpretation that makes it a plausible candidate for biological representation. Second, whereas in an amodal system a single amodal symbol typically represents a category, in a neural net multiple statistical

```
1110101000101
1100011000111
1100101010101
1110001010111
1100111000101
         .
         .
         .
```

FIGURE 4–9 Statistical patterns can represent the cake in the birthday scene

A 1 or 0 indicates whether a particular neuron in a population of neurons is firing (1) or not firing (0). Different statistical patterns can represent slightly different versions of the same thing (for example, a cake), although these patterns are usually highly similar to one another.

patterns can represent the same category, as in Figure 4–9. The flexibility offered by varying statistical patterns reflects the reality in the world: not all cakes are exactly the same. Because cakes differ, their representations should differ as well. And because even different cakes are more similar to one another than they are to tables, the representations of cakes should be more similar to one another than to the representations of tables. Although the representations that could stand for a cake differ to some extent, they should generally be highly similar. Statistical patterns capture these intuitions.

For these two reasons, statistical representations of knowledge have become increasingly interesting to researchers. Although amodal symbols are still used widely, models that rely on statistical approaches are increasingly plausible.

2.3. Multiple Representational Formats in Perception and Simulation

Some researchers have argued that an abstract descriptive representational format underlies all knowledge. But the brain is a complex system, and knowledge is used in many ways; representations play many roles in the myriad processes that constitute cognition. It is implausible that a single format would serve all these roles; it is much more likely that multiple formats—images, feature detectors, amodal symbols, and statistical patterns—are required.

Again imagine viewing your birthday party scene. On perceiving this scene, your brain constructs a somewhat patchy visual image of it, largely in the occipital cortex. As this image is developing, feature detection systems extract meaningful features from it in particular regions of the occipital, temporal, and parietal lobes. Finally, a statistical

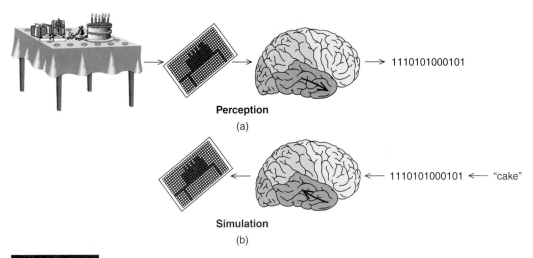

Perception

(a)

1110101000101

Simulation

(b)

1110101000101 ← "cake"

FIGURE 4–10   Perception and simulation processes

(a) The levels of processing that occur during the perception of a scene: a patchy image in the occipital lobes; feature extraction in the occipital, temporal, and parietal lobes; and the integration of this information using a statistical pattern, perhaps in the temporal lobes. (b) An example of the simulation process, which is thought to be the process in part (a) run in reverse. Hearing someone say the word *cake* may activate the statistical pattern used previously to integrate information about the cake in the birthday scene that is now in the past. In turn, the statistical pattern would partially reactivate the features extracted for the cake, along with the accompanying image.

pattern in the temporal lobes becomes active to stand for the image and feature information extracted previously, and to associate all this information (Figure 4–10a). Because the neurons representing the statistical pattern are conjunctive neurons (that is, they have a linking function), the neurons active in the image, along with the neurons active in the feature analysis, all became associated with the neurons that represent the statistical pattern. Each element in the statistical pattern develops associations back to the image and feature units that activated it. Together, this sequence of processing phases establishes a multilevel representation of the scene as it is perceived.

It is possible, as it were, to "run the film backward." In a process known as simulation, a statistical pattern can reactivate image and feature information even after the original scene is no longer present (Figure 4–10b). For instance, say the following day, a friend reminds you how great the cake was. Your friend's words activate the statistical pattern that integrated information stored for the cake at the time you saw and tasted it. Now, in a top-down manner, this statistical pattern partially reactivates features extracted from the cake, along with aspects of the image that represented it. The associative structure linking all this information allows you to simulate the original experience. Whereas bottom-up processing through a perceptual system produces a statistical representation, top-down processing back the other way reenacts, at least partially, the original visual processing. This top-down capability allows you to generate mental images and to remember past events. We shall have more to say about how mental simulations work in Chapter 11.

> ✓ **Comprehension Check:**
>
> 1. What representational formats are likely to exist in the brain? Why?
> 2. How might multiple representational formats work together in the brain to represent and simulate an object?

3. FROM REPRESENTATION TO CATEGORY KNOWLEDGE

The aim of an actor is to provide for the audience the "illusion of the first time"—the sense that what is happening now on stage has never happened before, neither in the real world nor in last night's performance. But the constant illusion of the first time in life would lead to chaos and confusion. When you arrived at your birthday party bereft of knowledge, the experience was bewildering. Representations are the means; the end is knowledge. The question before us now is how large assemblies of representations develop to provide knowledge about a category.

Category knowledge develops first from establishing representations of a category's individual members and second from integrating those representations. You have undoubtedly experienced members of the "cake" category many times. On each occasion, a multiformat representation became established in your brain. How might the representations of these different cakes have become integrated?

Consider the five different cakes in Figure 4–11a. Each cake produces a statistical pattern that integrates the results of its image and feature processing. Because the cakes are so similar, they produce similar statistical patterns, but because they differ to some extent, the patterns are not identical. If you study the five individual patterns, you can see that $11-0--10-01-1$ is common to all five (where – indicates a unit that is not shared across cakes). The eight units corresponding to the 1s and 0s in this shared pattern offer a natural way of integrating the five memories. Because all five memories share these units, all the memories become associated to this common "hub" (Figure 4–11b). The result is the representation of a category. At one level, all category members become linked by virtue of the common statistical units they share. At another level, these shared units constitute a statistical representation of the category, not just of one member. (As we note later, though, natural concepts are less neat than this simple example—it's hard to think of a feature that's true of *all* possible cakes.)

Furthermore, the shared units offer a means of retrieving category members from memory. Because all category members become associated with a common hub, the hub serves as a mechanism for remembering category members at later times. When the associative structure is run in a top-down manner (Figure 4–11c), the hub reactivates the image and the feature processing associated with a category member, thereby simulating it. Notably, this process may often mix memories of multiple category members together during retrieval to produce a blending (e.g., Hintzman, 1986). As a result, the simulated category member may often be more like an average category member than like a specific one (as shown in Figure 4–11c). This process of simulating average category members provides one mechanism for generating prototypes, as will be described later.

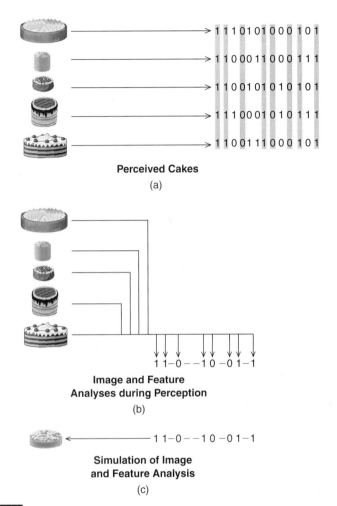

Perceived Cakes

(a)

**Image and Feature
Analyses during Perception**

(b)

**Simulation of Image
and Feature Analysis**

(c)

FIGURE 4–11 Individual memories of a category become integrated to establish category knowledge

(a) Five individual cakes perceived on different occasions are each represented with a unique statistical pattern; the conjunctive units common to all are highlighted. (b) The shared conjunctive units across statistical patterns establish a representation of the cake category. These shared units further integrate memories of the image and feature processing that occurred across cakes. (c) The shared statistical pattern becomes active in the absence of a particular cake, and produces a simulation of image and feature processing that is roughly the average of previously experienced cakes.

3.1. The Inferential Power of Category Knowledge

Armed with the concept of category knowledge, we can begin to understand what makes organisms more intelligent than cameras. The power of category knowledge comes from capturing and integrating diverse pieces of information about a category. When you encounter a new category member, you activate the relevant knowledge of that general category, which provides a tremendous amount of useful information for dealing with this new entity. You aren't like a camera that operates exactly the same way whether its subject is making a first time appearance or has been photographed a hundred times before. Despite your parents' best efforts, how you dealt with your cake at your 3rd birthday party probably left something to be desired, but your 20th birthday cake presumably didn't end up in your hair. And when you encounter a new birthday cake at your next birthday party, your category knowledge about birthday cakes makes you an expert on it. You know how to act—blowing out the candles, cutting the cake, eating a piece of it. You can predict what will be inside, and pretty much how it will taste. You can explain generally how it was made and predict what will happen if it is left out for a few days. All these inferences are possible because you have integrated diverse pieces of information about birthday cakes into a body of category knowledge.

Even simply hearing the phrase "birthday cake" when there's nary a cake in sight activates your category knowledge of birthday cakes; you may not know whether it's chocolate or angel food, but you understand what's being talked about. In each case, as you encounter something associated with the category, other knowledge becomes active. Because your category knowledge contains diverse kinds of information that goes considerably beyond what's immediately before your eyes, you can draw many useful inferences and perform various intelligent functions (Bruner, 1957).

3.2. The Multimodal Nature of Category Knowledge

Cakes are not only seen, they are also tasted, smelled, touched, and acted on; perhaps the one modality by which cakes are not experienced much is sound. Guitars, on the other hand, are heard, seen, touched, and acted on, but neither tasted nor smelled. Depending on the category, a different profile of information across the six modalities of vision, audition, action, touch, taste, and smell is salient (Cree & McRae, 2003). Emotion and motivation offer further modes of experience that enter into a category's representation. Cakes are associated with positive emotion, poor grades with negative emotion; restaurants are associated with feeling hungry, pillows with feeling sleepy. The very name of a category opens the door to category knowledge: either through hearing the name, seeing its sign-language form, or, for the literate, seeing its orthographic (i.e., written) form or feeling its Braille configuration.

Integration is obviously the key: how does the brain do it, combining category name and all the relevant information across modalities? One proposal is the convergence zone theory (Damasio, 1989; for a more developed account, see Simmons & Barsalou, 2003). A **convergence zone** (also known as an **association area**) is a population of conjunctive neurons that associates feature information within a modality. These patterns integrate information from image and feature analyses within a given modality, such as vision. For cakes, image and feature information would similarly be integrated within the taste modality and also within the modalities for smell, touch, and action. Much neuroscience research indicates that association areas store modality-specific information (e.g., Tanaka, 1997).

Damasio (1989) further proposes that higher order convergence zones in the temporal, parietal, and frontal lobes integrate category knowledge *across* modalities, together with the category name. (Note that a convergence zone is *not* modality specific, suggesting the importance of amodal "symbols."). In general, these higher order convergence zones integrate the conjunctive neurons that reside in the earlier convergence zones for specific modalities. Thus, a convergence zone in the parietal lobe might integrate conjunctive neurons in visual and motor areas, which in turn integrate specific visual and motor features. Alternatively, convergence zones in the left anterior temporal lobe might integrate the names of categories with category knowledge. Throughout the brain, convergence zones integrate category knowledge in various ways, such that category knowledge captures the multimodal character of category members. As a result, all the relevant features across modalities for a category become integrated, so that they can all be retrieved together. When you think of cakes, higher order convergence zones activate how they look, taste, smell, and feel, and how you eat them.

If the convergence zone account of category knowledge is correct, two predictions follow. First, simulations in the brain's modality-specific areas should represent knowledge. To represent knowledge of how a cake looks, the relevant convergence zones should reactivate features that have previously been used to represent cakes in visual perception. Second, the simulations that represent a category should be distributed across the particular modalities that are relevant for processing it. The simulations that represent "cakes" should arise not only in the visual system but also in the taste and motor systems. Both behavioral and neural findings increasingly support these predictions (for reviews, see Barsalou, 2003b; Barsalou et al., 2003; Martin, 2001).

3.3. Multimodal Mechanisms and Category Knowledge: Behavioral Evidence

If simulations in perceptual systems underlie knowledge, then it should be possible to demonstrate the contribution of perceptual mechanisms in the representation of categories. To investigate this possibility, investigators focused on the perceptual mechanism of **modality switching**, a process in which attention is shifted from one modality to another, as, say, from vision to audition (Pecher et al., 2003). Researchers have shown that modality switching takes time. In one study, participants had to detect whether a stimulus—which might be a light, a tone, or a vibration—occurred on the left or right (Spence et al., 2000). Because the various stimuli were randomly mixed, participants had no way of predicting which particular type of signal would occur on a given trial. When the modality of the signal switched between two trials, participants took longer to detect the second signal than when the modality stayed the same. For example, the time to detect a tone was faster when the previous stimulus was a tone than when it was a light or a vibration. Switching modalities carries a cost.

Pecher and colleagues (2003) predicted that the perceptual mechanism of modality switching should be found not only in perception but also in category processing. They reasoned that if simulations represent category knowledge, then switching costs analogous to those incurred while processing perceptual information should be incurred while processing information about categories. Participants in this study verified the properties of objects. On a given trial, the word for a category (for example, "cakes") was followed by a word for a possible property, both words presented visually. Half the time the property was true of the category ("frosting") and half the time it was false ("crust"). As in the earlier perception experiment, sometimes the properties referred to the same modality on two consecutive trials: a participant might verify that "rustles" is a property of "leaves" and on the next trial verify that "loud" is a property of "blenders." Most of the time, however, the properties across two consecutive trials referred to different modalities.

Pecher and colleagues (2003) found that switching modalities in this property verification task produced a switching cost, just as in the perception experiment by Spence and colleagues (2000). When participants had to switch modalities to verify a property, they took longer than when they did not have to switch modalities. This finding is consistent with the idea that perceptual mechanisms are used in the representation of category knowledge: to represent the properties of categories, participants appeared to simulate them in the respective modalities.

Many other behavioral findings similarly demonstrate that perceptual mechanisms play a role in the representation of category knowledge. The visual mechanisms that process occlusion, size, shape, orientation, and similarity have all been shown to affect category processing (e.g., Solomon & Barsalou, 2001, 2004; Stanfield & Zwaan, 2001; Wu & Barsalou, 2004; Zwaan et al., 2002). Motor mechanisms have also been shown to play central roles (e.g., Barsalou et al., 2003; Glenberg & Kaschak, 2002; Spivey et al., 2000). Across modalities, behavioral findings increasingly implicate modality-based representations in the storage and use of category knowledge.

3.4. Multimodal Mechanisms and Category Knowledge: Neural Evidence

When talking about modality-specific mechanisms, conclusions drawn from behavioral evidence, no matter how suggestive, have their limits: behavioral experiments don't measure brain mechanisms directly. But neuroimaging does, and much supportive evidence for the perceptual underpinnings of category knowledge comes from neuroimaging research. In these studies, participants lie in a PET or fMRI scanner while performing various category-related tasks, such as naming visually presented objects (for example, a dog), listening to the names of categories (for example, "hammer"), producing the properties of a category (for example, "yellow" for a lemon), or verifying the properties of a category (for example, answering the question "Does a horse run?").

For example, in a study by Chao and Martin (2000), participants were asked to observe pictures of manipulable objects, buildings, animals, and faces while their brains were scanned using fMRI. The investigators found that when participants viewed manipulable objects such as hammers, a circuit in the brain that underlies the

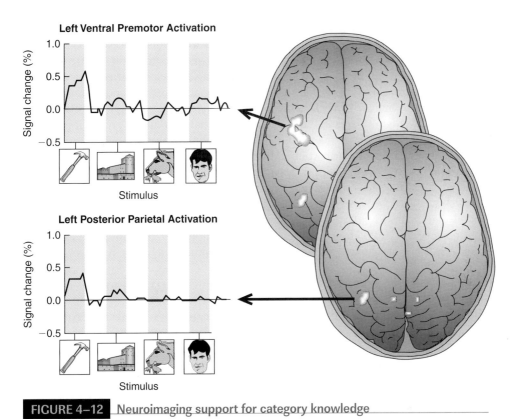

FIGURE 4–12   Neuroimaging support for category knowledge

The left-hemisphere grasping circuit (for right-handed participants) became active only while participants viewed pictures of tools, not while they viewed pictures of faces, animals, or buildings.

grasping of manipulable objects became active (Figure 4–12). This circuit did not become active when buildings, animals, or faces were observed. In much previous work, this grasping circuit has been found to become active while monkeys and humans perform actions with manipulable objects and while they watch others perform such actions (e.g., Rizzolatti et al., 2002). Even though Chao and Martin's participants were not allowed to move in the scanner, and even though they viewed no agents or actions, this grasping circuit nevertheless became active. From this result, the investigators concluded that activation of the grasping circuit constituted a motor inference about how to act on the perceived object. As participants viewed an object (for example, a hammer), they accessed category knowledge about it that included motor inferences (for example, "a hammer can be swung"). These inferences appear to be represented in the motor system, as we would expect if mental simulations are used to represent the objects and their categories.

Many further neuroimaging studies (reviewed by Martin, 2001; Martin & Chao, 2001; Martin et al., 2000) have shown that other modality-specific regions become active as other kinds of category knowledge are processed. In a striking correspondence, category knowledge about color, shape, and motion is processed near the respective brain areas that process this information in visual perception (Figure 4–13 on Color Insert B). When participants retrieve an object's shape properties, an area in the fusiform gyrus that overlaps visual shape processing areas becomes active during PET and fMRI scans. Similarly, when participants retrieve an object's color properties from category knowledge, an area in the occipital cortex that overlaps an area that processes color in perception (V4) becomes active. When participants think about performing actions on objects, motor areas become active. When participants retrieve an object's motion properties, regions in the posterior temporal gyrus that overlap motion processing areas in vision become active. When participants retrieve the sounds of objects, an auditory brain area becomes active (Kellenbach et al., 2001). And when they access knowledge of foods, gustatory areas in the brain become active that represent tastes (Simmons et al., 2005). Together these findings demonstrate that an object category's representation is distributed across the brain's perceptual and motor systems.

> ✔ **Comprehension Check:**
>
> 1. How might multimodal representations of a category's members become integrated in the brain to establish category knowledge?
> 2. What behavioral and neural evidence exists to support the hypothesis that the brain's modality-specific areas are involved in representing category knowledge?

4. STRUCTURES IN CATEGORY KNOWLEDGE

Category knowledge is not an undifferentiated mass of data; it contains many different structures, organized in many different ways. As we shall see in this section, exemplars, rules, prototypes, background knowledge, and schemata all play roles in creating the category knowledge that allows us to live lives cognizant of ourselves and the world around us. Furthermore, we possess powerful and dynamic abilities for using these structures.

4.1. Exemplars and Rules

The simplest structures that category knowledge contains are memories of individual category members; these are known as exemplars. The first time you see an unfamiliar type of dog and are told its breed, a memory of that dog is stored along with the name of the breed. As you see more of these dogs, a memory for each one similarly becomes associated with the breed name, and thereby with other memories of that breed. Over time, a collection of memories results for these category exemplars, all integrated in the appropriate memory store (as illustrated earlier in Figure 4–11a). This sort of content is relatively simple because each type of memory is stored independently of the others.

Much research has shown that exemplar memories are common in our category knowledge (e.g., Brooks, 1978; Lamberts, 1998; Medin & Schaffer, 1978; Nosofksy, 1984), and that they play a powerful role. For example, participants in a study by Allen and Brooks (1991) were told about two categories of imaginary animals; *builders* and *diggers*. Individual animals might have long or short legs, an angular or curved body, and spots or no spots. A rule—that is, a precise definition of the criteria for a category—determined whether a particular animal was a *builder* or *digger*:

> An animal is a *builder* if it has *two* or *three* of the following properties: *long legs, angular body, spots;* otherwise it is a *digger*.

Some participants were told the two-out-of-three rule. These participants were then shown pictures of the imaginary animals sequentially and instructed to indicate which were *builders* and which were *diggers*. Presumably they used the rule to do this, counting the number of critical properties for each animal. If they made an error, the experimenter told them the correct category. Once the participants demonstrated that they could apply the rule for the categories effectively, they received a surprise test. On each trial they saw an animal that they hadn't seen earlier. Again they had to say whether the animal was a *builder* or *digger,* but this time the experimenter didn't say whether their categorizations were correct or incorrect.

Allen and Brooks (1991) suspected that even though participants knew a rule for the categories, they might nevertheless be storing exemplar memories and using them in categorization. From earlier research, the investigators believed that the human brain automatically stores and uses exemplar memories, even when doing so is not necessary. But how to determine this? Figure 4–14 illustrates the clever technique that the investigators used. In the test phase of the experiment, participants were shown some of the animals they had seen before and some new ones. Two of the new ones were *builders*. One of these differed from a builder seen during training in only one characteristic; this type of correspondence, between two entities of the same category, is referred to as a *positive match*. The other new builder, while fulfilling the rule, differed in only one characteristic from a *digger* seen previously; this kind of correspondence, between two entities of different categories, is a *negative match*.

Here's the key prediction. If participants do not store exemplar memories and use only the rule, the positive- and negative-match animals should be equally easy to categorize: both fulfill the rule for builders. If, however, participants stored exemplar memories—even though they did not have to in order to make the call—then the negative-match animal, which shared more characteristics with the *digger,* should be harder to categorize correctly than the positive-match one.

Why? Think about what happens when participants encounter the negative-match animal. If an exemplar memory of its counterpart from training exists, it is likely to become active. If it does, then because the two animals are so similar, sharing as they do two characteristics, the negative-match animal is a reminder of the counterpart seen earlier. *But the counterpart was in the other category!* So if the exemplar memory is active, the temptation to miscategorize is strong; rule and exemplar memory conflict.

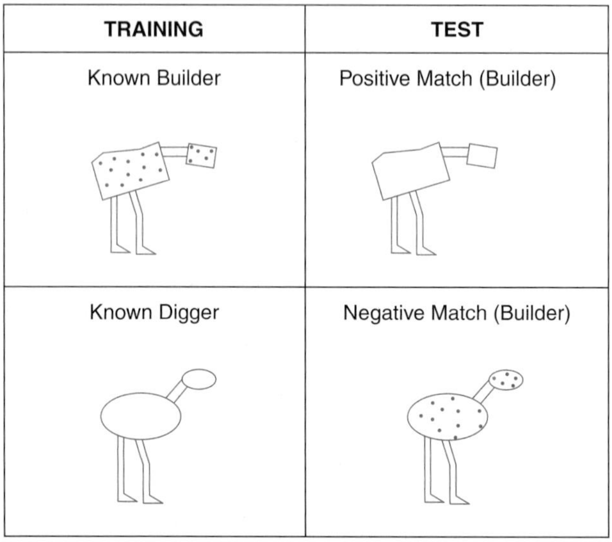

TRAINING	TEST
Known Builder	Positive Match (Builder)
Known Digger	Negative Match (Builder)

FIGURE 4–14 The original builders and diggers

Left column: A *builder* and a *digger* that participants studied while they learned the rule for *builders*. Right Column: Positive and negative test matches. A positive match was a *builder* that differed only by one property from a *builder* studied earlier; a negative match was a *builder* that differed only by one property from a *digger* studied earlier. If participants use only rules to categorize *builders,* the positive and negative matches should be equally easy to categorize, given that both have two of the three *builder* properties. Alternatively, if participants also use exemplars to categorize *builders,* the negative match should be harder to categorize because it is so similar to a member of the wrong category.

(Adapted from Allen, S. W., & Brooks, L. R. (1991). Specializing the operation of an explicit rule. *Journal of Experimental Psychology: General, 120,* pp. 3–19, Fig. 1, p. 4. Copyright © 1991 American Psychological Association. Adapted with permission.)

What happens when participants encounter the positive-match animal and exemplar memory is active? Again, they will be reminded of the similar animal they saw in training, which in this case is in the correct category. This time both the exemplar memory and the rule point to the right answer.

Numbers told the story: the results demonstrated clearly not only that exemplar memories had been stored but also that they had a profound impact on categorization. Participants correctly categorized the positive-match exemplars 81 percent of the time, but correctly categorized the negative-match exemplars only 56 percent of the time. Even though participants knew a good rule for categorizing all the test animals, their memories of earlier exemplars intruded on categorization of negative-match animals, causing 25 percent more errors than in the other condition. If exemplar memories hadn't been stored, there shouldn't have been any difference in categorizing positive- and negative-match animals, given that both satisfied the rule equally well. Many similar findings in the literature demonstrate that exemplars are ubiquitous structures in category knowledge.

Does this finding suggest that we store only exemplars and not rules? Before we can answer, we need to look at another side of the coin. A second group of participants received the same training, learning by feedback from the experimenter whether their categorizations were correct. The difference? This second group was *not* told the rule for categorizing *builders* and *diggers*. These "no-rule" participants then were shown the same series of positive- and negative-match animals at test as the "rule" participants in the first group.

Two findings are of interest. Like the rule participants, the no-rule participants were more accurate on the positive-match animals (75 percent correct) than on the negative-match animals (15 percent correct). For these participants, similarity to exemplar memories played the central role in categorization. The effect of exemplar memories was significantly larger in the no-rule condition (incorrect negative-match categorization, 85 percent) than in the rule condition (incorrect negative-match categorization, 44 percent). Rule participants had stored a rule in their category knowledge that made them less vulnerable to exemplar memories than were no-rule participants. By applying the rule on some occasions, rule participants were more likely to categorize negative-match animals correctly. These and other results demonstrate that we can store rules for categories, not just exemplars (e.g., Ashby & Maddox, 1992; Blok et al., 2005; Nosofsky et al., 1994).

Thus the Allen and Brooks (1991) study established that, depending on the training conditions, we acquire exemplar memories, rules, *or both* for the categories we learn. To corroborate these behavioral findings with neural evidence, neuroimaging was conducted while two groups performed the task, either in the rule condition or the no-rule condition (Patalano et al., 2001; see also E. Smith et al., 1998). The investigators made the following predictions. First, in the no-rule condition, the brain areas used should be those that store exemplar memories (because the exemplars were experienced only visually, the primary sites of brain activation should be in the visual system). Second, in the rule condition, the primary brain areas used should be those that represent rules. (Because people rehearse a rule to themselves while they assess its fit to exemplars, motor areas that implement the implicit speech actions for rehearsal should become active.)

The results of the brain scans bear out the predictions. In the no-rule condition, most of the active sites were in occipital areas where vision is processed. As predicted, when participants did not know a rule, they primarily used visual memories of exemplars to categorize. In the rule condition, there were active sites in frontal motor areas. Again as predicted, when participants knew a rule, they rehearsed it silently to themselves, and the actions of internal rehearsal engaged the motor system.

The conclusion? Different brain systems become active to represent exemplars and to represent rules. Furthermore, the particular systems that become active support the notion that category knowledge is represented in modality-specific areas: visual areas represent the content of exemplars, motor areas implement the process of rehearsing rules. (For other work that also localizes various category representations in the brain, see Ashby & Ell, 2001.)

4.2. Prototypes and Typicality

Prototypes offer a different way to summarizing a category's members. Whereas an exemplar offers a reference for direct comparison, and a rule is a rigid requirement about the properties required for membership in a category, a **prototype** simply specifies what properties are *most likely* to be true of a category. A set of nine new *builders* is shown in Figure 4–15. These new builders have various combinations of horns, tails, ears, and a hump, as well as the familiar long legs, angular bodies, and spots.

What structures could represent these nine creatures, no two identical but all *builders*? Nine exemplar memories would do the job, but that doesn't seem very economical. A rule could summarize their shared properties. What rule? One possibility, borne out by inspection of this herd of nine, is that a creature possessing at least two of the following four properties—long legs, angular bodies, spots, horns— is a *builder*. This rule is good, but complicated to apply.

Knowing the prototype—that is, knowing the combination of properties most likely to appear in a builder—seems the most efficient approach here. The prototype of the nine *builders* is the set of properties that occurs most often across builder-category members, excluding properties that occur rarely. Let's define a rare property as one that occurs less than 40 percent of the time, thus excluding tails, ears, and hump. All the remaining properties end up in the prototype, so the prototype of a *builder* is an animal with spots, angular body, long legs, and horns. Because the prototype summarizes statistical information about the category's most likely properties, the prototypical *builder* in Figure 4.15 results from combining the properties of spots

FIGURE 4–15 **An augmented builder category**

These *builders* can have the additional properties of horns, tail, ears, or hump, along with the usual properties of long legs, an angular body, or spots. The category prototype is a *builder* that has any property included in at least 60 percent of the population of nine *builders*.

(which appear in 78 percent of the population), angular body (in 67 percent,) long legs (in 67 percent), and horns (in 67 percent). Many theories assume that proto-types develop to represent categories. (For further discussion of prototype theories, see (Barsalou, 1990; Barsalou & Hale, 1993; E. Smith & Medin, 1981; J. Smith & Minda, 2002).

If a category has a prototype, category members similar to the prototype are viewed as typical category members, whereas category members different from the prototype are viewed as atypical. If the prototype for birds indicates that they tend to fly, nest in trees, and be small, then sparrows, which fit this prototype well, are typi-cal; ostriches, on the other hand, which have none of these properties, do not fit the prototype and are therefore atypical. Typicality is not an on–off condition. Eagles fit the prototype moderately well, and so they are moderately typical. In general, the members of a category vary continuously in how similar they are to the prototype; thus, different birds vary continuously along this continuum of typicality, from highly typical to highly atypical. Such *typicality gradients* occur universally across categories (Barsalou, 1987; Rosch, 1973). Every category ever studied has one, even categories with precise rules (e.g., Armstrong et al., 1983).

Typicality gradients have substantial effects on how we process categories. When learning categories, we tend to learn typical members of a category before atypical ones (e.g., Mervis & Pani, 1980). When we categorize individuals, we categorize typ-ical ones faster than atypical ones (e.g., Rosch, 1975), and with greater accuracy (e.g., Posner & Keele, 1968). When we draw inferences from category members, we draw stronger ones from typical than from atypical category members (e.g., Osherson et al., 1990; Rips, 1975). In general, typical category members enjoy a privileged status in the kingdom of categories.

Such typicality effects have been widely viewed as implicating prototypes in the representation of categories (e.g., Hampton, 1979; Rosch & Mervis, 1975; E. Smith et al., 1974). Typicality effects can arise, however, even if no prototype is stored for a category and only exemplar memories represent the category (Medin & Schaffer, 1978). Much research has attempted to identify whether typicality gradients result from prototypes, exemplars, or other types of representations (e.g., Barsalou, 1985, 1987, 1990; Medin & Schaffer, 1978; J. Smith & Minda, 2002). Whatever way typ-icality gradients happen to originate, there is no doubt that categories have them, and that typicality is one of the most important factors in the acquisition and use of category knowledge.

4.3. Background Knowledge

An implicit assumption underlying exemplar memories, rules, and prototypes is that the properties constituting them are processed in a vacuum. To establish an exemplar memory of a chair, for example, the perceived object is simply added to a set of memorized exemplars of the object. To update a rule or prototype, newly perceived properties are simply integrated into its previously established property information. In either learning process, properties accumulate in relative isolation. Increasingly, however, researchers have come to appreciate that properties typically activate **background knowledge** in memory that specifies how properties originate, why they are important, and how they are related to one another (e.g., Ahn & Luhmann, 2005; Goodman, 1955; Murphy & Medin, 1985). Rather than being processed in a vacuum, properties are processed within a larger context of associated knowledge.

For instance, suppose that someone tells you that an object has wheels and a large sheet of canvas. In representing this object to yourself, do you assume that it has *only* these two properties and imagine a set of stationary wheels linked by a canvas axle? No. You could probably draw the additional inferences that the cloth is a sail, that the object uses wind power to roll along the ground, and that this "land sailboat" contains other parts, such as a metal axle, a mast, and a seat. Where did this interpretation come from? Background knowledge about wind, rolling, and transportation became active to explain and integrate the two stated properties. This example illustrates how readily background knowledge becomes active in interpretation and how it complements perceived properties. Rather than perceiving the properties of an entity in isolation, we almost always bring background knowledge to bear on interpreting them. (For a review of findings, see Murphy, 2000).

Here's another illustration (Barsalou, 1983). Participants were presented with the names of several objects—rock, chair, brick, potted plant—and asked to identify a category to which they all belong. (Not so easy—what's your guess?) But here's some background knowledge. The day is hot and windy. You want to keep your door open, but it keeps blowing shut. You decide to do something about it, maybe hold the door open with . . . right. With this information, people often instantly see that rock, chair, brick, and potted plant all belong to the category of things that will hold a door open on a windy day. The category did not become apparent until you activated the relevant background knowledge, another demonstration of the central role of background knowledge in processing categories.

A structure for representing background knowledge is the **schema**, a structured representation that captures the information that typically applies to a situation or event (for reviews, see Barsalou, 1992; Barsalou & Hale, 1993; Rumelhart & Norman, 1988). Schemata are described as "structured" because they are not lists of independent properties but instead establish coherent sets of relations that link properties. Thus the schema for a birthday party (like yours) might include guests, gifts, and cake; the structure is that the guests give gifts to the birthday celebrant, and that everyone eats cake. Schemata are similar to rules and prototypes in that they summarize the members of a category. They differ from rules and prototypes in that they contain much information that is not essential for categorizing entities but that is important for understanding the events surrounding them. The schema for a birthday party provides useful background knowledge about birthday cakes; seeing a birthday cake activates the schema for birthday parties, so useful inferences can be drawn about why the cake is there and how it will be used.

Much evidence for schemata can be found across all aspects of cognition. When processing visual scenes, we expect to see particular configurations of objects (e.g., Biederman, 1981; Palmer, 1975). In a given social situation, we expect to observe (and engage in) particular relations among the those present (e.g., Fiske & Taylor,

1991). In the realm of memory, schemata produce strong expectations about what is likely to have occurred in the past, expectations that can distort our memories (e.g., Bartlett, 1932; Brewer & Treyens, 1981; Schooler et al., 1997). Schemata play central roles in aspects of reasoning such as analogy, problem solving, and decision making (e.g., Gentner & Markman, 1997; Markman & Gentner, 2001; Markman & Medin, 1995; Ross, 1996).

4.4. Dynamic Representation

As we have seen, many different structures can underlie the knowledge of a given category: exemplars, rules, prototypes, and schemata. When we think of a particular category, do all the structures representing it become fully active? Or does the cognitive system vary the most active information about a category dynamically, highlighting the information most useful on the current occasions?

Much evidence indicates that not all possible information for a category is activated when the category is accessed, but rather information relevant in the current context is preferentially activated. Dynamic representation refers to the ability of the cognitive system to construct, and call on as necessary, many different representations of a category, each emphasizing the category knowledge currently most relevant.

One source of evidence for dynamic representation comes from cross-modality priming studies. Participants listen to a sentence over headphones. Immediately following the last spoken word, they see a string of letters. Their task is to indicate as quickly as possible whether the string forms a word (for example, *yellow*) or a nonword (for example, *yeelor*). This basic task can be used to demonstrate dynamic representation (e.g., Greenspan, 1986; Tabossi, 1988). Here's how it works. Let's say that the last word of an auditorally presented sentence is *beachball* and that this word appears in one of two sentences:

> The swimmer saw the gently bobbing *beachball.*
> The air hissed out of the punctured *beachball.*

If *beachball* is represented dynamically in these two sentences, then the information active for it should vary, reflecting the most relevant property about beachballs in each situation. After presentation of the first sentence, the property "floats" should be more active than the property "is flat." But following the second sentence, "is flat" should be more active than "floats." If the representation of "beachball" is *not* dynamic, the activations of "floats" and "is flat" should not change across sentences. If all category knowledge is equally active for a category on every occasion, then the change of sentence should not affect the conceptual representation of "beachball."

Many experiments, using cross-modal priming and many other techniques, have consistently produced results that support dynamic representation (for reviews, see Barsalou, 1987, 1989; L. Smith & Samuelson, 1997; Yeh & Barsalou, 2004). The information that is most active varies from occasion to occasion. Furthermore, the most active information is typically relevant to the current context.

> ✓ **Comprehension Check:**
>
> 1. Do we use memories of individual category members to represent knowledge, or do we always summarize the properties of category members to do so? Justify your answer.
> 2. On a given occasion when the brain represents a category, describe what happens. Also address how this process might vary across occasions on which the same category is represented.

5. CATEGORY DOMAINS AND ORGANIZATION

For what domains in the world do we establish category knowledge? It seems we develop categories that reflect the kinds of things in the world—what philosophers concerned with ontology, the study of being or the essence of things, call *ontological types* (e.g., Sommers, 1963). Ontologists generally agree that important ontological types include living natural things ("kinds" in the language of ontology), nonliving natural kinds, artifacts, locations, events, mental states, times, and properties. Most ontologists believe that ontological categories are probably *universal;* that is, they are categories that every normal human knows regardless of culture. Psychologists believe that different domains of category knowledge develop for different ontological types (e.g., Keil, 1979).

Within each domain of category knowledge lie many more specific categories. "Living natural kinds" includes "mammals" and "trees." "Nonliving natural kinds" includes "water" and "gold." "Artifacts" includes "tools" and "clothes." "Locations" includes "oceans" and "parks." "Events" includes "meals" and "birthday parties." "Mental states" includes "emotions" and "ideas." "Times" includes "night" and "summer." "Properties" includes "green" and "expensive." Many of these more specific categories within domains also appear to be known universally across cultures (e.g., Malt, 1995). As categories become increasingly specific, though, they are less likely to be known in all cultures (for example, tank top, paper shredder, foods high in vitamin C).

5.1. Distinguishing Domains of Category Knowledge in the Brain

The various domains of category knowledge certainly seem different, at least intuitively: animals seem in their essence different from artifacts, objects seem different from thoughts. Are these intuitive differences realized in the brain's representational systems? Is knowledge of different categories stored in different regions of the brain? Or is all category knowledge stored in a single brain area? To address this question, researchers have assessed category knowledge in patients who have suffered brain lesions, seeking to learn which particular categories are lost and whether these losses can be associated with particular brain regions.

Typically when a brain-damaged patient loses category knowledge, only some knowledge is lost, while other knowledge is preserved. For example, Warrington and

Shallice (1984) described four patients with brain damage who exhibited a deficit for animal categories (such as "dogs" and "robins"). But, although these patients had difficulty naming and defining various animals, they had little trouble naming and defining artifact categories (such as "hammers" and "chairs"). More rarely, patients show the opposite deficit (e.g., Warrington & McCarthy, 1983, 1987), exhibiting less knowledge of artifacts than of animals. This double dissociation of animals and artifacts suggests that different localized brain areas represent these two kinds of categories. Various deficits for other categories have been reported as well, such as deficits for number categories and abstract categories (e.g., Thioux et al., 1998; Tyler & Moss, 1997).

How can these selective deficits in category knowledge be explained? Modality-specific representations of categories may provide a clue. Both behavioral and neural evidence suggest that the representation of a category is distributed across the modality-specific brain systems that process its properties. For example, in Western culture, at any rate, many people see animals (engaging the visual modality) far more often than they work with them (engaging the motor system). In contrast, knowledge of artifacts generally relies much more heavily on motor information than on visual information (try to describe a screwdriver while keeping your hands still). Given these different profiles of multimodal information, lesions to the visual system might produce larger deficits for living things than for artifacts, whereas lesions to the motor system might produce larger deficits for artifacts. Perhaps the multimodal profiles for different domains of categories interact with lesions in this way to produce different deficits in category knowledge when the corresponding brain area is damaged. Many theorists have reached this conclusion (e.g., Damasio & Damasio, 1994; Farah & McClelland, 1991; Gainotti et al., 1995; Humphreys & Forde, 2001; Pulvermüller, 1999). To the extent that this account is correct, it offers further evidence for the claim that category knowledge is distributed across the modality-specific systems that process it.

But the verdict is not in. Some researchers believe that this account is too crude to explain the subtle patterns of deficits that are often seen in patients with brain damage (Cree & McRae, 2003). Most typically, a patient does *not* lose just a single category but rather loses several. Foods can be lost along with living things, and so can musical instruments. Fruits and vegetables are typically lost together, and can be lost with either living things or nonliving things. Figure 4–16 presents seven patterns of category deficits that Cree and McRae identified in their review of the literature; there is no way that loss of either visual or motor processing could explain all these different patterns.

Cree and McCrae (2003) believe that deficits result from specific losses to a much wider variety of properties, for which the processing is distributed across the brain. To assess this hypothesis, they asked people to produce the properties for the kinds of categories that patients lose following brain lesions, such as the properties of birds, fruit, and tools. Once they had established each category's properties, they assessed what *types* of properties the various categories in each deficit pattern shared, along with the types that differed. Of central interest was whether the multiple categories in a particular deficit pattern had one or more property types in common—visual motion, say, or color? If so, lesions to areas that process a given property type could

Deficit Pattern	Shared Properties
1. Multiple categories that constitute living creatures	Visual motion, visual parts, color
2. Multiple categories that constitute nonliving things	Function, visual parts
3. Fruits and vegetables	Color, function, taste, smell
4. Fruits and vegetables with living creatures	Color
5. Fruits and vegetables with nonliving things	Function
6. Inanimate foods with living things (especially fruits and vegetables)	Function, taste, smell
7. Musical instruments with living things	Sound, color

FIGURE 4–16   Seven patterns of category deficits that result from brain lesions

These are sets of categories for which patients with brain damage simultaneously exhibit much poorer knowledge than normal. There is evidence that when a brain lesion compromises representations of particular properties, the categories that rely heavily on them are impaired.

cause categories that share it to be lost together. For example, if color areas are damaged, then categories for which color is important, such as animals and foods, might be compromised simultaneously.

The results were illuminating (see Figure 4–16). Cree and McRae (2003) found, for example, that the categories in the first pattern of deficits, living creatures, typically share many properties: they generally move, have interesting and salient parts, and have relatively informative colors. The categories in the fifth pattern (fruits, vegetables, and nonliving things) share properties for functions, in that all these things have roles in our life—fruits and vegetables in our diet, nonliving artifacts in our manipulation of the world around us. Thus, a more complicated formulation of the original theory might explain the patterns of category-specific deficits found in the literature.

As provocative as these conclusions are, the issue of how the brain represents categories is far from settled. Cree and McRae (2003) show that factors besides shared properties are important, such as property uniqueness. Alternative accounts for category-specific deficits in terms of amodal symbols have also been offered (e.g., Capitani et al., 2003; Caramazza & Shelton, 1998; Tyler & Moss, 2001), and it is likely that a variety of mechanisms produce category-specific deficits, not just one (e.g., Coltheart et al., 1998; Simmons & Barsalou, 2003). Furthermore, studies of patients with brain damage suffer from a variety of methodological problems, including difficulties in measuring behavioral deficits, along with difficulties in measuring lesions and fully understanding their implications for brain operation (see Chapter 1). Nevertheless, a conclusion emerging from this research is that different types of categories are represented primarily in different brain areas. Consistent with the multimodal-simulation view, a category's representation appears, at least in part, to be distributed across the modality-specific areas of the brain that process its members.

Further support for this conclusion comes from neuroimaging studies that have measured brain activity while participants process categories from different domains, particularly the domains of animals and artifacts. Different patterns of brain activity are observed for these domains. Consistent with findings from research with brain-damaged patients, for example, artifacts tend to activate premotor areas more than do animals (see Figure 4–12).

For the "animals" domain, studies of patients with brain damage and neuroimaging studies show an interesting difference (Martin, 2001). On the one hand, studies show that damage to the temporal lobes often produces a categorical deficit for animals; on the other hand, neuroimaging studies often show extensive activation for animals in the occipital lobes. Why do these different patterns occur? Martin suggests that the temporal lobes are *association areas* that work to integrate category knowledge. When there is damage to these areas, the statistical patterns stored there cannot trigger simulations in the occipital lobes that represent the properties of animal categories. When these association areas are intact, as they are for most participants in neuroimaging studies, the statistical patterns stored there can trigger simulations in the occipital lobes, which are then detected by neuroimaging. Thus, the differential pattern of results offers support for the idea that representations are distributed in the brain, as described earlier.

Neuroimaging studies also have found that using knowledge of object shape (for example, the shape of a cat) activates the fusiform gyrus, whereas using knowledge of object motion (for example, how a cat moves) activates the posterior temporal gyrus (Chao et al., 1999; Martin & Chao, 2001; Martin et al., 1996). Furthermore, these studies have found that accessing different kinds of categories activates somewhat different fusiform areas for shape, and somewhat different temporal areas for motion. Although the sites for shape are near each other, they differ. Whereas the shapes of animals, people, and faces tend to activate lateral fusiform areas, the shapes of tools tend to activate more medial ones. The same is true for motion sites. Whereas animals, people, and faces tend to activate superior temporal areas, tools tend to activate more inferior ones. These slightly different sites are a further indication that different domains of category knowledge rely on different brain systems. Increasingly, studies suggest that different domains of category knowledge are distributed differently across the brain's modality-specific areas. The intuitive differences that we experience for different domains indeed reflect important differences in the underlying neural implementations.

5.2. Taxonomies and the Search for a "Basic Level"

Within a domain of category knowledge, categories are not represented in isolation, but rather in various structures that link related categories. One important organizational form is the taxonomy, a set of nested categories that vary in abstraction, each nested category a subset of its higher order category (Figure 4–17). Thus, the category of objects includes living things and artifacts. "Artifacts" includes "tools," "vehicles," "clothing," . . . "Tools" includes "screwdrivers," "hammers," "saws," . . . "Screwdrivers" includes "slot," "Phillips," "ratchet" screwdrivers. . . . Taxonomies such as these examples sound like the result of formal education and,

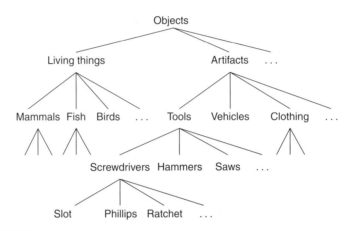

FIGURE 4–17   A taxonomy for objects

Increasingly specific categories are nested in more general ones.

certainly, to some extent they are. But in fact taxonomies are found universally throughout cultures and are not dependent on formal training. After reviewing anthropological work on biological categories, Malt (1995) concluded that all cultures studied so far, including traditional, nonindustrial ones, have taxonomies for plants and animals.

A central question in this area has been the search for a *basic level* in taxonomies, a level that is more central than others in human cognition. In Figure 4–17, for example, which levels—the lower ones? the middle ones? the higher ones?—are likely to be the most important for cognition?

In classic anthropological work on biological categories, Berlin, Breedlove, and Raven (1973) argued that the middle levels are the most important. For one thing, more words for categories exist at middle levels than at those above and below— more words such as "dog," "horse," and "lion" exist than words such as "mammal" (above) or "collie," "poodle," and "terrier" (below). Although it is logically necessary that more categories become possible as you go *lower* in a taxonomy, the important finding here was that more single-word names exist for categories at middle levels than at lower ones. Another important finding was that names for categories at middle levels are shorter than names for categories above and below (for example, "dog" vs. "mammal" above and vs. "poodle" below). *Zipf's law* in linguistics states that the more frequently a word occurs in a language, the shorter it becomes as the language evolves over many generations of speakers. Names for categories at middle taxonomic levels are shortest, suggesting that these are the names used most often and therefore most important.

Cross-cultural conclusions from Malt (1995) further demonstrate the importance of middle-level categories in taxonomies. Across all cultures, traditional and developed, there is high agreement in middle-level categories: names for middle-level categories such as "deer," "eagle," and "alligator" tend to be found wherever these animals are part of the environment. Furthermore, these names refer to essentially the same groups of entities in the environment—"deer," for example, refers to pretty much the same creature across cultures. Finally, cultures typically have names for these categories even when they play no role in people's lives. Across cultures, many plants and animals that have no function still have names at the middle level. Middle-level categories in biological taxonomies are sufficiently salient perceptually that members of nearly all cultures perceive and develop names for them (for example, in our culture, many wild animals).

Much psychological research further shows that the middle levels in a taxonomy are most important. Investigators found that categories at mid-taxonomic levels are processed faster than are categories at other levels (Rosch et al., 1976). When participants have to match a pictured object to a category name (for example, "poodle," "dog," "animal"), they match middle-level names fastest (in this case, "dog"). These investigators also found that children learn names for middle-level categories earlier than they do the names for categories at other levels. Much other research has reported similar results (for a review, see Murphy & Lassaline, 1997). On the basis of results like these, Rosch and colleagues called middle-level categories the basic level, the level of a taxonomy used most often, learned most easily, and processed most efficiently.

Names for categories at higher and lower levels show much less agreement across cultures (e.g., Malt, 1995). For example, cultures that eat butterfly larvae have many categories for different kinds of larvae; cultures that don't, don't. When similar categories at higher and lower levels do exist in two cultures, they often do not refer to the same sets of things in the environment. One culture might have a category for "trees," another might have a category for "firewood" that includes only those trees that are burnable. Furthermore, both high- and low-level categories are more likely to deviate from scientific taxonomies than are middle-level categories.

So what is it about middle-level categories? *Why* do they show these advantages? Why are they the most common; why are their names shortest? Why are these the categories most agreed on across cultures and the closest to scientific taxonomies? Why do we learn and process them most easily?

Although this issue is far from settled, a dominant account has emerged (e.g., Malt, 1995; Tversky & Hemenway, 1985). Middle-level categories are important because their members (unlike members of categories at higher and lower levels) typically share a common configuration of physical parts, and this configuration differs from that of other categories at the same level. For example, deer have four legs, two ears, pointed hooves, a tail, and other physical properties in a particular arrangement; most butterflies have a specific arrangement of head, body, antennae, and large flat wings. For hundreds of years, biologists have used these morphological descriptions to define natural categories. Evolutionary and genetic theories have made it possible to link the genetic histories of species directly to these morphological structures.

At higher levels, there is no common morphological structure within a category—lots of mammals are built nothing like deer. At lower levels, such as varieties of butterflies, the morphology is shared across different categories, making different varieties confusable. To discriminate the difference between categories, it is necessary to learn subtle visual features that are much less salient than the morphological characteristics that distinguish the deer and butterflies categories at the middle level.

Why is the morphology of middle-level taxonomies so salient? One explanation is that our visual feature-detection systems have become tuned over evolutionary time to the features that distinguish different morphologies from one another. Laboratory evidence for this conclusion can be found in Tversky and Hemenway (1985), Jolicoeur et al. (1984), and Murphy and Brownell (1985); Biederman (1987) presents a related theory of object recognition.

Still, many researchers are reluctant to adopt the construct of a "basic level." One reason is that middle-level categories are not always the dominant ones. In Western culture, for example, the dominant level for categories of plants and birds is not at a mid-taxonomic level. Many Westerners know little about different types of plants and birds and cannot name the middle-level categories for them; besides, they often find higher level categories of plants and birds sufficiently informative for their purposes (e.g., Rosch et al., 1976). As Western culture has increasingly lost touch with the natural environment, the dominant taxonomic level for natural living kinds has shifted upward. Wolff and colleagues (1999) counted the taxonomic terms for trees in the *Oxford English Dictionary* from the sixteenth through the twentieth centuries, and discovered that the number of words for tree categories generally increased over this period, as knowledge about the natural world increased. In the twentieth century, however, names for tree categories decreased precipitately—especially for middle levels—indicating an upward taxonomic shift in knowledge about the natural environment.

So, one difficulty with middle-level categories as a basic level is that many people simply use higher level categories instead (see also Mandler & McDonough, 1998, 2000). A related problem, at the other end of the scale, is that when people become expert in a domain, they become able to process lower level taxonomic categories as effectively as middle-level ones (e.g., Gauthier et al., 1999; Johnson & Mervis, 1997; Tanaka & Curran, 2001; Tanaka & Gauthier, 1997).

Furthermore, the most useful taxonomic level can vary with the current goal (e.g., Cruse, 1977). You want your dog with you on a once-in-a-lifetime trip to London? In this situation, your travel agent does *not* use the basic level and simply tell you that all "dogs" coming into the United Kingdom are subject to a six-month quarantine. Because the law actually applies to all non-human *mammals,* your travel agent tells you that all non-human "mammals" coming into the United Kingdom are subject to quarantine. Even though the basic level is normally more salient than the next level up, your travel agent moves up a level so that you understand the full extent of the law. Under these conditions, a non–basic level is most important.

Thus, although there is an overall tendency for middle-level categories to dominate categories at other levels in many important ways, so many exceptions exist that many researchers believe that referring to middle-level categories as "basic" confers on them an objective reality not warranted by the data. The relative importance of a taxonomic level reflects a wide variety of mediating factors and fluctuates with need and circumstance.

Comprehension Check:

1. How do we organize large systems of categories?
2. How do different profiles of modality-specific information represent different types of categories?

Revisit and Reflect

1. *What roles does knowledge play in cognition, and how is it represented in the brain?*

   It has been said you can't step into the same river twice, or in a sense, even once—it is constantly changing. If you were now to reread the description at the beginning of this chapter about the apparently bizarre birthday party—bizarre because you lacked all knowledge—all sorts of things may come to mind that didn't the first time. Your understanding has been changed by the knowledge that you acquired from reading this chapter.

   Knowledge permeates every aspect of cognitive activity. It completes perceptions and guides attention; it enables categorization and produces rich inferences that go beyond the information given. Knowledge interprets memories, confers the meanings of words, and produces the representations that underlie thought. Without knowledge we would be like cameras that represent images but cannot interpret or make use of them.

   Think Critically

   - If a camera had knowledge, how would its functionality change?
   - Does knowledge play the same roles in nonhuman species of animals as in humans? What might some similarities and differences be?
   - If a person really lost all knowledge, what sorts of social support systems would have to be implemented to help this person cope in the world?

2. *What representational formats are most likely to exist in the brain, and how do multiple representational formats work together to represent and simulate an object?*

   Knowledge can be represented in various formats, including depictive images, feature analyses, amodal symbols, and statistical patterns. Most likely, the brain uses multiple formats, with images, features, amodal symbols, and statistical patterns all playing a role in many tasks.

   On perceiving an object, representations in multiple formats become active, beginning with images in the brain's topographically organized areas. Feature detection systems then extract meaningful features that identify functionally important aspects of the object. Finally, statistical patterns in convergence zones integrate the information extracted from images and features. This process apparently can be run in reverse to simulate category members in their absence; by activating the statistical pattern for a once-perceived entity, a partial simulation of its image and features can be reenacted.

Think Critically

- How does the representation of knowledge in computers (documents, photos, music files, etc.) differ from the representation of knowledge in humans? How are they similar?

- How could multiple formats of representation be implemented and combined in cameras and computers to make them more sophisticated?

- What important roles does attention play in creating knowledge? Can you think of any further roles not discussed in Chapter 3 or in this chapter?

3. *How do representations distributed across the brain become integrated to establish category knowledge?*

Because different members of a category activate similar statistical patterns, they probably become associated to shared conjunctive neurons. As a result, bodies of category knowledge develop in the brain that can be used to produce useful inferences. Perceived aspects of a category member activate category knowledge, which then produces inferences about its as-of-yet unperceived aspects. Once category knowledge develops, it provides a wealth of inferential knowledge that helps us go beyond the information given.

Category knowledge also results from the integration of information experienced across modalities for category members. Information in all the relevant modalities for a category becomes integrated in higher order convergence zones. Because different categories are experienced in different modalities, the profile of relevant modalities varies from category to category.

Think Critically

- For many categories, no single feature is shared by all category members. How does the account of exemplar integration provided here explain the integration of exemplars for such categories?

- On perceiving a category member, why aren't all possible inferences generated? Would it be useful to generate all inferences? Why or why not?

- If categories are represented in the modalities that are used to process their members, then how are abstract categories such as "love" represented? (*Hint*: Think of the situations where love is experienced, and then think of aspects of those situations—both in the world and in the mind—that "love" refers to.)

4. *What different types of representational structures underlie category knowledge, and how are they accessed on particular occasions?*

Multiple types of structures underlie category knowledge. Most basically, the brain stores specific memories of category exemplars. The brain also summarizes these exemplar memories in rules and prototypes. Additionally, the brain situates category knowledge in background knowledge and schemata.

On a given occasion, only a small number of the structures associated with a category are activated. Depending on the current situation and goals, different subsets of background knowledge become active to represent the category.

As a result, the representation of a category may vary widely, with the representation on a given occasion being tailored to a person's current context.

Think Critically

- What constitutes an exemplar memory? Imagine seeing a particular member of a category, such as a chair in your living room. Is an exemplar an integrated representation of all the times you've perceived this chair, or does each occasion produce a different exemplar? What defines the spatiotemporal boundaries of an exemplar?

- What types of information reside in background knowledge and schemata? Can you suggest any particular kinds of information that are likely to be included? Likely to be excluded? Also, how are these structures likely to be organized?

5. *How are different domains of categories represented and organized?*

Different domains of category knowledge exist for the diverse components of human experience. Studies of patients with brain damage and neuroimaging studies suggest that each domain establishes a unique presence across the brain's modality-specific areas. The modalities used to process a category's members apparently are the ones used to represent knowledge about it.

Within domains, categories are organized by taxonomies that contain categories on multiple levels. Typically, middle-level categories are most important in everyday conceptual knowledge, often being shared extensively across cultures. Nevertheless categories at other taxonomic levels often become important for cultural and functional reasons.

Think Critically

- What kinds of other organizations of category knowledge exist besides taxonomies?

- How might organizations of category knowledge be acquired?

- How does an organizational structure affect the representations of the categories it includes? How might the representation of an individual category affect the representation of an organizational structure?

5

Encoding and Retrieval from Long-Term Memory

Learning Objectives

Y ou're walking down a hall. Coming toward you, at a distance of about 50 feet, are two people walking together. You recognize one of them immediately: you know her name, you met her at a political rally last term. On that occasion you discovered that you grew up in the same city and share a liking for Italian food. Her companion looks familiar, you have a vague sense you've met before, but you can't place him—you can't think what his name is, where you might have met, or any details about him. But now, as you all meet, he greets *you* by name. Your embarrassment at not knowing his name grows when the conversation reveals that he remembers you from an encounter only two weeks ago, just before you both took a physics exam. How is it that you can recall clearly a conversation you had months ago, and have no recollection of another that apparently took place relatively recently?

This chapter considers the nature of long-term memory, first describing two classes of long-term memory systems, declarative and nondeclarative. We then focus on the mechanisms that encode, consolidate, and retrieve declarative memories, consider how and why our memories are sometimes inaccurate, and explore why we sometimes forget. We conclude with a discussion of the forms of nondeclarative memory that allow the past to unconsciously shape our current thinking and actions. We specifically address five questions:

1. What are the characteristics of declarative and nondeclarative memory systems?
2. How do we encode new declarative memories, what processes affect encoding efficacy, and what brain mechanisms build these memories?
3. How are episodic memories retrieved, and why is it that sometimes what we retrieve is not an accurate reflection of our past?
4. Why do we sometimes forget?
5. What are the forms of nondeclarative memory, and how do they influence our behavior?

1. THE NATURE OF LONG-TERM MEMORY

The ability to remember the people, places, and things encountered in the course of daily life is a fundamental form of cognition that guides behavior. The frustration experienced in situations such as the hallway meeting described serves as a brief reminder of our dependence on **memory**, the internal repository of stored information. As we shall see in this chapter, memory relies on a set of processes by which information is encoded, consolidated, and retrieved. Although the consequences of memory failure are sometimes limited to social embarrassment, that is not always the case: memory is essential to the functioning and even the survival of human and other animals. Without memory, we could never learn from our experience and would operate aimlessly, without plans or goals. Motor skills and language ability would be lost. Even the sense of personal identity we all possess would be gone.

The kind of memory involved in these situations is **long-term memory**, information that is acquired in the course of an experience and that persists so that it can be retrieved long after the experience is past. As we will see, some forms of long-term memory can be consciously retrieved, so that we can use our remembrance of things past to guide present thought and action. William James (1890) described this kind of memory as "the knowledge of a former state of mind after it has once dropped from consciousness." By contrast, other forms of long-term memory influence our present thinking and behavior while operating outside awareness. In such instances, past experience unconsciously affects the present. Progress in understanding long-term memory has come from behavioral investigations of people with intact memories as well as of patients with memory deficits. Insights into the operation of memory also have come from lesion and recording studies in animals and neuroimaging studies in humans.

1.1. The Forms of Long-Term Memory

Theorists believe that there are multiple forms of long-term memory that differ in their basic information processing properties and in the brain structures that support them (Figure 5–1). These various forms of memory are thought to fall into two general classes, described as declarative and nondeclarative. Declarative memory (also known as explicit memory) refers to forms of long-term memory that can ordinarily be consciously recollected and "declared," or described to other people, such as memory for facts, ideas, and events. Declarative memory encompasses episodic memory, the memory of events in our own personal past, and semantic memory, our general knowledge about things in the world and their meaning, a distinction proposed by Endel Tulving in 1972. Tulving defined episodic memory as the conscious knowledge of temporally dated, spatially located, and personally experienced events or episodes.

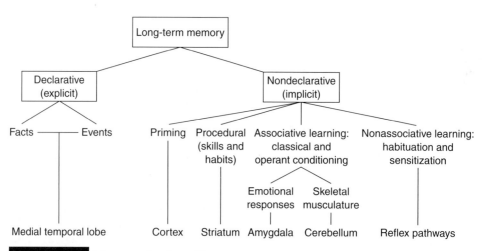

FIGURE 5–1   The organization of long-term memory

Forms of long-term memory can be classified as either declarative (explicit) or nondeclarative (implicit). Declarative and nondeclarative memory depend on different brain regions.

(Kandel, E. R., Kupferman, I., & Iverson, S. (2000). Learning and Memory. In: E. R. Kandel, J. H. Schwartz, & T. M. Jessell (eds.) *Principles of Neural Science*, pp. 1227–1246. New York: McGraw-Hill, Fig. 62-4. Reprinted with permission.)

He defined semantic memory as knowledge about words and concepts, their properties, and interrelations (Tulving, 1972). We are aware of the contents of both kinds of memory, but a difference between them is context, or the lack thereof. Episodic memory, which supports memory for individual life events, has a context: when you recollected details about one of the people you met in the hall—her political views, her tastes in cuisine—you engaged in a kind of "mental time travel" to your earlier meeting, and you were aware that the information you possessed about her was bound to that particular autobiographical experience. But when you retrieve your semantic memory of, say, the main ingredients of Italian cuisine, that memory is not bound to the specific context in which you acquired that knowledge because you likely accumulated the knowledge across multiple experiences in a variety of contexts. Tests that assess declarative memory are termed explicit memory tests because they require the retrieval of an explicit description or report of knowledge from memory. Declarative memory is highly flexible, involving the association of multiple pieces of information into a unified memory representation; thus, we may have different routes to retrieval of a given memory. Both forms of declarative memory, episodic and semantic, depend on the operation of the medial temporal lobes.

Nondeclarative memory (also known as implicit memory) refers to nonconscious forms of long-term memory that are expressed as a change in behavior without any conscious recollection. Tests of nondeclarative memory—termed implicit memory tests—do not require description of the contents of memory, but rather reveal memory *implicitly* through observed changes in performance, such as the gradual acquisition of a motor skill. In comparison to declarative memory, nondeclarative memory tends to be more restricted in the ways that this knowledge can be retrieved. The various forms of nondeclarative memory do not depend on the medial temporal lobe structures that are important for declarative memory. Rather, the various forms of nondeclarative memory are implemented in different brain regions (see Figure 5–1).

1.2. The Power of Memory: The Story of H.M.

Much of the research describing and classifying types of long-term memory has a very human foundation in the experience of a patient known as H.M. The pattern of catastrophic memory deficits observed in this man initiated a revolution in our understanding of memory, revealing that our ability to encode and retrieve new episodic and semantic memories depends on a particular set of brain structures in the medial temporal lobes—the hippocampus and surrounding entorhinal, perirhinal, and parahippocampal cortices (Figure 5–2). The story of H.M. highlights the centrality of memory to our mental lives, and shines a spotlight on the powerful role the medial temporal lobes play in documenting our experiences.

When he was 7, H.M. had a bicycle accident that left him unconscious for 5 minutes. By the age of 10, he was suffering minor epileptic episodes that ultimately progressed to include major seizures. For more than a decade, H.M.'s life was increasingly disrupted by his constant seizures: he had to drop out of high school for a time and had to quit working while he was in his twenties. Because the seizures could

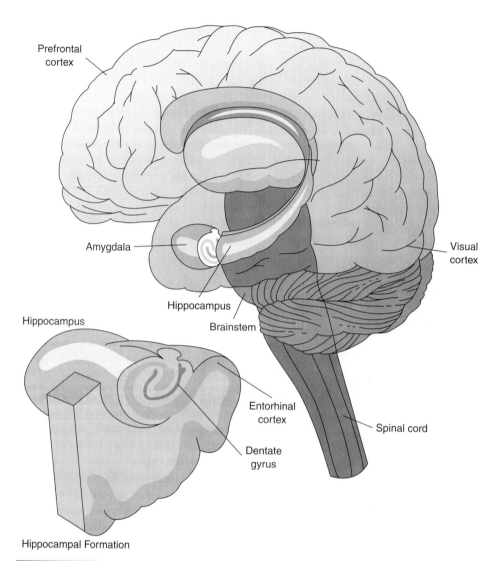

Prefrontal cortex

Amygdala

Hippocampus

Brainstem

Visual cortex

Hippocampus

Entorhinal cortex

Spinal cord

Dentate gyrus

Hippocampal Formation

FIGURE 5–2   The medial temporal lobe structures of the human brain, which are critical for declarative memory

The hippocampus is a structure located deep in the medial portion of the temporal lobe. Information flows into the hippocampal formation from the surrounding medial temporal cortices, including the entorhinal cortex.

(From Squire, L. R. & E. R. Kandel. *Memory: From Mind to Molecules*, p. 111. © 2000 Larry R. Squire & Eric R. Kandel. Reprinted with permission of the authors.)

not be controlled by medication, at 27 H.M. underwent bilateral removal of the medial temporal lobes, thought to be the site where his seizures originated. The surgery excised the hippocampus, amygdala, and much of the surrounding medial temporal cortices (Figure 5–3). The surgery effectively brought H.M.'s seizures under control, but it was immediately clear that this positive outcome was accompanied by an unexpectedly devastating loss of memory (Corkin, 1984; Scoville & Milner, 1957).

Tests of H.M.'s cognitive abilities reveal that his deficit is highly specific, as his intelligence and some memory functions are relatively preserved. For example, when presented with a short list of numbers and asked to remember them for 30 seconds, H.M. performs as well as those with intact medial temporal lobes. This observation indicates that *working memory* (discussed in Chapter 6), information that is maintained over a period of seconds or minutes, does not depend on medial temporal lobe structures. H.M. also has preserved long-term memory for information acquired well before his operation. He remembers his name and former occupation, and he retains a command of language, including vocabulary, indicating a preservation of previously

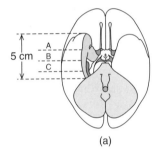

(a)

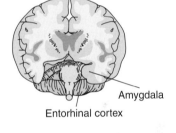

Amygdala
Entorhinal cortex

FIGURE 5–3 H.M.'s medial temporal lobe surgery

(a) A diagram of the brain, in ventral view (i.e., looking up from the bottom), showing the longitudinal extent of H.M.'s temporal lobe lesion. (b) Cross sections (seen from the front, with the locations of slices identified in panel a) showing the estimated extent of surgical removal of areas of H.M.'s brain. (Note the lack of brain tissue at the bottom left side, in fact the surgery was bilateral, but here the left side of the brain is shown intact to illustrate the structures that were removed.)

(Corkin, S., et al., 1997. H. M.'s medial temporal lobe lesion: findings from magnetic resonance imaging. *Journal of Neuroscience, 17,* 3964–3979.)

Hippocampus
Collateral sulcus   Entorhinal cortex

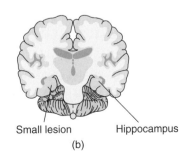

Small lesion   Hippocampus
(b)

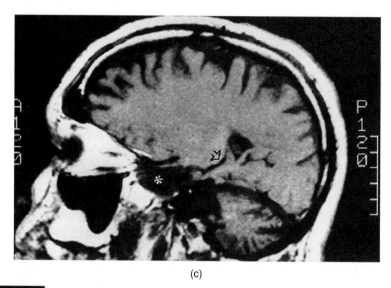

(c)

FIGURE 5–3 (contd.)

(c) An MRI scan of a parasagittal (i.e., seen from the side) section from the left side of H.M.'s brain. The resected, or removed, portion of the anterior temporal lobes is indicated by the asterisk. A remaining portion of the hippocampal formation is indicated by the open arrow.

(Corkin, S., Amaral, D. G., Gonzalez, R. G., Johnson, K. A., and Hyman, B. T. 1997. H.M.'s medial temporal lobe lesion: findings from magnetic resonance imaging. *Journal of Neuroscience*. Copyright © 1997 by the Society for Neuroscience. Reprinted with permission.)

acquired semantic memory. Remote episodic memories are also spared: he can recall childhood events in detail, including riding in a car with his parents when he had his first major seizure on his 16th birthday.

However, even though some memory functions are preserved, to this day H.M. suffers from a severe anterograde amnesia, the inability consciously to remember information encountered *after* brain damage. Thus, although H.M can briefly retain a short list of numbers (because his working memory is intact), he will immediately and completely forget them as soon as the information is lost from working memory. This catastrophic forgetting reveals an inability to form, retain, and retrieve new episodic memories. In essence, H.M. is frozen in time, and has been since the 1950s—he is unable to update his personal life narrative because of his inability to remember his daily experiences. H.M. himself has eloquently described this outcome:

> Right now, I'm wondering. Have I done or said anything amiss? You see, at this moment everything looks clear to me, but what happened just before? That's what worries me. It's like waking from a dream; I just don't remember (Milner, 1966).

Extensive testing indicates that H.M.'s anterograde amnesia is global; that is, he cannot consciously remember new events irrespective of their content or modality.

He cannot remember the people, places, and objects he sees, even after repeated encounters. He rapidly forgets both face-to-face conversations and songs heard on the radio, he cannot remember where he lives or who cares for him, and he even has difficulty recalling what he has eaten. It is clear that his amnesia does not reflect a perceptual deficit or a generalized impairment in intelligence; rather, H.M. suffers from a domain-general memory deficit. Moreover, H.M. has been unable to form new semantic memories following his surgery (an indication not appreciated until the late 1980s). Thus, when his semantic memory was tested for phrases such as "flower child" that had entered the language after his surgery but to which he had been repeatedly exposed, H.M. did not know their meanings (he guessed that "flower child" meant "a young person who grows flowers") (Gabrieli, Cohen, & Corkin, 1988). His anterograde amnesia applies to both episodic and semantic knowledge (O'Kane et al., 2004).

H.M. also demonstrates some retrograde amnesia, the forgetting of events that occurred *before* the damage to the brain. An important aspect of H.M.'s retrograde amnesia is that it is *temporally graded:* The closer an event had occurred to his surgery, the more likely it is to have been forgotten. In particular, he has greater difficulty remembering experiences that had occurred during the 11 years immediately preceding his surgery than in recalling more remote experiences from his childhood. This pattern of forgetting indicates that memories do not permanently depend on the medial temporal lobes; if this were the case, then even H.M.'s remote memories should have been forgotten. That remote memories were retained suggests that *over time* some process appears to lodge information in memory so that it remains even after medial temporal lobe damage. Nonetheless, the pattern of preserved working memory and impaired long-term memory following H.M.'s surgery is a powerful demonstration that the medial temporal lobes are critical for long-term memory (Squire, Stark, & Clark, 2004).

1.3. Multiple Memory Systems for Long-Term Learning and Remembering

The impact of the study of H.M. continued. Following the understanding that long-term memory depends on the medial temporal lobes, further tests of H.M.'s memory abilities initiated a second landmark insight into the organization of memory: the medial temporal lobes are not necessary for *all* types of long-term memory. Although suffering profound deficits of episodic and semantic memory after removal of his medial temporal lobes, H.M. nevertheless was able to form and retain other types of long-term memories.

The first evidence to this effect came in the 1960s with the observation that H.M. could acquire new motor skills at a normal rate, and that his level of long-term retention of these new skills was comparable to that of healthy controls (Milner, 1962). For example, H.M. was able to learn the skill of "mirror tracing." Given a picture of a star drawn with a double outline, H.M. was to draw a third outline of

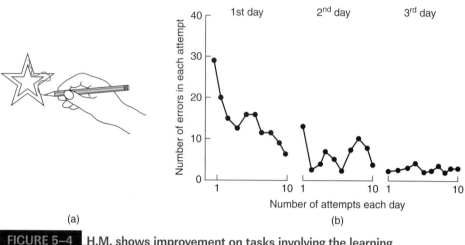

(a)   (b)

FIGURE 5–4   **H.M. shows improvement on tasks involving the learning of skilled movements**

(a) The task: to trace between two outlines of a star while looking at his hand in a mirror. (b) The graphs plot, over three days, the number of times during each attempt that he strayed outside the outlines as he drew the star. As with neurologically healthy participants, H.M. improved considerably across the multiple attempts, but he had no conscious recollection that he had ever performed the task before.

(Adapted from Brenda Milner, Larry R. Squire, & Eric R. Kandel, Cognitive neuroscience and the study of memory, *Neuron* 20 (1998): 445–468, Fig. 2. Found in Squire, Larry R. and Eric R. Kandel. *Memory: From Mind to Molecules.* W.H. Freeman and Company, New York, 2000, p. 13. Reprinted with permission from Elsevier.)

the star between the two already present—while looking only at the reflection of his hand and the star in a mirror (Figure 5–4). This task requires the remapping of visual perception onto motor actions because of the mirror-reversed nature of the visual input. Tested over a period of days, his improvement in performance—a measure of learning—was similar to that of participants with no memory deficit. H.M. became increasingly adept each day, tracing the star more quickly and more accurately, but at the outset of each day he had no conscious recollection of ever having done it before. These observations provided a clear demonstration that different kinds of long-term memory can be distinguished in amnesia.

The observation of intact skill learning following his surgery prompted careful reassessment of H.M.'s memory abilities, as well as those of other amnesic patients who suffered similar declarative memory deficits following damage to the medial temporal lobes. Investigations revealed that there is a whole class of long-term memories—now described as nondeclarative (implicit) memories—that operate outside awareness and that are preserved in the face of medial temporal lobe damage. For example, Warrington and Weiskrantz (1968, 1974) showed that amnesic patients could indirectly manifest evidence of recent learning in a perceptual domain. In their experiments, amnesic patients and controls were shown a list of words, such as ABSENT, INCOME, FILLY. Memory for the words was then tested.

However, instead of asking participants to recall or recognize the words on the list, Warrington and Weiskrantz instructed them simply to try to complete word beginnings (or "word stems"), taken from the original list, to make complete words (for example, ABS_____ could be completed to make either ABSENT or ABSTAIN). With these instructions, which made no explicit reference to the original list, both amnesic patients and controls were more likely to complete the word stems to make words that had been initially presented (ABSENT, not ABSTAIN). The presence of such a *priming* effect—which in this case is an increased likelihood of generating a particular response (for example, ABSENT) related to a stimulus previously presented—with amnesic patients was subsequently clarified. Graf and colleagues (1984) showed that amnesic patients demonstrate normal priming when the test instructions are to complete each word stem with the first word that comes to mind, but their performance is impaired when the instructions are to complete each stem by recalling a previously presented item.

Such reports of intact priming following medial temporal lobe damage indicate that the long-term memory capabilities of amnesic patients are not limited to motor skills such as mirror tracing. Amnesic patients are able to improve their performance on certain perceptual and conceptual tasks, even though they demonstrate deficient episodic memory for the earlier encounter with the material. Considerable evidence indicates that episodic memory and priming obey different underlying principles even in neurologically healthy people. We revisit such nondeclarative memory in more detail in the final section of this chapter.

Comprehension Check:

1. What are the differences between declarative and nondeclarative memory?
2. What are the two forms of amnesia?

2. ENCODING: HOW EPISODIC MEMORIES ARE FORMED

Some of life's episodes, central or trivial, may be remembered so well that we can accurately bring back to mind tremendous detail, even after considerable time has elapsed—you remember with pleasure an Italian dinner you shared with the friend you just met again in the hall. Other experiences may be poorly remembered or, worse yet, irretrievably lost—what *is* that guy's name? He's not in my physics section, is he?

What determines whether an experience will be remembered or forgotten? Early experimental studies of human memory in the late 1800s investigated this puzzle. Research during the past century has demonstrated that a complete understanding of how memories are formed requires appreciation of the many cognitive and neurobiological processes that constitute the three stages of memory processing—encoding, consolidation (the modification of representations in memory so that they become stable), and retrieval—and the interactions among these different stages.

Encoding is the term used for the various processes by which information is transformed into a memory representation. These processes are set in motion at the time of the experience, forming a mental representation that records some aspect or aspects of it. All forms of memory, declarative and nondeclarative, begin with encoding. But because episodic memory records the unique history of each person's life, it seems a suitable starting point for our discussion of how encoding works.

One way to uncover the fundamental properties of encoding is to try to determine what strengthens the process. This approach has revealed that encoding is influenced by a number of factors, including the degree to which we attend to information and the extent to which we "elaborate" on its meaning. **Elaboration** involves interpreting information, connecting it with other information, and mulling it over. Other influences that strengthen encoding are conscious retrieval of the information, and practice that is "distributed," or spaced out, in time. As suggested by studies of patients with amnesia, the medial temporal lobes play a critical role in episodic encoding. Neuroimaging and clinical data also indicate that the frontal lobes contribute to attention and elaborative processing and thus affect encoding.

2.1. The Importance of Attention

You're not alone if you've said things like "Where did I put my glasses?" or "Tell me *again* the name of the new teaching assistant!" This kind of forgetting of everyday events is not likely to be either an indication of a poor memory or a harbinger of decline with age. Many instances of forgetting are simply the natural consequences of ineffective encoding of an experience into episodic memory in the first place.

One of the more obvious and consequential reasons for poor encoding is failure to attend to an event while it is happening. When your attention to information is divided, for example because you are distracted, encoding is weaker and later attempts to remember are likely to fail. You may have forgotten where you put your glasses because you're still trying to remember the name of the physics student you saw in the hall. And you may have forgotten his name because when you met the first time your attention was focused on the impending physics exam.

The role of attention in encoding has been explored in the laboratory. In one set of experiments (Craik et al., 1996) participants were instructed to try to remember 15 auditorily presented words under one of two conditions. In the *full-attention* condition, participants were not given any task other than to try to remember the words. In the *divided-attention* condition, during word presentation participants were also instructed to monitor the position of an asterisk on a computer screen and press one of four buttons as the location changed. Participants remembered on average 9 of the 15 words when encoding was performed under full attention, but only 5 words when encoding was performed along with the secondary task. Many other experiments have revealed equally compelling evidence that attention is necessary for effective encoding.

Neuroimaging studies indicate that the pattern of neural activation during encoding under conditions of full attention differs from that when attention is divided. In one study, the brains of participants were scanned, using PET, while these people tried to encode category–exemplar pairs (for example, POET–BROWNING) (Shallice et al., 1994). This encoding was conducted while participants performed either an "easy" or a "difficult" secondary task, with "easy" defined as "requiring less attention." There were two significant findings. First, the behavioral performance of the "easy task" group was better than that of the "difficult task" group. Second, the brain images showed that regions in the left frontal lobe were more active when encoding was accompanied by the easy secondary task, indicating that the frontal lobes support the ability to attend during learning, and in so doing, affect episodic encoding (Uncapher & Rugg, 2005).

2.2. Levels of Processing and Elaborative Encoding

Evidence that attention is central to encoding might seem to suggest the conclusion that *intent* is required for effective memory formation. But not so fast: although intent to encode can motivate attention, intention per se is not required for effective encoding. Encoding is an automatic by-product of attending to and processing a stimulus (Craik & Lockhart, 1972). What influences encoding efficacy is the way the stimulus is processed, not the reason that processing was performed.

2.2.1. Levels-of-Processing Theory: Argument and Limitations

Consider the various kinds of cognitive operations you could perform when meeting someone for the first time. Looking at that person's face, you might observe some aspect of the structure of its appearance. Or you might note the phonology—the speech sounds—of the person's name. Or you might *elaborate* on conceptual details you learn at this first meeting, a political viewpoint, for example, relating it to your own. In this sense, elaboration consists of generating additional information.

Levels-of-processing theory draws on the fact that there are various aspects of any given stimulus that can be attended and processed. In this view, encoding is seen as a direct by-product of stimulus processing, the processing of particular aspects of a stimulus leaving a corresponding residue in the system that can guide later remembering. Different aspects of stimulus processing are thought to correspond to different levels of analysis that range from a "shallow" or superficial level of perceptual analysis to a "deep" (i.e., elaborative level) of semantic (i.e., meaning-based) analysis that actively relates incoming information to knowledge already stored in memory (Figure 5–5).

Shallow (perceptual aspects)

structural: "*She has shiny hair*"
phonological: "'*Jane*' rhymes with '*brain*'"
semantic: "*She supports the Republican Party*"

Deep (elaborated aspects)

FIGURE 5–5 Levels of processing illustrated

According to levels-of-processing theory, different aspects of stimulus processing are thought to correspond to different levels of analysis, ranging from a "shallow" level of perceptual analysis to a "deep" level of semantic analysis.

According to the theory, encoding efficacy heavily depends on the level of processing performed on a stimulus, with deeper processing producing a stronger, more durable representation and thus increasing the likelihood that the stimulus will be remembered.

Many behavioral studies have supported the hypothesis that episodic memory benefits from "deep" (i.e., elaborative) processing. In one of these studies (Craik & Tulving, 1975), participants viewed words and made one of three decisions about each word. For some words, participants were to say whether the words were in uppercase or lowercase letters—a "shallow" structural condition. For a second set of words, participants were asked whether each rhymed with a target word—an "intermediate" phonological condition. For words in a third set, participants were to decide whether each was a member of a particular category—a "deep" semantic condition. Consistent with the levels-of-processing hypothesis, a later memory test revealed that the percentage of words from each set that was subsequently recognized as having been studied differed markedly for the three sets: 78 percent of the words were recognized following "deep" encoding, 57 percent following "intermediate" encoding, and just 16 percent following "shallow" encoding. Episodic memory substantially benefits from elaboration of the meaning of a stimulus or event at the time it is encountered. Levels-of-processing theory suggests that the stimuli and events that we are likely to remember best are those that we actively process for meaning. Your recollection of meeting someone who also grew up in Des Moines, likes the same kind of food you do, and is a supporter of the Republican party is clear and detailed because of the elaboration provided by links to other representations of information already in memory and shared in conversation.

As in the Craik and Tulving (1975) experiment, most studies testing levels-of-processing theory have used instructions that reveal **incidental learning**, learning that occurs not as the result of a purposeful attempt but as a by-product of performing a task. In these instructions participants are not explicitly directed to learn, but rather are asked to perform a particular task with stimuli. Because participants are unaware that memory for the stimuli will be tested, they do not intentionally try to learn, and learning is incidental to performance of the task. The phenomenon of incidental learning helps us understand just how it is that we can remember our everyday experiences, which, after all, we don't usually deliberately attempt to encode into memory. It is unlikely that you tried to encode your meeting with your political bedfellow when it first occurred. Nonetheless, you do remember it, because encoding occurs whenever we process or attend to a stimulus or event while it occurs. (You didn't try to encode your first meeting with the physics student, either—but more to the point, you didn't particularly attend to it, so the encounter left only a weak memory, and you had difficulty remembering the event.)

Levels-of-processing theory has provided much insight into the processes that lead to episodic encoding, and thus it has considerable explanatory power. But the theory has a number of limitations. For example, as Shakespeare put it in another context, "Who hath measured the ground?" There is no way of measuring the "depth" or quantifying the "level" of processing required by a particular encoding task other than its impact on memory. The lack of an independent measure of depth makes it difficult to test the theory.

A more central question concerns interpretation: do levels-of-processing effects reflect differences in the strength and durability of encoding, or differences in which aspects of a stimulus are selected for encoding and the correspondence between the kind of processing performed at encoding and that performed at retrieval? Some investigators believe that the question is not one of level but of match between what is encoded and what is tested at retrieval. If retrieval demands recovery of semantic details about a past experience, then semantic processing at encoding will be more effective because it increases the likelihood that semantic aspects of the stimulus or event will be stored in memory; but if retrieval demands recovery of perceptual details, then perceptual processing at encoding will be more effective for the complementary reason. This principle—that processing at encoding is most effective to the extent that that processing overlaps with the processing to be performed at retrieval—is known as **transfer appropriate processing** (Morris et al., 1977).

In an important study testing the levels-of-processing and transfer-appropriate-processing perspectives, Morris and colleagues (1977) had participants encode words by making a rhyme decision or a semantic decision about each word. During retrieval, memory was probed in one of two ways. A task requiring recognition of words that had been previously studied revealed the standard levels-of-processing effect (superior memory following semantic encoding). By contrast, a task requiring recognition of words that rhymed with previously studied words revealed superior memory following rhyme encoding. The level of processing does not necessarily affect the strength or durability of the encoded memory, but rather influences *what* is encoded. Encoding processes yield superior memory to the degree that the features attended and processed during encoding overlap with those being sought at retrieval. For a more detailed discussion of this landmark work, see the accompanying *A Closer Look* box.

A related idea, proposed by Tulving and Thompson (1973) and referred to as the **encoding specificity principle**, states that our ability to remember a stimulus depends on the similarity between the way the stimulus is processed at encoding and the way it is processed at test. For example, if the word *bank* is interpreted as meaning "the side of a river" rather than "a financial institution" at encoding, then remembering will be superior if at retrieval *bank* is interpreted as "the side of a river."

2.2.2. The Brain, Semantic Elaboration, and Episodic Encoding

Because semantic processing tends to yield higher levels of memory performance (on standard tests) than does nonsemantic processing, it is reasonable to ask whether brain regions that are more active during semantic processing tasks are regions that support encoding processes that influence learning. A series of studies measured brain activity of participants while they encoded words under semantic or perceptual processing conditions (Gabrieli et al., 1996; Kapur et al, 1994; Wagner et al., 1998;

A CLOSER LOOK
Transfer Appropriate Processing

We consider the landmark work of C. D. Morris, J. D. Bransford, and J. J. Franks, reported in a 1977 paper titled "Levels of Processing versus Transfer Appropriate Processing," *Journal of Verbal Learning and Verbal Behavior, 16,* 519–533.

Introduction

The investigators hypothesize that the level of processing at encoding does not influence later memory performance in isolation, but rather later memory depends, at least in part, on the overlap between the processing engaged at encoding and at retrieval. Put another way, transfer appropriate processing proposes an interaction between encoding and retrieval, leading to the prediction that memory performance will be better when encoding processing overlaps with (and thus transfers to) retrieval processing.

Method

The investigators tested their hypothesis by examining the memory performance of undergraduate participants, using an experimental design that combined two encoding tasks (*semantic* and *rhyme*) with two retrieval tasks (*standard recognition* and *rhyming recognition*).

All participants studied 32 target words embedded in sentences. For all words, a sentence was initially read aloud by the experimenter, with the target word missing from the sentence (for example, "The _____ had a silver engine."). Following each sentence, a target word was presented to the participant, who had to decide whether the word fit the sentence. There were two types of sentences, *semantic* and *rhyme*, with 16 words studied in each type. For semantic sentences, participants had to decide whether the target word was semantically consistent or inconsistent with the sentence (TRAIN would be consistent with the example sentence, whereas APPLE would not be). For rhyming sentences (for example, "_____ rhymes with legal"), participants had to decide whether the target word was phonologically consistent (EAGLE) or inconsistent (CHAIR).

Following encoding of the 32 target words, memory was tested using either a *standard recognition* test or a *rhyme recognition* test; half the participants received the standard and half received the rhyme test. In the standard test, the 32 target words and 32 unstudied words were presented one at a time in a random order. Participants responded "yes" if they recognized the test word as having been studied, and "no" if they did not. In the rhyme test, participants were presented a random ordering of words that rhymed with the studied words and unstudied words that did not. Participants responded "yes" if they recognized the test word as rhyming with a studied word, and "no" if they did not.

By having two study conditions and two test types, the experimental design resulted in four critical conditions that combined encoding (semantic/rhyme) and test (standard/rhyme): semantic + standard test, semantic + rhyme test, rhyme + standard test, rhyme + rhyme test.

Results

The data of interest are the percentage of test trials on which participants correctly recognized either studied words (standard test) or rhymes of studied words (rhyme test), correcting for erroneous responses to unstudied words or to nonrhymes of studied words. The analysis focuses on memory for items that were consistent with the sentence context at encoding, and the key question is how performance varied across the four critical encoding + test conditions. The results are plotted in the following table:

	Standard Test	Rhyme Test
Semantic encoding mode	84%	33%
Rhyme encoding mode	63%	49%

These data reveal a striking interaction: when memory is probed using the standard test, performance is clearly better following semantic than following rhyme encoding, whereas when memory is probed using the rhyme test, performance is clearly better following rhyme than following semantic encoding.

Discussion

The transfer-appropriate-processing hypothesis is supported by the observed interaction: processing at encoding is particularly effective to the extent that it overlaps with processing at retrieval. These data support the interpretation that level of processing does not influence encoding strength per se, but rather influences what is encoded. When processing at study fosters encoding of information that will be desired at retrieval, then that processing will be particularly effective in enhancing later memory performance.

2005). Greater activation in the left inferior frontal lobe was observed during semantic compared to perceptual processing, and a similar pattern was observed in the left lateral and medial temporal lobes (Figure 5–6).

An interesting correspondence suggests itself. We know from the studies involving "easy" and "difficult" secondary tasks that divided attention diminishes left frontal lobe activation and episodic encoding during intentional learning, learning that occurs as the result of a purposeful attempt (Shallice et al., 1994). We also know that during *incidental learning* left frontal lobe activation is diminished at shallower levels of processing. This overlap of brain regions engaged during intentional and

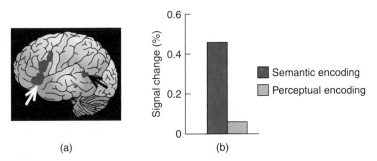

(a)   (b)

FIGURE 5–6   Brain activation in perceptual and in semantic processing

(a) The left inferior frontal cortex (*white arrow*) and left lateral temporal cortex (*black arrow*) are active when we attend to and elaborate on the meaning of stimuli.

(Wagner et al. (2001). Recovering meaning: left prefrontal cortex guides controlled semantic retrieval. *Neuron, 31,* 329–338 (Fig. 3b). Reprinted with permission from Elsevier.)

(b) When data are plotted, the graph shows that left frontal activation (expressed as signal change) is greater during semantic than during perceptual processing of words.

(Wagner et al. (2000). Task-specific repetition priming in left inferior prefrontal cortex. *Cerebral Cortex, 10,* 1176–1184. Reprinted with permission of Oxford University Press.)

incidental learning is consistent with the idea that intention per se does not determine learning. Rather, intentional learning affects encoding to the extent that it motivates elaboration and thus leads to processing at a deeper level.

To assess more precisely how experienced events are transformed into memories, researchers have sought to obtain tighter links between memory behavior and brain activity. A particularly powerful approach measures brain activity at encoding and correlates the results with participants' later successful or unsuccessful recollection. The key contrast is between neural responses during the encoding of events that are later remembered and neural responses during the encoding of events later forgotten. By identifying brain activity at the moment when memories are born, this method reveals neural responses that predict the mnemonic fate of an experience—that is, whether it will be remembered or forgotten.

A functional magnetic resonance imaging (fMRI) study using this approach scanned participants while they made semantic judgments about a series of words (Wagner et al., 1998). Participants' memory for the words was later tested and correlated with the fMRI encoding data. Analysis revealed greater activation in the left inferior frontal and medial temporal lobes during the encoding of words that were later remembered compared to words that were later forgotten (see Figure 5–7 on Color Insert C). Further, the regions predicting subsequent memory were those previously identified as showing a levels-of-processing effect. A related study of visual learning (Brewer et al., 1998) revealed a similar pattern, but this time in the right frontal lobe and both medial temporal lobes. These data indicate that greater engagement of frontal lobe attentional mechanisms increases encoding efficacy, with the left frontal lobe supporting the encoding of words and the right frontal lobe the encoding of nonverbal stimuli. These frontal lobe attentional processes appear to interact with medial temporal lobe learning mechanisms during effective learning.

2.3. Enhancers of Encoding: Generation and Spacing

The circumstances of the initial encounter with information influence the strength of encoding, as we have seen: it makes a difference if you're paying attention, it makes a difference if, at the time, you elaborate. Research has also uncovered other factors that enhance the strength of the encoded representation. One way makes use of the *generation effect*, where episodic learning is better if we can generate the target information from memory compared to when the information is presented to us by another person. The other employs the *spacing effect*, where encoding across multiple study trials with the same information is optimal following a particular pattern of temporal sequencing of the study trials.

2.3.1. The Generation Effect

Flashcards. You may have used them in elementary school: $9 \times 7 = ?$ on one side of the card, 63 on the other. Medical students use them to learn diagnostic symptoms, chemistry students use them to learn the formulas of compounds and alloys, language students use them to learn vocabulary. Formula on one side of the card, compound name on the other. And rather boring they are.

But the flashcard approach to learning is a highly effective way to learn, and there is an important reason why: the act of retrieving or generating information from memory is a powerful enhancer of encoding. "Generating" here does not mean "creating;" rather, it emphasizes the idea of active production of the information rather than passive study.

The term generation effect describes the observed phenomenon that you are more likely to remember information you retrieve or generate (during study) than information that you simply receive and attempt to "memorize." Thus you are more likely to remember the 12 cranial nerves from flashcards, which demand action on your part, than from studying a list. The effect is an experimental demonstration of the generally accepted idea that we often learn best by doing.

The generation effect was first described following an experiment (Slamecka & Graf, 1978) in which participants learned word pairs in one of two ways. In the "read" condition, word pairs were presented and participants decided whether the second word was a synonym of the first (as in UNHAPPY–SAD) or a rhyme of it (as in PAD–SAD). In the second learning task—the "generate" condition—participants were to generate a synonym (from, say, UNHAPPY–S_____) or a rhyme (from, say, PAD–S_____). Following learning, when participants were tested for memory of the second word (given the first word as a cue), two effects were revealed. Memory was better after semantic encoding, which depended on the meaning of the words, than after phonological encoding, which considered only their sound; this was a levels-of-processing effect. Further, overall memory was better when participants were asked to generate the second word themselves than when this word was presented by the experimenter and they had simply to read it (Figure 5–8).

Generating information from memory is thought to be a more powerful encoding event than merely processing externally presented information because both elaboration and greater attention are required for generation. Support for this interpretation comes from neuroimaging experiments, which have demonstrated that the left frontal lobe region, which shows a levels-of-processing effect, is also more active when generating than when reading words (Petersen et al., 1988). Transfer appropriate processing further suggests that generation is a particularly effective way to learn because the processes that are engaged during the initial generation at encoding are likely to overlap with those required to generate the information from memory at retrieval.

2.3.2. The Spacing Effect

Should you go over and over an idiom translation, or a chemical formula, flipping the card over and back time after time, and only eventually move on to the next item to be learned? Or should you go through a number of cards, and then go through them all again? The first approach, in which many trials with the same stimulus are undertaken without interruption, is known as massed practice; the second, in which the trials with the same stimulus are separated by other stimuli, as distributed practice. Which is more effective for learning?

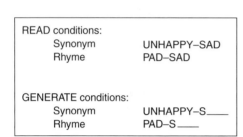

READ conditions:
  Synonym   UNHAPPY–SAD
  Rhyme   PAD–SAD

GENERATE conditions:
  Synonym   UNHAPPY–S____
  Rhyme   PAD–S____

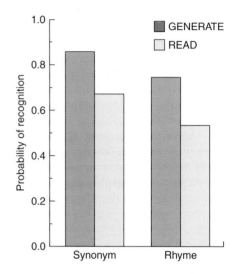

FIGURE 5–8   The effects of generation and processing level

Participants studied words by either reading presented words or generating words in response to a cue. In both the READ and GENERATE tasks, words were processed for meaning (synonym) or phonology (rhyme). As shown in the graph, the probability of later remembering the studied words was facilitated both by generation and by a deeper level of processing (synonym as opposed to rhyme, which was appropriate for the type of test).

(Slamecka, N. J., & Graf, P. The generation effect: Delineation of a phenomenon, *Journal of Experimental Psychology: Human Learning and Memory*, 4 (1978): Fig. 2, p. 595 (adapted) from Exp. 2. Found in: Anderson, John R., *Cognitive Psychology and its Implications* (4th ed.). W.H. Freeman and Company, New York, 1995, p. 192. Copyright © 1978 American Psychological Association. Adapted with permission.)

The German psychologist Hermann Ebbinghaus (1850–1909), whose work laid the foundations for modern experimental investigation of mental processes and particularly memory, was the first to study the effects of massed vs. distributed practice (Ebbinghaus, 1885/1964). In his pioneering experiments, he taught himself meaningless consonant–vowel–consonant syllables (such as WUG, PEV, RIC), using massed practice learning for some items and distributed practice for others. A later test of his memory revealed a spacing effect: that is, as Ebbinghaus himself put it, "with any considerable number of repetitions a suitable distribution of them over a space of time is decidedly more advantageous than the massing of them at a single time" (p. 89). So a word to the wise: for more effective encoding, go for distributed practice.

There are a number of reasons for the spacing effect. An obvious one is that when study trials are massed together, we are less likely to attend fully to each presentation. Rather, with each subsequent presentation we are likely to be deluded into thinking we've learned the item, and therefore allocate increasingly less attention to it. Moreover, when trials are spaced, the context in which the stimulus is processed is likely to have changed to a greater degree than in massed practice. The result is a richer memory representation and additional retrieval routes

Color Insert A

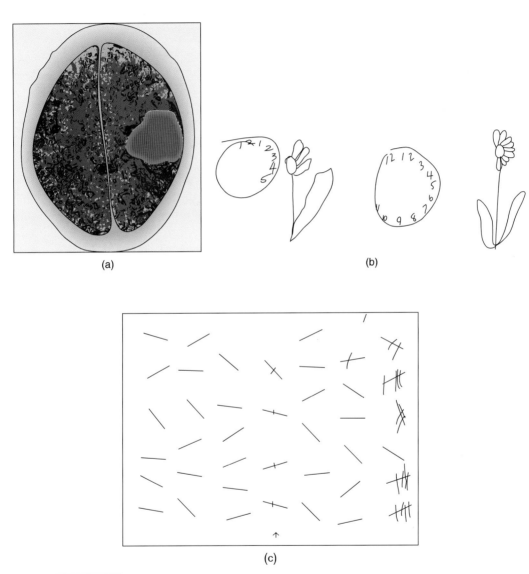

(a)

(b)

(c)

FIGURE 3–6 Hemispatial neglect, its cause and effects

(a) A brain scan of a patient with hemispatial neglect, showing brain damage, the [red] area, to the right side of the brain. (b) Drawings of a clock and a daisy by two patients with hemispatial neglect. (c) An example of line cancellation by a patient with hemispatial neglect.

Color Insert B

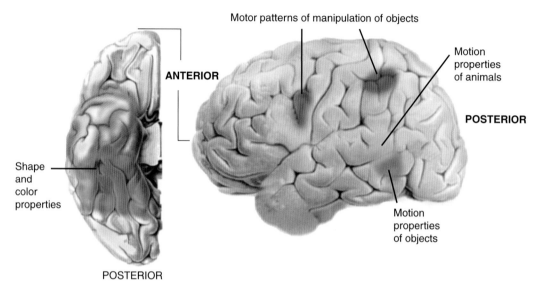

Motor patterns of manipulation of objects

Motion properties of animals

ANTERIOR

POSTERIOR

Shape and color properties

Motion properties of objects

POSTERIOR

(a) Left Ventral View

(b) Left Lateral View

FIGURE 4–13 Brain areas activated in processing various kinds of property information about categories

(a) Ventral brain areas, running from the occipital to the temporal lobes, become active to represent shape and color properties. (b) Areas in motor and parietal areas become active to represent knowledge about possible manipulations of objects, and posterior temporal areas become active to represent motion properties of objects. In all cases, the areas that represent property information for categories overlap the areas that represent these properties during the actual perception of objects.

(From Martin, A., & Chao, L., (2001). Semantic memory and the brain: structure and process. *Current Opinion in Neurobiology*, 11, pp. 194–201.)

Color Insert C

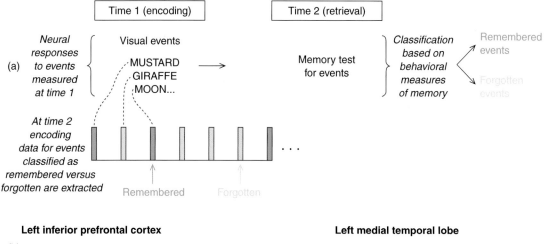

(a) *Neural responses to events measured at time 1*

Time 1 (encoding)

Visual events

MUSTARD
GIRAFFE
MOON...

Time 2 (retrieval)

Memory test for events

Classification based on behavioral measures of memory

Remembered events

Forgotten events

At time 2 encoding data for events classified as remembered versus forgotten are extracted

Remembered   Forgotten

(b) **Left inferior prefrontal cortex**

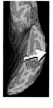

MR signal change

4
3
2
1
0
−1

0   4   8   12
Time (sec)

—— Remembered
······ Forgotten

Left medial temporal lobe

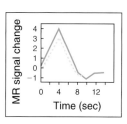

MR signal change

4
3
2
1
0
−1

0   4   8   12
Time (sec)

FIGURE 5–7 Links between memory behavior and brain activity

(a) Neural responses are recorded during event processing (in this example, visual word presentations). Memory is then probed and events are classified as later remembered or later forgotten. (b) Neural responses during encoding are analyzed based on subsequent memory, revealing neural correlates of encoding in various brain regions. The data show that during encoding subsequently remembered events (dark shade of blue) elicited greater responses than subsequently forgotten events (light shade of blue).

(From Paller, K. A. & Wagner, A. D. (2002). Observing the transformation of experience into memory. *Trends in Cognitive Science, 6,* 93–102. Data are adapted from Wagner, A. D., Schacter, D. L., Rotte, M., Koutstaal, W., Maril, A., Dale, A. M., Rosen, B. R., and Buckner, R. L. 1998. Building Memories: Remembering and Forgetting of Verbal Experiences as Predicted by Brain Activity. *Science, 281,* 118–1191. Reprinted with permission.)

Color Insert D

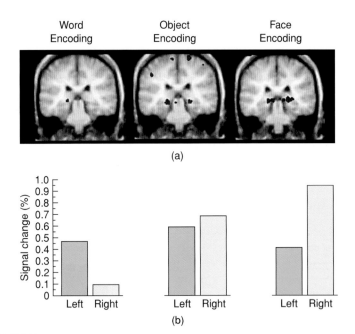

(a) Medial temporal lobe activation during the encoding of words, objects, and faces, shown by fMRI.

FIGURE 5–11 Activation in the left and right medial temporal lobes differs for verbal and nonverbal events

(a) Medial temporal lobe activation during the encoding of words, objects, and faces, shown by fMRI. (b) The magnitude of activation (as measured by signal change) is plotted for each case. Note the significantly greater signal intensity in the left than right medial temporal lobe for word encoding and significantly greater right than left for face encoding.

(Kelley, W. M., Miezin, F. M., McDermott, K. B., Buckner, R. L., Raichle, M. E., Cohen, N. J. Ollinger, J. M., Akbudak, E., Conturo, T. E., Snyder, A. Z., & Petersen, S. E. (1998). Hemispheric Specialization in Human Dorsal Frontal Cortex and Medial Temporal Lobe for Verbal and Nonverbal Memory Encoding. *Neuron, 20,* 927–936. Reprinted with permission from Elsevier.)

Color Insert E

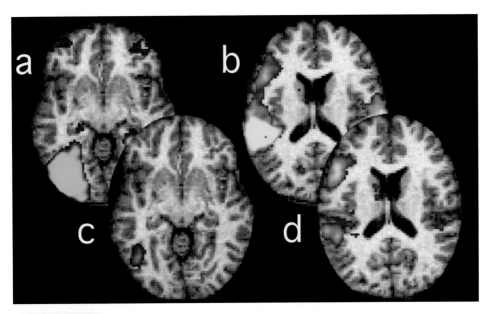

FIGURE 5–12 fMRI evidence for recapitulation during episodic retrieval

During encoding, participants studied words paired with either sounds or pictures; during retrieval, they were asked to remember whether a word had been previously associated with a sound or with a picture. fMRI images taken show regions of the brain active during *perception* of (a) pictures and (b) sounds, and regions active during *retrieval from memory* of the same (c) pictures and (d) sounds. Retrieval of pictures from memory was associated with reactivation of a subset of visual cortical regions that were active during picture perception—compare (c) to (a); retrieval of sounds was associated with reactivation of bilateral superior temporal regions that were active during sound perception—compare (d) to (b).

(Buckner, R. L., & Wheeler, M. E. (2001). The Cognitive Neuroscience of Remembering. *Nature Reviews Neuroscience, 2*, 624–634. Data are from Wheeler, Petersen and Buckner (2000). Memory's echo: Vivid remembering reactivates sensory-specific cortex. *Proceedings of the National Academy of Sciences, USA, 97*, 11125–11129. Reprinted with permission from Elsevier.)

Color Insert F

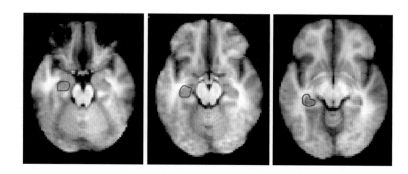

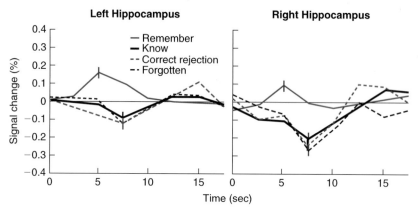

MRI scans show the location of the hippocampus (outlined in red in the left hemisphere). The graphs plotting brain activation show greater activation during recognition accompanied by recollection; activation during recognition based on stimulus familiarity ("knowing") did not differ from that during forgetting.

(Eldridge, L. L., Knowlton, B. J., Furmanski, C. S., Bookheimer, S. Y., Engel, & S. A. (2000). Remembering episodes: A selective role for the hippocampus during retrieval. *Nature Neuroscience, 3,* 1149–1152. Reprinted with permission.)

Color Insert G

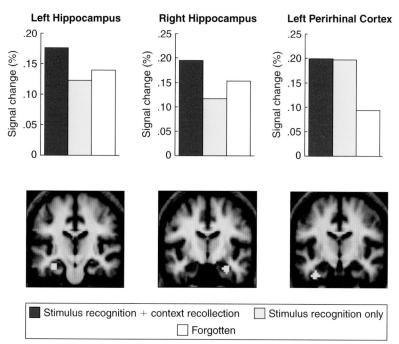

Left Hippocampus **Right Hippocampus** **Left Perirhinal Cortex**

■ Stimulus recognition + context recollection   □ Stimulus recognition only
□ Forgotten

Activation in left and right hippocampus during activation predicts later recollection of the context in which a recognized stimulus was encountered but does not predict differences in stimulus recognition versus stimulus forgetting. By contrast, activation in perirhinal cortex predicts whether or not the stimulus will be later recognized or forgotten, but does not predict differences in context recollection. The hippocampal and perirhinal regions are highlighted in yellow on the MRI scans below.

(Davachi, L., Mitchell, J. P., & Wagner, A. D. (2003). Multiple routes to memory: Distinct medial temporal lobe processes build item and source memories. *PNAS, 100,* 2157–2162. Reprinted with permission.)

Color Insert H

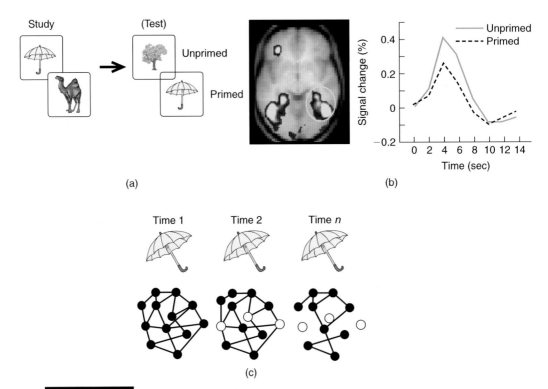

(a)

(b)

(c)

FIGURE 5–19 Priming and neural tuning

(a) The study and test items: some test items are primed, some are not. (b) A typical fMRI scan of a participant's brain showed reduced activation in left and right fusiform cortex when a primed object was processed. The graph plots the average fMRI signal from right fusiform cortex (circled).

(Wagner, A. D., & Koutstaal, W. Priming. In *Encyclopedia of the Human Brain,* Vol. 4. Elsevier Science, 2002, pp. 27–46, Fig. 2. Reprinted with permission from Elsevier.)

(c) Hypothesized changes in a neuronal network representing visual object features as a function of repeated experience. As an object is presented repeatedly, neurons coding features that are not essential for recognizing the object decrease their responses (shown as the change from black to white), thereby weakening connections with other neurons in the ensemble (from black, to open circles, to no connecting lines). As a result, the network becomes both sparser and more selective, yielding enhanced object identification.

(Wiggs, C. L., & Martin, A. (1998). Properties and mechanisms of perceptual priming. *Current Opinion in Neurobiology, 8,* 227–233. Reprinted with permission from Elsevier.)

back to the memory. That is, the processing performed for the initial encounter and for repeated trials in massed practice is likely to be highly similar. Distributed practice, on the other hand, fosters greater encoding variability, the encoding of different aspects of a stimulus as different features are selected for encoding in subsequent encounters. A stimulus is more likely to be remembered when it is processed in different ways across study trials.

2.4. Episodic Encoding, Binding, and the Medial Temporal Lobe

Encoding information into episodic memory involves attention and elaboration, which rely on the frontal lobes. Damage to the frontal lobes generally impairs episodic memory (Shimamura, 1995) because these cognitive processes are affected. These deficits are modest, however, compared with those resulting from damage to the medial temporal lobes, such as that suffered by H.M. Densely amnesic patients, such as H.M., are as it were "stuck in time" because they are unable to form new episodic memories.

The hallmark of episodic encoding is the binding together of the various features of a stimulus or event into an integrated memory representation (Tulving, 1983). When you first met the people you later encountered in the hall, you encoded various characteristics of each of them (with different degrees of success, for the reasons we've discussed). Perceptual aspects of visual appearance and sound of voice, the spatial and temporal context, phonological encoding of names, and the semantics of your conversation: each was processed by a different neural network in the brain. But in the same way that perception of an apple requires the binding together of disparate features (green color, round shape, sharp smell), memory of a life experience requires the binding together of the disparate elements that make it up: the people and things you encounter, the place and time in which these things are encountered, your thoughts during the encounter. And here is the crux of the problem: how does this binding occur?

The answer lies, literally, in the medial temporal lobe, the area excised in H.M.'s surgery (Squire et al., 2004). This region has been shown to be a convergence zone (a notion discussed in Chapter 4), that is, a region that receives highly processed input from many brain areas (Lavenex & Amaral, 2000; Suzuki & Amaral, 1994) (Figure 5–9). Information about a face, a name, and the context converges on the medial temporal lobe, and this region—in particular, the hippocampus—binds these multiple features into an integrated memory representation (Figure 5–10). Frontal lobe activity involved in attention and elaboration modulates encoding by favoring the processing of particular features, enhancing their input into the medial temporal lobe, and thus increasing the likelihood that those features are bound into the episodic memory representation. But this binding no longer can happen in H.M.'s brain, and he is left without the ability to construct episodic memories.

The anterograde amnesia that follows bilateral medial temporal lobe damage provides critical evidence that this region is necessary for episodic memory. Unilateral medial temporal lobe lesions also produce a deficit in episodic memory,

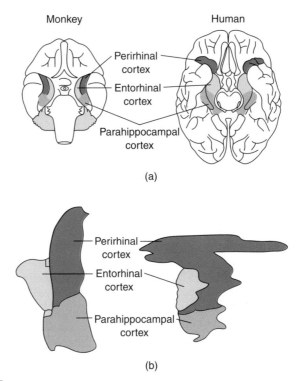

Monkey　　　　　　　Human

Perirhinal
cortex
Entorhinal
cortex
Parahippocampal
cortex

(a)

Perirhinal
cortex
Entorhinal
cortex
Parahippocampal
cortex

(b)

FIGURE 5–9 The medial temporal lobe memory system

(a) Ventral views (i.e., seen from the bottom, looking up) of the monkey and human brain show the borders of the entorhinal, perirhinal, and parahippocampal cortices.

(From R. D. Burwell, W. A. Suzuki, R. Insausti, & D. G. Amaral. Some observations on the perirhinal and parahippocampal cortices in the rat, monkey and human brains. In *Perception, Memory and Emotion: Frontiers in Neuroscience,* edited by T. Ono, B. L. McNaughton, S. Molotchnikoff, E. T. Rolls and H. Hishijo. Elsevier UK, 1996, 95–110, Fig. 1. Reprinted with permission from Elsevier.)

(b) Unfolded two-dimensional maps of these cortical areas, which, together with the hippocampal formation, make up the medial temporal lobe memory system on which declarative memory depends. (The brains are not drawn to scale.) The pathways into and out of the medial temporal lobe memory system are believed to be important in the transition from perception to memory.

(From Squire, L. R. & E. R. Kandel. *Memory: From Mind to Molecules,* p. 111. Originally appeared in Squire L. R., Lindenlaub, E., *The Biology of Memory*. Stuttgart, New York: Schattauer, 1990; 648. Reprinted with permission.)

although of lesser magnitude. Behavioral studies of patients with unilateral lesions indicate that there are hemispheric differences in medial temporal lobe function: lesions of the right hippocampus give rise to greater deficits in nonverbal episodic memory, whereas lesions of the left hippocampus give rise to greater deficits in verbal episodic memory (Milner, 1972). Neuroimaging studies of medial temporal lobe activation in neurologically healthy people have provided convergent evidence: right hippocampal activation is greater during the encoding of unfamiliar faces, whereas left

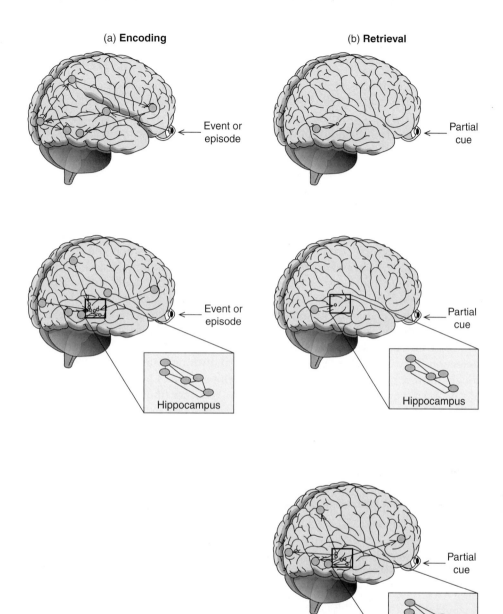

(a) Encoding

(b) Retrieval

Event or episode

Partial cue

Event or episode

Partial cue

Hippocampus

Hippocampus

Partial cue

Hippocampus

FIGURE 5–10 How the medial temporal lobe contributes to episodic encoding and retrieval

(a) During encoding, aspects of the stimulus or event are processed in different lateral cortical processing areas (*top*). These pieces of information converge on hippocampal neurons, and activated hippocampal neurons are bound together (*bottom*). (b) During retrieval, cues typically hold partial information about a past stimulus or event (*top*). As this partial information converges on the medial temporal lobe, it may trigger pattern completion in the hippocampus (*middle*). This medial temporal lobe process is thought to result in reactivation of information in lateral cortex (*bottom*).

hippocampal activation is greater during the encoding of words (Figure 5–11 on Color Insert D) (Kelley et al., 1998; Powell et al; 2005). Although such conclusions are well documented, it should be emphasized that the verbal and nonverbal mental representations are ultimately bound together within the medial temporal lobes, perhaps partially through cross-hemisphere interactions.

2.5. Consolidation: The Fixing of Memory

Encoded episodic memories undergo consolidation, a process that modifies these representations such that they become more stable over time and ultimately exist independently of the medial temporal lobes. Evidence for consolidation comes from the observation that H.M.'s, and other amnesic patients', retrograde amnesia is temporally graded: following removal of the medial temporal lobes, H.M. could still recall childhood memories, but he had difficulty remembering events that happened during the years immediately preceding the surgery. The preservation of his remote episodic memories implies that older memories are not stored in the medial temporal lobe—otherwise, those memories would have been lost following medial temporal damage. Rather, interactions between the medial temporal lobe and various lateral cortical regions are thought to store memories outside the medial temporal lobes by slowly forming direct links between the cortical representations of the experience (thus obviating the need for the bound representation in the medial temporal lobe). One hypothesis is that memory consolidation in cortex occurs through a process of reinstatement or recapitulation, wherein during sleep and during remembering the medial temporal lobe recapitulates the pattern of activation present during learning, thus strengthening the direct connections across the relevant lateral cortical regions (McClelland et al., 1995; Wilson and McNaughton, 1994). Thus the medial temporal lobes are necessary for retrieving unconsolidated memories but, once consolidated, memories can be retrieved directly from lateral cortical regions (McGaugh, 2000; Squire, 1992).

✓ Comprehension Check:

1. What are the major factors that affect encoding efficacy?
2. How does the medial temporal lobe support encoding and consolidation?

3. RETRIEVAL: HOW WE RECALL THE PAST FROM EPISODIC MEMORY

Our individual remembrances of times past depend on episodic retrieval, the processes by which stored memory traces are subsequently reactivated. It is the phenomenon of retrieval that produces the subjective experience of consciously remembering the past. Episodic retrieval depends on medial temporal lobe processes that support pattern completion, and frontal lobe processes that support strategic retrieval mechanisms.

3.1. Pattern Completion and Recapitulation

Episodic retrieval is a powerful cognitive event that transforms our current mental state such that the present makes contact with and reinstates aspects of the past. Before you unexpectedly saw those people in the hall, it's perfectly likely you weren't thinking about either of them. For reasons we've discussed, you didn't remember one of them very well at all. But simply upon perceiving the face of the other person, your mental state was transformed. The sight of her face was a *cue* that initiated a cascade of processes that brought back to mind a host of details about your earlier encounter. Moreover, you were aware that these retrieved details pertained to a particular moment in your personal past. In essence, it is as if episodic retrieval launched you back in time, to an earlier moment in your life (Tulving, 1983).

How does a retrieval cue—such as the appearance of a face—serve to bring back details about the past? Episodic memories are encoded by binding together the various features of a stimulus or event into an integrated representation, so an episodic memory consists of a conjunction of linked features. Why is this important to retrieval? For two reasons: (1) because any of those features is a possible route to the memory, multiplying the "ways in" to recollection, and (2) because it means we have access to our memories even when we have limited information. When a retrieval cue that corresponds to part of the encoded information, such as sight of a particular face, homes in on the stored representation, other features bound to the representation—a name, a restaurant sign, a conversation—are reactivated (see Figure 5–10). Because in this way a whole is built from linked parts, this retrieval process is known as pattern completion (McClelland et al., 1995; Nakazawa et al., 2002).

Perhaps not surprisingly in view of their role in integrating features, the medial temporal lobes are critical for pattern completion (at least for unconsolidated memories). Unconsolidated episodic memories are stored at least in part in the medial temporal lobes, and retrieval of these memories depends on the function of the medial temporal lobe circuit. Neuroimaging studies in neurologically healthy humans have provided evidence for a role of the medial temporal lobes in episodic retrieval. For example, it has been demonstrated that the hippocampus is active during retrieval attempts that yield successful recollection of contextual or event details, but not during attempts that result in retrieval failure (Eldridge et al., 2000).

The notion that episodic retrieval depends on pattern completion has led to the additional hypothesis that retrieval entails recapitulation, a reinstatement of the pattern of activations that was present during encoding. Recapitulation is a reversal of the direction of information processing between lateral cortex (where disparate types of information are processed) and the hippocampus (where this information is integrated). During encoding, cortical processing provides inputs to the hippocampus, which binds the inputs into an integrated memory. In retrieval, a partial cue to the hippocampus triggers pattern completion, and the hippocampus projects back to cortical areas and replays the pattern of activation that was present during encoding (see Figure 5–10). (This is similar to the notion of simulation discussed in Chapter 4.)

The pattern completion and recapitulation hypotheses make two predictions. First, if pattern completion occurs in the medial temporal lobes and serves to recapitulate activation patterns, redirecting them to the lateral cortices, then medial temporal lobe retrieval activation should precede the recovery of episodic knowledge. Such retrieval signals preceding knowledge recovery in lateral cortical neurons have been observed in nonhuman primates (Naya et al., 2001). Further, it has been demonstrated that medial temporal lobe lesions in nonhuman primates eliminate cortical knowledge recovery, indicating that medial temporal processes precede and are necessary for reactivating cortical representations (Higuchi & Miyashita, 1996).

The second prediction is that, if episodic retrieval in fact entails the recapitulation of representations that were present during encoding, the pattern of cortical activation during retrieval should resemble that seen at the time of encoding. Neuroimaging studies with human participants have shown patterns of activation in visual and auditory association cortices during the encoding of pictures and sounds that were strikingly similar to those observed during the retrieval of such episodes (Figure 5–12 on Color Insert E) (Nyberg et al., 2000; Wheeler et al., 2000). It seems clear that retrieval entails the recapitulation of encoding patterns. However, what is recapitulated is typically not an *identical* copy of the information that was present at encoding; memory, as we all have had occasion to know, is subject to distortion.

3.2. Episodic Retrieval and the Frontal Lobes

Episodic retrieval involves a complex interaction between the medial temporal lobes and other cortical regions (Johnson et al., 1997; Shimamura, 1995), and considerable evidence indicates the importance of the frontal lobes. In nonhuman primates, disconnection of the frontal lobes from posterior brain structures causes a deficit in the ability to retrieve information associated with a retrieval cue (Tomita et al., 1999). Similarly, human patients with damage to the frontal lobes have particular difficulties in recollecting the details of earlier personal events (Janowski et al., 1989; Schacter et al., 1984). For example, frontal patients have difficulty remembering from whom they learned a new fact even when they can remember the fact itself, thus revealing a specific deficit in recollecting context. (This deficit is called *source amnesia*.) Consistent with these findings, neuroimaging studies of neurologically healthy people have revealed activation in a number of frontal lobe areas when participants are asked to retrieve episodic memories (Buckner & Wheeler, 2001; Fletcher & Henson, 2001; Nolde et al., 1998; Nyberg et al., 1996; Wagner, 2002).

The frontal lobes are important when we develop a retrieval plan, which requires selecting and representing the cues that will be used to probe memory. In addition, when we attempt to remember details of a past experience, there is activation in left frontal lobe regions associated with semantic elaboration (Dobbins et al., 2002). This pattern suggests that we elaborate on retrieval cues, thereby generating additional cues that might trigger pattern completion. The frontal lobes also support mechanisms that resolve competition or interference between competing memories (more than one memory is retrieved from a single cue, and the memories compete to be fully retrieved). Interference during retrieval is a significant cause of forgetting, and studies of patients with frontal lesions indicate that these patients are particularly prone to interference-based forgetting (Shimamura, 1995). Finally, the frontal lobes are important for evaluating or monitoring retrieved information, permitting decisions based on the quantity and quality at what is remembered (Rugg & Wilding, 2000).

3.3. Cues for Retrieval

As with the investigation of encoding, researchers have gained insight into the mechanisms underlying episodic retrieval by noting the factors present on occasions when retrieval is successful. One of the fundamental conclusions reached as a result of this approach is that retrieval is **cue dependent**, that is, it is stimulated by hints and clues from the external and the internal environment—from the state of the world and the state of ourselves. When cues are not available or are not used, attempts at retrieval are less likely to produce pattern completion. Many instances of forgetting occur not because the information sought has been lost from memory but because the cues used to probe memory are ineffective.

Context provides particularly strong retrieval cues, a phenomenon you may have experienced in visiting your old elementary school or standing in the room you had as a child or for old times' sake having a snack at a deli that was a high school hangout. The memories thus produced are stronger and more detailed in such circumstances than when you simply reminisce without cues. This phenomenon reveals a **context-dependent effect** on retrieval: retrieval is typically better when the physical environment at retrieval matches that at encoding (this is similar to the encoding specificity principle). In a particularly creative experiment, the context dependency of retrieval was demonstrated by presenting word lists to four groups of deep-sea divers and testing recall (Godden & Baddeley, 1975). One group both encoded and retrieved the words on shore, another group while under water. The third and fourth groups, however, encoded and retrieved in different contexts (studying the lists underwater and recalling them on shore, and vice versa). The groups that encoded and retrieved in the same physical context had the most successful retrieval (Figure 5–13).

Thus context-dependent effects not only support the idea that retrieval is cue dependent, they also reveal another important characteristic of episodic memory: when a stimulus or event is encoded, features of the physical environment are typically bound into the resulting episodic memory representation, providing another route to recall. If those features are present in the environment at the time of retrieval, they serve as further cues to memory and increase the likelihood of retrieval of other details of the experience. Similarly, aspects of our internal states, as affected by drugs or mood, also are encoded in memory and provide important cues at retrieval. Research has demonstrated **state-dependent effects**—better retrieval when internal states at retrieval match those at encoding—that parallel context-dependent effects. For example, Eich and colleagues (1975) demonstrated that participants who learned a list of words after having smoked marijuana were better

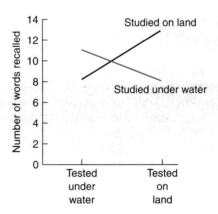

FIGURE 5–13   **Evidence for context-dependent memory**

In a test with deep-sea divers, the mean number of words recalled was affected by the match between the study and test contexts. Performance was better when words were recalled in the same environment in which they were learned.

(Data from Godden, D. R., & Bradley, A. D. (1975). Context-dependent memory in two natural environments: On land and under water. *British Journal of Psychology, 66:* 325–331. Reprinted with permission from Elsevier.)

able to recall the words if they smoked again just before retrieval. And if the learning was done without marijuana, retrieval was better without marijuana. As with external environmental features, internal states facilitate retrieval when the internal state at retrieval matches that encoded in memory at the time of the encounter with the stimulus or event. (Participants who did not smoke marijuana at either encoding or retrieval performed the best of all groups: both encoding and retrieval are impaired if you are "under the influence.")

3.4. The Second Time Around: Recognizing Stimuli by Recollection and Familiarity

A central function of memory is to permit an organism to distinguish between novel stimuli and those that have been previously encountered. The ability to recognize people, objects, and places can be based on two processes: *recollection,* the conscious recall of specific contextual and event details of the earlier encounter, and *familiarity,* the subjective (and unspecific) sense of having previously encountered a stimulus.

The distinction between recollection and familiarity is captured in your experience with those two people in the hall. You remembered one of them clearly, consciously recollecting details about your earlier meeting; on the other hand, you didn't doubt your impression that you'd met the other person before, but you could recollect nothing about him. In the first case, recognition was based on recollection; in the second, on familiarity in the absence of recollection. Dual-process theories of recognition assert that both recollection and familiarity can support recognition.

Recollection is thought to depend on the same pattern-completion mechanisms that allow the recall of episodic details associated with a retrieval cue. Familiarity, on the other hand, is thought to emerge from a different process, one that takes account not of detail but of overall similarity. A stimulus is matched against information in memory; if there is a match or a sufficient overlap, we can say "I *know* I've seen you before" without having any specific detail to bring to bear.

Behavioral research has provided compelling evidence that recollection and familiarity are distinct memory processes, with distinct modes of operation (Yonelinas, 2002). For example, recollection is a slower process than is familiarity. Thus, when we are forced to make a recognition decision very rapidly, we are more dependent on assessing the familiarity of a stimulus and less on recollection because recollected knowledge tends to arrive too late to inform our decision (Hintzman & Curran, 1994; Yonelinas & Jacoby, 1994). Also, recollection is particularly dependent on attention at the time of encoding and retrieval: if attention is divided, the contribution of recollection to recognition decisions is markedly decreased (Dodson & Johnson, 1996; Jacoby & Kelley, 1991).

Does neurological investigation support the inferences drawn from behavioral research? Are recollection and familiarity implemented differently in the brain? The medial temporal lobes are known to be crucial for recognition memory, but controversy remains on the question of differential contributions of specific subregions to recollection and familiarity (see Figure 5–9). There is some evidence, from both animal and human studies, that supports the hypothesis that different sub-regions of the medial temporal lobes mediate different memory processes (Brown & Aggleton, 2001). For example, lesions of perirhinal cortex in monkeys yield a more severe impairment in object recognition performance than does damage to the hippocampus (Murray & Mishkin, 1986; Zola-Morgan et al., 1989). Moreover, hippocampal neurons differentially signal memory for the conjunction between stimuli rather than for individual stimuli, whereas perirhinal neurons differentially signal stimulus familiarity (Brown et al., 1987; Sobotka & Ringo, 1993). In humans, studies of some patients believed to have damage limited to the hippocampus have revealed disproportionate deficits in recollection relative to familiarity (Holdstock et al., 2002; Yonelinas et al., 2002; cf. Wixted & Squire, 2004); however, studies of another group of amnesic patients with selective hippocampal damage revealed comparable deficits in recollection and familiarity (Manns et al., 2003a). Human patients with isolated hippocampal lesions are rare, however, and another avenue of investigation is neuroimaging of neurologically healthy people. Initial findings from these studies support the notion that recollection and familiarity differentially depend on hippocampal and perirhinal memory mechanisms, respectively (see the accompanying *Debate* box).

3.5. Misremembering the Past

We tend to regard retrieval as successful when we can say, "Yes, of course I remember that!" (Or even, "Yes, I remember that clearly!") But is what we remember an accurate reflection of past encounters, or is it distorted or even illusory? Almost a

"Remembering," "Knowing," and the Medial Temporal Lobes

The controversy surrounding the relative contributions of the hippocampus and the surrounding perirhinal cortex to recollection and familiarity has recently been explored by neuroimaging of neurologically healthy humans. In one study, hippocampal signals were examined while participants made recognition decisions about previously studied words (Eldridge et al., 2000). The investigators measured recollection and familiarity by asking participants to describe the basis for each recognition decision. Participants were asked to indicate whether each recognition decision was accompanied by "remembering," consciously recollecting particular details about a prior encounter with a stimulus; or by "knowing," feeling confident that a stimulus is familiar but being unable to recollect details about a prior encounter. The important outcome: hippocampal activation was observed during "remembering" but not during "knowing" or forgetting (defined as the inability to recognize a previously encountered item). This pattern suggests that the hippocampus may selectively support recollection (see also, Yonelinas at al; 2005).

Another neuroimaging approach is to measure hippocampal and perirhinal activation at encoding and to test subsequent memory to determine whether the neural encoding signals differentially predict whether recognition will be based on recollection or on familiarity. A study that employed this strategy examined the relation between hippocampal and perirhinal activation during encoding and the ability (1) later to recognize a stimulus as previously encountered (an index of stimulus familiarity) and (2) later to recollect specific contextual details about the prior encounter (an index of recollection) (Davachi et al., 2003). The fMRI data from this investigation revealed that encoding activation in the hippocampus predicted later recollection but was uncorrelated with later stimulus familiarity. In contrast, encoding activation in perirhinal cortex predicted later stimulus recognition but not subsequent recollection. These results suggest that the hippocampus and perirhinal cortex subserve complementary encoding mechanisms that build representations that support later recollection and familiarity, respectively (see also, Ranganath et al., 2004; Kirwan & Stark, 2004). Future neuroimaging investigations, in conjunction with continued study of human patients and of animals with lesions of specific medial temporal lobe structures, promise ultimately to resolve this debate. See figures on Color Insert F and Color Insert G.

---

century of behavioral research indicates that remembering is often not perfect and suggests why. Memories are occasionally distorted to match our expectations, and sometimes we "remember" events that never occurred. Investigating the similarities and differences between accurate and illusory memories at the neural level provides further insights into the operation of memory. Schacter (2001; Buckner & Schacter, 2005) argues there are multiple forms of memory errors, including *bias*, *misattribution*, and *suggestion*.

3.5.1. Bias

Experimental analysis of memory distortions began with the work of the British psychologist Frederic Bartlett. In the 1930s, Bartlett had English participants read and then retell complex stories from the folklore of other cultures. He observed that participants frequently misremembered the stories in a number of ways: they noticeably shortened them; they eliminated unfamiliar interpretations; and made the stories more coherent and conventional in the storytelling tradition of their own culture. Adopting a similar approach, Sulin and Dooling (1974) had participants read a brief passage about a violent and unruly young girl; some participants were told that the passage was about "Helen Keller," others that the girl was "Carol Harris." Nowhere in the passage did the words "she was deaf, dumb, and blind" appear. When memory for the story was tested a week later and participants were asked if those words were in the story, half the participants who were told the story was about "Helen Keller" said yes (as opposed to 5 percent of those who thought the story was about "Carol Harris"). These distortions and errors of memory suggest that cultural experience and other background knowledge influence our memories for stimuli and events.

This form of memory distortion is due to *bias,* the inclination toward a conclusion not justified by logic or knowledge. In belief bias, such as that observed in the studies just mentioned, background knowledge about the way of the world and personal beliefs unconsciously influences memory to reshape it in a form consistent with expectations.

Bias can operate retrospectively, as well as during encoding. For instance, in one study (Markus, 1986), participants were asked in 1973 to describe their attitudes about the equality of women and legalization of marijuana (and other social issues). A decade later, in 1982, the same participants were asked to rate their *current* attitudes, and also to try to recall their 1973 attitudes. The result? Memory of their 1973 attitudes was more similar to their 1982 beliefs than the beliefs they had in fact expressed a decade earlier; and they apparently sincerely believed they had thought that way all along. Similar consistency biases, biases resulting from the often erroneous belief that one's attitudes are stable over time, have been observed in personal relationships: memory for the degree of initial happiness with a relationship is typically distorted by beliefs about the current degree of happiness (Kirkpatrick & Hazan, 1994; McFarland & Ross, 1987). It has been argued that bias of this sort occurs partly because people tend to believe that their attitudes are stable over time, and memories are therefore unconsciously adjusted to bring the past in line with the present (Ross, 1989).

An important implication of memory distortions due to bias is that retrieval is often a reconstructive process—what we retrieve is not always a direct recapitulation of what happened at encoding. In reconstructive memory, we reconstruct the past during retrieval rather than reproduce it. We often experience reconstructive memory when our memories for the event are not clear; in such instances we may infer the way things "must have been" from our current thoughts and expectations.

3.5.2. Misattribution

Here's a list of 15 associated words: *candy, sour, sugar, bitter, good, taste, tooth, nice, honey, soda, chocolate, heart, cake, eat, pie* (Deese, 1959; Roediger & McDermott, 1995).

Don't look back at the list, and answer these questions: Was the word *taste* on the list? The word *sweet*? The word *taste* was, and an average of 86 percent of participants said so. The word *sweet* wasn't—but an average of 84 percent of participants said it was. (The false recognition rate for unrelated words, such as *point,* was an average of 20 percent.) What's going on here—beyond the demonstration that it is possible to "remember" something that never happened?

False recognition often occurs when a novel stimulus is similar to stimuli previously encountered. One hypothesis is that, in the example of word lists, seeing each word activates related words, and these related words spontaneously come to mind and thus also are encoded. Then at retrieval, memory for having *thought* the related word is confused with memory for having *seen* the related word. This is an instance of misattribution, ascribing a recollection to an incorrect time, place, person, or source (Schacter, 2001). Participants who said the word *sweet* was on the list misattributed self-generated information (their thought of the word) to an external source (the presented word list).

In particular, false recognition occurs when we encounter a stimulus that, although not previously encountered, is semantically or perceptually similar to previously encountered stimuli (Koutstaal et al., 1999). In the example of word lists, *sweet* is semantically similar to the words on the list. In such circumstances, because the stimulus is consistent with the gist of our past experiences, it may elicit false recollection or a false sense of familiarity, leading us to believe that we had encountered the stimulus even though we had not. In essence, the same mechanisms that allow us to remember stimuli accurately that we have encountered can be fooled into signaling memory for a novel stimulus when it is similar to encountered stimuli.

Neuropsychological studies indicate that amnesic patients show lower levels of false recognition than do neurologically healthy people (Koutstaal et al., 2001). This finding suggests that the structures in the medial temporal lobes that support accurate episodic memory are also involved in storing and retrieving the information that leads to false recognition. Neuroimaging studies reveal that the hippocampus is similarly activated during the accurate recognition of previously studied words and the false recognition of related words. However, some studies suggest that accurate recognition and false recognition activate different perceptual processes, an indication that there are subtle but perhaps important differences in the level of perceptual recapitulation underlying true and false memory (Slotnick & Schacter, 2004).

3.5.3. Suggestion

False memories can muddy the waters of criminal investigations, and courtroom testimony based on the memory error of an eyewitness can lead to wrongful acquittal or conviction. Mindful that the fallibility of memory can have serious social and political consequences, researchers have sought to determine whether false memories can be implanted at the time of retrieval by *suggestion,* wherein false or misleading information is introduced after the event or is elicited through the use of leading questions (Schacter, 2001; Loftus, 2005).

In the laboratory, memories have been implanted by asking participants leading questions about an event they had observed in a slide presentation. In a classic experiment, participants watched slides of a car accident and then were asked to remember particular details about the incident (Loftus et al., 1978). The questions used to probe participants' memory introduced new—and false—information. For example, some of the participants were asked, "Did another car pass the red Datsun while it was stopped at the stop sign?" when in fact the slide presentation showed that the car had been stopped at a yield sign. When memory was tested again later, participants who were offered this misinformation were more likely to claim to have seen the car stopped at a stop sign than were those who had not been exposed to misleading information.

What accounts for this misinformation effect, which produces misremembering of an original event in line with false information (Loftus, 2005)? One hypothesis is that by suggesting false information about a prior event, the misinformation provided in the question serves to overwrite the information that was encoded during the event (Loftus et al., 1978). In this view, information that was once in memory is supplanted by the new misinformation. Alternatively, subsequent presentation of misinformation may lead to misattribution; that is, although the original accurate details remain in memory, when the false details are suggested, the misinformation is also encoded into memory. When later tested, you may remember the accurate information and the misinformation, but fail to remember which was in the original event and which was presented by the questioner. A third account is that, because we often cannot remember details about the past, we are inclined to accept misinformation as accurate when provided by a questioner because we lack memory otherwise; that is, if you cannot remember whether it was a yield sign or a stop sign, you are likely to be inclined to accept the information suggested by the questioner as accurate even if it is not. (This is especially likely to be the case when the questioner is a person of authority, such as a police officer.) Research addressing these alternatives indicates that misinformation distorts memory through a combination of misattribution (i.e., failing to remember the source of false information) and acceptance of suggested misinformation when accurate memory is weak (Lindsay, 1990; McCloskey & Zaragoza, 1985).

In special circumstances we may not only accept suggested misinformation as accurate but may also "remember" other details beyond those suggested by a questioner (Loftus & Bernstein, 2005). Do you remember being taken to a wedding reception as a child and spilling punch on the bride's mother? No? Perhaps you will, if you are subjected to a skilled interviewer; behavioral studies have shown that repeated suggestions about an event that never took place can induce not only acceptance of the memory but also can elicit additional—and wholly imaginary—details (Hyman & Pentland, 1996; Hyman et al., 1995). It appears that inducing people to visualize experiences that never occurred can sometimes lead them to conclude that their representations for what they'd imagined were actually memories of real events. Neuroimaging data support this conclusion: we are more likely falsely to claim to have seen an object that we had simply imagined when our earlier imagination of the object elicited robust activation of brain regions that support object perception (Gonsalves & Paller, 2000).

Comprehension Check:

1. What are the major factors that affect retrieval efficacy and how are memories retrieved in the brain?

2. What are the ways in which memory can be distorted?

4. THE ENCODING WAS SUCCESSFUL, BUT I STILL CAN'T REMEMBER

Noël Coward wrote of a great romance, "What has been is past forgetting." Alas, not true. Although memory processes are operating at every moment of the day, typically we are not aware of the functioning of memory until attempts to remember are met with failure—that is, when we forget.

Forgetting is the inability to recall or recognize previously encoded information. Although some instances of forgetting are due to poor initial encoding, and others are due to the lack of the right cues at the right time, many instances of forgetting result from postencoding mechanisms. These mechanisms interfere with memory, so even if encoding was effective and the cues suitable, attempts to remember may be met with failure, as if the memory were lost.

4.1. Ebbinghaus's Forgetting Function

In his classic work *Memory* (1885/1964), Hermann Ebbinghaus systematically examined how memory for encoded stimuli and events changes as the retention interval—the time between encoding and retrieval—increases. He observed that his memory for meaningless, nonsense syllables declined as the retention interval increased (Figure 5–14). Subsequent studies during the decades since Ebbinghaus's report have consistently replicated this pattern. It is now believed that forgetting follows a power law, that is, the rate of forgetting slows with the passage of time: initially very rapid, it

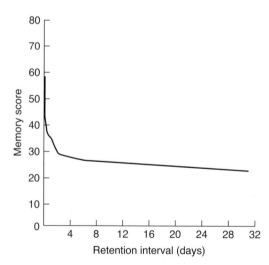

FIGURE 5–14 Ebbinghaus's forgetting function

Initially rapid forgetting is followed by a slow gradual decline.

(Data from Ebbinghaus, Hermann. Memory: A contribution to experimental psychology. Dover Publications, Inc., New York, 1964. Reprinted with permission.)

then settles into an extended, slow decline as the retention interval increases (Wixted & Ebbesen, 1991).

Because our ability to remember a stimulus or event systematically declines over time, the earliest theories held that forgetting was caused by the spontaneous weakening of memory representations with time. Such decay theories are attractive because they are simple and because they are intuitive. But they don't hold up; there is little direct evidence supporting decay. Indeed, some have argued that time alone cannot be the answer—*something must happen* (Lewandowsky et al., 2004). Consider a fading pair of jeans. Jeans do not fade spontaneously just because they've been around for a while. Their fading reflects a number of mechanisms that occur over time, such as repeated chemical interactions with sunlight and detergent. So it is likely to be for memory: time cannot operate directly on memory representations, which are neurobiological consequences of prior experience. Forgetting must be produced by some mechanism that play out in time.

4.2. Forgetting and Competition

Ample evidence indicates that many instances of forgetting are caused by interference. Interference theories hold that if the same cue is bound to a number of representations, these representations compete during retrieval, resulting in interference. Newer memories interfere with older ones, and older ones with newer ones; and the result is that neither old nor new stimuli or events are perfectly recalled—even though the information is still in memory, we have forgotten because retrieval attempts have failed.

4.2.1. Retroactive and Proactive Interference

Interference can work both ways: here's an example of retroactive interference, in which new learning results in the inability to remember previously learned information (McGeogh, 1942; Melton & Irwin, 1940). You have an old e-mail account, which you used on your home computer, with a password you once used daily; now you're on your school's system, with a new password. The school takes a generous view of personal use of the school account, so you haven't used your old account in some considerable time. But now you need to find some ancient message buried in that e-mail account and *you can no longer remember the old password, because the new password interferes with it.*

Retroactive interference has been demonstrated in the laboratory with pairs of stimuli (Barnes & Underwood, 1959) (Figure 5–15a). All participants first learned random word–word pairings, the A–B pairs. (This stage is analogous to the learning you did when you encoded an association between the concept "password" and a particular combination of characters to gain access to your earlier account.) Some of the participants were then asked to associate a second word (C) with each A word from the original pairs. (This A–C learning is akin to encoding the association between the concept "password" and the characters that make up your school password.) Other participants were not asked to form a second set of word associations, but were given a "filler" task that, although time consuming, did not require learning. Memory was then tested by presenting the A words as retrieval cues and asking

Retroactive Interference

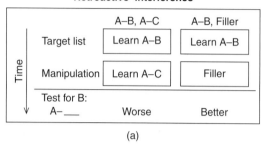

(a)

Proactive Interference

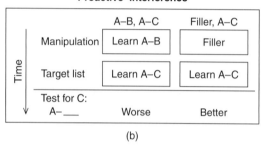

(b)

FIGURE 5–15   Experimental designs examining retroactive interference and proactive interference

(a) Retroactive interference is shown to produce worse subsequent memory for A–B associations because of A–C associations learned later. (b) Proactive interference is shown to produce worse subsequent memory for A–C associations because of A–B associations learned earlier.

participants to recall the word or words that had been paired with each. The first group, which had to learn A–C as well as A–B pairs, had worse memory for the A–B pairs than did the second group, whose second task did not require learning.

This result eliminated passive decay as a cause: the time between tasks and memory test was the same for both groups, and thus any decay should have been the same. The conclusion then was that the learning of the A–C pairs (or of your new password) interfered with the ability to remember the A–B pairs learned earlier (or your old password). Other research has shown that the degree to which later learned information interferes with memory for earlier learned information depends on the similarity of the two (McGeogh & McDonald, 1931). The more similar the later information is to that learned earlier, the greater the interference and thus the greater the forgetting.

Now let's reverse direction: previously learned information can interfere with memory for information learned later by **proactive interference** (Underwood, 1957). This phenomenon has been explored in the laboratory in the same way as retroactive interference (Figure 5–15b). Here's an example of proactive interference: many people would agree that it is more difficult to remember the location of your car after parking it in a lot that you use regularly than when you park it in a lot you use only occasionally. The many earlier instances of associating your daily lot with a parking location for your car compete—and thus interfere—during attempts to retrieve the memory for the most recent association.

4.2.2. Blocking and Suppression

Memory is associative: encoding entails the formation of associations between different mental representations, such as binding the concept "password" to a particular sequence of characters. Retrieval entails pattern completion: presentation of a retrieval cue (for example, the demand for "password" on a computer screen) reactivates the associated representation (your sequence of characters). Given the fundamental principles of binding and the cue dependence of pattern completion, it becomes clear that interference can lead to forgetting through a number of mechanisms.

Forgetting can be caused by the blocking of a memory representation, that is, by obstruction that can occur when multiple associations are associated with a cue and one of those associations is stronger than the others, preventing retrieval of the target information. Many theorists believe that the probability of retrieving a target memory depends on the strength of the association between the retrieval cue and the target representation *relative to* the strength of the association between that same cue and other representations. In the ensuing competition during retrieval, the representation with the strongest association "wins" and is remembered; ones with weaker associations "lose" and are "forgotten". There is an important contrast here to decay theories, which hold that the degraded memory representation is lost; blocking theory emphasizes that the forgotten information still resides in memory, but access to it is temporarily blocked by a dominant competing representation. This weaker representation can be unblocked if a better retrieval cue, one that is more strongly associated with it, is presented.

Blocking likely accounts for many instances of forgetting; the mental representation of the old password, unused for some time, could be considered a weaker representation than the new password, which is used daily (Figure 5–16). The phenomenon is possibly adaptive: it permits the updating of memories so that we remember the information most likely to be relevant (Bjork, 1989).

Blocking also partly explains a striking and counterintuitive characteristic of memory: that the mere act of remembering one stimulus or event can result in the forgetting of another. Suppose you idly start thinking about cataloguing your CDs, and you begin by making a mental list of them. The list grows quickly at first, but very soon your rate of retrieval slows. Your familiarity with all your CDs is about the same, so why should this be? What is happening is a phenomenon called output interference, in which the strengthening of memories provided by the act of initial retrieval blocks the retrieval of other memories. Retrieving the names of some of the CDs in your collection serves to strengthen the association between those representations and the retrieval cue; and in turn these newly strengthened representations serve to block access to other CD titles, temporarily decreasing your ability to remember them.

If representations can be strengthened, as by retrieval, can nonretrieved representations be *suppressed*—weakened in absolute, not relative, terms? In other

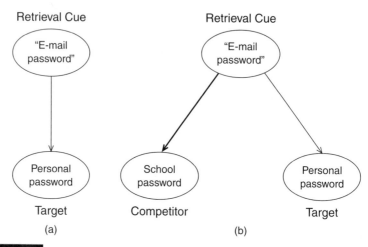

FIGURE 5–16   Cue overload and blocking

(a) The retrieval cue ("e-mail password") is associated with a single item ("personal password"). (b) The later learning and use of your new "school password" results in its also being associated with the cue "e-mail password," and thus begins to overload the cue. Because of its more recent use, the association between "school password" and the cue may be stronger (depicted by a thicker line) than the association between your earlier "personal password" and the cue. This stronger association may block retrieval of your earlier password.

words, does the competitive nature of memory actually cause some memories to weaken? (Is memory for your earlier password suppressed by repeated retrieval of your school password?) The answer appears to be yes, as shown by a phenomenon called **retrieval-induced forgetting**, forgetting that occurs when a memory is suppressed during the retrieval of another memory (Anderson & Spellman, 1995). **Suppression**, the active weakening of a memory, occurs because the act of retrieval is competitive: to retrieve a desired memory (your school password) you must not only strengthen its representation, you also must suppress the representations of competing associates (your earlier password).

Note the important difference between suppression and blocking: if memory for a competitor has been *suppressed*, one has difficulty retrieving it even when using a cue that has not been overloaded, which is not the case in *blocking*, which depends on multiple associations—that is, cue overload. In the password example, let's say your earlier password was "Batman Begins," the name of a movie. To the extent that the representation of this earlier password was suppressed during retrieval of your school password, then you should have increased difficulty retrieving it even when using an alternative cue ("movie names") rather than the trained cue ("e-mail password") (Figure 5–17). Anderson and Spellman demonstrated that retrieval of one representation associated with a cue results in the active weakening or suppression of other representations associated with that cue, as revealed by increased difficulty remembering the item when probed with an alternative cue.

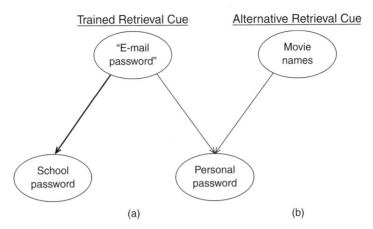

(a)   (b)

FIGURE 5–17   Two mechanisms that can explain interference

(a) *Blocking* posits that learning and using (that is, retrieving) your new school password with the cue "e-mail password" serves to hinder access to your earlier and less-used personal password (note the relative thickness of the lines). The *suppression* hypothesis states that retrieval of your new password serves actively to suppress (that is, weaken) the representation of your earlier password. (b) Testing memory with an alternative cue—one that is not overloaded, as is "e-mail password," which can apply to both passwords—provides evidence of forgetting that is not a result of blocking.

(Adapted from Anderson, M. C., & Green, C. (2001). Suppressing unwanted memories by executive control. *Nature, 410:* 366–369. Reprinted with permission.)

Comprehension Check:

1. What factors lead to forgetting?
2. How do blocking and suppression account for forgetting?

5. NONDECLARATIVE MEMORY SYSTEMS

The cognitive and neurobiological mechanisms that support declarative memory—and lead to forgetting—were best explored through our discussion of episodic memory, one form of declarative memory. We experience other forms of long-term memory quite differently. These other forms are known collectively as *non-declarative (or implicit) memory.*

In discussing nondeclarative memory systems, concepts such as "recollection" do not apply. Nondeclarative memory operates outside of awareness: we typically are unaware of the influences of nondeclarative memory on our behavior, and we cannot describe the contents of retrieved nondeclarative memories. Rather, their retrieval and influence are expressed implicitly, by changes in behavior. As we noted earlier, nondeclarative memory supports forms of learning (habits, for instance) and remembering (the ability to ride a bike) that are qualitatively distinct and functionally independent of declarative memory.

There are a number of nondeclarative memory systems, each with unique qualities and dependent on specific brain circuits (see Figure 5–1). The medial temporal lobes are not involved, and therefore amnesic patients such as H.M., who suffer devastating declarative memory losses, can still form and retrieve nondeclarative memories, such as learning and expressing new motor skills (see Figure 5–4).

5.1. Priming

The phenomenon of priming illustrates some of the central characteristics of nondeclarative memory systems. Through priming, we can be unconsciously influenced by our experiences in such a way that previously encountered stimuli and concepts become more readily available. Specifically, as observed in memory, *priming* follows an encounter with a stimulus—a word or a face or other object—and constitutes unconscious alterations in our subsequent response to that stimulus or a related one. These behavioral changes can include increasing the speed of response, increasing the accuracy of the response, or biasing the nature of the response.

Changing vocabulary can be an interesting example of priming. Are you using a particular expression or bit of slang more often than you used to? Perhaps you picked it up from a friend. You may have begun using this phrase unintentionally, without considering its source or the original influence. Your mimicking of your friend occurs unconsciously in conversation, because your memory of that expression has been primed by your friend's use of it, increasing the likelihood that you will use it spontaneously.

Although there are a number of forms of priming, most instances fall into one of two broad categories: perceptual and conceptual (Roediger & McDermott, 1993). Perceptual priming results in an enhanced ability to identify a stimulus; conceptual priming results in facilitated processing of the meaning of a stimulus or enhanced access to a concept.

5.1.1. Perceptual Priming

In what is known as the *perceptual identification task,* test words are presented on a computer screen for as short a time as 34 milliseconds, and the task is to identify each flashed word. Because the perceptual input is limited in such a brief presentation, participants typically can identify only a small proportion of the test words. However, when a test word is visually presented in a study list before the performance of the task, the probability of identifying that word increases, even though participants are unaware that they have been influenced by the study list. This difference in accuracy for studied and unstudied stimuli—the measure of priming—occurs even though participants often report that they are simply guessing the flashed test words, thus indicating that declarative memory is not guiding performance.

Perceptual priming reflects the consequences of perceptual learning, and thus is highly dependent on the degree of perceptual overlap between the initial encounter with the stimulus and repeated ones. The degree of overlap is greatest, of course, when both initial and subsequent encounters are in the same modality; seeing a word primes seeing it again, but does little or nothing for hearing it (Jacoby & Dallas,

1981). Perceptual priming has been observed in all modalities tested (vision, audition, and touch), suggesting that it reflects a general form of learning in perceptual representation systems (Tulving & Schacter, 1990).

Because patients whose amnesia results from injury to the medial temporal lobes show intact perceptual priming, this form of memory cannot depend on the mechanisms that support declarative memory. Rather, perceptual priming is thought to emerge from learning within sensory cortices. The experience of a patient known as M.S. is illustrative (Gabrieli et al., 1995).

Like H.M., M.S. suffered from epileptic seizures that could not be controlled with medication, although in M.S.'s case the epilepsy was due to abnormalities in the occipital cortex, not the medial temporal lobes. Surgery to remove most of M.S.'s right occipital lobe controlled his seizures, but also resulted in a remarkably subtle memory deficit of which he was unaware: although M.S.'s declarative memory is intact, he fails to show perceptual priming in the visual domain. For example, his ability to identify briefly presented visual stimuli is not improved by prior viewing of the stimuli (Figure 5–18). This memory pattern has two important implications. First, M.S.'s priming deficit allows us to rule out the possibility that intact priming

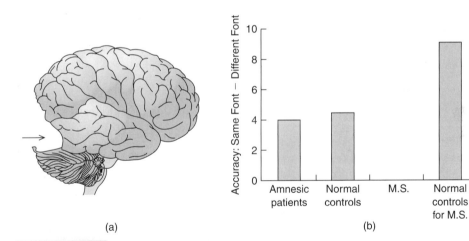

(a) (b)

FIGURE 5–18 Priming, memory, and brain damage

M.S. has intact declarative memory, but does not benefit by visual perceptual priming; amnesic patients do. (a) A three-dimensional MRI rendering of the right hemisphere of M.S.'s brain, showing the extent (*arrow*) of the removal of the right occipital cortex.

(Wagner, A. D., & Koutstaal, W. Priming. In *Encyclopedia of the Human Brain*, Vol. 4. Elsevier Science, 2002, pp. 27–46, Fig. 1. Reprinted with permission from Elsevier.)

(b) The magnitude of visual priming in amnesic patients and their age-matched normal controls, and in M.S. and his age-matched normal controls. In all groups, except M.S. himself, word-stem completion priming was greater when the font of the word stem matched the font of the studied word.

(Data from Vaidya, C. J., Gabrieli, J. D., Verfaellie, M., Fleischman, D., & Askari, N. (1998). Font-specific priming following global amnesia and occipital lobe damage. *Neuropsychology, 2:* 183–192. © 1998 American Psychological Association. Reprinted with permission.)

in amnesic patients simply reflects residual declarative memory function. To the contrary, because M.S. has impaired perceptual priming and intact declarative memory, which is the reverse pattern of that seen in amnesic patients, it seems clear that perceptual priming and declarative memory reflect different forms of memory that depend on distinct brain structures. Second, M.S.'s memory deficit provides compelling evidence that sensory-specific cortical processing is necessary for perceptual priming.

During the past decade, researchers have used neuroimaging to examine the neural correlates of perceptual priming in the intact human brain (Schacter et al., 2004). In the typical experiment, the activation level during the initial processing of visual stimuli is compared to that during the repeated (that is, primed) processing of the same stimuli. Such experiments have revealed that visual priming is accompanied by *decreased* activation in the regions of visual cortex that were engaged during the initial processing of stimuli (Figure 5–19 see Color Insert H). This finding has been seen across a variety of tasks and stimuli types, including words and objects, suggesting that it reflects a fundamental operating principle shared by sensory processing regions. Localization of visual priming to visual cortex is further evidence that modality-specific sensory cortices are central to perceptual priming.

Neuroimaging observations of priming in human sensory cortex bear a striking resemblance to the phenomenon of repetition suppression observed in studies of nonhuman primates and rats; that is, a reduced firing rate of neurons in visual regions with repeated exposure to a stimulus (Desimone, 1996). Perceptual priming in the human and repetition suppression in the nonhuman might reflect the operation of a single underlying learning mechanism that changes the response properties of sensory neurons that process perceptual features of a stimulus and, accordingly, affects behavior. One hypothesis is that this change consists of dampening down the responses of neurons that, though initially responsive to stimulus presentation, are not essential for stimulus identification. This process results in a sparser and more selective neural representation—fewer neurons fire in response to the stimulus, leading to reductions in the fMRI signal and neural firing rate—and enhanced stimulus identification (Wiggs & Martin, 1998; see Figure 5–19).

5.1.2. Conceptual Priming

Modifications of speech, such as incorporating a new expression into your everyday vocabulary, often occur outside conscious awareness, and do not reflect changes in perceptual representation systems. Rather, the form of priming that gives rise to an increased accessibility to concepts, such as slang terms, is thought to emerge as a result of learning in semantic representation systems. Conceptual priming, which results in facilitated processing of the meaning of a word, is demonstrated by the *category exemplar generation task*. Participants are presented a category cue, such as "fruit," and are asked to name the first few fruits that come to mind. Typically, the probability of spontaneously generating a given exemplar, such as "cherry," is higher if that word had appeared on an earlier (unrelated) study list. This increase does not reflect declarative memory, because amnesic patients show intact levels of conceptual priming even though they have impaired episodic memory for the study list as such. In other words, if asked to recall the words on a study list, they can't; nonetheless, they show improvement in the category generation task when they've seen the words before.

Neuroimaging studies of the healthy human brain during conceptual priming have revealed changes in frontal and temporal lobe activation. The typical study compares activation in response to initial and repeated conceptual decisions about words or objects (for example, deciding whether a word is "abstract" or "concrete"). In contrast to perceptual priming, which is associated with decreased activation in modality-specific perceptual cortices, neuroimaging studies of conceptual priming reveal that the left inferior frontal lobe and left lateral temporal cortex are less active during repeated conceptual processing of a stimulus. The left frontal lobe is thought to contribute to semantic retrieval when the sought information does not immediately come to mind upon cue presentation (Wagner et al., 2001). The increased accessibility of sought semantic information as a result of priming serves to decrease demands on this retrieval process. In this way priming decreases the cognitive effort required to retrieve relevant information.

5.2. Beyond Priming: Other Forms of Nondeclarative Memory

Although priming is arguably the best understood form of nondeclarative memory, there are other memory systems that operate independently of the medial temporal lobes to acquire and store knowledge that can be unconsciously or implicitly expressed. These other nondeclarative systems support skilled behavior, the acquisition of stimulus–response habits, and the formation and expression of conditioned associations. Learning within these systems is typically gradual and incremental.

5.2.1. Skill Learning

Humans are capable of acquiring remarkably skilled behavior. Skill learning supports our ability to become experts, to a greater or lesser degree, at things like snowboarding and typing. With practice, skilled behavior becomes more accurate and responses are made more quickly.

It has been proposed that skill acquisition entails three stages (Fitts & Posner, 1967). Learning begins with a *cognitive stage*, in which knowledge is declaratively represented, often in a verbal code, and attentional demands are high. When you begin learning to snowboard, you have to remember consciously a set of instructions on, for example, how to turn; and inattention is often followed by a spill. With practice, you gradually move to an *associative stage*. Behavior begins to be tuned and error rates and "verbal mediation"—that is, talking to yourself as you learn—decline as the visual information about the mountain's terrain and your motor responses that allow you to navigate the terrain come together, and the associations in memory required for snowboarding are formed and strengthened. Finally, you may reach an *autonomous stage*, in which behavior is highly accurate, rapidly executed, and relatively automatic, requiring little attention. If you've reached this stage, you may find it hard to explain to a novice exactly how you do what it is you do, because your knowledge now is typically expressed without awareness of the underlying memories that make it possible.

Skill learning is distinguished from priming on the basis of specificity of the memory change. Priming reflects a change in the perceptual or conceptual representation of a specific item; skill learning generalizes to new instances or exemplars that were not encountered during learning. You don't lose your ability to type when you're using someone else's computer keyboard.

Skill learning also is distinguished from priming, and from declarative memory, with respect to the brain regions that are ultimately necessary to acquire and express skills. In general, the acquisition of skills partially depends on the basal ganglia, a set of subcortical structures long known to be important for motor execution and more recently linked to memory and various cognitive processes. Particular skills also place additional demands on the cerebellum and on cortical regions. The importance of the basal ganglia for skill learning has been revealed in studies of patients with Parkinson's and Huntington's disease, both disorders of basal ganglia function. Basal ganglia dysfunction spares priming, but it differentially impairs skill learning relative to declarative memory. Consistent with these findings, neuroimaging of neurologically healthy people has revealed changes in the activation of the caudate and putamen, portions of the basal ganglia, as a skill is acquired (Grafton et al., 1995; Poldrack et al., 1999).

5.2.2. Habit Memory

Nondeclarative memory also encompasses the acquisition of stimulus–response habits, habits that emerge through the slow accumulation of knowledge about the predictive relation between a stimulus and a response. The acquisition and expression of habit memories has been assessed using the *probabilistic classification task,* in which participants learn to predict one of two possible outcomes from a set of cues, each cue bearing a probabilistic relation to the outcome. For example, participants may be asked to predict rain or sunshine from a set of cue cards. Because the cue–outcome associations are probabilistic—that is, a given card never perfectly predicts rain or sunshine— retrieving episodic memory for specific study trials is an ineffective learning strategy. Rather, through repeated presentation of cards and resulting outcomes, participants gradually accumulate implicit knowledge about the stimulus–response associations.

In contrast to patients with medial temporal lobe damage, patients with basal ganglia dysfunction are severely impaired in this task (Knowlton et al., 1994, 1996). Neuroimaging of neurologically healthy people has shown increasing basal ganglia activation and decreasing medial temporal lobe activation over the course of habit learning (Poldrack et al., 2001). Thus, the basal ganglia become increasingly involved across the course of habit learning, whereas the declarative memory system appears to shut down.

5.2.3. Conditioned Associations

Nondeclarative memory mechanisms support the learning and expression of conditioned associations such as those described by the Russian psychologist Ivan Pavlov early in the twentieth century. The simplest form of conditioning, referred to as classical conditioning, entails learning a predictive relationship between two successive stimuli such that a response that is triggered by an initial stimulus (the *unconditioned stimulus*) prior to learning comes to be triggered by a second stimulus (the *conditioned stimulus*) that predicts onset of the unconditioned stimulus. The formation of a conditioned association depends on the degree to which the presence of one stimulus predicts the occurrence of the other. Accordingly, effective learning occurs when one stimulus reliably and predictably signals the occurrence of the second stimulus. (Classical conditioning will be discussed further in Chapter 8.)

As with other forms of nondeclarative memory, the medial temporal lobes are not necessary for conditioning. Thus, H.M. and other amnesic patients can form a conditioned eye-blink response with the repeated pairing of a tone and a following puff of air to the eye. (H.M., like you, will soon start to blink when the tone is sounded.) This knowledge is nondeclarative: the patients cannot state the temporal relation between the tone and the air puff. The cerebellum is thought to be the site at which perceptual inputs (such as the sound of the tone and the sensation of the puff of air) are associated; it has been demonstrated that cerebellar lesions disrupt the acquisition of conditioned eyeblink responses (Solomon et al., 1989).

Comprehension Check:

1. How do perceptual and conceptual priming affect cognition?
2. What are the stages of skill learning?

Revisit and Reflect

1. *What are the characteristics of declarative and nondeclarative memory systems?*

   Declarative memory supports the encoding, consolidation, and retrieval of knowledge that can be consciously remembered and described, or "declared," to other people at the time of retrieval, such as memory for events (episodic memory) and for facts and concepts (semantic memory). When you recognize someone, you rely on episodic memory to remember details about your earlier encounter—perhaps her tastes in cuisine, her name, her politics—and you are aware of the contents of your memory and their relation to your past. To launch your new conversation you also rely on semantic memory to retrieve knowledge of relevant concepts—say, the views of her political party—and consciously use this knowledge to guide your discussion. Declarative memory depends on the medial temporal lobes.

   Nondeclarative memory supports forms of long-term knowledge that are implicitly expressed as a change in behavior rather than as conscious remembering. We are often unaware of the operations of nondeclarative memory and how such memories shape our thoughts and actions. Thus, your ability perceptually to process the face of someone you recognize is likely facilitated (that is, primed) by your having previously processed that face—and although you most likely do not notice the change, your second perceptual processing of a face is performed more quickly than was the first. Nondeclarative memory systems support skill learning, conditioning, habit memory, and priming, and all depend on brain structures outside the medial temporal lobes.

Think Critically

- Try to imagine what life would be like without the ability to form new declarative memories. What aspects of your life would change?
- Although we are typically not aware of when our behavior is being influenced by nondeclarative memory, can you think of three examples across the course of today where your actions were likely affected by one form of nondeclarative memory?

2. *How do we encode new declarative memories, what processes affect encoding efficacy, and what brain mechanisms build these memories?*

Declarative memories are encoded through medial temporal lobe processes that bind the various aspects of a stimulus or event into an integrated memory representation. Episodic encoding entails the binding of the elements of a stimulus or event with its context. Thus, to remember a past encounter with someone, you must initially encode the elements of that encounter—binding together perceptual information (for example, her face), verbal information (for example, her name), spatial information (for example, where you met), and semantic information (for example, her taste in cuisine and her political views). Semantic memories are thought to emerge when the regularity of the co-occurrence of elements across multiple contexts is extracted; thus those elements are divorced from context but still capture the central tendencies of a stimulus or event. Thus, knowledge of Italian cuisine emerges by pooling across the various experiences one has had that included Italian food.

Episodic encoding is facilitated by a number of factors: attention, semantic processing and elaboration, generating information from memory, and the spacing of encoding trials. For example, failure to attend to a person's name when being introduced because of distraction (for example, thinking about an impending physics test) will result in poor encoding (and future embarrassment!). Attention, semantic processing and elaboration, and the generation of information all partially depend on frontal lobe brain mechanisms, and thus the frontal lobes are in a position to influence how we learn and what we learn. Although each of these encoding factors affects later memory performance, encoding is not deterministic—rather our ability later to remember critically depends on the overlap between the processing and cues present at encoding and those engaged and present at retrieval.

Think Critically

- How should you study to improve your learning of course material and the likelihood that you will be able to retrieve this material when necessary?
- Consider a recent instance in which you failed to remember a prior event. Can you trace this memory failure to ineffective encoding? How might you have changed this memory outcome?

3. *How are episodic memories retrieved, and why is it that sometimes what we retrieve is not an accurate reflection of our past?*

Remembering events past depends on episodic retrieval, the process by which stored memory representations are subsequently reactivated. According to dual-process theory, retrieval can take either of two forms: recollection of a past encounter with a stimulus or the subjective experience that a stimulus is familiar. Recollection is thought to depend on pattern completion processes in the hippocampus that recapitulate information in lateral cortex that was present during encoding of the event; a topic of current debate is whether familiarity particularly depends only on the medial temporal cortex or also on the hippocampus.

Because pattern completion is triggered by retrieval cues, recollection critically depends on the cues used to probe memory and their overlap with the cues present at encoding—both external contextual cues and internal ones. Thus, you may fail to recognize someone you've previously met not because you have forgotten that person but because the contexts of the two encounters are different; many of the cues that may trigger pattern completion are not present when the context changes. The frontal lobes affect recollection partly because these brain regions serve to represent and elaborate on retrieval cues and to resolve interference between competing memories.

Memory is prone to distortion and error—what we retrieve is not always an accurate reflection of what we encountered. Biases at encoding can distort what is stored in memory—and even when memories are relatively accurately encoded, biases at retrieval can distort what is "remembered" as we reconstruct the past. Another common memory error is the misattribution of something remembered to the wrong source. Thus, you might become confused as to whether you actually performed an action that you'd simply thought about performing (did I lock the door?). We sometimes also mistakenly claim to have encountered stimuli that, though novel, are perceptually or conceptually similar to stimuli that we have previously encountered. Finally, memory can be led astray through suggestions by others: sometimes suggestion leads to error because it induces a misattribution, and at other times errors occur because we accept misleading information as true because we can't remember otherwise.

Think Critically

- In deciding whether or not a particular event happened just the way it was described to you by the sole eyewitness, what factors would you consider?
- What is the relation between binding in the medial temporal lobes and pattern completion? Is anterograde amnesia likely a failure of binding or of pattern completion? What about retrograde amnesia?

4. *Why do we sometimes forget?*

We forget for many reasons. Sometimes it is because we failed to encode the information effectively that we now are trying to remember. At other times it is because the cues that we are using to try to trigger remembering are ineffective; a change to other cues or elaboration on the cues we are using could help. Some theorists have hypothesized that forgetting can also occur because memories spontaneously decay over time; this hypothesis has been challenged, although it is difficult completely to discount decay as a possible forgetting mechanism. That said, there is strong agreement and extensive evidence that forgetting often is due to interference—memories compete (or interfere) with one another during retrieval, thus resulting in failure to recover the desired memory. Proactive and retroactive interference arise partly because having multiple associates to a cue serves to overload the cue, making it less effective for triggering remembering of any given associate. In addition, when one piece of information is more strongly associated with a cue than is another, our ability to retrieve the latter memory may be blocked by this competing stronger memory. Moreover, because memories compete during retrieval, the act of recovering one memory directly weakens or suppresses the representation of a related memory, resulting in retrieval-induced forgetting.

Think Critically

- Memory is critical for recording one's life narrative and thus for generating a sense of self. How should the knowledge that memory is fallible influence our confidence in what we know about our past and our sense of self?

- Often when we are having difficulties remembering something, a friend might try to lend a hand by suggesting possible answers. Although well intentioned, how might these efforts to be helpful result in the exact opposite outcome—decreasing the probability of remembering the desired information?

5. *What are the forms of nondeclarative memory, and how do they influence our behavior?*

The realization that the brain supports multiple memory systems makes a fundamental point: all regions of the brain change (or "learn") as they are engaged to perform some function or computation. What differs between declarative and nondeclarative memory systems are the particular kinds of processes or functions supported by different brain regions, and thus the particular kinds of memories that these regions can support. Whereas declarative memory depends on the unique ability of the medial temporal lobes to receive and bind inputs from elsewhere in the brain, nondeclarative memory typically depends on changes in local brain networks following previous engagement of these networks. Thus, priming reflects changes in perceptual and conceptual representation systems that follow prior perceptual or conceptual processing of stimuli; these changes are behaviorally expressed as facilitated performance. Skill learning, habit memory, and conditioning are other forms of nondeclarative memory that are gradually acquired and that ultimately shape our behavior in ways that we need not be aware.

Think Critically

- What are the implications of nondeclarative memory for the perspective that humans have free will—that is, that we make conscious choices on how to think and act?

- If you had a brain injury that resulted in impaired conceptual priming, how do you think this might impact your everyday functioning?

Working Memory

Learning Objectives

You're in the middle of a lively conversation about movies, one in particular. You and your friends have all seen it and have come away with different views. One friend says he felt that one of the leads was not convincing in the role; you disagree—you think the failing was in the screenplay, and want to make your case. But before you have a chance to get going, another friend jumps in and says she doesn't think this actor was miscast, just that he's not very good, and is prepared to argue chapter and verse. You think your point is a good one, and you want to make it; but you'll only offend this friend, who's now arguing her point with enthusiasm. Moreover, you find yourself agreeing with some of what she's saying. Your challenge is to manage two tasks at once: pay attention to what your friend is saying, both out of courtesy and to follow her argument so you don't repeat or overlook her points when you speak; and hold on to your own argument, which is forming in your head as you listen. Your working memory is getting a workout!

Working memory is widely thought to be one of the most important mental faculties, critical for cognitive abilities such as planning, problem solving, and reasoning. This chapter describes current conceptions regarding the nature of working memory, its internal components, and the way it works. We specifically address five questions:

1. How is working memory used in cognition?
2. How did the modern view of working memory arise?
3. What are the elements of working memory?
4. How does working memory "work" in the brain?
5. How might views of working memory change in the future?

1. USING WORKING MEMORY

Every day we have occasion to keep particular pieces of critical information briefly in mind, storing them until the opportunity to use them arrives. Here are some examples: remembering a phone number between the time of hearing it and dialing it ("1 646 766-6358"); figuring a tip (the bill is $28.37, call it $30; 10 percent of that is $3.00, half of that is $1.50, $3.00 plus $1.50 is $4.50, the 15 percent you're aiming for); holding driving directions in mind until you get to the landmarks you've been told to watch for ("take the first left, continue for one mile, past the school, bear right, left at the four-way intersection, then it's the third building on the left—you can pull into the driveway"). Sometimes a problem offers multiple possible solutions, such as when you must look ahead along various possible sequences of moves in a chess game, and sometimes, as when you must untangle the structure of a complex sentence like this one, it is straightforward but nonetheless requires holding bits of information in mind until you can put it all together.

In situations like these, not only do we need to keep certain bits of information accessible in mind, but also we need to perform cognitive operations on them, mulling them over, manipulating or transforming them. These short-term mental storage and manipulation operations are collectively called working memory. Think of working memory as involving a mental blackboard—that is, as a workspace that provides a temporary holding store so that relevant information is highly accessible and available for inspection and computation. When cognitive tasks are accomplished, the information can be easily erased, and the process can begin again with other information.

1.1. A Computer Metaphor

The computer, so useful a metaphor in cognitive psychology, offers an intuitively appealing model for thinking about the nature and structure of working memory.

Simplifying the workings of a computer, there are two means by which information is stored, the hard disk and random-access memory (RAM). The hard disk is the means by which information is stored permanently in a stable and reliable form; all software programs, data files, and the operating system of the computer are stored on the hard disk. To use this stored information you must retrieve it from the hard disk and load it into RAM. Now for the analogy: the information stored in the hard disk is like long-term memory, RAM corresponds to working memory.

The notion of working memory as a temporary workspace fits nicely: in a computer, RAM is cleared and reset when the task executed by the program is finished, or when the program is closed. The computer metaphor also suggests two further characteristics of working memory. First, RAM is completely flexible with regard to content. That is, there is no fixed mapping between the location of a part of RAM and the program that uses it; any program can access any part of RAM. Second, the more RAM a computer has, the more complex and sophisticated the programs that can be run on it, and the more programs that can be running simultaneously. Thus, if the computer-based metaphor of working memory holds, storage in working memory involves a content-free flexible buffer (the term in computer science for a limited-capacity memory store), and cognitive abilities are dependent on the size of the buffer.

How well does this metaphor fit with actual human working memory structure and function? The evidence is not all in, but cognitive and neuroscience approaches to the study of working memory have in many ways revolutionized the types of questions that can be asked and provided new insights into how working memory works.

1.2. Implications of the Nature of Working Memory

A better understanding of the nature of human working memory may have important implications for understanding why people differ in cognitive skills and abilities and why individuals have different degrees of success in their efforts to accomplish real-world goals. Research suggests that people vary widely in working memory capacity (also known as working memory span), the amount of information that can be held accessible (Daneman & Carpenter, 1980), and that these differences predict general intelligence (as measured by standard IQ tests), verbal SAT scores, and even the speed with which a skill such as computer programming is acquired (Kane & Engle, 2002; Kyllonen & Christal, 1990).

A test to determine working memory capacity is shown in Figure 6–1. (Why not take it yourself? Do the results accord with your view of your own working memory?) A relationship between working memory and cognitive ability is not surprising, given how pervasively working memory affects a wide range of complex cognitive tasks, not all of them as mundane as figuring out a tip. The more interesting questions remain: why do people differ so widely in working memory capacity, and where exactly do the differences lie? If we understood more precisely the components of working memory, and which aspects are the most critical for real-world cognitive

IS (5 × 3) + 4 = 17?　BOOK
IS (6 × 2) − 3 = 8?　　HOUSE
IS (4 × 4) − 4 = 12?　JACKET
IS (3 × 7) + 6 = 27?　CAT
IS (4 × 8) − 2 = 31?　PEN
IS (9 × 2) + 6 = 24?　WATER

FIGURE 6–1　A standard test of working memory capacity

To take this test yourself, cut out a window in a blank sheet of paper so that it exposes only one line at a time. For each line, determine whether the arithmetic is correct or not: say, out loud, "yes" or "no." Then look at the word that follows the problem and memorize it. Move through each line quickly. After you have finished all the lines, try to recall the words in order. The number you get correct is an estimate of your working memory capacity. Very few people have a working memory as high as 6; the average is around 2 or 3.

success, we might be able to develop methods to train and exercise working memory in a manner that could improve its function, and consequently enhance a person's cognitive repertoire.

Today's conceptions of working memory have evolved from earlier ideas in cognitive psychology, and current research stands, as so often in science, on the shoulders of predecessors. What the earliest workers did not have were the tools provided by modern neuroscience. Nonetheless, their work is a good place to begin.

✓ **Comprehension Check:**

1. Give an example of an everyday situation in which you would need to use working memory.
2. If working memory were a capacity of a computer, what component might it correspond to, and why?

2. FROM PRIMARY MEMORY TO WORKING MEMORY: A BRIEF HISTORY

The notion that there is a distinct form of memory that stores information temporarily in the service of ongoing cognition is not new, but ideas regarding the nature and function of short-term storage have evolved considerably during the last hundred years. The very terms for this storage system have changed over the years, from *primary memory* to *short-term memory* to *working memory*. How and why did this happen?

2.1. William James: Primary Memory, Secondary Memory, and Consciousness

The first discussion of a distinction between short-term and long-term storage systems was put forth by the pioneering American psychologist William James in the late nineteenth century. James called these two forms of memory *primary memory* and *secondary memory*, using these terms to indicate the degree of the relationship of the stored information to consciousness (James, 1890). In James's view, primary memory is the initial repository in which information can be stored and made available to conscious inspection, attention, and introspection. In this way, such information would be continually accessible. In James's words, "an object of primary memory is thus not brought back; it never was lost." He contrasted primary memory with a long-term storage system, or secondary memory, from which information cannot be retrieved without initiating an active cognitive process. The link between working memory and consciousness that James sought to describe remains a central part of most current thinking; the question of whether or not we are conscious of the entire contents of working memory is still open to debate. Some current models suggest that only a subset of working memory is consciously experienced (Cowan, 1995).

2.2. Early Studies: The Characteristics of Short-Term Memory

Despite James's early work regarding the system for short-term information storage, there were no experimental studies of the characteristics of this system until the 1950s. Part of the reason for this neglect was the dominance of behaviorist views in the first half of the twentieth century, which shifted the focus of investigation away from cognitive studies. Then George Miller, an early and influential cognitive theorist, provided detailed evidence that the capacity for short-term information storage is limited. In what has to be one of the most provocative opening paragraphs of a cognitive psychology paper, Miller declared: "My problem is that I have been persecuted by an integer. . . . [T]his number has followed me around, has intruded in my most private data, and has assaulted me from the pages of our most public journals. This number assumes a variety of disguises, being sometimes a little larger and sometimes a little smaller than usual, but never changing so much as to be unrecognizable" (Miller, 1956, p. 81). In this paper, titled "The Magical Number Seven, Plus or Minus Two," Miller suggested that people can keep only about seven items active in short-term storage, and that this limitation influences performance on a wide range of mental tasks.

What data supported Miller's claim? Tests of short-term memorization, such as repeating a series of digits, showed that regardless of how long the series is, correct recall of digits appears to plateau at about seven items (though for some people this plateau number is a little lower and for some it is a little higher; Guildford & Dallenbach, 1925). Miller made a further, and critical, point: that although there is a limitation on the number of items that can be simultaneously held in short-term storage, the definition of an "item" is highly flexible, and subject to manipulation. Specifically, Miller (1956) suggested that single items can be grouped into higher level units of organization he called chunks. Thus, three single digits could be chunked together into one three-digit unit: 3 1 4 becomes 314. What determines how much information can be chunked together? Miller suggested that chunking might be governed by meaningfulness. For example, if the numbers 3 1 4 are your area code, it is a very natural process to store them together as a chunk. These grouping processes seem to be ubiquitous in language, where we effortlessly group letters into word-chunks and words into phrase-chunks. Indeed, this may be why our ability to maintain verbal information in short-term storage is better than for other types of information.

The key notion of Miller's chunk idea is that short-term storage, though possibly subject to certain constraints, is not rigid but amenable to strategies, such as chunking, that can expand its capacity. This notion is still very much present in current thinking about working memory. However, although the notion of a "magical number" is still part of current ideas regarding short-term storage capacity, recent work has suggested that this number might not actually be 7 ± 2, as Miller suggested, but instead may be much less—3 ± 1. This revised estimate comes from a review of studies suggesting that storage capacity is much lower than seven when participants are prevented from using strategies such as chunking or rehearsal (Cowan, 2001).

Miller's (1956) work drew attention to the concept of short-term storage and its functional characteristics. However, other influential evidence suggesting the distinct nature of the short-term storage system came from studies of amnesics who, like H.M. (see Chapter 5), showed grossly impaired long-term memory but relatively intact performance on immediate recall tasks (Baddeley & Warrington, 1970; Scoville & Milner, 1957). As a result, a common view emerged that short-term storage was structurally and functionally distinct from long-term storage and could be independently studied. In particular, it seemed that short-term memory, as this capacity began to be called, could be uniquely defined in terms of its short duration and high level of accessibility. During the 1950s and 1960s much research was devoted to examining these characteristics.

2.2.1. Brevity of Duration

A central idea regarding short-term memory was that information would be available only for a very brief period if it were not rehearsed. An experimental technique for studying short-term memory called the Brown-Peterson task was developed to test that idea (Brown, 1958; Peterson & Peterson, 1959). Participants are typically given a string of three consonants to memorize and then prevented from engaging in active rehearsal (that is, from saying the consonants to themselves), perhaps by being asked to count from 100 backward by 3s. After variously set delays, participants would be asked to recall the string. Measuring recall accuracy in relation to the delay

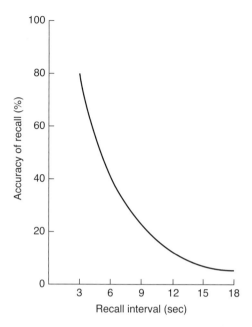

FIGURE 6–2 Short-term recall related to delay interval in the Brown-Peterson task
Typically, accuracy in recalling short consonant strings decays to about 50 percent by 6 seconds and
almost to zero by 18 seconds if rehearsal is blocked.
(Peterson, L. R., & Peterson, M. J. (1959). Short-term retention of individual verbal items. *Journal of Experimental
Psychology, 58,* 193–198, Fig. 3, p. 195 [adapted].)

interval showed the time course of forgetting. After a delay as short as 6 seconds, recall accuracy declined to about 50 percent, and by about 18 seconds recall was close
to zero (Figure 6–2). These findings suggested the shortness of short-term storage.
(About this time investigations were also being conducted on an even briefer form of
storage—termed *sensory memory*—that serves to keep a perceptual representation
of a stimulus persisting for a few hundred milliseconds after the sensory input is
gone; Sperling, 1960.)

However, in work that followed, a controversy arose as to whether the forgetting
of information was truly due to a passive decay over time, or rather due to interference
from other, previously stored information (similar to the controversy regarding long-
term memory, discussed in the previous chapter). The argument favoring the role of interference was bolstered by the fact that participants' recall performance tended to be
much better in the first few trials of the task (when proactive interference from the earlier trials had not yet built up). Moreover, if a trial was inserted that tested memory for
a different type of information than that sought in the previous trials (for example,
switching from consonants to vowels), participants' recall performance greatly increased on the inserted trial (Wickens et al., 1976). The debate over whether information is lost from short-term memory because of decay, in addition to interference, has
not been resolved, and the question is still studied today (Nairne, 2002).

2.2.2. Ready Accessibility

The high level of accessibility of information stored in short-term memory was demonstrated in a classic set of studies conducted by Saul Sternberg (1966, 1969a), which we briefly considered in Chapter 1. We now consider these findings in greater detail. A variable number of items, such as digits (the memory set), were presented briefly to participants at the beginning of a trial and then removed for a minimal delay. Following the delay, a probe item appeared and participants were to indicate whether or not the probe matched an item in the memory set. The time required to respond should reflect the sum of four quantities: (1) the time required to process the probe item perceptually, (2) the time required to access and compare an item in short-term memory against the probe item, (3) the time required to make a binary response decision (match–nonmatch), and (4) the time required to execute the necessary motor response. Sternberg hypothesized that as the number of items in the memory set increased, the second quantity—the total time required for access and comparison—should increase linearly with each additional item, but the other three quantities should remain constant. Thus, Sternberg hypothesized that when the response time was plotted against the number of memory set items, the result would be a straight line on the graph. Moreover, the slope of that line should reveal the average time needed to access and compare an item held in short-term memory. The results were as predicted—the plotted data formed an almost perfect straight line, and the slope indicated an access plus-comparison time of approximately 40 milliseconds (Figure 6–3). The hypothesis that information held in short-term memory could be accessed at high speed was certainly borne out by these findings.

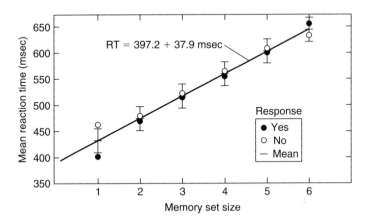

FIGURE 6–3   Recognition time related to memory set size in the Sternberg item recognition task

As the number of items to be memorized—the memory set size—increases from one to six, the time to evaluate a probe increases in a linear manner with about a 40-millisecond increase per additional item. The best-fitting line for the data obtained is plotted here; it is very close to the actual data points.

(Sternberg, S. (1969). The discovery processing stages: Extension of Donders' method. In W. G. Koster (ed.), *Attention and Performance II*. Amsterdam: North-Holland.)

More recent work, however, has called into question the fundamental assumption underlying Sternberg's interpretation of the results of this experiment: that short-term memory scanning proceeds sequentially, one item at a time. In particular, as discussed in Chapter 1, sophisticated mathematical modeling techniques show that similar linear curves could be found from a parallel scanning process that accesses all items simultaneously. In some of these models, the increase in response times is due to the decreasing efficiency of the parallel process as the number of items held in short-term memory increases (McElree & Dosher, 1989; Townsend & Ashby, 1983). But even assuming parallel scanning, the time to access information in short-term memory is very short indeed. Thus, even the more recent accounts retain the basic idea that information held in short-term memory is very quickly accessible.

2.3. The Atkinson-Shiffrin Model: The Relationship of Short-Term and Long-Term Memory

The notion that short-term and long-term memory are distinct modes of storing information was further articulated in the model proposed by Richard Atkinson and Richard Shiffrin (Figure 6–4) (Atkinson & Shiffrin, 1968). In this model, short-term memory serves as the gateway by which information can gain access to long-term memory. The function of short-term memory is to provide a means of controlling and enhancing, via rehearsal and coding strategies (such as chunking), the information that makes it into long-term memory. The Atkinson-Shiffrin

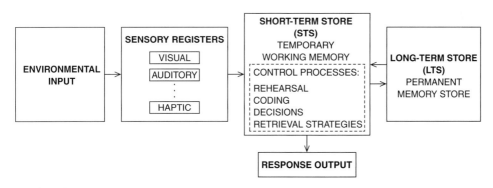

FIGURE 6–4 The Atkinson-Shiffrin model of memory

This model, also termed the modal model, suggests that the flow of information from sensory input to long-term memory must first pass through short-term memory. Information from the environment is registered by sensory receptors—visual, auditory, haptic (relating to touch), and others—and passed to short-term memory. Here it is rehearsed or otherwise manipulated before entering long-term memory; here also are strategies for retrieving information from long-term memory.

(R. C. Atkinson & R. M. Shiffrin, "The control of short-term memory." *Scientific American*, Aug. 1971, Vol. 225, No. 2. Reprinted with permission.)

model was highly influential because it laid out a comprehensive view of information processing in memory. In a nod to the statistical notion of the mode, it is still referred to as the modal model of memory, the model most frequently cited.

Yet today the modal model does not have the influence it once had, and most psychologists favor a different conceptualization of short-term storage, one that is not exclusively focused on its relationship to long-term storage and includes a more dynamic role than storage alone. This shift was reflected in the increasing use of the term "working memory" which better captures the notion that a temporary storage system might provide a useful workplace in which to engage in complex cognitive activities.

What caused this shift in perspective? For one thing, the Atkinson-Shiffrin model is essentially sequential: information passes through short-term memory before entering long-term memory. But neuropsychological data were showing that this assumption is not correct. Some patients with brain damage (typically to the parietal lobe) who showed drastic impairments in short-term memory nevertheless were able to store new information in long-term memory in a fashion comparable to that of neurologically healthy people (Shallice & Warrington, 1970). This finding demonstrated that information can gain access to the long-term memory system even when the short-term memory system was dramatically impaired. The Atkinson-Shiffrin model could not account for this result: with a poorly functioning short-term memory, according to Atkinson-Shiffrin, long-term storage should also be impaired.

Another strand of evidence, from behavioral experiments with neurologically healthy people, suggested that there is not a single system for short-term storage but multiple ones. Alan Baddeley and Graham Hitch (1974) asked participants to make simple true–false decisions about spatially arrayed letters: for example, shown "B A" they were to decide whether the statement "B does not follow A" was true or false. Before each trial, the participants were *also* given a string of six to eight digits (which according to Miller should fill the capacity of short-term memory) to repeat immediately after each true–false task. If the short-term memory store is critical for performing complex cognitive tasks and there is only one short-term store available, then performance on the reasoning task should drastically decline with the addition of the digit-memorization task. However, this was not the case. The participants took slightly longer to answer questions but made no more errors when also holding digit strings in short-term memory. From these results Baddeley and Hitch argued that there are multiple systems available for short-term storage and that these storage systems are coordinated by the actions of a central control system that flexibly handles memory allocation and the balance between processing and storage.

2.4. The Baddeley-Hitch Model: Working Memory

The dynamic concept of "working memory"—as opposed to the passive nature of a simple information store—is at the heart of the Baddeley-Hitch model, a system that consists of two short-term stores and a control system. Three important characteristics differentiate this model from the Atkinson-Shiffrin model.

First, the function of short-term storage in the Baddeley-Hitch model is not primarily as a way station for information to reside en route to long-term memory. Instead, the primary function of short-term storage is to enable complex cognitive activities that require the integration, coordination, and manipulation of multiple bits of mentally represented information. Thus, in the "A–B" reasoning problem described earlier, working memory is required to (1) hold a mental representation of the two letters and their spatial relationship to each other, (2) provide a workspace for analyzing the statement "B does not follow A" and deciding that it implies that "A follows B," and (3) enable comparison of the mental representations of the letters and statement.

Second, in the Baddeley-Hitch model there is an integral relationship between a control system—a **central executive**—that governs the deposition and removal of information from short-term storage and the storage buffers themselves. This tight level of interaction is what enables the short-term stores to serve as effective workplaces for mental processes.

Third, the model proposes (as implied earlier) at least two distinct short-term memory buffers, one for verbal information (the **phonological loop**) and the other for visuospatial information (the **visuospatial scratchpad**). Because these short-term stores are independent, there is greater flexibility in memory storage. Thus, even if one buffer is engaged in storing information, the other can still be utilized to full effectiveness. The supervision of these storage systems by a central executive suggests that information can be rapidly shuttled between the two stores and coordinated across them.

The three components of the Baddeley-Hitch model interact to provide a comprehensive workspace for cognitive activity (Figure 6–5). Applying the terms of the Baddeley-Hitch model to the "A–B" task, the phonological loop was occupied storing the digits, and the visuospatial scratchpad did much of the cognitive work in evaluating the spatial relationships in the true–false task. Coordination was supplied by the central executive, which transformed information from reading the statement (essentially in the verbal store) into a mental image on the visuospatial scratchpad. These interactions meant that performance on the reasoning task did not decline greatly when digit memorization was added.

FIGURE 6–5   **The Baddeley-Hitch model of working memory**

Two distinct storage buffers, one for verbal and the other for visuospatial information, interact with a central executive controller.

(Baddeley, A. D., & Hitch, C. J. (1974). Working memory. In G. Bower (ed.), The psychology of learning and motivation (Vol. VIII, pp. 47–89). New York: Academic Press. Reprinted with permission from Elsevier.)

The Baddeley-Hitch model was a major departure from earlier theories about short-term memory in that it emphasized neither its duration nor its relationship to long-term memory, but rather its flexibility and critical importance to ongoing cognition. In the years since his first work on the model, Alan Baddeley has been a major figure in working memory research, continuing to elaborate on the initial conception of the working memory model and providing a great deal of experimental support for its validity and usefulness.

✔ Comprehension Check:

1. What evidence suggested that information in short-term memory is very quickly accessible?
2. What distinguishes the Baddeley-Hitch model of working memory from the Atkinson-Shiffrin model?

3. UNDERSTANDING THE WORKING MEMORY MODEL

Baddeley's conceptualization of working memory is still highly influential and serves as a source of an enormous amount of research. The initial idea of a central controller interacting with dual short-term memory buffers has been retained over the years, and certain aspects of the model have been further elaborated by the work of a number of investigators. In particular, intense research has focused on storage within verbal working memory—the phonological loop—because so much of everyday cognition (especially for students and academics!) seems to rely on this cognitive function.

3.1. The Phonological Loop: When It Works and When It Doesn't

Read the digits below to yourself and then, immediately, close your eyes and try to remember the digits, silently. After a few seconds, repeat them aloud.

7   5   9   4   1   3   2

How did you do in recalling the numbers accurately? It's no coincidence that there were seven digits in the series. The demonstration was meant to mimic the ordinary experience of hearing and remembering a telephone number.

How did you accomplish the task? Many people report that when they read the digits silently they "hear" them in their head, in the sound of their own voice. Then, when their eyes are closed, they "rehearse" the sounds, repeating the words silently to themselves. The subjective experience seems to be of speaking the digits "in your mind." Does this experience match yours?

The idea that verbal working memory involves both a "mind's ear" (that heard the digits when you read them) and a "mind's voice" (that repeated them in rehearsal) is central to current thinking about the phonological loop. It has been proposed that the phonological loop system involves two subcomponents: a *phonological store* and an *articulatory rehearsal* process (Baddeley, 1986). When visually presented verbal information is encoded, the information is transformed into a sound-based, or "auditory-phonological," code. This code is something like an internal echo-box, a repository for sounds that reverberate briefly before fading away. To prevent complete decay, an active process must refresh the information, and this is where the idea of a "loop" comes in. The active refreshment comes via articulatory rehearsal, as you voice internally the sounds you heard internally. (The process seems very like our ability to "shadow"; that is, to repeat quickly something that we hear, whether or not we understand it—an indication that the phonological loop may be involved in language learning.) Once the verbal information is spoken internally by the mind's voice in rehearsal, it can then be again heard by the mind's ear and maintained in the phonological store. In this way a continuous loop plays for as long as the verbal material needs to be maintained in working memory. The first step of the process—translation into a phonological code—is of course necessary only for visually presented material. For auditory information, such as speech, initial access to the phonological store is automatic.

This idea sounds intuitive, because the experience of this kind of internal rehearsal seems universal, and that has been part of its appeal. For example, in your conversation about the movie, it is likely that you would be using the phonological loop to rehearse the key points you want to make and also time-sharing this same system to help process your friend's speech.

It is significant that this description of the phonological loop component of verbal working memory includes a number of characteristics that should be testable. First, verbal working memory capabilities should depend on the level of difficulty of both "phonological processing" (translating verbal information into a sound-based code) and "articulatory processing" (translating verbal information into a speech-based code). Second, because working memory is flexible, performance on verbal working memory tasks will not be catastrophically disrupted if for some reason the phonological loop component is unusable: in that case, other components, the central executive and the visuospatial scratchpad, kick in. Thus, in your movie conversation, if verbally processing your friends' ideas temporarily uses up too much capacity of the phonological loop, you might be able to use the visuospatial scratchpad to rehearse your ideas, possibly by using visual mental imagery—forming a mental image of your ideas rather than thinking of them in verbal terms. Third, the phonological loop model suggests that the two primary components of verbal working memory—phonological storage and articulatory rehearsal—are subserved by functionally independent systems, and hence should be dissociable. All these hypotheses have been tested in experiments, and all have held up.

Behavioral studies have suggested that phonological and articulatory factors significantly affect verbal working memory performance. One example is the phonological similarity effect: when items simultaneously stored in working memory have to be serially recalled, performance is significantly worse when the items to be maintained are phonologically similar—that is, when they sound the same (Conrad & Hull, 1964). The effect is thought to be caused by confusions that arise when similar sound-based codes are activated for the different items in the phonological loop. This finding can easily be informally appreciated. Try holding these two strings of letters in working memory, one after the other:

D   B   C   T   P   G   K   F   Y   L   R   Q

In the first string, the letters all have the "ee" sound; in the second list, all the letter sounds are distinct. Which did you find easier to remember and repeat? In these tasks, the typical error is substituting a phonologically similar item, such as "V" for "G."

The other part of the phonological loop, articulatory processing, or the "speaking" of presented items by the inner voice, is reflected in the word-length effect. Performance on a recall task is worse when the items to be maintained are long words, such as *university, individual,* and *operation,* than short words, such as *yield, item,* and *brake.* The key factor seems not to be the number of syllables per se, but rather the time it takes to pronounce them: performance is worse for two-syllable words that have long vowel sounds, such as *harpoon* and *voodoo,* than for two-syllable words with short vowel sounds, such as *bishop* and *wiggle* (Baddeley et al., 1975). The phonological loop model accounts for the word-length effect by the assumption that pronunciation time affects the speed of silent rehearsal, which requires speech-based processing. The longer it takes to rehearse a set of items in working memory, the more likely those items will have been dropped from the phonological store.

The relationship between pronunciation time and working memory performance was further tested in a study involving children bilingual in Welsh and English (Ellis & Hennelly, 1980). The names of the digits in Welsh have the same number of vowels as the English names but generally have longer vowel sounds and consequently take longer to say. As predicted, when performing digit-span tests in Welsh, the children scored significantly below average norms. However, when they performed the tests again in English their scores were normal. Follow-up studies have confirmed that the faster an individual's speech rate, the more items can be recalled correctly from working memory (Cowan et al., 1992).

What happens when the normal operation of the phonological loop is disrupted? The Baddeley-Hitch model suggests that the central executive and the visuospatial scratchpad take over and with the phonological loop out of operation phonological similarity and word length should no longer have an effect on working memory. Can this hypothesis be tested? Yes, by experiments based on dual-task interference. Participants are asked to maintain visually presented words in working memory while simultaneously producing overt and irrelevant speech, a task that interferes with phonological processing and rehearsal of the information. (Imagine that, in your movie conversation, while you are trying to keep in mind the point you want to make you also have to say the word *the* over and over again out loud; you can see how such conditions might make it almost impossible to rehearse your thoughts). Under these conditions, termed articulatory suppression, performance is significantly, although not catastrophically, impaired (demonstrating that although working memory is partially disrupted, it is still working). But critically, neither the phonological similarity nor the word length effect is present—which is as predicted because these effects are thought to be due to the phonological loop, which is rendered useless by the conditions of the experiment (Baddeley, 1986; Baddeley et al., 1984).

Converging evidence for the phonological loop model has come from the results of studies of patients with brain damage. One of them, P.V., was a woman, then 28 years old, who had suffered a stroke that damaged a large extent of her left hemisphere, especially the cortical regions thought to be involved in language processing (Basso et al., 1982; Vallar & Baddeley, 1984; Vallar & Papagno, 1986). Despite this damage, a number of P.V.'s language processing abilities remained intact. For example, she could clearly perceive and comprehend spoken speech. Nevertheless, P.V. suffered a dramatic decline in performance on verbal working memory tasks, especially those involving auditorily presented information. P.V.'s poor auditory verbal working memory—she had a span of only about two items—might be expected if the damage to her brain had selectively targeted the phonological loop; if that were the case, she would have become more reliant on the visuospatial scratchpad in attempting verbal working memory tasks.

And in fact, when performing verbal working memory tasks with visually presented items, P.V. showed no evidence of word-length effect or phonological similarity effect, thus suggesting that the visuospatial scratchpad rather than the phonological loop was engaged for storage. But for auditorily presented information the scratchpad is not much help: the information would first have to be processed phonologically before it could be translated to a visuospatial code. When doing tasks with auditorily presented words, P.V. did show a phonological similarity effect but no word-length effect. This suggested that P.V. was forced to use the phonological buffer—which was why she showed a phonological similarity effect—but because this buffer was defective, the information could not be appropriately transferred to the articulatory rehearsal system—which was why she did not show a word-length effect.

A number of patients have been identified who, like P.V., have selective auditory-verbal short-term memory deficits. Their common pattern of deficits and area of brain damage suggest that the phonological store component of verbal working memory has been damaged in these patients, and that this component relies on the left inferior parietal cortex (Vallar & Papagno, 1995).

Is there evidence that storage and rehearsal are functionally independent processes, as predicted by the phonological loop model? It should be possible to determine functional independence based on patterns of behavioral performance. If word length (which affects rehearsal) and phonological similarity (which affects storage) target independent components of the phonological loop, then manipulations of word length and phonological similarity should not interact with each other. That is exactly what behavioral studies showed: the magnitude of the phonological

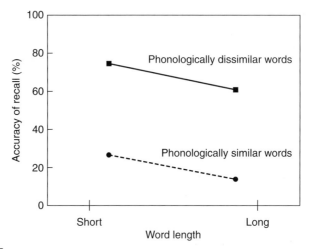

FIGURE 6–6 Independence of the effects of word length and phonological
similarity

An immediate recall task presented participants with five words that were either phonologically similar (such as FASTER, PLASTER, MASTER, TASTER, and LASTED) or dissimilar (such as FAMOUS,
PLASTIC, MAGIC, TEACHER, and STAYED), and were either short (two syllables) or long (four syllables). Both similarity and greater word length decreased recall performance, but the parallel slopes of
the lines indicate that the two effects are independent.

(Adapted from Longoni, A. M., Richardson, J. T. E., & Aiello, A. (1993). Articulatory rehearsal and phonological
storage in working memory. Memory and Cognition, 21(1), 11–22. Reprinted with permission.)

similarity effect on performance was not influenced by word length, and vice versa
(Figure 6–6) (Longoni et al., 1993).

Of course, behavioral data can provide only one kind of evidence for functional
independence. Results from brain-based studies provide a different kind of evidence,
showing that separate systems support phonological storage and rehearsal.

On the one hand, studies of patients with brain damage have documented a relationship between left inferior parietal damage and phonological storage impairments, and a relationship between left inferior frontal cortex damage and articulatory
rehearsal impairments (Vallar & Papagaro, 1995). (The left inferior frontal cortex,
also referred to as Broca's area, is known to be involved with language.) On the
other hand, neuroimaging studies have provided a means to examine these relationships in neurologically healthy participants. Such studies can show whether
these brain regions are in fact the ones engaged during normal processing conditions. For example, participants in one study were asked to memorize a series of
six visually presented items, either six English letters or six Korean language characters (none of the participants were speakers of Korean) (Paulesu et al., 1993). The
researchers assumed that the phonological loop system would be engaged to maintain the English letters but not utilized for the Korean characters (because the
sounds represented by the characters were unknown to the participants). This
assumption was validated by testing the effects of articulatory suppression—as

expected, articulatory suppression impaired memory performance for the English letters, but had no effect on memory for the Korean letters. PET images revealed increased blood flow in both left inferior parietal cortex (storage) and left inferior frontal cortex (rehearsal) only for the English letters (Figure 6–7a on Color Insert I). It is interesting that activation was also observed in brain structures associated with motor-related components of speech, even though the task did not require participants to speak overtly. The speech-related brain activity was thus thought to represent "internal speech" or subvocal rehearsal.

In a second experiment, Paulesu and colleagues (1993) attempted to dissociate regions associated with phonological storage from those involved in rehearsal. They asked the same participants to perform rhyme judgments on the English letters, deciding whether each letter in turn rhymed with "B." Here the researchers assumed that the rhyme task would engage rehearsal but not storage, and so it proved. In contrast to the results for the English letter group in the first experiment, in which there was increased blood flow in both brain regions, this time only the left frontal cortex was activated; the left parietal cortex was not active above baseline (Figure 6–7b on Color Insert I). Thus, behavioral and neuroimaging results converge to establish the dissociability of the storage and rehearsal components of verbal working memory.

However, additional neuroimaging studies suggest a more complex picture. For example, different subregions of Broca's area (which is crucially involved in producing speech) appear to be engaged at distinct points in time during the delay period of working memory tasks (Chein & Fiez, 2001). The investigators argue that the more dorsal region of Broca's area is active only during the first part of the delay period, and is involved in the formation of an articulatory rehearsal program; in contrast, the more ventral region of Broca's area is active during the remainder of the delay period, and is involved with the act of rehearsal itself. Neuroimaging studies continue to play an important role in refining and reshaping the verbal working memory model.

The larger question is what is the true function of the phonological loop in cognition? Surely it did not arise just to help us retain letter strings or telephone numbers! It seems intuitive that the phonological loop would have to play some role in language processing, because it is so clearly integrated with language comprehension and production systems. One hypothesis is that working memory—specifically, the phonological loop—is not critical for *comprehension* of familiar language, but it is essential for *learning* new language (Baddeley et al., 1998), a challenge experienced both by children learning their first language and by adults learning a second one or acquiring new vocabulary. It may be that evolution has imbued us with a specific expertise in repeating what we hear, even if we don't initially understand it. This form of imitation is something that even young infants can do, and it may provide a means for helping us learn new words via a linkage of sound and meaning.

Developmental data strongly support this claim: the level of children's ability to repeat nonwords strongly predicts the size of their vocabulary one year later (Gathercole & Baddeley, 1989). The patient P.V. was found to be completely unable to learn the Russian equivalent of any words in her native Italian despite extensive practice (Baddeley et al., 1988). Yet she could learn a novel association between two Italian words, indicating that her general learning abilities were intact when dealing with items that were phonologically familiar to her. But her impairment prevented her from being able to accomplish the short-term storage of phonologically unfamiliar items (in her case, Russian words) that apparently is needed to accomplish longer term learning. Thus, the data support the idea that the phonological loop has a primary function as a language-learning device, but that this functionality can be exploited to support a wide range of verbal working memory tasks.

3.2. The Visuospatial Scratchpad

Think of a familiar room (not the one you're in now!). What objects are on the walls? Name them in order, starting from the door and moving clockwise around the room. Now ask yourself, did you do this by "looking around your room with your mind's eye"? If so, you have just engaged your visuospatial scratchpad.

The ability to develop, inspect, and navigate through a mental image is thought to be a cardinal function of visuospatial working memory. (See Chapter 4 for a more extensive discussion of imagery.) A classic experimental study examined these memory functions by having participants answer questions about an outlined capital letter (Figure 6–8a) (Brooks, 1968). Participants were instructed to form a visual mental image of the letter and then navigate around it. At each corner, they had to answer yes or no to the question, is this corner at the extreme top (or extreme bottom)

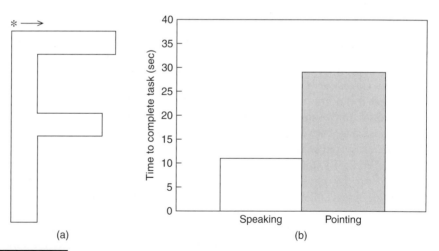

(a)   (b)

FIGURE 6–8   A visuospatial imagery and interference task

(a) As participants mentally navigated around the figure, starting at the asterisk, they were to answer yes or no questions about each corner as they reached it. (b) The time to respond was considerably longer when participants had to point to a printed YES or NO than when they spoke their responses, suggesting that the spatial movements interfered with the mental navigation.

(Brooks, L. R. (1968). Spatial and verbal components in the act of recall. *Canadian Journal of Psychology, 22*, 349–368.)

of the letter? To test whether the participants were using visuospatial representations to do the task, some participants were instructed to point to the word YES or NO printed irregularly on a page, and others had to speak the words "yes" or "no." The hypothesis was that if the classification decision depended on visuospatial representations, then requiring the pointing—a visuospatially based response—would interfere with performance. This is exactly what was found; participants took almost three times as long to perform the task when they had to point in response than when they had to speak (Figure 6–8b).

These results, and those of many other studies that followed, suggest that mental navigation is an inherently spatial process (Logie, 1995). The subjective experience of moving the mind's eye from one spatial location to another also suggests the possibility that visuospatial working memory depends on brain systems that plan movements of the eyes (or possibly other parts of the body), just as verbal working memory depends on brain systems involved with planning speech (Baddeley & Lieberman, 1980). Interestingly, this movement planning system might also be the basis for spatial rehearsal, the process of mentally refreshing stored locations to keep them highly accessible. The idea is that when you rehearse spatial locations in working memory (think of mentally visualizing driving directions to turn left at the next block, and then right at the stoplight), you are actually utilizing the same systems that would help you move your eyes or body toward that location. And just as rehearsal of verbal information does not require actual speech, it is thought that rehearsal of spatial information does not require actual eye (or body) movements. Instead, spatial rehearsal may involve *covert* shifts of attention to memorized spatial locations (Awh & Jonides, 2001).

In other words, just as we can keep our attention focused on a place in space without actually physically looking at it, we might also be able to keep remembered locations in memory by covertly focusing our attention on those remembered locations. An example: think of being at a party and talking with one friend, keeping your eyes focused on him, while also paying attention, out of the corner of your eye, to the gestures of another friend to your left.

This analogy leads to concrete predictions. It is thought that paying attention to a spatial location will enhance perceptual processing at that location. If the systems for spatial working memory are the same as those for spatial attention, then keeping a particular location in spatial working memory should also enhance perceptual processing of visual information that is physically presented at the remembered location. This prediction was tested behaviorally (Awh et al., 1998). In a spatial working memory task single letters (the cues) were briefly presented in varying locations on a display; after a short delay, another letter (the probe) was presented. In one condition, participants had to remember the location of the cue, and to decide whether the probe was in the same location. In another condition, it was the identity of the letter cue that had to be maintained, and participants had to decide whether the probe had the same identity. Additionally, during the delay participants had a second task—to classify the shape of an object appearing at different locations. On some trials the object appeared in the same location as the letter cue that was being maintained. It was found that the shape-classification decision was made more quickly when the shape's location matched that of the cue, but only when the information being maintained was the location of the cue. This result suggested that maintaining a location in working memory facilitates the orienting of attention to that location (which is what improved the speed of the shape-classification task).

Neuroimaging studies have provided even stronger evidence that rehearsal in spatial working memory and spatial selective attention draw on at least some of the same processes, by demonstrating that they both rely on the same right-hemisphere frontal and parietal cortex brain regions. Maintaining a spatial location in working memory produced enhanced brain activity in visual cortex regions of the opposite hemisphere, as expected because of the contralateral organization of these brain regions (Figure 6–9 on Color Insert J) (Awh & Jonides, 2001; Postle et al., 2004). These results suggest that spatial working memory is accomplished by enhancing processing in brain regions that support visual perceptual processing of those locations.

As the compound nature of its name implies, information processed by the visuospatial scratchpad is of two sorts: spatial, like the arrangement of your room, and visual, like the face of a friend or the image of a favorite painting. It seems that different types of codes may be required to maintain these two types of nonverbal information on the visuospatial scratchpad. For example, we seem to have the ability to "zoom in" on images like faces and paintings, magnifying particular features (Kosslyn, 1980). And we are able to decompose objects into constituent parts and transform them. We can, for example, imagine how a clean-shaven friend would look with a beard. These mental operations seem to be inherently nonspatial, yet nevertheless they require an accurate visual representation to be maintained and manipulated within working memory. Thus, visuospatial working memory may be composed of two distinct systems, one for maintaining visual object representations and the other for spatial ones.

The distinction between object and spatial processing is clearly in line with observations about the visual system: there is a great deal of evidence for distinct neural pathways involved in processing spatial and object visual features (respectively, the dorsal "where" and ventral "what" pathways) (Ungerleider & Mishkin, 1982; see discussion in Chapter 2). In monkeys it has been found that this distinction is also present for working memory: neurons in the dorsal region of the prefrontal cortex respond especially strongly to stimuli during a spatial working memory task, whereas neurons in the ventral prefrontal cortex respond especially strongly during an object working memory task (Wilson et al., 1993). In humans, some patients with brain damage have shown selective impairments on nonspatial mental imagery tasks (for example, making judgments about the shape of a dog's ears), but not on those involving spatial imagery (for example, rotating imagined objects) (Farah et al., 1988). The reverse pattern has been observed with other patients, demonstrating a double dissociation (Hanley et al., 1991). Neuroimaging studies have also tended to show dissociations between brain systems involved in spatial and in object working memory (Courtney et al., 1996; Smith et al., 1995), although these dissociations have been most reliable in posterior rather than prefrontal cortex (the region identified in monkey studies) (Smith & Jonides, 1999). The specific characteristics of object working memory, such as whether or not it involves a distinct storage buffer or rehearsal system, are not yet well worked out, and the question of a dissociation of object and spatial working memory remains a topic of continued study.

3.3. The Central Executive

The component that most strongly differentiates the idea of working memory from the earlier conceptions of "short-term memory" is the *central executive*. This part of the model (1) determines when information is deposited in the storage buffers; (2) determines which buffer—the phonological loop for verbal information or the visuospatial sketchpad for visual—is selected for storage; (3) integrates and coordinates information between the two buffers; and, most important, (4) provides a mechanism by which information held in the buffers can be inspected, transformed, and otherwise cognitively manipulated. These functions all depend on the central executive's controlling and allocating attention. The central executive determines both how to expend cognitive resources and how to suppress irrelevant information that would consume those resources (Baddeley, 1986). The central executive is what does the "work" in working memory. (And it does more; in fact, many of the functions associated with the central executive may be only indirectly related to working memory itself. See Chapter 7 for a discussion of the role of the central executive in other contexts.)

The notion of a central executive is supported by studies that show a dissociation between the functions listed above and the operation of the two storage systems. These investigations often involve the problem of **dual-task coordination**, that is, the process of simultaneously performing two distinct tasks, each of which typically involves storage of information in working memory. Participants are given two such tasks, one visuospatial and one auditory-verbal, to perform at the same time. (An example would be doing the "corners-of-the-F" task shown in Figure 6–8 while quickly repeating spoken words.) The assumption is that managing performance of the two tasks requires some sort of time-sharing. If the central executive is specifically required to manage the coordination—the time-sharing—of the two tasks, then it should be possible to find effects of dual-task performance over and above those present when each of the tasks is performed in isolation.

For example, one study examined patient groups with cognitive deficits, matching patients with early-stage Alzheimer's disease with healthy adults of the same age (Baddeley et al., 1991). The hypothesis was that much of the cognitive impairment exhibited by people in early stages of Alzheimer's disease is due to a dysfunctional central executive. In the single-task phase, participants performed each of two tasks, one auditory and one visual, separately. In the dual-task phase, participants performed the two tasks simultaneously. An important feature of the study was that the difficulty of each task could be adjusted for each participant individually to enable him or her to reach a fixed level of behavioral performance. Because all participants had the same level of single-task accuracy, any decrements in performance on the dual-task condition could not be attributable to difficulties in single-task performance. The results were clear in showing that the Alzheimer's patients were markedly worse than the healthy participants in the dual-task condition. The results support the idea that the coordination of storage demands requires the engagement of the central executive.

Neuroimaging studies as well as behavioral ones have explored whether executive functions can be distinguished from short-term storage. One test has been to compare

---

D E B A T E   **How Are Working Memory Functions**
                                         Organized in the Brain?

The Baddeley-Hitch model of working memory sug-
gests distinctions both in terms of the buffers used to store different kinds of information
(verbal or visuospatial) and in terms of different working memory processes (storage or executive
control). How do these distinctions map onto brain organization? Findings in both neuroimaging studies in humans and neural recording studies in monkeys suggest that the prefrontal cortex is an important
component of working memory. Yet these studies appear to suggest differences in the way that prefrontal
cortex is organized with respect to working memory.

In the monkey work, neurons in dorsal areas of prefrontal cortex were found to be specialized for spatial working memory, whereas ventral prefrontal cortex neurons were specialized for object working memory (Wilson et al., 1993). Thus, the monkey results suggested a **content-based organization** of working
memory in prefrontal cortex; that is, spatial and object information is maintained in different regions. However, the neuroimaging data in humans have not reliably supported such distinctions in the location of prefrontal cortex activity based on the content of working memory. Instead, the neuroimaging data have
tended to find that dorsal prefrontal cortex is engaged by working memory tasks that require manipulation
in addition to maintenance, whereas ventral prefrontal cortex is active even when the task requires only
simple maintenance. Thus, it has been argued that the human neuroimaging data support a **process-
based organization** (that is, storage and executive control processes are carried out in different regions).
The resolution to the controversy is not yet clear, but some researchers have suggested that the two sets
of findings may not be incompatible (Smith & Jonides, 1999).

maintenance versus *manipulation* in working memory, contrasting the brain activity occurring in tasks where the information only has to be briefly stored and then recalled
(maintenance) against a similar task in which the stored information also has to be
mentally transformed in some way (manipulation). Significantly increased activation
was observed when participants in such a study had to recall a sequence of letters in
alphabetical order, as opposed to simply recalling them in the order in which they were
presented (D'Esposito et al., 1999). A further point: the increased activation was observed in the dorsal regions of the prefrontal cortex. This result, and others, suggest
that different portions of the prefrontal cortex implement different processes used in
working memory: specifically, simple maintenance recruits ventral regions of prefrontal
cortex, and information is manipulated in more dorsal areas (Figure 6–10 on Color
Insert K) (Owen, 1997; Postle & D'Esposito, 2000). However, this view remains controversial; see the accompanying *Debate* box.

3.4. Are There Really Two Distinct Storage Systems?

It seems obvious that we use distinct mental representations for verbal and visual information while we perform tasks. But what about the storage of such information?
Must verbal and visual information be maintained in two distinct buffers, as the

working memory model has it—could they not be maintained in one? Alternatively, might there not be a multitude of buffers, each specialized for a distinct type of information? A number of theorists have proposed many-store accounts (Miyake & Shah, 1999), and this question is unresolved. Nonetheless, there is fairly good experimental evidence in favor of the distinction between verbal and visuospatial working memory.

Many of the behavioral studies demonstrating dissociations between the two working memory systems involve the dual-task methodology, and the results demonstrated the selective nature of interference with working memory. As we have seen, performance on the F-task (with participants instructed to respond verbally or by pointing) was better when participants could respond verbally. When participants then had to make judgments about words in a sentence, pointing produced the better performance (Brooks, 1968). In another study, participants were similarly asked to make judgments about words in a sentence, in this case while either manually tracking a light or repeating the word *the* over and over. The pattern of results was the same as in the F-task: when the interference with this verbal task was verbal, performance was more impaired than when the interference was spatial (Baddeley et al., 1973). The implication? Competition between two verbal (or two spatial) tasks produced more-impaired performance, which is evidence for separate resources or stores for each type of information.

Neuropsychological data support the functional and structural independence of visuospatial and verbal working memory, such as was seen with P.V., whose working memory, poor for spoken words, improved considerably when the test items were presented visually (Basso et al., 1982). P.V., and other patients with similarly impaired verbal working memory, had brain damage involving the left hemisphere. Patients have been studied who show the opposite pattern of deficits—selectively impaired visuospatial working memory (De Renzi & Nichelli, 1975)—and in these instances the brain damage involved the right hemisphere. Thus, the neuropsychological data are consistent with the idea that verbal and visuospatial working memory rely on distinct brain systems.

Moreover, neuroimaging studies have demonstrated dissociations between the two working memory systems in neurologically healthy participants. Many of these studies have also pointed to a pattern in which verbal working memory is associated with the left hemisphere, nonverbal working memory with the right (Smith et al., 1996). This fits the general finding that language-related functions are more associated with the left hemisphere of the brain, whereas spatial processing is more associated with the right. The neuroimaging studies have also indicated that the picture might be a bit more complicated than is indicated by the behavioral and neuropsychological investigations. Many of the working memory tasks that have been studied with neuroimaging involve storage over longer intervals, keeping track of temporal order, and maintenance in the face of distracting information. In these complex tasks, the brain areas activated by verbal and visuospatial working memory tend to be highly overlapping (D'Esposito et al., 1998; Nystrom et al., 2000). So the picture is more complicated, but not necessarily contradictory. Perhaps under more difficult conditions all parts of the working memory system are recruited to perform the task most effectively.

This kind of flexible use of the storage buffers—with their deployment controlled by the central executive—is a key characteristic of the working memory model.

✔ **Comprehension Check:**

1. What evidence suggests that working memory depends on both phonological processing and articulatory processing?
2. What working memory functions are thought to be handled by the central executive?

4. HOW WORKING MEMORY WORKS

We have looked at the boxes in the working memory model, which are the storage systems and the central executive; much of the research we have discussed provides evidence that these components are distinct and dissociable. The boxes may have sub-boxes: components of the verbal and visuospatial storage systems may be independent, and within each of these systems there may be distinct specialized mechanisms for storage and for the refreshment of stored items via rehearsal. Now the questions concern what is inside the boxes of the model: *What* powers them? *How* do these storage and control mechanisms actually work in the brain?

4.1. Mechanisms of Active Maintenance

A place to begin is to ask "What is the nature of the memory representation that is stored?" This question has been prominent throughout the history of psychology and neuroscience. Today there is fairly widespread agreement that long-term memory representations occur as relatively permanent strengthenings (or weakenings) of connections among neural populations. Using the vocabulary of neural net models, we can call these changes weight-based memory, since the memory representation takes its form in the strength or weight of neural connections. Although weight-based memories are stable and long lasting, we are not always aware of them because they reflect a structural change in neural pathways that is revealed only when those pathways are excited by input.

Short-term storage appears to rely on a different mechanism, which we can call activity-based memory, in which information is retained as a sustained or persistent pattern of activity in specific neural populations (O'Reilly et al., 1999). Activity-based memories are more highly accessible but less permanent. Activation signals can be continually propagated to all connected neurons, but once the activation level changes, the originally stored information is lost. Think about holding a thought in your mind, such as the point you want to make in the movie conversation. While the information is in this state, in your working memory, it is highly accessible, and so it can directly influence what words you choose to speak and you can make your point fluently. But what if instead your point was lost from working memory? In that case, you'd have to retrieve it from long-term memory. The information is probably still around, stored in your brain, but less accessible, until it is retrieved into working memory. In that interim, you are likely to be at a loss for words, even if you have a chance to jump into the conversation. These characteristics fit well with the functional distinctions between a rapid, on-line, and flexible working memory and the slower but more permanent long-term memory.

Much of what has been learned about how activity-based storage occurs in the brain has come from neuroscience studies utilizing direct neural recordings in monkeys as they perform simple working memory tasks. A typical experimental procedure is the delayed response task: a cue is briefly presented and, after a delay—during which presumably the information in the cue must be held in short-term storage—a response is required. Many of these studies are designed so that the response takes the form of eye movements. The animal is trained by rewards to keep its eyes fixated on a central location in a display screen. A brief visual cue, such as a spot of light, appears in one of up to eight spatial locations on the display, the animal still focusing straight ahead. After a specified delay of between 2 and 30 seconds, the animal is given a "go" signal to move its eyes to the exact location in which the light appeared. Again, this is accomplished by training, with rewards of juice or food for a correct response. Because the location of the cue varies randomly from trial to trial, the animal must rely on its working memory of the cue location in order to make the correct response.

Direct neuronal recordings suggest that the working memory representation used to perform this task relies on the activity patterns of single neurons. In particular, certain neurons in the dorsolateral region of prefrontal cortex have shown transient increases in their activity level (as measured by increased firing rate) during presentation of the cue, whereas others showed firing rate increases throughout the delay interval (Fuster, 1989; Goldman-Rakic, 1987). A critical finding was that activity during the delay was stimulus specific: a given neuron would show activation only in response to a cue in a particular location on the display (Figure 6–11) (Funahashi et al., 1989). These sustained responses could not be due to perceptual stimulation; there was no perceptual stimulation during the delay.

This evidence is correlational. Can it be strengthened to show that the activity in these neurons actually serves as the working memory representation? Well, what happens when the animal *doesn't* remember? (That is, it did not hold the location of the cue in short-term storage.) What about activity in the delay periods preceding *incorrect* responses? Would it be less than in the periods preceding *correct* responses? Yes, indeed; that is exactly what was observed. In trials when an error was made, the activation during the delay showed either no change from the baseline rate or a premature decay of activity in neurons thought to be coding for that location.

Intriguing evidence, but still correlational only. The changes in neuronal firing may have reflected a brain-wide lapse in attention or motivation rather than a specific loss of information. To address this concern, other animal studies have made direct interventions in neural functioning and observed the results. In one study, small areas of cortical tissue were removed from regions of dorsolateral prefrontal

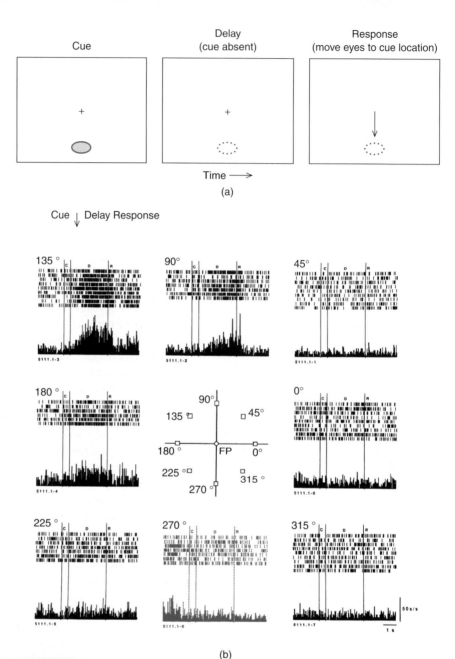

FIGURE 6-11 Neuronal activity in monkey prefrontal cortex during a delayed response task

(a) The task: a cue (the blue ellipse) is briefly presented in one of eight locations surrounding the fixation point (the plus sign). During a delay period the monkey must maintain this location in working memory. Following a go signal (removal of the plus sign), the monkey makes an eye movement to-ward the remembered location. (b) Averaged activity traces for a representative neuron in the prefrontal cortex. Each trace represents activity during the trial in which the cue was presented in the location corresponding to the layout shown. For this neuron, activity was selective to spatial location: it increased during the delay only when the cue was presented directly below the fixation point, the position shown in part (a).

(Funahashi, S., Bruce, C. J., & Goldman-Rakic, P. S. (1989). Mnemonic coding of visual space in the monkey's dorsolateral prefrontal cortex. *Journal of Neurophysiology, 61*(2), 331–349. Used with permission.)

cortex after the animals had learned the requirements of the experiment. After the lesioning, the animals made the correct responses to most locations, but failed miserably when the cues were presented in locations that normally would have been coded by the neurons in the lesioned area. The lesions had produced *mnemonic scotoma*, or memory blindspots (Funahashi et al., 1993). (The behavioral deficit was neither perceptual nor motor: the animals performed correctly in a control task in which the visual cue at the critical location was present throughout the delay.) Similar results have also been observed in procedures that cooled the neurons to a temperature at which they do not function normally (Bauer & Fuster, 1976). Such cooling procedures are important because they rule out effects due to new learning or functional reorganization following permanent brain damage. In these cooling studies the degree of impairment was related to the length of the delay: the longer the delay, the greater the impairment.

Do humans also show evidence that information storage in working memory occurs through sustained neural activity? Direct experimental single-cell neural recordings are not normally performed on humans (although they are sometimes made before medically necessary neurosurgical procedures). Instead, the research tool is neuroimaging, which can also provide information about how neural activity changes over time and in response to specific events, although at a coarser temporal resolution and only in terms of the activity of larger scale neural populations (rather than single neurons). Nevertheless, these studies have provided remarkably convergent evidence to that observed in single-cell research. Specifically, during the delay period of working memory tasks, dorsolateral prefrontal and parietal cortex show sustained increases in activity levels (Cohen et al., 1997; Courtney et al., 1997; Curtis, 2005).

These results are critical because they inform our notions regarding the nature of short-term storage in the brain. First, they suggest that the distinction between long-term memory and short-term memory—at least in many cases—is not so much in terms of structurally distinct brain systems, but rather in terms of the mechanisms by which the information is maintained. For short-term storage, information is maintained in the form of sustained neural activity, whereas for long-term storage this is unlikely to be the case. Second, for at least some brain regions, short-term memory storage is not like RAM in a computer at all, because RAM is completely flexible with regard to what information gets stored in different locations. Instead, in the brain some neural populations appear to be specialized for the storage of very selective kinds of information, such as a particular location on a screen in front of you. This result indicates a further degree of content-based organization of working memory, as discussed in the *Debate* box on page 260. Yet it is still not known how widespread such content-based organization is in the brain. For example, does it extend to more abstract forms of verbal information, such as meaning? Similarly, it appears as if the neural populations store information by a sustained increase of firing rate. But what happens when more than one item is being stored in working memory? How does the brain store the increased information?

In studies of nonhuman primates, these questions have been hard to answer, because it is very difficult to train an animal to maintain more than one item at a time. Humans, however, can be given more complex assignments. We know that multiple items can be stored in working memory simultaneously. Thus, it has been possible to examine brain activity when different numbers of items simultaneously must be maintained in working memory. Increasing that number could produce two possible effects on brain activity: (1) The number of active brain regions may remain constant, but the activity levels in at least some of those regions may increase with each additional item stored. (2) The number (or size) of active brain regions may increase, but the activity level of an already active region would not change with additional items. In fact, the studies to date have tended to show a mix of these two patterns: increasing the number of items to be stored appears both to increase the number of active brain regions and also the levels of activity in those regions.

The effect of changing the load on working memory is commonly studied by the N-back task, in which participants are presented with a continuous stream of items, such as letters, and instructed to decide, as each item is presented, whether it matches one that is N items back in the series, where N typically equals 1, 2, or 3. (The participant is also instructed to answer "no" if in a given case there are no preceding items or the number of preceding items is less than N.) The value of N is varied in order to examine how performance and brain activity varies with working-memory load. Thus, given the sequence

$$D \quad F \quad F \quad B \quad C \quad F \quad B \quad B$$

participants may be asked to say yes or no to a match when $N = 1$. Here the correct answers are no–no–yes–no–no–no–no–yes. In a three-back condition for the same series, that is, $N = 3$, the correct responses are no–no–no–no–no–yes–yes–no. An elegant aspect of the N-back task is that the experimenter can hold constant the identity and order of items presented; the only factor that is changed is the working memory load (1 in a 1-back task vs. 3 in a 3-back task). This means that the possibility of "confounding variables"—other, extraneous, factors that also change with the task condition—is eliminated.

Neuroimaging studies of participants engaged in the N-back task have generally found that brain activity in lateral prefrontal cortex (and parietal cortex as well) increases with the value of N in a linear relationship (Figure 6–12) (Braver et al., 1997). A common interpretation of this result is that maintaining each additional item in working memory places an additional demand on working memory storage buffers as they approach capacity.

Note, however, that the N-back task requires control or executive processes in addition to storage, and that these demands on the central executive also increase with N. Both the identity of an item *and its ordinal position* must be stored, and then the test item matched to the one in the appropriate position. More sequence "tags" for the items are needed as the number of items increases. The need for manipulation of information as the item changes means that it is not clear whether to interpret linearly increasing activity in a brain region in these N-back trials as reflecting maintenance processes or executive processes.

A number of studies have tried to address this issue by examining brain activity during simpler tasks, such as item recognition (the task studied by Sternberg, discussed earlier in Section 2.2.2). Here the demands on maintenance far outweigh

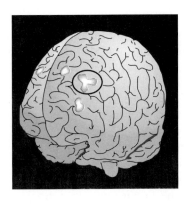
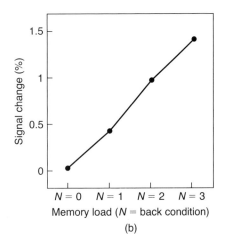

(a)   (b)

FIGURE 6–12 Working memory load effects in prefrontal cortex during the N-back task

(a) The image shows the surface of a participant's brain. Blue-white areas indicate regions of the prefrontal cortex that demonstrated increased activity with working memory load. (b) Change in activation in the region circled in the image as a function of N-back condition (N = 0, 1, 2, or 3). Activation increased linearly with N.

(Braver, T. S., Cohen, J. D., Nystrom, L. E., Jonides, J., Smith, E. E., & Noll, D. C. (1997). A parametric study of prefrontal cortex involvement in human working memory. *Neuroimage, 5*(1), 49–62. Reprinted with permission from Elsevier.)

those on control processes. Order of items is not an issue; all that is required is a simple match of the test item, and the number of items stored (varied in different trials) is well within the capacity of working memory. These studies have tended to confirm the findings of the N-back task: increases in memory load are associated with increased activity in the prefrontal and parietal cortex. An additional benefit of the item recognition task is that brain activity can be independently computed for each phase of the trial: encoding, maintenance, and retrieval. This fMRI work has demonstrated that the number of items influences the activity of the prefrontal and parietal cortex specifically during maintenance (Jha & McCarthy, 2000). The overall picture is still complex, however; a large number of items may result in greater activation during encoding and retrieval than during maintenance (Rypma & D'Esposito, 1999). This latter finding is consistent with the idea that prefrontal cortex is also important for executive control processes, such as influencing what information is selected for storage and also how the maintained information is used.

The neuroimaging and neuronal recording studies provide strong support for the idea that representations in working memory rely on sustained activity in selected neural populations. These findings are a critical first step in understanding the nature of working memory coding, but in and of themselves they do not tell us exactly how such sustained neural activity arises. What causes the neurons in prefrontal cortex to keep firing after the perceptual information has come and gone? In other words, what powers the maintenance process? An answer to this question is critical not only for understanding why information in working memory can be kept at a high level of accessibility for a short period of time, but also why there appear to be such strict limitations on both the length of time and number of items that can be stored. One hypothesis is that short-term maintenance occurs as connected neurons recirculate activity among themselves. That is, each neuron in the circuit participates in a reverberatory loop, holding onto the information by both "talking" and "listening"—by communicating the information to the other neurons it is connected to, and by later receiving that information from those same (or other) connected neurons (Hebb, 1949). Each time a neuron passes the information on, it provides an input signal to the other neurons it is connected to that allows those neurons also to "pass it on." Thus, the neurons in the circuit mutually support one another, each neuron contributing to the maintenance of the information.

Sounds good—but are brain neurons really equipped to form such a reverberating circuit? To begin to grapple with this question, psychologists and neuroscientists have built small-scale neural network models to investigate the mechanisms of working memory. In some of these models, the simulated neurons are implemented as computer programs with properties that attempt to capture closely what is known about the physiology and structure of real neurons and their organization within circuits. Now the question is, can the simulated neural circuit achieve short-term information storage with model neurons showing activity patterns that are comparable to those observed in experimental recordings of real neurons? The answer: models have been very successful in showing that short-term information storage can be achieved by means of recirculating activity in neural circuits, and the behavior of model neurons can approximate closely what has been seen in the experimental data (Durstewitz et al., 2000).

Moreover, such models have been used to demonstrate how the limits of storage capacity and storage duration might arise. When more than a few items are maintained simultaneously in overlapping reverberating circuits, they can interfere with each other to a great enough extent that circulating activity is disrupted during the delay period (Lisman & Idiart, 1995; Usher & Cohen, 1999). Similarly, if irrelevant signals leak into such a circuit, potentially from ongoing perceptual input, this can also interfere with the process of reverberation and lead to disruption of the sustained memory signal over time (Brunel & Wang, 2001; Durstewitz et al., 2000). Thus, the models can be used to predict the types of task situations that will be most vulnerable to the loss of information in working memory. A final benefit of these models is that they can be observed over time, to see how the behavior of the system evolves. A number of such models are publicly available as demonstrations on the Internet. If you are interested in looking at an example, try http://www.wanglab.brandeis.edu/movie/spatial_wm.html.

4.2. The Role of the Prefrontal Cortex in Storage and Control

Although the prefrontal cortex is not the only area of the brain that shows sustained activation during the delay in working memory tasks—other areas of increased activation observed in various studies have included, most notably, the parietal and temporal cortex (Fuster, 1995)—the prefrontal cortex appears to play a special role in the active maintenance of information. This was demonstrated most clearly in a study in which neuronal activity in nonhuman primates was recorded in both temporal and prefrontal cortex during performance of a delayed matching task (Miller et al., 1996). In this variant of an item recognition task, intervening distractor items were shown in the delay between presentation of the item and the subsequent probe. Both temporal and prefrontal cortex showed selective and sustained activation during the delay; however, when a distractor was presented, stimulus-specific activation disappeared in the temporal cortex but was maintained within the prefrontal cortex. This work is examined in greater detail in the accompanying *A Closer Look* box.

In studies that used a spatial variant of the task, the same pattern was observed between parietal and prefrontal activity; the distractors reduced parietal but not prefrontal response (Constantinidis & Steinmetz, 1996). Similar results in humans have been obtained through fMRI studies (Jiang et al., 2000). Taken together, these results suggest that there might be specializations within the brain not just for the type of material being stored in working memory, but also for different ways of storing the information. The prefrontal cortex might be specialized for maintaining information over longer intervals (but still in terms of the sustained activity characteristic of working memory) or in the face of distraction, whereas temporal or parietal brain systems might have different mechanisms for maintaining information over shorter intervals.

In addition to the data suggesting that the prefrontal cortex plays a role in maintaining information in the face of distraction, many human neuroimaging studies have suggested that it is also involved in executive functions such as dual-task coordination or manipulation of information within working memory. Moreover, experimental research conducted on patients with frontal lobe damage seems to indicate an impairment of central executive functions rather than of working memory per se (discussed in Chapter 7) (Stuss & Benson, 1986). What do such findings say about the Baddeley-Hitch model of working memory, in which there is a strict segregation of storage and control functions? In that model, the two buffer systems, the phonological loop and the visuospatial scratchpad, serve as "slave" systems that only maintain information, and the central executive, which controls the operation of the buffers, has no storage capability itself. How might the neuroimaging data be reconciled with cognitive theory? One possible resolution might be that different subregions of prefrontal cortex carry out storage and control functions. And indeed, as we have seen, some studies have shown prefrontal regions selectively involved in the maintenance (the ventral regions) and the manipulation (the dorsal regions) of information. However, these findings appear to be more a matter of degree than a clear-cut distinction and, moreover, they have not been consistently observed (Veltman et al., 2003).

There is another possibility: that the prefrontal cortex is the brain region where goal-related information is represented and actively maintained (Braver et al., 2002; Miller & Cohen, 2001). In this goal-maintenance model (Figure 6–13), the

A CLOSER LOOK
Mechanisms of Working Memory Storage in the Monkey Brain

We consider the work of Earl Miller, Cynthia Erickson, and Robert Desimone, who investigated neuronal activity in primates during performance of a delayed matching task. They reported their work in 1996 in a paper titled "Neural Mechanisms of Visual Working Memory in Prefrontal Cortex of the Macaque," *Journal of Neuroscience, 16*(16), 5154–5167.

Introduction

The investigators were interested in examining the activity of neurons in the prefrontal cortex during a working memory task in which distracting information was presented during the delay interval. The activity of prefrontal neurons was compared to the response observed from neurons in the temporal cortex. The hypothesis was that only the prefrontal neurons would maintain a sustained, stimulus-specific response in the face of distraction.

Method

To test responses of individual neurons, the investigators implanted tiny electrodes into neurons in the cortex of macaque monkeys. In one study, 135 neurons in the inferior temporal cortex were examined; in a second study, involving the same two monkeys, 145 prefrontal neurons were recorded. By measuring the change in voltage on the electrode, the electrical activity of the neuron was monitored to determine how strongly the neuron was responding (in terms of the number of action potentials, or electrical spikes, generated per second). Activity was recorded from each sampled neuron across a large number of trials of a delayed response working memory task. The task involved the presentation of a series of line-drawn objects. The monkey was instructed (through gradual, rewarded training) to release a lever when the presented object matched the sample, the first object presented in the trial. Between the sample and the match, anywhere from 0 to 4 intervening nonmatching drawings might be presented; these were to be ignored.

| Sample | Nonmatching test items (distractors) | Match |

The monkey's memory task, which required memorizing a sample and responding when a match appeared after a variable number of intervening distractor objects.

(Miller, E. K., Erickson, C. A., & Desimone, R. (1996). Neural mechanisms of visual working memory in prefrontal cortex of the macaque. *Journal of Neuroscience, 16*(16), 5154–5167. Copyright © 1996 by the Society for Neuroscience. Reprinted with permission.)

Results

In both the temporal and prefrontal cortex, many of the neurons were stimulus selective: they showed a greater response when one object was presented as the sample relative to other objects. It is important that this stimulus-selective response was retained when the sample was removed from the display (this is the memory representation of the sample). In the prefrontal cortex neurons the stimulus-selective activity persisted even when intervening distractor items were presented, and continued until the presentation of the match item. However, in the temporal cortex, the stimulus-selective response was abolished following the presentation of the first distractor.

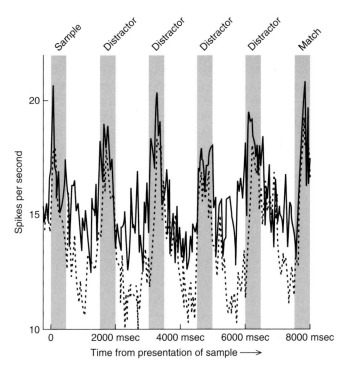

Average neuronal activity in the prefrontal cortex during distractor periods following presentation of sample objects (indicated by bars) that elicit a strong response (solid lines) or a weak response (dashed line). The heightened activity is maintained throughout each distractor and delay period, until the match object is presented.

(Miller, E. K., Erickson, C. A., & Desimone, R. (1996). Neural mechanisms of visual working memory in prefrontal cortex of the macaque. *Journal of Neuroscience, 16*(16), 5154–5167. Copyright © 1996 by the Society for Neuroscience. Reprinted with permission.)

Discussion

The finding that neurons in the prefrontal cortex and inferior temporal cortex retained a stimulus-selective pattern of activity during the delay period immediately following the sample suggests that both brain regions could be involved in activity-based short-term storage. However, the finding that only the prefrontal neurons retained this selective response across intervening distractor items suggests that the two brain regions serve distinct functions in working memory. One interpretation of the results is that the prefrontal cortex is critical for protecting actively maintained information from the disruptive effects of interference.

prefrontal cortex serves *both* a storage and a control function: the maintenance of information about a goal (storage) and a top-down influence that coordinates perception, attention, and action to attain that goal (control). The information stored in the prefrontal cortex may provide a context that aids the interpretation of ambiguous situations and the response to them. Just how might this work? Here's an example.

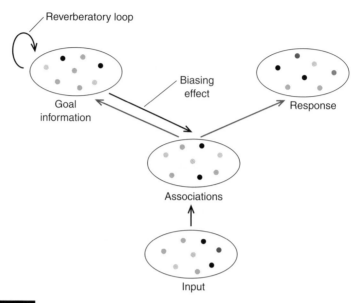

Reverberatory loop

Goal information

Biasing effect

Response

Associations

Input

FIGURE 6–13   The goal-maintenance model

In this model, goal information is represented in the prefrontal cortex as a pattern of activity. Reverberatory loops allow this activity to be sustained over delays, and feedback connections enable the maintained activity to bias the internal associations that are activated in response to perceptual input. In this way goal information is able to provide control over thoughts and behavior.

(Adapted from Braver, T. S., Cohen, J. D., & Barch, D. M. (2002). The role of the prefrontal cortex in normal and disordered cognitive control: A cognitive neuroscience perspective. In D. T. Stuss and R. T. Knight (eds.), *Principles of Frontal Lobe Function* (pp. 428–448). © 2002 Oxford University Press. Reprinted with permission of Oxford University Press.)

Suppose you have a regular route you drive, perhaps from a job to where you live. At an intersection, your route directly home is straight through, but you always get yourself in the leftmost lane because it has a left-turn arrow and so the traffic moves through faster, either turning left or going straight ahead, than from the other lanes. So ordinarily—the default pattern—you're in the leftmost lane but don't turn left. But, if you need to stop at the grocery store on the way home, as you do now and then, you must turn left at that intersection. Now you're stopped at the light: do you turn left or go straight ahead? That depends on your goal, which provides a context for determining your action: do you want to go home or to the store? You may very likely find that in the less frequent situation you have to keep the go-to-the-store goal active in working memory while you're waiting at the light, or you'll blow it and go straight ahead.

In the goal-maintenance view of the role of the prefrontal cortex in working memory, this is what's happening: As you wait at the stoplight, the goal of go-to-the-store is actively maintained in the prefrontal cortex, and this activation flows from the prefrontal cortex back to the brain systems serving perception, attention, and action to influence your response when the light turns green. Were the goal not actively maintained, you'd go straight ahead—your default route—and get home without the milk. The goal provides a context that influences your behavior, overriding your usual response in the situation.

The goal-maintenance theory of prefrontal involvement in working memory appears to be consistent with a wide range of both human and animal data (Miller & Cohen, 2001). For example, in studies with monkeys, careful analysis of the responses of prefrontal cortex neurons during behavioral tasks suggests that what is being maintained in their sustained activity patterns is not just a simple perceptual representation of the input, but rather something like the task-relevant features or behavioral rules of the situation (for example, if the light is red, then press the left button; Miller et al., 2002). Because the information being maintained in the prefrontal cortex is the most relevant for performing the task at hand, it could potentially be used to bias how new information is interpreted and how actions are determined. Is there a way to test such an idea?

In fact, the goal-maintenance theory has been implemented and tested in computational modeling studies in which the storage and control mechanisms could indeed work together to produce the patterns of performance that humans and animals exhibit in working memory tasks (Braver et al., 2002; O'Reilly et al., 2002; Rougier et al., 2005). The theory goes a long way toward demystifying the concept of the central executive in working memory by showing how control of behavior can occur in a neurobiologically plausible manner. Nevertheless, it is important to realize that there may be many possible executive functions related to working memory—updating, integration of information, transformation, buffer allocation, attention, and coordination—and it is not clear how these could arise solely from the goal-maintenance model. It is likely, as discussed in the next chapter, that executive processes other than goal maintenance are implemented in the prefrontal cortex.

Comprehension Check:

1. What evidence suggests that information is maintained in working memory through activity-based storage?
2. How have studies of the prefrontal cortex informed cognitive theories of working memory?

5. CURRENT DIRECTIONS

The Baddeley-Hitch model and the idea of a "mental workspace" took us a long way in the exploration of working memory. However, the close examination of the role of the prefrontal cortex, particularly the goal-maintenance model and the interaction of storage and control functions, leads to considerations of other hypotheses. The original model makes a structural distinction between storage and control; if that distinction is not rigid, other possibilities arise.

5.1. The Episodic Buffer

Even good models of cognition need an update after a while, and Baddeley (2000) recently refined his model of working memory to account for some limitations associated with the original Baddeley-Hitch model. The more recent version has added a third storage buffer, termed the episodic buffer, as a system that can serve as both an auxiliary store when the primary ones are overloaded or disrupted, and also as a site in which to integrate diverse types of information such as verbal and spatial content within working memory. Another key aspect of the episodic buffer is that it appears to be a place where short-term memories of complex information such as temporally extended events or episodes can be stored (hence, the name "episodic").

The inclusion of the episodic buffer into the working memory model appears to provide a nice solution to many peculiar findings that have accumulated over the years, findings that could not be easily accounted for by the original conception. As an example, read the following and then close your eyes and try to repeat it out loud: *The professor tried to explain a difficult cognitive psychology concept to the students, but was not completely successful.* You probably did pretty well at remembering most of the words. Now try this one: *Explain not but successful difficult a psychology the was to concept completely students cognitive to professor the tried.* Impossible, right? There is a huge difference between a meaningful 18-word sentence and one that has no meaning because the words are jumbled. What allows us to maintain such information in working memory when the number of words so vastly exceeds generally recognized capacity limits? One possibility, as Miller (1956) would have argued, is that we can chunk the information into larger, more meaningful units than single words. But how and where does such integration occur? At first blush, it seems that it might be in the phonological loop, because this holds verbal information. Yet the phonological loop is thought to use a sound-based code rather than a meaning-based one. Similarly, patients such as P.V., who are thought to have a completely damaged phonological loop, still show the sentence effect just described. P.V. has a word span of 1, but a sentence span of 5 words (Vallar & Baddeley, 1984). That is still lower than the normal range of 15 to 20, but it indicates that she might have been able to utilize a backup storage system that is more flexible with the type of information being stored. Perhaps the episodic buffer plays just such a role.

The episodic buffer is a relatively new idea, and so has not been put through many experimental tests as of yet. Moreover, the mixed nature of its function could indicate that it may actually be a part of the central executive rather than a storage component. Baddeley (2003) has indicated as much himself, which suggests that the separation of storage and control within working memory, so strongly advocated in the original version of the model, may be blurring in current conceptions. Such a view would fit well with the goal-maintenance account.

5.2. Person-to-Person Variation

A current focus of research on working memory is that of individual differences in working memory capacity. People vary widely in the ability to maintain items in working memory, and especially in maintaining these items under conditions of interference. Because working memory appears to be so important for mental processes such as problem solving and thinking, it is not surprising that these individual differences are associated with success in academic examinations (such as the SAT tests) and the learning of new and complex cognitive skills (such as computer programming). Indeed, some researchers have suggested that working memory capacity is related to general fluid intelligence, defined as the ability to solve problems and reason in novel situations (Kyllonen & Christal, 1990). An important question, then, is to determine more precisely what varying component of working memory is critical for predicting cognitive success and general intellectual ability.

A standard task for measuring working memory capacity, such as the one presented in Figure 6–1, essentially asks how many items a participant can store in working memory in the face of distraction (Conway et al., 2005). If working memory capacity is defined by number of items, and the ± 2 following the magic number 7 reflects individual variability, we might imagine that someone with a capacity of nine items might have a strong advantage in carrying out complex cognitive tasks over someone with a capacity of five items. That is, someone who can keep more information available in working memory might be more efficient, forget less, and be less reliant on the slower and less flexible long-term memory system.

An alternative, and more recent, idea suggests that what is being measured in tasks like this may not be storage capacity per se but rather the ability to keep goal-relevant information actively maintained in the face of interference (Engle, 2002). In this view, high working memory capacity can refer to the ability to keep even a single goal active under conditions of high interference. Researchers have shown that this ability is distinct from short-term storage capacity and that this function, not short-term storage capacity, correlates strongly with fluid intelligence and cognitive abilities (Engle et al., 1999). Further, these researchers suggest that this function is implemented in prefrontal cortex, a notion consistent with the role of prefrontal cortex in maintaining information in the face of distraction. Evidence suggests that this ability may be the component of working memory capacity that varies most strongly from person to person.

This idea was tested in a neuroimaging study that examined the brain response to distracting information occurring during performance of the N-back task (Gray et al., 2003). The distractors used were items that had recently been repeated but were not targets (for example, the second "F" in the sequence "B–T–R–F–T–F" where the task is to look for $N = 3$ matches). Participants measuring high in fluid intelligence were found to have a stronger activation response in the prefrontal cortex during distractor trials, even though there was no reliable difference among participants for nondistractors. Thus, people with high working memory capacities may be better able to keep goal-relevant information highly activated and ready for use when needed.

5.3. The Role of Dopamine

Researchers have found that patients suffering from certain forms of neurological or psychiatric illnesses have impaired working memory. These groups include patients with schizophrenia, Parkinson's disease, and Alzheimer's disease. Given the critical role of working memory in cognition, it is of clinical importance to determine whether there might be any drug treatments that could improve working memory in such populations. Interestingly, a number of studies in both animals and humans suggest that the neurotransmitter *dopamine* is especially important for working memory, and that drugs that increase levels of dopamine in the brain or facilitate the action of dopamine can enhance working memory capabilities (Luciana et al., 1998; Sawaguchi, 2001). Conversely, drugs that block the action of dopamine have the opposite effect and interfere with working memory (Sawaguchi & Goldman-Rakic, 1994).

In addition to the clinical relevance of this work, it also may influence our understanding of how working memory is normally implemented in the brain, and what can cause it to go awry at times, even in healthy individuals. Some theoretical accounts have suggested that dopamine may be critically important for helping to maintain ongoing information in the face of interference by signaling when information in working memory should be updated (Braver & Cohen, 2000; Durstewitz et al., 1999; Servan-Schreiber et al., 1990). Neurophysiological research suggests that dopamine can help to amplify strong signals and attenuate weak ones (Chiodo & Berger, 1986). Such a mechanism might be very useful in working memory if we assume that task-relevant information carries a stronger signal than the background noise of interference. It is suggestive that the anatomy of the dopamine system is such that dopamine-producing cells have a strong connection to the prefrontal cortex—the brain region that may be most important for protecting maintained information from distraction. Thus, a reasonable hypothesis is that dopamine input to the prefrontal cortex might play a key role in providing that region with interference-protection capabilities. Finally, there is some indication that dopamine levels and activity are highly variable, both over time within an individual (King et al., 1984) and across a population (Fleming et al., 1995). An intriguing possibility is that variability (possibly genetically based) in the dopamine system might be the neural source of differences in working memory seen in different people (Kimberg et al., 1997; Mattay et al., 2003).

✓ Comprehension Check:

1. How does the addition of an episodic buffer handle findings that are problematic for the original Baddeley-Hitch model?
2. According to the executive attention account, what is the source of person-to-person variation in working memory capacity?

Revisit and Reflect

1. *How is working memory used in cognition?*

   Working memory can be defined as the cognitive system that keeps task-relevant information stored in a highly active state so that it can be easily accessed, evaluated, and transformed in the service of cognitive activities and behavior. A potentially useful metaphor is the RAM of a computer. Working memory is used pervasively in everyday cognition. Not only is working memory used to keep a point in mind while listening to someone else talk, but it is also used in tasks as varied as calculating a tip in a restaurant, executing driving directions, parsing complex sentences, and planning a chess move. Because working memory is so pervasive in cognition, person-to-person variation in working memory capacity may be the fundamental component of individual differences in a wide variety of cognitive abilities.

Think Critically

- Imagine that your working memory was impaired. What aspects of your daily life do you think would be most disrupted?
- Do you think it is possible to "train" your working memory to be better? How might one go about doing this? Use the movie conversation as an example—how could you improve your performance in this kind of situation?

2. *How did the modern view of working memory arise?*

Early notions of working memory strongly linked it to consciousness; experimental research in the 1950s and 1960s focused on the characteristics of short-term storage and its distinction from long-term storage. Three primary findings emerged from this work: (1) 7 ± 2 chunks is the maximum capacity of short-term storage (although this number later proved to be an overestimate); (2) information may rapidly decay from short-term storage if not rehearsed; and (3) information in short-term storage can be very quickly accessed. The Atkinson-Shiffrin model provided a functional account of short-term storage as a necessary repository or gateway that enables efficient coding and access into long-term memory. However, later work revealed that normal storage in long-term memory can occur even with an impaired short-term memory system. The Baddeley-Hitch model reformulated the notion of short-term memory into the modern concept of working memory, which postulates multiple storage components and emphasizes the interaction with control processes.

Think Critically

- Do you think that working memory is just consciousness, and vice versa? Why or why not? Is "consciousness" the same kind of thing as information processing?
- Short-term storage is thought to be severely limited in both capacity and duration. Can you think of any advantages this limitation might confer? What might the world be like if both capacity and duration were unlimited?

3. *What are the elements of working memory?*

The Baddeley model has three components: the phonological loop (which stores and rehearses verbal information), the visuospatial scratchpad (which enables mental imagery and navigation), and the central executive (which directs information to one or the other of the storage buffers and coordinates, integrates, and manipulates that information). A number of lines of converging evidence from behavioral studies, neuropsychological patients, and neuroimaging data have suggested that visuospatial and verbal working memory involve distinct storage buffers.

Neuroimaging studies have provided some support for a distinction between maintenance and manipulation processes; manipulation of information seems to rely on lateral prefrontal cortex, whereas maintenance of information seems to rely more on ventral areas.

Think Critically

- How might studies of working memory in people who are blind or deaf (but who are fluent in sign language) inform our understanding of short-term storage buffers?
- One theory of the phonological loop suggests that it is based on our expertise at imitation. Can you think of any equivalent expertise we have that might be the basis for the visuospatial scratchpad?

4. *How does working memory "work" in the brain?*

The maintenance of information in working memory might be carried out through activity-based storage mechanisms involving the prefrontal cortex. Prefrontal neurons show sustained heightened activity during delay periods in working memory tasks. This prefrontal activity appears most critical in situations where the stored information has to be protected from sources of interference. Human neuroimaging studies have shown sustained prefrontal activity during the N-back task; moreover, this activity appears to increase in intensity with the number of items being simultaneously maintained. Detailed computational models have suggested that active maintenance in prefrontal cortex might arise from recirculating activity among local networks of neurons.

Think Critically

- Research using transcranial magnetic stimulation (TMS; see Chapter 1) has enabled studies to be conducted in which temporary and reversible "lesions" are produced in humans. What kind of effects might you predict if TMS were applied to the prefrontal cortex during different kinds of working memory tasks? How might this research be used to address unresolved questions regarding the nature of working memory?
- There have been reports of individuals with exceptionally large capacities for short-term storage, such as up to 100 digits (presumably due to increased chunk size). Imagine that you could scan the brains of such people while they performed working memory tasks such as the N-back or Sternberg item recognition task. What patterns would you predict?

5. *How might views of working memory change in the future?*

A wide variety of different models currently exist regarding the structure and components of working memory. Some, such as the Baddeley-Hitch model, focus on the storage side, emphasizing the distinctions between types of storage content (verbal, spatial) and the role of rehearsal in keeping information activated. Other models, such as the goal-maintenance account, focus more on the control side of working memory, emphasizing how active maintenance of goal-related information can be used to constrain attention, thoughts, and action. The control of behavior is multifaceted and likely to involve a variety of mechanisms. An important direction for future research will be to determine the precise relationship between executive processes and working memory.

Think Critically

- Working memory capacity predicts performance on tests such as the SAT and GRE. Thus, why not just replace the current standardized testing with a simple measurement of an individual's working memory capacity, using a short test like that illustrated in Figure 6–1? What might be the possible advantages, disadvantages, and implications of such a decision?

- Imagine that a drug becomes available that has been proven to enhance working memory function in healthy young adults. Would it be ethical to allow this drug to be made widely available? If you were involved in making this policy decision, what factors would influence you?

Executive Processes

Learning Objectives

You're on your own in the kitchen, preparing some pasta for dinner, music blasting in the background. The phone rings. It's a friend who wants you to do him a favor tomorrow and pick up a package when you're downtown. As you continue the conversation, your eyes go back to the stove and focus on the water to be sure that it's not boiling yet. Still chatting, you try to figure out how you'll fit your friend's errand into everything else you have to do downtown. Whoops, the water's boiling, and you realize you haven't started to heat the sauce—you blew it. Too many things to do going on at once!

To avoid domestic and social disaster in this situation—a ruined dinner, rudeness to your friend—in these few minutes you have to do five distinct things, some of them simultaneously: pay attention to getting the meal together, switch your attention to the phone call and continue to switch back and forth between phone and stove, ignore the background music while listening to your friend, plan how to schedule tomorrow's activities so as to include your friend's request, and monitor how the cooking is going. As you deal with the situation, at least five critical cognitive processes are in play:

- *The kind of selective attention that typically acts on the contents of working memory and directs subsequent processing so as to achieve some goal.* (You're focusing on tomorrow's schedule, which you've entered into working memory.) This kind of attention—often called **executive attention**—is to be distinguished from the kind that selects certain spatial positions in the outside world and determines what gets perceived in the first place (which is discussed in Chapter 3, *Attention*).
- *Switching executive attention from one activity, or process, to another* (from watching the pot to answering the phone).
- *Ignoring or inhibiting information that has already been perceived.* (Yes, you've been hearing the music—but now you hear it less while your friend is talking.)
- *Scheduling a sequence of activities.* (Can you postpone a planned coffee date for half an hour to give you time to make it downtown and back to campus?)
- *Monitoring your performance.* (How are you doing with that pot of salted water—will it never boil?).

These five processes are referred to as *executive processes;* the term comes from Alan Baddeley's (1986) influential model of working memory in which there are separate short-term storage systems for verbal and visual information and a central executive that operates on the contents in storage (discussed in Chapter 6, *Working Memory*). Executive processes organize our mental lives, just as a corporate executive coordinates a business's activities; in both cases the function is administrative, not "hands on." The corporate executive may reallocate resources to increase the size of the service department in the interest of improving quality control, but the actual repairs are made at a lower organizational level. Like the CEO, executive processes coordinate lower level processes (such as remembering words and adding numbers). If the phone rang right now, you'd be able to turn readily from the process of reading this line to the process of answering your phone because the executive process "switching attention" organizes the two activities.

More formally, we may define **executive processes** as processes that modulate the operation of other processes and that are responsible for the coordination of mental activity so that a particular goal is achieved. Processes that, like executive processes, operate on other processes are known as *metaprocesses.* (Although all executive processes are metaprocesses, not every metaprocess is an executive one, because it may not coordinate and control mental activity.)

This chapter addresses six questions about executive processes:

1. Are executive processes mediated by the frontal lobes?
2. What is executive attention, and how can it be modeled?
3. What is involved in switching attention?
4. What is response inhibition, and what is distinctive about it?
5. What mechanisms are used for sequencing information?
6. What is involved in monitoring our performance "on line"?

1. THE FRONTAL LOBE CONNECTION

One of the major reasons for thinking that executive processes form a distinct class of cognitive processes comes from relatively early studies of patients who had suffered frontal brain damage as a result of a closed head injury, injury caused by an external bump that does not pierce the skull. (Why do car accidents or other head-bumping incidents lead to damage in the frontal lobes more than to other places in the brain? Examine a skull sometime, and you will see that it has ridges on its inside surface; the sharpest and most protruding of these are adjacent to the frontal lobes, so a bang on the skull cuts deeper into the frontal lobes than elsewhere.) Of course, frontal damage can result from other events as well, for instance, from a stroke or from brief deprivations of oxygen. One of the oddest incidents—and most significant in its early influence on thinking about frontal lobe function—resulted from an accident to a railway worker, Phineas Gage, in 1848. Part of Gage's job was to pack explosives into drilled holes with a 3-foot-long rod called a tamping iron. When a charge went off prematurely, the tamping iron was driven into his head, entering below the left cheekbone and exiting through the top of his skull (Figure 7–1), and landing some distance away. Gage survived; but, although he

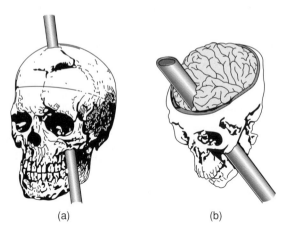

(a)   (b)

FIGURE 7–1   Phineas Gage, frontal-lobe patient

(a) This drawing of the reconstructed path of the tamping iron through Gage's head appeared in the 1868 account of the case by Dr. John M. Harlow, who treated Gage at the time of the accident and examined his skull after his death.

(Harlow, J. M. (1868). Recovery from the passage of an iron bar through the head. *Publ. Mass. Med. Soc.* 2:327–347. Found at: http://home.earthlink.net/~electrikmon/Neuro/artGage.htm.)

(b) A modern-day reconstruction, using computer techniques, that shows the areas of the brain that were destroyed. The study of Phineas Gage, who survived the accident and lived for another 13 years, marks the beginning of the systematic analysis of frontal-lobe function.

(H. Damasio, T. Grabowski, R. Frank, A. M. Galaburda & A. R. Damasio (1994). The return of Phineas Gage: The skull of a famous patient yields clues about the brain. *Science, 264,* 1102–1105. Found at: http://www.sciencemuseum.org.uk/exhibitions/brain/291.asp. Reprinted with permission.)

apparently recovered physically and suffered little intellectual damage, his behavior was radically changed. Before his accident he was trustworthy, hardworking, of calm demeanor; after it, he was irresponsible, impulsive, given to fits of temper and profanity. The physician who treated him at the time of the accident and later studied him, John M. Harlow, drew a connection between the area of greatest damage in the frontal lobes and the lack of social restraint that Gage showed subsequently.

In the twentieth century, Hebb and Penfield (1940) were the first to observe some of the most striking facts about frontal-lobe patients. Such patients perform relatively normally on an IQ test, yet are often incapable of leading anything like a normal life. It is as if they have all their cognitive components intact but have lost the ability to organize and control them. The obvious hypothesis was that the frontal lobes implement these control processes—the executive processes—and consequently damage to the frontal lobes leads to a breakdown in executive processes and a breakdown in normal life.

Consider the case of Dr. P., whose history is described in Lezak (1983) and adapted here. Dr. P. was a successful middle-aged surgeon who used the financial rewards of his practice to pursue his passions for traveling and playing sports. While undergoing minor facial surgery, he suffered complications that caused his brain to be deprived of oxygen for a short period. This led to damage in areas of the frontal lobes. This damage had profound negative consequences on his mental functioning, compromising his ability to plan, to adapt to change, and to act independently. Standard IQ tests administered after the surgery revealed Dr. P.'s intelligence still to be, for the most part, in the superior range; yet he could not handle many simple day-to-day activities and was unable to appreciate the nature of his deficits. His dysfunction was so severe that not only was returning to work as a surgeon out of the question, but also his brother had to be appointed his legal guardian. Previously Dr. P. had skillfully juggled many competing demands and had flexibly adjusted to changing situations and demands. Now, however, he was unable to carry out all but the most basic routines and those only in a rigid, inflexible manner. Furthermore, he had lost the ability to initiate actions and the ability to plan. His sister-in-law had to tell him to change his clothes, and his family managed to get him to do this on his own only after years of rule setting. He was able to work as a delivery truck driver for his brother's business, but only because his brother structured the day so that it involved minimal planning. His brother would give him information about one delivery at a time. After each delivery, Dr. P. would call in for directions to the next stop. Dr. P. was totally unaware of his situation. He seemed unconcerned and uninterested in how he was provided with clothes, food, and lodging, and was totally complacent about being a ward of his brother and sister-in-law. Formerly an outgoing man, he now spoke in a monotone and expressed little emotion. He did not initiate any activities or ask questions about his life, and was content to spend his free time watching television.

This is the story of a man in whom executive processes have broken down. Dr. P.'s inability to appreciate the nature of his deficits suggests a breakdown in self-monitoring; his inability to juggle competing demands implicates a deficit in attention-switching. And, most blatant, Dr. P. seemed to have completely lost the

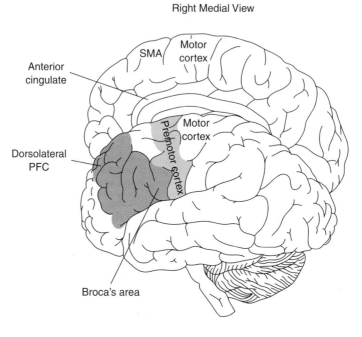

Right Medial View

Left Lateral View

FIGURE 7–2   Frontal lobe syndrome starts here

These views of the brain—a lateral view of the left hemisphere, and behind it a partial medial view of the right hemisphere—show the areas involved: the dorsolateral prefrontal cortex, the anterior cingulate, the premotor area, and, at the posterior end of the prefrontal cortex, Broca's area (note: SMA stands for supplementary motor area, to be discussed in Chapter 11).

(From *Fundamentals of Human Neuropsychology,* 5/E by Bryan Kolb and Ian Q. Wishaw. © 2003 by Worth Publishers. Used with permission.)

ability to sequence activities to achieve a goal. His condition is described as *frontal-lobe syndrome.*

Actually, the brain area involved is not the entire frontal lobe, but only the anterior part of it, the prefrontal cortex (PFC). Figure 7–2 is a simple schematic of the left side of the brain and distinguishes the PFC from the rest of the cortex. The PFC lies directly in front of the motor and supplementary motor areas. At the most posterior end of the PFC is Broca's area, which is known to be involved in speech (as described in Chapter 6). Portions of the premotor area may mingle with true PFC and are sometimes considered to be part of the PFC.

The PFC has many anatomical properties that make it suitable for implementing executive processes. For one thing, it is extremely large in humans, disproportionately so compared to most other primates. This suggests that the PFC may be responsible for some of the more complex activities that humans carry out, such as mentally sequencing a list of activities. For another, the PFC receives information from virtually all perceptual and motor cortical areas, and a wide range of subcortical structures as well. This mass of connections provides a good infrastructure for combining the diverse sources of information needed for complex behavior. The PFC also has multiple projections back to sensory, cortical, and motor systems that allow it to exert a top-down influence on other neural structures, including those mediating the perception of objects (Miller, 2000).

The idea that every executive process is primarily mediated by the PFC is the frontal executive hypothesis. This hypothesis has been widely accepted for a long time, and it has usefully stimulated a great deal of research. It also provides a conceptual framework for thinking that all executive processes are alike in critical ways. As we will see, the hypothesis is overstated, but there is indeed a special connection between executive processes and the frontal lobes.

Comprehension Check:

1. What evidence directly links executive processes to the PFC?
2. What properties of the PFC make it particularly suitable for mediating executive processes?

2. FRONTAL DAMAGE AND THE FRONTAL HYPOTHESIS

A number of tests that are used to diagnose frontal-lobe damage demonstrate the extent of deficits in executive processing. When administered to neurologically healthy people, these tests can also tell us something about the way executive processes work.

Perhaps the best known of these tests is the Stroop task (mentioned in Chapter 3), a classic psychological test of attentional function devised in the 1930s by J. Riddley Stroop and still widely used today in various forms (Stroop, 1935) (Figure 7–3). In the standard version the names of colors are presented in colored ink, and the participant's task is to name the ink color and ignore the color name. Sometimes the

BLUE   WHITE

BLACK   GRAY

GRAY   WHITE

BLUE   **BLACK**

FIGURE 7–3 A Stroop test for a two-color book

For both columns, state the color of the *ink* (don't read the word) as quickly as you can. Did you sense a difference in your performance on the two columns?

(From *Fundamentals of Human Neuropsychology*, 5/E by Bryan Kolb and Ian Q. Wishaw. © 2003 by Worth Publishers. Used with permission.)

name and print color are *compatible*, as when the word *blue* is printed in that color. At other times the color name and the print color are *incompatible*, as when the word *black* is printed in blue. Remember, the task is to name the *ink color*—so the correct answer in both examples here is "blue." With normal participants, accuracy is high even for incompatible trials, but it takes longer to respond to them than to compatible trials. It is as if participants have to do some extra processing on incompatible trials, but that such processing succeeds. Frontal-lobe patients who have damage to the PFC, particularly the dorsolateral (i.e., upper side) PFC, show a different pattern of results. Their accuracy level on incompatible trials is significantly lower than that of neurologically healthy participants. The standard interpretation of these results is that to succeed in the task, participants must selectively attend to the ink color or inhibit the color name (or both), and frontal participants are known to be impaired in selective attention and inhibition (Banich, 1997). Thus, we have some support for the idea that executive attention and inhibition are executive processes: they are clearly metaprocesses, and they are mediated by the PFC.

A word of caution: there's an intuitive sense in which attention and inhibition go together—it is hard to imagine focusing on something without at the same time ignoring something else. Put another way, it is hard to imagine processing some information without at the same time inhibiting the processing of other information. But can attention and inhibition be considered to arise from the same underlying process? This problem has bedeviled modern cognitive psychology since its inception. In Ulric Neisser's *Cognitive Psychology* (1967), a classic book that helped define the field, the author pointed out that the act of selective attention could be achieved by focusing on the to-be-attended representation or process, or by inhibiting all irrelevant representations and processes, and it is often difficult experimentally to tell focusing from inhibition. Recent models of executive attention (e.g., Cohen et al., 1996) contain both excitatory and inhibitory components. Although it is useful to begin our discussion with a concept of attention that includes either focusing or inhibitory components, we will later consider cases that clearly require inhibition of response. For now, when we talk of executive attention, keep in mind that inhibition may sometimes be involved as well.

The Wisconsin Card Sort task, illustrated in Figure 7–4, is another well-known test of frontal-lobe damage. Four stimulus cards are arrayed in front of the participant, each bearing a design with a distinctive value on each of three attributes: number, color, and shape (e.g., one white triangle; two bright blue stars; three light blue crosses; four circles of some other color—this text is limited in the number of colors it can present). From a deck of similar cards in which the values differ from those of the four stimulus cards (that is, the values are in different combinations, such as three white circles or one light blue triangle), participants must take each card in turn and match it to one of the stimulus cards. And here's the rub: participants are not told the criterion for matching—whether it is number, color, or shape—but only whether their match is "right" or "wrong." At first participants must guess the critical attribute, but since they receive feedback after every response they eventually home in on the right one. After they have sorted about 10 cards correctly, the examiner changes the critical attribute without warning. Normal participants soon figure out, from the feedback, first that the critical attribute has changed, and then what the new one is.

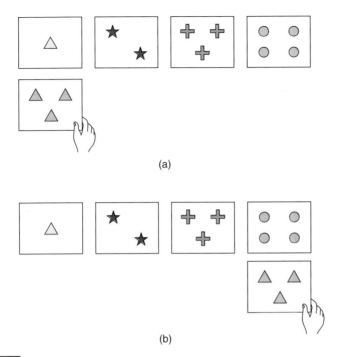

(a)

(b)

Interestingly, there is no difference between the performance of normal participants and that of frontal (PFC) patients in determining the first critical attribute, but there is a big difference in their ability to switch attributes—an example of switching attention. Normal participants switch critical attributes after a few trials of negative feedback, but frontal patients are far less able to switch attributes, and often keep going for many trials, continuing to sort in accord with the original critical attribute (Banich, 1997). Indeed, there are anecdotal reports of frontal patients who can tell you that the critical attribute has changed, but nevertheless continue to sort on the basis of the original attribute. This suggests that switching attention is another executive process that is compromised by frontal-lobe damage.

There is further systematic evidence that executive attention, inhibition, and attention-switching are involved in performance on frontal-lobe tests (see Miyake et al., 2000). For present purposes, it is sufficient to consider only one further frontal-lobe task, the Tower of Hanoi problem (Figure 7–5). (You might look on the Web for an electronic version of the Tower of Hanoi problem and play a few rounds; what's required in the task quickly becomes obvious.) In its simplest version the task involves

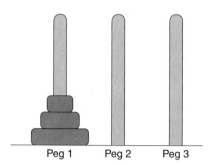

Peg 1   Peg 2   Peg 3

FIGURE 7–5   Three-disk Tower of Hanoi problem

At the outset all the disks are on the first peg, as shown here. The task is to move all the disks to peg 3, with the constraints that only one disk can be moved at a time and that a larger disk can never be placed on a smaller one.

three pegs and three different-size disks. At the outset, all the disks are on peg 1; the participant's task is to move all the disks to peg 3, with the constraints that only one disk can be moved at a time and that a larger disk can never be placed on a smaller one. A further wrinkle: participants are asked to solve the problem "in their head"—no objects to manipulate, no computer version, no paper and pencil. Once they've done this, participants are asked to show their solution (by actually moving the disks, or by the electronic equivalent). Behavioral experiments indicate one of the major strategies used: the participant represents the whole array in working memory, selectively attends to the top disk on peg 1, mentally moves it to peg 3, updates working memory with the new array, then selectively attends to the middle-size disk on peg 1, moves it to peg 2, updates working memory with a new configuration, and so on (e.g., Rips, 1995).

Frontal-lobe patients, particularly patients with damage to the dorsolateral PFC, perform poorly on the Tower of Hanoi problem, taking many more moves than do normal participants to achieve a solution (Shallice, 1982). In relation to executive processes, two points are critical. First, the Tower of Hanoi task involves attending to some disks while ignoring others, as well as switching attention between each mental move and updating working memory; thus, the usual suspects are involved. Second, the task involves goals ("get the big disk to the bottom of peg 3") as well as subgoals ("get the big disk on peg 1 out from under"). Thus, goals are decomposed into subgoals, and a big problem is broken into smaller ones, suggesting that analysis by subgoals and sequencing of steps are also executive processes. (These latter processes will be discussed in Chapter 10.)

We have emphasized patients with direct injuries to the frontal lobes, but other kinds of patient groups also share something of a frontal-lobe syndrome. Although the most dramatic symptom in early Alzheimer's disease (AD) is memory loss, another early symptom is poor performance on frontal-lobe tasks (e.g., Baddeley, 1986). One of the first brain areas affected in AD is the PFC. Thus, AD patients may have frontal-lobe syndrome. Further, many neurologists and neuropsychologists are now observing what they call *executive dysfunction* in children with learning disabilities and in adults who are markedly disorganized and failing in their careers. The fact that what appear to be the same functions—the executive processes—are all affected in various diseases and disorders provides further evidence that these processes form a distinct class.

Are there other executive processes beyond the five outlined at the beginning of the chapter? Possibly—analysis by subgoals and updating working memory may be viable candidates (see Banich, 1997; Gazzaniga et al., 1998)—but none of these other candidates has been as systematically studied as the five executive processes that we will consider in the remainder of this chapter: executive attention, attention-switching, response inhibition, temporal-coding-plus-sequencing, and monitoring. Furthermore, these five processes appear to be required in many real-life situations.

Comprehension Check:

1. Why is executive attention needed in the Stroop task?
2. What executive processes are needed to perform well on the Tower of Hanoi problem?

3. EXECUTIVE ATTENTION

Executive attention, which directs subsequent processing, is needed whenever multiple mental representations in working memory, or multiple processes operating on representations, compete for the control of cognition and behavior. When you play a game of chess, you attend to various pieces in sequence, as these players are doing in Figure 7–6. When you do a crossword puzzle, you attend to some spaces and

FIGURE 7–6 Executive attention required here

At least for the novices among these players, executive attention is needed at every move of a chess game. (Photograph by Lon C. Diehl. Courtesy of PhotoEdit Inc.)

words while inhibiting the others. When you hear an ambiguous sentence, you attend to some meanings while inhibiting others. Indeed, it is difficult to think of a complex mental event that does *not* require executive attention. Executive attention was certainly going on in the kitchen, when you had to attend both to your friend on the phone and your pasta water on the boil.

Executive attention determines which of the contenders will gain control. Let's take another look at the Stroop task of naming the ink color in which a color name is printed, because it is the task par excellence for understanding executive attention. The basic finding for normal participants is that it takes less time to say the print color when the color is compatible with the color name (*red* printed in red ink) than when it is incompatible (*blue* printed in red ink). In essence, when an automatic response (i.e., one that does not require conscious intention, such as saying "red" for the word *red* even when it is printed in blue) must be overcome, some other process must be brought into play so that behavior satisfies the goal. Over the years, many other tasks have been developed that have this character. For example, it is harder to report the color of a pictured banana when that color is anything but yellow (Klein, 1964). The Stroop effect thus applies to noncolor stimuli that, like a picture of a *banana*, refer to objects with a characteristic color.

Now consider a task that's a little further removed from Stroop, a *stimulus–response compatibility task* (Fitts & Deininger, 1954). Stimulus–response compatibility is a measure of the degree to which the assignment of the correct response to a stimulus is consonant with the way people would act naturally. The compatibility can be spatial, as in a head-up map (that is, one that is oriented in the same direction as the observer by rotating about its center), or symbolic (such as in using high pitch to signal upward movement and low pitch to signal downward movement).

In a typical version of a task designed to assess stimulus–response compatibility, a stimulus is presented on either the left or right side of a display. In the *compatible* condition, participants respond to the stimulus on the left by pushing a left-sided key, and to a stimulus on the right by pushing a right-sided key. In the *incompatible* condition, the stimulus–response assignments are reversed: now left-sided stimuli go with right-handed responses, whereas right-sided stimuli go with left-handed responses. Stimulus-response assignments are of course more natural in the compatible condition. Response times are faster in the compatible than the incompatible condition (Kornblum & Lee, 1995; Kornblum et al., 1990), a finding that has important safety applications in industrial design (Figure 7–7). This *compatibility effect* is one of the most easily demonstrated phenomena in cognitive psychology. Remarkably, one can get a similar result even when the position of the stimulus is irrelevant. Suppose participants have to make a right-handed response whenever a circle appears and a left-handed response whenever a square appears. Participants respond faster when the object—circle or square—appears on the same side as the required response, even though the object's position is irrelevant to the task (Simon, 1990).

What's going on in these tasks? There is either a relatively automatic connection between stimuli and responses (ink color goes with color name, stimulus position goes with response position) or an arbitrary connection (ink color is arbitrarily associated with a color name, response position is the opposite of stimulus position). When the connection is automatic, little executive attention is needed. (Even after his brain

FIGURE 7–7   Straighten up and fly right

With complex displays like this, it is important that the stimulus–response assignments, in the positioning of controls and the arrangement of displays, be compatible.

(Photograph by Tom Carter. Courtesy of PhotoEdit Inc.)

damage, Dr. P. could still carry out the most basic routines of surgery; presumably these were the automatic ones.) But when the two sources of information are not compatible, you must attend to the relevant information—"it is color that matters"—and perhaps inhibit the automatic connection. (Dr. P. apparently could not do this. He could carry out routines only in a rigid, inflexible manner.) This attention-and-inhibition amounts to some extra cognitive work, and we are usually aware of having to do it.

3.1. A Neural-Network Model of Conflict in Processing

Most researchers agree with the formulation of attention-and-inhibition described above, but the trick is to spell out the details. In the basic Stroop task, the participant must attend to the ink color and perhaps inhibit the color word. How exactly is this done—what representations and processes are involved? A number of proposals (e.g., Kornblum et al., 1990; Zhang et al., 1999) have been made, but perhaps the most influential one is a neural-network model that has been developed over the years by Jonathan Cohen and colleagues (1990, 1996). It is easier to understand this model if we build it in stages; Figure 7–8 presents the first stage.

This is a relatively simple model—information flows only in an upward direction—with three layers: the input layer, the hidden layer, and the response layer. (Neural-network models are discussed in Chapter 1; see Figure 1–14.) You can think of the nodes as representations, and the connections as associations between the nodes; these associations vary in weight, or strength. To keep things simple in the

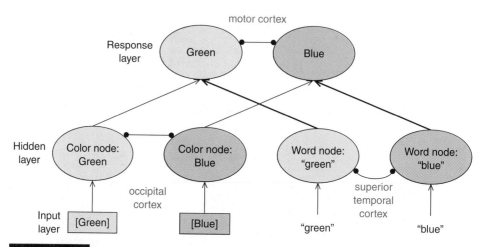

FIGURE 7–8 A three-layer neural-network model of the cognitive processing in the Stroop task

The bottom layer is the input layer, where both color and word information are encoded. From here information flows to the hidden level ("hidden" because there's no direct connection to the outside world): color information flows to the corresponding color nodes, and word information to the corresponding word nodes. (At this level, and elsewhere, because this text is limited in the number of colors it can present, nodes cooling blue are colored dark blue, whereas nodes coding green are colored light blue.) The top level is the response layer: both color and word information from the hidden level flow to corresponding nodes at the response level. Presumably the connections between the word nodes at the hidden level and their corresponding response nodes are stronger than the comparable connections between the color nodes and their corresponding response nodes (as indicated by relative line thickness). The word nodes should dominate at the response level, and the participant should make many errors on incompatible trials. The neural structures that likely mediate each cognitive component are indicated. Lines with arrowheads indicate excitatory connections; lines with filled circles indicate inhibitory connections. (See text for additional features of this model.)

figure, the relative weight of a connection is shown by the line's thickness, rather than by a number, and we have not bothered to designate the activation values for the representations—you can assume they are all equal (at the start). Connections with arrowheads are excitatory, which send activation from one node to another; connections with dark circles are inhibitory, which decrease the activation level of the recipient node. Note that within both the hidden and response layers, the connections are largely inhibitory (as in the Stroop task, where the stimulus can be only one color—"if it's blue, it can't be green"—and only one response can be made).

When input is presented during the Stroop task, e.g., the word "blue" printed in green, both the color representation and the word representation are activated (see the input and hidden layers in Figure 7–8). Because the word representation in the hidden layer has a stronger connection to its relevant response node—this connections is relatively automatic—the response node for the color word will usually be activated (*usually*, not *always*, because there's noise in the system). Thus, even normal participants should make many errors on incompatible trials, e.g., responding with blue even though the color is green. But they do not, so something is wrong with the model.

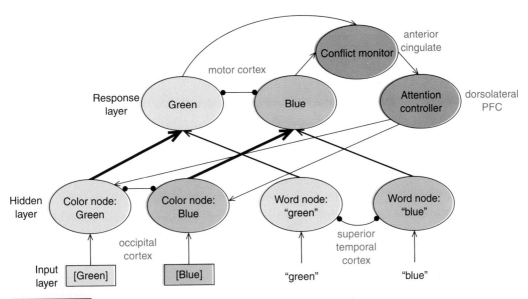

FIGURE 7–9 An amended model for the Stroop task

The critical additions to the model in Figure 7–8 are an *attentional controller*, which adds activation to all color nodes at the hidden level, so their connections to the corresponding nodes at the response level are now stronger than the connections between the word nodes and their corresponding response nodes; and a *conflict monitor*, which monitors the amount of conflict at the response level. The neural structures that likely mediate each cognitive component are indicated.

What's wrong is that the model does not contain an executive-attention component. This component (and another) has been added in Figure 7–9. Cohen et al. (e.g., 1996) refer to this component as an attentional controller. The attentional controller contains an indication of the current goal and adds activation to nodes relevant to that goal. Thus, continuing to use the Stroop task as an illustration, the attentional controller indicates the current goal—"respond on the basis of ink color"—and it adds activation to all the color nodes in the hidden layer, so that their connections to the nodes in the response layer are stronger than the well-learned (and hence strong) connections between the word nodes and their corresponding response nodes. The result is that participants now should be highly accurate even on incompatible trials, as they in fact are. Now when the word "blue" is printed in green, the connection between the color node and its corresponding response node will dominate processing. But why do incompatible trials take longer than compatible ones? Because some of the activations from the word nodes are still gaining access to their corresponding response nodes; on compatible trials this activation will just add to the activation of the correct response node, but on incompatible trials the irrelevant activation will compete with the relevant activation from the color node. (Competition occurs because there are inhibitory connections between the response nodes.)

The other additional component in Figure 7–9, which ties the whole model together, is a conflict monitor. This component monitors the amount of conflict between the nodes at the response level, and as conflict increases, the monitor engages executive attention. To the extent this conflict is high, the conflict monitor increases attention, via the attentional controller. (Conflict between two responses is high when they are roughly equally activated, less so when the difference in activation is greater.) So this is the overall picture: when the required response is automatic or straightforward, there is no conflict at the response level, and no need for the use of executive attention. (This is the case when participants are presented with color names printed in different ink colors and the task is simply to *read the words*, an automatic process for literate adults.) But when the required response is not automatic, measurable conflict will occur at the response level, which will be detected by the conflict monitor, which will turn on executive attention, which in turn imposes the requirements of the current goal on processing. (This is what happens when participants must name ink colors incompatible with the color name.) As for the breakdown in performance in patients with frontal damage, presumably this results from a deficit in executive attention. Thus, Figure 7–8, which lacks both a component for executive attention and a signal to engage it, provides a possible model of performance for patients with damage to the frontal lobes.

Progress has also been made in specifying the neural bases of the critical components in the neural-network model shown in Figure 7–9. Researchers have conducted many neuroimaging studies of participants performing the Stroop task and related tasks, and Jonides et al. (2002) surveyed a number of such studies to determine whether certain common regions were activated in all these tasks of executive attention. The results are shown in Figure 7–10. Each symbol represents an activation obtained in one of the studies. One significant cluster of symbols is in the anterior cingulate (which is known to be involved in monitoring processing), another is in a region that mingles with the anterior cingulate at its most ventral extent, and the third significant region is in the right-hemisphere dorsolateral PFC. This last area is

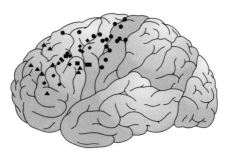

Left Lateral View

FIGURE 7–10   A summary of neuroimaging results on the Stroop task

Points on this schematic brain represent the major activations from different imaging studies on the Stroop task (represented by different symbols). The points form a large cluster that extends from the dorsolateral PFC to the anterior cingulate.

(Jonides, J., Badre, D., Curtis, C., Thompson-Schill, S. L., & Smith, E. E. (2002). Mechanisms of conflict resolution in prefrontal cortex. Adapted from *The Frontal Lobes,* edited by D. T. Stuss and R. T. Knight. Copyright © 2002 by Oxford University Press. Reprinted with permission of Oxford University Press.)

known to be important for working memory and executive processes (as discussed in Chapter 6), and it is highly interconnected with the anterior cingulate.

These results fit relatively well with the theory. Presumably the anterior cingulate mediates the conflict monitor, and the dorsolateral PFC mediates executive attention. Some striking imaging evidence exists for this proposal. The evidence comes from an fMRI experiment (MacDonald et al., 2000) that involved the Stroop task and a reading task. In part 1 of each trial an instruction was presented that told the participant whether the task will be to name the ink color or to read the word. Part 2 occurred several seconds later and presented a color name printed in a particular color ink. Consider what should happen during part 1: if participants are told that a reading task is coming (and if they are fluent readers), there's no need for executive attention; in contrast, if participants are instructed that a color-naming task is coming they know that they will need attentional help (presumably they know this from past experience, possibly their experience in practice trials). When they know that they need help, they initiate executive attention. Because executive attention is mediated by the dorsolateral PFC, the images of brain activity should reveal a difference between dorsolateral PFC activity in part 1 between the two instructions. But there should be no difference in the anterior cingulate, because there's no conflict yet—the actual task, which does involve conflict, has not yet been presented. This pattern of brain activity is exactly what was found (Figure 7–11a).

Now consider what should happen in part 2, those trials when participants have to name colors in the Stroop task. On incompatible trials, there should be conflict at the response level, which should be noted by the conflict monitor, which is mediated by the anterior cingulate. So the images of brain activity for color naming during part 2 should reveal different levels of activity in the anterior cingulate for compatible versus incompatible trials. Again, the results conform with the predictions (Figure 7–11b).

Another way of viewing this model and others like it (e.g., Polk et al., 2002) is shown in Figure 7–12. As you can see, in the Stroop task and other conflict tasks, activation travels from the PFC in the front of the brain to a region in the back. This front-to-back processing is the heart of models of executive attention. In the Stroop test, activation goes from the PFC to the fusiform gyrus, in the back of the brain, where color is processed. In tasks involving conflict in motor responses, such as making a left-handed response to a right-handed stimulus, activation from the PFC travels to areas involved in motor planning—the premotor cortex behind the PFC. Control is in the front of the brain; what gets controlled is farther back.

The monitor-plus-attention model we have been describing is consistent with behavioral data from frontal-lobe patients and behavioral data and neuroimaging evidence from neurologically healthy people. It is at present the dominant theory of executive attention. Still, the model is not without its critics. One challenge comes from researchers who have argued that there is more than one kind of attention–inhibition in play in the Stroop task and related tasks (e.g., Jonides et al., 2002). According to Milham and colleagues (2001), attention can be needed either at the response level or *earlier in the processing*, and only the response level activates the anterior cingulate. These claims are supported by experiments using our old friend, the Stroop task. Milham and colleagues used two kinds of incongruent trials. In the *incongruent–eligible*

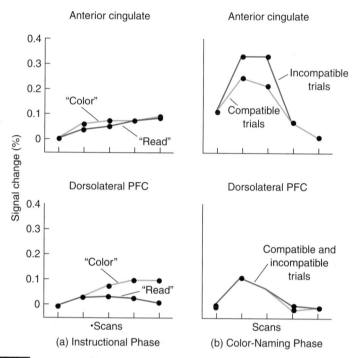

FIGURE 7–11 Neuro-imaging evidence for a dissociation of the attentional controller and the conflict monitor

The task includes an instructional phase, in which the participant is told whether the task will be to name the word ("Read") or the ink color ("Color"), as in the Stroop task, and a color-naming phase, in which the participant must sometimes name the color of the ink, which may or may not be compatible with the color word. (a) In the instructional phase, the anterior cingulate is unaffected by the nature of the upcoming task (it "cares" only about conflict); the dorsolateral PFC shows more activity when preparing for the Color task ("turn on the attentional controller") than for the Read task.
(b) In the color-naming phase, the anterior cingulate shows greater activity for incompatible than for compatible trials (because there is more conflict in the former). There is no difference in activation between incompatible and compatible trials in the dorsolateral PFC. (The attentional controller presumably is used for both kinds of trials.)

(Adapted from MacDonald, A. W., Cohen, J. D., Stenger, V. A., & Carter, C. S. (2000). Dissociating the role of the dorsolateral prefrontal and anterior cingulate cortex in cognitive control. *Science, 288,* 1835–1838. Reprinted with permission.)

condition, the color names (which have to be suppressed) could also occur as ink colors, and hence were possible responses. Thus, the ink colors to be named were blue, yellow, and green, and the words used were *blue, yellow,* and *green.* In the *incongruent–ineligible* condition, the color names could never occur as ink colors and hence could never serve as responses. Here the ink colors to be named were, again, blue, yellow, and green, but now the words were *red, orange,* and *brown.* When participants were imaged by fMRI while doing this task, the dorsolateral PFC was active on both kinds of incongruent trials, but the anterior cingulate became activated only on the incongruent–eligible trials, that is, only on trials that required inhibition at the

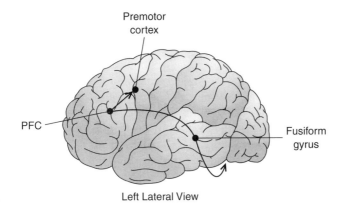

Left Lateral View

FIGURE 7–12   The front-to-back flow of brain activation when attention is required

During the Stroop task, the activation flows from the attentional centers in the PFC back to the fusiform gyrus, the area for color processing. During stimulus–response compatibility tasks ("respond right to a left-sided stimulus"), the activation flows from the attentional centers to the premotor cortex, behind the PFC.

response level. These results challenge the idea that the anterior cingulate is a conflict monitor, by suggesting instead that it mediates response inhibition (inhibition of a prepared or partially prepared response). In either case, however, the broad outlines of the model remain intact; it is clear that the details will continue to be determined by research just now being conducted—this is an exciting period in the history of cognitive psychology and cognitive neuroscience!

3.2. Executive Attention and Categorization

Executive attention is important in a mental process that you engage in many times a day: assigning an object to a category. That is what you're doing every time you recognize a particular creature as a dog (you've assigned the creature to the category of DOG), or when you identify a weird-looking bean-bag structure as a chair (you've assigned that object to the category of CHAIR). (Categorization was discussed at length in Chapter 4.)

Rips (1989) was interested in demonstrating that there is more to categorization than the similarity of the to-be-categorized object and the corresponding long-term memory representation. On each trial of his experiment, participants were presented with a brief description of a test object and the names of two categories; for example, the description might be "an object that is three inches in diameter" and the two categories PIZZA and QUARTER. Note that one of the categories, QUARTER, is fixed with respect to the dimension mentioned in the description—quarters are of a specific size, which is smaller than 3 inches in diameter; the other category, PIZZA, permits extensive variation on the relevant dimension. This distinction between *fixed* and *variable* categories turns out to be critical.

All participants were to decide which category better described each test object. However, different groups of participants were instructed to make their categorization decisions in different ways. The "similarity" group was instructed to base their decision on the similarity of a test object to the categories. Because the experimenter had chosen the descriptions to be approximately equally similar to each category—the 3-inch object of the example is roughly equally similar to pizzas (round, usually larger) and to quarters (round, always smaller)—one would expect a 50–50 split between fixed QUARTER responses and variable PIZZA responses, and this was roughly what was found (Rips, 1989; Smith & Sloman, 1994). In contrast, for the "reasoning" group similarity was not enough. This group was instructed that there was always a correct answer, and to think through their decision aloud. This emphasis should have induced participants to *attend* to the size dimension of the two categories, and realize that because quarters cannot possibly be three inches in diameter (as stipulated by the U.S. Treasury), the test object was more likely to be a member of the variable category (PIZZA) than the fixed category (QUARTER). Again, these were the obtained results (Rips, 1989; Smith & Sloman, 1994), showing that the critical difference between two basic categorization strategies is whether or not executive attention plays a role.

If executive attention is indeed mediated by the PFC, then one would expect that patients with frontal damage that includes the PFC would have particular difficulties in making categorization decisions based on reasoning but not on similarity (similarity mechanisms are presumably distributed throughout the cortex). Grossman et al. (2003) confirmed this prediction. On similarity-based categorizations, frontal patients were indistinguishable from normal participants of the same age. In sharp contrast, on reasoning-based categorization frontal patients continued to select the fixed category (QUARTER) as frequently as the variable category (PIZZA) whereas the normal participants favored the variable category. Presumably the frontal patients are compromised in executive attention and hence cannot successfully apply the reasoning-based strategy (see *A Closer Look*).

Furthermore, if executive attention is indeed mediated by the PFC, then this area should be activated in normal participants when they make reasoning-based categorizations but not when they make similarity-based categorizations. Using fMRI as the means of neuroimaging, Grossman et al. (2002) have confirmed this prediction.

Here three different types of evidence about the functioning of executive attention converge: (1) behavioral studies with normal participants (PIZZA–QUARTER) have found different categorizations with similarity and reasoning instructions; (2) comparable behavioral studies with patients with frontal damage have found that only reasoning-based categorization is compromised in the patients; and (3) a neuroimaging study found that the PFC is activated when normal participants carry out the same reasoning task, but not the similarity task. It is hard to imagine any complex cognitive process that does not involve executive attention operating on the contents of working memory.

3.3. The Role of Consciousness

We have repeatedly noted that cognitive conflict arises when the correct response must be determined by a nonautomatic process at the same time that an automatic process is competing with it. For literate adults, reading words is presumably an

A CLOSER LOOK
Prefrontal Damage, Reasoning, and Category Decisions

Researchers Murray Grossman, Edward E. Smith, Phyllis Koenig, Guila Glosser, Jine Rhee, and Karl Dennis sought to confirm predictions about prefrontal involvement in category decisions based on reasoning and on similarity. Their results were published in a 2003 paper titled "Categorization of Object Descriptions in Alzheimer's Disease and Frontotemporal Dementia: Limitation in Rule-Based Processing," *Cognitive, Affective, & Behavioral Neuroscience, 3*(2): 120–132.

Introduction

The investigators hypothesized that patients with damage in the prefrontal cortex would be impaired in making categorization decisions based on reasoning but not in making similarity-based decisions. This is because only reasoning-based decisions require the sort of processing mediated by the PFC, particularly, executive attention.

Method

Normal participants were compared with patients in the early stages of Alzheimer's disease (AD). Such patients are known to have atrophy in the PFC. The two groups of participants were matched on age and years of education.

The two groups of participants were tested on the two tasks used in the PIZZA–QUARTER experiments of Rips (1989) and Smith and Sloman (1994). In both tasks a trial starts with a brief description of a test object (or event), for example, "an object three inches in diameter," followed by two categories, PIZZA and QUARTER. In the similarity condition, participants were instructed to base their decisions on the similarity of the test object to the categories; in the reasoning condition, participants were told there was a correct answer and were encouraged to "think aloud," using reason in making their decisions (quarters are a fixed size, the size of pizzas is variable). If the hypothesis of the present investigators is correct, then AD patients should not differ from normal participants in the similarity condition, but should perform more poorly than normal participants in the reasoning condition (that is, they should choose the variable category less often).

Twenty-five different items were used, all having the same structure as the PIZZA–QUARTER example. Different groups of normal participants were used in the two conditions, similarity and reasoning, because memory for the response in the first condition might contaminate responses in the second condition. For the AD patients, it was possible to test the same participants in both conditions, as long as a month intervened between the conditions. (After a month's time, the AD patients had lost all memory of the first test; memory loss is the primary symptom of AD.)

Results and Discussion

The data of interest are the percentage of times each group of participants chose the variable category. For the similarity condition, the percentage choice of the variable category was 58 percent for normal participants and 59 percent for the AD patients. There was no difference between the groups when executive attention (and thus the PFC) is not involved. This finding is consistent with the hypothesis. For the reasoning condition, the percentage choice of the variable category was 78 percent for the normal participants and only 58 percent for the AD patients. Normal participants did better than AD patients when executive attention (and PFC resources) is required. This finding provides direct support for the hypothesis.

automatic process, whereas naming ink colors is not (and hence requires attention for help); this contrast would account for the results we have seen in the Stroop test. But what exactly do terms like *automatic* and *nonautomatic* mean? The answer may partly involve consciousness.

According to most views, an **automatic process** is one that can be initiated without intention (in Stroop, you read the word whether you want to or not), that operates very rapidly (it takes about half a second to read a word), and, most important for our purposes, that can operate without *consciousness* (you don't have to attend consciously to the word to get its name). In contrast, a nonautomatic process (often called a *controlled process*) is one that requires intention (you have to want to name the print color), is relatively slow, and requires consciousness for its operation (we have to attend consciously to ink color) (Posner & Snyder, 1974; Shiffrin & Schneider, 1977).

But what, exactly, do we mean here by the term *consciousness*? Consciousness is a state that is accompanied by a certain phenomenology—an experience—and that experience presumably reflects certain types of information processing. Philosophers distinguish between different types of consciousness (e.g., Block et al., 1997). At a low level is *awareness consciousness*, a state in which you aware of the stimuli and events presented to you. At a higher level is a kind of *introspective consciousness*, in which you are aware not only of external stimuli but also of internal representations and processes. The distinction is important in dealing with questions such as whether certain kinds of brain damage differentially affect different types of consciousness, and whether nonhuman species may have awareness consciousness but not introspective consciousness. Clearly the kind of consciousness that we have been talking about is of the introspective type, because we have considered models in which we monitor for internal conflict.

There is consensus that the information processing resources that give rise to consciousness are limited (as William James suggested more than a hundred years ago). Consequently, we can be conscious of only a limited number of things at a time. Indeed, some have placed this limit at one (McElree & Dosher, 1989). If limited resources are posited, the processing underlying consciousness seems a lot like attention, and indeed the two concepts are tightly intertwined. It may be that whenever we attend to some stimulus or mental representation, we are conscious of it (this has been assumed throughout much of this book). Just what the function of the phenomenology of consciousness is remains controversial.

Whereas nonautomatic processes seem to require the resources that give rise to consciousness, automatic processes do not. We are generally not aware of the processing involved in reading a word or reaching for a cup. In many cases, what once required conscious processing no longer does so after extensive practice. Sports provide some excellent examples. Beginning tennis players may be very conscious of the components of their strokes, reminding themselves to get to the destination of the ball first and then bring their racquet all the way back, but seasoned players perform these essential actions unconsciously.

What do we know about the neural basis of consciousness? One suggestion is that in conflict situations such as Stroop, the anterior cingulate comes on line only when the conflict is conscious (Jonides et al., 2002). A broader hypothesis has been offered by no less than Francis Crick (the co-discoverer of the structure of DNA), working with Christof Koch. On the basis of a number of cognitive-neuroscience results, Crick and Koch (1995) speculated that information cannot become conscious until it reaches the frontal lobe. Only time will tell whether the suggestion has merit.

Comprehension Check:

1. How do patients with frontal damage differ from normal participants on the Stroop task?
2. In the neural network model of the Stroop task, what two components come into play on incompatible trials?

4. SWITCHING ATTENTION

There you are in the hot kitchen, the phone ringing, the water coming to a boil, a favorite song coming over the speakers. You keep going in this crowded environment by executive attention, focusing on one or another aspect of what's going on as needed. How do you get there—how do you get from focus on phone to focus on pasta? To control internal processing, we not only have to be able to attend to some representations and processes, but must also be able to *switch* our attention from one representation or process to another. In switching attention, the focus of attention is moved from one entity to another, so it becomes possible for you to get dinner on the table.

4.1. The Costs of Switching

Switching attention has often been studied by having participants do one task on the first trial, another task on the next trial, then return to the first task on the third trial, the second task on the fourth trial, and so on until a set of trials is completed. For example, all trials may contain a digit and a letter, and on trial 1 the participant has to attend to the digit and decide as quickly as possible whether it is above or below 5, then on trial 2 the participant must attend to the letter and decide whether it is a vowel or a consonant, then back to digit decisions, then back to letter decisions, and so on (e.g., Rogers & Monsell, 1995). This alternation of tasks is compared to the case in which the participant performs the same task throughout an entire set of trials. The participant makes only "above-below 5" decisions for an entire set of trials, and then vowel–consonant decisions for an entire set. Sets with alternating tasks are called *alternating blocks;* sets with only one task are called *pure blocks.* To see whether the act of switching takes time, the time for the average of the pure blocks is subtracted from the time for the alternating blocks. The general finding, and it has been obtained many times, is that participants require more time to respond on alternating blocks than on pure blocks. This time difference, usually on the order of 100 to 300 milliseconds, is often referred to as the switching cost.

But wait a minute—the alternation condition does not seem to have much to do with what happens in life. You don't alternate between cooking and talking on the

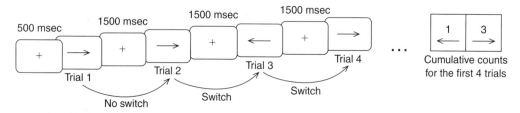

FIGURE 7–13   A sequence of trials in an attention-switching task

Participants must keep separate cumulative counts of left- and right-pointing arrows; on each trial, they push a button to indicate that they have updated the appropriate count. Between trials a fixation point (a plus sign) appears on the screen for 1500 milliseconds. In this example, there is no switch of counts between trials 1 and 2, but there are switches between trials 2 and 3 and between trials 3 and 4.

(Hernandez-Garcia, L., Wager, T. D., & Jonides, J. (2003). Functional brain imaging. In J. Wixted and H. Pashler (eds.), *Stevens Handbook of Experimental Psychology,* Third Edition, Vol. 4: Methodology in Experimental Psychology, pp. 175–221. New York: Wiley & Sons, Inc. Reprinted with permission.)

phone on some kind of schedule—and what if a third need screaming for your attention arises? What happens in life is that you tend to each need as required; you do each task as it is called for, and it is unpredictable which task is required moment to moment. Are there studies that capture this kind of ad hoc switching? Yes.

For example, an experiment by Garavan (1998) fits the bill, and a variant of it is illustrated in Figure 7–13. On each trial participants see, for instance, either a left-pointing arrow or a right-pointing arrow, and their job is to keep cumulative counts of the appearance of each type of arrow. Presumably, the two cumulative counts are held in a state of readiness in working memory. Once the stimulus is presented and the appropriate count updated, the participant pushes a button to bring on the next stimulus. As we will see, the time taken to press the button can be used to assess switching cost. At the end of a block of trials (about 15 to 20), the participant is tested on the two final counts; accuracy is typically high. High accuracy indicates that the switching process works—but at what cost?

When successive trials involve the same stimulus (for example, a right-pointing arrow followed by a right-pointing arrow), participants have to update the same count that they have just worked on. But when on other successive trials the stimulus changes (i.e., right-pointing arrow is followed by left-pointing arrow), participants have to switch from one count to the other to make the update. The time to press the button to bring on the next stimulus should be greater—and it is—when a switch in count is called for than when it is not; this difference in time is the switching cost. And the cost is substantial—on the order of 500 to 600 milliseconds. This difference is so large that it cannot be attributed to some kind of perceptual priming that might occur when identical stimuli are seen in succession. True, seeing the stimulus once might "grease the wheels" for seeing it again and thus contribute to participants' greater speed when the same stimuli appeared in succession (a kind of implicit memory); however, such visual priming effects are much smaller than the differential found here. Thus, switching costs are evident even in tasks that have the same unpredictable structure as natural situations.

4.2. A Framework for Understanding Task Switching

Strong evidence that switching attention is a metaprocess—a process that coordinates other processes—that also provides an information-processing framework for understanding task switching comes from a set of studies by Rubenstein et al. (2001). Participants were required to shift attention between different attributes of multidimensional stimuli. The task, based on the idea of alternation, was modeled after the Wisconsin Card Sort task. Designs on four target cards vary in the number, shape, color, and size of the pictured objects. Participants must sort each test card in a deck into one of four piles according to a particular attribute, and they always know what that attribute is. In the alternation condition, participants sort on the basis of one attribute, for instance, shape, on the first trial—that is, for the first card; then on the basis of a different attribute, for instance, number, on the second trial; switch back to shape on the third trial; switch back to number on the fourth trial; and so on for an entire block of trials. In other conditions, the participants sort on the basis of the same attribute for the entire block (that is, in pure blocks). The time to sort a card in the alternation condition takes longer than the comparable time in the various pure-block conditions. Again, switching attention takes time.

The same investigators provide a sketch of a simple information-processing model of what is going on in this and other switching tasks. The model is presented in Figure 7–14. Note first that there are two different levels of processing, task processing and executive processing, and the latter can influence the former (hence, again, the notion that executive processes are metaprocesses). The task-processing level requires the following sequence of processes: identify the value of the stimulus on the critical attribute ("It's the shape of a square!"), select the appropriate response

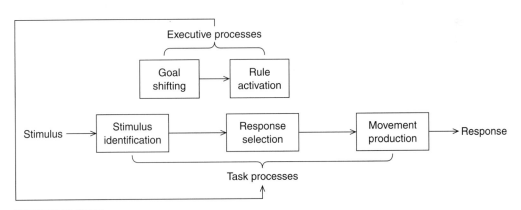

FIGURE 7–14   An information processing model for task switching

The model has two levels, task processing and executive processing, which differ in the kinds of operations they perform. Of particular importance, the executive processes include goal shifting (for example, "now sort according to number") and rule activation (for example, "selectively attend to numerosity").

(Adapted from Rubinstein, J. S., Meyer, D. E., & Evans, J. E. (2001). Executive control of cognitive processes in task switching. *Journal of Experimental Psychology: Human Perception & Performance, 27*(4), Fig. 1, p. 770. Copyright © 2001 American Psychological Association. Adapted with permission.)

("place this card in the square pile"), and then actually make the needed movement. The executive-processing level requires different processes. First, set the goal for the trial ("sort according to shape"), then activate the rules needed to implement the goal ("attend to shape"). In the alternation, or switching, condition, a new goal must be set on every trial ("sort by shape," "sort by number," "sort by shape," . . .), whereas in the pure conditions the goal need not be changed during a block of trials. This is one reason why switching attention takes time. Further, in the switching condition, the activated rules change from trial to trial, whereas in the pure conditions the rules stay the same throughout the entire block of trials. Changing rules takes time—this is the second reason why switching takes time.

Perhaps the best evidence for the model in Figure 7–14 is that Rubenstein et al. (2001) were able to show a double dissociation between the task-processing and executive-processing levels. In this double dissociation, a given variable affects one level of processing but not the other, whereas another variable shows the opposite pattern. The fact that one variable affects task processing but not executive processing implies that there must be some mechanism in the former that is not present in the latter, whereas the fact that another variable affects executive processing but not task processing implies that there must be some mechanism in the former that is not present in the latter. Hence, a double dissociation is strong evidence that two different mechanisms are involved.

Specifically, Rubenstein et al. (2001) used two arithmetic tasks—addition and subtraction—and participants either alternated between the two tasks or did just one for an entire block of trials. To influence the executive level, the researchers manipulated the ease of changing goals by either including the operator sign (+ or −) with the problem or not. Including the operator sign relieved the participants of having to remember which task they should be performing, and thereby should have speeded the changing of goals. This in turn should decrease the switching cost (the time difference between performance in alternating and in pure blocks), because this cost supposedly arises in part from goal changing. This is exactly what the researchers found. Furthermore, in the pure conditions, inclusion of the operator sign had no effect; so this variable—presence or absence of the operator sign—had no effect on the task-processing level, but it did affect the executive-processing level. This is half the double dissociation.

To complete the double dissociation, the researchers manipulated a factor that, in theory, should have an effect on the task-processing level but not on the executive-processing level. That variable was simply the discriminability of the numbers—they were either easy or difficult to see. As expected, low discriminability increased response times in all conditions but had no effect on switching time (because it had no effect on goal switching or rule changing). This is the other half of the double dissociation.

The framework depicted in Figure 7–14 is also consistent with another result in task switching: switching costs become greater as the two tasks become more similar. Suppose in one case that participants have to alternate between addition and subtraction, whereas in another they have to switch between addition and generating an antonym to a given word. Suppose further that the antonym task takes the same amount of time as the subtraction task, so the difficulty level in both instances is the same and any differences in switching costs therefore cannot be attributed to different demands of the individual tasks. Obviously, the two arithmetic tasks are more similar than are the addition and antonym tasks. Results in a number of studies show that the switching costs are higher in the first case than the second (e.g., Allport et al., 1994; Spector & Biederman, 1976). How does the model account for this? The more similar the two tasks, the more similar the relevant rules and the greater the opportunity for confusion in activating the rules; and the more confusion in these metaprocesses, the longer it takes to accomplish the switch. Thus, when trying to activate the rules for subtraction, you might have some difficulty in keeping them separate from the rules for addition, but no such difficulty should arise when activating the "rules" for coming up with an antonym.

Thus, the model depicted in Figure 7–14 has some behavioral support. But it does not look anything like the model for executive attention presented in Figures 7–8 and 7–9, in that the current model is a sketch of an information-processing model, whereas the models in Figures 7–8 and 7–9 are neural-network models that include detailed mechanisms.

4.3. The Neural-Switcher Hypothesis

Behavioral results, as we have seen, support the idea that additional mechanisms are brought into play when we must switch attention. Is there any neurological evidence for this? Yes, and much of it comes from neuroimaging studies. To start, participants have performed the attribute-shifting task employed by Rubenstein et al. (2001)—sort by shape, sort by number, sort by shape, and so on—while having their brains imaged by PET. When the patterns of activation for the pure conditions were subtracted from those for the alternation condition, the result—known as a *subtraction image*—showed a very substantial activation in the PFC, particularly dorsolateral PFC, as well as clear activation in the parietal cortex (Meyer et al., 1998). The attribute-shifting task is a close cousin of the Wisconsin Card Sort task, which is used to detect frontal damage—and no wonder, given that the card sort involves switching, that the dorsolateral PFC may underlie switching, and that this area is often compromised in frontal damage.

But these results also raise a number of new issues about task switching and executive processes in general. First, the neuroimaging results imply that regions of the parietal cortex are involved, suggesting that the neural mechanisms mediating switching are not confined to the frontal cortex. This is the first evidence we encounter against the strong frontal-executive hypothesis—that executive processes are mediated only by the frontal cortex. More such evidence will be presented later.

A second general issue raised by the neuroimaging results concerns the degree to which neural regions are dedicated to specific cognitive processes. One region associated with switching—dorsolateral PFC—is also involved in executive attention. How is it possible for one region to have two functions? Perhaps it does not—the problem may be methodological. The spatial resolution of PET is only about 10 millimeters, which means that it cannot discriminate between activations from two different brain regions—one doing attention and one doing switching—that are within 10 millimeters of each other. But this possibility is doubtful, given that other neuroimaging studies of switching that used fMRI, which has better spatial resolution than PET, also found that switching per se is associated with activations in the dorsolateral PFC and the anterior cingulate, both structures that have been activated in studies of executive attention. Another possibility is that the same neural mechanism mediates both executive attention and attention switching, but more of that mechanism's resources are typically needed when switching attention than when just attending. This possibility raises an important question about the neural bases of attention switching: Is there any evidence that there are neural mechanisms *dedicated solely* to switching?

An experiment by Sylvester et al. (2003) offers direct evidence on this issue of specificity. While being imaged by fMRI, participants worked on two different kinds of tasks: the cumulative-counts task described earlier ("How many left-pointing arrows?" and "How many right-pointing arrows?"), which is a good example of task switching, and a stimulus–response compatibility task, such as left-handed stimuli–right-handed responses and vice versa, which presumably taps executive attention and inhibition. In the count task, Sylvester et al. obtained the subtraction image—the difference in activations—for switch minus nonswitch conditions, which provided an indication of the neural location of the switching regions. In the stimulus–response compatibility task, the researchers obtained the subtraction image for the incompatible minus the compatible trials, which provided an indication of executive attention areas. Now the crux of the question: comparison of the two subtraction images. Do they show any substantial differences? Yes, they do. Areas distinct to switching include regions in the inferior parietal lobe and the extrastriatal visual cortex, whereas areas distinct to executive attention include two frontal areas, one in the anterior PFC and the other in the premotor cortex. (Are you wondering why the dorsolateral PFC did not show up? Activation in this area was cancelled out in the critical comparison in this experiment because PFC was activated roughly equally in both executive attention and switching executive attention). Because distinct neural processes suggest distinct cognitive processes, we have evidence that the process of switching executive attention is distinct from that of engaging executive attention. This work also provides further evidence for the role of the parietal lobes in attention switching, and further evidence against the strongest version of the frontal-executive hypothesis.

4.4. What Gets Switched?

You may have noticed that in all this discussion of switching we have been rather casual about what exactly gets switched. In addition–subtraction studies there is a switch in the actual task the participant has to carry out. In the cumulative-counts task, participants switch between different mental representations in working memory, but there is no real switch in task. In some tasks participants switch between different attended attributes of the same stimulus (sort by number–sort by color–sort by number); again, there is no real change in task. That is a total of three kinds of switches—switch of task, of representation, and of attended attribute—and there are other kinds of switches as well. The obvious question: does it make a difference what exactly is switched?

There is some relevant neural evidence on this point. The evidence is in the form of a *meta-analysis* (i.e., an analysis in which one pools the results of numerous studies, and tests statistically whether the studies are showing the same effects) of neuroimaging studies of switching (Wager et al., 2003). To conduct the meta-analysis, these investigators first put together on one schematic brain the peaks of the activations from switching studies that involved either attended attributes or tasks. (There were not enough studies on switching working-memory representations to include in the analysis.) Then they applied a *clustering algorithm*—a computer program that determines whether the peaks fall into clusters rather than being evenly distributed throughout the brain. In particular, the investigators wanted to determine: (1) whether the peaks for switching attributes fell into a few separate clusters; (2) similarly, whether the peaks for switching tasks fell into a few clusters; and (3) the extent to which these two sets of clusters overlap. The results are presented in Figure 7–15.

Figure 7–15 shows the brain as if it were glass. In Figure 7–15a, we are looking *through* the right lateral cortex. Thus, we can see *all* the clusters (but since we have essentially collapsed the brain horizontally, we cannot tell whether a cluster is in the left or the right hemisphere). What is abundantly clear in the figure is the substantial overlap between clusters for switching tasks and clusters for switching attributes. These results imply two conclusions: switching tasks and attributes seem to involve the same neural mechanisms, and many of the relevant neural mechanisms are located

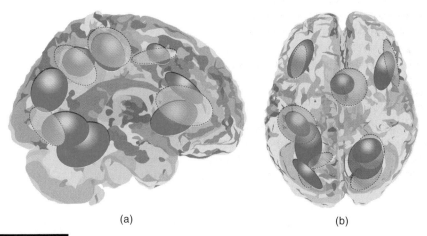

(a)   (b)

FIGURE 7–15 A meta-analysis of switching

Clusters of activations from studies that involved either switching attributes or switching tasks are shown on (and in) a "glass brain." (a) In this view, it is as if you are looking through the brain from the right side. As is evident, almost all the clusters for switching attributes (shown in dark blue, with solid outlines) overlap with the clusters for switching tasks (shown in light blue, with dotted outlines). This means that the regions activated when switching attributes are roughly the same as those activated when switching tasks—that is, there may only be one neural switcher. (b) In this view of the clusters, it is as if you are looking through the brain from top to bottom. The conclusions remain the same.

in parietal cortex, which again argues against the frontal-executive hypothesis. Figure 7–15b provides the same data from a different view. Now it is as if we are looking from the top, down through the brain, so now we can distinguish clusters on the left from those on the right. Our two conclusions remain unchallenged.

These results are relatively new, and they need to be backed up by at least two different kinds of studies. First, we need neuroimaging studies that compare two or more switching types *in the same participants*. The meta-analysis does not do this, because its input—activation peaks—was drawn from different experiments. Second, we need behavioral experiments that seek to determine whether or not switching in different ways is affected by different factors. At least one behavioral study indicates that there may be little difference in switching between attributes and objects (Wager, et al., 2006). As usual, we want converging evidence.

✓ **Comprehension Check:**

1. How can a switching cost be demonstrated?
2. According to the model of attention switching discussed, what are the underlying causes of a switching cost?

5. INHIBITION OF RESPONSE

How can we tell the difference between attending to something and ignoring everything else—in other words, the difference between focusing on one thing and inhibiting another? In the Stroop task, it is difficult to determine whether the basic phenomenon—the slowing on incompatible trials where color name and ink color conflict—is due to heightened activation of the ink color or to inhibition of word names, or both. Ditto for many other executive-attention tasks. But there is one case—*response inhibition*—in which inhibition, rather than attention, clearly is the key factor. Response inhibition is the suppression of a partially prepared response.

Distracted by the phone call, you reach to move the pot of boiling water off the electric burner and remember only in the nick of time that you haven't picked up a potholder—you have to inhibit your reaching response, whether it has only been programmed or in fact has been initiated. Or, listening on the phone to your slightly pushy favor-seeking friend, you are getting annoyed and are about to say something that will be hard to unsay. Again, you need to inhibit a partially prepared response. Though response inhibition is only one kind of inhibition, it is an important kind that occurs frequently in everyday life.

5.1. Representative Cases of Response Inhibition

A number of experimental tasks have been designed to study response inhibition and its neural underpinnings. One is the go/no-go task, a classic test that has been widely used to assess frontal-lobe functioning. Participants are presented with a sequence of stimuli, say, letters, and instructed to push a button at the appearance of every letter (a "go" response) *except* X ("no-go"). As long as X occurs relatively infrequently, when it does appear the task clearly requires the participant to inhibit a tendency to press the button. As the number of consecutive go responses increases, the more likely the participant will be to respond in error when an X finally shows up (Casey et al., 1997). Presumably, the longer the sequence of go trials, or the higher the probability of a go response, the more difficult it is for a participant to start an inhibitory response that will overturn the processing that underlies the go trials.

A number of fMRI studies of participants doing this task have been conducted, and the results are of considerable interest: they suggest that response inhibition is a separate executive process, distinct from those considered thus far. The critical contrast is between the regions activated on no-go trials (when response inhibition is required) and on go trials (when no inhibition is required). As frequently occurs in executive-processing tasks, our old friend the dorsolateral PFC is activated. But other brain areas get into the act as well. One such area is the anterior cingulate. Although some researchers have argued that the anterior cingulate plays a role in tasks requiring executive attention, others have provided suggestive evidence that the anterior cingulate is active in these tasks only when there is a need for inhibition at the response level (consider the distinction between eligible and ineligible responses, discussed on page 295). Perhaps most interesting, in response inhibition an additional PFC region is sometimes activated, the orbitofrontal cortex (which is below the dorsolateral PFC). Furthermore, activation in this other region is correlated with performance in the task: participants who show more activation in the orbitofrontal region produce fewer errors on the no-go trials of the task.

Studies with nonhuman primates provide evidence for orbitofrontal cortex involvement in inhibition (e.g., Iverson & Mishkin, 1970; Sakuri & Sugimoto, 1985). In these studies, lesions in the PFC, particularly the orbitofrontal cortex, have been shown to produce deficits in tasks that require the inhibition of strong response tendencies. Similarly, studies with human patients who have damage in this critical region also show that the patients are impaired on tasks requiring the inhibition of responses or response tendencies (Malloy et al., 1993).

Another task (performed by human participants) that relies on response inhibition is the stop-signal task developed by Logan (1983). In a typical version of this task, participants have to reply quickly to questions concerning category membership ("Is a pomegranate a fruit?") or rhymes ("Does *sleigh* rhyme with *play*?"). On some trials, a tone is sounded—the *stop signal*—which directs participants to stop their processing on that trial and not answer the question. The critical determinant of performance in these tasks is the *stop-signal delay,* that is, the length of time between question and stop signal. The longer this delay, the more processing the participant has completed, and the more likely it is that the response tendency cannot be aborted—and therefore the more likely it is that the participant will commit an error by answering the question despite the stop signal.

But how do we know that the inhibition observed is truly an inhibition of response, rather than an inhibition of some earlier process? Logan (1983) has some decisive evidence on this point. After the stop-signal experiment just described was completed,

Logan gave the participants a surprise memory test on the critical words in the test questions. If the inhibition engendered by the stop signal had affected earlier processes, then memory for the critical words should have been poorer on trials that included a stop signal than on trials that did not. In fact, there was no difference in memory for the two kinds of trials, which indicates that inhibition affected response processes after earlier processing was completed. In subsequent studies (de Jong et al., 1995), event-related potentials (ERPs) (electrical activity in the brain linked to a particular "event," that is, a particular stimulus or response) were used along with electromyograms (measures of electrical activity in motor systems) and behavioral measures to show that the inhibition of response could occur at any point in the preparation and execution of response. The ERP measures, which offer some rough information about brain localization, were consistent with a frontal localization of response inhibition.

Response inhibition is vitally important in normal life. If you said everything that came to mind, or performed every action that you thought of, you'd probably soon end up friendless or worse. And a number of psychiatric disorders appear to be marked by a lack of response inhibition: witness the bizarre speech and behaviors that often appear in schizophrenia, or the blatant lack of response inhibition in some obsessive-compulsive disorders, in which patients repeat nonfunctional responses again and again. Or consider the personality trait of being unable to delay gratification, which in adulthood is often a major handicap in dealing with real-life situations, and which may heavily involve a failure of response inhibition. A recent study shows that this trait, as indexed by tests performed during childhood, is associated with poorer performance on the go/no-go test, indexed in adulthood (Eigsti et al., 2006).

5.2. Development of Response Inhibition

"Kids say the darndest things"—possibly because impulsivity, and a lack of response inhibition, may be most widespread in children. How does it come about that at some point we know (pretty much) when to keep our mouths shut?

A substantial amount of behavioral and neural research has been conducted on the development of inhibitory processes. A good deal of this research is inspired by the belief that inhibition, particularly response inhibition, is mediated by the PFC, and by the fact that the PFC undergoes one of the longest periods of development of any brain region, taking almost two decades to reach full maturity in humans (Diamond, 2002). Thus we can expect young children to have great difficulty inhibiting their responses even in simple cases, and to progress systematically in their ability to inhibit responses as they grow up. (Because the PFC clearly seems to be involved in executive attention, and in at least some cases of task switching, we would expect similar developmental trajectories for these executive processes as well.)

One of the simplest and most widely used tasks with infants is the A-not-B task, which was introduced by Jean Piaget in 1954. Infants watch as a desired object is first hidden in one of two places that differ only in spatial location. Then follows a delay of a few seconds, after which the infants are induced to find the hidden object and are rewarded when they do. If the object is hidden in the same place on the first few trials, infants have no problem reaching for that same location. But when the desired object is switched to the other position, infants (younger than about 1 year old) still reach for the location rewarded earlier, even though they have seen the object placed elsewhere. It is as if infants cannot inhibit the previously rewarded response and select the new correct one (see, e.g., Diamond, 1985).

An alternative interpretation of these results is that the infants lack a sufficiently developed working memory to maintain the location of the desired object. Although this may be part of the story, it cannot be all, because in some trials in these experiments, when during the test phase the infant *looks at the correct location,* he or she *persists in reaching for the out-of-date location.* The infant is essentially attending to the correct choice, so this is not a problem in either attention or memory, but is reaching for the wrong place, which seems like a striking failure of response inhibition.

Children improve on the A-not-B task by the end of the first year of life, and by the time they are 3 to 5 years old they show some competency in tasks such as go/no-go. (By the time they are 7 to 12, their neural patterns of activation in go/no-go are almost identical to those of adults, although they are still not at adult levels of behavioral performance; Casey et al., 1997). Another task on which children show rapid improvement during the period of 3 to 5 years is the tapping task (Luria, 1966). On each trial, the experimenter taps either once or twice, and participants have to respond in reverse, tapping once if the experimenter taps twice, and twice if the experimenter taps once. On the face of it, the task appears to involve response inhibition (although it is awfully close to the executive-attention compatibility task discussed on pages 290–291). Neuroimaging studies with adults show that performance on the tapping task is accompanied by activation of the dorsolateral PFC (Brass et al., 2001), and it has long been known that adults with lesions in the PFC do poorly on such a task (Luria, 1966).

There is much more to the development of response inhibition (a useful starting point is Diamond, 2002), but enough has been said to make the major points response inhibition is a distinct executive process, and there is a striking correspondence between the development of response inhibition and the maturation of the PFC. The period of marked growth of the length of dendritic branches of PFC neurons—at about 7 to 12 months—exactly mirrors the period when infants first show improvement on the A-not-B task. A comparable correspondence is seen between improved performance on tasks such as go/no-go or tapping and neuronal developments in PFC. The density of neurons in dorsolateral PFC is highest at birth and declines with age, as if a pruning process (in which ineffective connections are removed) were taking place. At age 2, the density of PFC neurons is 55 percent greater than the adult number, but by age 7 it is only 10 percent above the adult number (Huttenlocher, 1990). And by age 7, children's patterns of results on tasks such as the go/no-go start to look more like those of adults. Although these correspondences do not prove that the PFC underlies response inhibition, they are certainly compatible with that hypothesis.

Comprehension Check:

1. What evidence indicates that response inhibition is a distinct executive process?
2. Why is response inhibition so important in daily life?

6. SEQUENCING

Planning: getting the pasta going before heating the fudge sauce for dessert; re-arranging your schedule to accommodate a friend's request; making that schedule in the first place—all these activities require the ability to sequence operations or events to accomplish a goal. The coordination of processes necessary for planning suggests that an executive process—sequencing—is involved.

6.1. Mechanisms for Sequencing

By sequencing we mean, in part, coding information about the order of events in working memory. You can't form a plan to accomplish a goal without coding the order of actions or events involved. Dr. P.'s inability to execute a sequence of actions was among his most striking deficits. So a fundamental question is, what mechanisms do we use to code the temporal order of a sequence of events?

To answer this question, we first need to show that coding the order of an item requires different mechanisms than coding the identity of that item (Estes 1972). A number of behavioral experiments suggest that it does. In one pair of studies (Sternberg, 1966, 1967), participants were tested on two related tasks, one requiring the storage in working memory only of item identity (Figure 7–16a), the other requiring the storage of order information as well (Figure 7–16b). In the item identity task, participants were presented with a series of items to remember followed by a probe item, and their task was to decide whether the probe occurred in the memory set, in any position; for this task only item information had to be stored in working memory. In the order task, participants were presented with a series of items, followed by a probe item from the series; here the task was to produce the item in the input sequence following the probe item. (For example, given the series A T G M and a probe item t, the response should be "g.") Clearly, participants had to store item and order information to accomplish this task.

In both the order and item tasks the number of items in the memory set is varied, and in both cases the time to respond to the probe increases with this variable. The data are plotted in Figure 7–16c. Look at the slopes of the lines relating response time to the size of the memory set: this relation tells us how long it takes to process each additional item (as described in Chapter 6). The graphs show striking differences between the two tasks. The slope for the order task is steeper than the slope for the item task. The most straightforward conclusion is that storing and retrieving order information involves additional processes than are required for storing and retrieving item information. Some of this difference could be due to the fact that the first task involves recognition whereas the second requires recall. But other data, as we will see, support the idea that item and order information are stored and processed differently.

Why think that coding order information—that is, sequencing—is an executive process? For one thing, it certainly is a metaprocess, because virtually any kind of items or events can be coded for order information. And it has long been known that patients with frontal-lobe damage are deficient in coding order information compared to item information. In a study by Corsi (cited in Milner, 1971) frontal-damage

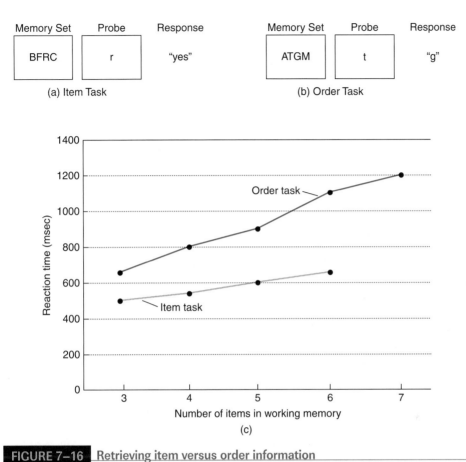

FIGURE 7–16 **Retrieving item versus order information**
(a) This task involves only item identity information: participants must decide only whether the probe occurred in the memory set. (b) This task requires the storage and retrieval of order information as well as item identity information. Now participants must report the item that *followed* the probe item in the memory set. In both tasks the probe is in a different case from the memory set to prevent participants from using a visual matching strategy. (c) The data plotted: these two tasks lead to sharp differences in the way that information is retrieved from working memory.

patients and parietal-damage patients were shown a series of pairs of items; occasionally the two items in a pair would appear with a question mark between them. The patient's task was to decide which of the two items had appeared more recently. When only one of the items had actually been presented previously, this was a test of item recognition; when both items had been previously presented, this was a test of order memory as well as item memory. The results showed a striking double dissociation. The frontal-damage patients were impaired on order information, but not on item memory, whereas the parietal-damage patients showed the opposite pattern—impairment on item memory but not order memory. These findings have been strengthened and extended in subsequent studies (B. Milner et al., 1991).

How might order information be represented? Three well-known possibilities are worth considering. To be specific, let's discuss these mechanisms in the context of an experiment in which participants are shown a short series of items to remember (for example, J G X R L B) followed by a pair of probe letters, both of which were in the memory set (for example, G L). The participant's task is to decide whether the probe letters are in the same order as they were in the memory set (they need not be adjacent; so the answer in the example is yes). One possible order mechanism is to form directed associations between every pair of successive items—J precedes G precedes X, and so on (e.g., Burgess & Hitch, 1999). With this mechanism, the farther apart two items are in the memory list, the longer it should take to determine that they are correctly ordered because more associations have to be traversed (G L should take longer than G R).

A second possible order mechanism is that we attach "order tags" to the items: J is tagged as the first item, G as the second item, and so on. With this way of representing order information, there is no reason for the time to decide on the order of the probe items to depend on the distance between the two items in the input list.

A third possibility is that you code order information on the basis of familiarity: perhaps when asked to decide whether G preceded L, the participant might simply check the familiarity of the two items; presumably the representation that is less familiar has decayed more than the other, is less strong, and hence likely occurred earlier (e.g., Cavanaugh, 1976). (In this way of coding, order information is represented continuously, rather than as discrete associations or order tags.) And when coding order by familiarity, we would expect that the farther apart two probe items are in the memory list, the less time it should take to determine that the items are correctly ordered because there will be a greater difference in strength (E. E. Smith et al., 2002).

There is behavioral evidence for all three mechanisms. The Burgess and Hitch (1999) model focuses on the serial recall of unrelated words. For example, the participant might see the words *table, lemon, rock, sheet, pen,* and *lunch,* followed by a brief delay, and then be given a signal to recall the words in order. Participants report rehearsing the items to themselves during the delay. This model assumes that successive elements are directly associated, and this model explains behavioral data on serial recall. Here's an everyday case of direct associations: when asked for the last four digits of their Social Security number, which are often requested by various security programs, many people find themselves going through the entire number to get to the fourth-from-last digit. Presumably, they have memorized the number as a sequence of direct associates (try it—have you?).

Other studies supply evidence for order tags. In one experiment, participants were first presented a short sequence of words, and after a brief delay had to perform one of two working memory tasks: recall the words in the order given, or recall the words in alphabetical order. Because the second task requires a reordering of the input order into an alphabetical order, it probably can be accomplished only by a mechanism that assigns alphabetical-order tags to items held in working memory, and then uses these tags to guide recall. Accuracy was high in the alphabetic-order task, which offers some indirect evidence for a direct tagging mechanism. Interestingly, when participants performing these tasks had their brains imaged, only the alphabetized-recall task activated the dorsolateral PFC; the simple input-order task did not result in such activation even though it required representation of the input order (Collette et al., 1999.)

Still other studies provide evidence for the use of familiarity to represent order information. In a representative study, participants were presented five letters in a particular order, followed by a brief delay. The probe that followed always consisted of two letters (Figure 7–17a). There were two tasks: an item task, in which the two probe letters were identical, and the participant simply had to decide whether that letter had appeared in the memory set; and an order task, in which the probe letters

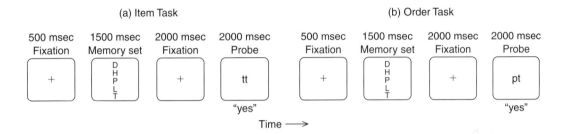

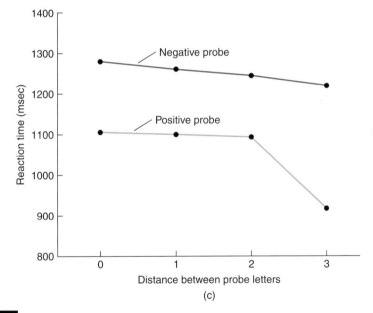

FIGURE 7–17 Distance effects in order judgments

(a) The item task and (b) the order task. In both tasks, participants were shown a fixation point (a plus sign) between trials. In a positive probe, the probe item or order matched the memory set; in a negative probe, it did not. Again, in both tasks the probe is in a different case from the memory set to prevent participants from using a visual matching strategy. (c) The distance effects obtained in the order task: the greater the distance between the two probe letters, the faster the response times.

(Marshuetz, C., Smith, E. E., Jonides, J., DeCutis, J., & Chenevert, T. L. (2000). Order information in working memory; fMRI evidence for parietal and prefrontal mechanisms. *Journal of Cognitive Neuroscience, 12,* 130–144. © 2000 by the Massachusetts Institute of Technology. Reprinted with permission.)

differed, but were both drawn from the memory set, and participants had to decide whether the letters were in the same order as in the memory set (they did not need to be adjacent for a yes response). In the order task, when the time to make a positive or negative decision is plotted against the distance between the two probe letters in the memory set, response times decrease with distance—a "distance effect"—as we would expect if relative familiarity or strength were used to make the judgments (Figure 7–17b) (Marshuetz et al., 2000).

When participants performed these same tasks while their brains were imaged by fMRI and the activations for item and order tasks were compared, two regions were more activated in the order than in the item task. One was the dorsolateral PFC, which of course fits with the frontal-executive hypothesis. But the other areas were in the parietal cortex, again showing that certain parietal regions are involved in some executive processes. Even more interesting, some of the parietal regions were in the intraparietal cortex, an area known to be involved in judgments of continuous quantities, such as comparisons of numerosity (Chochon et al., 1999). This fits with the behavioral data showing distance effects. In short, the neuroimaging data provide evidence that people can use two of the different representations of order: a familiarity-based representation that relies on the intraparietal cortex, and a direct temporal-coding representation that is mediated by the dorsolateral PFC (Marshuetz et al., 2000).

6.2. Sequencing Connected Items

Given some idea of how we code the order of arbitrary items, the next step is to consider the sequencing of connected items, as occurs in many real-life situations. It turns out that a critical distinction here is between familiar and novel item sequences.

A familiar real-life sequence is "going to a restaurant." Most adults, like the diners in Figure 7–18, have memorized the sequence of steps in this endeavor, which in the United States goes roughly like this: enter the restaurant, be seated, accept a menu, look over the menu and make a choice, place an order, receive the food, eat the food, ask for the check, pay the check (plus a tip), and leave the restaurant. So familiar is this sequence that Schank and Abelson (1977) dubbed it a *script,* and detailed a number of other scripts (among them "going to the movies," "washing clothes," and "starting a car"). Moreover, there is evidence that our representation of a script consists of direct inter-item associations. When you hear a story about going to a restaurant and some important steps are left out ("Herbie was seated and ate his steak"), the effect is disconcerting. The more steps that have been left out, the longer it takes to understand the story, as if you have to fill in the missing steps mentally before taking in the next one (Abbott et al., 1985).

Things are different when it comes to generating a novel sequence, say, the sequence of activities needed to open a beauty salon. Now you must do some problem solving rather than just rely on associations (Schank & Abelson, 1977). The goal of opening a beauty parlor must be broken down into subgoals, and plans and subplans must be generated. Normal participants have little trouble generating such novel sequences, but it is a very different story for patients with damage in the frontal lobes, particularly the dorsolateral PFC, as shown by the following experiment.

FIGURE 7–18   The restaurant script in action

These diners, at various stages of the restaurant experience, know what comes next, know what to do. Patients with frontal-lobe damage have difficulty with this.

(Photograph by Spencer Grant. Courtesy of PhotoEdit Inc.)

Three different groups of participants were tested on event-sequencing tasks. The three groups included patients with lesions in the PFC, particularly the dorsolateral PFC; patients with lesions in posterior cortical regions; and normal controls. The types of sequences they were tested on included scripts, such as starting a car, and novel sequences, such as opening a beauty parlor. In one study, participants were first asked to generate actions associated with the themes (for example, miming starting a car); then they ordered the generated actions into an appropriate sequence. There were no differences among the three groups of participants in the number or type of actions generated for familiar or unfamiliar themes.

In contrast, notable differences appeared when the participants had to order the generated items into a sequence. None of the normal participants nor the patients with posterior lesions made any errors on the script sequences (such as starting a car), whereas the frontal-damage patients made some errors in sequencing. This pattern was amplified when the sequence was unfamiliar (opening a beauty parlor). Now frontal-damage patients made substantially more sequencing errors than either normal participants or posterior-damage patients (the latter two groups did not differ). These findings show that the PFC is involved in sequencing actions as well as generating them. Exactly the same pattern of results was obtained in a second study, in which participants were given cards with actions for different themes written on them and were asked to order the actions for each theme. Frontal-damage patients made many errors, whereas normal participants and posterior-damage patients were almost perfect (Sirigu et al., 1995).

These results cannot be explained by assuming that sequencing unfamiliar items is more difficult than sequencing familiar ones and that patients with brain damage will show a deficit in performing a task to the extent the task is difficult. The posterior patients, like the PFC patients, had extensive brain damage, yet they performed relatively normally in sequencing unfamiliar items. So it matters where the damage is, and when it is in the PFC, sequencing processes deteriorate. This study provides good evidence that the PFC (particularly the dorsolateral PFC) is involved in sequencing actions. It also has the virtue of being closer to real-life concerns, given that the kind of sequencing that was studied captures much of the difficulties that frontal patients experience while trying to carry out a job or lead a normal life.

✔ **Comprehension Check:**

1. What are different ways in which order information may be represented?
2. What is the evidence that the PFC is involved in processing ordered sequences?

7. MONITORING

In the context of executive processes, monitoring is the assessment of one's performance on a task *while the task is being performed*. This is to be distinguished from the ability to assess (and improve) your performance *after* the task is completed, either from feedback received or your own view of how things went.

On-line monitoring occurs in a vast number of human activities—whenever you assess how you are doing while solving any kind of problem, intellectual or social (e.g., Metcalf & Shiamura, 1994), or when you check your understanding of the sentence you are reading as you go. Monitoring may be even more "meta" than the other executive processes we have considered; you can imagine situations where you assess whether you are attending well, or switching attention well.

7.1. Monitoring Working Memory

We have already seen a close connection between working memory and a number of executive processes. Some of the most influential work in this area involves the self-ordering task (Petrides et al., 1993a) illustrated in Figure 7–19. In this example of the task, trials are presented in blocks of six. On the first trial a set of six objects is presented, and the participant points to one of them. On the second trial the same six objects are presented, but in a different configuration, and the participant's task is to point to a different object from the one selected earlier. On the third trial, the same six objects are again presented in still a different configuration, and the participant's task is to point to an object that has not been selected before. According to Petrides et al. (1993a), participants accomplish the task this way: they store their

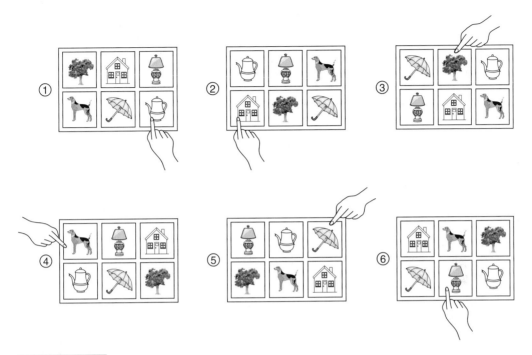

FIGURE 7–19 A correct performance on a six-item self-ordered pointing task

The participant must point to a different item on each page; the position of each picture varies from page to page.

first choice in working memory; then, before making the second choice, inspect (that is, monitor) the contents of working memory so as not to make an error; store their second choice in working memory; and so on. The task involves the constant updating and monitoring of working memory, and it is generally assumed that it is the monitoring part that is critical to success.

Normal participants have little trouble with this task, as long as the memory load is in the range of six (that is, within the capacity of working memory). For patients with frontal damage, it is a different story. Frontal-damage patients are impaired on this task, even when compared to patients with temporal-lobe damage; in contrast, frontal-damage patients are not impaired on a working memory task that requires only reporting the six items presented. Presumably the requirement to monitor the contents of working memory is mediated by the PFC, the left PFC in particular (Petrides & Milner, 1982). This result has wide generality. It holds with verbal items as well as visual ones, and essentially the same deficits can be produced in monkeys that have been lesioned in the region of the dorsolateral PFC (Petrides, 1986). Furthermore, when normal human participants perform the task while having their brains imaged (by PET), one of the major regions activated is—you guessed it—the dorsolateral PFC.

A comparable task is the generate-random task. The task sounds simple enough. Generate a string of, say, eight random numbers. Now, most people believe that a string of random numbers would have few or no immediate repeats and no discernible pattern (both beliefs are incorrect, by the way). The only way to meet these two constraints while generating "random" numbers is to store each digit produced in working memory, and then monitor working memory before generating the next digit so that you do not get a repeat or produce a pattern. In a PET experiment that compared generate-random to generate-in-order (for example, say the numbers 1 through 8 in order), only the former task activated the dorsolateral PFC (Petrides et al., 1993b). On the face of it, these studies suggest that monitoring is an executive process at least partly mediated by the dorsolateral PFC.

7.2. Monitoring for Errors

Another source of evidence for monitoring as an executive process comes from studies that focus on errors. For openers, there is a good deal of behavioral evidence that participants know when they commit an error in choice-response time tasks such as "push the left button when a circle appears, the right button when the square appears, and push the middle button if you make a mistake." Judging from these behavioral data, error detection can be quite slow, with some studies showing that it takes about 700 milliseconds (Rabbitt, 1998). These times are sufficiently slow that it is hard to take them as measures of on-line processing.

However, work using event-related potentials provides more convincing evidence that participants are detecting errors very soon after making them. Gehring et al. (1993) found a wiggle in the ERP response wave that followed incorrect responses. This component, called the *error-related negativity* (ERN), is a negative deflection in the ERP wave that begins about the time of an error, often slightly before it, and peaks roughly 100 milliseconds after the error. Given how quickly the ERN occurs, it probably reflects some kind of internal monitoring process. One interpretation of the results is that the ERN reflects a process that signals errors whenever it detects a mismatch between the response made and the correct response, where the latter is determined by information accumulating after the initial response has been selected (e.g., Gehring et al., 1993; see also Botvinick et al., 2001). Furthermore, although ERPs do not lead to fine-grained information about location in the brain, it appears that the ERN is being generated by a midline structure in the frontal cortex, presumably the anterior cingulate.

In discussing earlier the neural-network model of executive attention, we considered the proposal that what is being monitored is not errors per se but rather conflict at the response level. The evidence in favor of this position comes from a neuroimaging study. It showed that trials that engender substantial conflict, yet are responded to correctly, lead to increased activation in what appears to be the same region of the anterior cingulate activated in the ERP studies (Carter et al., 1998). The exact interpretation of how on-line monitoring is accomplished remains a hot topic of research, but the findings from both ERP and fMRI experiments leave little doubt that such an executive process exists.

An issue that has arisen repeatedly in this chapter focuses on the question of how many executive processes exist. In closing, we address this question in the *Debate* box.

We have assumed throughout the discussion that there are a number of executive processes and that this number is relatively small—fewer than 10. Although this assumption is shared by many researchers (see Stuss & Knight, 2002), there are other views. Some researchers hold that there is only one executive process, whereas others hold that there are hundreds.

When Alan Baddeley published his model of working memory in 1986 and introduced the notion of a central executive, he had in mind an attentional–inhibition system, similar to what we discussed under the heading of "executive attention." The basic idea (in line with Norman & Shallice, 1986) was that when stimuli are unambiguous or the required response is straightforward, no attention is needed; but when there is any kind of conflict, then executive attention—the central executive—must be brought into play. More recently, the neural-network model initially developed by Cohen and his colleagues (1990) posited only an attentional device as an executive process (the notion of a conflict monitor was added to the model more recently). Because the Cohen et al. model has inhibition naturally built into it, it is capable of accounting for much of the data presented in our discussion of executive attention and switching attention. This type of model clearly has parsimony on its side, but it also has some substantive problems. First, it cannot easily explain why a neuroimaging contrast between an executive-attention task and an attention-switching task has produced some notable differences in activation sites. Second, it is not obvious how this model could account for the sequencing data we presented.

Another argument for a single-executive-process view has been made (Duncan et al., 2000). These investigators imaged participants on a few different tasks that supposedly involved different executive processes, and found that all tasks activated the same general PFC region, the dorsolateral PFC. They concluded that only one process is in play, something like general intelligence (or what is called *fluid intelligence*, that is, the ability to reason about novel situations). Our discussion, too, has implicated the dorsolateral PFC in every executive process considered. But we have surveyed a far greater array of studies than did Duncan and his colleagues, and we have turned up evidence for the involvement of some different neural areas in different executive processes, for example, parietal regions in attention switching, orbitofrontal areas in response inhibition, and intraparietal regions in order judgments.

Those who argue for a multitude of executive processes often do so from the perspective of a computational model, although of the "boxes-and-arrows" information-processing type (e.g., Meyer & Kieras, 1997a, 1997b). Consider a close cousin to task switching; namely, doing two tasks at the same time. For example, a participant may be instructed to discriminate a light (red or blue) and a sound (high or low frequency) simultaneously, and to make the response about the light first. To implement this processing in detail (that is, computationally), one must posit "mini" metaprocesses such as "locking out" the response to the sound in case it comes in first, and then "unlocking" this response when the response to the light has been made. Given the plethora of mini-executive processes that have to be posited, this kind of approach may have the opposite problem from that faced by the unitary modelers. The executive processes in these multiple-executive-process models are often inserted to make the model sufficient to account for data, and it may prove very difficult to obtain independent evidence for their existence. So they explain much, but possibly at the expense of positing too much.

✓ Comprehension Check:

1. In tasks requiring the monitoring of working memory, what neural structure is routinely activated?

2. "We are quickly 'aware' of making an error." What is the evidence for this assertion?

Revisit and Reflect

1. *Are executive processes mediated by the frontal lobes?*

   Early studies indicated that many executive processes are impaired by injuries to the frontal lobes, particularly the PFC. Researchers developed a set of tests that presumably taps executive processes—among them the Stroop, Wisconsin Card Sort, and Tower of Hanoi tests—and showed that patients with PFC damage were selectively impaired on these tasks. These findings strengthened the frontal executive hypothesis, the idea that every executive process is primarily mediated by the PFC. Our review has shown that this hypothesis is too strong: although the PFC plays a role in executive processes, regions in parietal cortex appear to be as important in a number of executive processes, such as attention switching and scheduling.

   Think Critically

   - What anatomical properties of the frontal cortex makes it particularly suitable for mediating executive processes? Does this preclude there being another anatomical basis for executive processes?
   - What kinds of jobs could a person with frontal damage perform normally? What kinds of jobs could such a person not perform normally?

2. *What is executive attention, and how can it be modeled?*

   Executive attention is probably the one metaprocess that everyone would agree is necessary for controlling cognition. A huge number of behavioral experiments point to its role in biasing one source of information over another. Progress has been made both in modeling executive attention—as a neural network that includes an attentional controller and a conflict detector—and in determining its neural bases, the dorsolateral PFC and the anterior cingulate. The exact role of the anterior cingulate, however, remains controversial.

   Think Critically

   - How could software designers make use of stimulus–response compatibility in devising, say, a new e-mail system?
   - How does the neural network model of executive attention explain the poor performance on the Stroop task of patients with frontal lobe damage?

3. *What is involved in switching attention?*

Switching attention brings more processes into play. Behavioral experiments show that there is almost always a cost to switching, regardless of the task. This cost is presumably due to engaging additional cognitive processes; most of the neuroimaging results on switching attention indicate that additional neural areas are involved during the switch. Some of these additional neural areas are the same ones involved in executive attention—dorsolateral PFC and the anterior cingulate. (In the relevant studies on switching, these two areas were not involved when performing one task for an entire block.) Other additional switching areas are in the parietal cortex.

Think Critically

■ As discussed in Chapter 3, some researchers have proposed that attending to something is like shining a spotlight on it; if so, then switching attention would be like moving the spotlight. Consider a behavioral prediction about task switching that this analogy suggests to you.

■ Imagine an experiment in which on alternating trials participants had to do a Stroop task ("name the ink color") and a reading task ("read the word"). How would the information-processing model describe the underlying processing? How would the neural-network model describe it?

4. *What is response inhibition, and what is distinctive about it?*

Response inhibition, the suppression of a partially prepared response, can be isolated experimentally by tasks such as go/no-go and stop-signal. These tasks show that participants are sensitive to the probability of a go response or the time to delay a response. At the neural level, these tasks activate the dorsolateral PFC and the anterior cingulate. However, these tasks often bring an additional area on line, the orbitofrontal cortex. In addition, there is a remarkable parallel between the participant's ability to inhibit a response and the development of the PFC.

Think Critically

■ Can you think of any real-life situations in which it is adaptive to be impulsive, that is in which it is adaptive *not* to exercise response inhibition?

■ Suppose the PFC were fully developed by age 2. What would be some of the implications for child rearing?

5. *What mechanisms are used for sequencing information?*

Three different mechanisms may be used in sequencing unrelated items, including associations between adjacent items, direct coding of temporal order, and using relative familiarity to code order. Neuroimaging studies support the idea of different mechanisms: the dorsolateral PFC may mediate direct coding of order, whereas the parietal cortex may mediate the use of continuous information—such as the relative strength or familiarity—to code order. In sequencing related items, there is an important distinction between constructing familiar versus novel sequences; the operation of the PFC is sensitive to this distinction, as indicated by the fact that frontal-damage patients are far more impaired on generating a novel sequence than a familiar one.

Think Critically

- When might it be advantageous to code for order by using the relative familiarity of the items?
- What is the difference between sequencing and coding order?

6. *What is involved in monitoring our performance "on-line"?*

Work on monitoring as an executive process has followed two lines of research. One focuses on monitoring the contents of working memory; the PFC is clearly involved. The other focuses on monitoring for errors, a process that has been well studied in behavioral experiments. In addition, ERP and fMRI studies suggest that such monitoring is extremely rapid, occurring within 100 milliseconds of the response, and that the process is mediated by the anterior cingulate.

Think Critically

- Is there any difference between *monitoring* the contents of working memory and *attending* to the contents of working memory?
- What are some of the advantages of being able to monitor for errors on line?

Emotion and Cognition

Learning Objectives

On September 11, 2001, two planes crashed into the two buildings of the World Trade Center in New York. You watched television that day as the images were played over and over, and you clearly remember seeing both buildings hit. *But you didn't see that: there was no video available of the first plane until the next day. Emotion interacts with memory.*

You're driving on a highway. All of a sudden there are brake lights ahead of you as far as you can see and traffic has slowed to a creep. A wrecker passes on the shoulder, and you realize there's been an accident. You're scornful of the rubberneckers who are causing the delay by their ghoulish curiosity. After half an hour, you're at the crash site. *Although the road ahead is clear, you, too, pause to stare before driving on. Emotion interacts with attention.*

You know that the odds favor the house, but the thrill and the excitement of the possibility of a big payoff overcome common sense. *You bet the ranch. Emotion interacts with decision making.*

These common scenarios emphasize the importance of emotion in understanding a range of cognitive processes. In this chapter we discuss what is known about the interaction of emotion with cognition. We specifically address five questions:

1. How have researchers defined emotion to allow scientific investigations of the interaction of emotion and cognition?
2. What techniques are typically used to manipulate and measure emotion in the laboratory?
3. What are the means by which stimuli can acquire emotional properties and how is this emotional learning expressed?
4. How does emotion alter our ability to remember?
5. How does emotion change attention and perception?

1. THE CONNECTION

In spite of the intimate relationship between emotion and cognitive processes, which we often experience consciously—"I was so *furious*," we say, "that I couldn't think straight"—emotion was not considered an appropriate domain of inquiry within the study of cognition until very recently. Why has it taken so long for the study of cognition to include the exploration of emotion?

The idea, no longer tenable, that emotion and cognition are distinct and separable mental activities can be traced back to early philosophical thought. Plato, for example, believed that human beings have three "souls," corresponding to three aspects of human nature: the intellect, the will, and the emotions. The influence of this early philosophical thought laid the groundwork for debates over the centuries about cognition and its relation to emotion.

In modern times, the study of cognition has been greatly influenced by the development of the computer—so much so that we speak of the "cognitive revolution" to describe the new way of thinking about cognitive processes that was based on the model of the computer (as discussed in Chapter 1). The computer provides a useful tool, but it is obvious that studying human information processing solely by analogy to a technological device leaves little role for emotion. Thus, both historically and in contemporary work, the prevailing models have left little room for the investigation of the connection between emotion and cognition. Nonetheless, the link between emotion and cognition is undeniable, and some psychologists have sought to explore its nature. One of the more recent debates (in the 1980s), which opened the door to further investigation of the interaction of emotion and cognition, involved the question of whether or not an emotion could be experienced without *cognitive appraisal* (i.e., an interpretation of the reason for your feeling). On one side was research showing that emotional stimuli presented subliminally, without the participants' awareness, nonetheless influenced the way participants evaluated subsequent neutral stimuli (Zajonc, 1980, 1984). From this the investigator, Robert Zajonc, argued that affective ("affect" is a general term that includes emotions and preferences) judgments, such as how much you like a particular painting, occur before, and independently of, cognition. The other position, championed by Richard Lazarus (1981, 1984), held that emotion could not occur without cognitive appraisal. Sweating and an increased heart rate, both signs of arousal, may occur when you watch a horror movie, talk to someone you find attractive, or work out at the gym; but in each case your appraisal of your emotional response would very likely be different. Thus, your emotional response—disgust, say, or joy—depends on the reason you experience arousal, and this determination is part of cognition (Schacter & Singer, 1962). Zajonc, then, argued that emotion can occur independently of cognition, and Lazarus believed that emotion depended on a subset of cognitive processes; their writings helped to draw researchers' attention to the interaction between emotion and cognition.

But the single most influential factor in this new focus is our growing understanding of the neural systems underlying emotion. It now appears, from neuroimaging and other brain-based studies, that some brain structures are more or less specialized for processing emotional stimuli. One of these is the **amygdala,** a small, almond-shaped structure in the medial temporal lobe just anterior to the hippocampus (LeDoux, 1996) (Figure 8–1). This research is consistent with the idea that there are separate systems for emotion. However, these neural structures specialized for

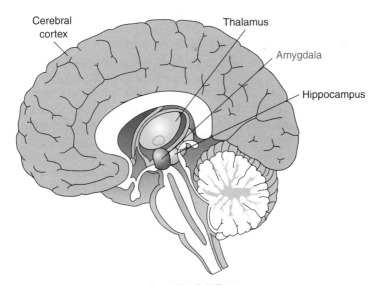

Right Medial View

FIGURE 8–1   The amygdala

The amygdala is centrally involved in the processing of emotional stimuli. Although the ancient Greeks and Hebrews (as well as the Elizabethans) believed the liver to be the seat of the emotions, the modern-day view is diffferent.

emotion both influence, and are influenced by, neural systems known to be important for cognitive behaviors (Dolan, 2002; Oschner et al., 2002); the inference is that emotion and cognition are interdependent.

It is no longer considered ideal to study emotion without considering cognition and vice versa. The neural systems, and behavioral expression, of emotion and of cognition are interdependent in many circumstances. The understanding of cognition is incomplete without exploration of the role of emotion.

✓ **Comprehension Check:**

1. In what sense is the relationship between emotion and cognition a very old question? In what sense is it new?
2. What is the key difference between Lazarus's and Zajonc's positions?

2. DEFINING EMOTION

Many have argued that the essential appeal of the arts is the subtlety and power with which emotion can be expressed by the artist and evoked in the spectator—it is the essence of Aristotle's conception of tragedy. Shakespeare certainly knew the intrigue of complex emotional lives; his aim, in his words, was "to hold, as 'twere, the mirror up to nature," and he portrayed those emotions in his plays. A great opera combines dramatic scenarios and sublime music to heighten the emotional experience of the audience. And a great rock song does more than get your feet tapping—it also tugs at your emotions. All of us, not just our artists, have a rich vocabulary for describing our emotional lives: *joyful, elated, contented, delighted, cheerful, pleased, jovial, exultant, glad, blissful* all describe subjective variations of the experience of "happiness." Art and language emphasize the complexity and subtlety of emotion. But how can we define emotion in a way that captures the range of emotional experience, yet is objective and therefore can allow scientific investigation?

Researchers and philosophers have struggled with this problem. Although most people have little difficulty describing their individual emotions, a single definition of emotion is elusive (Russell, 2003). Thus the term *emotion* has been used to refer to mental and physical processes that include aspects of subjective experience, evaluation and appraisal, motivation, and bodily responses such as arousal and facial expression. For the purposes of this chapter (adapted from Scherer, 2000), we will use the term emotion when referring to a relatively brief episode of synchronized responses (which can include bodily responses, facial expression, and subjective evaluation) that indicate the evaluation of an internal or external event as significant. Emotion refers to the range of reactions to events that are limited in time, such as experiencing joy, fear, or sadness in response to hearing some news. Mood, on the other hand, is used to refer to a diffuse affective state that is most pronounced as a change in subjective feeling. Moods are generally affective states of low intensity but relatively long duration, and sometimes without any apparent cause, such as a spontaneous feeling of gloom or cheerfulness. Two related concepts are attitudes and motivation. Attitudes are relatively enduring, affectively colored beliefs, preferences, and predispositions toward objects or persons, such as like, love, hate, or desire for a person or object. Finally, motivation refers to the propensity to action that is a component of some affective responses. When you watch a horror movie, at fearful moments you may hide your eyes to escape the image on the screen. A primary function of emotion is to motivate action (if the image on the screen had been real, your action in response might have been of larger scale, and you might have survived to see another day).

In an effort to establish a scientific framework for the investigation of emotion, researchers have focused on various aspects of affective experience (facial expressions, feelings of arousal, motivation), attempting to capture a range of emotion responses such as sadness, fear, and happiness. The two main current approaches classifying the range of emotional states are the attempt to define basic emotions and the attempt to explore their dimensions. Each approach is more or less useful, depending on the question being asked.

2.1. Basic Emotions

In his groundbreaking work "On the Origin of Species" (1859), Charles Darwin was one of the first to propose that there are a limited number of basic and universal human emotions. He derived this idea in part from colleagues who had studied different cultures around the world. When Darwin asked them about the emotional lives of people far removed from Western culture, they all reported similar emotional facial expressions. Darwin suggested that this universality of emotional expression implies a common emotional experience.

Nearly a hundred years later Paul Ekman and his colleagues studied the facial expression of emotion and suggested that there are six basic expressions of emotion, corresponding to anger, disgust, fear, happiness, sadness, and surprise (Ekman & Friesen, 1971) (Figure 8–2). Each of these expressions is characterized by a unique subset of facial muscle movements, and the ability to convey them appears to be innate. Infants display these facial expressions, as do people who have been blind since birth and so never had the opportunity to mirror them. These facial expressions appear to be universal and similar in range, appearance, and interpretation whether you are from Papua, New Guinea, or Buffalo, New York. More recently, researchers interested in the detection of deception have taken advantage of this detailed knowledge of characteristic muscle movements corresponding to genuine facial expressions to help determine when someone is lying (Gladwell, 2002).

Using these social, emotional facial expressions as stimuli in experiments, researchers have started to study the neural systems underlying the perception of basic emotional expressions. It has been shown that certain neural systems seem to be specialized for the perception of specific emotional expressions. For example, there are many reports of patients with bilateral damage to the amygdala who have a specific deficit in the perception of expressions of fear (Adolphs et al., 1999). More recently,

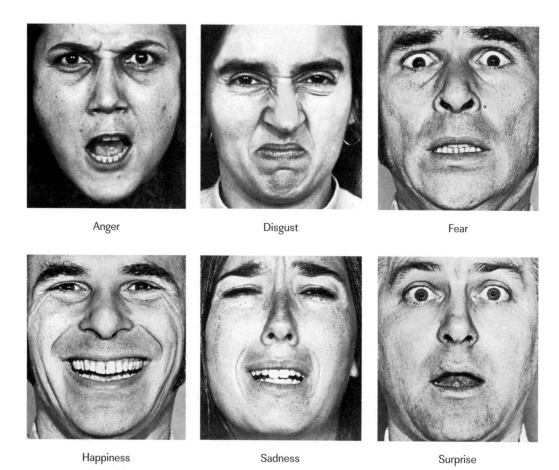

Anger	Disgust	Fear
Happiness	Sadness	Surprise

FIGURE 8–2   Expressions of emotion: unique and universal

The six emotional facial expressions found in virtually all cultures. Each is implemented by a unique subset of facial muscle movements.

(Photographs by Paul Ekman Ph.D.)

other neural structures—the insula and basal ganglia—have been shown to underlie the perception of disgust (Calder et al., 2001), and a neurotransmitter system (activated by dopamine) and a neural structure (the ventral striatum) are important for the perception of expressions of anger (Calder et al., 2003; Lawrence et al., 2002). Although there is not yet a complete understanding of the specific neural representations that underlie the perception of each of the six basic emotion expressions defined by Ekman, this research supports the idea that there are in fact distinct basic emotions, emotional reactions that are universal across cultures. However, it is important to acknowledge that Ekman's six basic emotions do not capture the range of human emotional experience. Several more complex emotions, among them guilt and love, are less clearly linked to specific facial displays.

2.2. Dimensional Approaches

Dimensional approaches to the exploration of emotion seek to classify the range of emotional states on certain specific scales. Our emotions are not "on" or "off," but are experienced on a continuum. The two primary dimensional approaches used by researchers emphasize, and attempt to measure, different aspects of emotional experience.

2.2.1. The Circumplex Model

Arousal is the overall term for the bodily changes that occur in emotion, such as changes in heart rate, sweating, and the release of stress hormones in response to a stimulus—the changes in your physical self when you're watching a horror movie or asking for a date. The intensity of the emotional reaction may be assessed by the strength of these responses. Valence, on the other hand, is the subjective quality, positive or negative, of the emotional response to a specific object or event. Both these dimensions can be put on scales: you can be asleep, relaxed, or highly excited, you can be terrifically pleased, indifferent, or highly turned off—and anything in between.

The circumplex model of emotion puts "arousal" on one axis and "valence" on the other (Barrett & Russell, 1999; Russell, 1980). "Arousal" refers to both the strength of the response to a stimulus and to activation, that is, the mobilization of resources. "Valence" (or "evaluation") reflects the degree to which the experience is pleasant or unpleasant. Using these two dimensions of emotional experience, the circumplex model creates a graphic framework in which a range of emotional states can be positioned. For example, "sadness," "fear," "excitation," and "nervousness" are considered discrete emotional states. These could be understood as varying along the dimensions of arousal and valence. "Sadness" and "fear" are both unpleasant, but "sadness" is not as arousing or activating as "fear." "Excitation" and "nervousness" are both arousing states, but "excitation" is relatively positive and "nervousness" is relatively negative. As more emotional responses are plotted, the reason for the name of the model becomes clear: the data fall in a circular pattern (Figure 8–3).

The dimensions of arousal and valence may have distinct representations in the human brain. For instance, one study examined brain activation patterns that result from the presentation of olfactory stimuli (A. K. Anderson et al., 2003). The amygdala responded primarily to the intensity of the smell whether it was pleasant or unpleasant to the participant, whereas different subregions within the orbitofrontal cortex (OFC) responded when the smell was either pleasant (medial OFC response) or unpleasant (lateral OFC response), regardless of the stimulus intensity. These results suggest that the amygdala, which also is important in our perception of expressions of fear in others, may code several different aspects of emotional experience.

2.2.2. The Approach–Withdrawal Distinction

Emotions may be classified along the dimension of *motivation*, which can be conceptualized as the propensity to action that is a component of some emotional

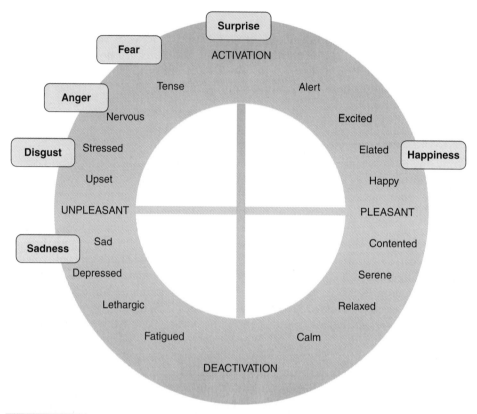

FIGURE 8–3 The circumplex model of emotion

This graph, on which arousal is plotted on the vertical axis and valence on the horizontal, permits the depiction of a range of emotional states. The basic emotions are noted in boxes.

(Russell, J. A., & Barrett, L. F. (1999). Core affect, prototypical emotional episodes and other things called emotion: Dissecting the elephant. *Journal of Personality and Social Psychology, 76,* pp. 805–819. © 1999 American Psychological Association. Reprinted with permission.)

responses. Different emotions lead to different goals for action. Some, such as happiness, surprise, and anger, are referred to as "approach emotions" in that they evoke the desire to approach the stimulus object or situation. In contrast, others, sadness, disgust, and fear, are referred to as "withdrawal emotions" in that they evoke the desire to withdraw from objects or situations linked to these emotions. The approach–withdrawal model characterizes the component of an emotional reaction that is the propensity to action—that is, motivation—as either a tendency to approach the object, event, or situation or to withdraw from it. Davidson et al. (2000) have provided evidence that there is a cerebral asymmetry in the neural representation of approach and withdrawal tendencies. Using EEGs, these investigators found that participants varied in the relative level of activity of the anterior left and right cerebral hemispheres when at rest, and linked this asymmetry to their various

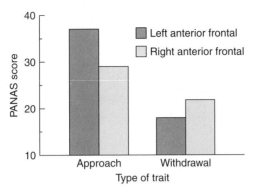

Participants with greater activity in the left anteriorfrontal region at rest (measured by EEG) rated themselves as higher on "approach" traits such as enthusiasm, pride, and attentiveness. Those with greater activity in the right anteriorfrontal region rated themselves higher on "withdrawal" traits such as irritableness, guilt, and fear. The rating scale is the Positive and Negative Affect Scale (PANAS); whether approach (positive affect) or withdrawal (negative affect) traits are being rated is shown on the horizontal axis.

(Adapted from Tomarken, A. J., Davidson, R. J., Wheeler, R. E., & Doss, R. C. (1992). Individual difference in anterior brain asymmetry and fundamental dimensions of emotion. *Journal of Personality and Society Psychology, 62*, pp. 676–682. Copyright © 1992 American Psychological Association. Reprinted with permission.)

dispositions. Participants who rated themselves higher on a series of positive affective traits such as enthusiasm, pride, and attentiveness ("approach" traits) showed relatively greater EEG activity over the left anterior frontal region at rest, whereas those who rated themselves higher on negative affective traits such as irritableness, guilt, and fear ("withdrawal" traits) showed relatively greater EEG activity over the right anterior frontal region (Figure 8–4).

This asymmetry also reflects emotional responses. In an intriguing study with infants, researchers found that infants with more dominant right-hemisphere EEG activity at rest were more likely to cry and fuss when separated from their mothers in comparison to infants with more dominant left-hemisphere EEG activity (Davidson et al., 2000). Although all healthy people are capable of both approach and withdrawal dispositions and emotional responses, the relative frequency and intensity of these emotional reactions in a given person may be related to the relative baseline asymmetry in the activity of the anterior right and left cerebral hemispheres.

Comprehension Check:

1. What evidence is used to support the idea that there are basic emotions that are universal across cultures? What are these basic emotions?

2. Describe an emotional reaction that would result in an approach response and another that would be linked to a withdrawal response.

3. MANIPULATING AND MEASURING EMOTION

As social animals, we often try to manipulate and measure the emotions, moods, and attitudes of those around us—that is what we are doing when we try to comfort a grieving friend or reassure a frightened child. But although manipulating and measuring affect is a part of human experience, it is a challenge to do so in a manner that can be assessed objectively and reliably. Researchers interested in emotion have met the challenge by using a number of techniques.

3.1. Manipulation by Mood Induction

As mentioned earlier, mood is a more stable and diffuse affective state than emotion, longer lasting and not necessarily linked to a specific event or object. In research, one method that has been used to manipulate affective experience is to change the participant's mood. This technique, called *mood induction,* focuses on changing the baseline state reported by the participants on arriving at the laboratory. Typical means of changing a participant's mood are to show the participant affective film clips (hilariously funny or grim and despairing, depending on the change sought by the experimenter), to play music (again, upbeat or solemn), or to ask the participant to focus on affective situations, real or imagined, that result in either positive or negative mood states. Mood induction is considered successful if the participant reports a shift of mood in the predicted direction.

3.2. Manipulation by Evocative Stimuli

The most common laboratory technique used to manipulate emotion (as opposed to mood) is the presentation of *emotionally evocative stimuli.* Typical stimuli used to elicit emotional responses in participants are pictures of faces with different emotional expressions; pictures of emotional scenes such as an appealing baby or the very unappealing muzzle of a revolver (Figure 8–5); words that vary in valence and arousal; money; loud noise; and mild shock. By presenting participants with stimuli that evoke emotional experiences, investigators can explore the impact this emotional experience has on mental and physical behaviors and neural responses.

3.3. Measuring Emotion Directly

How would you know whether you were being successful in your attempt to console a sad friend? You might simply ask: "How are you doing now?" Or you might look for an emotional reaction, such as a smile or the end of tears. Probably the most common technique used to assess affective states or responses, both inside and outside the laboratory, is self-report. If we want to know how someone feels, we ask. This is a form of *direct assessment,* in that participants explicitly report their emotional reaction, mood, or attitude. Although this is an often-used method for assessing affective states, it relies on introspection and is affected by cultural conventions.

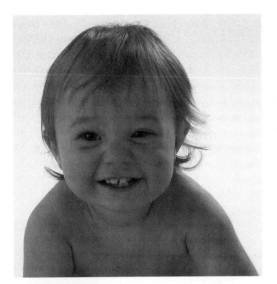 

FIGURE 8–5 Emotionally evocative stimuli

Examples of positive and negative emotional scenes from the International Affective Picture System developed by Peter J. Lang and colleagues.

(Left photograph courtesy of Jo Foord and Dorling Kindersley. Right photograph by John McGrail. Courtesy of The Stock Connection.)

Therefore, it is important to have a way to measure an affective reaction by *indirect assessment*, that is, by means independent of subjective report and language.

3.4. Measuring Emotion Indirectly

One way of making an *indirect assessment* is to ask the participant to choose among different options on the assumption that an emotional assessment of the options partly determines the choice. A second indirect measure of emotional assessment is the inhibition or facilitation of a behavior, such as response time or eye movements. The pleasure of seeing a joyful reunion between friends in the yard outside your classroom may cause you to linger your gaze and be slow to respond to a question. Emotion can influence our actions and the ease with which we respond by both inhibiting and facilitating behaviors.

A third technique of indirect assessment makes use of psychophysiology, the study of the relationship between mental states and physiological responses. One of the primary ways that emotion differs from other mental processes is that emotion typically results in substantial changes in our physical state. As described in Chapter 1, the autonomic nervous system, part of the peripheral nervous system, is concerned with maintaining the body's internal environment. Its sympathetic branch, which prepares the body for action in the face of, say, a threatening event, may become more activated and initiate a number of physiological responses, including pupil dilation, sweating, and increased heart rate and blood pressure. Correspondingly, the parasympathetic branch is dominant when the threat is past, and the body is at rest; its functions, which essentially conserve energy, such as by slowing heart rate, can also be measured (Figure 8–6). An underlying emotion may also be reflected in reflex responses and facial muscle movements. All these bodily responses can be assessed with psychophysiology.

Two important psychophysiological responses assessed by researchers interested in emotion are the *skin conductance response* and the *potentiated eyeblink startle*.

The skin conductance response (SCR) is an indication of autonomic nervous system arousal. Even a subtle emotional stimulus can produce a response from the sweat glands (controlled by the autonomic nervous system). The increased sweating creates

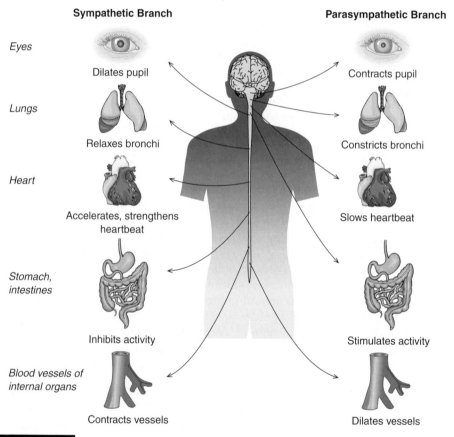

Sympathetic Branch   **Parasympathetic Branch**

Eyes
    Dilates pupil   Contracts pupil

Lungs
    Relaxes bronchi   Constricts bronchi

Heart
    Accelerates, strengthens   Slows heartbeat
    heartbeat

Stomach, intestines
    Inhibits activity   Stimulates activity

Blood vessels of internal organs
    Contracts vessels   Dilates vessels

FIGURE 8–6   The autonomic nervous system

The sympathetic branch prepares the body for action: the parasympathetic branch counteracts the sympathetic branch and maintains the body equilibrium at rest.

(Barry D. Smith, *Psychology, Science & Understanding*, p. 73. New York: McGraw-Hill, 1998. Reprinted with permission.)

a change in the electrical conductivity of the skin. The SCR is assessed by placing electrodes on the participant's fingers; the electrodes pass a small electrical current through the skin. Changes in resistance to the current, which occur with subtle changes in the sweating, are measured. You may already be familiar with the SCR because it is typically used as a component of the lie detector. Because it is often assumed that there is an emotional reaction related to guilt or anxiety when telling a lie, answers to questions that are known to be true (for example, your name or address) should yield less of an SCR than answers that are not true.

The strength of the startle reflex, the response that follows a sudden and surprising stimulus such as a sudden loud noise, can be measured. If you are walking down a relatively quiet street at midday and suddenly hear a car backfire, you might be startled. If you hear the same sound late at night on a deserted street when you're already feeling a little anxious, you might startle even more. Startle is a reflex that is *potentiated,* or enhanced, when we are in a negative emotional state. The degree of potentiation can be measured in the laboratory by examining the strength of the eyeblink response, a component of the startle reflex. The strength of this response is measured by electrodes placed on the skin over the eye muscles. The amount of muscle contraction reflects the strength of the startle reflex. We blink harder when startled more, which is called a potentiated eyeblink startle. A researcher interested in a participant's emotional responses to different scenes might present the scenes one at a time and unexpectedly present a loud click or popping noise. The difference in the strength of the potentiated eyeblink startle to the sound provides information about the emotional state evoked by the different scenes. Scenes that are more negative elicit a stronger startle reflex response than scenes that are neutral or more positive (Lang et al., 1990).

One of the interesting distinctions between SCR and potentiated startle measures is that the SCR reflects arousal that can occur in response to both negative and positive stimuli, whereas the startle reflex is modulated by valence—that is, it increases when the participant is in a negative emotional state and decreases when the participant is in a positive emotional state. Both measures provide an indirect, physiological assessment of an emotion, but they differ in the type of emotional information they register.

Comprehension Check:

1. Describe a technique that can be used to manipulate emotion in the laboratory.
2. Give an example of a direct assessment of an emotional response and an example of an indirect assessment of an emotional response.

4. EMOTIONAL LEARNING: ACQUIRING EVALUATIONS

Why do you like some movie genres and not others? Some brands of soap and not others? Some kinds of people and not others? In this discussion, the supposedly rational answer—in the case of movies, "because I enjoy the special effects"—does not suffice. What *underlies* these preferences? Here's another instance: have you ever felt uneasy, for no good reason, around someone you barely knew—and then realized that the person reminded you of someone who had once done you harm? What *underlies* this emotional reaction?

All these instances involve emotional learning—learning, one way or another (and not always on the basis of fact), that people, places, and things are not all neutral but often acquire some kind of value. Some people, places, or things are better or worse, comforting or scary, or simply good or bad. This value determines, in part, our emotional reaction to the person, place, or thing.

Some emotionally evocative stimuli are inherently positive or negative; there is no need to learn their value. A mild shock is aversive to all animals, from family pets to Nobel laureates. These types of stimuli are called primary reinforcers because their motivational properties occur naturally and do not need to be learned. Other stimuli are motivating only because we have learned that they represent positive or negative consequences. A bathtub full of hundred-dollar bills will not keep you warm (or at least not very warm), taste good, or provide safety—nonetheless, a bathtub full of hundred-dollar bills would be very nice to have. Money has value because we have learned to associate it with stimuli that are inherently motivating: with money we can buy things that keep us warm, taste good, and provide safety. Money is a classic example of a secondary reinforcer, a stimulus whose motivational properties are acquired through learning.

Understanding how stimuli acquire affective value is of interest to a wide range of professions, advertising and animal training among them. For psychologists, understanding how a stimulus becomes associated with an emotion is a central challenge in the investigation of the interaction of emotion and cognition. There are several means by which a stimulus can acquire emotional significance.

4.1. Classical Conditioning

The name most often associated with classical conditioning is that of Ivan Pavlov (1849–1936), the great Russian physiologist who discovered the principles of such conditioning. Pavlov was interested in digestion and intended to examine salivation in dogs in response to food. His studies became complicated when the dogs started to salivate *before the food was presented:* the salivation response was occurring when a researcher opened the door to the dogs' quarters. The dogs were salivating in response to an event *associated with* the presentation of food. Pavlov realized that reflexes such as salivation can be evoked not only by the appropriate stimuli (in this case, food), but also by events associated with these reflex-inducing stimuli. Further research has demonstrated that all sorts of reflexes and responses, including emotional responses, can be elicited by conditioning.

In the study of emotion, it has become clear that stimuli that are linked with positive or negative events themselves take on affective qualities and elicit affective reactions. For example, if you have been in a car accident, it would not be surprising if you were to feel uneasy the next time you found yourself at the intersection where the accident happened. The association between the previously neutral location and the negative accident results in a conditioned arousal response and a feeling of nervousness linked to that location. It is not uncommon for us to feel anxious or aroused around people, places, or things that have previously been connected with unpleasant experiences. This is the result of emotional classical conditioning, the learned association between a neutral event and an emotional event.

Emotional classical conditioning can be expressed in different ways. As *autonomic conditioning,* it can be expressed through bodily responses, such as an arousal response. As *evaluative conditioning,* it can be expressed through a preference or attitude: a stimulus that predicts a negative emotional event may be rated more negatively. Most studies of emotional classical conditioning examine either autonomic responses or subjective reports of evaluation, although these two types of conditioned responses are often acquired simultaneously.

One of the more widely studied forms of autonomic conditioning is aversive, or *fear conditioning*. Fear conditioning occurs when a neutral stimulus paired with an aversive or fearful event comes to elicit a fear response when the stimulus is presented alone. That is what is happening when the acquired arousal response is made to the site of the car accident. The experience is a familiar one: most of us could find examples in our lives to substitute for "car accident" and "intersection." Learning by aversive conditioning has been considered a model for fear learning in general, and it has been suggested that it may be specifically related to phobias (Ohman & Mineka, 2001).

Aversive conditioning has been studied extensively in both humans and nonhumans. Across species, it has been shown that the amygdala is a critical brain structure in both the acquisition and expression of aversive conditioning (LeDoux, 1996). Humans with damage to the amygdala do not acquire conditioned fear responses (Bechara et al., 1995; LaBar et al., 1995), but they show a normal ability to report that the neutral stimulus predicts the aversive or fearful event. For example, a patient known as S.P., who had sustained bilateral damage to the amygdala, and normal control participants were given several pairings of a blue square and a mild shock to the wrist (Figure 8–7). After a few trials, the normal participants showed a skin conductance response to the blue square presented alone, indicating autonomic conditioning. S.P., however, showed no evidence of arousal to the blue square alone, even though her arousal response to the shock was normal. When S.P. was shown her own data and asked what she thought about the results, she answered:

> I knew that there was an anticipation that the blue square, at some particular point in time, would bring on one of the volt shocks. But even though I knew that, and I knew that from the very beginning, except for the very first one where I was surprised, that was my response. I knew it was going to happen. I expected that it was going to happen. So I learned from the very beginning that it was going to happen: blue and shock. And it happened. I turned out to be right, it happened! *(Phelps, 2002)*

It is clear that S.P. understood fear conditioning and had episodic memory of the events of the study. The ability to acquire and report this explicit representation depends on medial temporal structures, the so-called hippocampal complex, that are close to the amygdala (see Chapter 5). Patients with damage to the hippocampus, who have an intact amygdala, show the opposite pattern of results; that is, they

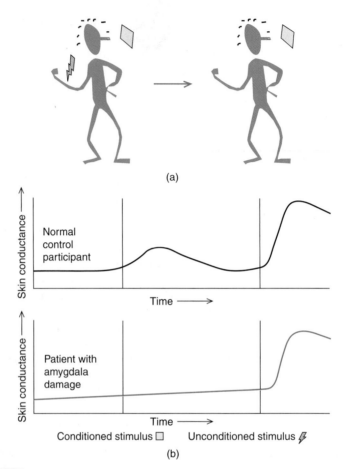

(a)

(b)

Conditioned stimulus ▢   Unconditioned stimulus ⚡

FIGURE 8–7   Fear conditioning: when it occurs, when it does not

(a) Fear conditioning occurs in normal participants: pairing a shock with a blue square results in a conditioned emotion response to the blue square when presented alone. (b) The graphs show the response of amygdala patient S.P. (bottom) and a normal control participant (top) in the blue square–shock experiment. Both show a skin conductance response (SCR) to the shock itself (far right), but only the normal participant shows an SCR to the conditioned stimulus. (Even though S.P. did not show a conditioned emotional response as measured by skin conductance, she demonstrated intact declarative knowledge of the fear conditioning procedure.)

show normal autonomic conditioning, as measured by SCR, but they are unable to report that the blue square predicts the shock (Bechara et al., 1995).

This double dissociation between direct (explicit report) and indirect (SCR) measures of emotional learning indicates that there are at least two kinds of learning systems that are operating independently: one (which relies on the hippocampus) mediates learning accompanied by awareness, namely, the declarative memory system described in detail in Chapter 5; the other (which relies on the amygdala) is necessary for conditioned autonomic responses. Additional support for the notion that awareness is not necessary for aversive conditioning comes from studies in which the stimulus linked with the aversive event is presented subliminally, so that the participant is unaware that it has been presented; this procedure can result in the expression of autonomic conditioning, as measured by SCR (Ohman & Soares, 1998).

Studies of autonomic conditioning have revealed the importance of learned physiological responses. Studies of evaluative conditioning, on the other hand, are more concerned with learned preferences or attitudes, the subjective, emotional responses that are acquired through classical conditioning. Evaluative conditioning is the goal of many (most) forms of advertising. Why do advertisers assume that pairing new products with attractive stimuli, such as popular athletes or celebrities, will alter our attitudes and, specifically, our purchasing decisions? We don't really think that using products endorsed by stars will confer stardom on us. Nonetheless, advertising works. It works because evaluative conditioning works. If we experience positive affect (for example, admiration of a celebrity endorser or amusement at clever ad copy) in the presence of a neutral stimulus (a deodorant, say) we may eventually come to prefer that stimulus. Evaluative conditioning manifests itself via a subsequent change in valence, that is, the degree to which the stimulus is regarded as pleasant (or unpleasant).

Like aversive conditioning, evaluative conditioning can occur without awareness (as can be the case with advertising). In other words, a preference is acquired and expressed, but we may be unaware of how this preference came to be. For example, in one study researchers paired a series of neutral pictures with either positive, negative, or other neutral pictures (Baeyens et al., 1990). Some participants were told to search for a relationship between the members of a pair; others were told simply to look at the pictures. Participants' awareness of the relationships between the neutral and emotional pictures was then assessed. Participants were considered "aware" if they correctly indicated which emotional picture was paired with a target neutral picture; if they indicated a different emotional picture of the same valence as the one actually paired with the target neutral picture; or if, although unable to indicate a particular picture, they correctly expressed the valence of the picture paired with the target neutral picture. Regardless of a participant's level of awareness of the relationship, similar levels of evaluative conditioning were observed.

Specifically, when participants were asked to rate how much they liked the neutral pictures, those who had been unable to report any knowledge of the relationship between the target neutral pictures and their respective pairs showed levels of acquired preferences similar to those of participants who were completely aware of the relationship between pictures. This attitude formation can occur independently of awareness. In addition, results consistent with this idea were obtained in two studies conducted with amnesic participants, who have deficits in declarative memory. Preference formation was demonstrated even though these patients were unable to report any memory for the conditioning procedures (Johnson et al., 1985; Lieberman et al., 2001).

It is likely that both types of emotional classical conditioning—autonomic conditioning and evaluative conditioning—occur simultaneously. For instance, a typical aversive conditioning study might pair an abstract pattern with a mild electric shock. After several presentations of such pairings the abstract pattern may come to elicit an arousal response when presented alone. This is an indication of autonomic conditioning. At the same time, if participants are asked to rate how much they like the abstract pattern compared to a similar pattern that was never paired with shock, they might rate the pattern paired with shock more negatively, thus indicating evaluative conditioning.

Even though autonomic and evaluative conditioning can occur simultaneously, there is some evidence that these two types of emotional classical conditioning can be dissociated. This evidence comes from studies of *extinction*. Extinction is the decrease in a learned emotional response that occurs when a stimulus is presented enough times without the occurrence of the emotional event that the participant learns that this conditioned neutral stimulus no longer predicts the occurrence of the emotional event. Your unfortunate car accident again: the first time after the accident you drive through the intersection where it occurred, you may feel nervous—this is a conditioned autonomic response to that particular location. Several months later, however, after you have driven through this intersection a number of times with no further mishap, your nervousness may fade; it has been extinguished. This is an example of the extinction of a conditioned autonomic response.

With autonomic conditioning procedures, extinction typically is rapid. After a few extinction trials in which the neutral event occurs without the aversive one, the conditioned autonomic response may no longer be expressed (e.g., LaBar et al., 1995; Ohman & Soares, 1998). Evaluative conditioning, on the other hand, is very hard to extinguish. Once a preference or attitude is acquired, this preference does not seem to diminish, even when there are twice as many presentations of the previously neutral stimulus without the occurrence of the emotional event and the participant is fully aware that the presentation of this stimulus no longer predicts the emotional event (De Houwer et al., 2001). Even if you extinguish your autonomic response when you pass the intersection where you had the accident, it is likely you will still dislike this intersection. This resistance to extinction for evaluative conditioning differentiates conditioned preferences from other types of classical conditioning.

4.2. Instrumental Conditioning: Learning by Reward or Punishment

Emotional learning can occur when certain actions and stimuli are paired with reward or punishment. Take, for example, gambling. For a gambler who bets on horses, actions such as going to the racetrack and placing the bet, and stimuli such as the racing pages and the morning line of probable odds, are paired with reward if the player wins. Although the bettor may lose (punishment), part of the reason gambling is so appealing to some people is that the thrill and excitement of an occasional large win is often more powerful than the many smaller losses that may occur.

Thus, liking to gamble may arise from instrumental conditioning. The principle underlying instrumental conditioning (which is also known as operant conditioning) is that a behavior or response will increase or decrease in frequency depending on the outcome of that behavior—on whether it yields a reward or a punishment. If we do something that leads to a good result (reward), we are more likely to repeat that behavior, and if we do something that leads to a bad result (punishment), that behavior is less likely to be repeated. Instrumental conditioning depends on our taking an action that can be rewarded.

In an effort to understand the nature of reward, researchers have explored the neural systems of reward learning and, to a lesser degree, of punishment learning (e.g., Bornhovd et al., 2002; Delgado et al., 2000). The neural system for reward is described in terms of both a neurotransmitter, dopamine, that is linked to reward and a neuroanatomical region, the striatum. The "mesolimbic dopamine pathway" links the ventral tegmental area of the medial forebrain bundle in the midbrain to the striatum, in the forebrain. It is this pathway that is activated in expectation of reward (Figure 8–8). If the ventral tegmental area is stimulated, activation of this pathway results in the release of dopamine to the striatum (Wise & Rompre, 1989). Neuroimaging studies have consistently shown activation of the striatum in response to a reward the participant perceives as such (e.g., Delgado et al., 2000; Knutson et al., 2001), and drugs that block the action of dopamine have been shown to lead to impairments in performance of rewarded learning tasks (Stellar & Stellar, 1984).

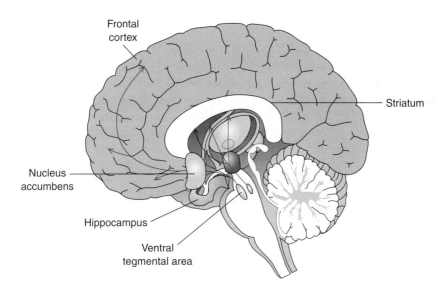

Right Medial View

FIGURE 8–8 The mesolimbic dopamine pathway—the reward circuitry of the brain
If the ventral tegmental area is stimulated, activation of this pathway results in the release of dopamine to the striatum and other regions, such as the frontal cortex. This sequence occurs in the presence of a reward.

(Figure 6.19 from *Psychological Science: The Mind, Brain and Behavior* by Michael Gazzaniga and Todd F. Heatherton. Copyright © 2003 by W. W. Norton & Company, Inc. Used with permission of W. W. Norton & Company, Inc.)

One of the most interesting findings to emerge from research on the neural basis of reward learning is that the neural system involved responds to all types of reward, whether it is a drug given to an addict (Breiter et al.,1997), a primary reinforcer such as food (Rolls et al., 1980), or a secondary reinforcer such as money (Delgado et al., 2000; Knutson et al., 2001). The fact that a common neural pathway mediates both primary and secondary reinforcers suggests that this system is important for coding perceived reward value. However, what is rewarding to one person may not be rewarding to another—and may be neither healthy, necessary, nor inherently valuable.

Instrumental conditioning requires action that can be reinforced. It is this action, and the stimulus prompting it, that acquires affective value. However, along with the action and stimulus, the affective value of a range of other, associated stimuli may be altered as well. An addict learns to associate taking the drug with reward. Drug taking is also linked to a number of other stimuli: the location where it usually takes place, the paraphernalia used, other people who use the drug with the addict, the dealer who sells the drug. All these stimuli, simply by their association with the action of drug taking, can acquire affective value by *classical conditioning*. Instrumental and classical conditioning can go hand in hand in an intimate relationship that makes changing behaviors such as taking drugs so challenging.

4.3. Instructional and Observational Learning

Both classical and instrumental conditioning depend on emotional experience for learning to occur—you must receive a stimulus that you perceive as positive–rewarding or negative–punishing. There are other means of emotional learning that do not require direct emotional experience, but depend instead on instruction or observation. Why, for instance, are some people afraid of germs and why do most people try to avoid them? Outside a research facility or academic setting—and for English majors not even then—most people have never seen a germ. And as far as our unassisted perceptual systems are concerned, germs are an imaginary concept. However, we have been told about the negative value of germs (and admonished from childhood, and in signs in restrooms, to wash our hands to avoid them). This is an example of *instructional learning*. (If the instruction is threatening enough, and not modulated by experience, the healthy avoidance of germs can become an unhealthy phobia.)

Unlike other species, we can learn about the emotional significance of events and stimuli through symbolic means such as language. We do not have to experience directly negative or positive consequences to know whether a stimulus is good or bad. Learning through instruction is a common means of emotional learning in humans, and it is highly effective. Learning emotional responses to neutral stimuli that are directly linked to aversive consequences (conditioning) is similar to learning through verbal communication (instruction) (Hugdahl & Ohman, 1977).

In fact, learning to fear through instruction and through classical conditioning activate some of the same neural pathways. In particular, the amygdala is not only important in aversive conditioning, but also plays a role in the physiological expression of instructed fear learning. This finding resulted from a study designed to be as similar as possible to the fear conditioning study described earlier in which patient S.P. participated. The difference is that shock was paired with the blue square only through verbal instruction. Patients with right or left amygdala damage as well as normal participants were told that they might receive a mild shock to the wrist when a blue square is presented ("threat"), but they would never receive a shock when a yellow square was presented ("safe"). Even though none of the participants in fact received a shock, the normal participants and those with *right* amygdala damage showed a potentiated startle response during presentations of the blue square, indicating a negative emotional response to the blue square–threat stimulus. The participants with *left* amygdala damage, however, did not demonstrate potentiated startle to the blue square (Funayama et al., 2001), indicating that the left amygdala is involved in instructed learning to fear. Although only the left amygdala plays a role in the expression of instructed fear, perhaps because of the verbal nature of instructed learning, these results suggest that the amygdala plays a role in the expression of fears that are imagined and anticipated, but never actually experienced. A related study using fMRI data from normal participants was reported by Phelps et al. (2001). Both these studies are examined in the accompanying *A Closer Look*.

Like instructional learning, *observational learning* does not rely on direct experience with positive or negative consequences. If we observe someone being rewarded or punished for a behavior, or enjoying or avoiding an event, we may learn something about the value of that behavior or event. A teacher who "makes an example" of a disruptive pupil and administers a reprimand in front of the entire class is hoping that the other pupils will engage in some observational learning.

Some nonhuman animals also learn by observation. For example, monkeys raised in a laboratory free of snakes can learn to fear them by observing monkeys raised in the wild who have an intense fear of snakes (Mineka et al., 1984) (Figure 8–9). The neural systems for learning through observation may involve "mirror neurons." Mirror neurons, discovered in monkeys, are neurons that respond both when an action is observed and when that action is performed (see Chapter 11). Mirror neurons in the premotor cortex of a monkey fire when that animal performs a motor response and also when it observes another monkey performing that response. In humans, it typically is not possible to study responses in single neurons, but by the use of neuroimaging techniques, mirror responses have been reported similar to those observed in the monkey (Gallese & Goldman, 1998; Rizzolatti et al., 1996). Moreover, researchers have discovered mirror responses for emotion. Watching someone else experience pain results in activation of parts of the pain circuitry in the observer (Singer et al., 2004). In an effort to extend this finding to observational learning, participants were told to watch a film clip of a confederate of the investigator undergoing classical conditioning in which a blue square is paired with a mild shock to the wrist. The participants were then presented with blue squares, but never actually received a shock. The amygdala, which we know

Two related studies that investigated, in different populations, the neural mechanisms underlying imaginary fears are considered together; both were published in 2001. Elizabeth A. Phelps, Kevin J. O'Connor, J. Christopher Gatenby, John C. Gores, Christian Grillon, and Michael Davis reported their results in a paper titled "Activation of the Left Amygdala to a Cognitive Representation of Fear," *Nature Neuroscience, 4,* 437–441; E. Sumie Funayama, Christian Grillon, Michael Davis, and Elizabeth A. Phelps reported theirs in "A Double Dissociation in the Affective Modulation of Startle in Humans: Effects of Unilateral Temporal Lobectomy," *Journal of Cognitive Neuroscience, 13,* 721–729.

Introduction

Do symbolically communicated and imaginary fears rely on the same neural mechanisms as fears acquired through direct, aversive experience, as in fear conditioning? This question was addressed in two studies (Funayama et al., 2001; Phelps et al., 2001).

Both groups of investigators were interested in how verbally communicated fears are represented in the brain and whether expressing this type of emotional learning depends on the amygdala, which has been shown to be critical in fear conditioning.

Method

Two techniques were used to assess human brain function: functional magnetic resonance imaging (fMRI) in normal participants (Phelps et al., 2001) and physiological responses of patients with amygdala lesions (Funayama et al., 2001). In each of the studies, participants were told that the presentation of a colored (for example, blue) square would indicate the possibility that a mild shock to the wrist would be delivered: this was called the "Threat" stimulus. Participants were also shown a square of another color (for example, yellow) and were told that this stimulus indicated that no shock would be delivered: this was called the "Safe" stimulus. In the fMRI study, normal participants were presented with the Threat and Safe stimuli while responses in the amygdala were assessed. Skin conductance responses were also measured to obtain a physiological indication of a fear response. In the patient study, normal controls as well as patients with left, right, and bilateral amygdala damage participated in an experiment of similar design in which eyeblink startle to the Threat and Safe stimuli was assessed as a measure of fear learning. In both the fMRI and patient study, none of the participants actually received a shock to the wrist.

Results

In both the fMRI and patient studies, normal control participants exhibited a physiological response consistent with fear in reaction to the presentation of the Threat (relative to Safe) stimulus. In autonomic measures taken during the fMRI study, the participants showed increased SCR to Threat versus Safe. In the patient study, the normal control participants showed a potentiated startle reflex response to Threat versus Safe. These results suggest that simply instructing someone about the potential aversive properties of a stimulus can elicit a fear response. Both the fMRI and patient studies also found that the left amygdala is important for this expression of instructed fear. In the fMRI study, activation of the left amygdala was observed in response to the Threat versus Safe stimulus, and the magnitude of this activation was correlated with the magnitude of the SCR response. In the patient study, patients whose damage included the left amygdala failed to show potentiated startle to the Threat stimulus.

Discussion

These results suggest that the left amygdala responds to verbally instructed fears and plays a critical role in their expression. The left amygdala may be particularly important because these fears require linguistic interpretation, which is known to rely on the left hemisphere in most people. Animal models of the neural mechanisms of fear learning have relied on fear conditioning, in which learning occurs through direct aversive experience. These results suggest that similar neural mechanisms may underlie fears that are uniquely human—that is, fears that are linguistically communicated and are imagined but never actually experienced.

FIGURE 8–9 An example of observational learning

Two sets of monkeys were required to reach past a snake to get food. Monkeys raised in the labora-tory showed no fear of the snakes and would reach for food—until they saw other monkeys, raised in the wild, that refused to reach for the food and displayed fear of the snake. The laboratory-raised monkeys then also demonstrated a fear response to the snake and refused to reach for food. (Courtesy of Susan Mineka, Northwestern University.)

is important for fear conditioning and instructed fear, also responded when partici-pants observed the confederate respond to the shock paired with the blue square. The magnitude of amygdala activation during observation was the same as when the participants were presented with the blue square and were anticipating the shock themselves (Olsson et al., 2004).

4.4. Mere Exposure

All the types of emotional learning described thus far rely on linking a stimulus or action to something that is "good" or "bad." When a preference or attitude is ac-quired through mere exposure, no linkage is required; just the simple repetition of a stimulus can make it likable. The *mere exposure effect* is based on familiarity, and so only the (repeated) presentation of the stimulus is necessary. In a typical mere expo-sure study, participants are shown neutral stimuli, such as abstract patterns. Some patterns are presented perhaps 10 times, others 5 times or once, and some patterns are not shown at all. After the exposure procedure, participants are asked to rate how much they like these abstract patterns. They are more likely to give high ratings to the patterns that they have been exposed to more frequently than to those they have been exposed to less frequently or not at all. Mere exposure effects have been observed with a range of stimuli, including Chinese ideographs, musical tunes, and nonsense syllables (Zajonc, 1980).

Although the mere exposure effect results from familiarity, it does not require recollection of previous experience with the stimulus. A study examining preferences for novel musical tunes found that the mere exposure effect was equally strong for tunes the participant could and could not identify as having been previously presented (Wilson, 1979). Similar effects have been observed for other types of stimuli. The factor that predicted the formation of a preference for the tunes and other stimuli was the amount of previous exposure, not awareness of that exposure (Zajonc, 1980). The notion that mere exposure effects can be obtained independent of awareness receives further support from studies demonstrating the mere exposure effect for stimuli presented subliminally (Bornstein, 1992). The next time you find yourself humming along with a song on the radio, remember: the more you hear it, the more you'll probably like it.

✓ **Comprehension Check:**

1. Describe an emotional learning situation in which there is evidence for both evaluative conditioning and autonomic conditioning.
2. In what ways can you learn to like or dislike something even when no conditioning occurs?

5. EMOTION AND DECLARATIVE MEMORY

Day to day, we tend to use our memory to answer questions such as "Where did I leave the keys?" But on the scale of a life, your lasting memories are not of the pocket in which you left your keys. Memories for events that are emotional and important seem to have a persistence and vividness that other memories lack. Memory for emotional public events, such as the destruction of the World Trade Center, will persist, although imperfectly. Memories for emotional private events, such as the birth of a baby, also are imbued with special qualities. How, exactly, does emotion influence memory?

As discussed in Chapter 5, one of the primary advances in memory research during the past 40 years has been the growing recognition that memory is not a unitary concept: different forms of memory, conscious and unconscious, relate to different neural systems. Declarative memory is long-term memory that can be consciously recollected and described to other people. It includes episodic memory, the "first-hand" memory of our own individual past histories, and semantic memory, knowledge about objects and events in the world. Both forms of memory can be influenced by various aspects of emotion in several possible ways.

5.1. Arousal and Memory

Regrettably for our peace of mind, memories for embarrassing situations may not fade. It would be nice to forget those occasions when our ignorance or social awkwardness was on full display. But we don't forget these events, and sometimes other people don't either. Why are these moments when you'd like to sink through the floor selected to last (and last vividly) and others are not? One reason is that embarrassment, an emotional reaction, leads to arousal, and arousal enhances our ability to store memories.

It is well known that emotional arousal can enhance recollection. This has been shown for a number of different types of stimuli and a range of memory tasks, both in and out of the laboratory (Christianson, 1992). In a classic study, Hueur and Reisberg (1992) showed each of two groups of participants a different slide show with a corresponding narrative. Both shows depicted a mother and son going to visit the father at work. The slides and narrative at the beginning and end of each show were the same and represented neutral events, such as the mother and son leaving the house and the mother making a phone call. In one of the slide shows, the emotion condition, the middle section of the story showed the father, identified as a doctor, responding to a gruesome accident. In the other slide show, the neutral condition, the father was a car mechanic. After seeing the slide show, participants were asked to recognize details of the slides and narrative. For both groups, there was no difference in the ability to remember details of the early and late portions of the show, which depicted neutral events. Participants in the emotion condition, however, were much better at remembering details from the middle, emotional portion of the slide show they saw compared to participants in the neutral condition, who saw a middle part that carried no emotional weight.

It is a well-documented finding that there is better declarative memory for arousing, emotional stimuli. How does this happen? To understand how this works, we can look at the neural mechanism underlying the influence of emotional arousal on memory.

A number of studies have shown that the amygdala, which is critical for the acquisition and expression of aversive conditioning, also has a secondary role in memory. Patients with damage to the amygdala do not show arousal-enhanced memory (Cahill et al., 1995; LaBar & Phelps, 1998). Neuroimaging studies reveal a correlation between the strength of the amygdala response to an emotional stimulus at encoding and the likelihood of successful recollection of that stimulus at a later time (Cahill et al., 1996; Hamman et al., 1999). These results suggest the amygdala can influence declarative memory for emotional events. But it is neighboring medial temporal lobe structures, in and around the hippocampus, that underlie the acquisition of declarative memory: the amygdala has its influence by interacting with the hippocampus.

Hippocampal consolidation is a slow process by which memories become more or less stable over time. A series of studies has demonstrated how the amygdala, through arousal, can influence hippocampal processing, modulating the consolidation of hippocampal-dependent memories (McGaugh, 2000). By enhancing hippocampal consolidation with arousal, the amygdala alters the storage of new information in memory (McGaugh et al., 1992).

To demonstrate that the amygdala modulates storage, investigators have disrupted or enhanced amygdala processing in rats *after* memory encoding. In one study rats were given a maze-learning task, which depends on the hippocampus for normal learning. Immediately after learning, some of the rats were given a pharmacological agent that induced an excitation response in the amygdala; the other rats were given a (nonactive) saline injection. Those rats whose amygdalas were artificially excited after learning showed better memory for the maze than the rats that received saline (Packard & Teather, 1998). The mechanism by which the amygdala modulates consolidation relies on activation of the *β-adrenergic system* in the amygdala. *Beta-blockers* (drugs that block the action of the β-adrenergic system by blocking β-adrenergic receptors) also block the effect of arousal on declarative memory (Cahill et al., 1994; McGaugh et al., 1992). It has been suggested that one of the adaptive functions of having a long consolidation process for the storage of declarative memories is to allow time for the arousal response to enhance the retention of events linked to emotional consequences.

If arousal, via the amygdala, modulates the storage of declarative memories, there should be different forgetting curves for arousing and nonarousing stimuli. This has been demonstrated in a number of studies. In an early experiment, participants were presented with word–digit pairs (Kleinsmith & Kaplan, 1963). Half the words were emotional and arousing, half were neutral. Participants were then presented with the word alone and asked to recall the paired digit. Some participants were given this memory task immediately after encoding, others a day later. Participants who were asked to recall the digits immediately showed somewhat better memory for the digits paired with neutral words, although this difference was not significant. Participants who were tested 24 hours later showed significantly better memory for the digits paired with high-arousal words. Comparing across the groups, there was evidence of forgetting over time for the neutral word–digit pairs, whereas memory for the arousing word–digit pairs did not diminish over time (Figure 8–10). Consistent with the idea that the amygdala enhances consolidation or storage processes, patients with damage to the amygdala show similar patterns of forgetting for arousing and neutral words (LaBar & Phelps, 1998).

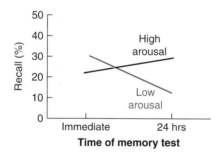

FIGURE 8–10 Memory and arousal I

Memory for digits paired with high- and low-arousing words was assessed both immediately after encoding and 24 hours later. Digits paired with low-arousal words were forgotten over time; digits paired with high-arousal words were not forgotten.

(Adapted from Kleinsmith, L. J., & Kaplan, S. (1963). Paired-associated learning as a function of arousal and interpolated interval. *Journal of Experimental Psychology, 65* (2): 190–193. © 1963 American Psychological Association. Adapted with permission.)

5.2. Stress and Memory

The effect of arousal on memory storage can help to explain why those events that are most exciting, embarrassing, or nerve wracking may receive preferential treatment in memory. However, prolonged stress and extreme arousal can have the opposite effect, impairing memory performance. The effect of arousal and stress on declarative memory can be characterized by an inverted U-shaped curve (Figure 8–11). Mild to moderate arousal enhances memory performance, but if the arousal response is prolonged or extreme, memory performance suffers.

The mechanism underlying this stress-induced memory impairment is related to hormonal changes that occur with long-term stress. Glucocorticoids, a group of stress hormones released by the adrenal gland, are the primary culprit. In studies with rats, researchers have shown that extended exposure to stress leads to increased levels of glucorticoids that can reduce the firing rate of hippocampal neurons, impair memory performance, and, if exposure is long enough, lead to hippocampal atrophy (McEwen & Sapolsky, 1995). The hippocampus has two types of glucocorticoid receptors, which are affected by different levels of glucocorticoid exposure. The existence of these two types of receptors may help to explain why different levels of exposure to arousal and stress hormones lead to either an enhancement or an impairment of memory.

The research examining the effect of stress on human memory is limited: the ethics of psychological investigation preclude inducing in humans the levels of stress necessary to impair memory performance. However, there is some evidence that patients who suffer from stress-inducing disorders, such as depression or post-traumatic stress disorder, have impaired memory, and that patients who suffer from these

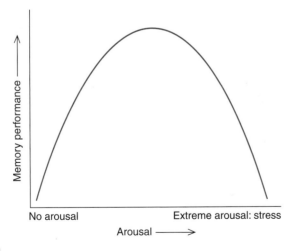

FIGURE 8–11 Memory and arousal II

An inverted U-shaped curve depicts the relationship between declarative memory performance and arousal. Mild or moderate arousal improves memory, but stress—that is, prolonged and extreme arousal—impairs it.

disorders for a number of years show signs of hippocampal atrophy (Bremner, 2002; Nasrallah et al., 1989).

Although it is difficult to test the effects of stress on human memory in a controlled laboratory study, it has been possible to demonstrate in humans the glucocorticoid influence observed in rats. For instance, in one study participants were daily either administered a drug that artificially increases the level of glucocorticoids or given a placebo. After four days, participants who had taken the drug and who had elevated glucocorticoid levels showed impaired memory performance relative to participants who took the placebo (Newcomer et al., 1994). These results support the conclusion that stress hormones can impair memory if exposure is prolonged.

5.3. Mood and Memory

Mood reflects a lasting and diffuse affective state that is not necessarily linked to any specific event. Have you ever noticed that when you are in a bad mood, you are more likely to recall negative and unfortunate events, whereas when you're in a good mood, happy occurrences come to mind more readily? This common experience reflects an influence of mood on memory known as the mood-congruent memory effect (Bower, 1981).

Mood induction—the deliberate attempt to change a participant's mood—is used to assess the mood-congruent memory effect. In a typical study, participants are first asked to fill in a mood questionnaire that asks them to rate how happy, sad, positive, or negative they are feeling at that moment. A mood-induction procedure follows: for example, participants may be shown a movie and told to try to feel whatever mood the movie seems designed to elicit. A second questionnaire is administered to determine whether mood induction was successful. Following successful mood induction, participants are given stimuli to remember, such as positive words (for example, *humor*), neutral words (for example, *cloth*), or negative words (for example, *failure*). Memory for the words is then assessed, typically by free recall (i.e., participants are not given specific cues but simply instructed to recollect as many of the words as possible). The mood questionnaire is administered a third time, to ensure that the induced mood was in place at the time of test. If in fact it was, participants will show better recall for words whose valence is congruent with the mood state (for instance, they will remember more positive words when in a positive mood) than words whose valence is incongruent with the mood state (for instance, they will remember fewer negative words when in a positive mood).

Mood-congruent memory effects are not always found. For example, tests of recognition memory ("Did you see this word before?") are less likely than tests of recall ("What was the word you just saw?") to elicit mood-congruent memory effects (Bower & Cohen, 1982). In addition, although mood-congruent memory effects have been found for both positive and negative moods, they are stronger for positive moods. This may reflect a tendency toward more creativity and generative activity with positive moods (Fiedler et al., 2001).

Mood-congruent memory effects can be observed when memory encoding occurs before or after mood induction. Therefore, the mood-congruent memory effect is the result of altering the retrieval, rather than the encoding or storage stage of memory. Two hypotheses have been proposed to explain the influence of mood on memory retrieval. The first suggests that mood creates a bias in responding: the memory representations for the mood-congruent and mood-incongruent stimuli are equally accessible, but participants are biased to respond to the mood-congruent stimuli (Schwarz & Clore, 1988). The second hypothesis suggests that mood actually changes the accessibility of the memory representation during retrieval, so that a given mood leads to greater activation of memories for stimuli whose valence is consistent with that mood. For this reason, memories of mood-consistent stimuli are more easily retrieved (Bower, 1981). With most memory tests using free recall, it is difficult to distinguish a tendency or bias to respond with mood-congruent stimuli from a change in the accessibility of these stimuli to retrieval. However, in a clever study using a modified recognition memory test, investigators were able to demonstrate that the primary mechanism by which mood alters memory is the greater accessibility of mood-congruent memories (Fieldler et al., 2001). In other words, mood can actually determine which memories are most available for explicit retrieval at any given time.

5.4. Memory for Emotional Public Events

There is only so much that can be done to manipulate emotion in a controlled and ethically responsible fashion. Because emotional reactions studied in the laboratory are therefore mild and constrained, some researchers have chosen to study emotion and memory in "natural experiments." An area that has been investigated in this way for its psychological, historical, and cultural importance is memory for emotional public events. Although these studies cannot be nearly as controlled or detailed as laboratory research, they nevertheless provide a window through which we can have another view of the link between human memory and emotion.

One of the first emotional public events studied by psychologists was the assassination of John F. Kennedy in 1963. This event shocked the nation, and reactions to it were highly emotional. Two psychologists, Roger Brown and James Kulik (1977), studied the qualitative aspects of memory for this event, asking people to recall incidental details of their experience of the event, such as where they were and whom they were with when they heard about it. Many respondents had detailed recollections and believed their memory to be extremely accurate, almost like a photograph that recorded every aspect of the scene. Brown and Kulik introduced the term flashbulb memory to describe memory for surprising and consequential events; the phrase reflects the vivid and detailed nature of the recollections reported. Brown and Kulik suggested that there are special mechanisms for the formation of memories for highly charged events and that they elicit a "print now" response from the memory system, which ensures that the memory remains accurate and not forgotten.

This groundbreaking study highlighted the qualitative nature of memory for emotional public events and seemed to imply that such memory is different and more detailed than other kinds of declarative memory. But the study was not particularly concerned with assessing the accuracy of these flashbulb memories and such a study was not conducted until more than a decade after the assassination. Despite respondents' confidence, the accuracy of flashbulb memories has been called into question. Since this initial study, there have been investigations of memory for a number of emotional public events in various parts of the world, including the 1981 assassination attempt on Ronald Reagan (Pillemer, 1984), the *Challenger* space shuttle catastrophe (Neisser & Harsch, 1992), the assassination of the Swedish prime minister, Olaf Palme (Christianson, 1989), the Loma Prieta earthquake in California (Neisser et al., 1996), the Hillsborough, England, soccer disaster (Wright, 1993), the resignation of the British prime minister, Margaret Thatcher (Conway et al., 1994), and the death of King Baudouin of Belgium (Finkenauer et al., 1998). Studies examining memory for the attack on the World Trade Center in New York in 2001 have also been reported (Begley, 2002; Talaricho & Rubin, 2003). Taken together, these studies suggest that even though memory for emotional public events may be more accurate than most ordinary memories, they do not have the type of photograph-like accuracy implied by the term *flashbulb memory*—despite the confidence of respondents.

One of the first studies to demonstrate significant errors and distortions in memories for emotional public events examined memory for the *Challenger* explosion in 1986 (Neisser et al., 1992). Within a few days of the event, students were asked to recollect what they knew and how they heard about it. Three years later, they were again asked to recall this event. When comparing the early and later recollections, the investigators found significant differences between them. For example, a few days after the explosion, most respondents reported hearing the news from someone before seeing the television reports. After a few years, however, most respondents stated that they had been watching the *Challenger* flight on television and saw the explosion as it occurred. But despite the distortions of most of the second reports, all respondents were extremely confident in the accuracy of their memories. Similar results have recently been reported for memories of the 9/11 terrorist attack (Talaricho & Rubin, 2003). It seemed as if the powerful nature of these events overrode any doubt.

In a study designed to discover factors that may be related to accuracy and confidence for memory of emotional public events, researchers examined memory for the O. J. Simpson murder trial verdict in 1995, a "hot-button" political and social event for many people (Shmolck et al., 2000). A little more than a year after the verdict, respondents were still fairly accurate in their recollections of the personal details surrounding the event (where they were, who was with them). After three years, however, many showed significant distortions in their memories. As in the *Challenger* study, all respondents, including those whose memory was faulty, gave detailed accounts of their experience and were confident of their accuracy. In the Simpson verdict study, the only factor that emerged as predicting better accuracy after three years was the level of emotional involvement of the respondent at the time of the verdict. Those who reported higher levels of emotional arousal to the verdict had more accurate memories for the event when questioned three years later. These results are consistent with the idea that higher levels of arousal (at least up to a point) may help guard against some distortions of memory.

Although memory for emotional public events is often inaccurate in detail, it is nonetheless long lasting and compelling. The respondents in the *Challenger* study remembered that the event had occurred; their inaccuracies concerned their own connection to it. Similarly, although many people are confident that on September 11, 2001, they saw television pictures of two planes striking the World Trade Center (Pedzek, 2003), they couldn't have: no video of the first plane was available until the following day. (A moment's thought will suggest why: no television station, network or otherwise, was photographing the buildings that morning before the first attack—they had no reason to. Video of the first plane came from another source, and it took a certain amount of time before it was available.) Again, people obviously remember what occurred, but have forgotten details about their connection to it. Nevertheless, iconic images of emotional public events—John Kennedy smiling in an open car moments before the shots, the heartbreaking arc of the damaged *Challenger* against the blue sky—the image of billowing smoke from the World Trade Center (Figure 8–12) have left a lasting impression.

FIGURE 8–12   An emotional public event

The destruction of the World Trade Center in New York City, September 11, 2001.

(Photograph by Chris Collins. Courtesy of Corbis/Stock Market.)

Some large-scale studies are under way examining memory for the World Trade Center disaster (Begley, 2002). These studies should help clarify whether, as Brown and Kulik (1977) proposed, special mechanisms exist for the formation of memories for emotional public events or, as the results from the Simpson verdict suggest, these memories are the result of ordinary memory mechanisms, likely interacting with arousal. It is clear that the recent advances in our understanding of the influence of emotion on memory will help us interpret results from these studies in light of both cognitive and neural mechanisms.

✔ **Comprehension Check:**

1. What does the inverted U-shaped curve describe, when referring to the impact of emotion on memory?
2. What evidence supports the idea that mood can influence memory?

6. EMOTION, ATTENTION, AND PERCEPTION

Emotional events are distracting—despite your opinion, only moments before, about the drivers in front of you who slowed traffic to look at the accident, the car crash seized your attention, compelling you to pause and look before you returned your concentration to the road ahead. In some circumstances an emotional stimulus may break through to awareness. You may be reasonably successful at tuning out the conversations around you at a party—until someone mentions an emotionally evocative topic or word.

Emotion can influence attention and perceptual processing by different means. Most of the studies that have examined the influence of emotion on attention or perception have reported effects for negative, arousing, or threat-related stimuli—often in combination. It is proposed that these stimuli, because of their potential importance for survival, may receive priority in attention and perception (LeDoux, 1996; Ohman et al., 2001a; Whalen, 1998).

6.1. Emotion and the Capture of Attention

Emotion captures our attention and makes it hard to respond to nonemotional stimuli. This was demonstrated in an emotional version of the Stroop test, a classic measure of attention (see Chapter 7). As in the original version, participants are presented with words printed in different ink colors and asked to report the color of the ink and ignore the words. However, in this modified version the words are not color names but either emotional words (for example, *rape, cancer*) or neutral words (for example, *chair, keep*). When the words are emotional, participants find it more difficult to ignore the words and name the color of the ink (Pratto & John, 1991). This effect can be exaggerated for stimuli that are specifically relevant to a given person, such as the word *snake* for someone with a phobia for snakes (Williams et al., 1996).

In an effort to determine the precise mechanism underlying the capture of attention by emotion, researchers (Fox et al., 2001) employed the exogenous cueing technique developed by Posner (1980; see Chapter 3). The investigators suggested that emotion could capture attention by one of two mechanisms: it could either *draw* attention or *hold* attention. Participants were asked to respond as quickly as possible when a dot appeared either to the right or left of fixation and indicate by pressing a button on which side of the screen the dot appeared. The location of this dot probe was cued by a stimulus that was presented in the same location 150 milliseconds before the dot appeared. Most of the time, the cue predicted the correct location of the dot, but sometimes it predicted an incorrect location. As cues, the investigators used emotional and neutral words and faces to differentiate two components of attention (Figure 8–13).

The researchers reasoned that if emotion can enhance the automatic orienting or shifting of attention to the cue location, then the participants should be faster for valid emotion cues than for valid neutral ones. This pattern of performance would support the interpretation that emotion *draws* attention. However, if emotion makes it difficult to withdraw or disengage attention from an inappropriate cue, then the participants should perform similarly for the valid emotion and neutral cues, but should respond more slowly for invalid emotional than for invalid neutral cues. In other words, it should take the same amount of time for participants to shift attention to both emotional and neutral cues, but longer to stop looking at an emotional cue and shift attention to another location in order to respond on the invalid cue trials. This pattern would be consistent with the idea that emotion *holds* attention and makes it difficult to disengage from an emotional stimulus. The findings supported the idea that emotion holds attention: the primary effect of the emotion cue was to make it more difficult to respond when the cue was invalid. These results suggest that the capture of attention by emotion makes it hard to disengage in order to focus on nonemotional aspects of the task at hand.

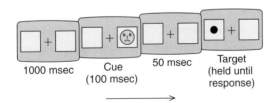

1000 msec   Cue (100 msec)   50 msec   Target (held until response)

FIGURE 8–13   Emotion holds attention

When, as here, a cue is invalid—it does not predict the location of the target—the participants take longer to respond if that cue is emotional (here, an angry face) than if it is neutral. Attention is being held by emotion.

(Fox, E., Russo, R., Bowles, R., & Dutton, K. (2001). Do threatening stimuli draw or hold attention in visual attention in subclinical anxiety? *Journal of Experimental Psychology: General, 130,* 681–700. © 2001 American Psychological Association. Reprinted with permission.)

6.2. Facilitation of Attention and Perception

Emotion can capture attention and impair performance on a task; and, as we see in this section, it can also facilitate attentional processing. How is it that emotion can both impair (or "capture") and enhance (or "facilitate") attention? The effect of emotion on attention depends on the specific demands of the task. In the studies considered so far, successful completion of the task required the participants to focus on and process the nonemotional aspects of the task; in the emotional Stroop task, for instance, participants are told to ignore the content of the words and to process the color. The attention tasks that demonstrate facilitation due to emotion usually require the participants to respond to or process the emotional stimuli directly or to respond to or process a stimulus that is cued by emotion.

"Finding the face in the crowd" is an example of a task in which performance is enhanced by emotion (Hansen & Hansen, 1988; Ohman et al., 2001b). This is a visual search task in which participants must locate a target among distractors as quickly as possible. In this variation, the targets are either neutral faces or faces with emotional expressions, such as angry or happy. When the target faces are angry, participants take less time to find the target than when the target faces are neutral or happy. Similar results have been observed for other negative stimuli, such as pictures of spiders and snakes among other natural stimuli (Ohman et al., 2001a). This is a "valence-asymmetric" effect: facilitation is apparent for negative stimuli, but not for positive ones.

In addition, a series of studies has demonstrated that the time needed to detect negative stimuli is not influenced by factors such as the number of distractor items (Ohman et al., 2001a, 2001b). These results are reminiscent of other findings on attentional search tasks in which certain visual features "pop out" so that identifying these target stimuli among distractor items is relatively easy and does not require that each stimulus in the display be examined (see Chapter 2). It has been suggested that visual features that pop out during search tasks are more elementary and may be processed more easily without attention (Treisman & Souther, 1985). On this basis, it is proposed that negative faces (and other natural emotional stimuli) receive priority in processing and their enhanced detection on the visual search task is due to a mechanism that operates without requiring attention (Ohman et al., 2001a).

The face-in-the-crowd effect is thought to result from enhanced early processing of the emotional faces (Ohman et al., 2001a). Neuroimaging studies have suggested that the amygdala plays a role in this initial processing of emotional faces. Researchers have demonstrated that the amygdala shows robust activation to fearful, relative to neutral, facial expressions, and that this occurs even when the faces are presented so quickly that participants are unaware of their presentation (Whalen et al., 1998). In addition, a number of studies have found that manipulating attention does not influence the amygdala's response to "fear faces" (expressions of fear in others) (A. K. Anderson et al., 2003; Vuilleumier et al., 2002; Williams et al., 2004). In most cases, the amygdala shows a similar response to fear expressions whether or not they are consciously detected or the focus of attention (see the accompanying *Debate* box for a further discussion of this topic). These results are consistent with the idea that the emotional content of faces is processed before attention is deployed.

Is the Detection of Threat Automatic?   DEBATE

The *affective primacy hypothesis*, originally proposed by Wundt (1907) and reintroduced by Zajonc (1984), suggests that the processing of emotional stimuli does not depend on limited cognitive resources. Zajonc argued that detecting emotional salience occurs prior to, and independent of, awareness and appraisal. Stimuli that can be processed irrespective of attentional resources and in an obligatory manner—that is, the processing cannot be "turned off"—are said to meet the criteria for *automaticity* (see Chapter 7). Automaticity is characteristic of many perceptual functions: we can't help detecting the edges, objects, and scenes that we see. Reading is a skill that becomes automatic: once you are adept at reading, it is not possible to see a string of letters and not perceive the word they spell.

Evidence from neuroscience indicates that specialized brain systems may ensure that some emotional stimuli, specifically those indicating threat, are processed automatically. The evolutionary reasons for this are clear: even if the alarm is false, it is certainly better to be safe than sorry if the potential consequence is physical harm or death. Evidence that there may be special neural mechanisms for detecting a threat is derived in part from research on classical fear conditioning in rats. This research shows that there are two pathways by which information about the emotional significance of a conditioned stimulus can reach the amygdala (LeDoux, 1996). The cortical pathway allows the stimulus to go through all stages of normal perception before reaching the amygdala; the subcortical pathway skips some perceptual stages and allows the amygdala to make a fast and crude assessment of the emotional significance of a stimulus. It is suggested that this subcortical pathway provides an early warning system in the presence of potential danger (LeDoux, 1996).

There are clear differences in the complexity and range of affective experience across species; however, for fear in particular there appears to be significant overlap across species between basic "flight or fight" responses and their corresponding neural circuitry (Davis & Whalen, 2001; LeDoux, 1996). A number of neuroimaging studies in humans have shown that the amygdala's processing of faces showing fear meets the principles of automaticity: the processing is irrespective of attentional focus (A. K. Anderson et al., 2003; Vuilleumier et al., 2004) and awareness (Whalen et al., 1998), and it appears to be obligatory in the presence of fear stimuli (A. K. Anderson et al., 2003; Williams et al., 2004). Although these findings do not necessarily implicate a subcortical pathway for perception, neuroimaging studies have attempted to demonstrate that a subcortical pathway for the detection of threat stimuli by the amygdala underlies its automatic response to fear faces in humans.

Specifically, fMRI studies have reported a lack of activation in visual cortex when fear faces are processed without awareness (Pasley et al., 2004; Williams et al., 2004). The amygdala seems to respond preferentially to a fear face, even if the visual cortex does not. In addition, Vuilleumier and colleagues (2003) took advantage of the fact that a visual subcortical pathway should respond preferentially to crude, less detailed visual information, whereas the visual cortex should respond preferentially to highly detailed visual information. They found that the amygdala, pulvinar, and superior colliculus (components of a proposed subcortical pathway) show a greater response to less detailed versions of fear faces relative to neutral ones, whereas the visual cortex showed a greater response to fine details of these fear faces. Finally, two studies have reported amygdala activation to fear in patients whose visual cortices are damaged, resulting in an inability consciously to identify stimuli (Morris et al., 2001b; Pegna et al., 2005). The amygdala's enhanced response to fear faces in the absence of awareness, highly detailed information, or an intact visual cortex supports the existence of a subcortical pathway for the detection of threat stimuli by the amygdala.

However, another study (Pessoa et al., 2002) arrives at a different conclusion. Using a demanding attention task in which participants are asked to attend to the orientation of lines in the periphery while a fear or neutral face is presented in the center of the screen, these investigators did not observe amygdala activation in response to fear faces in the absence of attention. In this situation, the amygdala's response to fear faces is not automatic. Pessoa et al. argue that the presence of a subcortical pathway for detection of threat by the amygdala should result in an obligatory response to a fear face, regardless of how demanding the attentional task. In other words, the amygdala's response should *never* be dependent on attention. In addition, there is not yet any anatomical evidence in primates verifying the existence of a subcortical pathway for the detection of visual information by the amygdala (Pessoa & Ungerleider, 2004). The evidence to date for such a pathway has been limited to rats (LeDoux, 1996; Romanski & LeDoux, 1992).

The finding that attention can modulate the amygdala's response to a fear face clearly demonstrates that activation of the amygdala can depend on attention in *some* circumstances and is not *completely* automatic. Although these results indicate limitations on the automaticity of the amygdala's response to fear faces, they do not rule out the possibility of a subcortical pathway. A limitation in interpreting fMRI results in humans is that the signal observed is not an absolute measure of neural function, but rather a relative measure indicating the degree of difference between conditions (for example, fear versus neutral faces). It is not possible to conclude that there is no amygdala response, but only that there is no significant difference in observed activation. Of course, fMRI results used to argue in favor of a subcortical pathway by pointing to the lack of activation in visual regions in normal participants suffer from the same limitation (Pasley et al., 2004; Williams et al., 2004). It is unclear whether fMRI, when used without other techniques, can provide sufficient evidence that a subcortical pathway for the detection of visual threat stimuli by the human amygdala does, or does not, exist. (More generally negative evidence from neuroimaging—no significant difference in activation—is not as diagnostic as positive evidence.)

Whether or not a subcortical pathway for the detection of threat stimuli by the amygdala exists in humans is still a matter of debate. However, whether or not the amygdala receives input about the emotional significance of a stimulus via a cortical or subcortical pathway, amygdala activation to fear faces meets most of the principles of automaticity—that is, it is independent of attention and it is obligatory—with certain limitations for highly demanding attention tasks (Pessoa et al., 2002). Future research will need to determine the characteristics and range of these limitations. To date, most, but not all, of the available research supports the affective primary hypothesis, at least for the processing of threat stimuli. In most situations, the amygdala enables preferential processing of stimuli that are emotional and potentially threatening, thus ensuring that information of importance to the organism is more likely to influence behavior.

Another study seeking to determine whether the amygdala modulates the facilitation of attention with emotion made use of the phenomenon known as the *attentional blink* (discussed in Chapter 3). The attentional blink is a brief loss of attention that occurs when a second visual stimulus appears very quickly, perhaps a few hundred milliseconds, after the first one (Chun & Potter, 1995). (Proofreaders must guard against attentional blink, or they will miss a second error that falls soon after an earlier one.) An attentional blink test might employ a string of 15 words as stimuli that are presented very quickly, about one every 100 milliseconds. If the experimenter tells participants that they only have to attend to and report two of the words, which are printed in a different color of ink from the rest of the words, participants are generally successful—unless the second target word is presented soon after the first target word. It is almost as if noticing and encoding the first target word creates a temporary refractory period during which it is difficult to notice and report the second target word. It is as if attention blinked.

To investigate the role of the amygdala in the facilitation of attention, the emotional salience of the second target word was altered. When the second target word was an emotional, arousing word, participants were more likely to report it (Anderson et al., 2005). In other words, emotion facilitated processing and decreased the attentional blink. Consistent with the "face in the crowd" studies reported earlier, this result suggests that when attentional resources are limited, emotional stimuli reach awareness more readily than non-emotional stimuli. This study was also conducted with patients who had suffered damage to the amygdala (A. K. Anderson & Phelps, 2001). These patients showed no difference in the attentional blink effect for emotional words versus neutral ones, which offers further evidence that the amygdala is modulating this enhanced awareness for emotional stimuli.

The idea that specific neural systems give rise to the enhanced attentional and perceptual processing of emotional stimuli is consistent with a psychological model suggested in the early years of the twentieth century (Wundt, 1907). This is the affective primacy hypothesis, which proposes that emotional stimuli are processed relatively automatically, making fewer demands on limited cognitive resources than do other types of stimuli. The findings from the attentional blink study, as well as recent research demonstrating enhanced detection of emotional stimuli in the neglected field of patients with attentional neglect (Vuilleumier & Schwartz, 2001; see Chapter 3), provide support for this early psychological theory.

Although the amygdala appears to be involved in the facilitation of attention by emotion, it must interact with brain systems underlying attention and perception to accomplish this. Two mechanisms have been proposed to explain the amygdala's influence on attentional and perceptual processes. The first suggests that through learning the actual cortical representation of emotional stimuli is altered to allow for enhanced perception of emotional events (Weinberger, 1995). Evidence for this effect has been demonstrated with fear conditioning in rats by showing that the processing of neurons that have receptive fields for different tone frequencies is altered to enhance perception of the frequency used as the conditioned fear stimulus. In humans, neuroimaging studies have reported enhanced auditory cortex activation for a tone used as a conditioned stimulus during fear conditioning (Morris et al., 2001a). In addition, words that have an emotional meaning elicit greater activation in the lingual gyrus (A. K. Anderson, 2004), a region thought to be involved in the representation of words (Booth et al., 2002). Although these neuroimaging studies in humans do not prove that emotion, via the amygdala, plays a causal role in creating lasting changes in the cortical representation of stimuli, they are consistent with the studies in rats observing this effect (Weinberger, 1995).

The other proposed mechanism for the facilitation of attention by emotion is a faster, more transient modulation of perceptual processing. There are connections to and from the amygdala and sensory cortical processing regions, such as the visual cortex (Amaral et al., 1992) (Figure 8–14). It is hypothesized that the amygdala, which receives input about the emotional significance of a stimulus early in processing, provides rapid feedback to sensory cortical areas of the brain, thus enhancing further perceptual and attentional processes. Consistent with this model, several neuroimaging studies have demonstrated enhanced activation in visual cortex for

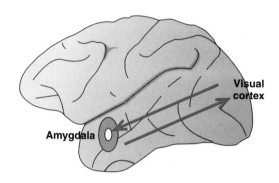

FIGURE 8–14   The amygdala has connections to and from sensory cortical regions
The amygdala may receive input about the emotional significance of an event early in visual processing and project back to sensory cortical regions to modify further perceptual and attentional processing.

emotional stimuli (e.g., Kosslyn et al., 1996; Morris et al., 1998). The strength of
this activation response in the visual cortex is correlated with the strength of amygdala activation to these same stimuli (Morris et al., 1998). Researchers have attempted to determine whether the enhanced response in the amygdala for fear faces
is causally related to the enhanced response in the visual cortex. Neuroimaging
techniques demonstrated that damage to the amygdala eliminates the enhanced visual cortex response normally observed for fear faces (Vuilleumier et al., 2004). By
combining neuroimaging and studies of patients with brain damage, researchers
have provided strong support for the conclusion that the amygdala's transient modulation of visual processing regions underlies some of the effects of emotion on attention and perception.

Through these two mechanisms—a lasting change in the cortical representation
for stimuli linked to emotion and a transient enhancement of sensory cortical processing—the amygdala can alter the processing of incoming information to produce
increased vigilance in the presence of threat (Whalen, 1998). Both these mechanisms
highlight emotion's influence on perceptual regions, such as visual and auditory cortex, as opposed to other brain regions that are thought to underlie the allocation of
attention (Corbetta & Shulman, 2002). A growing body of evidence suggests that
many observed effects of attention are linked to enhanced perception (Carrasco,
2004) and enhanced processing in perceptual brain regions that occur with attention
(Polonsky et al., 2000). Consistent with the notion that emotion enhances activation
in visual processing regions, thus facilitating awareness and identification of emotional stimuli, a recent study found enhanced contrast sensitivity for stimuli cued
with a fear face (Phelps et al., in press). Contrast sensitivity—the ability to detect
subtle gradations of gray—is known to arise from the functioning of the primary visual area (Carrasco, 2004). These results suggest that emotion can actually enhance
how well we see.

The studies showing that emotion can facilitate attention demonstrate that the
line between attention and perception can be fuzzy. The facilitation of attention by

emotion apparently is the result of mechanisms by which emotional stimuli receive priority in perception. Models of the neural mechanisms underlying emotion, attention, and perception support this interpretation.

Comprehension Check:

1. What are two ways in which emotion can influence attention?
2. Describe how the amygdala may play a role in the modulation of attention or perception by emotion.

Revisit and Reflect

1. *How have researchers defined emotion to allow scientific investigations of the interactions of emotion and cognition?*

   Although we all have an intuitive sense of what emotion is, finding a precise definition of emotion is challenging. Emotion is often described as the range of relatively brief reactions (including facial expression, bodily responses, and subjective evaluation) that occur in response to a significant internal or external event. In this way, emotion has been differentiated from mood, attitudes, and motivation—all of which involve affective responses and can influence cognition. Researchers interested in studying the impact of emotion on cognition have generally considered either basic emotions or the dimensions of emotion. Basic emotions are reflected in distinctive in facial expressions, in happiness, sadness, disgust, fear, anger, and surprise. Dimensional accounts reflect either specific qualities of the emotion response (valence and arousal) or the motivational state (approach versus withdrawal) elicited by an event.

   ### Think Critically

   - Can either the "basic emotions" or the dimensional approach to emotion capture the complexity of emotion you experience in your life?
   - How would you know whether an animal or insect is experiencing an emotion? What kind of behavioral cues would lead to your conclusion?

2. *What techniques are typically used to manipulate and measure emotion in the laboratory?*

   Researchers have used a range of different techniques to invoke and assess emotion. The most common way to manipulate emotion is to present emotionally evocative stimuli. Techniques to measure emotion include both direct and indirect assessments. An affective response can be assessed directly by simply asking the participants to indicate their subjective experience. Two common indirect, physiological measures of emotion are the skin conductance response, which measures mild sweating that occurs with autonomic nervous system arousal, and potentiated startle, which reflects a reflex response that is modulated by emotion. In the brain, these different assessments of emotion have been shown to reflect distinct neural pathways. Although direct and indirect measures of an emotional reaction may be similar, they reflect (at least partly), distinct components of emotion.

Think Critically

- Reflecting on your experience in the past week, how have you tried to manipulate or assess emotion in a social situation? What did you do?
- To what extent do you think your body's response to an emotional event is consistent or inconsistent with your subjective emotional experience? Why do you think this is so?

3. *What are the means by which stimuli can acquire emotional properties and how is this emotional learning expressed?*

Although there are some stimuli in the environment that naturally elicit an emotional reaction, such as an electric shock, most stimuli and events that elicit an emotional reaction have acquired their emotional properties through learning. These secondary reinforcers are neutral stimuli that acquire emotional properties by being associated with an emotion event (money is a classic example of a secondary reinforcer). This association can occur through a number of means. Directly pairing neutral and emotional events, without any action by the participant, is classical conditioning. Instrumental conditioning occurs when a neutral stimulus signals an action that will lead to reward or punishment. We can also learn about the emotional properties of an event without actually experiencing positive or negative outcomes through social means, by verbal instruction or by observation of another's experience. Emotional learning can be expressed directly, through the subjective evaluation of stimuli paired with emotional events (for example, how much do you like this person?), or indirectly, through autonomic reactions to these stimuli (for example, does your heart race when you see this person?). Studies of both normal people and patients with brain damage suggest that direct and indirect measures may reflect partially independent emotional learning mechanisms.

Think Critically

- If you were to run into someone with whom your relationship ended badly, what range of emotional reactions might you expect to have? How might you expect these different reactions to change if you ran into this person every day for a week?
- What are some cultural symbols (money is one) that have come to acquire emotional properties? How did these symbols become emotional?

4. *How does emotion alter our ability to remember?*

It has long been known that emotion can influence memory; recently, researchers have helped to specify exactly how this occurs. Probably the most widely investigated effect of emotion on memory is arousal's influence on memory accuracy. Through the amygdala's modulation of memory consolidation in the hippocampus, an arousal response helps ensure that emotional events are likely to be remembered. However, if this arousal response becomes prolonged (extreme stress), emotion can have the opposite effect; that is, it can impair memory performance through changes in the hippocampus.

In addition, researchers have found that mood during memory retrieval can alter which information is likely to be retrieved. And research on memory for emotional public events suggests that emotion can have an independent effect on the subjective sense of remembering. Emotional events are often recollected with a high sense of confidence and detail, even when these recollections are not completely accurate. These studies suggest that our sense of how accurate our memories are for emotional events may not reflect actual accuracy to the same degree as do our memories for neutral events.

Think Critically

- What were you doing on a specific day of high significance, public or private? How confident are you in the accuracy of your memory? If you can, check the details of your memory with someone also involved. Do both of you have the same memories of the events of that day?

- The last time you were sad, what kind of things did you remember? Are they different from memories that came to mind when you were in a better mood? How so?

5. *How does emotion change attention and perception?*

Emotion can influence attention in two different but related ways. Emotional events in the environment are more likely to enter awareness than are neutral events. The evolutionary reasons for this are clear: emotional events may signal threat, and so we should be especially attuned to these events. However, when something emotional is in the environment, this stimulus might capture attention and make it harder to focus on nonemotional aspects of the situation. In this way, emotion can sometimes impair performance on attention tasks, specifically when the task requires attention to nonemotional aspects of the stimulus. The brain mechanisms underlying the influence of emotion on attention highlight the role of the amygdala in modulating processing in the visual cortex. This modulation of processing in perceptual areas of the brain may result in enhanced perception for emotional stimuli.

Think Critically

- Mr. Spock in the *Star Trek* television series was supposed to be half human and half Vulcan—and his Vulcan side, governed solely by reason and logic, dominated. He was uninfluenced by emotion. How did his interactions with the environment differ from yours? In an emergency situation how might Spock perform better than you? How might his reactions suffer?

- If emotion influences perception and attention, how would you expect other cognitive functions, such as memory and reasoning, to be altered as a consequence?

9 Decision Making

Learning Objectives

Home alone, and the question is, pick up the phone or not? You have a new lab partner. Your new lab partner is interesting and attractive. Call and suggest meeting for coffee? Maybe. Did your new lab partner like you? Seemed to. Is your new lab partner involved with someone else? Who knows. Will your new lab partner accept your invitation? Well, nothing ventured, nothing gained. Then again . . . you have an exam tomorrow. Considering your plans for after graduation, it would be a good idea to go to the library and review the optional reading, a move that would very likely boost your score. You can't do both. What's your decision?

In this chapter we address the following questions about decisions and the way we make them:

1. What are the components of a decision?
2. How do human decisions compare to the ideal model for decision making, called the "expected utility" model?
3. How do we determine the values of the consequences of our decisions?
4. What is the role of emotions in decision processes?
5. What major heuristics do we rely on in estimating the likelihood of uncertain events?
6. How do decisions change when situations become uncertain, ambiguous, and more complex than those in simple laboratory experiments?

1. THE NATURE OF A DECISION

Essentially, a decision is a choice among possibilities. It involves assessment of the courses of action available and a determination of the action (or nonaction) to take. A decision occurs when a person with an unfulfilled need takes an action to satisfy that need or desire. Intuitively, a "good" decision is one that selects the best available course of action in the face of uncertainty about the consequences. Why is there uncertainty? Because, decision making does not necessarily have all the relevant information in hand. You can't by logic alone weigh the coffee date against the library session. Will the coffee date end on a pleasant note for the future? Will the reading prove relevant to what's asked on the exam? You can't know the definitive answers to these questions at the time you have to make your decision.

Some decisions are easy to make and, indeed, may not even feel like "decisions" because the choice seems so obvious. There is often a dominating option that is clearly better than the others in regard to the factors important to you. You don't spend much time in decision making when you order a favorite dish at a familiar restaurant, or take a better paying, more interesting job in preference to a less well paid, boring one. Decisions like these are easy because we know what we want (our values) and what we will get (the consequences). Of course, many decisions are much more difficult, and the stakes are much higher—some, like the response to disease or injury or the choice of a mate—are fundamental to the survival and propagation of our genes. But for both hard and easy decisions, these two factors, the *value to us of each option* and the *likely outcome,* are crucial in decision making.

1.1. The Science of Decision Making

A practical method of decision analysis was described by Benjamin Franklin in a letter to his friend Joseph Priestley in 1772:

> My way is to divide half a sheet of paper by a line into two columns; writing over one Pro, and over the other Con. Then . . . I put down under the different heads short hints of the different motives, that occur to me, for or against the measure. When I

have thus got them all together in one view, I endeavor to estimate their respective weights; and where I find two, one on each side that seem equal, I strike them both out . . . and, thus proceeding I find at length where the balance lies; and if nothing new that is of importance occurs on either side, I come to a determination accordingly. And, although the weight of reasons cannot be taken with precision of algebraic quantities, yet, when each is thus considered, separately and comparatively, and the whole lies before me, I think I can judge better, and am less liable to make a rash step, and in fact I have found great advantage from this kind of equation, in what may be called moral or prudential algebra.

In modern times, the earliest theories of decision making used in behavioral research come from economic and mathematical models developed in the middle of the twentieth century; they were intended to provide a framework for making the best possible decision in a given set of circumstances (Edwards, 1954). As normative (or prescriptive) theories of decision making—that is, as theories that tell us how we *should* decide—they stand as some of the most successful ever invented by human beings. They were also used as *initial* hypotheses to describe actual human behavior. Presumably our ancestors' evolutionary success depended in part on their being better decision makers than other members of our own and competing species; If so, then our brains presumably were influenced by natural selection to make good decisions—which means following the best decision-making policy we know which relies on weighting relevant factors and making the rational choice. Or so researchers hypothesized.

However, rational choice may in fact be an unreachable goal. As Franklin said, ". . . the weight of reasons cannot be taken with the precision of algebraic quantities. . . ." How do we actually make decisions in the face of uncertainty, incomplete information, and biases? Since the 1970s, descriptive theories, which focus on how we *actually* make decisions, not on how we *should* make them, have increasingly informed our understanding of decision making. These theories have led to research that has revealed how human behavior departs from the prescriptions of entirely rational choice.

The result has been the creation of descriptive psychological models that are useful in predicting and accounting for human decision behavior. Decision making has a lot in common with other complex cognitive skills such as problem solving (see Chapter 10) and reasoning, and so psychological theories of decision making propose an interesting mix of rational and cognitively plausible mechanisms.

To explore the scientific research on decision making today requires first an understanding of the traditional, normative models and the psychological models built on them. Further contributing to our knowledge is research that has investigated the neural systems that underlie decision processes. Both behavioral and neural studies rely heavily on casino-style gambles as experimental problems because they are well defined, interesting to participants, and provide a sound, but highly abstract, analogy to many everyday situations. The key ingredients in the gambles, or choices, as in important decisions made outside the laboratory, are desired outcomes (usually, in the gambles, money), more than one course of action to obtain those outcomes, and uncertainty about the likelihood that an outcome will be achieved if one or another course of action is chosen.

The primary cognitive activity in decision making is the evaluation of each possible choice and the determination of the one most likely to achieve current goals. Life presents many goals and more choices; in the laboratory participants are often asked to choose among possibilities that offer nothing more than monetary payoffs. This is done to simplify the "What-do-I-want?" and "How-do-I-balance-the-good-and-bad-features-of-every-possibility-available-to-me?" parts of any realistic decision. The experimenter is generally safe in assuming that all participants would like to win money, and that they would rather have more money than less. Although the gambling metaphor and gambling tasks are limited in some ways, they have dominated research to date on the behavioral and, especially, on the neural bases of decision processes.

1.2. The Decision Tree

The components of a decision are conveniently summarized in a graphical display known as a decision tree. Decision trees represent the courses of action or options under consideration, the likelihood of what we will get if we choose each course of action, and the consequences that follow each choice. We could represent the coffee date–library dilemma in a decision tree like the one shown in Figure 9–1. This tree represents two courses of action: invite your new lab partner out for coffee versus a study session in the library. One of the options involves little uncertainty

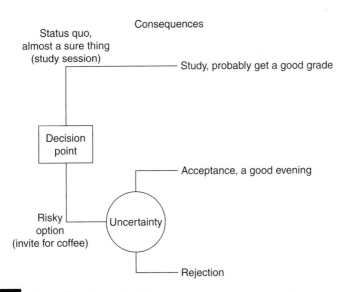

FIGURE 9–1 The coffee date decision tree

Decision trees provide an intuitive, useful way to visualize decisions, summarizing optional courses of action, outcomes and consequences, and uncertain event contingencies. They can be used to analyze personal and professional decisions, and they are a good way to keep track of decisions presented to participants in experiments.

about the consequence; it is highly likely, though not certain, that reviewing the optional reading will improve your performance on the exam. The "go out for coffee" option involves much more uncertainty: your new lab partner may be pleased at your invitation and accept; or may be unreceptive—and if unreceptive and the conversation is awkward, you may forfeit your current low-key friendship as well as the prospect of an enjoyable evening with a possible mate. If your invitation is accepted, the decision tree could be extended further into the future to show more distant possible consequences: abiding love, rejection, enduring friendship, embarrassment, a difficult working relationship in the lab. So of the two options, one of them—going out for coffee—is the more uncertain option, and thus involves greater risk or potential loss.

The decision tree is a useful practical aid to representing the aspects of a decision. Any situation that we would call a decision consists of *alternatives, beliefs* (about likelihoods) and *consequences*—elements that can be described as the ABCs of the decision.

Alternatives are different courses of action, options, choices, and strategies available to the decision maker and they are represented as branches of the tree. In the example decision tree there are only two: study session versus coffee date. Of course, this is a simplification of the situation, because in fact a number of other possibilities are open to you: you might call someone else and go to a movie, you might blow the evening watching television, you might just go to bed early. . . . The discovery and articulation of alternatives involves many of the skills usually described as "problem solving;" here is an instance of the close relationship between decision making and other aspects of cognition. When we make a deliberate decision, we usually consider only a few of the many conceivable actions we might take. The decision tree, even though vastly simplified, is probably a good approximate description of the cognitive state in the decision maker's head.

A belief, as the term is used in the context of decision making, is our estimate of the likelihood that a particular outcome will occur if we choose a particular alternative. The library alternative carries virtually no uncertainty about outcomes; you're confident—you *believe*—that doing the reading will improve your performance on the exam. Improved performance is for all practical purposes a "certain event." The events proceeding from a telephone call to suggest a coffee date are much less certain. These beliefs are quantified as mathematical probabilities in Figure 9–2.

Most theories of decision making suppose that we reason about uncertainty in some manner analogous to the calculations prescribed by the mathematical theory of probability, although realistic descriptive theories have rules that differ from those prescribed by probability theory in important ways (see, for example, Rottenstreich & Tversky, 1997; Tversky & Koehler, 1994). In formal decision analysis, the goal is to get human decision makers to think more rationally, so information about beliefs is added to the decision tree in the form of numerical probabilities that events will occur. If the decision maker believes that the alternative leads to a certain outcome—the study session branch in our example—the probability is 1.00 (see Figure 9–2).

The other alternative, "coffee date," carries uncertainty. To depict that in the diagram, a circle is inserted from which possible events are shown as further branches:

Color Insert I

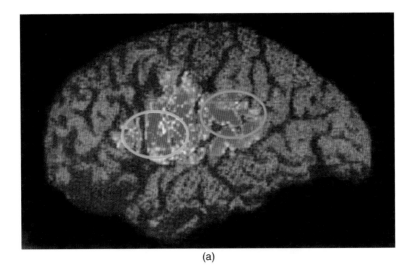

(a)

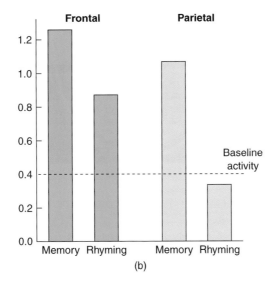

(b)

FIGURE 6–7 Brain activation during verbal working memory

(a) Activation in left inferior frontal cortex, that is, in Broca's area (green ellipse) and in inferior parietal cortex (blue ellipse), for English letters.
(b) The left frontal activity was above baseline during both a verbal memory task and a rhyming task. The parietal activity was above baseline only for the memory task, suggesting that the activity might be selective to phonological storage.

(Paulesu, E., Frith, C. D., & Frackowiak, R. S. J. (1993). The neural correlates of the verbal component of working memory. *Nature, 362,* 342–345. Reprinted with permission.)

Color Insert J

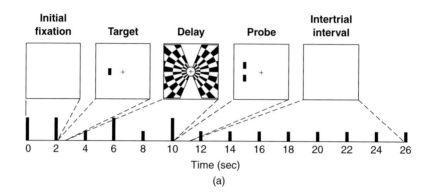

Time (sec)

(a)

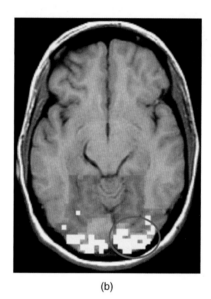

(b)

FIGURE 6-9 Enhanced activity in visual brain regions during a spatial working memory task

(a) The spatial working memory task performed by participants, which required memorizing the location of a vertical bar in order later to judge whether it was to the left or right of two probe bars presented after a delay period. During the delay the visual system was stimulated with a flashing checkerboard. (b) Visually sensitive brain regions that increased in activity (the white areas) during the delay. Activation, indicated by the blue ellipse, was reliably greater in the hemisphere opposite to the side of the display where the cue was shown (in this example, the right hemisphere), reflecting the contralateral organization of the brain.

(Postle, B. R., Awh, E., Jonides, J., Smith, E. E., & D'Esposito, M. (2004). The where and how of attention-based rehearsal in spatial working memory. *Brain Res Cogn Brain Res., 20*(2), 194–205.)

Color Insert K

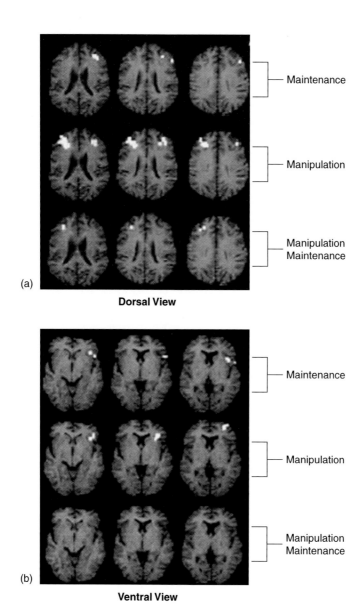

(a)

Dorsal View

— Maintenance

— Manipulation

— Manipulation
  Maintenance

(b)

Ventral View

— Maintenance

— Manipulation

— Manipulation
  Maintenance

FIGURE 6–10 Maintenance versus manipulation in working memory

These images of brain slices from a representative participant in a maintenance–manipulation study show active regions (white) in the prefrontal cortex. Ventral prefrontal cortex was active in both maintenance and manipulation, but dorsal prefrontal cortex was active only in manipulation.

(D'Esposito, M., Postle, B. R., Ballard, D., & Lease, J. (1999). Maintenance versus manipulation of information held in working memory: An event-related fMRI study. *Brain and Cognition, 41*, 66–86. Reprinted with permission from Elsevier.)

Color Insert L

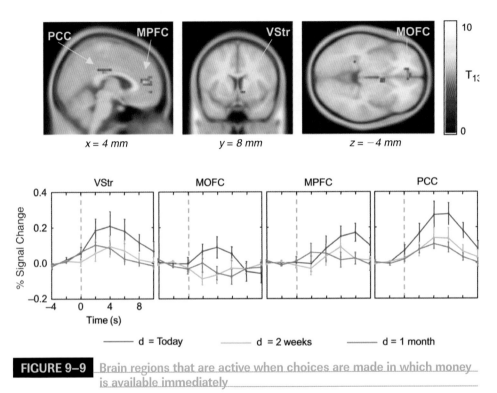

FIGURE 9–9 Brain regions that are active when choices are made in which money is available immediately

Four regions that were specifically active when an immediate money outcome was evaluated: the ventral striatum (VStr), medial orbitofrontal cortex (MOFC), medial prefrontal cortex (MPFC), and the posterior cingulate cortex (PCC). These areas are hypothesized to be substrates for the immediate-reward emotional component of the evaluation process. (B) fMRI activity in these four regions over time from the point at which the choice options are first presented (0 on the abscissa) until 8 seconds after presentation with separate curves for different delays (immediate, 2 weeks, and 4 weeks). It is clear that the immediate outcomes produce a distinctive difference in activity while the outcomes are being considered.

(McClure et al., *Science, 15,* October 2004, Vol. 306, p. 504. www.sciencemag.org. Reprinted with permission.)

Color Insert M

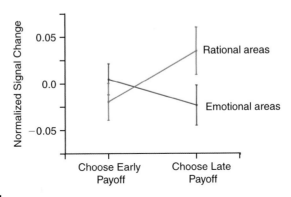

FIGURE 9–10 Predicting the choice—small–early reward versus large–late reward—from brain activity

An summary of the relationship between brain activity and choices. This graph shows that the choice made (choose the early payoff versus choose the later payoff) can be predicted by the amount of activity in rational versus emotional areas of the brain.

(McClure et al., *Science, 15,* October 2004, Vol. 306, p. 506. www.sciencemag.org. Reprinted with permission.)

Color Insert N

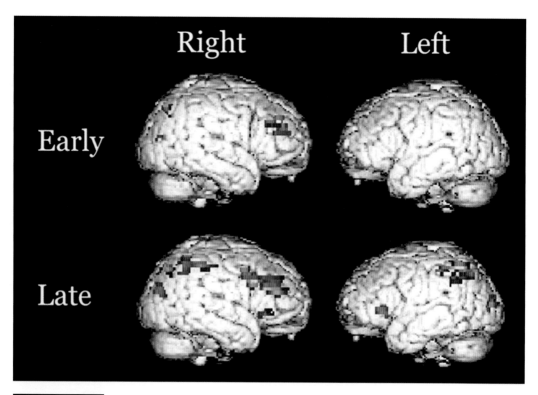

FIGURE 10–11 fMRI data on a classification task

Activation in the classification task—sorting abstract drawings—relative to the baseline task was limited to right-hemisphere areas of the frontal and parietal lobes in the early trials. During later trials, however, regions of the left dorsolateral prefrontal cortex and the right parietal cortex began to be recruited. This later left-hemisphere recruitment may indicate that participants were learning a verbal rule of classification.

(Seger, C., Poldrack, R., Prabhakaran, V., Zhao, M., Clover, C. & Gabrieli, J. (2000). Hemispheric asymmetries and individual differences in visual concept learning as measured by functional MRI. *Neuropsychologia, 28,* 1316–1324. Reprinted with permission from Elsevier.)

Color Insert O

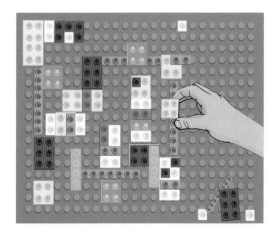

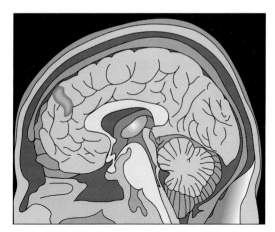

FIGURE 11–8 Does the end justify the means?

When participants observed someone building a Lego construction (*top*) in order to imitate the actions performed, but the goal of the actions—the final pattern of the blocks—was not known, activation was observed in the right medial prefrontal cortex, a region consistently involved in tasks that require an understanding of the mental states of others (in this case, presumably the intention to assemble something—even if the specific nature of the end goal is not known).

(Chaminade, T., Meltzoff, A. N. & Decety, J. (2002). Does the end justify the means? A PET exploration of the mechanisms involved in human imitation. *Neuroimage, 12,* 318–328. Reprinted with permission from Elsevier.)

Color Insert P

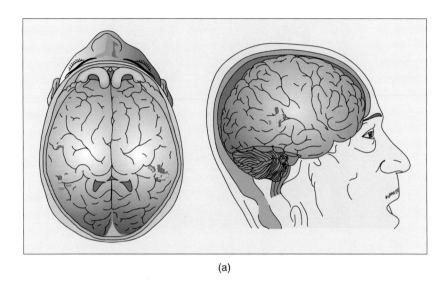

(a)

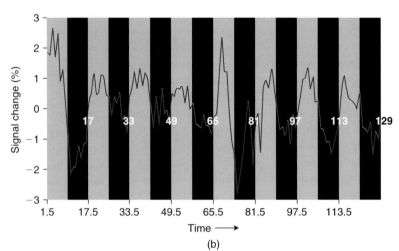

(b)

FIGURE 11–10 fMRI evidence: biological motion and the brain

(a) The perception of biological motion activates the superior temporal sulcus (STS), as shown in these fMRI images. (b) When results are plotted, increased activation (indicated by the gray bars) is seen on the occasions when the participants viewed biological motion, as opposed to the times they saw "scrambled" motion (black bars). The x-axis represents cumulative time in seconds from the beginning of the experiment, and the numbers on the axis indicate the specific times when biological motion sequences were presented.

(Grossman, E. E. & Blake, R. (2001). Brain activity evoked by inverted and imagined biological motion. *Vision Research, 41,* 1475–1482. Reprinted with permission from Elsevier.)

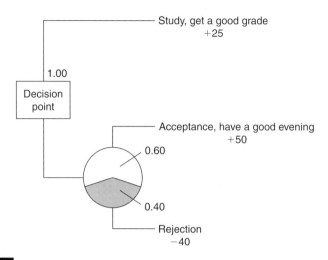

FIGURE 9–2 The coffee date decision tree—with numbers

Decision trees can help keep track of the details of decisions, such as numerical probabilities (1.0, 0.60, and 0.40) and payoffs (+25, +50, and −40). Here the tree shows the probabilities and payoffs that might be acceptable to the decision maker choosing between coffee date and study session. The tree sets up the calculations required in order to apply the expected utility model.

the two immediate possibilities, neither of them certain, are acceptance or rejection. Each branch is assigned a number, based on the belief of the decision maker, that indicates the likelihood of its occurrence. Faced with the coffee–study decision, you would probably not actually estimate numerical probabilities of accept–reject if you extend the invitation; but you would very likely think about what might happen, or might not, before you pick up the phone, and your thoughts would include a rough estimation of the chances the invitation might end well or badly.

Consequences are the benefits or losses that you receive or experience from the choice of a particular alternative and the events that follow from that choice. In the vocabulary of decision theory, these are described as outcomes, values, or utilities. The *outcome* is the result; the *value* is its net worth; and the *utility* is the desirability of that value to you. (Learn these terms well; we will use them repeatedly in the rest of this chapter.) Most likely you would feel best if you went out for coffee and had a splendid evening; feel the worst if you made the invitation and were rejected; and feel OK about hitting the books. Obviously, your evaluations depend on your goals and personal values, so the consequences of a decision are subjective. If you are a pre-med student, the decision is easy: "My goal is to get into med school, so I will study no matter what." If you are in school only to satisfy your parents, if you hate studying, and your goal is merely to pass the course, again the decision is simple: "When faced with studying, do anything else."

But if your goals are at neither of these extremes, you would be in a dilemma: the uncertain alternative (make the invitation) has various consequences, some higher and some lower in value than the certain alternative (study for the exam). Of course, evaluations can vary: if you're confident of a high score on the exam without further work, or if you're in danger of a low course grade, you might put a different value on a library session this evening.

Decision theorists signify the decision maker's evaluations of consequences in terms of utilities, numbers that, at the time you are faced with the decision, express the strength of your like or dislike of the outcomes that might occur. But life does not always follow the numbers. People's natural judgments under uncertainty are not captured by the rules of mathematical probability theory, nor does a formal theory that prescribes an ideal relation between values and utilities provide the full answer. Psychologically descriptive models are necessary, and these, as we will see, have been developed. Even so, the valuation process is especially mysterious. This is one reason why many experiments on decision making use monetary outcomes: people react to money in a very predictable fashion. (And, it is why so many neuroscience studies of decision making have focused on valuation.) The traditional *expected utility model* of rational decision making, despite its limitations, is a good starting point for an informed view of human decision making.

✓ Comprehension Check:

1. In what sense are other cognitive capacities and skills—executive processes, perception and attention, memory, problem solving, reasoning—involved in decision making?

2. Construct a decision tree to capture a recent decision that occupied your thoughts: Which job? Which major field of study? Which vacation? etc. How did you reason about the alternatives, beliefs (uncertainties), and consequences in your personal decision? Could constructing a decision tree have helped you think more clearly about the decision?

---

2. RATIONAL DECISION MAKING: THE EXPECTED UTILITY MODEL

In analyzing the coffee date–study session dilemma, we have considered the likelihood of various possible outcomes (beliefs) and arrived at evaluations of those outcomes (consequences). The **expected utility** is the utility of a particular outcome, weighted by the likelihood of that outcome's occurring. The expected utility model, which has provided the framework for most models of decision making, assumes rational behavior on the part of the decision maker in evaluating the likelihoods of alternatives, assessing the consequences, assigning utilities, weighting or multiplying the utilities by the liklihoods, and then finally choosing the option with the highest expected utility. The utility involved is inherently subjective; the breezy question "What's it worth to you?" sums up the idea of *subjective utility*. The central issue is not simply value, but value to *you*, the decision maker. Unlike the face amount on a dollar bill, subjective utility varies from person to person, circumstance to circumstance.

2.1. How the Model Works

Formal decision theory, in the form of the (subjective) expected utility model, proposes that we combine information in a three-step process: (1) Evaluate each course of action under consideration ("I'll make the telephone call") by *multiplying* the utility of each of its consequences (accept; reject) by its probability of occurrence (0.6; 0.4). To get the utilities, you'd have to estimate how much you care about being accepted or rejected. (2) *Add* these weighted values—the expected utilities—to create a summary evaluation of each alternative. (3) *Choose* the course of action with the highest *expected utility*, that is, the one with the largest sum of probability-weighted utilities. The expected utility would not be the same for everyone in the situation—the art student would, perhaps, assign different utilities to the consequences than you would; a more confident person might assign higher probabilities to the more desirable outcomes. It is in fact a *subjective* process; one size does not fit all. Your decision, in this model, is to take the course that has the greatest expected utility for you.

This "maximize utility" decision rule is the core of modern economic theories of rational behavior and it can be summarized in a succinct equation that represents the evaluation of each course of action. Put in words, the equation states that the (subjective) expected utility of an action is equal to the sum (Σ) of the probabilities (p) of each possible outcome (x_i, where the subscript i is a variable representing each possible outcome) multiplied by the utility (u) of that outcome. Thus,

$$\text{Expected utility} = \Sigma p(x_i)u(x_i)$$

You may have seen versions of this model in the form of expected value calculations in courses in elementary probability theory.

An example: if you are presented with a choice of two bets, a 0.45 probability of winning \$200 versus a 0.50 chance of winning \$150, your calculation would determine that the expected values are \$90 (0.45 × \$200) versus \$75 (0.50 × \$150), and you'd go for the bet with the higher expected value—that is, the higher *average payoff* if the gambles were played many times.

As we've mentioned, rational analysis and the idea of expected utility are often studied in terms of bets and money; in these situations, values are not as hard to quantify as, say, the enjoyment of a pleasant evening. The calculation is simple (although the subjective element must be accounted for here too): the probability of winning × the payoff. If there is a penalty if the bet is not won—that is, if the result is a loss, not just the continuation of the present situation—that downside must be included. So expected value for a simple bet is (Probability of winning × Payoff) − (Probability of losing × Amount of the loss). It is not as simple to put a number on the "payoff" of a successful coffee date. But for the sake of argument (if not practicality), the principles involved can be applied to the coffee date–study session dilemma. Probabilities and utilities can be assigned to the events and outcomes in this situation (Figure 9–2).

Suppose your utilities are +25 for studying, +50 for acceptance and a pleasant evening over coffee, and −40 for rejection. We assume that you believe that studying will definitely get you a good score on the exam (probability of a good score = 1.00). Also, suppose that you are not very confident about the likelihood that your invitation will be accepted: you estimate the likelihood of acceptance as 0.60 (a 60 percent chance), which of course means that the likelihood of rejection is 0.40. Then, the "study" option would have a summary expected utility of +25, that is,

Probability of good score × Utility of studying = 1.00 × +25 = +25

On the other hand, the coffee date would have a summary expected utility of +14, that is,

Probability of acceptance × Utility of a pleasant evening = 0.60 × +50 = +30
Probability of rejection × Utility of rejection = 0.40 × −40 = −16
… so the *expected utility* of the uncertain coffee date would be (+30) + (−16) = +14

The score stands at 25 versus 14; if you make the rational decision, you'll put on your coat and go to the library—but this was indeed a tough decision.

2.2. The Expected Utility Model and Behavioral Research

The earliest behavioral research on decision making, in the 1950s, relied heavily on gambles as stimuli and used the expected utility model as a hypothesis about human judgments and decisions. The *alternatives* in the decisions in these studies were usually monetary gambles. Participants' *beliefs* (about likelihoods) were based on information provided by the experimenter about the probabilities of receiving various payoffs. The *consequences* were the cash payoffs.

Many of these early studies aimed to convert objective stimulus numbers, such as dollar values and numerical probabilities, to subjective values—for example, factoring in the worth to a participant of a given amount of money in a given situation. Participants were responsive to the expected value (or expected utility) of gambles, paying attention to both probabilities and payoffs and predominantly choosing the "better bet." Figure 9–3 shows the results of an experiment in which college students were asked to value various gambles by putting a selling price on each (Shanteau, 1975; see also Tversky, 1969). For example, participants would be asked to put prices on gambles that had a .2 or .4 or .6 or .8 probability of winning 30 cents. The fanning-out pattern of curves in the graphs indicates that the participants assigned greater prices to gambles of increasing value, which shows that the participants evaluated the gambles in accord with the expected-value multiplying rule (Value = Probability × Payoff) that is at the heart of expected utility theory. Similar multiplicative patterns have been observed in college students' evaluations of the attractiveness of potential dates (Shanteau & Nagy, 1976).

Monetary gamble stimuli have been used in neuroimaging experiments in many laboratories, and participants' behavioral judgments repeatedly support the hypothesis that the expected-value multiplying principle underlies their evaluations. Converging evidence comes from research using single-cell recording techniques with nonhuman primates, which has identified small clusters of neurons that appear to serve as probability and value "meters" when monkeys assess simple gamble-type prospects to win rewards of juice (Glimcher, 2003; Newsome, 1997). That is, some clusters increase in activity when the probability of reward increases, whereas other

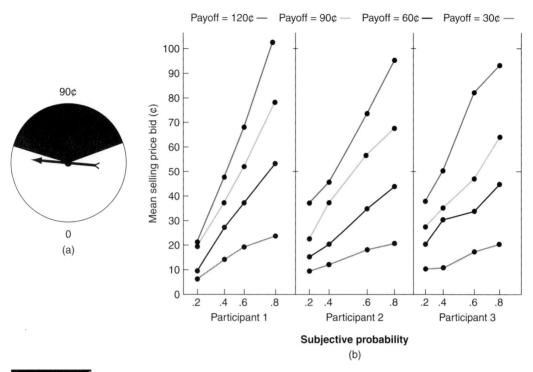

FIGURE 9–3 What's it worth?

(a) The wheel of fortune presented to participants, who were asked to "sell" the opportunity to bet for payoffs of 120¢, 90¢, 60¢, and 30¢ at different probabilities. Only the opportunity for the 90¢ opportunity is shown here; the ratio of dark to light area indicates the probability of winning.

(Shanteau, J. (1975). An information-integration analysis or risk decision making. In M. F. Kaplan and S. Schwartz (eds.) Human judgement and decision processes (pp. 109–137). New York: Academic Press. Reprinted with permission from Elsevier.)

(b) The graphs plot the results for three participants. All the graphs show a clear "fan" pattern, indicating that the participants are responding as though they are multiplying the probability and the payoff terms and order the gambles in a manner like that prescribed by the expected utility model. But note that they are not just setting expected *value* selling prices on the gambles: most of the prices are less than the corresponding expected values, indicating that the participants are risk averse, that is, the uncertain gambles are worth less to the participants than their expected values.

clusters increase in activity when the expected amount of reward increases. Several laboratories are now searching for neurons responsible for the multiplicative integration of probability and value information.

Both economists and psychologists also predicted and discovered that in addition to expected value or utility, the *variance* of a gamble matters in decision making. The variance of a gamble is a formulaic calculation that describes the range between possible payoffs. Variance preferences, sometimes called *risk attitudes*, differ from person to person. Some people prefer gambles with a small range in possible payoffs; others choose high-variance gambles, with high potential wins and high potential losses. For example, some people (who are known as risk-averse) would prefer the certain gain of approximately $100, whereas others (the risk-seeking ones) would prefer the chance to win almost $200, even at the risk of getting virtually nothing.

There are also individual differences in the willingness to choose gambles that may entail a loss—that is, an actual decrease in assets. Some people avoid a gamble with any potential loss outcome, no matter what the expected value and variance of the gamble are. People with this inclination, observed to a greater or lesser degree, are described as showing loss aversion.

In traditional economic theory, these characteristics of individual behavior in risky situations are summarized by *utility curves*. Such a curve relates the subjective evaluation—the utility, (plotted on the vertical y-axis)—to an objective measure such as dollars (plotted on the horizontal x-axis). A utility curve shows the *marginal utility*—that is, the change in utility, whether up or down—as a function of change in the relative payoff.

In Figure 9–4, we can see the marginally decreasing impact of both gains and losses in the concave (upper right) and convex forms (lower left) of the curves—the curves begin to flatten. A loss of $110 compared to a loss of $100 is subjectively

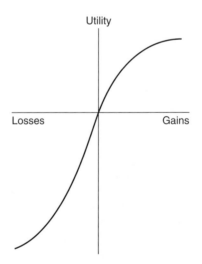

FIGURE 9–4   A utility curve

Relating objective outcomes to subjective utilities or values, the shape of the curve summarizes some important insights into the manner in which we put values on outcomes. On the gains side, the curve flattens out, reminding us that the perception of values shows a "diminishing marginal utility effect:" more is better, but additional gains are less valued than the same amounts of earlier gains. Similarly, on the loss side, the curve also flattens: more loss hurts more, but the "pain" diminishes as losses accumulate. Finally, the curve includes a "loss aversion" component: the loss curve is more than twice as steep as the gain curve, indicating that an equal-magnitude loss "hurts" more than twice as much as a gain.

(Based on Figure 3 in Kahneman, D., & Tversky, A. (1979). Prospect theory: An analysis of decision under risk. *Econometrica, 47,* 263–291. Reprinted with permission.)

much less significant than the difference between losing $20 and losing $10, though the absolute dollar amount is the same in both instances. (This shows clearly the difference between utility and value: the value of $10 is always $10.) The same diminishing impact applies to gains. Most people can sense this characteristic of utilities. Imagine a day at the races, and how delighted you would be to win $10 on the first race. Your winning streak continues: after the fifth race you've won a total of $100. You win yet again, on the same bet, so now you have $110 instead of $100. Now, how much happier do you feel? Most participants say the first change in this hypothetical situation, from $0 to $10, is much more satisfying than the later change from, $100 to $110. Or consider the possibility of saving $10 off the price of a $30 pocket calculator at a store on the other side of town versus saving $10 on a $130 pocket calculator, again with a drive across town. Would you make the drive to save on the more expensive calculator but not make the drive for the less expensive item?

The degree of curvature of the gain and loss functions corresponds to risk attitudes: the concave shape in gains implies risk aversion, whereas the convex shape for losses implies risk seeking. The utility curve in Figure 9–4 tells us that people should prefer certainty when it comes to gains, but prefer uncertainty when it comes to losses. This, in fact, captures peoples' preferences.

To appreciate this difference between gains and losses, consider the following pairs of gambles. Given a choice, would you prefer gamble 1 or gamble 2?

> *Gamble 1.* You win $10 if a head is tossed or win $50 if a tails is tossed.
> *Gamble 2.* You receive $30 for certain.

Most participants take the sure $30, indicating they are risk averse for gains. Now, let's make the payoffs losses:

> *Gamble 3.* On the toss of a coin, you lose $10 for heads and lose $50 for tails.
> *Gamble 4.* You lose $30 for certain.

Though the dollar amounts are the same as in gamble 1 and gamble 2, now most participants take gamble 3: when losses are involved, people are generally risk seeking—that is, in preference to the certain loss of a given amount, they accept the chance of a greater loss if a lesser loss is also a possibility.

In the graph shown in Figure 9–4, the slope of the loss section of the curve is much steeper than the gain portion; the utility of a $10 loss is much further below the starting point (zero) than the utility of a gain of $10 is above it. Many people will not play a gamble that involves a gain of $200 if heads is tossed and a loss of $100 if tails is tossed, even though the expected value of this bet is $50—that is, $(0.5 \times 200) + (0.5 \times -100) = 50$. For many people, losses apparently "hurt" at least twice as much as gains "please:" for about 50 percent of participants, the possibility of a $200 gain is not enough to compensate for the possibility of a $100 loss.

The tendency toward loss aversion appears in many everyday decisions. In the simplest form of "riskless choice," we tend to feel that the loss of utility in giving up something in our possession is greater than the gain of utility in obtaining that possession in the first place—that somehow the object acquires added value simply by belonging to us. This effect, known as the endowment effect, was first demonstrated in a classroom experiment (Kahneman et al., 1991). One-half of the students were given a new possession (for example, a coffee mug or a pen) and asked to assign a price to the object, a price at which they would be willing to sell the object to another student. The remaining half of the students, the buyers, were asked to state a price that they would be willing to pay to buy the object, thus establishing a market value for, say, a mug. All students were told that after they assigned their prices, a market would be held in the classroom and the objects would be exchanged between sellers and buyers. If a buyer offers a price equal to or greater than a seller's price, the mug will be exchanged for the money. All students, buyers and sellers, are faced with the same question: What is the mug worth? And each of them will end up either with a mug or with cash.

Note, however, that the two groups have different perspectives on the problem. The sellers are evaluating a loss: how much cash is sufficient to compensate me for losing my mug? The buyers are evaluating a gain: how much cash am I willing to spend to gain a mug? The loss aversion principle—that losses have a bigger impact than gains of equal magnitude—predicts that the sellers will value the mugs more highly than the buyers—and that is indeed what happened in the classroom market. This prediction has been confirmed in dozens of studies and classroom demonstrations with many different commodities and several different methods of assessing the true values of the objects to their owners. Typically, the sellers' values are about twice the buyers'. (It is important to note that in this classroom market there is no haggling over prices, otherwise we might interpret the "endowment effect" as due to strategic bargaining.)

Loss aversion also explains many financial habits on a grander scale. For example, economists have been puzzled by an investment phenomenon dubbed the "equity premium paradox" (Mehra & Prescott, 1985): why do so many investors put so much of their capital into bonds and other low-variability–low-payoff investments when they could be investing in the more volatile, but more profitable, stock market? Researchers hypothesized that what is happening is that the high-variability investments are avoided because of loss aversion (Benartzi & Thaler, 1995). Because losses are felt more deeply than gains, frequently checking a high-variability portfolio—a stomach-churning roller-coaster ride anyway—would produce some especially unpleasant moments when the painful losses were experienced; and there would be more of these moments the more often the portfolio was checked. Follow-up research in controlled laboratory markets replicated the experiences of actual stock market investors and provided strong support for the loss aversion interpretation. Simply increasing the frequency with which current assets were reported shifted investors from high-variance to low-variance investment instruments.

The general effect of loss aversion is the tendency to favor the status quo over change. As in the mug-trading demonstration, it can hinder the operation of markets, making even mutually advantageous trades sluggish and inefficient. It also appears to play a role in negotiations where each party is likely to frame a settlement as a personal loss (and conversely as a gain for the other side). Courses on bargaining strive to teach negotiators to represent and re-represent situations so that solutions can be evaluated more objectively, without the distortions created by a one-sided gain–loss frame of reference.

2.3. General Limitations of the Expected Utility Model

Of course, even when we know better, we make "bad decisions"—that is, decisions that are irrational according to the expected utility model. If you are offered a 0.45 probability of winning $200 or a 0.50 chance of winning $150, the expected-value calculation—$(0.45 \times 200) = 90$; $(0.50 \times 150) = 75$—suggests taking the first bet, and that's what most participants do. But what would you do if you were offered the choice between a 0.90 chance of winning $200 and a certain payoff of $150? Although the expected value of the first bet is higher—180 as opposed to 150—most participants choose the second bet. This preference highlights both the special attraction of a certain outcome despite the expected-value calculation, and a weakness in the expected utility model, which predicts that if you prefer the higher-expected-value option in the first pair of bets, you will choose the higher-expected-value option in the second. But apparently people do not do this.

Other experimental results have shown that participants tend to assess value according to the expected utility model but not the probabilities of consequences. In assigning decision weights—our estimates of the likelihood of various outcomes of a decision—we apparently have a general tendency to over-weight small probabilities, to be insensitive to middle to high probabilities, and to over-weight certain outcomes (as in the last example). For example, when asked to estimate the likelihood of various causes of death, participants tend to overestimate extremely unlikely events (tornadoes, earthquakes) and underestimate more common ones (heart disease) (Lichtenstein et al., 1978). This pattern reflects the difference between the actual probability of an event and what we imagine that probability to be. Such subjective beliefs in cases in which the outcome is uncertain contradict some of the basic laws of mathematical probability theory and are an irrational aspect of human reasoning (Figure 9–5). For example, if the probability of tossing a head is under-weighted and the probability of tossing a tail is also under-weighted, preferences based on gambles decided by simple coin tosses will violate the basic rule of probability theory—that the probability of an event (heads, p) plus the probability of its complement (tails, $1 - p$) must sum to 1.

Although the expected utility model is not a perfect psychological model, it provides a good first approximation of human (and much nonhuman animal) decision behavior (Bateson & Kacelnik, 1998; Krebs & Kacelnik, 1991). If an organism is highly motivated (a hungry rat or monkey; a human faced with making or not making a $100,000 investment), and if the situation is simple and provides full relevant information (the animal has been foraging for food over many days in this neighborhood; the investor has a good deal of experience in the market), the model is likely to make accurate predictions of behavior.

Comprehension Check:

1. Suppose that you bet $5 on red to come up on an American casino roulette wheel. If red comes up, you double your money (win $10), otherwise you lose your $5. There are 18/38 chances of winning on red. What is the *expected value* of your $5 bet?

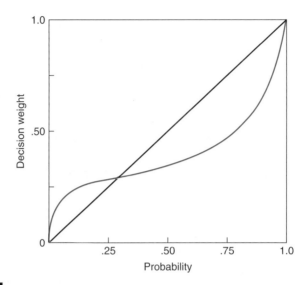

FIGURE 9–5 A decision weight curve

The curve relates objective probabilities to subjective probabilities—that is, to decision weights. The steep parts of the curve near zero (0) and certainty (1.0) indicate that we are very sensitive to small changes in probabilities at those points: "possibility-hood" and certainty have a big impact on our decisions. The relatively flat portion of the curve, between 0.15 and 0.75, indicates that we are relatively insensitive to differences in probability in that range—the difference between 0.40 and 0.49 just doesn't matter much to us, whereas the difference between 0.90 and 0.99 matters a lot.

(Based on Figure 1 in Tversky, A., & Kahneman, D. (1992). Advances in Prospect Theory: Cumulative representation of uncertainty. *Journal of Risk and Uncertainty, 5,* 297–323.)

2. Now, consider the *expected utility* of your roulette bet on red: How is the expected utility different from the expected value? How could expected utility explain why people gamble on casino bets of this type?

3. NEURAL BASES OF EXPECTED UTILITY CALCULATIONS

In his fascinating book, *Decisions, Uncertainty, and the Brain: The Science of Neuroeconomics* (2003), Paul Glimcher makes a compelling case for the expected utility model (see also Schall, 2001). Glimcher and several other researchers have found brain sites that exhibit neural activity correlated with performance of the calculations prescribed by expected utility model. These investigators, using single-cell recordings of monkey brains, have discovered neurons in the lateral inferior (i.e., side, lower) parietal cortex in which activity directly tracks the probability and the magnitude of reward. The early focus of this research was on experienced utility, that is, the reactions (in terms of their value or worth) to rewarded events when they are received. There has since been a gradual shift to the investigation of decision utility, the anticipation, at the time the decision is made, of the expected value or worth of a particular outcome. In a well-adapted organism, anticipatory decision utility should predict experienced utility to some degree, and probably both evaluations would involve some of the same brain structures.

The basic experimental task, developed in the 1980s by William Newsome, required monkeys to make discriminations between dots moving in different directions (up–down, right–left) (Newsome, 1997). The monkeys were rewarded when they correctly chose a direction of movement, responding with eye movements that indicated their decision. The task is analogous to the gamble-choice tasks that dominate laboratory research with human participants. On each trial the monkeys are choosing between two uncertain prospects (the discrimination is often difficult); they have to learn from experience the probabilities of receiving a reward (in their case, juice), and they receive their reward as an outcome of a prudent (and lucky) decision.

These investigators discovered anticipatory activation of neurons in the monkeys' lateral intraparietal area and the superior colliculus (which is a subcortical structure involved in shifting visual attention); other researchers found activity also in the dorsolateral prefrontal cortex (Kim & Shadlen, 1999). Neurons in these brain structures fired more frequently in the milliseconds just before the monkies indicated their decisions by eye movements. Two aspects of the findings are especially important. First, the result was obtained on some test trials, inserted among regular trials, on which the dots moved in random directions. Thus, on those "random dot trials" the stimulus was unrelated to the outcome of the monkey's decision. Second, the relevant neurons are not located early in the visual perception part of the neural circuit, nor in a motor control segment of the circuit. They are right in the center, at a junction connecting the perceptual and motor systems. In fact, electrical stimulation of neurons in these brain structures biased the monkey's decisions (Salzman et al., 1990), a result that provided a convincing demonstration of the causal role of these structures in the decision.

Other researchers quickly followed up Newsome's path-breaking experiments with further investigations of the eye movement–decision system. Glimcher and collagues (summarized in Glimcher, 2003) searched for neural mechanisms that might perform utility calculations like those prescribed by the subjective expected utility equation. A monkey in Glimcher's experiments learned to move her eyes to the right or left following a color signal indicating which direction was likely to pay off with a sip of juice (Figure 9–6a). The probability of receiving a sip and, if there was a reward, the amount of juice received were systematically varied. Single-cell recordings showed individual neurons in the lateral intraparietal cortex that, *before* the outcomes, tracked the changes in probability (Figure 9–6b) and magnitude of reward (Figure 9–6c) over a full range of values. The investigators searched for correlated activity in this area because it is one of the "neural bottlenecks" in a vast system of links between visual input and motor control of the monkey's eye movements (Platt & Glimcher, 1999).

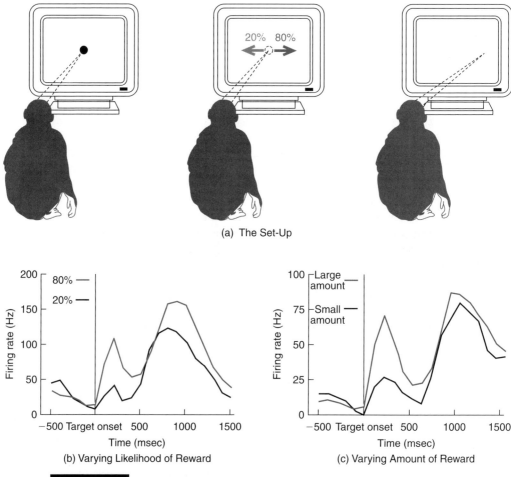

(a) The Set-Up

(b) Varying Likelihood of Reward

(c) Varying Amount of Reward

FIGURE 9-6 The monkey and the juice

(a) The monkey begins a trial by fixating on a central dot on the screen. The dot changes to one of two colors, each color indicating the direction of gaze (left or right) that will likely be rewarded. The probability of reward was varied over a range from 0.20 to 0.80, so that the investigators could assess whether some neurons were "anticipating" the probability of reward.

(Gimcher, P. (2003). Decisions, uncertainty and the brain: The science of neuroeconomics. Cambridge, MA; MIT Press. Figures 10.11, 10.12, 10.13; pp. 257–263. © 2003 by the Massachusetts Institute of Technology. Reprinted with permission.)

(b) A recording of a single lateral inferior parietal neuron across time, demonstrating a clear separation of activity when there was low probability (20%) that the direction corresponding to the neuron's visual receptive field would be rewarded versus a high probability (80%) that it would be rewarded. A summary of many calculations such as these demonstrates that monkeys appear to compute prior and subsequent probabilities in a rational manner. (c) Results when the researchers manipulated the amount of juice received—that is, the utility or value of the reward. Again lateral inferior parietal neurons serve as meters for anticipated (and received) rewards.

(Platt, M. L., & Glimcher, P. W. (1999). Neural correlates of decision variables in parietal cortex. *Nature, 400,* 233–238, Figures 1 and 2. Reprinted with permission.)

In addition to investigating neural areas that compute and use utility measures, researchers are also attempting to discover how these utility values are encoded in the brain. There is some suggestion that the dopamine system may play an important role in this. The activity of individual dopaminergic neurons—that is, neurons activated by dopamine—in monkey ventral midbrain areas was recorded in a classical conditioning task with juice as the unconditioned-stimulus reward. Researchers presented a visual signal to the monkey that indicated the probability (and amounts) of a juice reward (Fiorillo et al., 2003). Recordings of single dopaminergic neurons sampled in the monkey's ventral midbrain areas showed systematic responses directly related to the probability of receiving a juice reward. Furthermore, these same neurons showed post-reward responses that could be interpreted as "surprise reactions"—high response rates when a reward was in fact received despite a low probability (Figure 9–7).

One important experimental result has yet to be reported. Researchers have found neural "meters" for reward magnitude and for reward probability (and there are probably more to be found). But, it would be especially significant if neural structures could be identified that reflect a quantity representing the summary expected utility of potential consequences, that is, *the product* of Value × Probability, as displayed in Figure 9–3.

What about people? Research with human participants has pursued the quest for neural correlates to calculate uncertainty and utility with neuroimaging techniques. Some studies have found activation in the nucleus accumbens (a dopamine-using system) associated with the prospect of monetary gains (Gehring & Willoughby, 1999; Knutson et al., 2001). Other researchers also observed activation of the nucleus accumbens, as well as an extension of the amygdala and part of the orbital frontal cortex, in anticipation of monetary gains and losses (Breiter et al., 2001). In all these results, increasing activation was correlated with the magnitudes of the anticipated consequences.

Perhaps the most interesting result from the Breiter study is the observation that brains are responsive to the relative, not absolute, amounts to be gained or lost. One comparison from Breiter et al. (2001) is between three lotteries that all involve the potential outcome of $0 (at least on the surface, a neutral, null amount) with a probability of one-third. Three variations of a basic lottery were created with $0 ($p = 1/3$) paired with two wins ($10, $2.50), a mixture of win ($2.50) and loss ($1.50), or two losses (−$2.50 or −$6.00). The fascinating result was the reaction to receiving $0 in the amygdala was either positive or negative depending on "what else might have happened." The brain registered "disappointment" (less neural activity) when the alternative outcomes were better than $0 and "rejoicing" (more neural activity) when $0 was the best of the three possible outcomes.

Thus, there is accumulating evidence that the brain performs utility calculations like those prescribed by the expected utility equation, that gains and losses are not treated exactly the same, and that there may even be a distinct neural route for the evaluation of monetary consequences. However, the relativism of the Breiter et al. results is a big problem for the expected utility model as we will see later in our discussion of "value framing effects."

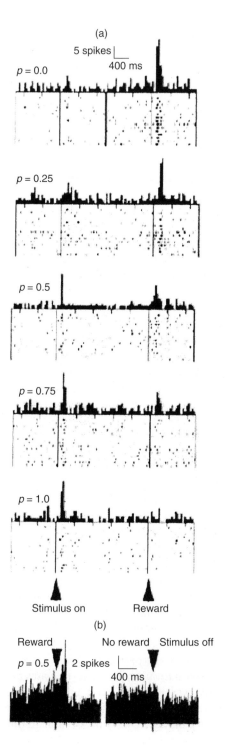

(a)

5 spikes

400 ms

$p = 0.0$

$p = 0.25$

$p = 0.5$

$p = 0.75$

$p = 1.0$

Stimulus on   Reward

(b)

Reward   No reward   Stimulus off

$p = 0.5$ 2 spikes

400 ms

FIGURE 9-7   A monkey, juice, and surprise

(a) The activity of a single representative neuron in a monkey's ventral midbrain region when the monkey received a signal indicating the probability of receiving a juice reward and after receiving the reward (ranging from 0.0 to 1.0). Activity immediately after the signal stimulus reflected the probability indicated by the signal—more activity for higher probabilities. (b) Activity after the reward was received mirrored the earlier activity, essentially indicating how "surprised" the monkey was to receive the reward: the greatest activity after being rewarded followed a low-probability signal.

(Fiorillo, C. D., Tobler, P. N. & Schultz, W. (2003). Discrete coding of reward probablity and uncertainty in dopamine neurons. *Science, 299,* 1898–1902, Figure 1, parts A and B only.)

1. What is the difference between experienced utility and decision utility? Can you think of a personal example where you observed a large difference between the two types of utility? Why would that difference be important?

2. What are the key experimental results that support the claim that the brain computes expected utilities?

4. HUMAN DECISION MAKING AND THE EXPECTED UTILITY MODEL: HOW CLOSE A FIT?

We have said that the expected utility model provides a good first approximation to human behavior, and so it does. But it is not a completely satisfactory psychological model. In the early years of research (1950–1970), however, the few results that contradicted the theory were treated as anomalies and ignored as problems for the overarching theoretical framework. (They were labeled *paradoxes* because the expected utility model was held to be so self-evidently true that any exception was regarded simply as an "apparent" contradiction.) But during the 1970s and 1980s the trickle of anomalies became a flood of contradictions of the expected utility model.

4.1. Preference, Transitivity, and Procedural Invariance: Behavioral Violations

In behavioral studies, two closely related principles of rational decision making are consistently violated, despite the fact that we should "know better." Both transitivity and procedural invariance are unassailable hallmarks of the expected utility model, yet we ignore them.

4.1.1. Transitivity

If the red ball is larger than the yellow ball, and the yellow ball is larger than the green ball, then the red ball is larger than the green ball. This is the principle of transitivity, which states that if a "greater-than" relation holds between a first element and a second one and between that second element and a third one, then it must also hold between the first element and the third one. (We've mentioned this principle before.)

Transitivity of preferences as expressed in choices is perhaps the most fundamental principle of rational choice: if I prefer X over Y, and Y over Z, then I should prefer X over Z. If you prefer fish to chicken, and like chicken more than steak, you won't choose steak over fish; if people did typically exhibit such a pattern of choice, they could be turned into "money pumps" by enterprising sellers who offered sequences of choices, but with a premium paid to the seller on each transaction. You want to go to the Rolling Stones concert? Fine, here's a ticket for $50. Oh, you'd rather hear Madonna? OK, just trade me the Stones tickets plus a $10 exchange fee and you're all set with Madonna. Wait, you say it's Eminem? Fine, give me back the Madonna ticket plus the customary $10. Happy now? Great! What, now you want

Gamble	Probability of winning	Payoff	Expected value
A	7/24	5.00	1.46
B	8/24	4.75	1.58
C	9/24	4.50	1.69
D	10/24	4.25	1.77
E	11/24	4.00	1.83

(a)

(b)

FIGURE 9–8 Gambles that produce intransitive choices

(a) Participants were given pairwise choices of which of these gambles they wished to play by spinning a wheel of fortune (b). Because the payoff amounts are easy to comprehend, the amounts controlled the pairwise choices and participants consistently preferred the higher payoff gamble in any *adjacent* bets. But the gambles were cleverly designed so that as payoffs went up (from $4.00 to $5.00), probabilities went down (from 11/24 to 7/24), so that the discrepancy between the expected value for the $4.00 bet and the $5.00 bet was dramatic ($1.83 versus $1.46). Participants faced with a choice between the *extreme* bets reversed the preference ordering implied by their pairwise choices, choosing the $4.00 (11/24) bet over the $5.00 (7/24) bet—and showed consistent, and irrational, intransitivities. (Tversky, A. (1969). The intransitivity of preferences. *Psychological Review, 76,* 31; 48, Table 1 and Figure 1. © 1969 American Psychological Association. Reprinted with permission.)

to go to the Stones again? Well, OK, we'll just exchange Eminem for the Stones, at the usual fee, and you're all set. . . .

Nonetheless, there have been many laboratory demonstrations of the intransitivity of preferences in human decision making. In one such study, participants were to choose between pairs of gambles shown in Figure 9–8 (Tversky, 1969). The probabilities of winning changed slightly (in units of 1/24) between adjacent gambles. In making their choices, participants typically ignored those differences and based their decisions on payoffs alone, choosing E over D, D over C, C over B, and B over A. But when gambles that were far apart in the ordering were paired, the difference in probability was much larger, as was the resulting difference in expected values. Now a typical participant preferred A over E, violating transitivity. The participants, penitentiary prisoners, were highly motivated; they were playing for cigarettes and cash, much valued commodities in prison. They seemed to understand the principle of transitivity in the abstract, but most did not notice that they had violated it in their choices, and some vehemently denied that they had.

4.1.2. Procedural Invariance

Two ways of asking the same question about preferences should produce the same answer—this is the principle of procedural invariance. For example, people can be asked to indicate their preferences by choosing between two options: "Which of these two gambles would you prefer to play?" Or they can be asked, "How much would you be willing to pay to have an opportunity to play each of these gambles?"

Presumably, any gamble that is deemed worth more money would also then be preferred in a pairwise choice. However, procedural invariance is consistently violated under some conditions. Consider a choice between the following pair of gambles:

Gamble 1 (P bet). Probability of 8/9 of winning $4; otherwise nothing.

Gamble 2 ($ bet). Probability of 1/9 of winning $40; otherwise nothing.

When asked which gamble they'd prefer to play, most participants choose the *P* bet; they seem to focus their attention on the likelihood of the payoff and choose the gamble with the higher probability of winning. But when asked to set a cash selling price for the gambles ("Suppose you own the rights to play these gambles. What would you sell them for"?), most people set a higher price on the $ bet than on the *P* bet. Now the amount of the payoff is more important than the probability of its occurring. The instruction to set a cash price apparently directs participants' attention first to the two outcomes ($40 and $4), and only then do they adjust their price down or up according to the probability. Such adjustments are typically insufficient to reflect the actual mathematical situation; they are heavily biased by the initial value set, the "anchor" value, which considered primarily the contrast between the payoffs and not the probability of either. Thus, the adjustment down from the $40 anchor on the $ bet did not reach the price set by adjusting up from the $4 outcome for the *P* bet.

These reversals of preference are a blatant contradiction of any model that seeks to demonstrate consistent preference ordering by exclusively rational methods of valuation. The original results included a replication in a casino with gamblers wagering with their own money (Slovic & Lichtenstein, 1979); nonetheless, some economists were so sure that the effect was spurious that they conducted 11 variations on the original method to prove that preference reversals could be produced only under unusual laboratory conditions (Grether & Plott, 1979). To their surprise, they found preference reversals in their studies as well, and concluded that this phenomenon is a fundamental obstacle to the claim that human decision making is fully rational. Subsequent research has shown preference reversal in experimental markets where participants could trade gambles with one another, and have even found that the effect could be exploited to pump money out of investor-participants (Berg et al., 1985; Knez and Smith, 1987).

4.2. Rationality—Up to a Point

Looking at the terms of the gambling choice studies, it is not hard to see why, at some point, the expected utility model fails: we are not perfect calculators, and in these choices there can be a fair amount to calculate. Intransitivity and preference reversals may be consequences of our limited attention and working memory systems. The expected utility model is both rational and descriptive of behavior only with well-defined goals in simple situations (Chater et al., 2003), and the model makes no claims about the cognitive abilities that may be necessary to implement calculations of subjective expected utilities of all the options being considered. Because it is obvious that considerable information-processing capacity is needed to approximate those calculations, a common theoretical tactic has been to assume people are as rational as they can be *within* the limits of our capacities for attention, working memory, and executive control.

4.2.1. Bounded Rationality and the Satisficing Algorithm

The Nobel prize–winning psychologist and economist Herbert Simon proposed the idea of *bounded rationality;* that is, choice processes that are as rational as they can be, given cognitive limitations on the amount of information we can process (Simon, 1955). He suggested that our information-processing systems develop adaptive strategies that make trade-offs between, on the one hand, the cognitive effort of searching for and processing information and, on the other hand, the choice of the absolutely best alternative. He described one such strategy as satisficing, a method that finds not necessarily the best of all possibilities, but one that is good enough to meet the desires of the decision maker (Simon, 1955).

Satisficing is an *algorithm,* a step-by-step recipe for making a decision. Say you're looking for an apartment. First, determine what characteristics of an apartment are important to you (rent, distance from school, number of rooms, and so on). Then, set criteria for acceptability on each important attribute (not more than a third of your budget, walking distance, three rooms, and so on). Finally, consider the available choices one at a time until an option is found that is "good enough" on the important attributes—and quit the search. The winner is the first candidate that is satisfactory—that meets your minimum requirements—in all respects. Note that this process will not produce the ideal apartment (unless you're very lucky indeed), but it will give you what is important to you and save a lot of time.

The cognitive processes required for satisficing are very different from those required by an expected utility calculation, and they generally require much less effort. Satisficing produces good, but often not optimal, outcomes, and it is biased by the order in which the possible options are searched. But considerable evidence from experiments and field studies indicates that satisficing strategies provide a more valid description of everyday decision-making behavior than does the expected utility model. Consumer choices are often made by satisficing. You know that if you keep searching for an apartment for another week—or month—you may well find one you like even better. Instead, as consumers, we usually stop with a "good enough" option because of the prohibitive costs in time and effort of continuing the search. It is usually simply not worth it to expend more effort to improve the outcome by a small amount. In fact, someone who obsessively seeks optimal solutions in a modern commercial environment could be described as maladaptive, if not downright irrational (see the *Debate* box).

4.2.2. The Cognitive Toolbox: How We Choose the Way We Choose

Satisficing is a practical, dependable, and computationally realistic strategy in human decision making; it is also not the only one by which people seem to balance cognitive effort and desirability of outcome. Another, for example, is elimination by aspects, a strategy that successively evaluates a possible choice on a number of attributes, eliminating the choices that do not measure up to the decision maker's criteria for each attribute. For instance, say you want to buy a car. Here's how it works: First, decide which attribute of the candidate options is most important to you (cost, color, four-wheel drive, and so on). Then, run through the options now available to you and decide where the options are on that attribute, eliminating all options that

DEBATE

Are Humans Rational Animals?

Most economists, some philosophers, and a few psychologists (e.g., J. R. Anderson, 1990) argue that we are essentially rational; for example, an expected utility model for choice is a good hypothesis about how humans will think and behave when they are well informed. One version of the debate compares human performance to the calculations of models from logic and probability theory: these are the best hypotheses our civilization has come up with about what it means to think in a rational manner. Here, there seems to be little question that we are often far from the rational standard. The many demonstrations of violations of logic and probability theory provided by Tversky and Kahneman (1974) have been enormously influential in convincing most scientists that humans are not fundamentally rational—at least by a textbook definition of "theoretical rationality" (Harman, 1996).

However, the debate is not this simple. When the stakes are high and people are well informed and have time to learn their environments, rationality is a good first hypothesis about how they will behave. Economists have long defended this view, and point out that the many rational paradoxes—demonstrated by, among others, Allais, Ellsberg, Tversky, and Kahneman—seem to diminish when stakes go up and problem solvers are well informed. In a related argument, the psychologist Gerd Gigerenzer has been an effective proponent of "ecological rationality," arguing that the shortcut judgment and decision heuristics that we rely on are tuned to specific, important environments and that they sometimes outperform theoretically rational calculations—and with a small cognitive investment.

Another complication in the debate about rationality is that any analysis has to postulate the decision maker's goals: what is the decision maker trying to maximize? Evaluations of rationality require much more thought than the simple demonstration that a participant makes logical or statistical errors. The issue is complicated by the fact that people want to maximize many more goals than simple selfish acquisitive objectives (which is the only goal considered in many discussions of rationality). It is now well established that many values, beyond selfish greed are important to decision makers: altruism, fairness, reciprocity, and others. Researchers can certainly create miniature experimental environments, minimize nonselfish motives, and give participants ample time to learn the environments before testing whether behavior is optimal. Such analyses have been done with non-human species, and have led to the general conclusion that many nonhuman species are remarkably well adapted to their environmental niches (Krebs & Davies, 1997).

At present, we would say that the best conclusion from behavioral research is that people frequently fail to meet standards of "theoretical rationality," that specified by logic, probability theory, and the like. However, the field is wide open for answers concerning "practical rationality" (rational for some goals and contexts). Our best judgment is that evolution and culture have prepared us to perform close to optimally in many environments (especially when it comes to primordial, survival decisions concerning diets, choice of habitats, and choices of whom to associate with and whom to trust). But, because humans seem to reinvent their environments frequently (think about recent changes in consumer and financial markets caused by the rise of the Internet), it is unlikely we are fully "practically rational," and we probably do not even have the learning capacities necessary to adapt to some modern artificial, but hugely important, environments.

are significantly worse in this respect. Then consider the second most important aspect and eliminate again. Keep this up until only one winner is left.

Simon (1955) and other investigators have envisioned a cognitive system with a "toolbox" of such strategies as well as utility calculations; these are variously brought into play as required to solve everyday intellectual problems. Some of these "tools" are computational algorithms learned by instruction, such as arithmetic skills and social decision strategies (e.g., imitating the choices of an expert); others are idiosyncratic, based on the personal learning experiences of the decision maker. When we run into an intellectual problem, we select or create an algorithm to solve it from the procedures in our "cognitive toolbox." Other "tools" we have available to us are heuristics, simple and efficient rules of thumb that work well in most circumstances.

The *adaptive decision maker model* is based on these principles (Payne et al., 1993). In this model the "cognitive toolbox" for decision making includes satisficing and several other practical but not quite optimal procedures, as well as the theoretically optimal expected utility equation. The fundamental assumption of the model is that people are adaptive, their choice of strategies is based on a reasonable, perhaps even rational, consideration of the trade-offs in cognitive effort and ease of execution, time, and consequences. Very important decisions (Should I buy this car? Should I move to Chicago?) are addressed with "more expensive" tools—ones with greater cognitive demands—that will produce close to optimal solutions; less important decisions (should I rent *Batman Begins* or *Rambo IV* tonight? Should I buy the Dell or the Gateway computer?) are solved with "cheaper" rule-of-thumb heuristic tools.

Our choice of algorithms or heuristics is adaptive: we rely on strategies that fit our needs at the time and that capitalize on the specific structures of the current environment (Gigerenzer et al., 1999; Payne et al., 1993). For example, Gerd Gigerenzer has shown that we can make surprisingly accurate judgments, relying on as little as one piece of information, if we know the right piece. So, the interesting hypothesis is that experience "tunes" us to the most important cues in our environments and thus allows us to rely on simple and not obviously optimal judgment and choice strategies. These so-called fast-and-frugal strategies often perform as well as more demanding rational algorithms. Furthermore, adaptive, fast-and-frugal strategies provide more valid descriptions of human decision behavior than does the expected utility model.

As we have seen, even when choosing between gambles to play in the laboratory, participants often do not perform a utility calculation. Instead, they focus on only one (or a few) of the attributes of gambles (probability of winning or the amount at risk) and ignore others—resulting in intransitivity and preference reversal in certain laboratory environments. Many studies have shown that much laboratory decision making with gamble stimuli follows a nonrational process based on specific information-processing strategies, such as satisficing and elimination by aspects.

4.3. Framing Effects and Prospect Theory

In traditional expected utility theory, the way the choices are described is irrelevant. This principle, known as *description invariance*, implies that a decision problem described by different but logically equivalent statements nonetheless should lead to the same choices. Note that such an invariance is not true of human perception: a single visual scene may be viewed from different perspectives, leading to different mental representations and different actions. The same turns out to be the case for situations that face decision makers. Consider the following problems (Kahneman & Tversky, 1982); what would you prefer in each case?

PROBLEM 1. You have just won $200. The casino now offers you a choice between (A) a sure gain of $50 or (B) a 0.25 chance of winning $200, with a 0.75 chance of winning nothing.

PROBLEM 2. You have just won $400. The casino now offers you a choice between (C) a sure loss of $150 or (D) a 0.75 chance of losing $200, with a 0.25 chance of losing nothing.

Most participants like option A in the first problem and option D in the second. This follows the pattern that people are usually risk averse when offered moderately likely gains but risk seeking when offered moderately likely losses, as discussed earlier. But notice that the payoffs in options A and C are identical (in each you end up with a sure $250), and so are options B and D (in each, 75 percent of the time you end up with $200, 25 percent of the time you end up with $400). The changed description has affected participants' choices, a violation of description invariance. In problem 1 participants view the problem from a "gain perspective," but in problem 2 from a "loss perspective." Demonstrations such as this one show the importance of framing effects, the influence of the various ways a problem may be put. Framing effects have long been of concern to pollsters, because the answers to survey questions depend on the exact form of the question put to respondents. "To what degree do you support the president's plan . . . ?" usually gets a very different estimate of support than the equivalent "To what degree do you oppose the president's plan . . . ?" (Tourangeau et al., 2000). Responses to advertisements are also frame sensitive; hamburger sells at a much slower rate when described as 90 percent lean versus 10 percent fat.

The most famous such demonstration involves a hypothetical medical scenario (Tversky & Kahneman, 1981):

PROBLEM 1. The nation is preparing for the outbreak of a disease that is expected to kill 600 people. Two alternative programs to combat the disease have been proposed by public health officials; which would you support?

PROGRAM A. Two hundred people will be saved.

PROGRAM B. There is a one-third probability that 600 people will be saved, and a two-thirds probability that no one will be saved.

In fact, the two programs have equal expected values (200 saved), but because of the tendency to be risk averse for gains, most participants choose program A. Now consider another problem:

PROBLEM 2. The nation is preparing for the outbreak of a disease that is expected to kill 600 people. Two alternative programs to combat the disease have been proposed by public health officials; which would you support?

PROGRAM C. Four hundred people will die.

PROGRAM D. There is a one-third probability that nobody will die, and a two-thirds probability that 600 people will die.

In problem 2, most participants like program D, in accordance with the tendency to be risk seeking when losses are involved. Look again: programs A and C have identical outcomes—400 deaths, 200 survivors. Similarly, programs B and D are identical in outcome—the language has been flipped, but the probabilities and outcomes are the same in both. Nonetheless, there is a strong shift in participant choices from problem 1 to problem 2. Framing effects such as these are not restricted to artificial laboratory brainteasers: investigators have replicated these results with practicing physicians who were asked to choose between medical treatments, the outcomes of the treatments framed in terms of survival rates (gains) versus mortality rates (losses) (McNeil et al., 1982).

A fundamental tenet of cognitive psychology is that our actions are determined by our mental representations of situations, not directly by the situations themselves. The implication of research on framing effects is that decision making, like any cognitive activity, depends on our view of the situation that confronts us. Our perception of that situation is a primary determinant of our behavior (Hastie & Pennington, 2000). This cognitive principle of representation is a basic assumption of prospect theory, currently the most influential theory of decision making in the face of risk and uncertainty (Kahneman & Tversky, 1979; Tversky & Kahneman, 1992).

Prospect theory proposes that the first stage in decision making is comprehending the prospects ahead by framing the terms of the decision. Framing involves simplifying and combining some quantities, and evaluating prospective gains and losses in relation to a reference point. This reference point, or anchor, is usually the current situation, before the decision is made. A novel assumption of prospect theory is that this reference point is not fixed, but rather is frequently updated. Thus, prospect theory explains the endowment effect—the added value we confer on something in our possession over something we have not yet acquired—by our updating of our reference point as a new possession is obtained. Or, consider a week's trip to Las Vegas. When you enter the casino the first day your reference point is the sum you've decided to gamble. Suppose you win $250 dollars that day. The next day, when you return to the tables, it is likely that your new reference point is $250 higher—the amount of your initial stake plus $250. Of course, after the ups and downs of a week's gambling, on your last day in Las Vegas your reference point may revert to the amount of your initial stake on your first day, and you may take risks in the hope of getting back in the black or at least breaking even before you leave town. Throughout the occasionally tension-filled week your reference point for the gambling decisions you make has moved, thus framing the outcomes you expect and experience.

According to prospect theory, once values and decision weights—our subjective estimates of probabilities—are mentally represented for the prospects under consideration, an expected-value calculation is performed on each prospect that combines values and decision weights into a summary evaluation (see Figures 9–3 and 9–4). Although the central computation in prospect theory is directly analogous to the calculation of an expected utility, both framing effects and decision weights violate mathematical and economic principles of rationality. Prospect theory describes many of the behavioral patterns seen in decision making, but it does not provide a specific account of intransitivity and preference reversal.

4.4. The Role of Emotions in Valuation: The Allais Paradox

Further difficulties for the expected utility model come from another source entirely: emotion. It comes as no surprise that emotions affect decision making—a wealth of anecdotal experiences (perhaps including some of yours) attests to the many bad decisions made in moments of anger or elation. Emotion has played a role in decision theory as well since the early days of the discipline: economists began with the assumption that decision making is performed in the service of achieving goals and that the goals are either essentially emotional ("the pursuit of happiness") or strongly associated with emotions (especially guilt, regret, rejoicing, and disappointment). There was also a general notion that emotions usually interfere with rational decision making. You might decide to save your money for retirement, but be diverted by momentary impulses and spend your savings on frivolous entertainments; you might decide to diet or to resist sexual seduction, but then succumb to temptation in moments of craving or passion. In modern views, however, the emotions play adaptive as well as dysfunctional roles in the decision-making process (DeSousa, 1987; Frank, 1988; Rottenstreich & Shu, 2004). One early demonstration, the *Allais paradox*, pointed to the role of anticipated regret. The Allais paradox is the apparent contradiction observed when the addition of the identical event to each alternative has the effect of changing the preference of the decision maker (Allais, 1953; 1979). What would you do in each of the following situations?

Situation 1. Choose between

Gamble 1. A certain gain of $500,000.

Gamble 2. A 0.10 chance of $2,500,000; 0.89 chance of $500,000; 0.01 chance of nothing.

Situation 2. Choose between

Gamble 3. An 0.11 chance of $500,000; 0.89 chance of nothing.

Gamble 4. A 0.10 chance of $2,500,000; 0.90 chance of nothing.

Most participants prefer gamble 1 to gamble 2. Even though the probability in gamble 2 of missing out on becoming rich by either a substantial or a whopping amount is very small (0.01), the potential regret at losing the larger amount looms so large that most people choose the certain $500,000. But participants also prefer gamble 4 over gamble 3: in this situation, the large difference in consequences ($500,000 versus $2,500,000) dominates the same small difference between the probabilities of winning the two amounts ($0.11 - 0.10 = 0.01$).

Although this paradox was treated as a minor anomaly in decision-making habits when it was described by the Nobel laureate Maurice Allais more than 50 years ago, it foreshadowed some of the most important new directions in current decision-making research, which are exploring the specific roles of emotions in decision making.

Probably the best interpretation of what's happening with the choices in the Allais paradox is that the decision maker confronted with the first pair of gambles just cannot stop thinking about the distinctively devastating consequence of ending up with nothing after being offered a sure $500,000. This anticipated regret drives the decision maker toward the certain payoff. In the second pair of gambles, however, both gambles will likely result in nothing, so none of the consequences "feels" as devastating, and the decision maker goes for the prospect with the higher expected value.

This innocent pair of choices—gamble 1 and gamble 4—contradicts the fundamental assumptions underlying the expected utility model. Gamble 1 has an expected value of $500,000 (that is, $1 \times 500,000$), whereas gamble 2 has an expected value of $695,000, or $(0.10 \times 2,500,000) + (0.89 \times 500,000)$. Thus, the preference in the first choice is, contrary to the model, for the gamble with the *lower* expected value.

Subsequent research has broadened our conceptions of the role of emotion in decision processes. A *decision affect theory*, in which anticipated emotions, especially regret and disappointment, replace utility as the carriers of value, has been proposed (Mellers, 2000; see also Bell, 1982, 1985; Loomes & Sugden, 1982, for variations). A great deal of work has been done on the confusing habits we exhibit when evaluating personal risks. Why are we so much more afraid of flying than of driving an equal distance, when we all know that driving is more dangerous? It seems that we can understand these apparently irrational reactions to natural and societal hazards as "head versus heart" contests—which the "emotional heart" often wins (Slovic et al., 2002).

The differences in valuation for emotion-laden versus monetary outcomes have been demonstrated in clever experiments (e.g., Rottenstreich & Hsee, 2001). In one study, participants were asked to choose between prospects involving an "opportunity to meet and kiss your favorite movie star" or $50 in cash. When the outcomes were certain, 30 percent chose the chance for a kiss. But, when there was only a 0.01 chance of receiving the outcome, 65 percent chose the chance for a kiss. For in between probabilities, the percentage choosing the kiss did not vary much with the actual probability. The investigators replicated this pattern with a trip to Europe versus college tuition payment, and electric shocks versus lost cash. In every case, the emotional outcomes, unlike the practical ones, were almost completely insensitive to variations in probability. It seems that the emotion-laden stimuli reduce the impact of information about probabilities; it is as though emotion-laden outcomes draw attention to consequences and away from other facets of the situation (as described in Chapter 8). Thus, the nature of the outcome can determine whether or not the probability information influences the choice; this is an interaction between value and probability that is profoundly contrary to the expected utility model.

4.5. The Role of Emotions in Valuation: Temporal Discounting and Dynamic Inconsistency

Compared to other animals, humans have a remarkable capacity to delay gratification (Rachlin, 1989). We are able deliberately to deny ourselves the immediate pleasure of a rich dessert (much of the time, anyway) because we know that we will enjoy it more tomorrow; we can decide to undergo a painful medical procedure because we know it will improve our physical state or prolong life. But we also exhibit lapses of self-control and appear to act contrary to clear intentions to abstain or save. One moment we behave like the prudent, hard-working ant in the fable, and the next we more resemble the lazy, self-indulgent grasshopper. The general conclusion is that although people are pretty good at acting prudently in planning for the future, the best laid plans can fall prey to impulsive and irrational behavior when we are confronted with immediate temptations. We have a tendency to devalue outcomes that occur further in the future, and this tendency is known as temporal discounting.

One controlled method of studying these anomalies of human behavior requires researchers to measure how much people value immediate versus delayed gratifications. In a typical temporal discounting experiment, participants are offered choices between immediate outcomes versus delayed outcomes. Their patterns of choices reveal the relative values of, for example, receiving $15 today versus $15 six weeks from now. A specific type of apparent irrationality has emerged in these studies. Consider the following choice: receive $10 immediately versus receive $15 in one week. Most participants choose the $10 today—their reaction is almost visceral, they are already savoring the consumption of the $10 treat they imagine. Now, consider a choice involving the same amounts of money, but to be received in five weeks versus in six weeks—$10 in 35 days versus $15 in 42 days. For most participants, the delayed choice is a no-brainer; wait for the $15. Why the reversal? This type of dynamic inconsistency—reversed preferences between identical outcomes depending on time—is contrary to a rational analysis, where the standard economic models predict consistency. In these models, although the value of a fixed outcome ($10) is expected to drop with distance in time (as a result of temporal discounting), there is no "crossover point" at which an initially preferred outcome reverses with a nonpreferred one (as in our $10 versus $15 example).

One interpretation of dynamic inconsistency is that when an outcome is immediate, an emotional system controls our behavior and leads us to choose the immediately available gratification. However, when gratification is not immediately available, our cooler, rational system takes over and we choose wisely (Loewenstein, 1996; Thaler & Shefrin, 1981). This interpretation is consistent with our subjective experience when faced with a rich dessert, a chance to slack off during a workout, an opportunity for a sexual hookup or a quick buck (as in the above experimental choice). It also makes sense of the common experience of being of two competing minds when choosing between temptation and a prudent course of action. It also helps us understand why we sometimes resort to various precommitment strategies to "do what is best for us" (e.g., joining a Christmas Club for savings).

Although, the "two systems" account fits our intuitions well, it has been devilishly difficult to test with behavioral data. McClure et al. (2005a) reported a novel test that combines behavioral and neuroscience measures. Participants made choices between immediate and delayed money rewards while their brains were scanned by fMRI. The hypothesis was that when both choice outcomes were delayed, only the cortical, deliberative systems would be active—calculating a more-or-less rational solution to the choice dilemma. However, when one or both of the outcomes was immediate, a second, emotional system would also be active, simultaneous with the cortical system. Their results provided remarkably clear support for the "two systems" hypothesis (see the accompanying *A Closer Look* box for more details of this work).

A CLOSER LOOK
Separate Systems Value Immediate versus Delayed Rewards

One of the most sophisticated studies to date of decision-making processes, which relied on both behavioral and neural data, was conducted by a multidisciplinary team of researchers. The results were reported by S. M. McClure, D. I. Laibson, G. Loewenstein, and J. D. Cohen in a 2005 paper titled "Separate Neural Systems Value Immediate and Delayed Monetary Rewards," *Science, 306,* 503–507.

Introduction

The investigators were interested in testing the hypothesis that the differences between choices made with immediate rewards versus delayed rewards is due to the operation of two independent valuation systems in the brain: a visceral, emotional evaluation system versus a deliberative, rational system. This hypothesis was grounded in more than 50 years of behavioral research.

The researchers sought to find different areas of brain activation when immediate versus delayed rewards were evaluated and, in particular, to find correlations between the amount of "emotional brain" activation and the preference for immediate outcomes. The hypothesis implied that areas of the brain known to be associated with emotional responses would be activated specifically when immediate rewards were considered.

Method

Princeton University students made choices between pairs of money rewards to be received immediately or at delayed time intervals (up to six weeks in the future), while lying in an fMRI scanner. Some of the rewards would actually be paid out at the point in time when they had been promised (as Amazon.com gift certificates), so participants were motivated to make careful choices that reflected their true valuations of the outcomes. Participants were presented with pairs of money payoff options (e.g., $25 in one week versus $34 in one month); on the left was a smaller earlier reward, on the right a larger delayed reward. They pressed a button to indicate their choice and, after a brief rest, another pair was presented.

fMRI methods were used to record brain activity during the 4 seconds preceding the choice response and 10 seconds following it. The time series graphs, summarizing activity in key brain areas are shown in Figure 9–9 along with brain images indicating which areas were active.

Results

The neuroimaging results were clear. Figure 9–9 shows the results for regions of the brain that were specifically active when an immediate outcome was presented as one option in a choice pair. The ventral striatum, medial orbitofrontal cortex, medial prefrontal cortex, posterior cingulate cortex, and the left posterior hippocampus were all significantly more active when immediate options were compared to options with a two-week or one-month delay. These areas are all good candidates to support the hypothesized emotional processes. There were six additional brain regions that exhibited significant elevation in activity when choices were being made, regardless of whether they involved immediate or delayed outcomes. Some of these areas involve perceptual and motor areas and are not likely to be associated with choice processes per se. But others, involving the lateral orbitofrontal cortex, the ventrolateral prefrontal cortex, and the dorsolateral prefrontal cortex, are probably involved in the deliberative, rational processes (see Chapter 7)—these are the "rational" areas in contrast to the "emotional" ones mentioned earlier.

Another noteworthy aspect of this study is the relation between the behavioral and the brain data. Figure 9–10 on Color Insert M shows a nice differential activation of emotional and rational regions for choices for immediate versus delayed rewards—more "rational" activation predicts choice of the delayed option.

Discussion

This study is an elegant illustration of how neuroimaging measures can complement and enhance the implicational power of behavioral analyses. Not all neural-behavioral collaborations are this successful, but this one was supported by several key ingredients: (1) the availability of a thorough behavioral analysis of temporal discounting and (2) the prior specification of potential neural components—specifically, the association of the emotional process with visceral-emotional systems and the rational process with a more deliberative-cognitive system.

The most important results from the neuroimaging data were differential activation of four areas of the brain when immediate versus delayed rewards were compared: there was more activation with immediate rewards in the ventral striatum, the medial orbitofrontal cortex, the medial prefrontal cortex, and the posterior cingulate cortex. The first three of these areas are clearly involved in emotion. When either immediate or delayed choices were contemplated, visual and motor areas were active (probably not involved in the choice process), along with areas of the left and right intraparietal cortex, the right dorsolateral prefrontal cortex, the right ventrolateral prefrontal cortex, and the right lateral orbitofrontal cortex. Although the association is not perfect, immediate choices generally activated areas of the brain associated with emotional responses, whereas areas associated with deliberate reasoning were active for both immediate and delayed choice pairs. It is also notable that "two systems" interpretations of moral decisions and consumer choices also have been supported by similar differential activation patterns (Greene et al., 2001; McClure et al., 2005b). Distinctive limbic and cortical areas are activated when emotion plays a central role in the decision.

4.6. Judgments in the Face of Ambiguity

Shortly after the expected utility model was introduced as the ultimate depiction of rationality, Daniel Ellsberg, then a graduate student, posed a challenge to its assumptions about judgments in the face of uncertainty. The Ellsberg paradox— the choice of certainty over ambiguity even when the result is an inconsistent pattern of choice—is demonstrated by choices in two pairs of gambles in which the outcome is determined by a random draw from an urn containing red, black, and yellow balls. The urn contains a total of 90 balls, 30 of which are red, and the remaining 60 balls are an unknown mixture of black and yellow balls (Figure 9–11). Thus, the probability of drawing a red ball is 0.333, but the probability of drawing a black ball or the probability of drawing a yellow ball is unknown, that is, *ambiguous;* it could be any value from 0.011 (1 out of 60) to 0.656 (59 out of 60).

FIGURE 9–11 Ellsberg's ambiguous urn

Daniel Ellsberg proposed to his research participants this urn, which contains balls of three colors. Participants are told the exact probability of drawing a red ball (30 reds out of 90 balls or $p_{red} = 0.33$) (represented here by blue), but the probabilities of drawing yellow (represented by white) or black balls are ambiguous. The participants know that the total is 60 balls (out of 90, or $p_{yellow\ or\ black} = 0.67$), but not the specific proportions.

Now consider the following gambles based on draws from this urn:

Situation 1. Choose between

Gamble 1. You win $100 if a red is drawn, nothing if a black or yellow is drawn.

Gamble 2. You win nothing if a red is drawn, $100 if a black is drawn, and nothing if a yellow is drawn.

Situation 2. Choose between

Gamble 3. You win $100 if red or yellow is drawn, nothing if black is drawn.

Gamble 4. You win $100 if black or yellow is drawn, nothing if red is drawn.

Most participants choose gamble 1 in the first situation and gamble 4 in the second. The explanation is intuitively obvious: even when there is massive uncertainty about what's going to happen, people prefer as much precision as possible. In gambles 1 and 4, it is possible to know the exact proportion of winning balls (0.33 and 0.67), whereas there is much ambiguity about the proportions in gambles 2 and 3. But the expected utility model is being violated, as can be seen more clearly in the table in Figure 9–12. In each pair of gambles, there is a common outcome, no payoff for yellow (situation 1) and $100 payoff for yellow (situation 2), which should be ignored. But because the remainder of the table entries (the left-hand and middle columns) are identical in the two situations, the strong preferences for gamble 1 in situation 1 and gamble 4 in situation 2 contradict the expected utility model, which would predict consistent choices of gambles 1 and 3 or gambles 2 and 4.

The neural events that underlie our reactions to ambiguity have been tracked with PET imaging (K. Smith et al., 2002). Participants were presented with ambiguous gambles such as Ellsberg's, as well as unambiguous gambles with a possibility of loss. The investigators found that when unambiguous gambles with losing outcomes were presented, there was activation of prefrontal (dorsomedial) cortex. However,

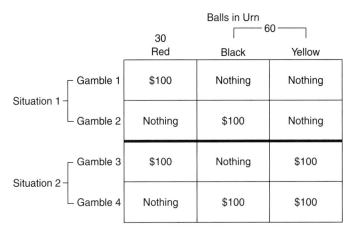

FIGURE 9–12   The underlying structure of Ellsberg paradox gambles

As in the Allais paradox, some columns discriminate between the gambles in each pair, but in a consistent manner, so that a reasonable person who favored gamble 1 over gamble 2 would have no rationale for choosing gamble 4 over gamble 3. In column 1, the difference between gamble 1 and gamble 2 is identical to the difference between gamble 3 and gamble 4; and again in column 2, and in column 3. Hence, although there are differences on which to make a choice in each pair, the differences are the same for every column within a pair, so there is no reason to reverse a 1 versus 2 choice made in situation 1 in a 3 versus 4 choice in situation 2.

for all ambiguous gambles and unambiguous gambles with winning outcomes, the dorsomedial system was not active, but rather an orbitofrontal (ventromedial) system was engaged. Other neuroimaging studies and behavioral studies with brain-damaged patients have also demonstrated that ventromedial regions play a key role when a person decides between gambles (Rogers et al., 1999a, 1999b). These same ventromedial areas have also been implicated in many studies that show a prominent role for emotional factors in decision making, suggesting the importance of these areas in integrating outcomes and values.

An important insight into our reactions to ambiguity was provided by investigators who presented each of Ellsberg's gambles in isolation and asked participants to set money values on them (Fox & Tversky, 1995). Now the effects of ambiguity vanished. Thus, it is only when the gambles are considered jointly in the context of one another, as in Ellsberg's pairs, that ambiguity aversion appears. It is comparative ignorance that matters, not some absolute sense of ambiguity.

4.7. Judgments about Likelihood in the Face of Uncertainty

The primary focus of early research on judgments in the face of uncertainty was this: in situations in which exact probabilities are not explicitly given, how do our intuitive judgments about likelihoods diverge from the prescriptions of mathematical probability theory? (The latter tells us the best way to capture our belief about likelihoods.) Dozens of ways in which our judgments violate the laws of probability were found (Gilovich et al., 2002; Kahneman et al., 1981). The essential message of this research is that people are not naturally endowed with intuitions that obey the laws of mathematical probability theory. Rather, in dealing with uncertainty we rely on cognitive capacities for retrieval from memory, for similarity assessment, and for figuring out causes for events (Tversky & Kahneman, 1974). Usually, these *judgment heuristics* yield useful, that is, adaptive, decisions. But under some conditions, we show biases in judgment. Our judgments about likelihoods in the face of uncertainty can be likened to the performance of our perceptual systems (Tversky & Kahneman, 1974). In most everyday environments, our visual systems do a good job of producing accurate models of the geometric space through which we navigate— but not always. The visual illusions demonstrated in Chapter 2 demonstrate that the visual system does not provide a perfect representation of our environment. And just as we suffer visual illusions, we are subject to judgment illusions.

One kind of judgment illusion is due to the effects of *availability* of information. When we try to assess the likelihood that a particular event will occur (the possibility we will get a cold, get a date with our new lab partner, be in a plane crash), we often rely on the ease with which relevant exemplars can be retrieved. Thus, we substitute *ease of recall* for a systematic assessment of the probability of occurrence. This might be an effective strategy *if* our memories gave us unbiased records of events occurring in our environment. But memory is biased by recency, vividness, personal relevance, and many other factors; and popular media and everyday gossip present a distorted reflection of the true frequencies of events. So, we overestimate the likelihood of overreported events such as dramatic dangers, negative social behaviors, and familiar events (for example, the proportion of Americans who graduate from college).

Here are a couple of demonstrations of availability at work (based on original studies reported by Tversky & Kahneman, 1974). Participants were told that the frequency of appearance of letters in the English language had been studied. A typical text was selected, and the relative frequency with which various letters of the alphabet appeared in the first and third positions in words was recorded. Words of less than three letters were excluded from the count. Consider the letter "K": is it more likely to occur as the first letter in such words, or as the third letter?

If you are like most participants, you judged that "K" is more likely to occur in the first than the third position; but, in fact, "K" is about three times more likely to occur in the third position. It is obvious you were relying on the ease with which you could recall words beginning with "K," which was much easier than recalling words with "K" in the third position. In other words, you showed an *availability bias*.

Here is another example: considering all fatalities in the American population, which is a more likely cause of death, homicide or suicide?

Here again, availability biases our judgment. Most people estimate homicides to be more frequent, but in fact, suicide is about twice as likely. Notice that the bias occurs this time because our experience (and hence our memory) is biased—the media floods us with reports of homicides. Murder stories are more than 20 times more common than suicide stories in print and television news. This is clearly an important bias; this is the kind of judgment we make when we decide whether to fly or drive, what kind of insurance to purchase, or whether to vote for a referendum to put more money into law enforcement, highway construction, or medical services.

A second heuristic we rely on to judge likelihoods is based on our ability to make rapid similarity judgments and our habit of thinking in terms of representative events or cases. *Representativeness* is judging by prototypes, and we all do it. We infer a person's social category from the similarity between that person's appearance and our prototype of a category member. Jane is always fashionably dressed and coifed, wears makeup, and has manicured nails so we guess she belongs to a campus sorority; Jack is big, taciturn, and wears sweat clothes and so we think he's a jock. Again, such habits of judgment are sometimes adaptive, *if* our prototypes are accurate *and* we consider other relevant information besides prototype-similarity when we make our final judgment. But, just as we too often rely on a quick availability-from-memory assessment, we rely on a quick similarity-to-prototype assessment and make biased judgments of the probability that an event or person represents a category.

Consider the following scenario. Linda is 31 years old, single, outspoken, and very bright. She majored in philosophy. As a student, she was deeply concerned with issues of discrimination and social justice, and also participated in antinuclear demonstrations. Rank the following statements by their probability, using 1 for the most probable and 8 for the least probable.

Linda is a teacher in an elementary school.
Linda works in a bookstore and takes yoga classes.
Linda is active in the feminist movement.
Linda is a psychiatric social worker.
Linda is a member of the League of Women Voters.
Linda is a bank teller.
Linda is an insurance salesperson.
Linda is a bank teller and is active in the feminist movement.

If, like most participants, you ranked "Linda is active in the feminist movement" high and "Linda is a bank teller" low, then you have relied on "representativeness" or a quick, intuitive assessment of how similar Linda is to your prototypes of the social categories of "feminists" and "bank tellers"; she sounds like a "typical feminist," but she doesn't sound like a bank teller.

But what about the "conjunction" category, "Linda is a bank teller *and* active in the feminist movement"? The natural inclination is to rely on similarity again and most of us conclude that the probability she is a feminist bank teller is intermediate between the probabilities of feminist (high) and bank teller (low). However, this judgment violates the logic of set relations: How could it be less likely that Linda belongs to a superordinate category (all bank tellers), than to one of its subset categories (bank tellers who are also feminists)? After all, every feminist bank teller is a bank teller! Some people—especially professorial types who felt embarrassed by their apparently illogical judgments—object that the wording of the problem is misleading; that when presented "Linda is a bank teller" they thought they were judging "Linda is a bank teller *and not* active in the feminist movement." But, when the problem was reworded to be unambiguous, there were still substantial violations of logic.

Violations can be reduced by asking the question in terms of frequencies, not more abstract probabilities, "Of 100 women like Linda, how many are . . .?" The "frequency format" is an effective reminder about the superset–subset relationships in the problem (feminist bank tellers is a subset of bank tellers), and, accordingly, people become more logical. In fact, restating any probability problem—in the classroom or on the street—in frequency format terms will help you adhere to the laws of probability theory. But, in spite of the fact that we can reduce these logical errors in the Linda problem, most of us will sheepishly admit that we made an error in our original judgment, and that similarity was what misled us (not the problem wording).

Let's look at a third heuristic for judging likelihood, reliance on causal relationships and simple causal models, known as the *simulation heuristic*. What about the following genetics question: Which is more likely, that if a mother has blue eyes, then her daughter has blue eyes; or that if a daughter has blue eyes, then her mother has blue eyes? The strong intuition is that it is more likely that if the mother has blue eyes, then the daughter will too. After all, it is the mother's genes that *cause* the daughter's blue eyes. But, again, the intuition is wrong. Under conditions that hold in most human populations, the probability is the same for the blue-eyed trait, mother–daughter or daughter–mother.

One last demonstration of the appeal of causal stories (adapted from Tversky & Kahneman, 1984): which is more likely, that during the next 12 months a massive flood will occur in California, causing more than 1,000 people to drown, or that during the next 12 months an earthquake will occur in California, causing a massive flood in which more than 1,000 people drown? Participants judging the likelihood of the second event assigned it a higher probability than a separate sample who judged the first event. Again, a conjunction (earthquake and flood) was judged more likely than one of its component events (flood alone) again violating the logic of set relations. This time it is not similarity that underlies the effects, but causal simulation—the earthquake is a good reason for the unlikely flood to occur, therefore the cause–effect combination is judged more likely than the unexplained effect alone.

Research on biases in judgments of likelihood led to the development of support theory, which specifies how we combine beliefs about likelihood derived from multiple sources and based on several underlying cognitive capacities, into a summary "strength of belief" for decision-making purposes. According to support theory, a possible event described as "My car won't start this morning" receives a different strength of belief (judged likelihood) from one described as "My car won't start this morning because of a mechanical failure or because it is out of gas or because of the weather or for some other reason." In general, "unpacked" events such as the second formulation with its explicit list of multiple possible causes recruit more belief support, receive a higher likelihood in the view of the decision maker, and have a greater impact on decisions, than "packed" events. So, p(car won't start) is given a lower probability estimate than p(won't start because of misfiring OR weather OR gas OR for another reason).

Support theory complements prospect theory and is consistent with the decision-weight function depicted earlier in Figure 9–4 (Fox, 1999). Taken together, these two theories provide a general behavioral theory of belief-based decision making (Tversky & Fox, 1995). Prospect theory is the general framework for both assessments of value (value function) and judgments about likelihood (decision-weight function); support theory provides a more detailed description of some of the cognitive processes underlying the decision-weight function.

In contrast to the large amount of behavioral research on rewards, punishments, and valuation processes, little neuroscientific research is available on our judgments about the likelihoods of events. However, research on mental calculation abilities may guide investigations in this field. The relevant ideas include the suggestion that intuitive judgments may be performed by a different neural system from the one that implements deliberate numerical estimations. It has already been shown that numerical calculation involves frontal-lobe activation, whereas approximate estimation recruits bilateral areas of the parietal lobes, areas generally associated with visuospatial processing (Dehaene et al., 1999). It is likely that judgments of frequency play a special role in many evaluations that correspond to probabilities (Cosmides & Tooby, 1996; Gigerenzer, 1994), and studies of patients with brain damage suggest that the frontal lobes are involved in frequency estimates (M. L. Smith & Milner, 1984, 1988).

Judgments about likelihood may be made by a "toolbox" of cognitive heuristics, probably the same "toolbox" hypothesized to contain various choice strategies. These heuristic tools are based on various memory, similarity, and inference capacities. It is therefore also likely that judgments under uncertainty are performed by a diverse collection of neural systems, recruited to perform the specific functions underlying each heuristic strategy.

Comprehension Check:

1. This section included a number of systematic errors and biases observed in laboratory judgment tasks. Which of them do you think play important roles in success (or nonsuccess) in everyday life outside the laboratory?

2. The text described two common short-cut choice strategies, satisficing and elimination by aspects. Can you think of any personal choices you have made recently in which you relied on one of those strategies—for example, when renting an apartment, purchasing something on the Internet, or renting a video?

5. COMPLEX, UNCERTAIN DECISION MAKING

In life, of course, we sometimes do not have the clearly presented descriptions of outcomes and their probabilities that enable useful valuation and sound judgments. Nonetheless, we generally do make adaptive decisions, even when information about outcomes and event probabilities is only implicit and must be learned from experience. How do we do it? This question was explored by Antonio Damasio and colleagues at the University of Iowa.

The investigation began with consideration of the behavior of patients who had sustained injuries to areas of the prefrontal cortex. The most famous patient of this type was Phineas Gage, who was injured in 1848 when an iron rod penetrated his prefrontal cortex in an explosion. (His case was discussed in Chapter 7, in the context of executive processes.) Careful inspection of the path of the rod through Gage's skull has implicated lesions to orbitofrontal (ventromedial) cortex. The behavioral changes exhibited by Gage can be characterized largely as maladaptive decision making, and similar behavior has been observed in other patients who have suffered damage to the prefrontal cortex.

Gage's was the first well-documented case of a victim of brain injury who, having made an apparently miraculous recovery, appeared on closer examination to be lacking something that impaired his capacity to make everyday decisions. A responsible, trusted employee before his accident, he underwent a remarkable personality change, becoming irresponsible, profane, and indifferent to the social conventions of the time. In his physician's memorable phrase, "Gage was no longer Gage." In general, patients with ventromedial prefrontal cortex lesions exhibit normal cognitive abilities as measured on standard tests of memory, language aptitude, and general intelligence. However, as in Gage's case, such patients frequently become bad decision makers, and their families and friends often complain of something "missing" in the patient's postinjury personality. The patients are described in phrases such as "emotionally flat," "decides against his best interest," "doesn't learn from his mistakes," "impulsive," and "decisions lead to negative consequences."

Until recently these descriptions were the only evidence available of a breakdown in the decision making of patients with ventromedial prefrontal cortex damage. The situation changed when Damasio and his group constructed a controlled task, now known as the Iowa gambling task. In this task, participants search for monetary payoffs in an uncertain environment composed of four card decks, A, B, C, and D (Bechara et al., 1994). The participant's goal is to earn "money" (play money) by selecting cards from the decks that were associated with gain and loss outcomes. On each trial, the participant chooses a card from one of the decks and receives the outcome printed on its hidden side. Each of the decks had a tendency to yield either high or low gains or losses, and the participant must learn that tendency by experience over several trials of sampling cards from the decks. The investigators called decks A and B "disadvantageous" because both had negative expected values: a player who sampled frequently from those decks would lose money over time and end up in the red. The C and D decks were "advantageous" because they had positive expected values, and repeated choices of those decks would win money for the player over time.

However, it was far from obvious at first which decks were good and bad. Specifically, each of the cards in the disadvantageous decks (A, B) paid a positive gain of $100 on every trial; but some of the cards (1 or 5 out of every 10, depending on the deck) *also* included losses, losses large enough to produce a net loss of $250 for every 10 cards sampled from those decks. Each of the cards in the advantageous decks (C, D) also paid a constant gain on each choice, but of only $50, but the intermittent, unpredictable losses on some of the cards were also smaller, so that the

	Deck A	Deck B	Deck C	Deck D
Reward amount (on every card in deck)	$100	$100	$50	$50
Punishment amounts (on only some cards)	$150–350	$1,250	$25–75	$250
Probability of punishment	0.5	0.1	0.5	0.1
First punishment appears at card:	3	9	3	9
Expected value	−$25	−$25	+$25	+$25

FIGURE 9–13   The Iowa gambling task

When a card is chosen and turned over it always reveals a gain payoff ($100 for decks A and B; $50 for decks C and D); but some cards reveal a loss (losses ranging from −$25 to −$1,250) in addition to the gain on that card. The payoffs are arranged so that the high-gain decks (A and B) also contain the highest loss cards. The losses outweigh the gains, so the expected values for decks A and B are negative—repeated choice of decks A and B result in the participant losing money. Decks C and D, however, carry lower gains on every card, but also lower losses, and these decks have positive expected values.

net for every 10 cards sampled was a gain of $250. The task was designed to be confusing: the *losing decks* consistently had larger positive amounts on every card ($100), and the winning decks consistently had smaller positive amounts on every card ($50). (A summary of the statistical characteristics of each deck appears in Figure 9–13.) Solving the game—that is, making profitable decisions—required learning the unpredictable pattern of losses.

The game was played by a group of patients with ventromedial prefrontal damage and a control group of participants with no ventromedial prefrontal damage. All players were initially attracted to decks A and B with their apparent high gains. But, after a while (typically 20 to 40 trials), the control participants shifted away from the A and B decks and chose instead from the advantageous C and D decks. The ventromedial prefrontal patients, however, persisted in their preference for the losing decks. Moreover, in *anticipation* of choosing cards from the disadvantageous decks, the patients showed flat skin conductance responses, whereas control participants gradually developed elevated skin conductance levels, associated with emotional reactions. It was as though an emotional "alarm bell" were signaling the nonpatients to avoid the losing decks. In contrast, the ventromedial prefrontal patients did not develop anticipatory emotional responses, and they did not learn to avoid the disadvantageous decks.

Damasio and his colleagues (1994) drew a bold conclusion from these results, hypothesizing that normal adaptive decision making in complex, uncertain environments depends on "somatic markers," emotional signals that warn us that important events are about to occur. Probably established by primitive conditioning processes, somatic markers warn us about exceptional threats or opportunities, or at least interrupt processing of other events and give a "heads up" warning that something important is about to occur. In routine decision making, somatic markers may help us winnow down large choice sets into manageable smaller sets. Extremely bad options are quickly eliminated from consideration because somatic marker signals quickly tell us to avoid them, so that we can reason about the serious contenders with our deliberate, conscious thought processes.

The hypothesis has led to some controversy in a decade of vigorous, sometimes critical, follow-up research (Bechara et al., 2000a, 2000b; Krawczyk, 2002; and see critical comments by Leland & Grafman, 2005; Maia & McClelland, 2004; Rolls, 2000; Tomb et al., 2002). The development of additional tests and further analyses of the underlying neural system are needed, as it is unlikely that Damasio's original version of the somatic marker hypothesis was exactly correct (e.g., Sanfey et al., 2003a). In particular, part of the problem that patients with ventromedial prefrontal damage have on the gambling task may result from the fact that they have difficulty shifting their choices when the rewards change; initially (the first few trials) the disadvantageous decks provided larger positive gains (and no losses) than the disadvantageous decks, and the patients may have had trouble shifting strategy when those once-good decks started leading to large losses (e.g., Fellows & Farah, 2003).

Nevertheless, Damasio's basic insight may be valid: many of the decisions we make are based on highly uncertain, partly understood situations. When our deliberate, controlled strategies cannot lead us to make a decision, they will be supplemented or replaced by more automatic, implicit, "intuitive" systems. In the Iowa gambling task, the cognitive systems underlying both our deliberate and "intuitive" processing "know" about the gains as every card in each deck gives consistent payoffs of $100 or $50. But learning the sporadic, unpredictable pattern of the losses may be beyond the deliberate system's capacity (at least in 100 trials of play). This means that effectively responding to the bottom line determined by both gains and losses requires players to rely on what is learned by the intuitive system. Because the ventromedial prefrontal patients appear to have deficits in the operation of this intuitive system, they fail to choose adaptively. A parallel result with amnesic patients underscores the role of intuitive processes in predicting the occurrence of uncertain events (Knowlton et al., 1994).

✓ **Comprehension Check:**

1. Why can studies of patients with brain damage sometimes support stronger *causal* inferences about brain–behavior relationships than can neuroimaging studies?

2. Damasio and his colleagues (1994) claim that the deficit underlying differences between patients with damage to the ventromedial prefrontal cortex and normal control participants reflects the inability of the patients to learn emotional responses to certain situations (experimental card decks). Can you think of other cognitive deficits that might also explain the patients' difficulties?

Revisit and Reflect

1. *What are the components of a decision?*

   A decision is the choice of a particular course of action from among those available. It is difficult to draw a sharp line between explicit, deliberate decisions and implicit, automatic decisions, but research has concentrated on deliberate decisions in which the decision maker consciously weighs the costs and benefits of alternative actions.

   A "good" decision is one that leads to the outcome that best satisfies the decision maker's goals at the time the decision was made. A method of analyzing decisions in terms of expected utilities, using a decision tree as a tool, is generally accepted as the rational method of making an ideal decision. Often construction of the tree initiates a search for information to reduce uncertainties about what consequences will occur, how they are related to the decision maker's goals, and the likelihoods that the decision-relevant event will occur.

   The expected utility model for rational, optimal decision making, derived from economics, underlies decision-making techniques that are often taught in medicine, business, and government.

   Think Critically
   - Do you think aliens from another planet would agree with this definition of a "good" decision? Can you think of a better definition?
   - Suppose you conduct an analysis of a personal decision and discover that the result of the analysis disagrees with your "gut feelings" about what you want to do. What should you do to reconcile the two conflicting conclusions?

2. *How do human decisions compare to the expected utility model for decision making?*

   In most situations, especially when the consequences are important and there is time to be well informed, people make adaptive, close-to-rational decisions. This is why the expected utility model is so successful in accounting for many behaviors. But behavioral scientists have been collecting "anomalies," behaviors that demonstrate departures from the expected utility model.

   Some anomalies illustrate fundamental violations of commonsense reasoning about consequences and values. For example, under some conditions, people show intransitivities, preferring A to B, B to C, but C to A—an irrational pattern. In addition, people are sensitive to the specific manner in which values are elicited—that is, to framing effects—which may cause preference reversals. Other anomalies involve violations of the rules of probability theory, and we have a natural aversion to ambiguous, uncertain courses of action that can produce paradoxical choices under some conditions. Finally, some anomalies, such as the *Allais paradox* and the *Ellsberg paradox*, seem to violate rules for rational thinking about uncertainties and consequences combined.

So there is plenty of evidence that we are not perfectly rational according to the rules for decision making prescribed by mathematical probability theory and the expected utility model. However, to date, psychologists have not been able to make a strong case that irrationality is rampant in important nonlaboratory decisions.

Think Critically

- Is simply receiving an undesirable consequence sufficient to conclude that the decision process was flawed? What are the most convincing arguments that can be made to prove that an actual, nonlaboratory decision is a bad one?
- How would you evaluate the goals of a decision maker? Do you think it is possible to have "bad goals"?

3. *How do we determine the values of the consequences of our decisions?*

To scientists and to decision makers, valuation of consequences is the most mysterious of the processes involved in making decisions. Researchers have side-stepped this deep problem by keeping the consequences in experiments simple—money payoffs for human animals, juice squirts for thirsty nonhuman ones. Certainly valuation depends on the decision maker's current goals. It is also certain that emotions play a central role in most valuation processes—this is evident from our subjective experience of the many emotions we experience when we anticipate consequences at the time we make decisions and when those consequences occur. Furthermore, regions of the brain associated with emotional reactions are active when human participants are evaluating consequences, including money payoffs.

Neuroscientific data are sure to play a major role in future studies of valuation. It seems clear that the brain computes relative values for consequences by "using" neural systems that originally evolved to assess the values of basic experiences: food, heat–cold, pain, sex. Already, fascinating results have been obtained that demonstrate that parts of the limbic system play some role in evaluations of immediate compared to delayed money payoffs (and even in reactions to brand names and moral judgments).

Think Critically

- How do people predict the value of future consequences when they make decisions? How accurate do you think these predictions are?
- How would you increase the accuracy of your personal predictions of the value of future consequences?

4. *What is the role of emotions in decision processes?*

The central role of emotions in decision making is doubtless in the valuation process, when we evaluate how much we want (or don't want) a consequence to occur. Almost all evaluations, even for "cold" consequences like cash, involve a significant emotional component. And when we consider "hotter" consequences, such as the outcomes of social interactions, outcomes that include visceral pleasures and pains or that are significant to our self-esteem, emotions are the dominant element in valuation.

Some researchers had thought that emotions evolved to support quick fight-or-flight responses or to interrupt ongoing activities for special problems or opportunities, but in modern environments they usually interfere with rational decision making. However, results from studies of brain-injured patients with damage to the orbitofrontal prefrontal cortex suggest that emotions may play an important positive role in decision making. Emotions may often support wise choices, even "out-thinking" more deliberate decision processes; and when deliberation is useful, emotions may facilitate deeper analysis by helping the decision maker zero in on the most promising alternatives in large choice sets, which is especially helpful in modern environments where the variety of choices can be bewildering and frustrating.

Think Critically

- Do you think, on balance, that emotions play a positive, adaptive role in our decision processes, or do you think that we would make better decisions if we had no emotions?
- Do you think emotions can play a positive role in all phases of decision making? Why or why not?

5. *What major heuristics do we rely on in estimating the likelihood of uncertain events?*

We have learned or invented many judgment and choice heuristics, quick, cognitively easy, usually adaptive reasoning strategies that provide close-to-optimal solutions with relatively little effort. Many of these heuristics are virtually automatic and are used to make likelihood judgments and valuation assessments almost without awareness. These fundamental heuristics involve avoiding difficult (perhaps impossible) deliberate reasoning processes, and instead using memory retrieval (the availability heuristic), similarity (the representativeness heuristic), and causal reasoning (the simulation heuristic). More elaborate, and hence more conscious, heuristics resemble simple inference rules: anchor-and-adjust, satisficing, and elimination-by-aspects.

Think Critically

- The current list of heuristics or decision habits is surely incomplete. What other judgment or choice heuristics do you rely on when you make personal decisions?
- How would you test how well a heuristic judgment process functions?

6. *How do decisions change when situations become uncertain, ambiguous, and more complex than those in simple laboratory experiments?*

There is no sure answer to this question without conducting additional studies in the natural setting that is of interest. The field of decision making is very practice-oriented (and there are major societies supporting applications in medicine, policy analysis, and business), so we do know something about the validity of laboratory results in field settings.

First, when complexity goes up, people rely heavily on heuristics that simplify the decision process. But, there seems to be a good balance between the importance of a decision and the amount of cognitive effort that is expended to make it, so that important decisions get more thorough and closer-to-rational strategies.

Second, learning becomes much more important outside the laboratory. Some heuristics depend on extensive pre-learning because they require knowing which cues are the best predictors of the events under consideration. Valuation is usually influenced by prior experiences with similar consequences, which also depends on learning and memory for information about those outcomes.

Third, emotions play a bigger role outside the laboratory: the consequences are usually more important and emotion laden; the pressures of time and environmental complexity introduce stress. Some of the most provocative recent findings come from studies of brain-injured patients' choices in a complex emotional task. These patients, who seem unable to connect emotional warnings to the situations in which they choose, choose unwisely; whereas uninjured control participants seem to rely on quick emotional conditioned responses to make better choices. This last result has been especially influential, and controversial, because it suggests the positive value of emotion in decision making.

Think Critically

- Consider the choices among pairs of casino gambles that are the staple of the most basic studies of decision making, then think about an important personal decision. How good is the analogy between the gambling choice and your decision situation? Is life really a sequence of gambles?
- What makes a decision subjectively difficult? What makes a decision likely to be a bad one? How are the two types of difficulty related?

Problem Solving and Reasoning

Learning Objectives

You're lucky—it's a quick, relaxing, and pleasant walk from your front door to the psychology building, where an exam awaits you this morning. Past the running track, across the small park, around the administration building, and you're there. You've crossed the park, but now, with the psychology building in sight, you also see barricades and police vehicles and officers. Your way is blocked: what's going on? Ah—you remember—the governor is coming today; protests must be expected. You'll have to find another way. You figure out that you can reach the psych building by first turning away from it and looping around on another path, avoiding the administration building entirely—and you won't lose much time. Success! Now for success on the exam. . . .

   Human animal that you are, you have just engaged in problem solving and reasoning. "I think, therefore I am"—with this simple statement the French philosopher René Descartes (1596–1650) famously captured what many believe is the essence of what it is to be human. But what does it mean to think? Philosophers have grappled with this profound question for millennia; in recent decades it has come under the scrutiny of cognitive psychologists and neuroscientists. **Thinking** is usually considered to be the process of mentally representing some aspects of the world (including ourselves) and transforming these representations so that new representations, useful to our goals, are generated. Thinking is often (but not always) as a conscious process, in which we are aware of the process of transforming mental representations and can reflect on thought itself. Problem solving and reasoning are two key types of thinking. **Problem solving** encompasses the set of cognitive processes that we apply to reach a goal when we must overcome obstacles to reach that goal. **Reasoning** encompasses the cognitive processes we use to make inferences from knowledge and draw conclusions. (Reasoning can be part of problem solving.)

These are not isolated sets of cognitive processes, but build on and give input to each other and to other cognitive processes, including those involved in categorization (Chapter 4), imagery (Chapter 11), and decision making (Chapter 9). Furthermore, problem solving and reasoning depend on attention (Chapter 3), long-term memory (Chapter 5), working memory (Chapter 6), executive processes (Chapter 7), and language (Chapter 12). Although problem-solving research and reasoning research are often carried out independently of each other, they are obviously related and, as such, we will cover them both in this chapter. This chapter sets out to describe how we deal with complex situations using a variety of problem-solving and reasoning tools. The successful use of these cognitive tools relies on many brain networks, and especially rely on the frontal and parietal cortices. We specifically address six questions:

1. What is the nature of problem solving?
2. How do we use heuristics or "mental shortcuts" to solve problems?
3. How do we use analogies to solve new problems?
4. What is the difference between inductive and deductive reasoning?
5. How do our knowledge and beliefs influence "logical" reasoning?
6. How do our brains coordinate the vast amount of processing involved in problem solving and reasoning?

1. THE NATURE OF PROBLEM SOLVING

In the context of cognitive psychology, a *problem* is a situation in which there is no immediately apparent, standard, or routine way of reaching a goal. The determination of the goal and the degree of difficulty you face are both important: if you don't care whether you get to the psychology building in time for the exam, or if a satisfactory detour is obvious, no problem faces you. Some problems, such as those that arise between parents and children as they try to get along with one another, may have emotional content; others, such as mathematical problems, are less emotional, but may involve emotions (e.g., anxiety) in certain circumstances (such as when math problems appear on an exam). Research on problem solving generally makes use of problems that are less emotional in nature, but it is thought that the types of strategies we use are similar for both emotional and nonemotional problems.

Problem solving, then, requires of surmounting obstacles to achieve a goal. Knowing how to get the lights on in your apartment is not a problem when there is power, but it is a problem when there is a power outage. So, routine situations with routine answers are not regarded as problems. There must be novel or nonstandard solutions that the problem solver must discover. Because problem solving is such an ubiquitous part of our lives, it has become an important area of research that is of both theoretical and practical importance.

The overarching goal of research on problem solving has been to identify the strategies we use when we are confronted by a novel situation and must decide on a course of action. The problem solver must identify the problem, find a way of representing it, and choose a course of action that will make it possible to achieve the goal. Because many different types of cognitive processes, including those drawn upon by memory, attention, and perception, are involved, many parts of the brain are involved in problem solving.

Research has been conducted on various aspects of problem solving and by various methods, both behavioral and brain based. Investigators have studied scientists such as Albert Einstein (Figure 10–1) as they solved problems (Wertheimer, 1945), molecular biologists as they made discoveries (Dunbar, 2000), artists such as Picasso

FIGURE 10–1   A famous problem solver

The Gestalt psychologist Max Wertheimer initiated one of the first investigations of problem solving by scientists in his landmark book, *Productive Thinking* (1945). Wertheimer spent a considerable amount of time corresponding with Albert Einstein, attempting to discover how Einstein generated the concept of relativity. This photograph shows Einstein around the time he developed relativity theory, about a century ago. (Photograph by Science Photo Library. Courtesy of Photo Researchers, Inc.)

as they paint (Weisberg, 1993), and participants as they solved puzzles and problems in logic (Greeno, 1978; Klahr, 2000).

1.1. The Structure of a Problem

At its most basic level a problem can be thought of as having three parts. First is the goal state: this is where you want to be, at the solution to the problem (such as arriving at the psychology building). Second is the initial state (or start state): this is where you are now as you face the problem that needs to be solved. Third is the set of operations that you can apply—that is, the actions (frequently mental ones) you can take—to get from the start state to the goal state (such as planning an alternate route). A simple example problem that has been frequently used in problem-solving research is the Tower of Hanoi task (Figure 10–2), also described in Chapter 7. In the initial state, all the disks are on peg 1, in increasing order of size from top to bottom. In the goal state, all three disks are on peg 3 in the same size order. The only operation permitted is the moving of a disk from one peg to another. The rules: you may move only one disk at a time, and you may not put a larger disk on a smaller one. To add

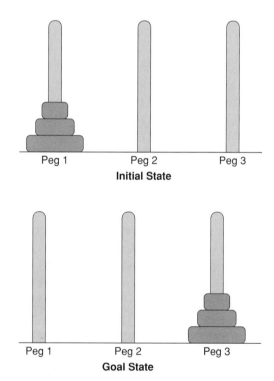

Peg 1   Peg 2   Peg 3

Initial State

Peg 1   Peg 2   Peg 3

Goal State

FIGURE 10–2   The Tower of Hanoi

This famous puzzle was invented by the French mathematician Edouard Lucas in 1883 and has been frequently used in problem-solving studies. In the three-disk version of the task, disks must be moved from peg 1 (the initial state) to peg 3 (the goal state) under specific constraints: only one disk may be moved at a time, and a larger disk may never be put on a smaller one.

to the challenge, try to solve the problem in your head, as in a typical experiment, with the minimum number of moves.

Try one of the playable electronic versions of the Tower of Hanoi on various Web sites that tally your moves, or you can use paper and pencil. How many moves did it take you to get to the goal state? Is there another set of moves that would have been successful? The Tower of Hanoi is thought to be representative of many types of problems because the solution is not obvious, many different strategies can be used to solve the problem, and many of the same problem-solving strategies are used in real-life problems (such as finding an alternative route to the psychology building).

Problems in which (as in the Tower of Hanoi) the initial state and the goal state are clearly defined and the possible moves (and the constraining rules) are known are called well-defined problems. Many games, no matter how complicated the rules and how great the number of operations, are well-defined problems; chess is a good example.

But sometimes it is not possible to be sure about the rules, the initial state, the operations, or even the goal of a problem; such a problem is described as ill defined. A Hollywood producer looking to win next year's Oscar has an enormous ill-defined problem: Which of the thousands of scripts to choose? Go with a star or a brilliant unknown? What's the likely public reaction? Will production be too costly to do the story justice? Many real-world situations present ill-defined problems, in which there are no clearly defined initial or goal states, and the types of operations that are used to reach a goal are not highly constrained by rules. The solution of ill-defined problems presents an additional challenge to the problem solver: finding the *constraints* (i.e., the restrictions on the solution or means whereby it can be achieved) that apply to the particular situation.

A special case of an ill-defined problem is known as the insight problem, to which, despite all the unknowns, the answer seems to come all of a sudden in a flash of understanding. Many scientists and artists have reported working on a problem for months or years, making no progress; then, when they are relaxing or their attention is elsewhere, they suddenly arrive at the solution. Insight problems are often used in problem-solving research; anagrams and riddles are examples of insight problems. Try this one: by moving only three dots, invert the triangle

```
   •   •   •   •
     •   •   •
       •   •
         •
```

so it looks like this:

```
         •
       •   •
     •   •   •
   •   •   •   •
```

1.2. Problem Space Theory

Today, the main theory underlying research on problem solving is *problem space theory*, developed by Allen Newell and Herbert Simon and described in their book, *Human Problem Solving* (1972). Problem solving, in this view, is a search within a problem space, which is the set of states, or possible choices, that faces the problem solver at each step in moving from an initial state to a goal state. The problem solver moves through the space from state to state by various operations. Thus, the problem space includes the initial state, the goal state, and all possible intermediate states. The problem space for the three-disk Tower of Hanoi problem, shown in Figure 10–3, consists of 27 possible states. Two things are apparent from the diagram: there are a number of routes that can take you from the initial state to the goal state, and the shortest requires seven operations (this is the path along the right-hand side of the diagram—is it the one you took?). If two disks are added, so the tower is five disks high, the problem space includes 64 possible states.

In Figure 10–3, the states are numbered in order to identify them and to provide a total count of states; they do not indicate a sequence. Nor is the spatial layout important. What is important is the distance between states—for instance, that state 5

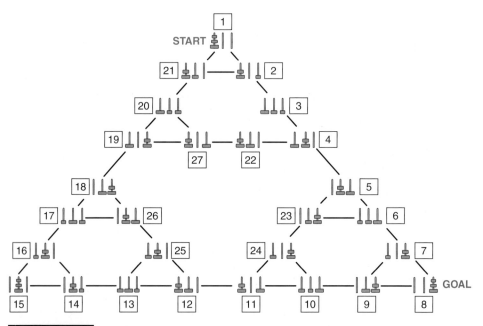

FIGURE 10–3 Problem space for the three-disk version of the Tower of Hanoi task

This figure depicts all possible states in the Tower of Hanoi task—but only seven moves are in fact necessary to get from the start state at 1 to the goal state at 8. The numbers are for identification of the various disk arrangements only; they do not always indicate a sequence or an ideal spatial layout between steps, although the path 1–8 provides the simplest solution to the problem. Rather, this figure shows how many operations are required between given states.

is one operation away from state 6, 23, or 4. Newell and Simon's original work on problem solving consisted of writing computer programs that calculated the best moves to make on the basis of nonspatial criteria such as the similarity of the selected move to the goal state, and comparing the output of these programs to the moves made by human participants attempting to solve the problem.

Problems such as the Tower of Hanoi and chess are highly constrained, with specific rules and clearly defined initial and goal states. Does problem space theory apply in less constrained domains—that is, can solving more complex problems and more ill-defined problems be characterized as searching a problem space? Much of the more recent research on problem solving has explored complex areas such as science, architecture, and writing (Dunbar, 2002; Klahr, 2000). The results indicate that in complex domains, such as molecular biology and cancer research, problem solvers search in more than one problem space. Thus, when working on scientific problems, for example, the problem space theory of problem solving has been expanded to include spaces such as a hypothesis space to formulate theories, an experiment space to design experiments, and a data space to interpret results (Klahr, 2000). Less constrained domains are more akin to situations in the real world than the Tower of Hanoi, and one of the goals of researchers who study problem solving is to understand the different types of problem spaces that we use in different tasks in real-life circumstances.

1.3. Strategies and Heuristics

A surefire way to solve a problem is to use an *algorithm* (discussed in Chapter 9), a set of procedures for solving a given type of problem that will always, sooner or later, produce the correct answer. The rules for finding a square root or performing long division are algorithms; so is a recipe for chocolate cake or a detailed set of directions that indicate the paths and turns to take the shortest route to the psychology building. But algorithms are often very time consuming, and they make great demands on both working memory and long-term memory.

Researchers using problems such as the Tower of Hanoi task in their studies have found that rather than using algorithms, participants often use specific strategies or heuristics when trying to solve problems. A heuristic is a rule of thumb that usually gives the correct answer—but not always. (Heuristics were also discussed in Chapter 9.) A commonly used heuristic in problem solving is "always move toward the goal." This approach often provides the solution, but sometimes—such as when you're trying to get to the psychology building in the face of a temporary obstruction—it is necessary to move away from a goal and then move back toward it to arrive at the correct solution. (Folk wisdom recognizes the truth of this in the saying "The longest way round is the shortest way home.") The twistable puzzle known as the Rubik's cube is a problem for which the heuristic of making moves that are similar to the goal state will not work. Each side of the cube is made up of nine colored squares (six colors are used). In the goal state, all the squares on a side are the same color. (There are playable electronic versions of Rubik's cube on the Web.) The cube is an interesting problem to examine because many steps are required to solve it, and because it is often necessary

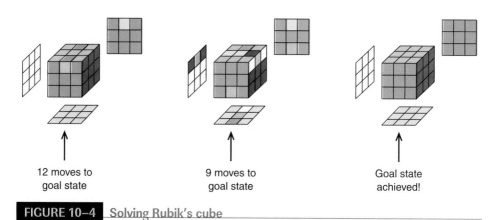

| 12 moves to | 9 moves to | Goal state |
| goal state | goal state | achieved! |

FIGURE 10–4   Solving Rubik's cube

Sometimes you have to move away from the goal in order to achieve it. The three same-color sides shown at the left will all have to be broken before all six sides of the cube can be made uniform.

to move away from the goal state before finally achieving it. In the initial state of play shown in Figure 10–4, for example, when you are 12 moves from the goal, three of the six sides are of uniform color; but to arrive at the goal from this configuration, all six sides will have be scrambled before you achieve success in 9 more moves.

Other commonly used problem-solving heuristics are *random search, hill climbing,* and *means–ends analysis.* The simplest and cognitively least demanding of these three is random search (also known as *generate and test*), which is essentially a process of trial and error: the problem solver randomly picks a move and tests to see whether the goal state is achieved. Researchers in the behaviorist tradition, among them E. L. Thorndike (1874–1949), proposed that animals and people solve problems by trial and error and randomly select moves until they achieve the goal state. Although random search appears to be a really inefficient and often unsuccessful strategy, we frequently resort to it when everything else has failed. It is hard to resist randomly pressing keys when your computer freezes and none of the known solutions work—and *sometimes* it does the trick. Random search is a fall-back heuristic that we use when other heuristics either do not work or are cognitively too demanding.

More often, we use other, more knowledge-dependent heuristics, such as hill climbing, in which the problem solver looks one move ahead and chooses the move that most closely resembles the goal state. As in climbing an actual hill, each step seems to move you closer to the goal; but if you are in thick fog (as you are figuratively if you can see only one move ahead), you may end up at the top of a small rise and not the big hill that you are trying to climb. What happens if you apply hill climbing to the three-disk Tower of Hanoi task? Look at Figure 10–3 again and imagine yourself at state 5. Your only possible choices are state 23 and state 6. State 23 more closely resembles the goal state than does state 6—there are more disks on peg 3 in state 23 than in state 6—so if you're using hill climbing you'd move to state 23. But state 23 is actually further away from the goal state than state 6, so hill climbing in this case is not an effective problem-solving strategy. Hill climbing is often a more reliable heuristic than random search, but sometimes it can lead the problem solver astray.

A classic problem that often leads participants to use the hill-climbing strategy is the water jug task (Atwood & Polson, 1976; Colvin et al., 2001). You have three water jugs of different capacity—8 ounces, 5 ounces, and 3 ounces. In the initial state the 8-ounce jug is full, the other two are empty. Your task is to transfer water from the large jug to the others so that you end up with 4 ounces of water in the large jug, 4 ounces of water in the medium-size jug, and the small jug is empty—this is the goal state. Moreover, whenever you pour water into another jug, you must fill it completely. The task and the problem space for possible moves are shown in Figure 10–5.

If you use the hill climbing strategy you might select a move that will put water in the large and medium jugs in amounts close to the goal state. So you pour water from the large jug into the medium one, and now you have 3 ounces of water in the large jug and 5 ounces of water in the medium jug (identified as R(3, 5, 0) in Figure 10–5). This is certainly closer to the goal than was the initial state, but now hill climbing fails you. Whatever move you take next will take you, as it were, *down* the hill, farther away from the goal state than your current state. Often at this point participants attempt to start the task again, this time moving farther away from the goal state in their next move by pouring water from the large jug into the small one. Thus, the hill climbing strategy, like the random search strategy, is an easy but often inefficient way of trying to solve a problem.

A more demanding, but more successful, strategy is means–ends analysis, in which the problem is broken into subproblems. If a subproblem at the first stage of analysis is not solvable, then the problem can be further broken into other subproblems until a soluble subproblem is found. Applying means–ends analysis to the three-disk Tower of Hanoi task, you would define your main goal as getting all three disks on peg 3 (look again at Figure 10–2). To accomplish this you must get the large disk properly arranged on peg 3, but in the initial state you can't move it: the medium disk is in the way. Try a further subgoal: get the medium disk out of the way; but again the move is not possible, this time because the small disk is in the way. The next subgoal? Move the small disk. This can be done: nothing blocks the small disk. But where should it be moved—to peg 2 or to peg 3? You must look ahead to the consequences of each of those moves. If you move the small disk to peg 3 (state 2 in Figure 10–3), then the medium disk can be moved to peg 2 (state 3), and so on. What you are doing in this process is setting up goals and subgoals until the entire problem is solved.

Until neuroimaging techniques became available in the late 1980s, three main methods were used to understand how we solve problems. First, and most obvious, is to record problem-solving behavior (as long as the moves are not being made "in your head"). Researchers can record, in sequence, every move that a problem solver makes in the course of arriving at a solution. Using this method, in each case researchers can chart how long it takes to solve a given problem and the different types of moves that problem solvers take.

A second behavioral approach, developed in the 1970s, is verbal protocol analysis, which is the analysis of the thought process of the problem solver as described aloud by the solver in the course of working on the problem (Ericsson & Simon, 1984). The problem solver is recorded in video, audio or both. Researchers then transcribe

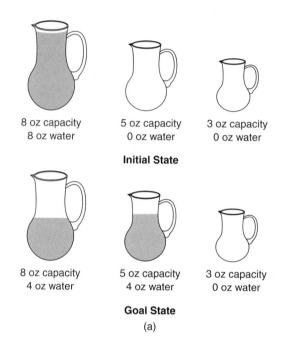

8 oz capacity   5 oz capacity   3 oz capacity
8 oz water   0 oz water   0 oz water

Initial State

8 oz capacity   5 oz capacity   3 oz capacity
4 oz water   4 oz water   0 oz water

Goal State

(a)

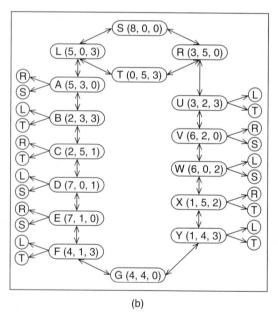

(b)

FIGURE 10–5   The water jug task

(a) Initial and goal states for the water jug task. (b) The problem space: the possible moves between start and goal. The notation gives the amount of water in each container as shown left to right: thus the start state is indicated as S(8, 0, 0) and the goal as G(4, 4, 0). The letters to the left of the parentheses identify the current state; the letters that follow the arrows from a current state name the possible following states, for example, from current state B(2, 3, 3), possible moves are to L(5, 0, 3) or to T(0, 5, 3).

(Mary Kathryn Colvin, Kevin Dunbar & Jordan Grafman, The Effects of Frontal Lobe Lesions on Goal Achievement in the Water Jug Task, *Journal of Cognitive Neuroscience, 13*:8. (November 15, 2001), pp. 1129–1147. © 2001 by the Massachusetts Institute of Technology. Reprinted with permission.)

the protocol and analyze the transcript to determine the ways in which the problem solver represented the problem and the sequence of steps employed, to infer the participant's problem space.

A third approach looks to computers, building programs that embody the strategy that people presumably use to solve a problem, and then comparing the computer output to the moves made by a person. Computer models make it necessary to state explicitly every step in the problem-solving process, and have been used to simulate all three problem-solving heuristics: random search, hill climbing, and means–ends analysis. Many researchers, particularly the late Herbert Simon (himself a Nobel prize winner) and his colleagues at Carnegie Mellon University, have used all three methods of investigation to understand problem solving. The problems that they have explored range from the Tower of Hanoi to the discovery of the urea cycle (by an analysis of the laboratory notebooks of the discoverer, the Nobel prize–winning biochemist Hans Krebs) (Kulkarni & Simon, 1988; Newell & Simon, 1972).

1.4. The Role of Working Memory and Executive Processes

What specific sets of representations and processes might be involved in problem solving? Using PET, ERP, and fMRI techniques (see Chapter 1), and studying both brain-damaged and unimpaired participants, investigators have sought to gain insight into the nature of the cognitive procedures used in problem solving working memory. Consider the different processes that seem to be used in a task such as the Tower of Hanoi. The problem solver must determine what operations are required to reach the goal state. This requires keeping in the goals and subgoals. Such a task places considerable demands on working memory, and so we would expect significant activations in areas typically involved in working memory (for example, dorsolateral prefrontal cortex; see Chapter 6). This prediction is confirmed by neuroimaging research. Using a modified version of the Tower of Hanoi task with healthy participants, investigators found that brain activation in the right dorsolateral prefrontal cortex, bilateral parietal cortex, and bilateral premotor cortex increased as the task became more complex (Finchan et al., 2002) (Figure 10–6). These regions have been strongly implicated in working memory and executive processes (see Chapter 7), thus underscoring the strong relationship among these systems and problem solving.

Several studies have also examined problem solving in patients with localized brain damage. Patients with frontal-lobe lesions have great difficulty using means–ends analysis to solve the Tower of Hanoi problem (Goel & Grafman, 1995). Frontal patients also have difficulty in applying the hill climbing heuristic to the water jug task: they find it hard to remember the moves that they have already made and cannot learn the moves that they must avoid (Colvin et al., 2001). Because these patients do not learn the moves to avoid, they cycle through the same moves again and again, never coming closer to a solution. From these studies, it is clear that the frontal lobes are involved in the long-term memory and working-memory processing during problem solving, and in the execution of plans to solve a problem.

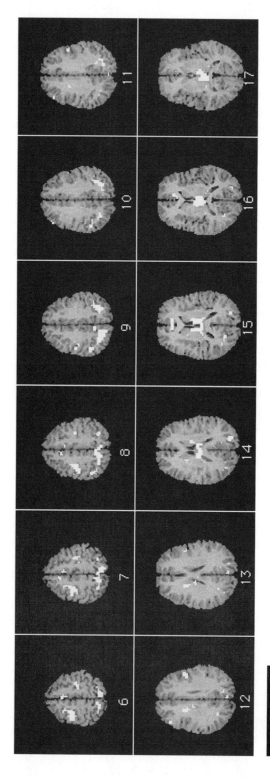

FIGURE 10–6 fMRI data on goal-directed processing

Goal-directed processing is distributed among prefrontal cortex, parietal cortex, cingulate gyrus, and subcortical structures (right caudate nucleus and thalamus). The slices of the brain shown are ordered from top (#6) to bottom (#17); the left side of each image is the right side of the brain and the right side of each image is the left side of the brain. Activation increased as the problems became more complex.

(Fincham, J. M., Carter, C. S., van Veen, V., Stenger, V. A. & Anderson, J. R. (2002). Neural mechanisms of planning; a computational analysis using event-related fMRI. *Proceedings of the National Academy of Sciences, 99,* 3346–3351. Reprinted with permission.)

1.5. How Experts Solve Problems

A considerable amount has also been learned about problem solving by comparing experts and novices. Experts know more than do novices in their field of expertise, and presumably that's a big help in solving problems in their field. An interesting question is whether expertise provides more than simply additional information; that is, do experts have specialized problem-solving strategies that novices don't? The answer is yes.

The first additional information is experts' organization of knowledge in their field, which is different from that of novices. Novices in a field often organize concepts in terms of surface features of the problem, whereas experts organize their knowledge in terms of deeper abstract principles. In a classic study of expertise (Chi et al., 1981), beginning and advanced physics students were presented with a variety of physics problems and asked to sort the problems into similar categories (Figure 10–7). The novice physics students grouped problems that involved the same physical characteristics, putting tasks with blocks in one category and tasks involving springs in another. The graduate physics students performed the task very differently: they sorted the problems in terms of physical concepts, such as conservation of energy.

A second sort of additional information used by expert problem solvers is seen in encoding: experts and novices do not encode information in the same way. In an important study of expertise, chess players of various proficiency were presented, for 5 seconds, with a chessboard with chess pieces in various positions; then the board was removed and the players were asked to reconstruct the arrangement of the pieces on a second board (Chase & Simon, 1973). The investigators found that experts were better than novices at reconstructing the arrangement only when the original configuration of pieces was taken from a real game; experts were no better than novices when the chess pieces were arranged randomly. Also, chess experts were able to recall positions from a real game much better than chess pieces that had been arranged randomly. Beginning chess players, however, did not perform any better on

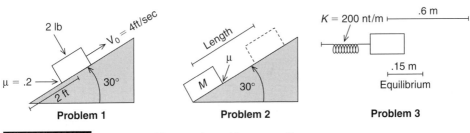

FIGURE 10–7   Which problem is the odd man out?

"Novices" (physics undergraduates) grouped problems 1 and 2, based on the superficial visual similarity to "blocks" on an "inclined plane" in both drawings. Graduate physics students, however, cut to the chase and recognized that problems 1 and 3 are the ones to be grouped: both deal with the conservation of energy.

(Chi, M. T. H., Feltovich, P. J. & Glaser, R. (1981). Categorization of physics problems by experts and novices. *Cognitive Science, 5,* 121–152. Reprinted with permission.)

real positions than on a random layout. The investigators argued that chess experts performed better because they were able to encode the position of many pieces as a unit or "chunk"—and they were able to do this because arrangements from a real game "make sense" in terms of the rules of chess, whereas random layouts do not. This ability to chunk information is a hallmark of experts, from architects to zoologists. Experts chunk information and can access related chunks of knowledge from long-term memory, thus making their problem solving more efficient.

Yet another difference between expert and novice problem solvers involves the direction of the search through the problem space. Experts tend to employ a forward search, that is, they search from the initial state to the goal. An experienced physician, for example, works from the symptoms to diagnosis. A medical student generally uses a backward search, from the goal of diagnosis to the symptoms that constitute the initial state (Arocha & Patel, 1995). It is also possible for both people and computers to work simultaneously from both the goal state (backward search) and the initial state (forward search). Many computer programs such as the IBM chess program Deep Blue use a combination of search strategies to choose a move.

 Comprehension Check:

1. What is the difference between using a hill climbing versus a means–ends problem-solving strategy?
2. What is a problem space?

2. ANALOGICAL REASONING

People do not always try to solve a problem by using the sort of heuristics described in the preceding section. Instead people sometimes try to think of a solution to a similar problem. If you go to use your laptop, which has a physical lock, but you have lost your key, what do you do? Do you try a random search, or do you notice the similarity between the computer lock and a bicycle lock. Then you remember that bicycle thieves are using ballpoint pen tubes to open bicycle locks. Aha, you think, I'll try a pen—and presto, you have your computer unlocked. This is *analogical reasoning*. In analogical reasoning, rather than beginning from scratch using heuristics such as means–ends analysis, you try to think of a problem with similar characteristics that has been solved before and use or adapt that solution in the present instance. Here the question is "Can a solution that worked for one problem map onto another?" Thus, analogical reasoning is often a process of comparison, using knowledge from one relatively known domain ("the source," such as the bicycle thieves in the earlier situation) and applying it to another domain ("the target," or your locked computer) (Clement & Gentner, 1991; Spellman & Holyoak, 1996). A famous analogy in science, though in some of its aspects now outdated, is shown in Figure 10–8.

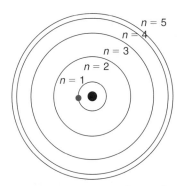 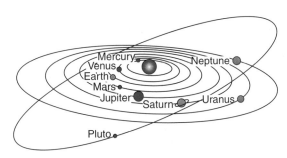

The Bohr Model of the Hydrogen Atom   The Solar System

FIGURE 10–8   The atom and the solar system

Perhaps one of the most famous scientific analogies is the comparison of the atom to the solar system, originally formulated by the Danish physicist Niels Bohr (1885–1962). He explained the hydrogen emission spectrum by picturing the hydrogen atom as a solar system with the nucleus—a sole proton—as the sun and its electron as a planet orbiting the nucleus at various fixed distances and energies; energy is emitted as the electron leaps from an outer to an inner orbit. (Modern quantum mechanics has replaced the orbits with energy levels, but the power of Bohr's analogy transformed scientific thinking about the atom.)

2.1. Using Analogies

Let's take an example from the world of computers that provides a good understanding of how analogical reasoning works. Consider the problem of developing a way to protect computers from viruses. Vaccines have been developed to protect humans from viral infections; might it be possible to develop a vaccine for computers? The answer is yes: reasoning by analogy with the action of biological viruses, computer scientists have done just that. There are of course differences between computer viruses and biological ones: a virus doesn't give a computer a runny nose or a fever. But, in their underlying, or structural, characteristics, computer viruses and biological viruses have important elements in common: they are contagious or infectious, they can self-replicate by means of the host, and they can cause damage to the host. (Structural information typically specifies a relation between different entities, such as between a virus and its host.) Thus, analogical reasoning involves identifying and transferring structural information from a known system (in this example, biological viruses) to a new system (in this example, computer viruses). Many researchers have argued that this structural similarity is one of the defining features of analogy (Gentner & Markman, 1997).

Analogical reasoning is generally thought to comprise five subprocesses:

1. *Retrieval:* Holding a target (such as the computer virus) in working memory while accessing a similar, more familiar example (such as a biological virus) from long-term memory.

2. *Mapping:* While holding both the source and the target in working memory, aligning the source and the target and mapping the features of the source (such as "contagious," "replicating," and "harmful") onto the target.

3. *Evaluation:* Deciding whether or not the analogy is likely to be useful.

4. *Abstraction:* Isolating the structure shared by the source and the target.

5. *Predictions:* Developing hypotheses about the behavior or characteristics of the target from what is known about the source (for example, predicting from the behavior of biological viruses that computer viruses can change their surface features to avoid detection).

These five components of analogical reasoning have been extensively investigated during the past 25 years and have led to many important experiments and computational models. One of the first cognitive investigations of analogical reasoning was that of Mary Gick and Keith Holyoak, carried out in 1980. These investigators presented participants with a problem, and its solution, in the form of a story. A few minutes later, after an intervening, irrelevant task, students were given a second story problem, but this time the story contained no solution. The first story was about a general who was planning to lead his army to attack a dictator who lived in a fortress. A number of roads converged on the fortress, but the dictator had mined all of them so that any large army traveling on a road would be blown up. The attacking general broke his army up into small groups that were not heavy enough to set off the mines and sent one of these small units along each of the roads. Arriving safely at the fortress, the soldiers converged, regrouped to full force and captured the dictator.

The second problem story was about a patient with a stomach tumor. Doctors have a powerful laser beam that can burn the tumor out, but the beam is so strong that it will burn the healthy tissue as well. Participants were asked to suggest a solution for the doctors that would spare the healthy tissue but destroy the tumor. (What's your suggestion? Of course, the fact that mention of this study appears in a discussion of analogical reasoning provides a considerable hint, one that was not available to the participants.) The solution that Gick and Holyoak (1980) were looking for was a convergence solution analogous to that in the first problem story: just as the general broke his army into smaller units so as to be able to travel swiftly and then regroup into a powerful force, the laser beam might first be broken up into a set of less powerful rays, all focused on the diseased spot, where they converge to burn out the tumor. Only 20 percent of the participants who read the army–dictator problem judged the radiation–tumor problem as similar and came up with the convergence solution. On the surface, dictators and tumors may not seem very similar. When the surface features of the source story were more similar to those of the target problem, 90 percent of the participants came up with the convergence solution (Holyoak & Thagard, 1995). It seems that when a source problem shares only structural similarity (i.e., similarity with respect to the relations among parts) with the target, far fewer participants recognize the analogy; when surface features also are similar, many more participants are able to retrieve a relevant analog.

Another approach to the study of analogy, used by Dedre Gentner and her colleagues, has been to investigate the factors that influence the retrieval of sources from memory. For example, participants are given a series of stories to read (Gentner et al., 1993). In one of them a hawk is attacked by a hunter but befriends the hunter by giving him some of her feathers. After this generous act, the hunter spares the hawk. A week later the participants read other stories. Some of these new stories had the same underlying structure, others shared only superficial features with the original story. One of the structurally similar stories was about a country, "Zerdia," that is attacked by the country of "Gagrach;" "Zerdia" offers to share its computers with "Gagrach" and the two countries become allies. One of the stories that was superficially similar, but structurally dissimilar, to the hawk–hunter story was about a hunter who loved to fish and eat wild boar. When participants were asked which stories reminded them of the original one, most of them chose the stories sharing superficial features, not the ones that shared underlying sets of structural relations. But when the same participants were asked which stories were analogically similar, they named the stories with similar underlying structures.

Dunbar and Blanchette (2001) have found that scientists, politicians, and students can use both structural and superficial features of a problem, but are more likely to use structural features when they generate their own analogies, and superficial features when they receive ready-made analogies. Furthermore, Blanchette and Dunbar (2002) have found that students will make analogies automatically and without awareness.

2.2. Theories of Analogical Reasoning

A number of influential theories of analogical reasoning have been proposed, all of which can be implemented in computer models that make explicit the mechanisms thought to be involved. Two of the most important are the structure mapping theory (SMT) (Falkenhainer et al., 1989; Gentner, 1983) and the learning and inference with schemas and analogies (the LISA) model (Hummel & Holyoak, 1997, 2003). Both models treat analogical reasoning as the mapping of elements from a source to a target, and both propose a search of long-term memory for a source that has a similar underlying structure to that of the target.

The *SMT model* has two stages. In the first stage, long-term memory is searched for potential sources that have a superficial feature that is contained in the target. For example, in the computer virus–biological virus analogy, memory might be searched for items such as *keyboard, mouse, not working, electrical,* and *infectious.* The second stage is evaluation: how good a match exists between what was retrieved in the first stage and the target. The SMT model as simulated by a computer behaves much like human participants: there will be many superficial matches, most of them having to do with functioning and nonfunctioning computers, and possibly a useful one such as *infectious.* The main assumption of the SMT model is that although structural similarity is the key component of analogical reasoning, the human cognitive system looks for superficial matches when searching memory for possible sources, and we find it difficult to retrieve true relational analogs.

The *LISA model* accounts for the same type of data, but uses very different computational mechanisms that are like the neural networks discussed in earlier chapters, in that features of both source and target may be considered as nodes in a network.

Thus, the target is represented in terms of the activations of features of the source: *computer virus* would activate, for example, the features *malfunctioning, harmful,* and *self-replicating*. This simultaneous activation of a number of features in working memory results in the activation of similar constellations of features in long-term memory, leading to the retrieval of a source analog such as *flu virus*.

There are a number of other models of analogical reasoning. It is difficult to determine what types of models most accurately capture analogical reasoning, but brain-based research may provide the answer.

2.3. Beyond Working Memory

From behavioral analyses, we now know that analogical reasoning is highly demanding of attention and memory. First, we must attend to the appropriate superficial and structural similarities between source and target; then we must maintain a representation of the target in working memory, and search long-term memory for the appropriate analog. Are brain regions that are involved in attention, working memory and searching long-term memory—specifically, the prefrontal cortex—highly involved in analogical reasoning? A PET scanning study was designed to answer this question (Wharton et al., 2000).

On each trial, participants were presented with, first, a source picture, and then a target picture. There were two conditions, *analogy* and *literal comparison*. In the analogy condition, participants were to decide whether the target picture was an analog to the source picture. On each trial in which source and target were indeed analogous, the pictures contained different objects but shared the same system of relations. In the literal comparison condition, participants were simply asked to decide whether the source and the target pictures were identical. When the researchers compared activations in the analogy condition to those in the literal condition, they found significant activations in the middle frontal cortex and the inferior frontal gyrus (both of which are portions of prefrontal cortex), as well as the anterior insula and the inferior parietal cortex. The prefrontal cortex and parietal cortex are known to be highly involved in tasks that require attention and working memory.

But is analogical reasoning simply a product of attention and working memory and nothing more? How could we answer this question? One way would be to look for a specific neural correlate that dissociated the relational component of analogical reasoning from working memory. This approach was taken by investigators who conducted an fMRI study in which working-memory load and the structural complexity of an analogy were varied independently (Kroger et al., 2002). As expected, increasing the working-memory load resulted in increased activations in the dorsolateral prefrontal and parietal cortices. Further, significant and unique activations in the left anterior prefrontal cortex were found when structural complexity was increased while the working-memory load was held constant. These data demonstrate that the relational component of analogical reasoning represents a cognitive capacity that recruits neural tissue over and above that of attention and working memory. Here is a nice example of how neuroimaging technology can provide us with new and informative data about cognition. By examining the neuroanatomical correlates of the subcomponent processes of analogical reasoning (that is, working memory and abstraction, which is required to discover structural relations), we can begin to decompose how such reasoning is accomplished.

1. What are the five subprocesses of analogical reasoning?
2. What is the role of working memory in analogical reasoning?

3. INDUCTIVE REASONING

Any thought process that uses our knowledge of specific known instances to draw an inference about unknown instances is a case of inductive reasoning. Common types of inductive reasoning often rely on category-based induction: either generalizing from known instances to *all* instances (which is a general induction), or generalizing from some members of a category known to have a given property to other instances of that category (which is a specific induction). If you have seen three violent football games and conclude that all football games are violent, you have made a *general induction*. If you see Alma Mater College play a violent game this weekend and therefore believe that College of the Gridiron, on the schedule for next Saturday, will also play violently, you have made a *specific induction*.

No inductive process can ever be certain: we cannot know all the instances that may exist, any of which may disprove the generalization. In both these types of induction, we are using our inference to add new knowledge, *which though plausible may be incorrect,* to our existing knowledge.

3.1. General Inductions

In the early 1980s, medical researchers were trying to identify the cause of a mysterious new disease soon called AIDS. It attacked a number of very different populations: young gay men, intravenous drug users, hemophiliacs, Haitians, infants, and recipients of blood transfusions. The only common factor among all these patients was a dramatic decrease in T lymphocytes, a type of white blood cell (Prusiner, 2002). From these instances, the prediction was made that all AIDS patients have decreased numbers of T cells, and it was proposed that the cause of the disease is an infectious agent that attacks these T lymphocytes. The researchers' approach to solving the AIDS problem employed a general induction from a number of instances. This type of induction occurs in solving very different sorts of problems, from drawing a generalization about a friend's honesty (of necessity—you can't possibly have knowledge of all circumstances) to scientific discovery. Cognitive psychologists have investigated both the strategies we use to make such generalizations and the errors we may fall into when we do.

Research on general induction began in earnest during the 1950s. In groundbreaking study, investigators devised a task much like the game Mastermind: from feedback provided by the experimenter, participants had to discover rules for the game, thereby making general inductions (Bruner et al., 1956). (To get a feel for the task, you might want to try a few rounds of Mastermind; there are playable versions available on the Web.)

The task employed a deck of cards that varied along four dimensions, with three possibilities for each attribute: color (white, black, or blue); number of items on a card (one, two or three); shape of item (circle, cross, or square); and number of borders (one, two, or three). Thus, there were $3 \times 3 \times 3 \times 3$ possible combinations of attributes, and so the deck consisted of 81 cards, or instances (Figure 10–9).

In one version of the task, the cards were laid out face up and the experimenter arbitrarily determined a rule—for instance, "red and square"—but did not tell it to the participant. Instead, the experimenter pointed to a card that was red and square and told the participant that this card was an example of the rule. The participant then pointed to various cards in turn and the experimenter would state in each case whether or not that card was an example of the rule. With each choice of card, the

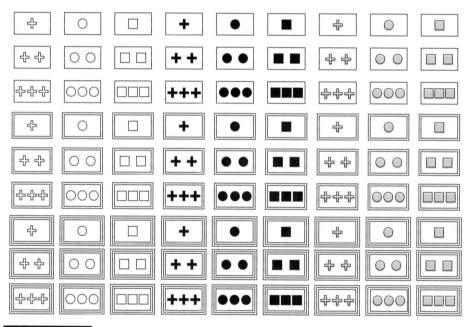

FIGURE 10–9   "Pick a card . . . discover a rule"

This is the deck of 81 cards, varying in the shape, color, and number of pictured objects, and in the number of borders, that was used in one of the first studies exploring how we perform general inductions. Participants either selected, or were presented with, one card at a time. The rule for a positive or negative instance was known only to the experimenter. For each trial participants stated their hypothesis and were told only whether they were right or wrong—not what the rule was. They then moved on to the next trial. The goal: to announce a hypothesis that corresponded to the rule.

(Bruner, J. S., Goodnow, J. J. & Austin, G. A. (1956). A study of thinking. New York, NY. Science Editions. Reprinted with permission.)

participant must offer a hypothesis as to the general rule. The experimenters varied the (unstated) rules, and found that simple rules (such as "red") were very easy for participants to discover, conjunctive rules (such as "red and square") were a little harder, and disjunctive rules (such as "red or square") were difficult. Negative rules, such as "not red," were very difficult to discover, and disjunctive negative rules, such as "not red or cross," were the most difficult of all.

Why did participants find some general rules easier to discover than others? The contribution of Bruner and colleagues (1956) was to present an explanation in terms of the different inductive reasoning strategies that participants used. In the *successive scanning* strategy, participants picked cards that differed by only one feature from the example card given by the experimenter ("red and square"). For instance, the example card might contain three red squares and one border; on the first trial the participant might pick a card with three red squares and *two* borders. If that card fulfills the rule, the participant knows that the number of borders is not relevant and that attribute may be disregarded; if it doesn't, the participant must continue to look at combinations of all four attributes when suggesting a card. Another approach, the *focus gambling* strategy, maintains one feature while changing all the others. A participant who knows from the experimenter that a card with three red squares and one border fulfills the rule might next choose a card with two green squares and one border. If the experimenter says "yes," then the participant knows that rule is based on the number of borders; but if the experimenter says "no," then the participant has not gained any new knowledge about the rule. Because both strategies involve first testing for single features, it is not surprising that participants found it easier to discover simple rules (such as "red") than conjunctive rules (such as "red and square").

The work of Bruner and colleagues (1956) led to two major developments in cognitive psychology. The first was concerned with the nature of categories. By focusing on rules, Bruner's work led to an examination of category formation that was relevant to categories that we use in real life (E. E. Smith & Medin, 1981). Bruner's work also led to investigation of the way we test a hypothesis. A hypothesis is an idea or proposition that we can evaluate or test by gathering evidence to support or refute it. How does a participant who has inferred a rule through general induction discover whether or not that rule is correct? What strategies are used to test a hypothesis? These questions became a central focus of research (Tweney et al., 1981).

A well-known task used to investigate the way we test hypotheses is the Wason 2–4–6 task, devised by the English psychologist Peter Wason (1924–2003). The task is structurally simple and easy to administer; try it on your friends. The experimenter states that the sequence 2–4–6 is a triad of numbers that is consistent with a rule. The participant's goal is to discover the rule by generating hypotheses about it, as well as generating new triads of numbers to test the hypothesis. The experimenter tells the participant whether or not each proposed triad is consistent with the rule. The participant may announce an induced rule at any time, and is told by the experimenter whether the rule is correct. If it is, the experiment is over. If it isn't, the participant is told to generate more triads of numbers. This procedure continues until the participant either announces the correct rule or gives up.

Participants typically begin by hypothesizing that the rule is "even numbers increasing by 2," and most test the hypothesis by generating triads of numbers that are consistent with it, suggesting, for example, the triad 8–10–12. Generally, participants propose three or four more such triads and are told that they are correct; they then announce, "even numbers increasing by 2" as the rule. But they then are told that this rule is not correct. Most participants then induce a more general hypothesis: "any set of numbers increasing by 2," suggesting triads like "1–3–5" or "7–8–10." But when they announce this new hypothesis they are told that this also is incorrect. At this point something interesting happens: most participants switch from trying to *confirm* their hypothesis to trying to *disconfirm* it (i.e., switch from generating triads consistent with their hypothesis to generating triads inconsistent with it) (Gorman et al., 1987). They might propose the triad 2–6–4; if so, they are told that this triad is inconsistent with the rule. Once participants have negative feedback to work with, they usually discover that the correct rule is simply "numbers of increasing magnitude."

Participants are sometimes resistant to taking into account information that is inconsistent with the rule that they have formed. For instance, if they are told that there is a probability of error in the feedback that they receive, then they attribute to error all feedback that is inconsistent with the rule they have induced (Gorman, 1989). Furthermore, even when participants are encouraged to look for disconfirming evidence when performing the 2–4–6 task, their performance is not significantly improved (Tweney et al., 1981).

How representative is the 2–4–6 task of real-world situations in which we must make a general induction over a set of instances? Participants often show a **confirmation bias**, the predisposition to weight information in ways consistent with preexisting beliefs (Figure 10–10), when they are given an arbitrary rule to discover (Dunbar, 1993). But there are situations in which people can overcome this bias. In studies of scientists' reasoning, little evidence was found that these participants attempted to confirm their hypotheses by not considering other possibilities, or by ignoring inconsistent data (Dunbar, 1997, 1999).

3.2. Specific Inductions

To assume that if one member of a category has a particular feature another member will also have it is to make a specific, category-based induction. Of course, there's an obvious trap: the feature involved may not be common to all category members. Nonetheless, specific, category-based induction often allows us to make useful inferences about a new or unknown category member. In this way we can update our knowledge without having to find out, instance by instance, whether this particular information is true of all category members. If you hear that crows in the northeastern United States have been dying of West Nile virus, you might induce that robins will die of West Nile virus; that would be making a specific, category-based induction. (The starting fact—in this case what you hear about crows—is often called the *premise*, analogous to the premise of an argument; the inference, which is about robins in this case, is the *conclusion*.) Would you also think that flamingos, pheasants, and ducks would die from the virus? Ornithologists did, and in August 1999, that is exactly what happened in the Bronx Zoo. The West Nile virus killed many species of birds.

FIGURE 10–10 Under a full moon . . .

Confirmation bias is a near-ubiquitous phenomenon: we tend, preferentially, to find evidence of what we already believe. Someone who believes that the crime rate increases when the moon is full will notice news reports of crimes committed then, but be less attentive to crime stories at other times. The result? "What did I tell you? Three burglaries this weekend—and I know why!"

Cognitive psychologists have been investigating specific, category-based induction since the mid-1970s (e.g., Rips, 1975). Such research has shown that we follow a number of heuristics in making category-based inductions. First, the more similar the premise instance is to the conclusion instance, the greater the likelihood that the feature mentioned in the premise will be attributed to the conclusion. Second, the more typical the premise instance is of its category, the more likely the conclusion instance will be judged to have the feature of interest. A third heuristic was identified by investigators who found that if the category involved is thought to be relatively homogeneous (for example, cats), we are willing to make stronger inferences by projecting the feature (for example, tails) from one instance to other instances of the category (although in this case, we would be wrong—Manx cats have no tails). If, however, the category is thought to be more heterogeneous (for example, animals), then we are unwilling to make strong inferences to other instances of the category (Nisbett et al., 1983). Variability within the category containing the premise and conclusion instances can have a large effect on judgments (see also Heit, 2000).

A model of category-based induction, known as the *similarity-coverage model*, has been developed (Osherson et al., 1990). It applies to general inductions as well as specific ones. In this view, the similarity of members of categories is not sufficient to explain all phenomena observed in category-based induction. Rather, the model proposes that underlying the typicality effects observed in inductive reasoning—that the more typical the premise instance, the more readily its feature is mapped to the conclusion—is the notion of coverage. "Coverage" is defined as the *average* maximum similarity between the instances in the premise and each exemplar of that category in the conclusion. To illustrate, consider the following two cases:

Premise:	Dogs have a liver.	*Premise:*	Dogs have a liver.
Premise:	Cats have a liver.	*Premise:*	Whales have a liver.
Conclusion:	Mammals have a liver.	*Conclusion:*	Mammals have a liver.

Which argument do you think is stronger? If you are like most participants in the original experiments, you chose the argument on the right. The investigators explained the effect by pointing out that, although the argument on the left contains terms ("dog" and "cat") that, to the non-zoologist, are more typical members of the category "mammal," the argument on the right contains terms that, between them, have more coverage of the category—that is, at least one of the exemplars should be relatively similar to *any* other instance of that category (and it is the *maximum* of the two similarities that determines induction).

Clearly, working memory is involved in the inductions: we must hold in memory the information from which we generalize. Induction also involves the executive functions needed to propose the induced rule, such as are required to switch attention from one exemplar to another. These observations lead us to expect the frontal lobes to play a dominant role in inductive inference—a possibility we consider in the following section.

3.3. Critical Brain Networks

Both studies of patients with various types of brain damage and neuroimaging studies of neurologically healthy participants point to the role of the frontal lobes in inductive reasoning. A standard test for frontal-lobe damage, discussed in Chapter 7, the Wisconsin Card Sort test (WCST) is a test of inductive reasoning in that the goal is to induce a rule. Participants are asked to match test cards to reference cards according to the color, shape, or number of stimuli on the cards. Feedback is provided after each trial, enabling the participant to learn (or induce) the correct rule for classifying the cards (e.g., sort the cards on the basis of color). After 10 or so correct trials, the rule is changed. Unimpaired, normal participants have little difficulty noting that the rule has changed. However, frontal-lobe patients, particularly those with damage to the left dorsolateral prefrontal cortex, have great difficulty switching rules even when they have overwhelming evidence that the rule they are continuing to use is incorrect (Dunbar & Sussman, 1995).

These data have been corroborated by fMRI investigations with unimpaired, normal participants, such as that reported by Monchi et al. (2001). In their study, participants responded to a computer-based WCST that was similar to the traditional version. They found significant activations in the mid-dorsolateral prefrontal cortex when participants received positive and negative feedback while performing the card sorting task. The researchers argued that these regions of the prefrontal cortex were activated because the participants had to selectively attend to a specific attribute, and to compare the current feedback information to prior trials held in working memory. These data are consistent with the notion that generalize induction, at least with respect to that used in the Wisconsin Card Sort test, involves the active monitoring of events in working memory. In addition, the researchers found that a combined cortical/subcortical network of regions, including the ventrolateral prefrontal cortex, caudate, and thalamus, was activated when participants received only negative feedback. These regions have been shown to be involved in a number of tasks that require the updating and modification of behavior on the basis of negative feedback.

Several studies using PET and fMRI have examined the neural underpinnings of category-based induction. In one of these, participants were asked to judge the probability of a stated conclusion from a given set of premises, similar to other studies we have described (Parsons & Osherson, 2001). The investigators found activation in portions of the left hemisphere, including in the medial temporal and parahippocampal regions and in large sections of the frontal lobes. These data extend the observations in the patient studies, showing that the frontal lobes are part of a more distributed network of brain regions that together support inductive inference. As discussed in Chapter 5, it is widely agreed that the medial temporal lobes are involved in memory, including both storage and retrieval. Given this information, we can then envision how category-based induction demands the active retrieval of relevant information from long-term memory and holding of that information in working memory, and these processes demand resources supported by the frontal and temporal lobes.

A further question focuses on the influence of experience: a key characteristic of inductive inference is that the underlying cognitive processes can change with experience. In the 2–4–6 task, for example, participants began in ignorance of the rule. As they worked on the task, proposing triads of numbers and rules and receiving feedback, they began to develop specific hypotheses, and some participants learned the rule. How does the brain change during this type of learning?

To answer this question, investigators presented unimpaired, normal participants with a simple task: they were required to sort abstract drawings into two groups, according to their two unseen, but strongly related, prototypes (Seger et al., 2000). (As discussed in Chapter 4, the prototype is the "central" member of a category.) The investigators found that during early trials brain activations were limited to frontal and parietal regions in the right hemisphere. As learning progressed, activation in left-hemisphere regions began to be seen, specifically in the left parietal lobe and left dorsolateral prefrontal cortex (Figure 10–11 on Color Insert N). What does this suggest? It appears that when the participants began to classify the drawings, they did so by processing the visual patterns of the stimuli. As learning progressed, however, they probably began to formulate an abstract rule. Reasoning from abstract rules is generally thought to be the realm of the left hemisphere. Like the neuroscience research discussed in the section on analogical reasoning, this is a nice example of how the use of neuroimaging technologies can inform our understanding of complex cognition.

Through the use of neuroimaging, researchers have recently been able to probe deeper into the underlying mechanisms involved in scientific hypothesis testing. For example, Fugelsang and Dunbar (2005) conducted an fMRI experiment examining the mechanisms by which we integrate data when testing specific hypotheses. Participants were asked to test specific hypothesis about the effect of various drugs designed to influence mood. The hypotheses could either be plausible or implausible. For example, the plausible hypotheses contained descriptions of drugs known to affect mood, for example, anti-depressants, whereas the implausible hypotheses contained descriptions of drugs known to have little to no effect on mood, for example, antibiotics. Data relevant to these hypotheses were then provided to participants in a trial-by-trial format, in which they viewed multiple trials of evidence for each type of drug. This evidence could be consistent or inconsistent with the hypothesis being tested. The researchers found that when participants were examining data relevant to a plausible hypothesis, regions in the caudate and parahippocampal gyrus were preferentially recruited. In contrast, when participants were examining data that were relevant to an implausible hypothesis, regions in the anterior cingulate cortex, precuneus, and left prefrontal cortex were selectively recruited.

What do these activations of different brain networks tell us about hypothesis testing? Let's consider first the caudate and parahippocampal gyrus activations, found with plausible hypotheses. These regions of the brain are typically thought to be involved in learning, long-term memory, and the process of integrating information. Given that, these data suggest that we may be more inclined to learn and integrate new information if it is consistent with a plausible hypothesis. The anterior cingulate cortex, one of the regions activated when participants were examining data that were relevant to an implausible hypothesis, has been largely implicated in detecting errors and conflict (as discussed in Chapter 7). Do participants treat data relevant to implausible hypotheses as error? These data suggest this may be the case! Taken together, the findings of Fugelsang and Dunbar (2005) suggest that during inductive reasoning the human brain may be specifically tuned to recruit learning mechanisms when evaluating data that are consistent with preexisting hypotheses, and to recruit error detection mechanisms when evaluating data that are not consistent with hypotheses.

This is an example of how the use of neuroimaging technologies can suggest new hypotheses about the cognitive processes involved in reasoning. By understanding the underlying brain networks that are involved in various complex tasks, we can begin to understand how the subcomponents of inductive reasoning (for example, attention, error processing, conflict monitoring, and working memory) interact.

✓ Comprehension Check:

1. What is the difference between general and specific category-based induction?
2. What are the proposed roles for the frontal cortex and temporal lobes in category-based induction?

4. DEDUCTIVE REASONING

You've decided to move, and soon will not be able to walk to campus. Thus, you're in the market for a new car. Lucky you, money is no object—but speed is. You go to the nearest Porsche dealership. You see that Porsche has developed a new model called the Boxster. From your knowledge of automobiles, you have come to the conclusion that all Porsches are reliable automobiles. Given that the Boxster is a Porsche, you expect the new Boxster to be reliable. So you take the new Porsche Boxster out for a test drive and it breaks down after only 10 minutes on the road. The only logical conclusion you can make is that one of your premises must be false: either premise 1—"all Porsches are reliable"—is false (which is possibly the case), or premise 2—"the Boxster is a Porsche"—is false (which is highly unlikely). You have just done a fine piece of deductive reasoning. In a deductive argument (unlike an inductive one), if the premises are true, the conclusion *cannot* be false.

Many theorists, from Aristotle on, have believed that deductive reasoning represents one of the highest achievements of rational thought. Deductive reasoning tasks are therefore one of the fundamental tools used by cognitive psychologists in the quest to understand human rationality.

One tool used to study deductive reasoning is the syllogism, an argument that consists of two statements and a conclusion. The conclusion may be either true or false. A conclusion that follows from given premises by the laws of deductive logic is a *valid* conclusion. Your conclusion that the Boxster is a reliable vehicle was valid; nonetheless, it turned out not to be true, because one or the other of your premises was false. In studies of deductive reasoning, a participant is given two premises and a conclusion and then asked to state whether the conclusion necessarily follows—in other words, whether it is valid. The basic idea of deductive reasoning is that a valid conclusion follows from the premises as a matter of logical necessity (which is not the case in inductive reasoning, where the conclusion is not *necessarily* true).

4.1. Categorical Syllogisms

The relations between two categories of things can be described by a categorical syllogism. Stated formally, your reasoning at the Porsche dealership looked like this:

Premise 1:   All Porsches are reliable.
Premise 2:   The Boxster is a Porsche.
Conclusion: The Boxster is reliable.

In the language of logic, premise 1 is the major premise, premise 2 is the minor premise. The categorical syllogism can be generalized:

Premise 1:   All A are B.
Premise 2:   C is an A.
Conclusion: C is B.

The relationship between two terms in a categorical syllogism can be described by four types of statements:

Universal affirmative (UA): All A are B.
Universal negative (UN): No A are B.
Particular affirmative (PA): Some A are B.
Particular negative (PN): Some A are not B.

These relationships between two terms are often represented in Venn diagrams, named for the English mathematician and logician John Venn (1834–1923). The diagrams are graphical depictions, by means of overlapping circles, of the relationship between two or more terms. The terms are represented as circles, and the categorical relationship between them is denoted by the degree of overlap. Figure 10–12 shows the four types of categorical syllogisms as Venn diagrams.

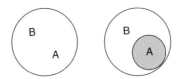

Universal affirmative (UA): All A are B.

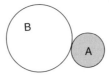

Universal negative (UN): No A are B.

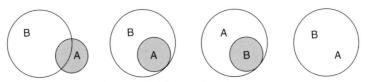

Particular affirmative (PA): Some A are B.

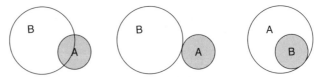

Particular negative (PN): Some A are not B.

FIGURE 10–12 Venn diagrams

The possible categorical relationships between the variables A and B are shown here as Venn diagrams. The universal negative has only one representation, but note that the other assertions can be expressed in more than one way. Seeing the various possibilities makes it clear why premises containing particulars are much more difficult to reason with than premises containing universals.

Note that there are two possible ways to represent the universal affirmative assertion "all A are B." A might represent a subset of B: the assertion that all jellybeans are red does not necessarily imply that there are no other things in the universe that are red. Alternatively, A and B might be equivalent, in which case everything that is red is a jellybean. Similarly, there are multiple ways to represent a particular affirmative and a particular negative. A total of 512 syllogisms can be constructed from all possible combinations of the quantifiers "all," "some," and "none," two premises, and a conclusion. Of these 512 possible syllogisms, only 27 have been found to be valid (Johnson-Laird & Steedman, 1978).

4.2. Conditional Syllogisms

The occurrence of an event may be conditional on the occurrence of another: this relationship between events can be described in a conditional syllogism. Like categorical syllogisms, conditional syllogisms consist of two premises and a conclusion. The first premise of a conditional syllogism is a statement of the form "if p, then q," where p is some antecedent condition and q is some consequent condition. The second premise can take one of four forms:

Affirmation of the antecedent (AA): p is true.
Denial of the antecedent (DA): p is not true.
Affirmation of the consequent (AC): q is true.
Denial of the consequent (DC): q is not true.

Your car-buying reasoning can be cast as follows in the form of a conditional syllogism:

Premise 1: If the automobile is a Porsche, then it is reliable.
Premise 2: The Boxster is a Porsche.

Conclusion: The Boxster is reliable.

Premise 1 is of the form "if p then q," "Porsche" is the antecedent and "is reliable" is the consequent; premise 2, in this case, affirms the antecedent; the conclusion, "is reliable," logically follows.

One of the most common tasks used to study conditional reasoning is the Wason selection task, a deceptively simple task in which typically fewer than 10 percent of participants make logically correct responses. An example problem in the task is shown in Figure 10–13. Four cards are laid out before the participant, bearing the letters A and D and the numbers 4 and 7. The participant is given this conditional rule: "If a card has a vowel on one side, then it has an even number on the other side." The task: to determine whether the rule is true or false by turning over the least necessary number of cards. All right, try it: Which cards do you think you will need to turn over to decide whether the rule is true? Think about this. You could flip over card A to see whether there is an even number on the other side; if there is an odd number on the other side, then the rule has been falsified. But if you find an even number on the other side, the rule has been affirmed—so far.

Are we finished now? Well, you could turn over the 4 card to make sure there was a vowel on the other side—and if you chose this option, you responded like 46

The rule: If a card has a vowel on one side,
then it has an even number on the other side.

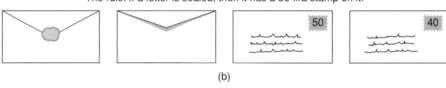

(a)

The rule: If a letter is sealed, then it has a 50-lira stamp on it.

(b)

FIGURE 10–13 The Wason selection task

(a) An abstract version and (b) one closer to life experience. The problem is the same in both: what is the least necessary number of cards (or envelopes) you have to turn over to establish whether or not the rule is true? Which ones would you turn over? Try both versions of the task; which one is easier?

percent of the participants in Wason's original experiment, if that's any comfort. Because where does this get you? The rule you were given made no reference to what you should expect on the other side of a card with an even number on it—*it doesn't matter what's on the reverse,* and you've wasted a move. Similarly, flipping over the D card will provide no useful information because the rule provided no information about what cards with consonants should have on the other side; so it doesn't matter. The correct inference is to choose the A card and the 7 card. Why the 7 card? Because turning over the 7 card allows you to test the negative of the if–then statement that was offered as the rule: if you find a vowel on the other side of the 7 card, then, and only then, could you know whether the rule is true or false.

The finding that typically fewer than 10 percent of participants perform logically on the Wason selection task paints a relatively bleak picture of our ability to reason logically. The version of the Wason task that is presented here, however, is very abstract: asking someone to make decisions about cards with even numbers and vowels does not draw on any relevant real-world knowledge. When versions of the task with "real-world" scenarios and combinations are presented ("If you borrow my car, then you have to fill up the tank with gas"), performance improves considerably (see the second row of Figure 10–13).

4.3. Errors in Deductive Thinking

Reasoning deductively is not always a simple matter. In fact, most of us make erroneous judgments when reasoning both categorically and conditionally. The types of errors we make have provided a wealth of information to researchers interested in developing theories of deductive reasoning.

We make two main types of errors when reasoning deductively: *form errors* and *content errors*. Form errors result from errors in the structural form or format of the premise–conclusion relationship. Content errors result when the content of the syllogism is overly influential.

4.3.1. Form Errors

A common form error in categorical reasoning is to accept a conclusion as valid if it contains the same quantifier—"some," "all," or "no"—as appears in the premises. This error is called the **atmosphere effect**: the use of these terms in the two premises conveys an overall mood, or atmosphere, that leads participants to accept a conclusion containing the same term (Woodworth & Sells, 1935). For example, it is easy to see that the conclusion "all As are Cs" necessarily follows from the two premises "all As are Bs" and "all Bs are Cs." Consider now what happens when we replace the previous quantifier "all" with "no" or "some":

Premise 1:	No As are Bs.
Premise 2:	No Bs are Cs.
Conclusion:	No As are Cs.

It may not be intuitively obvious that this conclusion is invalid. Let's replace the abstract A, B, and C with some concrete terms and see what the categorical syllogism looks like:

Premise 1:	No humans are automobiles.
Premise 2:	No automobiles are doctors.
Conclusion:	No humans are doctors.

It is apparent now that the conclusion is invalid.

A related form error, in conditional reasoning this time, is known as **matching bias**, that is, accepting a conclusion as valid if it contains the syntactic structure of the premises or some of the terms of the premise. For example, in the Wason selection task (Figure 10–13), this error occurs when people erroneously turn over the 4 card because it is referred to in the stated rule ("If a card has a vowel on one side, then it has an *even number* on the other side.") Both the atmosphere effect with categorical syllogisms and the matching bias with conditional syllogisms point to the strong impact of syntactic structure. In both cases, we are strongly influenced by the quantifiers used in the premises. Why might this be the case?

One possibility is that certain objects in categorical and conditional statements—such as the formal quantifiers—draw our attention. It has been argued that we simply expect the information we receive to be relevant (Evans, 1989), and so we expect the quantifier to be critical. Thus, the bias to attend to the quantifier words in the premises and accept them in the conclusion arises because in fact most of the time the salient information we are given *is* relevant. Another reason we may have difficulty in reasoning with more complex categorical and conditional statements has to do with the troublesome nature of negative quantifiers. We do not always spontaneously convert negative statements (for example, "not an even number") to positive statements (for example, "an odd number"). Finally, limitations on working memory could be at the root of many of the errors we make in deductive reasoning, and indeed, all contemporary theoretical accounts of deductive reasoning recognize the significant role that working memory plays in such reasoning.

4.3.2. Content Errors

Logical deductions should be influenced only by the structure of the premises: the laws of logic are abstract and are independent of the content of the syllogism. But we human beings are embedded in a world where the content—the information conveyed—is often important. A common content error is to focus on the truth or falsity of individual statements in the syllogism (while ignoring the logical connection between statements). This error was demonstrated in a study in which participants were presented with a number of invalid syllogisms whose conclusions sometimes contained true statements (Markovits & Nantel, 1989). Consider the following two examples:

Premise 1:   All things that have a motor (A) need oil (B).
Premise 2:   Automobiles (C) need oil (B).
Conclusion: Automobiles (C) have motors (A).

and

Premise 1:   All things that have a motor (A) need oil (B).
Premise 2:   Opprobines (C) need oil (B).
Conclusion: Opprobines (C) have motors (A).

Is either of these two conclusions valid? Which one? Most participants said that the first example was valid; in fact, they are both invalid. The first two premises do not specify a relationship between C and A, which is what the conclusion is about. Nonetheless, participants accepted the first conclusion as valid more than twice as often as they did the second. We are apparently more likely to accept as logically valid an invalid conclusion if the premises and conclusion are true statements.

The belief-bias effect—the tendency to be more likely to accept a "believable" conclusion to a syllogism than an "unbelievable" one—is perhaps the most prevalent content effect studied in deductive reasoning (for a review, see Klauer et al., 2000). Consider the following.

Premise 1:   No cigarettes (A) are inexpensive (B).
Premise 2:   Some addictive things (C) are inexpensive (B).
Conclusion: Some addictive things (C) are not cigarettes (A).

About 90 percent of participants presented with this syllogism judged the conclusion to be valid. The conclusion is both logical (it necessarily follows from the premises) and believable (there are many addictive things that are not cigarettes). What happens when we rearrange the content of the syllogism?

Premise 1:   No addictive things (A) are inexpensive (B).

Premise 2:   Some cigarettes (C) are inexpensive (B).

Conclusion: Some cigarettes (C) are not addictive (A).

Only about 50 percent of participants recognize this conclusion as valid. But of course it is: the conclusion logically follows from the premises. The conclusion, however, is no longer believable. The unbelievable content of the problem influences the ability of many participants to make a valid logical deduction.

Much research has found that both belief and logical validity influence our judgments of validity in an interactive fashion. By presenting participants with prose passages containing categorical syllogisms that varied in terms of validity and believability, Evans et al. (1983) found that the effects of logic were greater for unbelievable than for believable conclusions—that is, participants were more likely to ignore the logical structure of the syllogism if the conclusion was believable (see the accompanying *A Closer Look* box). This interaction between logical structure and content is one of the most tested phenomena in deductive reasoning, and contemporary theories of deductive reasoning generally take great care to address it.

4.4. Theories of Deductive Reasoning

There are several important theoretical accounts of deductive reasoning. One prominent class of theories of deductive reasoning proposes that deduction depends on formal rules of inference akin to those of a logical calculus (Braine & O'Brian, 1991; Rips, 1994). These theories propose that humans naturally possess a logical system that enables us to make deductions. In this view, we evaluate deductive syllogisms by constructing and verifying a "mental proof" in working memory. In other words, we attempt to solve deductive reasoning problems by generating sentences that link the premises to the conclusion and then determine whether the conclusion necessarily follows from the premises. That is, we assess the validity of the premise and conclusion by linking their representations in working memory with the logical rules we naturally possess. Rule-based approaches do very well at accounting for certain effects of logical form in reasoning. For example, the time it takes to solve conditional and categorical problems in deductive reasoning increases with the number of inferential steps needed and increases when more complex rules are required to solve the problem.

Rule-based approaches also acknowledge content effects in deductive reasoning. How might knowledge or expectations influence the application of internalized logical rules? One possibility is that reasoning that ignores logical rules may occur because of limitations on working memory (Rips, 1994). As noted earlier, we commonly use heuristics to solve problems, and in deductive reasoning, for better or worse, we use many heuristics to aid in making logical inferences that put too much of a load on working memory. One such heuristic—developed because we have experienced arguments with valid believable examples in the past—may lead to the belief-bias effect: that believable conclusions are more likely to be valid than unbelievable ones (Rips, 1994).

A CLOSER LOOK
Logic and Belief

An influential study by Jonathan Evans, J. L. Barston, and P. Pollard examined the relationship among logical processes, beliefs, and expectations; the results were reported in 1983 in a paper titled "On the Conflict between Logic and Belief in Syllogistic Reasoning," published in *Memory and Cognition, 11,* 295–306.

Introduction

The investigators were interested in examining how one's beliefs and expectations influence our adherence to the rules of logic. Do we reason "rationally," ignoring the content of a given problem and focusing only on the logical structure of the arguments?

Method

In the experiment, 24 participants were presented with 80-word prose passages containing categorical syllogisms that were (1) logically valid and had a believable conclusion, (2) logically valid but had an unbelievable conclusion, (3) logically invalid but had a believable conclusion, and (4) logically invalid and had an unbelievable conclusion. The logical structure for the valid arguments had the following form:

Premise 1:	No A are B.
Premise 2:	Some C are B.
Conclusion:	Some C are not A.

The invalid arguments had the form:

Premise 1:	No A are B.
Premise 2:	Some C are B.
Conclusion:	Some A are not C.

The content of the arguments contained either believable conclusions (for example, "Some religious people are not priests") or unbelievable conclusions (for example, "Some deep sea divers are not good swimmers"). Each participant evaluated four passages, one for each believability-by-validity condition.

Results

The data are plotted in the graph. First, as is evident, acceptance of a conclusion as valid was influenced by the logical validity of the categorical syllogism: when a conclusion was logically necessary, the proportion of participants who accepted it as valid increased. Second, acceptance of a conclusion as valid was also influenced by its believability: when a conclusion was believable, the proportion of participants who accepted it as valid increased. It is important to note, however, the interaction between logical validity and belief: the effects of logic were greater for unbelievable (46 percent versus 8 percent) conclusions than for believable conclusions (92 percent versus 92 percent); in fact, the participants in this experiment appeared to ignore completely the logical structure of the arguments when they considered the conclusion believable.

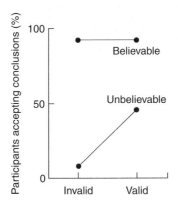

Whether participants accepted a conclusion as valid appeared to be unaffected by the validity of the conclusion if they regarded it as believable.

(Evans, J. St. B. T., Barston, J. L. & Pollard, P. (1983). On the conflict between logic and belief in syllogistic reasoning. *Memory & Cognition, 11,* 295–306.)

Discussion

The finding that beliefs strongly influence deductive reasoning challenges traditional views that argue that we humans reason purely on the basis of abstract, "content-free" rules of logic.

Another view is the theory of *mental models* (Johnson-Laird, 1983; Johnson-Laird & Byrne, 1991). Mental models are internal representations of real or imaginary situations that can be derived from information such as that in syllogisms. Deductive reasoning, in this view, occurs in three stages. First, a mental model is constructed that best represents the information in the premises. This requires comprehension of the terms in the premises and of the relationship between them. For example, being told "All As are Bs" and "All Bs are Cs," you might construct a model in which three mental objects are labeled "C," two of them are also labeled "B," and one of the latter is also labeled "A." Second, a tentative conclusion is generated and evaluated so it can be determined whether it is consistent with the model derived in the first stage. In our example model, a tentative conclusion would be "All As are Cs." Third, and this is the most controversial aspect of the theory, the conclusion must be validated. This involves the search for alternative models that are consistent with the premises but not with the conclusion. (In our example, any alternative model is consistent with the premises and conclusion.) If such an alternative model can be generated, then the conclusion is invalid and an alternative conclusion must be generated and evaluated, and so on. A conclusion is valid only if there are no alternative models available to falsify it.

The mental models theory provides a good account for both form and content errors in deduction. For example, the extent to which we have difficulty in evaluating conditional and categorical syllogisms has been shown to be directly related to the number of models required—a matter of logical form (Johnson-Laird, 1983).

Errors and Evolution

DEBATE

Why do we make errors in deductive reasoning? Most theories of deductive reasoning are based on the assumption that errors in reasoning are due to limitations of core components of the cognitive system, such as limited working memory capacity. Another theory, however, suggests that social and evolutionary factors are the cause of some deductive reasoning errors (Cosmides & Tooby, 1992). This view starts with the idea that humans are sensitive to rules for social reasoning—that is, the interpretation of social situations—because we have adapted, through evolution, to be sensitive to certain aspects of our social environment. In particular, this theory posits that humans possess a specialized brain "module" (i.e., self-contained system) for detecting those of their species who cheat in social exchanges (Stone et al., 2002).

This hypothesized evolutionary adaptation can account for performance on certain deductive reasoning tasks. For example, researchers studied a patient, R.M., who had severe damage to the basal ganglia and the temporal pole, a brain structure that is a source of input into the amygdala, which is critical for processing emotional and social information (as discussed in Chapter 8). The lack of a functional temporal pole renders the amygdala largely disconnected and incapable of processing this information. R.M. was given different versions of the Wason selection task. He performed normally on tasks that required him to determine whether someone was breaking a precautionary rule (such as "if you engage in hazardous activity X, you must take precaution Y"), but performed poorly on logically identical tasks that required him to determine whether someone was cheating on a social contract (such as "if you receive benefit X, you must fulfill requirement Y"). The researchers argue that R.M.'s unique pattern of correct and erroneous reasoning could not occur if detecting cheaters depended solely on the application of general reasoning rules. Instead, his selective deficit suggested that detecting social cheaters requires specialized neural circuitry.

The evolutionary hypothesis stands in contrast to accounts that suggest that we solve different deductive reasoning problems (such as precautionary rules versus social contracts) by applying logical rules. In all these cases, detecting cheaters would require no privileged circuitry above and beyond other reasoning domains. Again, more research is needed; the jury is still out on this issue.

The theory also provides an explanation of how knowledge or expectations influence reasoning: the believability of a conclusion, a product of knowledge and experience, may determine the extent to which alternative models are generated and verified. If the initial conclusion is believable, we may not search for alternative models and thus run the risk of accepting a believable but invalid conclusion.

4.5. Linguistic versus Spatial Basis

Work with patients who have brain damage, and neuroimaging of normal healthy brains has made it possible to study the neural underpinnings of deductive reasoning. This research has provided new insights into fundamental questions that have perplexed cognitive psychologists for decades. One such question that has received much attention is whether deductive and inductive reasoning are linguistically or spatially based. A linguistic model would propose that, because deductive reasoning involves language-like properties of representations, we should see activation of the left-hemisphere language structures such as the frontal and posterior temporal regions (see Chapter 12). A spatial model of deductive reasoning, on the other hand, would suggest that in order to reason we create spatial representations (i.e., particular types of mental models) of linguistic information. In that case, we would expect to see activation of the visual–spatial perceptual structures, such as those in the parietal and occipital lobes, particularly in the right hemisphere.

To date, the results of research have been mixed. On the one hand, researchers have provided data that support linguistic models. For example, patients with left-hemisphere brain damage were found to be severely impaired in a simple deductive reasoning task, whereas patients with damage in comparable regions in the right hemisphere were only minimally impaired relative to unimpaired, healthy controls (Read, 1981). Furthermore, right-hemisphere patients sometimes have been shown actually to perform better than left-hemisphere patients and controls (Golding, 1981). These patient studies provide some support for a linguistic model of deductive reasoning. In addition, a neuroimaging study with unimpaired, healthy participants found significant activations for deductive reasoning in the left inferior frontal gyrus (as well as the left superior occipital gyrus) (Goel et al., 1998). These findings also support the hypothesis that deductive reasoning is linguistically mediated. On the other hand, however, researchers found significant activations in the *right* middle temporal cortex and right inferior frontal gyrus for a similar task of deductive reasoning (Parsons & Osherson, 2001). These findings are more consistent with spatial models. Why the difference?

To begin at the beginning: these two neuroimaging studies differed in both the types of syllogisms used and the content of those syllogisms. In the Goel et al. (1998) study, which showed left-hemisphere activation and thus supported a linguistic model, categorical syllogisms were taken from a military context and employed terms not necessarily familiar to the participants (for example, *officers, generals, privates*). The Parsons and Osherson (2001) study, which showed right-hemisphere activation and thus supported a spatial model, presented participants with conditional arguments that contained more generally familiar material (for example, *doctors, firefighters, teachers*). Could these differences in materials result in different patterns of brain activation? The answer is yes: it has been suggested that deductive reasoning with highly familiar material recruits relatively more neural tissue from the right hemisphere, whereas content-free deductive reasoning recruits neural tissue predominantly in the left hemisphere (Wharton & Grafman, 1998). This fact alone can explain some of the discrepancy. But neuroimaging work examining reasoning is still in its infancy, and much research remains to be done.

Comprehension Check:

1. What are the differences between form errors and content errors in deductive reasoning?
2. What are the similarities and differences between the rule-based and mental-model theories of deductive reasoning?

Revisit and Reflect

1. *What is the nature of problem solving?*

   Problem solving is a process of surmounting obstacles to achieve a particular goal. To do this, we must identify what the problem is and choose a course of action that will make it possible to achieve the goal. At its most basic level a problem can be thought of as having three parts. First is the goal state: this is where you want to be, at the solution to the problem. Second is the initial, or start, state: this is where you are now, facing the problem that needs to be solved. Third is the set of operations that you can apply—that is, the actions you can take—to get from the start state to the goal state. This all sounds relatively straightforward; however, some problems (known as ill-defined problems) are hard to define and represent because their operations and constraints are unclear. On the other hand, *well-defined problems,* which have operations and constraints that are clear (no matter how complicated), are typically easy to define. The initial state, goal state, and the intermediate operations are all thought to occur within a defined problem space, which is the set of states, or possible choices, that face problem solvers at each step as they go from an initial state to a goal state.

   Think Critically

   - Are well-defined problems always easier to complete than ill-defined problems? Why or why not?
   - Can the solution of all problems be characterized in terms of search in a problem space? Are there key aspects of solving a problem that this approach leaves out? For example, are the start state and set of operations necessarily specified completely from the outset?

2. *How do we use heuristics or "mental shortcuts" to solve problems?*

   A heuristic is a rule-of-thumb that may offer a shortcut to solving a problem. Typically, a heuristic can help the reasoner to achieve the goal state faster than an algorithm, which is a set of procedures for solving a given type of problem that will always produce the correct answer (for example, the steps in taking a square root or performing long division). One heuristic is *random search,* a process of trial and error, such as randomly hitting keys on the keyboard when a computer freezes. A problem solver using the *hill-climbing* heuristic looks ahead one move and chooses the move that most closely resembles the goal state. In solving the Tower of Hanoi, the hill-climbing problem solver may try to select each move so that it most closely resembles the final state when the three disks are on the third pole. In the means–ends analysis heuristic, the problem solver breaks the problem into a series of subproblems, for example, completing one side of a Rubik's cube as the first stage in solving the puzzle.

Think Critically

■ Can you think of situations in which certain heuristics might lead a reasoner astray?

■ Which heuristics might work better for solving a well-defined problem? An ill-defined problem?

3. *How do we use analogies to solve new problems?*

When solving a novel problem, we often try to think of a solution to a similar problem—that is, we reason by analogy. Specifically, *analogical reasoning* involves using knowledge from one relatively known domain (the source) and applying it to another, less familiar, domain (the target). Analogical reasoning is generally thought to comprise five subprocesses: (1) *retrieval* of relevant (source) information, (2) *mapping* features of the source onto the target, (3) *evaluating* whether or not the analogy is valid, (4) *abstracting* the relevant feature shared by the source and the target, and (5) *predicting* behavior or characteristics of the target from what is known about the source.

Think Critically

■ Can you think of an example when you used an analogy to solve a novel problem?

■ Can analogies sometimes lead to faulty assumptions about the underlying nature of objects or events?

4. *What is the difference between inductive and deductive reasoning?*

Reasoning can be loosely defined as the ability to draw conclusions from available information. The processes that we adhere to when reasoning can be subdivided into two main inferential processes, inductive reasoning and deductive reasoning. Inductive reasoning involves using known information to draw new conclusions that are likely to be true. Inductive reasoning frequently involves categories, generalizing from known instances to all instances, or from some instances to another instance. *Deductive reasoning,* on the other hand, involves using known information to draw conclusions that *must* be true. Categorical reasoning (reasoning about the relations between two categories of things) and conditional reasoning (determining the degree to which the occurrence of an event may be conditional on the occurrence of another) are forms of deductive reasoning.

Think Critically

■ Can you think of specific scenarios that would demand both inductive and deductive reasoning?

■ Can you imagine a situation in which deductive logic leads you to a valid conclusion but your knowledge of the world tells you that this conclusion is not true? What is the reason for this discrepancy?

5. *How do our knowledge and beliefs influence "logical" reasoning?*

   Evidence from Wason's 2–4–6 inductive reasoning task has indicated that we typically show a confirmation bias when asked to discover a rule. In a variety of tasks reasoners have been shown to spend the majority of their efforts trying to confirm a rule that they believe to be correct as opposed to trying to disconfirm it. Much research on deductive reasoning has shown that we often focus on the truth or falsity of individual statements in the syllogism while ignoring the logical connection between statements.

   Think Critically

   ■ Is the finding that our beliefs influence our logical reasoning process necessarily a discouraging result?

   ■ How might any of a host of cognitive processes—attention, executive processes, working memory—contribute to the interaction between beliefs and logical processing?

6. *How do our brains coordinate the vast amount of processing involved in problem solving and reasoning?*

   Many of the brain areas linked to attention and memory are also highly involved in reasoning and problem solving. There is a very good reason for this—reasoning and problem solving are typically highly demanding of attention and memory. You must determine the goal of the current problem and keep it active; you must attend to the relevant properties of the current stimulus that will assist you to meet this goal; and, while keeping the current goal active in working memory, you must determine how the current features of the stimulus relate to the current goal and which operations to perform next. Depending on the outcome of this third step, you may need to modify your short-term goal in order to meet your desired end state. Such processing involves attention and working memory, thus invoking resources in the dorsolateral prefrontal cortex, the parietal cortex, and anterior cingulate (among other areas). The requisite preliminary visual feature analyses, object identification, and object location analyses would utilize resources in the occipital, temporal, and parietal lobes, respectively. The interplay between the analyses of the current features of the problem and the current goal state of the problem solver would invoke a feedback loop between the attention/working memory–related brain structures (in particular, prefrontal and anterior cingulate cortices) and the perceptual/object identification/location–related structures (in particular, occipital/temporal/parietal cortices).

   Think Critically

   ■ How does neuroimaging inform theories of problem solving and reasoning?

   ■ One of the most interesting findings about the brain and problem solving is that many regions of the brain that are involved in attention and memory are also involved in thinking and reasoning. Why is this the case?

Motor Cognition and Mental Simulation

Learning Objectives

It's late at night. You've taken a break from a demanding reading assignment and picked up a detective story . . .

> In front of us as we flew up the track we heard scream after scream from Sir Henry and the deep roar of the hound. I was in time to see the beast spring upon its victim, hurl him to the ground, and worry at his throat. But the next instant Holmes had emptied five barrels of his revolver into the creature's flank. With a last howl of agony and a vicious snap in the air, it rolled upon its back, four feet pawing furiously, and then fell limp upon its side. I stooped, panting, and pressed my pistol to the dreadful, shimmering head, but it was useless to press the trigger. The giant hound was dead.

It's Watson who hears the frightful cries, Watson who is running with Holmes across the moor, Watson who is panting—and the hound of the Baskervilles is no threat to you, safe in your room. But as you come to the climax of the story you realize that *your* pulse is racing, *your* heart is pounding; physical, motor responses are being evoked by imaginary stimuli. What's going on?

What's going on is that imagining the actions of another person, even a fictional other person, and taking that person's perspective of events recruit some of the same mental processing and activate some of the same neural networks as would be activated if you really were experiencing the imagined situation. In the previous chapter we discussed problem solving and reasoning of the sort that largely rely on conceptual analyses; in this chapter, we discuss another way in which thinking occurs that relies on mentally simulating possible actions or events. Historically it was thought that such simulations were used by young children prior to conceptual thought, and thus much of the relevant research we consider in this chapter will focus on development.

What would you have done if you were Watson? To answer this question, you might "put yourself in his shoes," imagining how you would react if you were in his place. Such thinking relies on motor cognition; **motor cognition** is mental processing in which the motor system draws on stored information to plan and produce our own actions, as well as to anticipate, predict, and interpret the actions of others. Throughout this chapter we investigate and provide evidence for the claim that some sorts of reasoning and problem solving rely on motor cognition, which often uses mental imagery to run "mental scenarios" that allow you to "see what would happen if. . . ." We specifically address these overarching questions:

1. What is the nature of motor cognition?
2. What is a mental simulation of action?
3. Why and how do we reproduce the actions of others?
4. What is the role of motor cognition in perception?

1. THE NATURE OF MOTOR COGNITION

You may never have thought much about how you plan and control your movements, but even a moment's reflection should make you aware that your actions typically are not reflexes, triggered by an external stimulus (such as occurs when you yank your hand back from a hot stove), but rather are the visible manifestation of a series of mental processes. A key idea is that these same mental processes can be used in cognition, even when they do not result in a specific movement. To see how the processes used to plan and guide movement can also be used in reasoning and problem solving, we must begin by considering the nature of motor processing.

Many contemporary researchers assume that there is a continuity between planning and enactment. In this view a **movement** is considered to be a voluntary displacement of a body part in physical space, whereas an **action** is a series of movements that must be accomplished in order to reach a goal. Indeed, actions are planned with respect to a specific goal. For example, if you are thirsty and want to take a sip of coffee, you might look at your coffee mug, reach toward it, wrap your fingers around the handle, lift the mug, and bring it to your lips. Motor cognition encompasses all the mental processes involved in the planning, preparation, and production of our own actions, as well as the mental processes involved in anticipating, predicting, and interpreting the actions of others.

1.1. Perception–Action Cycles

A key to understanding the nature of motor cognition is the concept of the perception–action cycle, which is the transformation of perceived patterns into coordinated patterns of movements. For example, you casually notice how high each step in a stairway rises, and you lift your feet accordingly (Gibson, 1966). As we shall see, even this seemingly very simple sort of movement planning—unconsciously figuring out when and how high to lift your feet—relies on a sophisticated set of neural processes. Evolutionarily speaking, perception exists not just to recognize objects and events, but also (as noted in Chapter 2), to provide guidance and feedback for the many different movements that animals make, so that a given movement is efficient and successful in its aim. Moreover, it is not just that perception exists partly in the service of planning movements; our movements allow us to perceive, which in turn allows us to plan our subsequent movements. Animals move so that they can obtain food, and eat so that they can then move; they move so that they can perceive, and perceive so that they can move. Perception and action are mutually intertwined and interdependent—and motor cognition lies at the heart of how the two interact. We plan so that we will reach an action goal, and what we perceive lets us know whether we are getting closer to that goal, or are on the wrong track.

What is the mediating link between perception and action? Neurophysiological and behavioral evidence suggests that the link is representation: that there is shared coding in the brain of perception and action, and that the contents of both perceptions and intentions—mental plans designed to achieve a goal through action—depend on neural processes with both perceptual and motor aspects (see Haggard, 2005).

1.2. The Nature of Motor Processing in the Brain

We have stressed that motor cognition is grounded in the systems used to control movement. A fundamental fact is that different brain areas support different motor processes. We focus on three motor areas; evidence for their roles in information processing comes in large part from the effects of experimental lesions in animals (Passingham, 1993) and clinical observations of humans with brain damage. Area M1 (discussed in Chapter 1) is the "lowest level" motor area; neurons in this area control fine motor movements, and send fibers out of the brain to the muscles themselves. The premotor area (PM) is involved in setting up programs for specific sequences of actions (and sends input to M1), and the supplementary motor area (SMA) is involved in setting up and executing action plans. Thus, these areas are often regarded as forming a hierarchy, with M1 at the bottom and SMA at the top. For our present purposes we cannot go too far wrong by considering the areas as processing increasingly abstract sorts of information, from specific movements (M1)

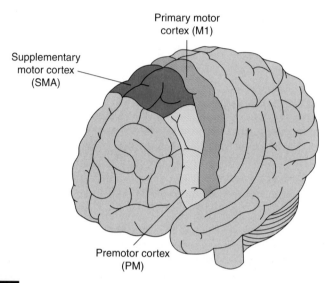

FIGURE 11–1   Key cortical motor areas

Three brain areas used in motor control and motor cognition.

(Figure based on http://www.brainconnection.com/med/medart/1/motor-cortex.jpg showing only primary motor cortex (M1), premotor cortex (PM) and supplementary motor cortex (SMA).)

to less precisely specified sets of movements (PM), to overarching plans for action (SMA). These three areas are illustrated in Figure 11–1.

Here is some evidence for the distinct roles of the three areas. Several studies have compared neuronal activity in M1, PM, and SMA during preparation of motor responses to investigate the distinction between processing of externally generated tasks (for example, reaching to turn off your alarm clock) and internally generated ones (for example, setting your alarm clock). In the latter case, you need to plan in advance; in the former case you do not. Mushiake and colleagues (1991) recorded single-cell activity in M1, PM, and SMA of monkeys immediately before and while they were carrying out a sequential motor task. The key to the experiment was that a movement sequence was either visually triggered (VT) or internally triggered (IT). In the VT condition, monkeys were required to touch three pads on a panel as they were illuminated in a random sequence. In the IT condition the monkeys were required to remember a predetermined sequence and press it on a keypad without visual guidance.

The results showed that most M1 neurons exhibited similar activity during both premovement and movement periods, in both the IT and VT conditions. This makes sense, because the same movements ultimately were produced in the two conditions. However, in SMA more neurons were active in the IT condition than in the VT condition during both the premovement and movement periods, which suggests that having to formulate a plan involves SMA. In contrast, in PM more neurons were active during the VT than the IT condition in both periods, which suggests that this area is involved in setting up specific movement sequences. These findings show that motor production as a whole—premovement and movement—exists at a number of levels of processing; moreover, neural processing differs when you are formulating a plan in advance and when you are simply responding to an environmental cue.

The discovery that these three brain areas operate on increasingly more specific information might suggest that the areas always operate strictly in sequence; specifically, it might be tempting to think that SMA finishes processing and only then directs PM, which finishes its processing and only then in turn directs M1. But this apparently is not the case. Instead, other neural evidence suggests that the three brain areas do not always operate in this sequence, but instead interact in complex ways. Nevertheless, different brain regions play different roles in the conception, initiation, and control of action. We have already seen that the SMA is involved in the organization of motor sequences based on plans, and that PM is involved in the preparation of a specific action. But that is not all there is to it: the prefrontal cortex is involved in the initiation and in the temporal organization of action (as described in Chapter 7), and the cerebellum is involved in the temporal control of action sequences. All these regions show anticipatory activity in relation to a forthcoming action. In fact, connections from one area to another typically are mirrored by feedback connections from the "receiving" area to the "sending" one; information is running in both directions, which presumably allows the areas to coordinate their processing.

In short, motor cognition relies on a multicomponent system, with many distinct processes that occur simultaneously, and these processes occur in different brain regions that support different neural networks.

1.3. The Role of Shared Representations

In the realm of motor cognition, the concept of shared motor representations refers to our ability mentally to represent actions made by other people. As we shall see, the same kinds of motor representations are formed when we observe someone else act as when we ourselves perform the same action. Thus, by observing, we can acquire representations that later allow us to think about actions. These shared representations are critical in motor cognition because they allow us to learn by observing the experiences of others (just as we can learn affective reactions by observing others, as discussed in Chapter 8). The notion of shared representations is widely used in social psychology, especially in the field of communication. For a successful conversation to take place, speaker and listener have to ascribe similar meanings to words and must have the same concept of the topic of communication (Krauss & Fussell, 1991). When you say "What I mean by that is . . ." you're making sure that the representation you hold is in fact shared by your listener, so that your responses "make sense" to both of you and advance the conversation. Such shared representations of the meaning of words and social interactions become internalized, that is, represented so that they can be used in mental processing even in the absence of an on-going social interaction. In the same way that shared linguistic representations enable a conversation, shared motor representations make it possible for us to interpret the meaning of the actions of others and respond appropriately. Shared motor representations were presumably elaborated early in our evolution by interactions with the physical and social environment.

As with your response to Watson's encounter with the hound of the Baskervilles, your ability to identify with the protagonist relies in part on the physical and motor responses that the character's behavior triggers in you, the reader.

✓ **Comprehension Check:**

1. What is motor cognition?
2. What are the major motor areas of the brain and what sorts of functions do they support?

2. MENTAL SIMULATION AND THE MOTOR SYSTEM

The moment Holmes emptied his gun was the final stage of a set of processes by which his action was planned in response to the dramatic event he witnessed. Do you think his reasoning processes relied on the kinds of logical deductions and inductions we discussed in Chapter 10? In fact, there is evidence that a different sort of cognition underlies our reasoning in action situations. Specifically, one way we reason is by forming and transforming mental images of possible actions, and "observing" the consequences of those actions. This makes sense because imagery and perception share most of the same neural mechanisms (Ganis et al., 2004; Kosslyn et al., 1997; Kosslyn et al., 2006). Thus, "watching" the events in a mental image can change our behavior, much as can watching another person's behavior. Indeed, many athletes believe that mentally rehearsing their movements before executing them on the field helps them to perform better, and research supports this belief. It has been demonstrated that motor imagery—mentally simulating an intended action without actually producing it—has a positive effect on subsequently performing that action (Feltz & Landers, 1983).

Not only can motor imagery guide our motor cognition, but our motor cognition in turn can affect our motor imagery. Converging evidence from several sources indicates that motor imagery involves processes involved in programming and preparation of actual actions. The essential difference is that in the case of motor imagery, the action is not performed. Still, the processes underlying motor cognition can direct the way mental images are transformed. In this section, you will see that the mechanisms that allow us to produce actions also allow us to anticipate the likely consequences of performing an action.

2.1. Motor Priming and Mental Representation

Mental simulations must be guided by specific types of mental representations. We gain insight into the nature of such representations by considering a type of priming. Priming, as we've discussed before, is the facilitation of processing that results from performing a previous process. In the investigation of motor cognition, motor priming is the effect whereby watching a movement or an action facilitates making a similar motor response oneself. Motor priming provides evidence for shared representations when we observe a movement or an action and when we produce the corresponding movement or action ourselves. The existence of these shared representations suggests that mental simulations are particularly useful for reasoning about possible actions that you or someone else could take. Consider the results of three studies that have explored perception–action cycles.

To examine the effect of perception on motor production, investigators designed an experiment based on reproducing observed motion (Kerzel et al., 2000). Participants were instructed to watch a "launching event" on a computer screen in which a disk (object A) collided with another disk (object B) and appeared to set object B into motion. The researchers varied the velocity of both object A and object B. Immediately after watching a launching event, participants were asked to reproduce the velocity of object A by moving a stylus from left to right on a tablet. The researchers found that not only did the perceived speed of object A influence participants' reproduced velocities but, even though participants had been asked to reproduce *only* the speed of object A, their velocity reproductions were also influenced by the speed of object B. Simply having perceived object B primed the participants, influencing the speed at which they later moved object A.

A more complex task, which echoes the Stroop effect, was required of participants in a study that investigated the relationship between perception of another person's movements and production of movement oneself. The investigators presented participants with views of two manual gestures, hand spreading and hand grasping (Sturmer et al., 2000), as shown in Figure 11–2. Participants were instructed to spread or clench their own hands according to the *color*, not the position, of the stimulus hand: red meant "grasping," blue meant "spread." The researchers observed that the speed of the response was quicker when the position of the stimulus hand matched the required response—for example, grasping when the stimulus hand was red *and* grasping; the grasping response was slower if the stimulus hand was red and spread. The perception of the stimulus hand position—although irrelevant to the

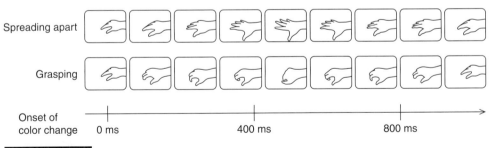

FIGURE 11–2 Hand position research

Sturmer, Aschersleben, and Prinz (2000) showed participants these hand positions. The color changed to red or blue, which cued the participants to grasp or to spread their own hand. The participants responded more quickly when the position of the stimulus hand matched the required response.

(Sturmer, B., Aschersleben, G. & Prinz, W. (2000). Correspondence effects with manual gestures and postures: A study of imitation. *Journal of Experimental Psychology: Human Perception and Performance, 26,* 1746–1759.)

task—clearly influenced the production of the movement itself. We cannot ignore the actions of others, and these actions prime corresponding actions in ourselves.

In addition, Castiello and colleagues (2002) explored the nature and specificity of motor priming by studying behavioral responses to actions by a robotic arm and by a human arm. Consistent with the conclusions we drew in the previous section, in four separate experiments these researchers found a priming advantage for a human arm over a robot arm—that is, the participants' responses were faster when the model was human. The human model also produced more specific and subtle responses in the participants than did the robot model: for example, viewing a human model led participants to adjust the width of their grasp depending on the grasp of the observed model, but no such effect occurred when participants watched a robot model.

Taken together, the findings in these investigations suggest that simply observing a movement or an action can prime a similar response in the observer. These results provide support for the inference that observing a movement or an action and performing the corresponding action share a representational system. These representations can be triggered in many different ways, including by reading the words of a master storyteller. Now it is less of a surprise that your body responded to Watson's dreadful experience when you read *The Hound of the Baskervilles*.

2.2. Motor Programs

You're at the wheel of a car, waiting at a traffic signal for the light to turn green. If you anticipate the signal change, you will be quicker to respond to the light when it turns green. This is because when you anticipate, you (sometimes unconsciously) set up a **motor program**, the representation of a sequence of movements that is planned in advance of actual performance, necessary to accomplish releasing the brakes and stepping on the gas pedal. Motor programs underlie motor cognition; you can run them not only to produce a movement, but also to reason about the consequences of moving in specific ways.

Studies of response time (RT) have contributed extensively to the investigation of motor programs. One way to study the nature of motor programs is to observe what happens right before a person must perform an action. In the framework of information-processing models, the concept of **motor anticipation** refers to the set of processing operations required to prepare a motor program. Such processing occurs after the stimulus is identified and before the response is executed. During the first part of the preparation process, the electrical activity that would be recorded when a muscle is contracted is not evident, whereas later in the process, the muscle is activated, but before the movement begins. This contrast is strong evidence in favor of mental processes being used to set up motor programs. Such findings demonstrate that there are two distinct stages to motor anticipation: the planning processes—which can also be used to create mental simulations—and the processes that initiate production of the response. Furthermore, it has been demonstrated that the time to begin a response after a cue increases with the complexity of the action, a relationship that suggests that a more complex action requires more time to plan.

What exactly is happening in the brain during motor anticipation? In humans, brain electrical activity can be measured by electroencephalography (EEG). Electrical negativity is related to cortical activity, and it is well known that before a movement there is a slow buildup of such an electrical signal over the central regions of the cortex. This electrical signal, called the *readiness potential,* appears to originate in the SMA. Another such signal, originating from the prefrontal cortex, precedes voluntary action by a longer time than does the readiness potential. In addition, fMRI studies have demonstrated that anticipation is not restricted to an increase in activation in the SMA, but also includes the parietal cortex, the thalamus, and the cerebellum (Decety et al., 1992). These findings suggest that motor anticipation takes into account not only the desired movement itself (the output of the system), but also its context and means. Such representations could be useful not simply to control movements, but also in many forms of reasoning and problem solving.

As we mentioned earlier, to use motor representations in reasoning and problem solving, you need to prevent yourself from actually moving (at least until you are ready). Motor anticipation has inhibitory effects at the spinal level, the level of reflexes that—to be useful—must take place very quickly, in less time than would be necessary for the stimulus to reach the brain for processing and response. It has been demonstrated that during preparation for a movement, inhibition occurs at the level of the vertebra corresponding to the relevant set of muscles. Preparing to kick a soccer ball, for example, would involve inhibition relatively far down the spinal cord, whereas preparing to throw a baseball would involve inhibition farther up. This mechanism allows the blocking of the movement by massive inhibition acting at the spinal level to protect motor neurons against a premature triggering of action. It is this inhibitory mechanism that enables you to keep from dropping a hot cup of boiling water when the water sloshes over onto your hand.

Here's an interesting twist, which provides insight into how motor cognition can be used for more than reasoning about our own actions: the representations that underlie our own motor programs are also used to anticipate the actions of others. This was demonstrated by a neuroimaging study in which participants were shown a black dot on a screen, moving as if someone were hand-writing a letter or, alternatively, as if someone were beginning to point to either a large or a small target (Chaminade et al., 2001). In both conditions perception of the first part of the movement of the dot influenced participants' expectation of the next. For example, seeing a dot move as if someone were hand-writing produced activation in cortical areas used to produce hand-writing. By the same token, studies have shown that people can visually anticipate the consequence or outcomes of actions. Flanagan and Johansson (2003) investigated participants' eye movements while they watched another individual perform a task. The observers' eye movements were similar to those that occurred when participants actually performed the task.

We have been discussing motor programs largely in the context of guiding ongoing actions, but we humans can also use such programs to anticipate and plan our future actions. One way to do that is by imaging how we would behave in various contexts.

2.3. Mental Simulation of Action

It is now a small step to see how we can set up "mental simulations" of actions. We build the same motor programs that could control action, but stop them from engaging the neural structures that actually produce movements. Instead, we use the motor programs to guide movements in mental images, which allows us to "see" the consequences of certain actions. For example, you can note the precise angle at which you should hold your hand in order to shoot one of that giant hound's vital organs. Unlike the situation with motor programs, we are aware of our mental simulations.

If the same motor programs that guide movements in mental images also guide actual movements, then we would expect that practicing with mental imagery should help a person learn to perform the corresponding activity. And, in fact, much behavioral and neurophysiological evidence has shown that motor imagery has significant positive effects on motor skill learning, that is, on the mastery of a complex action sequence such as putting a golf ball. Indeed, researchers have demonstrated that changes in motor programs induced by mental training may actually make a person stronger. For example, Yue and Cole (1992) compared finger strength in two groups, one that performed repeated isometric muscle contractions and one that received motor imagery training alone, learning to imagine making the movements without actually making them. Both groups increased finger strength, the isometric contraction group by 30 percent, the imagery group by 22 percent. Thus, strength increases can be achieved without repeated muscle activation.

One reason why motor imagery allows us to plan actual actions is that the constraints of the physical world shape our imagery in a manner similar to how they shape our actions. For example, when participants are asked to mentally walk toward targets placed at different distances, the amount of time it takes to perform this task varies according to the distance of the target. Moreover, the time it takes participants actually to walk toward the target is highly correlated with the time it takes them to imagine doing so. And when asked to imagine themselves walking toward a target while carrying a heavy load, participants reported longer times to reach the target than when asked to imagine walking the same distance while carrying a light load (Decety, 1996). In addition, Parkinson's patients (who experience a slowing of movements), when asked to produce and to imagine sequential finger movements, are slowed at *both* tasks (Dominey et al., 1995). Taken together, these findings suggest that motor imagery and motor production exploit the same representations and that the physical characteristics of objects and events exert an influence on both imagined and performed actions.

The neural difference between motor performance and motor imagery seems essentially to be a matter not of "what" but of "how much." The motor regions in the brain are activated not only during actual performance, but also in imagery, but less strongly than during actual performance. An fMRI study in which participants were requested to actually or mentally execute a finger–thumb opposition task found that the contralateral motor cortex was activated in both tasks (the imagery results are shown in Figure 11–3). In the mental execution task, however, the activation was never more than 30 percent of that found during actual execution (Roth et al., 1996).

Running across a dark moor to rescue a friend from the attack of a monstrous dog—as Watson is doing in the lines from *The Hound of the Baskervilles* quoted

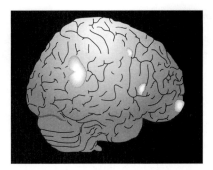

FIGURE 11–3 The power of motor imagery

Actually performing and consciously imagining an action—in this case, repeatedly touching thumb and finger—recruit similar sets of cortical areas: the premotor, motor, and parietal cortex and the cerebellum.

(Roth, M., Decety, J., Raybaudi, M., Massarelli, R., Delon, C., Segebarth, C., Morand, S., Decorps, M. & Jeannerod, M. (1996). Possible involvement of primary motor cortex in mentally stimulated movement: an fMRI study. *NeuroReport, 7:* 1280–1284. Reprinted with permission of Lippincott, Williams & Wilkins.)

at the beginning of this chapter—is a pretty dramatic situation, and the anecdotal evidence of many readers of thrillers suggests that a character's hard breathing and elevated heart rate can be mirrored in readers' responses. To find specific evidence for this kind of relationship, researchers investigated (in less hazardous circumstances) the idea that mental simulation taps the same neural processing as does actual experience, as reflected at the level of autonomic functions such as heartbeat and respiration (not generally under voluntary control). In a study that has been replicated by several research groups, measurements of cardiac and respiratory activity were made in healthy volunteers asked to perform a treadmill exercise at speeds of 5, 8, and 10 kilometers per hour (Decety et al., 1991). They were also asked to mentally simulate walking or running on the treadmill, coordinating their effort to the noise of the treadmill recorded during the actual exercise session. Both heart rate and pulmonary ventilation varied with the degree of imagined effort, although not to the point of equivalence with the physical exercise. The degree of actual autonomic activation of a participant mentally running at 12 kilometers per hour was comparable to that of a participant actually walking at 5 kilometers per hour. Nevertheless, imagery alone changed heart rate and breathing rate, which is powerful evidence that imagery can engage the autonomic nervous system.

What is the relationship between imagining your own actions via a mental simulation and anticipating seeing someone else's actions? To investigate this issue, Ruby and Decety (2001) asked volunteers either to imagine specific familiar actions such as brushing their teeth or stapling papers, or to imagine another person doing the same things. For a more detailed look at this work, see the accompanying *A Closer Look* box. The results indicated that both imagining themselves and imagining others performing a given action produced activity in the premotor cortex, the SMA, and the precuneus. These regions of the brain may account for shared motor representations between self and other. However, the overlap is not complete. When participants imagined their own actions, there were specific activations in the inferior parietal and

A CLOSER LOOK
Taking Perspective

Perrine Ruby and Jean Decety investigated the neural underpinnings of the phenomenon of taking another's perspective, that is, imagining someone else performing an action. They reported their results in 2001 in a paper entitled "Effect of Subjective Perspective Taking during Simulation of Action: A PET Investigation of Agency," *Nature Neuroscience, 4,* 546–550.

Introduction

Researchers have demonstrated a striking similarity between the neural networks involved in producing an action and in imagining ourselves performing this action. This network includes, in right-handed people, the inferior parietal and premotor cortex, the supplementary motor area (SMA) on the left side, and the right cerebellum. The present investigators asked "What processes are engaged when we imagine not ourselves acting, but rather someone else acting?"

Method

The investigators scanned the brains of individuals while they mentally simulated various everyday, familiar actions (for example, winding a watch); the participants were asked to simulate these actions either from their own perspective (imagining themselves performing those actions) or by adopting the perspective of observing another person (imagining the other person performing those actions). All actions selected for the study required the use of the right dominant hand. The participants (right-handed) were trained in the tasks before neuroimaging. In the scanner, these two perspectives were initiated either from photographs of familiar objects or from sentences describing familiar actions. Two baseline conditions were also performed (photos and spoken sentences). Each stimulus was presented for 5 seconds.

Results

Both the self-perspective and other-perspective mental imagery conditions evoked common activation in the SMA, premotor cortex, and the occipitotemporal region. However, the overlap between the two conditions was not complete. Adopting the perspective of another individual to simulate his or her actions resulted in selective activation of the frontopolar cortex and right inferior portion of the parietal lobe.

Discussion

This study demonstrates that imagining oneself acting and imagining another individual acting involve common neural resources. This finding is compatible with the idea that the same neural code is used in action production, imagination, and perception (Decety & Sommerville, 2003). The researchers also propose that the specific activation of both right inferior parietal cortex and frontopolar cortex when imagining the other acting provides a means whereby we can determine agency—whether an action should be attributed to ourselves or to another agent.

somatosensory cortices in the left hemisphere. When participants imagined the actions made by another person, additional activations were detected in the right inferior parietal lobule, the posterior cingulate, and the frontopolar cortex. These regions play a role in *distinguishing* the self from the other within the shared neural motor representation.

Finally, you might wonder whether *all* mental simulations rely on motor cognition. The answer is no. First, consider a classic finding reported by Shepard and Metzler (1971), illustrated in Figure 11–4. In this task, participants are asked whether the two objects in each pair are identical or are mirror images (try it yourself). Participants report that they "mentally rotate" one object until it lines up with the other, and only after this *mental rotation* do they compare the two objects. And, in fact, the further the object on the right needed to be rotated to line up with the one on the left, the longer the participants required to answer the question. The findings indicate that people not only can rotate objects in two dimensions, as if watching a CD spin, but also can do so in depth.

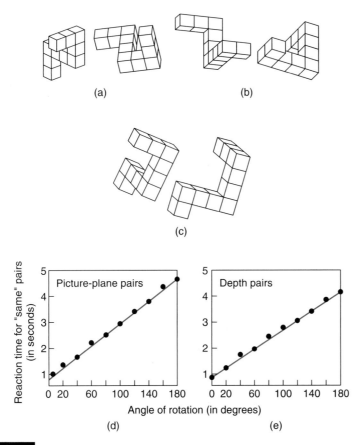

FIGURE 11–4   Mental rotation

When deciding whether the objects in each pair are identical or are mirror images, participants report mentally rotating one until it lines up with the other. And, in fact, the more rotation that is necessary, the more time the participants require (as shown in the graphs). This occurs both with picture-plane rotations (which occur in only two dimensions, such as occurs when a CD is spun around on a table-top) and depth rotations (which occur in the third dimension).

(From "Mental Rotation of Three-Dimensional Objects," by R. N. Shepard & J. Metzler, 1971, *Science, 171,* pp. 701–703. Reprinted with permission.)

How is such mental rotation accomplished? Research findings have shown that there is more than one way we can perform this task. For example, Kosslyn and colleagues (2001) asked participants to perform the Shepard and Metzler task while their brains were being scanned, and gave them specific instructions about how to imagine the objects rotating. In one condition, the participants were asked to imagine physically rotating objects (by twisting them in their hands). In this case, the primary motor cortex and other motor areas were activated—which is good evidence that motor cognition was at work. In the other condition, the participants were asked to imagine that an electric motor rotated the objects. In this case, the motor areas of the brain were not activated (but other frontal and parietal areas were)—which speaks against the involvement of motor cognition.

Many additional research findings have converged to show that although some types of mental simulations are guided by motor information, other types are guided by perceptual information about how objects appear when they move or interact in specific ways (Stevens, 2005). As we discussed in Chapter 4, mental simulations may be grounded in perceptual representations. Nevertheless, there is considerable evidence that motor cognition can also guide our mental simulations (which is why the two types of simulations are presented in the same chapter of this book).

✓ Comprehension Check:

1. What does motor priming tell us about motor cognition?
2. What is a motor program, and how are motor programs used in cognition?

3. IMITATION

How do we know which movements will achieve a certain goal? Without such knowledge, mental simulations could not operate. A fundamental idea is that we acquire such information partly by observing others. In fact, our cognitive systems are tailor-made to allow us to acquire knowledge of the consequences of actions by observing other people.

Specifically, we benefit from observing others and imitating them. Unlike mimicry, which is the tendency to adopt the behaviors, postures, or mannerisms of others without awareness or intent (Chartrand & Bargh, 1999), imitation is the ability to understand the intent of an observed action and then to reproduce it. Mimicry is highly present in nature; imitation is largely restricted to humans. This immensely useful attribute is even acknowledged to play an important role in cultural learning (Tomasello, 1999).

3.1. The Development of Imitation

The ability to imitate has been of interest to developmental psychologists for many decades. Initially, researchers thought that imitation was a sophisticated and late-developing ability. The famous developmental psychologist Jean Piaget (1953)

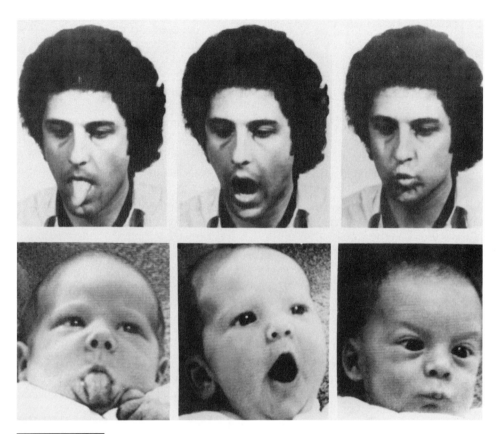

FIGURE 11–5   The power of imitation

Even newborns can imitate facial expressions.

(From: A. N. Meltzoff & M. K. Moore, "Imitation of facial and manual gestures by human neonates." *Science,* 1977, 75–78.)

claimed that infants' capacity to imitate does not emerge until approximately 8 to 12 months of age. Younger infants were thought to lack the ability to match observed movements with their own internally generated movements.

Studies during the last three decades have challenged this view. In a landmark study, Meltzoff and Moore (1977) demonstrated that imitation occurs even in newborn infants. Newborns shown simple facial gestures such as lip protrusion, mouth opening, and tongue protrusion are able to reproduce these gestures (Figure 11–5). Moreover, imitation is observed even after a delay is introduced between the stimulus and the response, ruling out reflexes as an account for the infants' reflection of the gesture.

Whereas initially infants imitate actions that are bodily directed, such as sticking out their tongues, by 6 months of age they can also imitate actions on objects, such as shaking a rattle (Butterworth, 1999). In addition, with age infants develop the ability to engage in deferred imitation over increasingly longer periods of time

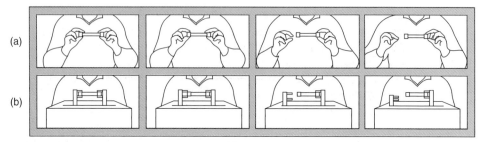

(a)

(b)

Time ⟶

FIGURE 11–6   What—or whom—do we imitate?

Eighteen-month-old children watched either (a) a human actor or (b) a mechanical device attempting to pull apart a dumbbell. All the children watched with interest, but only the children who watched the human actor imitated the action.

(Andrew N. Meltzoff, Understanding the Intentions of Others: Re-Enactment of Intended Acts by 18-month-old children. *Developmental Psychology,* 1995, vol. 31, no. 5, fig. 2, p. 844. Copyright © 1995 American Psychological Association. Reprinted with permission.)

(Barr et al., 1996). Moreover, even early imitation is not restricted to bodily movements but also includes facial emotional expressions (e.g., Field et al., 1982).

Meltzoff and Gopnik (1993) argued that infants' imitation of emotional facial expressions creates an internal feeling state in the infant that matches the partner's feeling state. A compelling demonstration of normal infants' self–other connection is illustrated by studies that show that infants imitate actions of people but not of objects (Legerstee, 1991). This result has been further explored with the reenactment procedure used by Meltzoff (1995), which makes use of toddlers' natural tendency to pick up behavior from adults, reenacting or imitating what they see. For example, in one study, two groups of 18-month-old children were shown either a human demonstrator or a mechanical device, both of them attempting to pull apart a dumbbell (Figure 11–6). The human actor never succeeded; a hand always slipped off one end of the dumbbell. The mechanical device failed in a similar fashion, its pincers sliding off the object. All the children were visually riveted by both displays, but only the children who had watched the human actor tried to dismantle the dumbbell themselves. Children apparently mentally represent the behavior of others in terms of goals and intended acts, instead of purely physical movements or motions. It may also be that children identify more closely with humans than with machines and unconsciously assume that they have competencies similar to those of other humans.

Furthermore, infants imitate what they understand. For example, fifteen-month-olds are happy to imitate an adult putting a bird to bed, but they are less willing to imitate an adult putting a car to bed (Mandler & McDonough, 2000). They not only represent actions as goal directed, but also seem to be able to have beliefs about what constitutes plausible goals.

In sum, these findings provide further evidence that the perception–action cycle is part of our built-in machinery for reasoning and problem solving; even young infants rely on comparable mental representations for their own and others' actions. Moreover, these findings fit neatly with the idea that we use our action system as a model to understand others's actions, which allows us to acquire motor representations from others, which we then can use to guide our own behavior.

3.2. The Cognitive Components of Imitation

If imitation were simply an automatic response like mimicry, it would not be of much use to us. After all, humans are not parrots. Our needs are far more diverse, and complex imitation is not reducible to mere perception or to a direct connection between perception and action. Instead, imitation includes having a plan to observe and then reproduce the observed movements, achieving the goal of the action, and reproducing the means by which the goal is achieved.

As we have seen in previous chapters, our goals and intentions affect how we process stimuli in the world. In fact a series of neuroimaging studies (Decety et al., 1997; Grèzes et al., 1998, 1999) has demonstrated that the *intention* to imitate actions has a top-down effect on the brain regions involved in the *observation* of actions (Figure 11–7). In these studies, adult participants were instructed to watch carefully actions performed by a human model either for later recognition or for imitation.

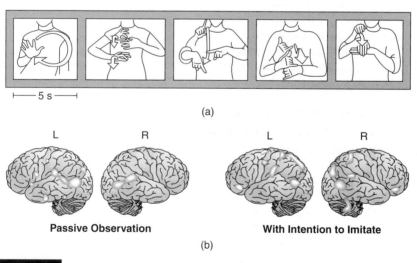

├── 5 s ──┤

(a)

L   R   L   R

Passive Observation   **With Intention to Imitate**

(b)

FIGURE 11–7   The power of intention

(a) Participants were shown a human model performing these actions, each for 5 seconds. (b) When they observed the actions for later imitation, as compared with passively observing the same actions, additional brain activation was detected in the supplementary motor area (SMA), the middle frontal gyrus, the premotor cortex, the anterior cingulate gyrus, and superior and inferior parietal cortices in both hemispheres. ("L" and "R" stand for left and right hemispheres.) Thus, the intention to imitate has a top-down effect on the information processing recruited when we observe actions.

(Decety, J., Grezes, J., Costes, N., Perani, D., Jeannerod, M., Procyk, E., Grassi, F., & Fazio, F. (1997). Brain activity during observation of actions. Influence of action content and subject's strategy. *Brain, 120:* 1763–1777. Reprinted with permission of Oxford University Press.)

When participants observed actions for later imitation, activation was detected in the SMA, the middle frontal gyrus, the premotor cortex, the anterior cingulate, and the superior and inferior parietal cortices in both hemispheres. A different pattern of brain activation was found when participants were passively observing the actions for recognition (in that case, the parahippocampal gyrus in the temporal lobe was the chief region activated). Thus, intention to imitate has a top-down effect on the information processing involved in action observation. Observing another person in order to imitate serves to tune regions involved in action generation. These studies strongly support the view that observing an action with the intention to imitate it involves neural regions similar to those engaged during actual production of the action.

In addition, the mechanisms that allow us to imitate depend on whether we observe meaningful or meaningless actions. Although normal adults and children have the ability to imitate both types of actions, evidence from research with apraxic patients suggests that the reproduction of meaningful and meaningless actions are mediated by different neural systems. Apraxia is a neurological disorder that impairs the ability to make voluntary movements, especially in the manipulation of objects. The left hemisphere, which when damaged impairs imitation, is dominant for the control of action and for language in most people, and it is often the case that apraxic patients have language as well as movement dysfunctions. Researchers have observed that in patients with apraxia the ability to imitate meaningful gestures is relatively spared, whereas the imitation of meaningless gestures is impaired (Goldenberg & Hagmann, 1997). On the basis of clinical observations, Rothi and colleagues (1991) postulated the existence of at least two partially independent processing routes. One route passes via long-term memory representations of familiar (and therefore meaningful) gestures. The other route, which can be used for the imitation of both meaningful and meaningless gestures, provides a direct link from perception to movement production.

Studies with normal participants showed that they too are better at imitating meaningful actions than meaningless ones: they were able to hold more meaningful than meaningless actions in working memory (Rumiati & Tessari, 2002). Also in normal participants, different brain regions are activated in imitation of the two types of action. In fact, different brain regions are involved when participants merely observe the two kinds of actions. For example, a PET study of participants observing meaningful actions showed strong engagement of the left hemisphere in frontal and temporal regions, whereas observation of meaningless actions involved mainly the right occipitoparietal pathway (Decety et al., 1997). These results support the view that meaningless and meaningful actions are processed via different routes.

What is acquired when we imitate? Not just the behaviors themselves. Rather we acquire the means to generate a motor program to achieve a goal. Humans have the ability to reproduce the goal state of an action (such as picking up a coffee cup), even when it requires reaching in a different way from what was observed, and to vary the means of achieving the goal (such as sliding—ever so carefully—a napkin on which the cup rests in order to bring the cup within reach before picking it up); and we can do this even in the absence of the model we initially observed (Tomasello, 1999). In one study, 14-month-old infants saw an event in which a human actor activated a light panel using her head, not her hand. When the reason the actor did not use a hand to manipulate the light panel was clear (if, for example, she was holding a blanket around her body with both hands), the toddlers imitated only the goal of the event, turning on the light panel by any available means. In contrast, when it was not apparent why the actor used her head to turn on the light, the toddlers reenacted both the means and the goal, using the head as did the model (Gergely et al., 2002).

Chaminade and colleagues (2002) used neuroimaging to attempt to identify to what extent, if any, the neural processing of goal and means differs. (In the language used in the problem-solving chapter, it's the difference between a "goal state" and a series of "operators".) In this experiment participants saw a human model making Lego constructions. The goal was defined as placing a block in a specified position and the means was defined as the motor program—the specific series of movements—used to achieve the goal. Participants were shown either the means and the goal (the whole action performed by the model, ending with block in position); the goal only (the block in the specified position); or the means only (the sequence of movements). All the participants were asked to imitate what they observed. When participants imitated either the goal or the means, there were partially overlapping clusters of activation in the right dorsolateral prefrontal cortex and in the cerebellum. This implies that these regions are involved in processing both the goals and the means of the action with the intention to imitate. Moreover, specific activity was detected in the medial prefrontal cortex during the imitation of the means, whereas imitating the goal was associated with increased activity in the left premotor cortex. Clearly, the processing of means and of goals is not identical. The act of imitation appears to involve two components (means and goals) that are at least partially dissociable.

Interestingly, an activation of the right medial prefrontal region was found only in the imitation of the means (Figure 11–8 on Color Insert O). This region is known to play a critical role in inferring others' intentions, and is consistently involved in tasks that require an understanding of the mental states of others (Blakemore & Decety, 2001). Its activation during imitation supports the idea that imitation involves inferring or identifying the intention of an action.

3.3. Simulation Theories of Action Understanding

Imagine yourself as Holmes. Seeing your friend attacked, you would probably have the same intention and consequently generate an action plan similar to Holmes's— disable the beast as fast as you can. When we put ourselves in another's place, either by observation or pure imagination, we can understand their plans (and later use such plans ourselves). How is it that we can come to understand the plans of others, if we must take into account unobservable, private, internal mental states?

Considerable speculation has surrounded this question for centuries (see the accompanying *Debate* box). Many researchers have speculated that our own actions, and their accompanying mental states, serve as a rich source of information for understanding the actions of others. In modern times, at least as far back as James Mark Baldwin (1861–1934), an early leading figure in experimental psychology, theorists have suggested that our experience as agents helps us to understand others

How Do We Know Whose Plan It Is?   DEBATE

The evidence indicates that we represent others' plans for actions in much the same way as we represent our own. Taken at face value, evidence for a shared representational system for actions of the self and actions of the other implies a paradox: if representations are in fact shared, how can a distinction between self and others be preserved? At first glance the answer may seem straightforward: we have a representation of the "self" and know when that representation is associated with plans. However, speculation on the nature—indeed, on the very existence—of the self is an age-old question. Perspectives have ranged from viewing the self as a tangible unified mental entity (Descartes, 1641/1985), to seeing the self as an illusion arising from various perceptions and sensations (Hume, 1739; James, 1890), to seeing the self as a mythical entity (Kenny, 1988). Twenty-first–century research findings can shed light on this classic debate.

Certainly it is true that sometimes we misreport actions performed by another as performed by the self and vice versa (Frith et al., 2000). Nevertheless, neuroimaging experiments have failed to find a "self center" in the brain (although there is some evidence for a role of the right prefrontal cortex in self-processing; see Keenan et al., 2000); instead, they have identified a set of areas, including the inferior parietal cortex, the insula, the posterior cingulate, and the prefrontal cortex, that—among other roles—play a role in the distinction between one's own action versus actions performed by others (Blakemore et al., 1998; Decety et al., 2002; Farrer & Frith, 2002; Farrer et al., 2003; Ruby & Decety, 2001). We all are usually readily able to attribute an action to its proper agent, we all have a "sense of ownership," and we all have the subjective experience of a sense of self. How is this accomplished?

There is accumulating evidence that the brain contains internal "models" that represent aspects of one's own body and its interaction with the environment (e.g., Frith et al., 2000). This interaction can be described by a feed-forward model of the general sort summarized by Decety and Sommerville (2003), which enables us to recognize the sensory consequences of self-generated actions. Every time a motor command is issued to make a movement, a copy of the motor command, known as an *efference copy,* is produced. This efference copy is then used to predict the sensory consequences of that movement (Greenwald, 1970). This sensory prediction is then compared with the actual sensory consequences of the act and the results of the comparison are used to determine the source of sensory events. This is why you cannot successfully tickle yourself: the sensory consequences of that action are predicted and cancelled. The sensory predictions associated with a wide variety of motor actions can be stored, providing a bank on which to draw.

This kind of model has been proposed to account for our awareness of ourselves as the source of our thoughts, desires, and beliefs (e.g., Frith, 1992). Investigators have explored how this feed-forward model could be used to predict what another person will do (Blakemore & Decety, 2001). When you see someone else perform an action, the forward model is reversed. You recruit the sensory consequences of the other person's action from your own model, use them to "estimate" what your own intentions would have been for that action, and attribute those intentions to the other person. The parietal cortex and the insula play a pivotal role in the comparison between one's own and another's intentions.

However, an alternative explanation for distinguishing self versus other within the shared representation network hinges on the timing of activation in a number of cortical areas, with no use of an efference copy. Grèzes et al. (2004) showed participants videoclips of themselves and of other, unfamiliar people lifting boxes of different weights. They asked the participants to decide whether the actor they watched had a correct or false expectation of the weight. When participants made this judgment, action-related structures in the frontal and parietal lobes were activated. But more than this, the neural activity started earlier when participants made judgments about their own actions than when they made judgments about others. This latter finding shows that the dynamics of neural activation within the shared cortical network provide a way to distinguish one's own actions from the actions of others. But they do not show that this is all there is to it. Only after future research is conducted will we come to understand exactly how we know when a plan is ours and ours alone, or whether it is in fact being evoked by our understanding of what another person is doing or intending to do.

as agents as well. Baldwin himself believed that imitation was the means by which children come to understand others:

> Now as he proceeds with these imitations of others, he finds himself gradually understanding the others, by coming, through doing the same actions with them, to discover what they are feeling, what their motives are, what the laws of their behavior. (Baldwin, 1897, p. 88)

In the early twentieth century, the social theorists Charles Horton Cooley and George Herbert Mead shared the notion that our understanding of other persons is based on analogy to the self. This idea has been taken up by philosophers of mind and psychologists in the form of *simulation theory,* which posits that we gain insight into the plans, beliefs, and desires that motivate others' actions by covertly simulating those same actions in ourselves, without actually performing them (e.g., Goldman, 2002; Gordon, 1986; Harris, 1989; Heal, 1998). Interestingly, this view is also compatible with the simulation theory in the field of physiology, as developed by Hesslow (2002), which is based on three assumptions about brain function: (1) behavior can be simulated by activating motor structures as is done during an overt action but suppressing the execution of that action; (2) perception can be simulated by internal activation of sensory cortex, without external stimuli; (3) both overt and covert actions can elicit perceptual simulation of their normal consequences—for example, by imagining twisting an object, you can produce a mental image of what you would see if the object were rotating (Kosslyn et al., 2001, 2006).

Proponents of the simulation view suggest that the behavior of others can be understood by simulating the same behavior in oneself and reflecting on the mental or internal states that accompany this simulation. The actions of others can also be predicted in this manner: you can put yourself in someone else's shoes, simulate the presumed mental states of the other person, and then deduce a likely action. Such simulations may help us gain access to knowledge stored in implicit representations, which otherwise would remain inaccessible.

3.4. Mirror Neurons and Self–Other Mapping

Until recently, the speculation that our understanding of the actions of others may be based on an analogy to ourselves had received scant empirical support. As we discussed earlier, plenty of research now suggests a common representation for the perception and production of actions (e.g., Prinz, 1997). Work with adults has documented perception-to-action transfer, which is part of the perception–action cycle: watching an action facilitates the later ability to plan and perform that action (well after priming effects affect such behavior; e.g., Hecht et al., 2001). Moreover, studies have documented perceptual interference during action planning (e.g., Müssler & Hommel, 1997), an effect that should be expected if action and perception share common representations and these similar representations are confused with one another.

We have seen that research reveals a shared neural basis for the observation and performance of action in both human and nonhuman primates. In addition electrophysiological recordings have shown that specific neurons in the ventral premotor cortex of monkeys discharge during execution of hand and mouth movements. But more than this, the same researchers discovered that most of these neurons discharge not only when the monkeys performed an action, but also when they observed the experimenter making a similar action (Rizzolatti et al., 1996). Neurons that behave this way are called mirror neurons (see Chapter 8). A subset of these mirror neurons also responds when the final part of an observed action, crucial in triggering the response, is hidden, and can therefore only be inferred (Umilta et al., 2001). Mirror neurons may play a central role in bridging what you see to what you can plan to do.

Evidence for mirror neurons in humans comes from various studies using different techniques. The first one, conducted by Fadiga and colleagues (1995), demonstrated with transcranial magnetic stimulation (TMS) that there is an increase in excitability of the motor system during the perception of actions performed by another person. This enhancement is selective: it was reflected by activity only in the muscles that the participants would use for producing the action observed (see also Fadiga et al., 2005). Converging evidence was reported in a study that used EEG as participants watched movies of objects in movement, animals in motion, gymnastic movements executed by a person, and still shots of these same events (Cochin et al., 1999). The results suggested the specific participation of the sensorimotor cortex during the observation of human motion. Magnetoencephalographic recordings have also shown activation of the motor cortex (Area M1) during the observation of action (Hari et al., 1998). These findings provide evidence that self and other actions are similarly coded in the brain. As such, they form the foundation for a system in which we can not only understand the actions of others on the basis of the production of our own actions, but also can then use others' actions as the basis for our own future actions.

Moreover, some researchers have proposed that this shared representational basis for self and other actions may serve as a powerful engine in development (Frye, 1991; Tomasello, 1999). If infants use information from their own actions to understand the actions of others, one might expect infants' ability to understand or interpret an action to be related to their own ability to perform that action. To test this hypothesis, Sommerville and Woodward (2005) examined how 10-month-old-infants responded to a simple cloth-pulling sequence, one in which an actor pulled a cloth to retrieve an out-of-reach toy. The researchers were interested in the relation between infants' ability to solve this cloth-pulling sequence in their own behavior and their ability to interpret the cloth-pulling sequence—that is, to identify the goal—when it was performed by another person. The results showed that the infants who were the most successful at generating goal-directed solutions in their own cloth-pulling behavior were the ones who recognized that the actor's actions on the cloth were in fact directed toward the ultimate goal of the sequence: the toy. In contrast, the infants who infrequently used goal-directed strategies to solve the cloth-pulling sequence in their own behavior appeared to misidentify the goal of the sequence in another person's actions. Follow-up analyses revealed that neither age (a proxy for developmental level) nor information-processing capacity (a proxy for intelligence) could account for the differences in action interpretation between the two groups.

In subsequent studies, it has been demonstrated that by 3.5 months infants detect a goal of another person's action better when the infants are given self-reaching experience (Sommerville et al., 2005). These findings provide support for the idea that plans for action and the perception of the actions of others are intimately connected, that they begin in infancy, and that infants' own developing capacities for action may provide them with important information about the actions of others.

However, we must close this section with a caveat: Just as not all mental simulations rely on motor processes, not all cognition about other people relies on motor processes. Motor cognition cannot reveal every aspect of the complex tangled web of beliefs and desires that motivate human beings—either in ourselves or in others (for a critique, see Jacob & Jeannerod, 2005).

Comprehension Check:

1. What are the two "processing routes" we can use in order to imitate? What are their relations to plans, previously stored or newly acquired?
2. What are mirror neurons and why are they important for understanding motor cognition?

4. BIOLOGICAL MOTION

The role of mirror neurons in imitation suggests that what we perceive is influenced by how we can move. If so, then our motor cognition systems may help us see subtle patterns of motion, specifically those that signal the presence of another living organism that plans and intends to carry out specific actions. This notion relies on the fact that all animals, human and nonhuman, produce unique patterns of motion. These patterns, no matter how distinct from one another, are all different from the motion of inanimate objects, and so are collectively called biological motion. As illustrated in the fictional, but possible, opening narrative, the ability to perceive biological motion from minimal visual cues can mean the difference between life and death, and we humans are very good at it.

In this section you will see that we humans are sensitive to biological motion, that we can readily distinguish among various types of motion that are on the surface very similar, and—crucially—that our motor cognition mechanisms are involved when a perceived motion is one that also can be produced. These findings are consistent with our conclusions from the previous section; actions are coded in a common framework for production and perception, both for the self and others.

Thus, we are able to observe others' actions and use that information later, when we ourselves are engaged in motor cognition and mental simulation.

These are the conclusions we will reach in this section. Let's now see why these conclusions are justified.

4.1. The Perception of Biological Motion

Like that of any other animal, our survival depends on the ability to identify, interpret, and predict the actions of other creatures. Perception of others' motion, in particular, plays a major adaptive role, important for our ancestors in distinguishing between prey and predator, friend and foe. To serve this purpose, the ability to detect biological motion must be fast, precise, and automatic.

Much behavioral evidence demonstrates that the human visual system is finely attuned to the perception of biological movements. The Swedish psychologist Gunnar Johansson (1973) developed the "point-light technique," attaching small light sources to the wrists, knees, ankles, shoulders, and heads of actors who were asked to perform various movements, such as walking, dancing, and running, in darkness (all that was visible to an observer were the moving lights). When asked to describe what they saw, participants readily identified human figures in motion and recognized the various types of actions performed by the actors. Several other research groups using this technique confirmed that the **kinematic pattern**—that is, the pattern of motion—that emerges from the moving lights is sufficient to convey a vivid and compelling impression of human movements, although the percept collapses to a jumble of meaningless lights when the point-light actor stands still (Figure 11–9).

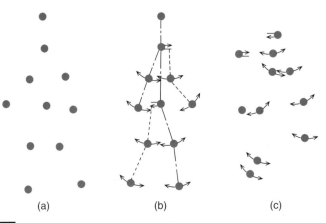

(a)   (b)   (c)

FIGURE 11–9   Our perception of point-light displays

(a) This static display is not usually seen as representing a human form. (b) When the same display moves coherently, it is easily seen as a person walking. (c) If the display moves randomly, it is often perceived as a swarm of bees.

(Bertenthal, B. I. (1993). Perception of biomechanical motion in infants: intrinsic image and knowledge-based constraints. In Carnegie symposium on cognition: visual perception and cognition in infancy. C. Granrud (ed.), pp. 174–214. Mahwah, NJ: Lawrence Erlbaum Associates. Reprinted with permission.)

For example, Kozlowski and Cutting (1977) showed that observers can make very precise discriminations when watching point-light displays, including recognizing the sex of the actors. Even more remarkable, this visual information is sufficient for observers, when filmed themselves as point-light actors, to distinguish themselves from other familiar people. However, when the films were presented upside-down, observers did not report seeing an upside-down human figure. Moreover, our ability to detect and identify biological motion is influenced by the specific kind of action made. Dittrich (1993) showed participants locomotory actions (walking, going upstairs), instrumental actions (hammering, stirring), and social actions (greeting, boxing). Participants recognized locomotory actions more accurately and faster than social and instrumental actions.

Even babies are sensitive to biological motion. Researchers have found that infants as young as 3 months prefer to look at a coherent display of point-lights that is produced by an upright walking person than a display of point-lights produced by an upside-down walking person. This implies that they are detecting the structure of the display (Bertenthal et al., 1984). How is this possible? Several physical constraints allow perception of human biological motion as distinct from object motion. For instance, the wrist can move back and forth and up and down relative to the position of the elbow, but it is always at a fixed distance from the elbow. Bertenthal (1993) proposed that infants' implicit knowledge of such constraints may reflect hard-wired characteristics of the visual system.

The development of infants' ability to detect biological motion provides an intriguing clue to the operation of how we plan our actions. As just noted, infants of 3 months discriminate between an upright and an upside-down point-light walker, as do older babies. But 3-month-old infants also discriminate between an upside-down point-light walker and a random pattern of lights, whereas 5- to 7-month-olds do not. Bertenthal's interpretation of this change is that by 5 months infants are responding to the perceived familiarity of the displays; that is, as a result of experience and accumulated knowledge, they recognize the upright display as a human walker, whereas they perceive the inverted and random displays equivalently because both are alien to their experiences. By the age of 5 months, infants are responding to these sorts of displays at a more complex level of processing as prior knowledge interacts with perception.

Because it seems that observational experience molds infants' developing perception of biological motion, an interesting question is whether the perception of biological motion is limited by an observer's experience of his or her own movement abilities. A fascinating case study is that of A.Z., who was born without limbs (Brugger et al., 2000). A.Z. was asked to judge whether she was viewing a left or a right limb (hand or foot) presented at a range of rotation angles. Normal control participants required more time when they would have to rotate their own limb greater amounts to line it up with the stimulus limb (engaging in a kind of mental rotation). In spite of never having had limbs, A.Z.'s perceptual judgments showed these same physical constraints. Thus, it seems that the perception of biological motion (at least locomotion) does not depend on motor experience per se, and that its core neural mechanism is hardwired.

4.2. Processing Biological Motion

The rapid recognition of a few moving point-lights as depicting the human form suggests that the correct grouping of the point-lights is accomplished by a specific neural network. In fact, researchers have reported a few cases of patients with brain damage who are impaired in the ability to detect biological motion but have few, if any, other deficits (Schenk & Zihl, 1997). The reverse dissociation, where perception of biological motion is intact while other types of perception are impaired, has also been reported (Vaina et al., 1990). The patient in this study suffered an impairment in the ability to discriminate different speeds of motion, and required more than the normal amount of organized information to detect biological motion, and yet had no difficulty in recognizing human activities other than locomotion portrayed by point-light displays.

In addition, Pavlova and colleagues (2003) have examined the visual sensitivity to biological motion in adolescents who were born preterm and had periventricular leukomalacia (PVL). This disorder, a softening of white matter near the ventricles of the brain (possibly caused by insufficient flow of blood to the brain before or at birth), produces early motor disorders. The researchers found in this group that the greater the extent of PVL lesions in the parieto-occipital region, the less the sensitivity to biological motion. These findings suggest that the parieto-occiptal region plays a role in the detection of biological motion.

More detailed evidence has come from several neuroimaging (fMRI) studies, which have identified a region in the posterior portion of the superior temporal sulcus (STS) that is active when participants are presented with Johansson-like point-light displays (Figure 11–10 on Color Insert P) (Grèzes et al., 2001; Grossman & Blake, 2001; Howard, 1996). This region lies anterior and superior to the visual area V5 (also called area MT), which is involved in the perception of motion. Another region, in the anterior part of the intraparietal sulcus (part of the parietal lobe) in the left hemisphere, has been found to be engaged during the perception of real human actions (Grafton et al., 1996; Grèzes et al., 1998; Perani et al., 2001). Consistent with our earlier discussion of mental simulation, the mere imagination of biological motion is sufficient to activate the region of the STS, although the activation is weaker than during actual perception of point-light displays (Grossman & Blake, 2001). When you read about the hound jumping onto its intended victim, those words were translated into representations of visual motion—and such representations are processed by cortical areas devoted to processing observed motion.

4.3. Motor Cognition in Motion Perception

When you read about Watson's terrifying experience, you did not confuse his movements with those of the giant hound. Our ability to perceive biological motion goes beyond merely distinguishing the movements of people and animals from those of cars and balls. In one study of children between 29 and 94 months, researchers showed that different cortical areas are involved in perceiving human, animal, and virtual human movements (Martineau & Cochin, 2003). Moreover, neuroimaging experiments have revealed neural activations that are specific to human actions

(a)

(b)

FIGURE 11–11   At the races

(a) *The Derby at Epsom* (1821), by Théodore Géricault. A beautiful painting—and physically impossible. In reality, the moment in a horse's gait when all four legs are off the ground comes not when the legs are extended but when they are collected under the body, as in (b), a photograph of the Preakness winner, 2003.

(a) ("The Derby at Epsom," Theodore Gericault (1821). Musee du Louvre, Paris.)
(b) (Photograph by Gary Hershorn Courtesy of Corbis/Reuters America LLC.)

(such as grasping a coffee mug) and that are not elicited by movements with similar visual properties, such as actions in virtual reality displays or actions produced by a robot (Decety et al., 1994; Perani et al., 2001; Tai et al., 2004). Now, let's consider the key question: Why do we perceive motion with such great specificity?

Human movements are the only ones that we produce as well as perceive. Our anatomy places constraints (i.e., limitations) on the actions that we perform, which in turn constrain the way that we can imagine and perceive action—and the way we can imagine actions plays a crucial role in our ability to plan our own actions. Thus, unless we have particular equine knowledge we don't immediately see what's "wrong" in the painting in Figure 11–11. It has been hypothesized that our perception of human movement in others is mediated by *tacit* knowledge of how our bodies work; such knowledge is truly unconscious—we typically do not even know that we have it. And such knowledge plays a key role in guiding our mental simulations—in making them behave in ways that mimic reality.

A compelling demonstration of the involvement of tacit motor knowledge in detecting biological movements is provided by studies making use of the phenomenon of **apparent motion**, the illusion created when visual stimuli in nearby locations appear in close succession. Apparent motion is the effect that makes the blinking lights on a theatre marquee seem to be moving around the frame, and the two lights on a construction warning sign appear to be a single light moving back and forth. It's what makes flipbooks and movies possible.

In a series of elegant studies, Shiffrar and Freyd (1990) showed participants alternating series of photographs of a human body in different postures. In one series, the postures were such that the direct transitions between any two sequential photographs corresponded to possible movements. The direct transitions between photographs in the other sequence violated the "solidity constraint" (that one solid object cannot pass through another solid object) and thus were impossible. When participants viewed the two series, the apparent motion they saw between two sequential photographs changed with the amount of time between the presentation of one photograph and the presentation of the next. This time between the onsets of two stimuli is called the *stimulus onset asynchrony,* or SOA. At short SOAs, participants reported seeing the shortest—but impossible—motion path, whereas with increasing SOAs they saw the motion path consistent with human movements (Figure 11–12). Paths of biological actions are more likely to be seen at SOAs that match the time in which the action could actually be performed. In contrast, when participants are shown photographs of inanimate objects, they consistently perceive the same shortest path of apparent motion, regardless of the SOA (Shiffrar & Pinto, 2002).

Neuroimaging investigations confirm that differences between perceiving object motion and human motion are due to the fact that there is direct involvement of motor areas in human motion but not in object motion. In one such study participants were presented with static images of a human model in different positions as well as objects in different spatial configurations (Stevens et al., 2000). Members of the pairs were presented in sequence, so that one position seemed to move into the other. The participants were asked to rate the trajectories of the perceived motion path. For the human model, the perceived motion was either a possible or impossible path. The results indicated that the left primary motor cortex, the parietal cortex in both hemispheres, and the cerebellum were activated specifically when participants perceived possible paths of human movement. In contrast, no selective activation of these areas was found during conditions of physically impossible movement paths. Instead, viewing impossible motion paths resulted in a dramatic increase of activity in the ventromedial prefrontal cortex, a region researchers previously found to be involved when people try to comprehend incoherent pairs of sentences (Ferstl & von Cramon, 2002) and social conflicts (Bechara et al., 2000a).

These findings provide evidence that the perception of human apparent motion relies not only on visual processes but also on motor processes, and also that perceiving object motion and human motion rely on different neural networks. Furthermore, the results are consistent with an idea discussed earlier: that we may understand the actions of others in terms of our own motor system and the way that we would plan our own actions (Shiffrar & Pinto, 2002; Viviani, 2002).

But wait a moment—there seems to be a contradiction between the neuroimaging findings using point-light displays and those based on apparent motion. Recognition of human movement in point-light displays is not affected by lesions in the motor production areas, and neuroimaging studies have consistently shown that brain activation is restricted to the temporo-occipito-parietal junction and the interparietal sulcus, not motor areas per se. The apparent-motion studies, however, have shown that the perception of biological movements is constrained by the motor

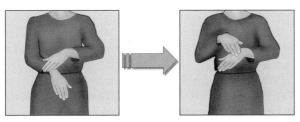

SOA: 150–350 ms

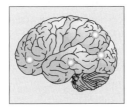

○ = Site of activation

(a)

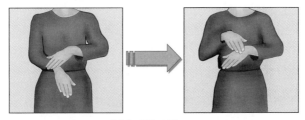

SOA: 550–750 ms

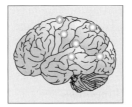

○ = Site of activation

(b)

FIGURE 11–12   The phenomenon of apparent motion

(a) A direct path—although physically impossible—is perceived when the interval between presentations of stimuli (the SOA) is short: the hands seem simply to exchange positions. Activation is detected in the frontal lobe, middle temporal gyrus, and posterior parietal lobe. (b) At longer SOAs, an indirect (and possible) path is perceived, one that corresponds to human movements. There is activation in the motor cortex, superior temporal sulcus, and inferior parietal cortex.

(From "The Visual Analysis of Bodily Motion" (pp. 381–399), by M. Shiffrar and J. Pinto, in *Common Mechanisms in Perception and Action,* edited by W. Prinz and B. Hommel, (2002), New York: Oxford University Press. Copyright 2002 by Oxford University Press. Reprinted with permission.)

capacities of the participants, and neuroimaging research has shown that brain areas involved in producing motor actions are activated during visual processing of plausible movements (Grèzes & Decety, 2001; Stevens et al., 2000). How do we account for this apparent conflict?

The explanation for this apparent inconsistency may rest in part on the fact that studies using point-light displays to investigate biological motion often are based on the detection of *locomotion*. Locomotion has a fundamental evolutionary and functional significance and its neural processing is fast and automatic; for those reasons the posterior, superior temporal sulcus alone may be enough to act as a detector, without the involvement of specifically motor areas. On the other hand, studies that investigate apparent motion often use more complex stimuli that, unlike the point-light displays, depict the shape of a human body and the movements depicted are not confined to locomotion. The processing used for these stimuli is thus far more complex than that used for point-light displays.

 Comprehension Check:

1. Why is human sensitivity to biological motion relevant for understanding how we reason about actions?
2. What is special about our perception of biological motion?

Revisit and Reflect

1. *What is the nature of motor cognition?*

   Motor cognition relies on internal representations that are used to plan and predict our own actions as well as to anticipate and understand the actions of others. As such, these representations are present early in life, elaborated through interactions between the self and others, and can be shared across individuals.

   Think Critically
   - What is the role of motor cognition in long-term planning (e.g., planning a vacation you'll take in 3 months)?
   - There are constraints on motor cognition and planning that correspond to the way in which the human body is constructed. Research findings suggest, however, that even people with atypical bodies incorporate these constraints in their action perception. If this is the case, what is the role of learning or experience in motor cognition?

2. *What is a mental simulation of action?*

   We can create and run motor programs, and "observe" how they affect mental images. We may run such mental simulations in order to achieve a goal, or in an effort to understand another person's actions. In some cases, however, mental simulations are guided not by motor information, but rather by perceptual and conceptual information.

Think Critically

- What sorts of problems are best solved with mental simulations? What sorts of problems are likely to be difficult to solve with mental simulations?
- Does all motor cognition involve mental simulations? (*Hint:* We are aware of having mental images—are we aware of all motor cognition?)

3. *Why and how do we reproduce the actions of others?*

The mental representations used in motor cognition are based in part on our observations of others. The ability to imitate is present very early in life, and plays an important role in understanding others. There is ample evidence to suggest that imitation involves more than simply reproducing observed behavior; rather, we infer others' intentions and goals. When later planning to achieve the same goal, we can use a range of possible actions.

Think Critically

- Does the fact that we humans are capable of imitation imply that we never engage in mimicry? What is the relation between motor priming and mimicry?
- What sorts of plans may not involve actions? Are there any plans that in principle can never lead to actions?

4. *What is the role of motor cognition in perception?*

Motor cognition not only depends in part on representations created during perception, but also actually affects the case of engaging in some forms of perception. The brain has evolved specific neural mechanisms that detect and process the motion of other animals, including humans. In addition, human actions are processed differently than other types of biological motion. Crucially, the motor system is involved when we perceive actions that we can produce, which thereby makes it easier for us to use memories of previously observed actions to produce our own actions in the future.

Think Critically

- If a capacity is innate, does this mean that learning plays no role? If learning plays a role in detecting and processing biological motion, what role might it play?
- If you were temporarily paralyzed, do you think you could still perceive actions even if you couldn't produce them? If so, would this disprove the idea that the motor system is involved when we perceive actions?

CHAPTER

12

Language

Learning Objectives

The sidewalk is full of jostling people, the traffic in the street busy with midday cars and trucks. Through the crowd you spot a friend you haven't seen in a while, wave, and catch up to her. She's wearing a t-shirt (not her style) printed with the words "The Happy Pig" and a cartoony picture of a pig wearing an apron and carrying a tray of food. You ask her about this fashion statement. "Oh, it's where I work now," she says. "It's, well, a ... um, sort of Asian-fusion-deli place. They have terrific sesame noodles, totally awesome." A bus roars by during the last of this, and you don't actually hear all of your friend's last sentence, but somehow you understand it anyway. "Where is this place?" you shout as another bus comes up. "It's at the corner of—" Again, you can't hear, and this time you have no idea what she said. Your friend fishes a takeout menu out of her backpack and shows you the address. "Great, I'll try it!" you call as you're swept away by the crowd.

Since the days of your early education, reading or hearing a sentence and comprehending its meaning has ordinarily been effortless and essentially instantaneous. (Fully appreciating the underlying concepts, of course, may pose more difficulty!) As the expert reader and listener that you are now, you may find it hard to recapture the sense of struggle you may have had as a young child. In fact, the production and comprehension of language are tremendously complex activities. In this chapter we will address these questions:

1. What are the different levels of language representation and how do they fit together?
2. How does language comprehension proceed at these different levels?
3. What are the similarities and differences in comprehension processes for spoken language and for reading, and what are the similarities and differences in comprehension processes for words and for sentences?
4. How do language users plan and produce language?
5. What is the relationship between language and thought?

1. THE NATURE OF LANGUAGE

Whenever you hear or read a sentence, you're focusing on the meaning and relating it to information stored in your long-term memory. Despite the ease with which you now accomplish this, the cognitive processes that you perform to figure out the meaning of that sentence are actually very complicated. The discipline that explores the comprehension of language and the mental processes underlying it is **psycholinguistics**, the study of the comprehension, production, and acquisition of language. As its name suggests, the field draws both on psychology and on linguistics, the study of language and language structures.

1.1. Levels of Language Representation

Every sentence you hear or read is composed of many different kinds of information, among them sounds or letters, syllables, words, and phrases. These pieces of language fit together rather like an interlocking puzzle, so that the many components contribute to the overall meaning of a sentence. Language researchers refer to the pieces as different *levels* of language representation, and together they make up the grammar of the language. The term *grammar* often suggests rules of usage based on ideas like the *parts of speech*. Linguists and psycholinguists use the term differently. They use the term **grammar** to refer to the sum of knowledge that someone has about the structure of his or her language. Most of this grammatical knowledge is unconscious, but it underlies our ability to speak and comprehend a language with ease. Figure 12–1 diagrams the different levels of language representation that underlie the ability to understand the sentence "The chef burned the noodles."

At the top of the diagram is the level of **discourse**, which refers to a coherent group of written or spoken sentences. This level mentally represents the meaning of the entire sentence, beyond the meaning of the individual words. In the sentence "The chef burned the noodles," an important part of the discourse representation is that "chef" is the agent performing the action and that "noodles" are the things being acted on. One way to represent this relationship is through **propositions**, assertions

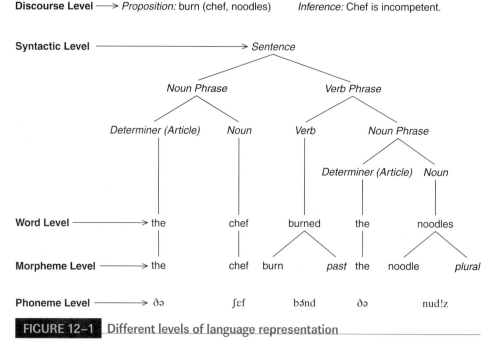

Discourse Level ⟶ *Proposition:* burn (chef, noodles)   *Inference:* Chef is incompetent.

Syntactic Level ⟶ *Sentence*

Noun Phrase   *Verb Phrase*

Determiner (Article)   *Noun*   *Verb*   *Noun Phrase*

Determiner (Article)   *Noun*

Word Level ⟶ the   chef   burned   the   noodles

Morpheme Level ⟶ the   chef   burn   *past*   the   noodle   *plural*

Phoneme Level ⟶ ðə   ʃɛf   bɔ̃nd   ðə   nud!z

FIGURE 12–1 Different levels of language representation

Shown here are the levels of representation for the sentence "The chef burned the noodles" and the relationships between them; this notation is known as a phrase structure tree.

made in clauses in sentences (Kintsch, 1998), as diagrammed as *burn(chef, noodles)* in Figure 12–1. A propositional representation (as shown also in Figure 1–4) concisely relates the action, the one doing the action, and the thing being acted on. A key part of language comprehension is arriving at this basic understanding of who did what to whom. The discourse representation also links the sentence meaning to the context in which it occurs (the conversation you're having or the text you're reading) and to information in long-term memory. This linkage allows you to relate the information in the sentence to prior knowledge ("The noodles were burned the last time we ate here, too!") and to generate inferences ("Hmm, maybe we should try another restaurant.").

Beneath the discourse level in the diagram is the level of syntax, which specifies the relationships between the types of words in a sentence (such as between nouns and verbs); syntax is a way of representing sentence structure, and many psychologists and linguists believe that it is part of our mental representation of a sentence as well. Here the sentence is composed of both a subject noun phrase ("the chef"), which at the discourse level maps onto the role of doer of the action; a verb phrase ("burned"), which describes the action; and another noun phrase ("the noodles"), which serves as the direct object and maps onto the role of the thing acted on. A standard way of representing the syntax of a sentence is a phrase structure tree, a diagram of a sentence that illustrates its linear and hierarchical structure (Figure 12–1). A phrase structure tree is a convenient way to talk about different components of a sentence but it's also much more than that. Many linguists and psycholinguists believe that in the process of understanding a sentence, we build a mental representation of the tree's hierarchical representation of word relationships, and that this process is a key step in determining the meaning of the sentence. It is at the syntax level that comprehenders work out how the word order will relate to discourse information such as "doer of action." For example, *The chef burned the noodles* and *The noodles were burned by the chef* both have the chef as the doer of the action at the discourse level, but the syntax of the two sentences is different.

A dramatic example of the importance of the syntactic level in language comprehension comes from studies of patients with brain damage. Patients who have had a stroke or other damage that affects parts of (typically) the left hemisphere of the brain may have aphasia, a language or speech disruption (so called from Greek words meaning "without speech"). Aphasia manifests itself in many different ways; one of them, which disrupts the syntactic level of representation, is called nonfluent aphasia or Broca's aphasia, named for the French physician Paul Broca (1824–1880), who first described an aphasic patient with damage to a left frontal area of the brain now known as Broca's area. This region is shown in Figure 12–2, which also shows

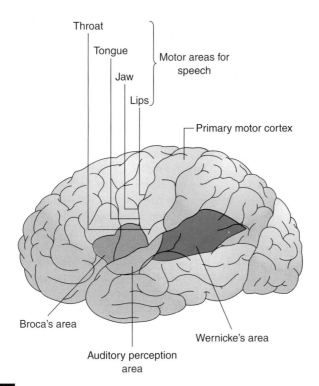

Throat
Tongue
Jaw
Lips
Motor areas for speech
Primary motor cortex
Broca's area
Auditory perception area
Wernicke's area

FIGURE 12–2 Key areas of the brain important for language

Broca's area and Wernicke's area are named for nineteenth-century neurologists, who each documented the language impairments of patients with damage to the respective region. The areas of the motor cortex that send information to structures important in speech production are also shown, as is the auditory perception area, where speech is perceived.

other key areas important in language. Broca hypothesized that the region that now bears his name was the location of language representations in the brain. We now know that many other areas are important for language, and that the behavioral syndrome called Broca's aphasia is not always tied to damage to Broca's area, but the names *Broca's area* and *Broca's aphasia* persist in part to honor this pioneer who sought to link language and brain.

Patients with Broca's aphasia have difficulty relating the discourse and syntactical levels of representation. Thus, they may have a great deal of difficulty distinguishing the meanings of *The chef burned the noodles, The noodles burned the chef,* and *The noodles were burned by the chef.* Their difficulty is not in the meaning of the individual words—these patients typically still know the meanings of words such as *chef* and *noodles*—but with the relationships among them in the sentence. Because their knowledge about how the world works is unimpaired, they would tend to interpret *all* these sentences according to the most likely combination of the words *chef, noodles,* and *burned,* and thus interpret all three sentences to mean that the chef burned the noodles. The language disruption experienced by these patients highlights an important feature of syntax, that recombination of words can produce sentences with different meanings—sometimes even unexpected meanings, such as *The noodles burned the chef.*

Moving to the next level of the diagram in Figure 12–1, below syntax, are the *word* and *morpheme* levels. These levels encode word meanings: for example, *chef* refers to "someone skilled in cooking food." Morphemes, the building blocks of words, are the smallest unit of meaning in a language. Some words, such as *the* and *chef,* are composed of only a single morpheme, whereas others are built up from several morphemes. *Noodles,* for example, is composed of two morphemes, the morpheme *noodle* plus the plural morpheme, which we typically write as *-s;* and *burned* is also composed of two morphemes, *burn* plus the past tense morpheme, typically written as *-ed.*

Compared to many other languages, English has a very simple morphological system and very few morphemes, such as the plural and past tense forms, that attach onto other morphemes (these are called *bound morphemes*). An example of a language with a much richer morphology is American Sign Language (ASL), the language typically used by the deaf in the United States. Figure 12–3 shows the verb meaning *give* in ASL in its bare state (equivalent to the infinitive form *to give* in English) and with several different bound morphemes added. The bound morphemes change the path of the gesture used in signing the verb, and as you can see from the last example in this figure, several bound morphemes can be combined during the production of the verb.

As well as classifying morphemes as bound or free, it is also useful to distinguish morphemes that carry a good deal of meaning from ones that have relatively less meaning but convey relatively more information about sentence structure. Morphemes such as *chef* and *burn* that convey meaning but do not indicate much about the structure of the sentence are called content morphemes. On the other hand, function words and function morphemes, such as *the* and the *-ed* past tense ending in English, convey less meaning, but convey a relatively large amount of information about relationships among words and about the syntactic structure of a sentence. For example, *the* signals that a noun is coming up, and the past tense morpheme *-ed*

(a) GIVE (uninflected)   (b) GIVE [durational] (give continuously)   (c) GIVE [exhaustive] (give to each)   (d) GIVE [[durational] exhaustive] (give continuously to each in turn)

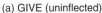

FIGURE 12–3   American Sign Language has a rich morphology

(a) The uninflected form of the verb *give,* without any bound morphemes. (b) Adding a *durational* morpheme, yielding the meaning *give continuously.* (c) Adding an *exhaustive* morpheme, meaning *give to each in turn.* (d) Adding both these morphemes yields the meaning *give continuously to each in turn.*

(Based on *What the Hands Reveal About the Brain* by H. Poivner, E. S. Klima and U. Bellugi, MIT Press, 1987. © 1987 by the Massachusetts Institute of Technology. Reprinted with permission.)

signals that, in this sentence, *burn* is a verb. Function morphemes (some of which are bound and some of which are free) link the levels of word and syntax. Interestingly, patients with Broca's aphasia, who have difficulty with syntax, also have difficulty perceiving and producing function morphemes. The speech of Broca's aphasics is halting and typically contains very few function words or morphemes. For example, when asked to describe the scene shown in Figure 12–4, a patient with Broca's aphasia said "Boy . . . cookie . . . down . . . taking . . . cookie" (Goodglass & Geschwind, 1976). The only function morpheme here is the *-ing* suffix on the verb; other function words, such as *a* and *the,* are omitted.

In contrast, patients with **Wernicke's aphasia,** also known as **fluent aphasia,** have a very different set of problems, which are at the word and morpheme levels. This type of aphasia often results from damage to Wernicke's area, also shown in Figure 12–2, which is named for Carl Wernicke (1848–1904), the Polish-German neurologist and psychiatrist who described a patient with damage to this area.

Patients with Wernicke's aphasia have generally good use of function morphemes, and their speech is typically fairly grammatical, with nouns, verbs and other parts of speech generally in the correct places in the sentence. But these patients can no longer produce content morphemes correctly, and the resulting speech is often nonsensical. In this example, a patient is attempting to describe the picture shown in Figure 12–4: "Well this is . . . mother is away here working her work out o' here to get her better, but when she's looking in the other part. One their small tile into her time here. She's working another time because she's getting, too" (Goodglass & Geschwind, 1976). Patients with Wernicke's aphasia also have great difficulty comprehending content morphemes, with the result that they often have very little understanding of what is said to them.

FIGURE 12–4   The "cookie theft picture"

This picture is often given to aphasic patients to describe because its rich mix of people, objects, actions, and disasters provides the opportunity for many different kinds of descriptions.

The distinctions between Broca's and Wernicke's aphasias show two important points about how language is organized. First, the differences between the impairments of the two kinds of patients emphasize the distinct levels of how language is represented mentally and in the brain, and demonstrate how different levels can be affected to varying degrees. Second, the nature of patients' impairments shows the degree to which these levels are interconnected: problems at one level, such as the disruption of function morphemes suffered by Broca's aphasics, can contribute to difficulties at other levels, such as interpreting sentence syntax—which can then lead to difficulties in the comprehension of sentence meaning.

Look back one more time at Figure 12–1. The last level in the diagram shows phonemes, the smallest distinguishable units of speech sound that make up the morphemes in a given language. Spelling is not a precise enough system for representing speech sounds for a number of reasons. For one thing, writing systems vary in different languages (think of a page of the same text in Russian, Chinese, English, Hindi, and Arabic); for another, spelling rules in many languages have a number of exceptions that do not affect pronunciation (think of *bear* and *bare*, *feet* and *feat*); and, moreover, even native speakers of the same language may pronounce words differently. The solution is an alphabet of symbols for speech sounds—a phonetic alphabet—in which the speech sounds of all languages can be represented, independent of how they are spelled in any word or writing system. These are the symbols used to represent phonemes, as in Figure 12–1; you may be familiar with some of them from studying a foreign language or drama (many dialect coaches use the phonetic alphabet to help actors perfect an accent), or from the pronunciation key in a standard dictionary.

Like phrase structure trees, phonemes provide useful notation; they also lead to another claim about how language is represented mentally. Many language researchers believe that our knowledge of words includes representations of their phonemes. That is, while we are consciously aware of breaking a word down into letters for spelling, we also unconsciously represent words in terms of phonemes.

Patients with Broca's aphasia offer further demonstration of how many of these different language levels relate to one another. We have seen that Broca's aphasia is associated with poor comprehension and production of syntax, and also with poor comprehension and production of function morphemes. Some research links these deficits with the phoneme level, indicating that Broca's aphasia may also include impairments in *perceiving* the function morphemes. Pairs of words were played to Broca's aphasia patients (Bird et al., 2003). Some of them, such as *pray* and *prayed,* were identical except that the second member of the pair contained the past tense function morpheme -*ed;* in the phonetic alphabet, they are represented as [pɹey] and [pɹeyd]. Other pairs, such as *tray* and *trade* (in the phonetic alphabet [tɹey] and [tɹeyd] also sounded very similar, but were two different words with unrelated meanings. For each pair, the patients were asked whether they heard two different words or the same word said twice. The patients had great difficulty hearing the difference between *pray* and *prayed;* very often when they heard such pairs they thought the same word was being repeated. The patients were equally inaccurate in distinguishing *tray* from *trade.* The patients' difficulty seems to be linked specifically to poor perception and comprehension of certain sequences of speech sounds, which in turn can lead to poor comprehension of function morphemes, and thence to problems interpreting syntax and ultimately understanding sentence meaning. The point is not simply that Broca's patients have difficulty perceiving speech, but that language representations are interlocking, and failure at one level can have consequences that spread throughout the language system.

1.2. Language versus Animal Communication

There are more than 5,000 human languages in the world, representing a huge reservoir of phonemes, morphemes, words, and syntax. With all this variety, what do human languages share that the communication systems of other animals lack? Answering this question would be an important step in the search to define what it means to be human. Many animals that live in social groups, including songbirds, many species of monkey, and honeybees, have complex systems of communication. The American linguist Charles Hockett (1916–2000) compared animal communication systems and human languages and identified a number of key and unique characteristics of human languages (Hockett, 1960). These include duality of patterning, that is, the property that *meaningful* units such as morphemes are made up of *meaningless* units such as phonemes, which can be recombined over and over again to make different words. For example, the phonemes [t], [k], and [æ] (æ is the phonetic symbol for the short-a sound) can be arranged in different ways to make three different English words: [kæt], [ækt], and [tæk] (spelled *cat, act,* and *tack*). Animal communication systems, such as the alarm calls of vervet monkeys, do not have duality of patterning: vervets have one call for a leopard predator and another for an eagle, but they cannot recombine the sounds in the calls to make new calls.

Another important characteristic of language is its **arbitrariness**: in general, the relationship between the sound (or spelling) of a word and its meaning is not predictable. There is nothing about the sound [kæt] (cat) that intrinsically means a feline—the word does not sound like a cat or look like a cat, and the fact that we use [kæt] to mean a small mammal with whiskers that purrs is an accident of the history of English.

Perhaps the most important feature of human languages is their **generative capacity**: we humans can recombine morphemes, words, and sentences to convey a potentially infinite number of thoughts. Your waitressing friend's t-shirt had a drawing that you described to yourself as *cartoony*, a combination of the morphemes *cartoon* and *y*, an ending that often signifies "like." Even if you had never seen or heard this combination before, your own generative capacity would allow you to create it. And if you were to write about this encounter, describing the picture as "cartoony," your readers' generative capacity to understand new combinations of morphemes would allow them to determine the intended meaning.

Similarly, words can be combined over and over to make an endless variety of sentences. An important component of this generative capacity in syntax is **recursion**, that is, the embedding of pieces of a sentence (or an entire sentence) inside other pieces or sentences. Figure 12–5 shows the syntactic structure of a sentence with recursion, in that the relative clause *whom the manager hired yesterday* is

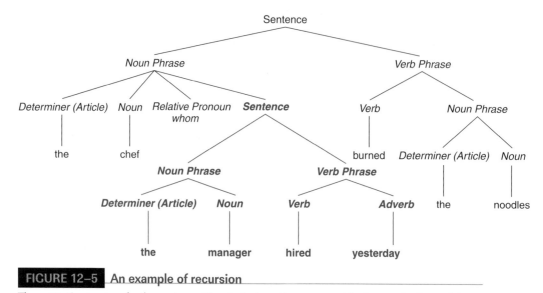

FIGURE 12–5 **An example of recursion**

The syntactic structure for the sentence *The chef whom the manager hired yesterday burned the noodles.* This sentence demonstrates *recursion*, the embedding of pieces of a sentence inside other pieces or sentences. In this example, the embedded portion is shown in blue.

embedded inside the simple sentence *The chef burned the noodles.* Although we typically keep our sentences fairly short, the use of recursion gives us the ability to make sentences that have many embeddings and could in principle be indefinitely long. For example, you could easily keep adding clauses onto the end of a sentence, as in *The chef burned the noodles that were made from the wheat that was grown on the farm that sat on the hill that was near the forest that. . . .*

The property of recursion has played an important role not only in psycholinguistics but generally in the development of cognitive psychology. Behaviorists, most notably B. F. Skinner, suggested that the syntax of sentences could be described as a chain of associations from one word to the next. Skinner suggested that behaviorist principles such as operant conditioning could explain how children learned language by being reinforced for adult-like speech. The linguist Noam Chomsky (1959) strongly criticized the behaviorist approach to language, arguing that the property of recursion could not be captured by any chain of associations. For example, in the sentence *Any chef who burns the noodles gets fired*, the verb *gets* and its subject (*chef*) are not adjacent because there's an embedded clause about burning noodles in between. A simple chain of association between adjacent words or phrases would incorrectly associate the noun *noodles* with *gets* rather than the real subject, *chef*. Chomsky's position, that the behaviorist account is inherently incapable of accounting for human linguistic abilities, was a crucial step in the rejection of behaviorist accounts of all aspects of human abilities. (Operant conditioning does explain some aspects of emotional learning, though, as discussed in Chapter 8.)

Even though the communication systems of highly intelligent nonhuman animals do not have the properties that Hockett observed in human languages, a number of researchers have asked whether chimpanzees could learn a language system if it were taught to them. Because the chimpanzee **vocal tract** (the parts of the anatomy needed for making sounds, including the vocal cords, mouth, and nose) is incapable of making most human speech sounds, researchers have taught chimps sign languages (Gardner & Gardner, 1969; Terrace, 1979) or communication systems using shapes on computer keyboards (Savage-Rumbaugh et al., 1986). Researchers found that chimps were good at using symbols or signs to make requests for food or other desires (for example, "strawberry," "tickle me"). However, many researchers agree that these animals' linguistic behavior does not go much beyond this, and it pales in complexity even with that of a 2-year-old human child.

Figure 12–6 dramatically demonstrates the contrast between the utterances of the chimpanzee Nim, who was taught a sign language, and the utterances of several hearing children who learned English and deaf children who acquired American Sign Language. The graph shows growth of utterance length over time in all the human children, whereas Nim's sign usage did not grow in length or complexity. Exactly why chimpanzees can be so intelligent in some respects and so unlike humans in their ability to use language is a source of continuing investigation and debate.

Some language researchers have suggested that syntactic recursion is the crucial property that separates human language capacities from other communication systems (Hauser et al., 2002). This approach places the crucial difference between humans and apes at the syntactic level of representation, but other suggestions have

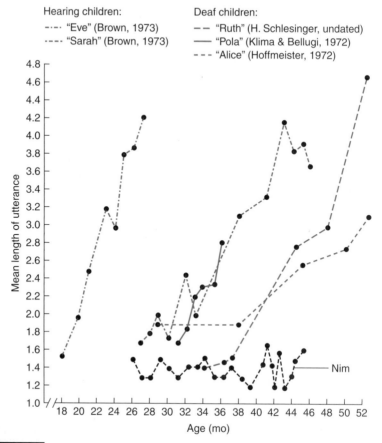

Hearing children:
---·- "Eve" (Brown, 1973)
----- "Sarah" (Brown, 1973)

Deaf children:
-- -- "Ruth" (H. Schlesinger, undated)
——— "Pola" (Klima & Bellugi, 1972)
- - - "Alice" (Hoffmeister, 1972)

FIGURE 12–6 Utterance length in children and in a chimpanzee

The utterance length of Nim, a chimpanzee who was taught a signed language, appears initially comparable to that of an 18-month-old speaking human child; however, utterances of both speaking and signing children rapidly increased in length with age, but Nim's did not.

(From *NIM* Herbert S. Terrace. Copyright © 1979 by Herbert S. Terrace. Reprinted with permission of Alfred A. Knopf, a division of Random House, Inc.)

been offered. For example, Seidenberg and Petitto (1987) argued for a difference between humans and chimps at the word level. They noted that chimps clearly can relate symbol use and getting a reward, but they do not seem to understand symbols as *names* for things. For example, a chimp can learn that pressing the symbol for "strawberry" on a keyboard often results in getting a strawberry to eat, but it does not realize that "strawberry" specifically names the tasty red fruit and does *not* refer to eating, nor to the location where strawberries are kept, nor to other objects and events associated with getting a strawberry. The chimps' behavior clearly is an example of communication, but it does not fit the criteria of human languages that Hockett and others have identified.

Comprehension Check:

1. What are the levels of language representation, and how do they interact?
2. What features distinguish human language from animal communication systems?

2. PROCESSES OF LANGUAGE COMPREHENSION

The different levels of language representation illustrated in Figure 12–1 reflect information that we know implicitly about language. How is this knowledge put to use in comprehending what we hear and read, and in producing language? How can we look at the letters *C*, *A*, and *T* together and realize that this sequence of letters indicates a small feline mammal? Our mental representations of words are a key component of a wide range of processes: speech comprehension, reading, writing, typing, and speaking. The first question then to explore is how the representations of words are maintained and accessed in the service of comprehension and production.

2.1. The Triangle Model of the Lexicon

Language researchers use the term lexicon to mean the entire set of mental representations of words. (The word is derived from a form of the Latin word *legere,* "to read," an obvious connection with meaning.) Often a lexicon has been described as a mental dictionary, a repository of what each of us knows about words, what they stand for, and how they are used. This comparison, though it can be useful, is not quite right: our mental representations are not lists of facts about a word's pronunciation, part of speech, and meaning—and they are certainly not in alphabetic order, a key characteristic of dictionaries! In fact, for some time researchers have pointed out that the list-structure idea of word representation fails to capture the degrees of similarity among word meanings, such as the fact that a robin and a cardinal are more similar to each other than either is to a duck (Collins & Quillian, 1969). These investigators instead promoted the idea that mental representations of words could be better described as networks. Reading researchers pushed these ideas further, observing that reading can be thought of as relating spelling to sound and spelling to meaning; again, the emphasis is on lexical knowledge as *mappings* between one level of representation and another (Seidenberg & McClelland, 1989). These and other considerations have led many researchers to conceive of word representations as networks comprising at least three major components: spelling, sound, and meaning.

In this triangle model (Figure 12–7), speech perception involves relating the sound representation—the phonology—of a word (the bottom right point of the triangle) to its meaning representation, at the top. Similarly, reading involves relating the spelling, or orthography, of a word (at the bottom left), to its meaning. Producing language involves relating the meaning of a word to its sound representation for speaking it aloud, or to its spelling representation for writing.

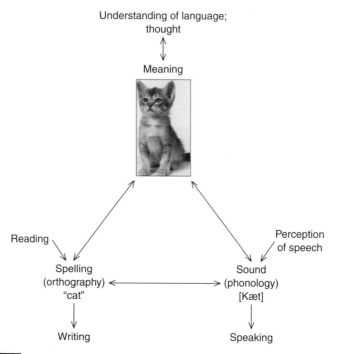

Understanding of language;
thought

↕

Meaning

Reading

Perception
of speech

Spelling
(orthography)   ⟷   Sound
(phonology)
"cat"   [Kæt]

Writing   Speaking

FIGURE 12–7   The triangle model of the lexicon

This model reflects researchers' current beliefs that information about words is represented in a network that relates meaning, sound, and spelling.

The triangle model shows how researchers have hypothesized how different aspects of word knowledge are linked, but it does not explicate the actual processes involved in language comprehension and production. What it does, however, is provide a framework for exploring several different kinds of comprehension processes in terms of relating one part of the triangle (such as sound representations) to another (such as meaning representations).

2.2. Ambiguity: A Pervasive Challenge to Comprehension

Comprehension is a complex business. Part of the reason is that most of the relationships among sound, meaning, and spelling are arbitrary—nothing about the spelling or sound of the word "cat" is inherently feline. Another feature of language that contributes to the difficulty of relating different levels of linguistic representation is ambiguity, which in language is the property that permits more than one interpretation of a sound, word, phrase, or sentence.

Language carries a huge amount of ambiguity at every level (Table 12–1), and the ambiguities at each of these levels have to be resolved before we can understand the meaning of what someone is saying. Let's consider ambiguity at just one level,

TABLE 12–1   Ambiguity in Language

Type	Perception	The Ambiguity
Word boundaries	You hear αɪ **skrim**	"Ice cream"?
		"I scream"?
Spelling/pronunciation and word meaning	You read "wind."	"Wind" like a breeze?
		"Wind" like a clock?
Spelling and word stress	You read "permit."	"PERmit" as in a license?
		"perMIT" as in "allow"?
Word meaning	You hear or read "bark."	The outer layer of a tree?
		The sound a dog makes?
Sentence structure	You hear or read "Mary read the book on the *Titanic*."	Was Mary reading about the *Titanic*?
		Was Mary reading a book while aboard the *Titanic*?
Pronouns	You hear or read "Susan told Mary that she was going to win."	Does Susan think Mary will win?
		Does Susan think Susan will win?

word meaning. Take a look at the objects around you right now: you'll certainly see this book, and probably a chair, a light, and a pen. All four of these words, *book, chair, light,* and *pen* have both noun and verb uses, so that every time you hear or read these words, you must determine whether the speaker is referring to an object (noun) or an action (verb). Some words, such as *pen,* have even more meanings, in this case as two nouns (a writing implement and an animal enclosure) and two verbs (to *pen* a sonnet, to *pen* up the pigs). Look around you again: you'll likely see more objects with ambiguous names (maybe *table, floor,* and *page* among them) than objects with names that seem to have only one clear meaning.

This exercise demonstrates a basic characteristic of words: ambiguity is rampant in the common words of the language; and those words that do not have multiple meanings—for example, *ozone, comma,* and *femur*—are typically technical terms and other relatively unusual words. How does this relate to the triangle model? It means that a single spelling or sound maps on multiple word meanings at the top of the triangle. As a result, for most words most of the time, we must sort through multiple alternative meanings, even though we typically become aware of only one interpretation. (Puns and similar jokes are a rare exception: the humor depends on making us aware of another meaning of an ambiguous word.)

Studies of how we resolve ambiguities in language are important for several reasons. First, these ambiguities are much more prevalent than we often realize. Research that explores the conditions in which resolving ambiguity is easy and the conditions in which it is not may help to improve communication in difficult situations, such as when using walkie-talkies, cell phones, or other static- or interference-prone devices. Second, a better understanding of why we are so good at resolving ambiguity may help in the development of computer language programs, such as speech recognition systems. Third, and most important, studying how we cope with ambiguity provides a good testing ground for understanding how language is mentally represented and processed. Language comprehension is naturally so fast and accurate that it is often very hard to gain insight about the process from direct observations, even with the simplest forms of language. If instead we can create experimental situations in which participants misinterpret ambiguities, we may gain some insight into how we typically integrate the various levels to understand language correctly.

A common theme running through all the research on ambiguity resolution is the integration of bottom-up and top-down information (first discussed in Chapter 2). *Bottom-up information* comes directly from what we perceive. Right now, as you read, one source of bottom-up information is the print on this page. In the triangle model, bottom-up information moves from the two bottom points on the triangle, spelling and sound information, to the top point, meaning. *Top-down information* comes from information in the long-term memories of each of us that helps us interpret what we perceive, and from information in the context in which the bottom-up information occurs. In the triangle model, top-down information also includes influence from meaning to spelling representations during reading. Because bottom-up information, such as printed text, is a very different thing from top-down representations of meaning, context, and other information in long-term memory, it is not entirely clear how two such different forms of information are integrated with each other to aid perception. Indeed, different claims about how such information is integrated form some of the major controversies in language research today. In what follows, we look at the roles of bottom-up and top-down information in speech perception.

2.3. Speech Perception

When someone speaks to you, fluctuations in air pressure strike your ear, and somehow you're able to turn these sound waves into an understanding of what the speaker is saying. One key step in this remarkable feat consists of identifying the boundaries between the words the speaker is saying. This is an area in which reading and speech perception are dramatically different: in English and in most other writing systems there are clear white spaces between the printed words on the page, whereas in the speech signal boundaries between words are not marked by pauses. You may have the conscious perception of hearing individual words in speech, but in reality you're hearing something that's more like this: thewordsareallconnectedinacontinuousspeechsignal. Jamming the print together on the page gives you some sense of the effect; an example of what speech actually looks like is shown in the sound spectrogram in Figure 12–8. A spectrogram is a two-dimensional visual display of speech in which time is shown on one axis, the frequency of the sound (which corresponds to pitch) on the other, and the intensity of the sound at each point of time and frequency is indicated by the darkness of the display (and thus white space indicates silence). The spectrogram in Figure 12–8 shows the spoken sentence "We were away a year ago." Most of the words in the sentence are not separated by spaces, and there are some spaces in the middle of words, as in "ago."

Without pauses to guide us, how do we find word boundaries? It appears that when we hear speech we unconsciously make educated guesses based on a mix of bottom-up and top-down information (Altmann, 1990). The bottom-up information

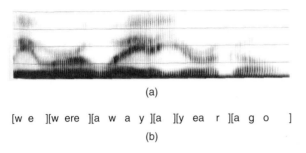

(a)

[w e][w ere][a w a y][a][y ea r][a g o   ]

(b)

FIGURE 12–8 *"We were away a year ago"*

This sentence is represented by (a) a spectrogram with (b) the approximate location of the words indicated below. In spectrograms, silence (pauses) in the speech signal appears as blank vertical bands; note that this sentence has no pauses between words, and the only silence is actually within a word, occurring at the "g" in the word "ago."

includes cues from the speech signal directly, such as occasional stretches of silence when the speaker pauses to think. Top-down information includes knowledge about typical phoneme patterns, for example, that [b] and [k] do not typically occur next to each other in English words (so if you hear the sequence [bk], the [b] is probably ending one word and the [k] is starting the next) (McQueen, 1998). We have very detailed knowledge of this sort about our native language (or any other language that we speak well), but this knowledge is not helpful when we listen to someone speaking a language with unfamiliar patterns. Speakers of foreign languages seem to be speaking very fast in a jumble of sounds with no clear boundaries between the words. (The ancient Greeks referred to foreigners as *barbaroi,* "barbarians," not because they were crude—they weren't, necessarily—but because they spoke something that sounded like "barbarbar" instead of Greek.) In contrast, when we hear a language we do know well, we do not perceive the speech signal as a continuous stream, because our speech perception system is doing such a good job of guessing word boundaries; the result is the illusion that the boundaries, in the form of pauses, are actually in the physical signal.

A second key problem in speech perception is identifying the phonemes in the speech signal. There is a huge amount of variability in the way each phoneme is produced: every speaker has a different voice and a slightly (or not so slightly) different accent; and the clarity of articulation—the production of speech sounds—varies depending on the rate of speech, the speaker's mood, and many other factors. The articulation of a phoneme also depends on what other phonemes are being articulated just before or just after it. Think about how you say the [k] sound in *key* and *coo.* Try preparing to say each word in turn, stopping just before you let the [k] sound come out of your mouth. How are your lips shaped in each case when you're about to say the [k]? You'll find the shapes are quite different, because even before you've gotten any sound out for the [k], your lips are already preparing to produce the following vowel. When the vowel is the "ee" of *key,* your lips are spread wide, but when the "oo" of *coo* is coming up, your lips are rounded. This overlapping of phonemes in speech is called coarticulation, and it has a large effect on the sound of each phoneme. If you say the [k] in *key* and *coo* without the vowels but with your lips spread or rounded as if you were going to say each of these words, you will probably hear that the [k] in *key* is higher in pitch and sounds different from the [k] in *coo*. The phenomenon of coarticulation means that each phoneme is articulated differently depending on which phonemes precede and follow it.

The combined effects of coarticulation, variation across speakers, variation with speaking rate, and many other changes in the way people can speak mean that each phoneme is probably never articulated exactly the same way twice. This enormous amount of variation means that, in principle, it is extremely hard to identify which phonemes are in the speech signal. Nonetheless, we routinely accomplish this feat—how? Once again, part of the answer seems to be the use of top-down information, particularly information about the context in which a phoneme is pronounced. In this way a badly articulated, or even missing, phoneme is supplied through the phoneme restoration effect (Warren, 1970).

In deceptively simple studies of this effect, participants listened to spoken sentences on audiotape and reported what they heard. Unknown to the listeners, the experimenters had spliced out a small portion of the tape corresponding to a single phoneme in a word and inserted in its place a recording of a cough of exactly the same duration. (In the sentence "The state governors met with their respective leg*slatures convening in the capital city," the asterisk indicates such a replacement.) Participants understood the sentences perfectly. Most did not notice that anything had been removed from the sentences; a common perception was that someone in the room had coughed during the recording. This illusion is even more dramatic in sentences such as the following (again, * indicates where a single phoneme has been spliced out and replaced by a cough):

> It was found that the *eel was on the orange.
> It was found that the *eel was on the axle.
> It was found that the *eel was on the shoe.

In these cases, the sound *eel is ambiguous among many different words, among them peel, wheel, and heel. Participants had no difficulty in comprehending the sentences, however, and they perceived *eel as a different word in each different context—they heard "peel was on the orange," "wheel was on the axle," and "heel was on the shoe."

This result provides powerful evidence for the role of top-down information in phoneme perception. The word at the end of the sentence (*orange, axle,* or *shoe*) can influence the perception of *eel only after it has been partly recognized, its meaning partly retrieved, and its relationship to various words that end with a sound like *eel* considered. These sentences all start exactly the same way, and it is the top-down context occurring four words after *eel that biases listeners' perceptions. These results also emphasize a point that has been confirmed in many studies: even though our conscious perception is that we instantaneously recognize the words we hear, very often in reality all the relevant information for recognizing a word does not arrive until after we hear it (Grosjean, 1985). Speech perception is extremely rapid, but it is not always quite as instantaneous as we feel it to be (see the *Closer Look* feature).

A CLOSER LOOK
Multiple Hypotheses during Spoken Word Recognition

We consider an experiment by Richard Shillcock that investigated how we perceive words in fluent speech (Shillcock, R. [1990]. Lexical hypotheses in continuous speech. In G. T. M. Altmann [Ed.], *Cognitive models of speech processing* [pp. 24–49]. Cambridge, MA: The MIT Press).

Introduction

Words are not separated by silence in the speech signal, and thus the listener is faced with the problem of identifying the boundaries between words. One possible way to find the boundaries between words in speech is to try out many different hypotheses for words and word boundaries simultaneously. For example, someone who hears the sound sequence "rek-uh-men-day-shun" might briefly hypothesize that this corresponds to five separate words, *wreck, a, men, day, shun,* or three words, *recommend, day, shun,* but ultimately rejects these nonsensical combinations in favor of a single word, *recommendation*. However, except for occasional misperceptions, we do not have any conscious awareness of considering words that turn out to be wrong. Thus, it is important to seek experimental evidence for these unconscious processes in speech perception.

Method

Participants performed two tasks simultaneously: they listened to spoken sentences and at some point during every sentence, they saw a letter string on a computer screen and had to push a key indicating whether or not the letter string was a real word or not (a *lexical decision* task). Unknown to the participants, some of the spoken sentences and printed words had a particular relationship that was designed to address the question of whether listeners consider several hypotheses during speech perception. On these critical trials, participants heard spoken sentences containing a two-syllable word in which the second syllable formed a real word. For example, for the sentence *He carefully placed the trombone on the table,* the second syllable of *trombone* is the real word *bone*. For half of these sentences, the printed word in the lexical decision task was related to the embedded second syllable word (*rib*, which is related to *bone*), and on the other half of the trials, the word was unrelated (*bun*). If listeners were temporarily considering *bone* as a possible word in the sentence while they were trying to find word boundaries and recognize words, then activating *bone* as a possible word should prime related words such as *rib*. This priming of *rib* from *bone* would result in faster responses to *rib* than to the unrelated word *bun* in the lexical decision task. Neither *rib* nor *bun* is related to *trombone*, so if listeners immediately settle on *trombone* and do not consider *bone* during speech comprehension, then there should be no priming of *rib* and thus no difference in response times to *bun* and *rib*.

Results

In the lexical decision task participants evaluated words related to embedded second syllables (like *rib*, related to *bone*) faster than they evaluated unrelated words (*bun*).

Discussion

This result suggests that even though perceivers are not aware of considering several different word boundaries and words during speech recognition, they do activate possibilities (such as *bone* during recognition of *trombone*) that they rapidly reject. These results support the claim that speech recognition is a process of unconsciously trying out many alternatives and rapidly homing in on the one that is the best fit.

Another kind of contextual information in speech perception comes not from what we hear but from what we see. Someone who is hard of hearing may say, "I hear you better when I can see your face." Someone who is not hard of hearing may say the same thing: whether we're hearing impaired or not, a certain amount of our comprehension comes from lip-reading. Being able to see the speaker's face provides additional information about which phonemes are being uttered because many phonemes are produced with characteristic mouth shapes. Mismatches between the speech sounds you hear and visual cues to articulation can be confusing—think of watching bad animation or a foreign film dubbed into English.

This confusion between what you see and what you hear is called the *McGurk effect,* after Harry McGurk, who discovered it by accident (Massaro & Stork, 1998; McGurk & MacDonald, 1976). McGurk and his research assistant, John MacDonald, were using video and audio tapes of mothers speaking to study speech perception in infants. When they dubbed the audio of a mother saying "ba" onto a silent video of her saying "ga" and played back the video tape, they were surprised to hear the mother on the tape suddenly saying a third sound, "da." Eventually they realized that the problem wasn't in the dubbing: if they closed their eyes and listened to the audio recording, they clearly heard "ba." The perception of "da" when they watched as well as heard the tape was an illusion that arose because their perceptual systems combined cues from both the video and the audio recordings. The video tape conveyed "ga," in which the consonant [g] is made by moving the tongue in the back of the mouth, and the audio conveyed "ba," in which the consonant [b] is made with the lips in the front of the mouth. Speech perception processes combined these two conflicting signals to yield the intermediate perception of "da," in which the consonant [d] is made in the middle of the mouth.

These examples of information integration explain why you could understand that your friend was saying that The Happy Pig's sesame noodles are "totally awesome" even though the noisy traffic drowned out much of those last two words. You were able to supplement a very poor speech signal (the bottom-up information) because you were able to integrate top-down information from a variety of sources. You were getting some extra information from looking at your friend's mouth during articulation—the [m] in *awesome,* for example, is made at the front of the mouth and is easily visible. You were also getting help from context (it seemed likely that she was going to offer some description of the noodles, which makes *awesome,* or another adjective, likely), and perhaps from long-term memory as well (maybe, irritatingly, she says "awesome" a lot). These sources together allowed your speech perception system to put together a very good guess about what was actually said. A minute later, however, when your friend was trying to describe the restaurant's location, top-down information was scarcer. Mouth shapes might have helped a little, but there was little context—she could have been mentioning any of a number of streets or landmarks. As a result, when her speech was again masked by the traffic noise, you had no idea what she was saying.

Results we have discussed indicate the importance of integrating top-down and bottom-up information during speech perception, but they do not suggest how that information is integrated. It is thought that much of the recognition component of integration works via an unconscious process of elimination in which we consider a number of possible words, called a cohort, that match the speech signal we hear, and then gradually weed out those that don't match the available bottom-up or the top-down information (Marslen-Wilson, 1984a). Thus, when you recognized the word *awesome*, you might have started out with a set of possibilities that contained words beginning with the same initial vowel sound: *awe, awesome, awful, author, audition, awkward, authentic, Australia, Austin,* . . . As soon as you heard the [s] in *awesome*, some of the words in the cohort no longer matched the speech signal (the bottom-up information) and dropped out of the cohort, leaving *awesome, Australia, Austin,* . . . At the same time, you were also guessing about word boundaries, so your cohort may also have included a pair of different words, *awe* and *some* (Shillcock, 1990). Very rapidly, as more of the speech signal is perceived and as top-down information suggests that some possibilities don't make sense (e.g., *Austin* is not an adjective), the remaining non-matching words drop out, and only one word, *awesome*, remains in the cohort.

Two key pieces of evidence support the view that speech perception involves a consideration of many possibilities from which the incorrect ones are weeded out. The first derives from the nature of the set of familiar words: although some words very rapidly diverge from other possibilities as more of the speech signal is heard, other words are similar to many other words throughout much of the speech signal. In the example of *awesome*, by the time you hear the *aw* vowel and the *s* consonant, there are very few possibilities left in the cohort—*awesome, Australia, Austin, awe*, plus the start of a new word beginning with *s*, and not much else. However, the first two sounds of *totally*, the *t* consonant and the *o* vowel, leave many more possibilities in the cohort—*totally, toast, tone, toe, told, Tolkien, toll, taupe, Toby, token, toad*, and many others. Speech researchers describe these differences in terms of neighborhood density, the number of similar sounding words in the language. *Awesome* has fairly few neighbors, whereas *totally* is in a dense neighborhood of many similar sounding words.

If researchers are right in believing that we recognize words by initially considering a cohort of possibilities and eliminating incorrect ones, it stands to reason that the more neighbors a word has, the longer it is going to take to eliminate them and get to the point of recognizing the word that was actually spoken. This has been demonstrated experimentally: many studies have shown that participants are faster at recognizing words, such as *awesome*, that have few neighbors, than words such as *totally*, that have many neighbors—which thus confirms the neighborhood density effect (Luce & Pisoni, 1998).

A second piece of evidence about cohorts and the elimination process comes from observation of our involuntary responses. We have no conscious feeling that we are considering many possibilities during speech perception, but the cohort model suggests that the candidates in the cohort must evoke a greater degree of activation than words that are not considered. If so, we should be able to observe some consequence of this activation, and that, too, has been demonstrated experimentally. For example, in one study participants were shown objects on a table and told to follow the instructions they heard, such as "Pick up the beaker" (Allopena et al., 1998). In some conditions, the objects on the table included a beaker, a toy beetle (*beetle* overlaps with the first sounds of *beaker*), a toy stereo speaker (*speaker* rhymes with *beaker* but does not overlap in the first sound), and various other objects that had no sound overlap with *beaker*. The investigators monitored the participants' eye movements to the various objects on the table, which indicated that while recognizing *beaker,* participants were also considering (glancing at) both *beetle* and *speaker* (but not objects that had no sound overlap with *beaker*). Similarly, other researchers found that when hearing words such as *trombone* that contain another word (*bone*), both words (*bone* and *trombone*) are considered (Shillcock, 1990). These results indicate that even though we have no conscious awareness of weighing alternatives during speech perception, we do in fact activate a cohort of possibilities on the way to recognizing words.

Why would we overlook mismatches at the start of a word and consider alternatives such as *speaker* for *beaker* or *bone* for *trombone*? One possible reason is the difficulty of recognizing word boundaries. We must guess about word boundaries at the same time we are developing candidates for the words we hear. If we are not sure about word boundaries, then we cannot be sure which phonemes are actually at the start of a word. Thus, it makes sense to consider many partially overlapping words in the cohort, even ones that have different initial sounds. The process of speech recognition is like working on several different intersecting answers in a crossword puzzle at the same time—you're guessing word boundaries, which words you're hearing, and which phonemes you're hearing, all at the same time. A good guess in one of these areas can rapidly make guesses in the others much easier.

2.4. Representing Meaning

Identifying words is only the beginning of comprehension, and getting to the actual meaning of what the speaker is saying is the ultimate goal. In the triangle model (see Figure 12–7), computing the meaning of individual words is represented as the mapping between the phonological level and the meaning representation. Researchers often think of the mental representation of meaning as a network of interconnected features.

Some evidence for this non-"dictionary" view of lexical meaning comes from studies of patients who have sustained damage to the temporal lobes of the brain. These patients previously had normal language abilities, but their temporal lobe damage (typically either bilateral or predominantly in the left hemisphere) leaves them with impaired knowledge of word meaning (Figure 12–9). Some of these patients have category-specific impairments, that is, they have more difficulty activating semantic representation for some categories than for others (mentioned in Chapter 4). Researchers who study these participants ask them to indicate the meaning of pictures, either by naming the object in the picture or in some other way, such as by choosing among a set of pictures in response to an instruction like "Point to the banana." Many different kinds of pictures have been used in these studies, spanning a range of living and nonliving things—animals, birds, plants, tools, musical instruments, vehicles, and others. Researchers have found a striking result: some patients are much worse on pictures in some categories than in others, and across patients, it is not always the same pictures or categories that prove to be especially difficult. Patients with this kind of brain damage tend to fall into two broad categories: those who are relatively more impaired at recognizing living things (animals, fruits, birds) and those who are relatively more impaired at recognizing

Left Lateral View

Regions of the brain involved in representation of word meaning

Damage to these areas affects understanding the meanings of certain words, sometimes in the form of category-specific impairments. The patterns of impairment suggest that words are represented in semantic networks that include various types of information, including perceptual aspects. Some of this information is also represented in similar areas of the right hemisphere.

manufactured objects (tools, vehicles, musical instruments). Occasionally patients have difficulty with a narrow category, such as fruits and vegetables, and less difficulty with other kinds of living things; see also Figure 4–16 and the accompanying discussion.

Some researchers have suggested that these patterns of impairments imply a *semantic representation* (a mental representation of meaning) that rests on various combinations of perceptual information (especially visual information) and functional information—information about what the thing is used for (Warrington & McCarthy, 1987; Warrington & Shallice, 1984). In this view, there is a broad division between living things and manufactured objects on these two dimensions. To the nonzoologist, living things are distinguished from one another mainly by perceptual features—a zebra has black and white stripes, an antelope and a deer have different shapes of horns or antlers. Manufactured objects, such as tools, writing implements, and furniture, have some important perceptual properties, but their *function* is typically more important. A pencil or a hammer or a car can be any color or pattern and still be a pencil or a hammer or car, but if you altered a picture of a zebra to remove its stripes, most people would think it was some type of horse and not a zebra at all. Patients with greater impairment to the parts of the brain that process perceptual information thus will have more difficulty recognizing living things compared to manufactured objects, whereas greater impairment to brain areas processing functional information will produce greater difficulty in recognizing manufactured objects as opposed to living things. One exception to this pattern is musical instruments—patients who have difficulty identifying living things often also have difficulty with musical instruments. But the exception may not be so "exceptional": true, musical instruments are manufactured objects, but fine detailed perceptual information is important in distinguishing them (think about how you would be able to know whether a picture is of a guitar or a violin).

The patterns of impairments argue against a semantic representation in which each word is its own distinct lexical entry, or even a scheme in which each category is stored in a separate brain area. Those sorts of organization do not predict what has been observed: particular semantic clusters become impaired together; for example, difficulty identifying musical instruments often accompanies difficulty identifying animals. Instead, the patterns of impairment suggest that the meanings of words are represented by combinations of perceptual information, functional information, and probably other types of information as well. The problems of the patients just discussed suggest that such networks of functional and perceptual information may be represented in different parts of the brain. That is, patients with greater difficulty recognizing living things would be expected to have more damage to areas of the brain that involve integrating perceptual features such as color and shape, whereas patients with greater difficulty recognizing objects would be expected to have more damage to areas of the brain related to function, particularly to motor areas, (because the function is often implemented by the way we manipulate an object).

Support for this hypothesis comes from neuroimaging studies of normal participants while they accessed semantic representations. In one such study, participants were presented with words and asked to think silently of color words appropriate to the presented words (such as *yellow* for the word *banana,* thus activating perceptual information), or action words (such as *eat* for *banana,* activating functional information) (Martin et al., 1995). The investigators found that thinking about color activated an area near brain regions involved with color perception, and thinking about related action activated an area near brain regions that control movement. These results, and others, suggest that meaning representations are distributed across multiple brain regions in networks coding various aspects of meanings, including perceptual features, movement features, and emotional associations. (A similar study was described in Chapter 4.)

If words are represented through networks of features, what happens when a word has several different meanings? Virtually every common word in English has more than one meaning. The problem is not so great in the "mental dictionary" account of meaning representations; a dictionary entry lists all the different meanings of an ambiguous word. If we think about meaning as emerging from feature networks, however, how are the different meanings of a word represented, and how do we activate the right meaning when we encounter an ambiguous word?

A study that sought to answer this question presented participants with words that have equally frequent noun and verb meanings, such as *watch* and *tire* (Tanenhaus et al., 1979). These ambiguous words were presented in contexts in which the syntax of the sentence forced either a noun interpretation of the word (for example,

I bought the watch) or the verb interpretation (for example, *I will watch*). The ambiguous word was always the last word of the sentence. Participants heard sentences of this sort, and after each sentence, they saw a word on a screen to read aloud. Sometimes the word to be read aloud was related to the noun meaning of the ambiguity, such as *clock* for the noun meaning of *watch*, and other times it was related to the verb meaning, such as *look* for the verb meaning of *watch*. The investigators compared reading times in three conditions: (1) when the onscreen word was consistent with the meaning of the ambiguous word as used in the sentence (for example, *clock* following *I bought the watch*), (2) when the onscreen word was consistent with the other meaning of the ambiguous word (*clock* following *I will watch*), and (3) a control condition in which the word that appeared on the screen was unrelated to *either* meaning of the ambiguous word. The investigators also varied the elapsed time between participants' hearing the ambiguous word at the end of the sentence and the appearance of the (related or unrelated) word to be read aloud.

When the word to be read appeared immediately following the ambiguous word, the result was surprising: reading times for *both* of the related words (in this example, *clock* and *look*) were shorter than when the word was unrelated to either meaning of the ambiguity—even though one of the two related words made no sense in the sentence context. When the word to be read aloud appeared 200 milliseconds after the sentence ended, however, the participants read the appropriate related word faster than the inappropriate word: for example, the participants read *clock* faster following *I bought the watch* than following *I will watch*.

These results provide information about the relative timing of bottom-up and top-down information in the resolution of lexical ambiguity. It appears that immediately after an ambiguous word is heard, several of its different meanings are activated, but within 200 milliseconds top-down information from context has suppressed all but the meaning that matches that context. Some researchers have interpreted these results to imply that the resolution of ambiguity relies on a two-stage process: first, there is a bottom-up stage in which all meanings of an ambiguous word are accessed independent of context; then a second stage, in which top-down information about context is used to pick the correct meaning (see, for example, Swinney, 1979).

Subsequent studies manipulated variables such as the strength of the context and the relative frequencies of alternative meanings of ambiguous words (*bank* as a financial institution, for example, is more frequent than *bank* as in "bank of the river"), and the results have shown that these and other factors affect the extent to which multiple meanings are activated for ambiguous words.

A neural-network model has been devised to interpret these findings: in this model the activation of each meaning of an ambiguous word depends on the strength of its connection to the spelling or sound of the word (Kawamoto, 1993). For instance, two meanings of *watch* are initially activated because there are strong pathways from the spelling and phonology of *watch* to the two different meanings. Thus, activating either the spelling or phonology in the triangle model rapidly activates the two meanings. For words with one frequent and one relatively rare meaning, however, such as *bank*, the higher frequency meaning has been perceived and produced more often, and thus has a stronger connection between the meaning and the spelling and phonology. The result is that the higher frequency meaning is activated more quickly than the lower frequency meaning.

In addition, top-down context effects are slower than these bottom-up effects when the contexts are not strongly associated with one or the other meaning. In the sentence *I bought the watch*, there is nothing about the context *I bought the* that is particularly associated with timepieces; rather, only after the word *watch* appears can the context have a role in the interpretation of this ambiguous word. Other contexts, such as *I thought the alarm clock was running fast, so I checked my watch*, are more strongly associated with the concept of time even before the word *watch* is encountered, and the effects of context are seen more rapidly in cases like this one.

This discussion of lexical ambiguity resolution in context has emphasized the timing of different kinds of information activation from bottom-up and top-down processes. It also relates, however, to the idea that words are represented by overlapping networks encoding different aspects of word meanings, such as the perceptual and functional features of a noun, such as *banana*. *Banana* is certainly not an ambiguous word in the sense that *watch* and *bank* are, yet activation in completely different brain regions was observed when participants were asked to think of the perceptual or the functional aspect of its meaning. Thus, every word has different aspects of meaning that can be emphasized to greater or lesser degrees in different contexts, and there is variation in the extent to which these different meanings are related. At one end of this distribution are words like *watch*, which have various meanings that are distinct from one another. At the other extreme are highly specific technical words like *ozone*. Because context can dramatically emphasize different aspects of word meaning, most words fall somewhere in between. Even for words with single definitions, such as *banana*, there may be no core aspect—function or perceptual characteristic—of the object that is activated *every time* the word is heard. And although words, such as *watch*, that can signify different things show some early activation of different meanings, after the first few hundred milliseconds, sentence context contributes greatly to determining the features of the word that are active during comprehension.

2.5. Sentence Comprehension

Sentences provide contexts that can shade the meanings of individual words; they also of course have meaning themselves. Part of this meaning comes from the meanings of the words contained in the sentence, part from the syntax of the sentence—the relation of those words to one another. "Man bites dog" means something different from "dog bites man." But nothing is simple: sentences as structural wholes, as well as the words within them, can carry ambiguity. For example, consider the sentence "The spy saw the cop with binoculars." This sentence can be interpreted in two ways, depending on which of two possible sentence structures is assumed. Each of the possible structures (indicated by brackets) leads to a different meaning. If the sentence structure is "The spy saw [the cop with binoculars]," the prepositional phrase "with binoculars" is describing something about the cop, namely, that this is a cop who has some binoculars. But if the sentence structure is "The spy saw [the cop] with binoculars," then "with binoculars" is describing something about the manner of seeing, namely, that the spy is using the binoculars as an aid to seeing.

This example illustrates **structural ambiguity**: the linear string of words that is heard or read is consistent with more than one syntactic structure and sentence meaning. The speaker or writer intended only one structure and meaning, and the listener, or reader, must figure it out, reconstructing it from the string of words. Structural ambiguities are extremely common in speech and writing, but nonetheless we generally manage to find our way to the correct interpretation. How do we do it? The occasional failures are quite revealing about how comprehension works. These failures are often the basis of jokes, in which the humor comes in part from lulling the listener (or reader) into one interpretation of a sentence and then springing another—the intended—interpretation on him or her. The great comedian Groucho Marx was a master at this. One of his most famous jokes of this nature is his line in the movie *Animal Crackers*: "One morning I shot an elephant in my pajamas. How he got in my pajamas, I don't know." The joke works because of a structural ambiguity in the first sentence, the same ambiguity as in the *binoculars* sentence above. The audience initially interprets the first sentence as "I shot [an elephant] in my pajamas" and is caught when the following context reveals the structure to be "I shot [an elephant in my pajamas]." This kind of ambiguity is called a **garden path sentence** because the listener or reader is first "led down the garden path" to an incorrect interpretation before being allowed to reanalyze the sentence and find the correct interpretation.

Garden path sentences reveal a very basic property about sentence comprehension: its immediacy—we interpret words as we encounter them (Just & Carpenter, 1980). In principle, you could avoid dealing with many ambiguities by waiting until you'd heard the entire sentence, or even more sentences, before making any decisions about what the words mean and what the sentence structure is. That way you wouldn't be surprised however an ambiguity resolved, because you would delay your interpretation until you had heard enough so that the context resolved any ambiguity. The fact that garden path sentences surprise us shows that comprehension proceeds as soon as we can make a reasonably good (unconscious) guess about what we're perceiving. This means that we often have to make these guesses about correct interpretations from only partial information. Presumably we get to the right interpretation of ambiguities most of the time without ever being consciously aware of alternative meanings because these early guesses are either often right or are fixed very rapidly, before we have a chance consciously to notice alternative interpretations. We previously observed this same phenomenon in the phoneme restoration effect, in which people did not notice when a phoneme in a word was replaced by a cough, as in "the *eel on the orange." The context from *orange* was integrated so rapidly that listeners believed that they had clearly heard the word *peel*. The same sort of rapid integration operates to resolve syntactic ambiguities.

Whereas ambiguities in the speech signal must be investigated with spoken language stimuli, researchers studying syntactic ambiguity resolution typically use measures of reading time to test their hypotheses about how we arrive at the right interpretation of ambiguities. By presenting written sentences, researchers can measure reading time at each word (for example, by using a device that measures readers' eye movements) and thereby track at which point a sentence becomes difficult to comprehend (the eye pauses). Having a measure of difficulty at each point in the sentence is important in understanding ambiguities, because patterns of reading can reveal *when* readers have misinterpreted an ambiguous sentence. As we have just seen, structural ambiguities are temporary, lasting only until a later portion of the sentence makes the intended interpretation clear. This is typically the case in language comprehension. For example, consider these sentences:

1. Trish knows Susan. . . . (structure: ambiguous)
2. Trish knows Susan from summer camp. (structure: subject–verb–direct object–prepositional phrase)
3. Trish knows Susan is lying. (structure: subject–verb–[sentence [subject–verb]])

Sentence 1 contains a temporary structural ambiguity concerning the interpretation of *know* and therefore of any words that might come after it. *Know* can mean "be acquainted with" and we can interpret the word that way, in which case the material that comes next in the sentence is simply a noun indicating who is known. Sentence 2 assumes this interpretation: *Susan* is the direct object of *know,* and the sentence means that Trish is acquainted with Susan. Alternatively, *know* can mean to be aware of the truth of something, in which case what follows *know* is generally an entire embedded sentence stating that truth. Sentence 3 is of this sort, and *Susan* is the subject of the embedded sentence "Susan is lying."

The point in the sentence at which the structure and, therefore, the intended interpretation are made clear is known as the **disambiguation region**. In sentence 2, the disambiguation region is "from summer camp"; in sentence 3, it is "is lying." Observations of reading times in the disambiguation region can reveal comprehension difficulties caused by ambiguities. Participants who read an ambiguous sentence and then encounter a disambiguation region that does not match their initial interpretation slow down in the disambiguation region (their eyes fixate on this region for an extended amount of time). At this point they realize that they have been led down the garden path and have to reanalyze the sentence, which takes more time (Rayner & Pollatsek, 1989).

Researchers have considered two general hypotheses about how we make early guesses about temporarily ambiguous sentences and, as in other problems of comprehension we have discussed, they involve different amounts of bottom-up and top-down information. One hypothesis holds that a syntactic structure is chosen first with only bottom-up information, and only later checked against top-down information (Frazier, 1987). According to this idea, a component of the language comprehension system, the *parser,* takes the written or speech input and builds a syntactic organization for the incoming sentence, much like the tree shown in the syntactic level of Figure 12–1. When a structural ambiguity is encountered, the tree could be built in two or more ways, so the parser chooses the simplest option, the one with the fewest possible nodes and branches. In the case of the ambiguous sentence about Trish and Susan, sentence 1, the first interpretation is the direct-object structure like that in sentence 2, because it is simpler than the embedded-sentence structure in sentence 3. As a result, when *Susan* is encountered, it is immediately interpreted as a direct object. This choice is initially made without regard to any context or even to the meanings of the words in the sentence. In a second stage of comprehension, if the meaning does not makes sense with the structure chosen by the parser, we realize we have been led down the garden path and hastily beat a retreat.

The parser hypothesis suggests that the strategies for resolving ambiguities of sentence structure are very different from lexical ambiguity resolution. Only one sentence structure is considered at a time, whereas we saw good evidence earlier that several different interpretations of an ambiguous word are activated during lexical ambiguity resolution. The difference comes from different conceptions of the lexicon and syntax—word meanings are stored in the lexicon, but syntactic structures are generated anew each time a sentence is heard. Thus, it is not computationally taxing to activate several alternative meanings of a word, but building several alternative structures simultaneously is thought to be too difficult to accomplish in the time we generally take to understand a sentence.

The alternative hypothesis is that we cope with ambiguities in sentence structure in basically the same way that we cope with lexical ambiguities (MacDonald et al., 1994; Trueswell & Tanenhaus, 1994). In this view, syntactic ambiguity resolution is a guessing game guided by both top-down and bottom-up information. Advocates of this view make the point that structural ambiguities also involve lexical ambiguities, as in "be acquainted with" and "have a belief about," alternative meanings of *know* in sentences 1–3. This kind of lexical ambiguity, just like other lexical ambiguities, should yield activation of alternative meanings of the word that depend partly on the frequency of these alternative meanings and the context. And just as with lexical ambiguities, context effects on the resolution of structural ambiguity will in normal circumstances tend to be weaker than bottom-up information. This view is appealing because it emphasizes the interlocking nature of the word and syntactic levels of language representations, and it allows a consistent characterization of ambiguity resolution at many different levels: whether it is an ambiguity at the level of the speech signal, word meaning, or sentence structure, or some combination of these, the comprehension system unconsciously rapidly integrates whatever information it can to interpret the input in a way that fits best with the available evidence.

Researchers are currently working on testing these two hypotheses, but as of this writing the jury is still out.

2.6. Figurative Language

Figurative language is by definition ambiguous, in that it is the deliberate use of one word to mean another, by metaphor or simile. Your friend "fished" a takeout menu out of her backpack, but the use of this word is not meant to suggest that she produced a fishing rod, baited the hook, and made a spectacular cast in the middle of a busy sidewalk. Instead, it concisely evokes a picture of rummaging around in a container to look for something. Figurative language presents another problem of comprehension: we must decide whether a literal meaning or a figurative meaning is intended. Like other kinds of ambiguities, figurative language is amazingly frequent in ordinary speech; some analyses suggest that speakers use figurative language about six times per minute of speech (Pollio et al., 1977), and figurative language is especially common in descriptions of emotions and abstract concepts (Gibbs, 1994).

Very often we do not even consciously realize that our language *is* figurative. Suppose someone says to you, "Registration was such a zoo—I spent two hours in line and then they said I didn't have the right forms." What's the figurative language here? *Zoo,* of course, used as a metaphor to evoke a crowded and chaotic situation. But in this sentence there's also a second, less obvious metaphor: in the phrase "spent two hours," time is described as if it were money. Metaphors of this sort pervade our thoughts and emerge in a number of different expressions—in the case of time and money, we have metaphoric expressions about wasting time, spending time, saving time, spare time, and investing time.

Figurative language fills our speech to such a large degree that it is tempting to consider it as just another example, albeit a special case, of the multiple meanings of words and sentences. However, evidence from neuropsychology tells us that there is something more to the story. Although several sites in the left hemisphere are crucial for most aspects of language comprehension, the interpretation of figurative language appears to rely to a much greater degree on processing in the right hemisphere. Patients with right-hemisphere damage often have particular difficulty understanding figurative language, and neuroimaging studies have shown that normal participants have more right hemisphere activation while comprehending metaphors than while comprehending literal language (Bottini et al., 1994).

The exact role of the right hemisphere in the comprehension of figurative language is not yet well understood, but it may have to do with the interpretation of sentence intonation, the "melody" of a sentence—the rise and fall of pitch, the variations in stress. Consider the sentence "Jim's a really nice guy": by uttering it with different intonations, you can make this sentence a statement of literal fact, a question, or a sarcastic comment indicating that you think that Jim is really not nice at all. The right hemisphere is highly involved in interpreting sentence intonation (Buchanan et al., 2000). The connection? Sarcasm, irony, jokes, and some other types of figurative language often rely on intonation. But the right hemisphere's role in the interpretation of figurative language interpretation cannot rest entirely in fine-grained analyses of intonation, given that it plays a similar role in the interpretation of spoken and written speech (and there is no intonation of written speech).

2.7. Reading

When you couldn't understand what your friend was saying, she gave you a takeout menu so you could see the address of the restaurant where she worked. The restaurant's name, The Happy Pig, and the picture of the pig were at the top of the menu. You identified the picture as a pig very rapidly, and you read the words *The Happy Pig* very rapidly too. The processes that allowed you to identify the pig—that is, object recognition processes described in Chapter 2—include putting together perceptual information from the picture such as areas of light and dark and the location of angles so as to identify the object. In other words, you used visual information in the picture to activate semantic information—in this case the meaning "a pig wearing an apron and carrying a tray of food." As with interpreting a picture, the goal of reading is to translate visual information—the words on the page—into semantic information about the meaning of the words and the text.

2.7.1. Reading Pathways

In thinking about the task of translating print to meaning, it's useful to refer again to the triangle model of the lexicon in Figure 12–7. Notice that there are two possible routes from the printed word to its meaning. The first is spelling→meaning, the route from the spelling of the printed word at the bottom left of the triangle up to meaning at the top, a route much like that for the recognition of objects. In both cases, you take information about patterns of light and dark on the page, angles, and other features and relate this visual input to stored representations of meaning. The alternative route is spelling→phonology→meaning: the print is first related to the phonological representation (that is, there is mapping between the two bottom points of the triangle), and then the phonological code is linked to meaning, just as in speech perception. When you read, you may have the sense that a voice in your head is saying the words to you; this effect appears to be the result of activating phonological codes from print as we read. Clearly, this phonological route is used when we sound out an unfamiliar word—the spelling is translated into a pronunciation. The phonological route is the basis of the "phonics method" of teaching reading. If you remember being explicitly told to sound out words when you were learning to read, this is how you were taught. Now that you are a skilled reader, do you still sound out words, or do you skip the pronunciation and use the spelling→meaning route? How much information flows through each of these two alternative routes?

It is hard to answer these questions just by thinking about them, because reading is so fast and automatic by the time most readers reach adulthood. The questions are therefore a topic of research, and answers to them have shifted dramatically during the past several decades (Rayner et al., 2001). Many researchers initially thought that skilled readers were, or at least should be, using only the spelling→meaning route. They thought that once readers had sufficient practice and no longer needed to sound out words, reading via the spelling→phonology→meaning route added a needless extra step that would slow them down.

Other researchers have taken a very different view of the reading process. They have noted that although the spelling→meaning route looks conveniently short in the triangle model, in fact the mapping between spelling and meaning is arbitrary. Again, there's nothing about the letters C, A, T that look anything like a cat. Computing these arbitrary mappings is relatively hard, but the mapping between spelling and pronunciation has many regular patterns that make this mental computation easier. For example, the letter C is very often pronounced like the [k] sound, as it is in *cat*. Once this computation is complete, all that remains is the mapping between phonology and meaning. It's true that this relationship also is arbitrary, but it is a route that is already highly practiced and is already used for speech perception in children who are beginning to learn to read.

According to this view, then, there is no reason to believe that reading via the phonological route is any slower than reading through the direct route from spelling to meaning. It is also important to remember that the "routes" here are not mutually exclusive, and in neural network models that implement the ideas behind the triangle model, the meaning representations can receive activation directly from spelling and through the spelling→phonology routes simultaneously (Seidenberg & McClelland, 1989). Thus, it is possible to integrate these two positions and suggest that both routes may be used to varying degrees, and the extent to which one route or the other dominates at any given time may depend on various factors, including the skill of the reader and the properties of the word being read.

Of course, the arguments for different routes are difficult to assess without data. One study designed to investigate the extent to which phonology is used in reading had participants make judgments about the meanings of words (Van Orden, 1987). The task was set up in such a way that the fastest and most accurate way to perform it was to use the spelling→meaning route, ignoring phonology. The logic of the experiment was that if effects of phonology appear in a task for which they are not helpful, and possibly even counterproductive, then this is good evidence that readers routinely rely heavily on the spelling→sound→meaning route. Specifically, participants first read the name of a general category, such as FOOD or ANIMAL, on a screen. The category name was then removed from the screen and a new word appeared. Participants were instructed to press a key as quickly as possible to indicate whether or not the new word was a member of that category. For example, for the category FOOD, participants would press a key labeled YES for the word *meat*; but if the word *heat* appeared, they would press a key labeled NO. On some trials, homophone words such as *meet* appeared. (These are words that are pronounced in the same way as another word but are spelled differently.) Participants who saw the category FOOD and the word *meet* should answer NO, but some participants pressed the YES key, and most took a long time to make their judgments. The results points to participants' use of the spelling→phonology→meaning pathway: the spelling *meet* activated the phonology of the word, and the phonology was used to activate meaning. Because the phonology maps to two different meanings, one of which is a food and one of which is not, participants had more difficulty producing a correct answer.

This result shows the importance of the spelling→phonology→meaning pathway in reading, but it does not mean that the spelling→meaning pathway is not also used. It is possible that pathway use can vary to some degree across readers or for different words, a hypothesis that was tested with a meaning judgment task similar to the one just described (Jared & Seidenberg, 1991). The investigators found that homophone interference, such as that illustrated with *meet*, was limited to relatively infrequent words in the language and did not occur for higher frequency words. They interpreted this result to indicate that the degree to which the spelling→meaning pathway is used depends on the amount of practice readers have had with this pathway. For high-frequency words, for which readers have a great deal of experience, the spelling→meaning pathway becomes heavily used; readers have had far less practice with lower frequency words and thus for these words they rely more on the spelling→phonology mapping and go from there to meaning.

Neuroimaging studies have produced corroborating evidence for this theory of how people use the different reading pathways. fMRI has been used to examine the amount of brain activity in readers of many ages and with many different levels of

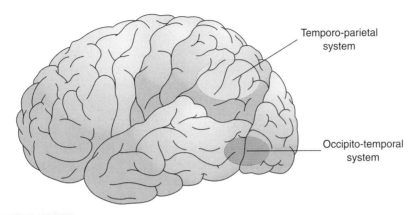

Temporo-parietal
system

Occipito-temporal
system

FIGURE 12–10   Regions of the brain important for reading

Reading—that is, mapping spelling to phonology and meaning—depends on a temporoparietal brain system, where spelling→phonology→meaning relationships are learned, and an occipitotemporal system, developed later as reading skill increases, which relates visual information (spelling) to meaning. (Shaywitz, B. A., Shaywitz, S. E., Pugh, K. R. et al., Disruption of posterior brain systems for reading in children with developmental dyslexia. *Biol Psychiatry,* 2002; *52,* 101–110. Reprinted with permission from Elsevier.)

reading skill as they read many different types of words (Pugh et al., 2001). These studies indicate that two different areas in the left hemisphere are crucial for fluent reading. One of these is in the temporoparietal areas of the brain, near regions that are important for word meaning and phonology, and the other area is the occipitotemporal system (Figure 12–10). The researchers suggest that when we learn to read, the temporoparietal system initially predominates and is responsible for learning the relationships in the spelling→phonology→meaning pathway. The occipitotemporal system develops later and becomes more important as reading skill increases. This system appears to relate visual information (that is, spelling) to meaning information directly. It is too soon to tell how definitively these brain regions relate to the spelling→phonology→meaning and spelling→meaning pathways as laid out in the triangle model, but fMRI research offers an exciting way to gain insight into the nature of the information processing that underlies reading.

2.7.2. Connected Text

A major part of reading is the recognition of individual words and the interpretation of sentences, but reading involves more than that if you are to make sense of this or any other connected text. What you see before you is not one sentence, but many connected sentences. How do we take in large amounts of text?

The first point we must make is that there is a motor aspect to the act of reading: you're moving your eyes across the page so that you can see all the words. These eye movements come in quick jumps, called saccades, that alternate with periods in which your eyes are still while you're fixating on some specific point in the text. About 90 percent of reading time is spent fixating, and you make two or three saccades each second to new parts of the text.

When you are fixating on a word, the image of that word falls on the fovea, the part of the retina with the greatest visual acuity. The farther away from the fovea the image falls, the poorer the visual acuity. The sentence set off below has one word printed in boldface type. When you fixate directly on this word, its image will fall on your fovea. Now, *still keeping your eyes only on the boldface word,* try to identify the other letters in the sentence.

Tyc amksp birxu roz ulvdp **walk** gehd thc pqzy gvlwn ckg.

If you were careful to keep your eyes on **walk** and not fixate anywhere else on the line, you probably found that you could identify or make a good guess about the letters just before or after this word, but more distant letters were just a blur. An obvious question about this example: why were all the letter combinations other than **walk** nonsense words? The reason is that most participants in demonstrations like this tend to glance at the entire display while looking for the one boldface word. If you had done that and the sentence had made sense, you would have been able to use top-down processing to help you guess the letters on either side of **walk**. Having nonsense on either side of **walk** reduced the use of top-down information and gave you a good sense of how poor your visual acuity really is outside the fovea.

Many studies suggest that skilled readers fixate on most but not quite all words when they are reading material of roughly the same difficulty as this textbook. Some words, especially long ones, are fixated more than once, and some short words can be perceived even when they are not directly fixated. The word *the* is very often not fixated; it is short enough (and frequent enough) that it can be perceived even if the fixation is nearby. Moreover, when a word is fixated the eye movement to it is often precisely planned so that the fixation is in the middle of a word, so that all or most of the word is clearly visible in a single fixation. This brings up the interesting question of how you are able to plan your eye movements to skip certain words and focus precisely in the middle of others if you haven't read the text yet and don't know what's coming up. In other words, how can you skip *the* if you haven't seen it yet?

The answer is that in some cases you use top-down information from your accumulated general knowledge of English vocabulary and sentence structure to guide your planning of eye movements. And you also get quite a lot of bottom-up information from the text. It has been shown that even though readers have a clear image of only about six characters around the point of fixation, they can get some gross visual features of letters and words that are seven to twelve characters away. Look again at the nonsense sentence above. While fixating on **walk,** try to see the shape of the second "word" to the right. You probably found that you could identify, if not the actual letters, then at least that this was a short "word" that began with some tall letters. This sort of partial information is not enough for perfect identification of upcoming words, but it is enough to allow eye movement programming processes to guess that the word *the* may be coming up, and sometimes skip it.

2.7.3. Speed Reading

As a skilled reader, you read very quickly, every *second* identifying several words. Many people who must do a great deal of reading often wish they could read even faster, and they invest in "speed-reading" courses. Does speed reading instruction work? No, not really.

Every speed-reading program is a bit different, but most make similar assumptions about how reading does or should work. One common—and outdated—assumption relates to the triangle model: speed-reading programs often suggest that efficient reading should relate spelling directly to meaning, avoiding the pronunciation route. These programs suggest that readers have got into the lazy habit of activating pronunciations while reading and could greatly improve their reading speed if they eliminated this "extra" step and read via the direct route of spelling→meaning. As we have seen, this view previously dominated the teaching of reading to children, but there is now good evidence that activation of pronunciation is in fact a natural component of skilled reading.

Most speed-reading instruction also encourages readers to move their eyes across the page faster. Because it is impossible to program and execute saccades any faster than our natural rate, the only way to get across a page faster is to make longer saccades. But this doesn't help: because words outside the foveal region are not well perceived, the consequence of longer saccades is that some words will never be fixated, or may even never be near the point of fixation, and thus won't be seen. In other words, speed reading is a lot like skimming: you zip through some parts of the text and skip over others.

The reading patterns and comprehension abilities of trained speed readers have been compared with those of college students who had no speed-reading experience (Just & Carpenter, 1987). The college students read texts in two different ways. In one condition, they were instructed to read the text; in the other, they were instructed to skim. The investigators found that the speed readers' eye movements were very similar to those of the college students who were skimming.

The study also explored the effect of skimming on the participants' understanding of the material. (An important claim of speed-reading programs is that reading speed can be increased by their techniques without sacrifice of comprehension.) With easy texts, all three groups—speed readers, skimmers, and normal readers—were fairly accurate. With more difficult material, however, the skimmers and the speed readers had poorer comprehension than the college students who were reading normally. These results reinforce everything that we have seen about comprehension: essentially, that it is a multifaceted process in which many different levels of information are integrated with one another. Skipping over pieces of the material, whether by informal skimming or by following a speed-reading method, inevitably leads to missing key portions of context and other information that are crucial to developing an accurate meaning representation of the material.

✔ Comprehension Check:

1. Why do researchers believe that when hearing speech, we initially consider many possible words (a cohort) and then reject possibilities that don't fit?

2. What is the relationship between the triangle model of the lexicon and the phonics and whole-word methods of reading instruction?

3. PROCESSES OF LANGUAGE PRODUCTION

You're taking an exam and your pen drops and rolls into the next row of seats. You tap the person sitting in front of you and say, "Could you please get my pen? It's under your chair." You've again effortlessly completed a complex feat. You've taken a goal to have your pen back, an abstraction that doesn't initially have any language associated with it, and you've turned that goal into a linguistic representation and then into series of muscle movements to utter the words. (This is similar to how we convert a motor goal—lifting a pen—into a series of movements, as discussed in Chapter 11.) There are a host of other ways you could have translated this thought into language—perhaps "My pen fell under your seat. Could you please get it?" or "Would you please give me the pen that rolled under your seat?"—but for some reason you made this particular choice of wording. Studying language production means studying the processes by which we turn nonlinguistic thoughts into language and then develop an actual plan for the utterance.

Compared to what we have learned about language comprehension, we know relatively little about how humans produce language, primarily because of several methodological challenges. In studies of comprehension, researchers typically present language stimuli and measure variables such as comprehension time, accuracy, and patterns of brain activations. Measurements of these variables can be very precise, in part because we can control exactly when the stimulus is presented, and we can time our measurements from that moment. In language production, however, the start of the process is the creation of a set of nonlinguistic internal representations, such as those that underlie your desire to have your pen back. This different kind of starting point is a real challenge for investigators, because it is much harder to have precise experiment control. Indeed, much of the early research in language production was not experimental at all but instead observational, recording speakers' errors in production. It is also possible to examine errors during production of signed languages and during written language production (handwriting or typing). However, the vast majority of research has been on errors during speaking, owing in part to the ease with which speakers' errors can be observed.

One of the first researchers to use this method was Victoria Fromkin (1923–2000), a linguistics scholar who argued that the patterns of errors that speakers make are informative about the underlying processes of language production (Fromkin, 1971). She carried a small notebook with her everywhere, and whenever she heard an error in speech, she'd whip out her notebook and write down the error and the intended utterance. The collections of errors that Fromkin and other researchers gathered revealed that the patterns of speech errors are not random but group together in specific ways. These error patterns formed some of the first data on language production processes.

Exchange errors occur when two elements of a sentence are transposed. In word-exchange errors, such as *I wrote a mother to my letter*, and *tune to tend out*, words in a phrase or sentence exchange places. The exchanged words are typically from the same grammatical class, so that nouns exchange with nouns, verbs with verbs, and so forth. The exchanged words are often fairly far away from each other in the sentence.

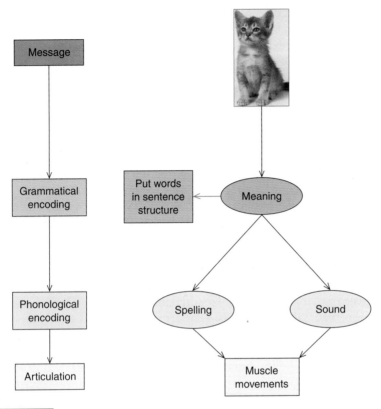

FIGURE 12–11 Stages of language production

The stages are named on the left. The right side of the figure shows the information that is represented in these stages and actions that take place during them. Note that the triangle model of the lexicon (with arrows showing only language production processes) is contained in grammatical and phonological encoding.

In contrast, sound exchange errors, in which two sounds exchange places, typically occur in nearby words, from similar positions within the words. These errors are often called *spoonerisms* after the Rev. William Archibald Spooner, head of New College, Oxford University, from 1903 to 1924, whose speech was peppered with these errors. They include these possibly apocryphal reprimands to students: "You have hissed all my mystery lectures!" and "You have tasted the whole worm!"

The very different characters of word and sound exchange errors were important early evidence in the development of language production models, such as the one shown in Figure 12–11 (Garrett, 1975; Levelt, 1989). In this model, production processes proceed through three distinct levels before arriving at articulation. First, at the message level, the speaker (or writer) formulates the message to be conveyed. At this point the message is still nonlinguistic, with no words or sentence structure attached to it: an example is your desire to have your pen back. The next stage, grammatical encoding, contains two different processes. One process involves choosing words with which to convey the message, the other involves developing the syntactic structure of the sentence to be uttered. All this information is then passed to another stage, phonological encoding, in which the phonological representation of the utterance is developed. Finally, the message is articulated. Let's take a more detailed look at some of these stages.

3.1. Grammatical Encoding

The process of choosing words during language production, one aspect of grammatical encoding, involves relating semantic information from the message level to individual words in the lexicon. Research in language production has focused on how those semantic representations are translated into particular word choices. For example, when you're trying to get your pen back, you could describe it as being either under the *seat* or under the *chair* in front of you. Both are reasonable choices given the furniture and the message you're trying to convey. This suggests that the meaning of your message partially activates both these word choices, and typically the one with the greater activation is selected. Occasionally two words are both selected, resulting in an error that is a blend of two different words, as in "My pen is under your cheat—I mean seat." (Freud believed that errors of this sort reflected suppressed thoughts or desires, perhaps in this case a belief that the person in front of you—or you yourself—might try to cheat on the exam. Embarrassing mistakes like this one are often called Freudian slips. Some of these errors do seem to stem from thoughts that speakers don't intend to utter, but most reflect the basic workings of the language production system more than our hidden motives.)

The other aspect of grammatical encoding is the development of a syntactic structure for the spoken or written utterance. As with word choices, myriad different sentence structures will do the job of conveying most messages. How do you settle on a single choice? It turns out that a great deal of the unconscious decision making for sentence structures depends on your word choices, specifically on how rapidly you are able to determine the various words that will go in the sentence. The process of choosing words starts for many words at once, so that while *chair* and *seat* are both being activated, so is *pen,* and probably *get* and *give* are competing with each other.

But even though the word-choice process starts for a number of words at about the same time, it is not necessarily completed at the same time for all the possibilities. There are a variety of reasons why word choice may be faster or slower at different times or for different words. For instance, certain parts of the message may be more important than others and thus the corresponding representations may be activated more strongly. Also, rare words may take longer to activate. These variations in lexical accessibility—the ease with which a word can be retrieved and readied for production—have a large effect on choice of syntactic structure for an utterance. The words that are chosen first are put toward the start of the sentence to be uttered, and the syntactic structure that develops is one that can accommodate these word choices.

This influence of lexical accessibility on structure choice was demonstrated in a series of ingenious language production studies that were disguised as memory

FIGURE 12–12   Why do we say things the way we do?

Pictures like this one were used in studies of sentence production; this picture can be described either actively ("Lightning is striking the church") or passively ("The church is being struck by lightning"). The participants' choice of the first noun in the sentence—and thus of active or passive voice—depended on the priming word, which was either *storm* or *worship*.

(Bock, J. K. (1982). Toward a cognitive psychology of syntax: Information processing contributions to sentence formulation. *Psychological Review, 89*(1), 1–47. Copyright © 1982 American Psychological Association. Reprinted with permission.)

experiments (Bock, 1982). In one study, participants described simple pictures; they were told that saying a sentence out loud about each picture would help them to remember the pictures better. The syntactic structure that participants used in the picture descriptions was the behavior of real interest in the research. An example picture, shown in Figure 12–12, could be described with an active sentence such as "The lighting is striking the church" or a passive sentence such as "The church is being struck by lightning." Bock hypothesized that the relative accessibility of the words *lightning* and *church* would affect the choice of active or passive syntactic structure, and she manipulated the accessibility of these words by briefly presenting a priming word, which the participant simply had to read aloud, before the picture appeared. (Participants were not aware of the connection between the task of word reading and that of sentence production.) In one condition the priming word *worship* appeared on the screen, in another condition the priming word *storm* appeared. Picture descriptions using passive sentences, such as "The church is being struck by lightning," were more frequent when the prime word had been *worship* than when it had been *storm*. The prime word had preactivated some meaning information, so that when the picture appeared and participants began planning their utterance, choosing a word for the primed concept was completed more rapidly than for the unprimed concept. This first-chosen word was then placed into an early position in the developing sentence, resulting in the choice of active or passive sentence structure as needed.

Putting the more accessible words first has real advantages in conversation, allowing speakers to set up the plan for the utterance early, before all words have been selected. As the beginning words are selected and the structure of the sentence starts to be developed, these early words move into the next stage of language production, phonological encoding. Speakers can therefore plan many different parts of the sentence at once. Because the earliest parts of the sentence are the ones in the lead in planning, these parts will be ready to be uttered while the speaker is still working on later parts. This has the conversational advantage of speeding up turn-taking: you don't have to wait until the last detail of a sentence is planned before you begin uttering it.

The complicated interleaving of lexical selection and sentence structure planning sometimes goes awry. One of the consequences can be word-exchange errors such as *I wrote a mother to my letter.* Errors of this sort appear to result from a mistake in inserting words into the sentence structure, and therefore these misassignments are not completely random but typically happen within a particular word type. Nouns (such as *mother* and *letter*) exchange with each other, verbs exchange with verbs, and so on.

Another breakdown can occur if the speaker finishes uttering all the planned parts of the sentence before later parts are fully ready to be uttered. For this reason, speakers may find themselves suddenly at a loss for words (a common experience), at which point they often slow down or add filler words and vocalizations like "um" at this point. Remember your friend's saying, "It's, well, a . . . um, a sort of Asian-fusion-deli place"? Here the speaker was having trouble choosing words that adequately described this novel restaurant. She started uttering "It's" before word selection and planning were complete, leading to the insertion of pauses and fillers while she planned the rest of the sentence and made it ready for articulation.

3.2. Phonological Encoding

As words are selected and pieces of the sentence structure are planned, these pieces of the utterance are sent off to the next stage of language production, phonological encoding. Here speakers retrieve the pronunciation representations that are necessary for articulating the words in the utterance. Remember that pronunciation representations are distinct from meaning (the triangle model of the lexicon again).

Indeed, there is a great deal of evidence in language production that choosing a word and retrieving its pronunciation are distinct stages. Usually these two processes happen so quickly that they are difficult to distinguish, but it is occasionally possible to isolate each stage. One way to do this is to study what happens when a speaker is having trouble thinking of a name or other word, in a "tip-of-the-tongue" state. We all have been in these states at one time or another, and a little reflection about

Definition	Your Answer of Hint
1. A Japanese robe with a wide sash.	
2. An illusion in which a non-existent pool of water seems to be visible in the desert.	
3. A device used to keep time in music.	
4. A mammal that kills snakes, the main character in Kipling's "Rikki Tikki Tavi."	
5. A large upholstered footrest.	
6. A type of giant redwood tree that grows in northern California.	
7. A single lens placed over one eye to improve vision.	
8. A single-celled organism that moves by means of temporary pseudopods.	

FIGURE 12–13 On the tip of your tongue

These definitions may elicit in you tip-of-the-tongue (TOT) states. Try to say the word that fits each definition. If you feel that you know the answer but can't think of the word, write in what you think you know about the word, such as its first sound or number of syllables, or a word that sounds like it. (Answers appear on page 531.)

what's going on in these situations reveals that "can't think of the word" isn't an accurate description—what you can't access is the *pronunciation* of the word. When you can't think of someone's name, you know perfectly well whom you're talking about. You have accessed the semantic component of the word quite satisfactorily, but for some reason you're having trouble getting from the semantic representation to the pronunciation.

These tip-of-the-tongue (TOT) states thus slow down a process that is usually too rapid to be observed easily, and they therefore provide researchers with valuable evidence about how phonological encoding proceeds. Obviously, following participants around and waiting for them to enter a tip-of-the-tongue state is a very inefficient way to collect this information, and so researchers have developed a procedure to induce these states. (If you want to try out a short version of this procedure yourself, or try it out on some friends, use the instructions and definitions in Figure 12–13.) In these studies, participants read or hear definitions of rare words and try to say the word that's being defined. Sometimes they know the word right away, and sometimes they have no idea what word is being defined. But other times the experimenter gets lucky: the participant says, "Oh that's a . . . um . . ." and is clearly in a tip-of-the-tongue state. The experimenter then asks the participant questions such as "Can you tell me what sound the word starts with?" or "How many syllables do you think it has?" People in a TOT state often can report several things about the word's pronunciation, such as the first or last phoneme of the word or the number of syllables, or can name some other word that sounds similar. This partial knowledge of a word is not unique to spoken languages: deaf users of signed languages occasionally find themselves in a "tip-of-the-fingers" state. Like users of spoken languages, the signers in this state cannot quite come up with the sign they want, but can report partial information about it (such as the basic handshape of the sign they are trying to produce), without being able to demonstrate the movement required to produce the sign (Thompson, Emmorey & Gollan, 2005). These results suggest that someone in a TOT (or tip-of-the-fingers) state certainly knows the word and has some small amount of the phonological representation activated; they also demonstrate that the choice of a word and the activation of its phonological form (whether for speaking or signing) are distinct processes.

For most people, TOT states are just an occasional annoyance; a more devastating form can emerge from certain kinds of brain injury. In contrast to the patients with semantic impairments discussed earlier, other patients with brain damage may appear to have normal semantic information but severe difficulty retrieving the phonological representation of words they have selected for an utterance (Kay & Ellis, 1987). This deficit in naming things is often termed anomia, from Greek words meaning "without" and "name." Anomia is a common consequence of injury to many language-related areas of the brain. Patients with anomia may look at a picture and be unable to retrieve the phonological representation, although they can demonstrate their understanding of the meaning in other ways: for example, a patient who sees a picture of a hammer and cannot retrieve the pronunciation for the word will readily mime hammering a nail. The deficit is more frequent for rare words, suggesting that the frequency with which the meaning→phonology pathway is used for a given word affects the ease of phonological retrieval. Like tip-of-the-tongue studies with unimpaired speakers, observation of anomic patients' difficulties serves to underline the distinction between word choice and phonological encoding.

Phonological encoding, not surprisingly, is the birthplace of spoonerisms and other sound exchange errors. The exchanging sounds typically are in nearby words and are often located at similar positions in words (such as the first sounds of two words), and so they appear to represent slight glitches that occur when several words are planned simultaneously.

3.3. Integrating Grammatical and Phonological Stages

We know that information from grammatical encoding flows to phonological encoding; is there any evidence that phonological encoding can affect grammatical processing? Originally researchers assumed that such feedback didn't happen. One reason for this belief was the nature of the error patterns that researchers observed in speech. Word exchanges seemed to occur over long distances and to depend on word type, not pronunciation, whereas sound exchanges occurred between sounds in nearby words, without regard to whether the words were nouns, verbs, or other word types. These patterns suggested that word exchanges happened before phonological encoding, and that sound exchanges happened only within phonological encoding, independent of grammatical encoding.

More recently, however, evidence has emerged that supports a more interactive system in language production. It is becoming clear that although there is a clear initial ordering of events in language production, so that speakers, signers (of American Sign Language), and writers begin to assemble sentences and choose words before they do much work on planning the motor movements that will enable them to speak, sign, write, or type, there is also some interaction between the later processes and the earlier ones. Some of the first evidence for this interaction again came from analysis of speech errors. Investigators examined a collection of word exchange errors and noted whether or not the exchanged words contained similar phonemes (Dell & Reich, 1981). For example, *writing a mother to my letter* is an error in which the exchanged words (*mother* and *letter*) sound fairly similar, whereas the error in *The shirts fall off his buttons* is an exchange between two phonologically dissimilar words (*shirts* and *buttons*). This examination revealed that the exchanged words contained similar phonemes more often than would be expected by chance—as though the similarity of sounds adds confusion and leads to misassignment of words into the sentence. This result indicates first that the process of phonological encoding of the words was well under way while the words were being arranged into their sentence, and second that phonological encoding was affecting the arrangement of words in the syntactic structure. Thus, this result argues for some interaction between grammatical and phonological encoding, because these phonological effects on word exchange errors should not happen if grammatical encoding proceeds completely independently of phonological encoding.

Similar evidence comes from experiments that try to induce speakers to produce exchange errors. In one such study, participants saw short phrases such as *darn bore* on a computer screen (Baars et al., 1975). The participants' task was to prepare to say this phrase if in a few seconds it was replaced by a GO signal. However, if the phrase was replaced by a different phrase on the computer screen (such as *dole bean*), participants were to ignore the previous phrase and say the new one. In some cases, participants saw many phrases before they got a GO signal.

The phrases that appeared before the GO signal all began with the same pair of letters (e.g., da_bo_). Then came a GO signal, and a phrase appeared with the same initial letters, but this time reversed (e.g., what were the initial letters of the first word were now the initial letters of the second word and vice versa). After planning their responses on the basis of the initial series, participants found it difficult to switch, and this is where the sound exchange errors appeared. Sometimes the reversed sounds produced another pair of words: *darn bore* would become *barn door*. Sometimes the sound exchange produced nonsense, as when *dart board* became *bart doard*. Here's the interesting wrinkle: sound exchange errors occurred 30 percent of the time with *darn bore*—and only 10 percent of the time with *dart board*, which reverses to nonsense. This result provides more evidence for the interactive nature of language production: if phonological encoding were operating independently of other levels, then the rate of speech errors shouldn't vary as a function of whether the result is a real word or nonsense. Because speech errors that make real words are more common than errors that make nonsense, researchers have concluded that the phonological encoding level is interacting with the word selection processes.

Language production processes (like the general motor production processes considered in Chapter 11) are complex and multilayered. The data illuminating these production processes initially consisted largely of analyses of speech errors, but more recently experimental methods have been developed to study production in the laboratory. Data from both analyses of errors and results of experiments show clearly that speakers and signers accomplish a great deal of planning before beginning an utterance, and after beginning, they are still planning upcoming parts of an utterance while actually uttering the earlier parts. This simultaneous planning at multiple levels results in some interaction between the different levels.

✓ Comprehension Check:

1. What are the stages of language production?
2. Why has it traditionally been more difficult to study language production in an experimental context than to study language comprehension?

4. LANGUAGE, THOUGHT, AND BILINGUALISM

Imagine that there are three students sitting in the row in front of you, one from the United States, one from Mexico, and one from Korea. Do they think about the world exactly as you do? Of course not. How much of that difference is from the accidents of language, that one is a native speaker of English, one of Spanish, and one of Korean? How much is from other differences in experience? Moreover, for the two students who have learned English later in life, how has the experience of learning a second language changed them?

4.1. Language and Thought

Languages differ dramatically from one another in terms of how they describe the world. Because language is the major vehicle for expressing our thoughts, scholars since the time of Aristotle have tried to understand to what extent the languages we speak shape the way we think. This question is most closely associated with the writings of Benjamin Lee Whorf, who argued that languages strongly shape the way their speakers perceive and conceive of the world (Whorf, 1964). Although not all differences between languages result in differences in thinking, researchers have found striking differences in how people who speak different languages perform a number of cognitive functions, such as how they navigate in and reason about space, perceive colors, and reason about objects, substances, events, time, numbers, and other people (e.g., see Gentner & Goldin-Meadow, 2003; Levinson, 2003). Many of the studies have found cross-linguistic differences even in surprisingly elementary processing (e.g., the ability to orient in space, judge duration, or perceive differences between different shades of colors). Beyond showing that speakers of different languages think differently, these studies have found that linguistic processes are pervasive in many fundamental domains of thought. That is, it appears that 'thinking' is a complex set of collaborations between linguistic and non-linguistic representations and processes (Papafragou, Massey, & Gleitman, 2006).

4.2. Bilingualism

The experiments designed to assess claims about the relationship between language and thought are faced with many complications: for instance, people who speak different languages also come from different cultures, making it hard to attribute any observed differences in thought to language differences alone. One "natural experiment" is the study of bilinguals, people who speak two (and despite the name, sometimes more than two) languages. The question here is whether one's thought processes in one language are influenced by the ability to comprehend, produce, and think in another language. The question of bilingual language representations actually extends well beyond questions of language and thought. For every language process discussed in this chapter—speech perception, reading, ambiguity resolution, language production, and all the others—researchers have asked whether these processes operate in the same way for bilingual and monolingual speakers. For example, do bilingual speakers have one lexicon or two, one for each language? There seem to be some situations in which bilinguals' two languages appear to be quite separate, and others in which they interact and even interfere with each other. Working out the factors that govern when two languages interfere and when they do not may help language researchers understand not only bilingualism but also all aspects of language representation in the brain.

In the United States, many people know little or nothing of any language except the one they grew up speaking, although this is changing. In most other parts of the world, however, most literate people speak two or more languages with some fluency. What are the consequences of being able to produce and comprehend in two languages instead of only one? The answers to this question can depend on how early the two languages are learned (see the accompanying *Debate* box) and how much each language is used—children need to hear and speak a language at least 25 percent of the time in order to become really proficient in it (Pearson et al., 1997).

Let's consider the case of children who grow up hearing and using two languages roughly equally often and compare their situation to that of monolinguals. The bilingual child must learn to map each concept (such as *dog, run, yellow*) onto two different phonological forms and must learn the syntactic structures for two different languages, whereas the monolingual child is learning only one. This additional learning burden initially results in slower vocabulary development in each language in bilingual children when each language is considered individually. For example, consider a typical group of bilingual English–Spanish children, a group of monolingual English children, and a group of monolingual Spanish children. If we tested the vocabulary scores of the bilingual children and the monolingual children, the bilingual children would tend to have smaller vocabularies—they would know fewer English words than the monolingual English children and fewer Spanish words than the monolingual Spanish children. However, if we added up the total

DEBATE

Are There Sensitive Periods for the Acquisition of Language?

Unlike so many other skills, learning a second language is easier when begun in childhood. Why is this? The answer may lie in the notion of a *sensitive period* for language learning: a period during development during which a child readily acquires an ability; before or after this limited period, acquisition is notably more difficult. Claims about a sensitive period raise many additional questions that do not yet have firm answers. For example, it is unclear exactly why the window of opportunity closes: is it because of a biological change, much like puberty, or is it an environmental effect—does the very act of learning one language thoroughly create interference for learning another?

We can ask how long the sensitive period is—when do you have to start learning a foreign language in order to be as fluent as someone who began learning it at birth? Researchers have offered various answers, some suggesting that you could wait until the age of 13 to start learning a language and still become as fluent (and accentless) as a native speaker. It's unlikely that there is any one magic age cutoff, however, but most research suggests that for complete fluency without any trace of a foreign accent, it's important to start learning a second language very early in childhood. It has been shown, for example, that although 6-month-old babies can perceive phonemes from many languages that they have never heard, they start to lose this ability by the age of 10 months (Werker & Tees, 1984).

Relating perceptual abilities that have a sensitive period to actual language mastery is complicated, however. An obvious experiment is to compare individuals who begin to learn a foreign language at different ages; immigrant populations offer a pool of potential participants for experiments of this sort. We could, for example, select people who first started learning English at age 10 and compare them to those who started learning at age 20, and test them after all the participants had been in the United States for the same number of years. This has been done, and essentially all studies of this sort show that the group that started learning English earlier performs much better in knowledge of English phonology and syntax (Flege et al., 1999; Johnson & Newport, 1989). However, it is difficult to know how to interpret these data, because the two groups likely have had very different language experiences and amounts of language practice: people who came to the United States at age 10 typically enroll in English-language schools, make friends with English-speaking classmates, and tend to get much more practice using English than do people who arrive in the United States at age 20. Compared to children, adult immigrants are overall less likely to spend time speaking and listening to English, so that even though the two groups have been in the United States the same length of time, the quality and amount of their English experience tend to differ.

Analyses of language skills in immigrant populations that have tried to take these differences into account (Flege et al., 1999) have found that the sheer amount of language use, not the age at which language learning starts, is the best predictor of syntactic knowledge. Thus, the studies noted above may not be clear evidence for a sensitive period for learning syntax. By contrast, knowledge of phonology, as measured by accent, does appear to have a sensitive period, in that people who begin learning a second language early have better accents than those who learn late, even when amount of practice is very carefully equated in the two groups.

If there is a sensitive period for acquisition of language phonology, we can also ask whether the limits of the period are hard and fast. Researchers have investigated whether even a little early experience with a foreign language can stave off later declines in the ability to perceive and pronounce phonemes like a native speaker (Au et al., 2002; Oh et al., 2003). One study tested groups of English speakers who had spoken Korean for a few years before switching to speaking English full time; another tested English speakers who had spoken no other language but who had heard Spanish frequently in childhood from the conversation of some of the adults around them. The results? The early Korean-speaking experience and even the early Spanish-overhearing experience resulted in better phoneme perception and production abilities for those languages, compared to English speakers with no comparable exposure.

However, another study yielded very different results (Pallier et al., 2003). This study investigated adults who had been born in Korea but were adopted between the ages of 3 and 8 by families in France. All of the adoptees reported that they had forgotten everything about Korean, and their French was judged to be perfect. They were no better at perceiving or remembering Korean speech than were monolingual French speakers, and their brain activations while listening to Korean, measured by fMRI, did not differ from those of monolingual French speakers.

What accounts for the striking difference between these results, in which all early experience of Korean seems to have been completely lost, and the studies by Au and colleagues (2002) showing that early experience had an effect in adulthood? The answer seems to rest in the degree to which the early language experience was replaced by another language. Pallier and colleagues (2003) studied Korean children adopted in France, where they essentially never heard Korean again. By contrast, Au and her colleagues tested early Spanish and Korean learners in southern California, a highly diverse community in which Korean and Spanish are both frequently heard. This continued exposure to another language may have supplemented the early experience, allowing the California group to retain some proficiency in a way that the experience of the adoptees in France did not. These studies reflect both the interest in and the complexity of research in bilingualism and foreign language acquisition. The studies show that the timing of the start of language learning, as well as the amount and nature of the experience using a language, influences the degree to which a late-acquired language will resemble an early-acquired one.

number of phonology–meaning mappings that the bilingual children know in both Spanish and English, their total vocabulary scores would tend to be at least as high as those of the monolingual children (Pearson et al., 1993). Similar results have been found for learning the syntax of a language: the burden of having to learn two different sentence structures initially slows down bilinguals' syntactic development in each of the languages (Muller & Hulk, 2001). Thus, children whose language comprehension and production experience is spread across two languages at least initially pay some price compared to children whose experience is concentrated on one language.

Although bilinguals eventually acquire both their languages extremely well, it is interesting to ask about the consequences of bilingualism in adulthood. A bilingual who routinely uses both languages will on average have half as much practice producing and comprehending each language as a monolingual. The effect of this split practice can be seen in word production, and bilinguals have been shown to have more tip-of-the-tongue experiences than monolinguals (Gollan & Acenas, 2004), even when the bilinguals are tested in the language that they use more often.

Another difference between bilinguals and monolinguals is that bilinguals must (consciously or unconsciously) choose which language to produce every time they speak or write, whereas monolinguals have no such choice to make. Whenever a bilingual uses one language, the other language must be inhibited, or language production could turn into an incoherent mix of two different vocabularies and sentence structures. Several studies have suggested that this constant need to inhibit one language and focus attention on the other increases the effectiveness of executive processes (the topic of Chapter 7). Bilingual children and adults appear to do better on nonverbal tasks that draw heavily on memory and cognitive control resources, such as playing a game in which a sequence of lights and sounds must be remembered and reproduced (Bialystok et al., 2004; Bialystok & Martin, 2004). Thus, the experience of being bilingual has many consequences, both in and beyond language use itself.

✔ Comprehension Check:

1. What is the Sapir-Whorf view on the influence of language on thought? What is a more moderate position?
2. How do bilinguals differ from monolinguals in their rate of language acquisition?

Revisit and Reflect

1. *What are the different levels of language representation and how do they fit together?*

   The levels of mental representation of language discussed are the discourse, syntax, word, morphology, and phoneme levels. These fit together in a complex way because the various levels are distinct from one another (a phoneme is clearly not the same thing as a proposition at the discourse level), yet the levels are not completely independent. For example, certain sentence structures (syntax) are used to convey certain kinds of propositions in discourse, certain kinds of morphemes occur with certain kinds of sentence structures, and so on. Moreover, all elements of language can be recombined over and over; for example, the phonemes and the morphemes can be recombined to generate new words and sentences.

   Think Critically

   - Broca's aphasics have difficulty comprehending and producing function morphemes. Many European languages, such as Italian and Russian, have more bound function morphemes (appearing as suffixes on words) in a typical sentence than does a typical sentence in English. Might this difference in the rate of function morphemes affect the nature of Broca's aphasia in the different languages?
   - The generative capacity of language implies that we can produce literally a potentially infinite variety of sentences, and that any sentence could in principle be indefinitely long. In practice, however, even long sentences don't go beyond a few dozen words in length. Why do we seem to use only this small fraction of our generative capacity? Does the limitation seem to be in our production ability, in our comprehension ability, and/or in other types of cognitive processing?

2. *How does language comprehension proceed at these different levels?*

Language comprehension is a specific example of the perceptual processes discussed more generally in Chapter 2, and the same principles that emerged in that chapter can be seen in language as well. For example, language comprehension has both bottom-up and top-down processes. A key component of language comprehension is ambiguity resolution, because ambiguity is everywhere in language—such as in words, sentences, word boundaries, and phonemes. The ambiguities can interact, so that decisions about where a word boundary is can affect interpretation of what phonemes were heard and vice versa. We appear to cope with these multiple ambiguities by unconsciously making decisions that favor the most likely choice given all available information.

Think Critically

- How are the problems of ambiguity in understanding language similar or different to the problems of ambiguity in other perceptual processes that were discussed in Chapter 2?
- We appear to be able to activate multiple meanings of ambiguous words. Is this finding another example of a cohort—activating many possible words that partially match the speech signal? If so, could there be a kind of neighborhood density effect (perhaps the number of alternative meanings) in the interpretation of ambiguous words?

3. *What are the similarities and differences in comprehension processes for spoken language and for reading, and what are the similarities and differences in comprehension processes for words and sentences?*

An obvious difference in spoken and written language is that listeners must identify word boundaries in the speech signal, whereas in many writing systems, including that of English, the word boundaries are marked with spaces. Another important difference between hearing and reading is that the speech signal is fleeting, whereas readers can reread text if necessary. A final major difference is that reading is a skill that is taught, whereas spoken-language comprehension is acquired at a very young age without explicit instruction. Still, reading and speech comprehension have important similarities, in that we appear to interpret both speech and writing through a process of integrating top-down and bottom-up information to arrive at the most likely interpretation of the material.

Comprehension of words and sentences appears to rely on many of the same processes, which is not surprising given the fact that sentences are themselves made up of words. In particular, both words and sentences contain a great deal of ambiguity, and a substantial amount of research suggests that in both cases ambiguity resolution involves integrating top-down and bottom-up information to develop the most likely interpretation given what has been heard or read up to that point in the sentence.

Think Critically

- Some writing systems, including Chinese, do not put spaces between the words in writing. Do you think that reading in Chinese might be more similar to listening in Chinese than reading English is to listening to English?
- In the Groucho Marx joke that begins *I shot an elephant in my pajamas,* either the person doing the shooting is in the pajamas or the elephant is in the pajamas, but not both. How is this like the duck–rabbit ambiguity discussed in Chapter 2?

4. *How do language users plan and produce language?*

Language production involves translating a nonlinguistic message (a thought or goal that does not yet have any language attached to it) into an utterance. The planning of the utterance begins with grammatical encoding in which representations of words are selected to encode the message, and a syntactic structure is chosen to allow the most accessible words (those the language user is most ready to articulate) to go first. Next comes phonological encoding, in which the pronunciation of the words is retrieved and a plan for articulation is developed. The basic flow of information is from message to grammatical encoding to phonological encoding, but there is also some evidence for interaction between the levels, so in some circumstance planning articulation can affect grammatical encoding.

Think Critically

- What is the relationship between the accessibility of words and the tip-of-the-tongue (TOT) state?
- Think of some common phrases or titles that have two nouns joined by *and* or *or,* such as salt and pepper, "The Pit and the Pendulum," or *Pride and Prejudice.* How often is the second noun longer than the first? Could the length of a word affect its accessibility and choices for word order in these phrases?

5. *What is the relationship between language and thought?*

Researchers have long debated to what degree one's language shapes thought. The strongest position, most closely associated with the work of Sapir and Whorf, is that the language you speak shapes many of your thoughts. A more moderate position is that language shapes primarily your language-based thoughts, but it does not have a strong influence on early perceptual processes or cognitive processes that do not rely extensively on language.

People who grow up bilingual are initially slowed in their language development in each of their languages compared to monolingual children. This stands to reason, because a bilingual child will on average get only half the amount of practice with each language compared to a monolingual child. These effects of different amounts of language practice extend into adulthood, and both positive and negative effects of being bilingual have been found that can be traced to the different language comprehension and production experiences that bilinguals and monolinguals have.

Think Critically

■ Eyewitness memories of events have been shown to be susceptible to leading questions, so that we will tend to "remember" a blue car as green if someone asks, "How fast was the green car going when it hit the tree?" (see Chapter 5) How does the fallibility of eyewitness memory here relate to the influence of language on thought?

■ Bilinguals often engage in *code switching*, the use of some words from one language while speaking another language. For example, Spanish–English bilinguals who are speaking Spanish may include an occasional English word in the conversation. Could code switching in this way be related to lexical accessibility during utterance planning?

Answers to TOT definitions, page 521
1. kimono
2. mirage
3. metronome
4. mongoose
5. ottoman
6. sequoia
7. monocle
8. amoeba

Glossary

achromatopsia (acquired): color blindness resulting from brain damage (typically to visual area V4); color vision and memory of color are lost.

action: a series of organized movements that is accomplished in order to reach a goal.

activity-based memory: a form of memory storage that occurs through a sustained or persistent increase in activity within specific neural populations.

affective primacy hypothesis: the idea, first proposed by Wundt (1907) and later elaborated by Zajonc (1984), suggesting that emotional stimuli are processed relatively automatically, making fewer demands on limited cognitive resources than do other types of stimuli.

agnosia: the inability to recognize familiar objects, even though there is no sensory deficit.

akinetopsia: motion blindness; that is, the loss of the ability to see objects move.

algorithm: a step-by-step procedure, invoking one process after another, that guarantees that a certain input will produce a certain output.

Allais paradox: in decision making, the apparent contradiction observed when the addition of the identical event to each alternative has the effect of changing the preference of the decision maker.

alternatives: in decision making, the different courses of action that are available.

ambiguity: in language, the property of having more than one interpretation of a sound, word, phrase, or sentence.

analogical reasoning: reasoning that involves using knowledge from one relatively known domain (the source) and applying it to another domain (the target).

anomia: a disturbance, caused by brain damage, in retrieving the name of an object or person.

anterograde amnesia: the inability consciously to remember information encountered *after* damage to the medial temporal lobes.

aphasia: a disruption in language or speech caused by brain damage.

apparent motion: the illusion created when visual stimuli in different locations appear in close succession.

approach–withdrawal model: a dimensional model that characterizes the component of an emotional reaction as either a tendency to approach the object, event or situation or to withdraw from it.

apraxia: a neurological disorder that impairs the ability to make voluntary movements.

arbitrariness: in language, the lack of direct resemblance between words and their referents.

arousal: the physiological responses (for example, heart rate, sweating, stress hormone release), the subjective assessment of intensity, and the mobilization of energy in response to an emotional stimulus.

articulation: the production of speech sounds.

articulatory rehearsal: the subcomponent of the phonological loop of working memory that is responsible for actively refreshing information in the phonological store.

articulatory suppression: the disruption of the phonological loop of working memory, and in particular the articulatory rehearsal process, caused by overtly producing irrelevant speech while maintaining information.

association: the case in which effects of an activity or variable on one task are accompanied by effects on another task. See also **dissociation**.

association area (convergence zone): a population of conjunctive neurons that associates feature information.

Atkinson-Shiffrin model (modal model): a model of memory based on information processing, first developed in the 1960s, that emphasizes the role of short-term memory as an entryway for information to pass through before entering long-term memory.

atmosphere effect: in reasoning the tendency to accept a conclusion as valid if it contains the same quantifier—"some," "all," or "no"—as appears in the premises.

attention: the process that, at a given moment, enhances some information and inhibits other information.

attentional blink: the decrease in performance in reporting a second piece of information if it appears within a certain period of time after the appearance of a first piece of information.

attentional controller: a component of a neural-network model of conflict phenomena that adds activation to representations related to the current goal.

attitudes: relatively enduring affectively colored beliefs, preferences, and predispositions toward objects or persons, such as like, love, hate, or desire for a person or object.

automatic process: a process that can be initiated without intention and that can operate without attention.

background knowledge: knowledge that specifies how properties originate, why they are important, and how they are related to one another.

backward search: in solving a problem, moving from the goal state to the initial state.

Baddeley-Hitch model: the currently influential model of working memory; it emphasizes the need for short-term storage of information to enable complex cognitive activities, employing two short-term storage buffers and a control system.

basic emotions: six basic types of emotional reactions that appear to be universal across cultures: happiness, sadness, anger, fear, disgust, and surprise.

basic level: the level of a taxonomy used most often, learned most easily, and processed most efficiently.

behavioral method: a technique that measures directly observable behavior, such as the time to respond or the accuracy of a response.

belief bias: bias resulting when background knowledge about the world and personal beliefs influence memory to reshape it in a form consistent with expectations.

belief-bias effect: in reasoning, the tendency to accept a "believable" conclusion to a syllogism than an "unbelievable" one.

binding problem: the question of how we associate different features such as shape, color, and orientation so that we perceive a single object.

binocular rivalry: competition between individual images seen by each eye.

biological motion: the pattern of motion that is uniquely produced by living organisms.

bistable perception: the perception of alternating interpretations of ambiguous stimuli.

blocking (of memory): obstruction preventing retrieval of target information when other information is more strongly associated with the retrieval cue.

bottleneck: a restriction on the amount of information that can be processed at once, necessitating a selection of information to pass through the bottleneck.

Broca's aphasia (nonfluent aphasia): a form of aphasia characterized by nonfluent speech, often with fairly good comprehension but deficits in processing complex sentences.

Brown-Peterson task: a task to examine the duration of storage within short-term memory.

categorical syllogism: a syllogism in which the premises and conclusion relate different categories.

category-based induction: a form of induction that relies on the category of the instances involved.

category-specific impairments: in agnosia, the selective inability to retrieve certain categories of words, such as fruits or vegetables, while retaining the ability to recognize other word categories.

central executive: the control system component of the Baddeley-Hitch working memory model, which governs operations on information in the two storage buffer systems.

change blindness: the failure to detect changes in the physical aspects of a scene, thought to arise from the inability to select at any one time all the information present in a scene.

chunks: groupings of information in working memory, which increase the effective storage capacity by enabling multiple bits of information to be treated as single units.

circumplex model (of emotion): a model that describes the range of emotional responses as varying along the dimensions of arousal and valence.

classical conditioning: the process wherein a response that is elicited by an initial stimulus (the unconditioned stimulus) prior to learning comes to be elicited by a second stimulus (the conditioned stimulus) that predicts the onset of the unconditioned stimulus.

closed head injury: a brain injury caused by an external blow to the head that does not pierce the skull.

coarticulation: the overlapping in time of the articulation of speech sounds.

cocktail party effect: hearing your name or some other salient or relevant information above a din of background noise that would mask other information.

cognition (mental activity): the internal interpretation and transformation of stored information.

cohort: in language, the initial set of lexical candidates activated by the comprehender during the recognition of spoken words.

computer simulation models: computer programs that are designed to mimic specific aspects of mental processing.

conceptual priming: facilitated processing of the meaning of a stimulus, due to processing a related stimulus (priming is a form of nondeclarative memory).

conditional syllogism: a syllogism that represents the condition relationship between variables; the first premise is of the form "if p, then q."

confirmation bias: in reasoning the predisposition to seek out, interpret, and weight information in ways that are consistent with preexisting beliefs and expectations.

conflict monitor: a component of a neural-network model of conflict phenomena that monitors the amount of conflict in processing.

conjunctive search: a type of visual search in which the target differs from the distractors in the display by at least two features; for example, if the target is a shaded circle, some distractors may be shaded squares and others unshaded circles.

consequences: the eventual benefits or losses that are incurred by a decision maker choosing a particular alternative.

consistency bias: bias resulting from the (often erroneous) belief that one's attitudes are stable over time; memories are therefore unconsciously adjusted to bring the past in line with the present.

consolidation: the process that modifies memory representations such that they become more stable over time.

content errors: errors in deductive reasoning that result when the content of the scenario in the syllogism is used instead of logical form.

content morphemes: morphemes that convey meaning but do not convey information about the structure of a sentence (e.g., *cat, run*).

content-based organization: a theoretical account in which maintenance in working memory is thought to occur in different regions of the prefrontal cortex according to the type of information (e.g., visual, spatial, or object) being stored.

context-dependent effect: the phenomenon that memory retrieval is typically better when the external or physical environment—the context—at retrieval matches that at encoding.

convergence zone (association area): a population of conjunctive neurons that associates feature information.

converging evidence: different types of results that imply the same conclusion.

critical periods: biologically determined periods early in life during which the animal is ready to develop particular abilities or responses; if a critical period is missed, the abilities or responses cannot be learned or can be learned only with great difficulty.

cue dependent: relying on hints and clues from the external and internal environment.

decay theory: the hypothesis that forgetting is caused by the spontaneous weakening of memory representations with time.

decision: the selection of one option or course of action from a number of possible alternatives.

decision utility: the anticipation, at the time a decision is made, of the expected subjective value or worth of a particular outcome.

decision tree: a graphical tool for decision making showing the available various courses of action, the likely outcomes, and the potential consequences of each possible choice.

decision weights: a decision maker's estimates of the likelihood of various outcomes of a decision.

declarative memory (explicit memory): form of long-term memory that can be consciously recollected and described ("declared") to other people; includes memory for facts and events.

delayed response task: a task used to study simple forms of working memory: a briefly presented cue is followed by a short delay period, during which the cue information must be held in short-term storage in order to enable the appropriate response to a later signal.

descriptive theories: theories of decision making that focus on how people actually make choices, regardless of how well the decision conforms to rational principles.

disambiguation region: the point in a sentence at which the structure and intended interpretation are made clear.

discourse: a coherent group of written or spoken sentences.

disjunctive (or feature) search: a type of visual search in which the target differs from the distractors in the display by a single feature.

dissociation: the case in which an activity or variable affects the performance of one task or aspect of a task but not another; a dissociation is evidence for the existence of a specific process. See also **association.**

distractors: items that appear (such as in a visual search experiment) that are not the target item that is being sought.

distributed practice: study trials separated by other stimuli.

divided attention: focusing on more than one source of input at any one time.

dorsal pathway: a visual pathway from the occipital lobes to the parietal lobes, which processes spatial information, such as where items are located.

double dissociation: the case in which an activity or variable affects one process but not another and a second activity or variable has the reverse effects.

duality of patterning: a feature of a communication system that enables a small number of meaningless units to be combined into a large number of meaningful units.

dual-process theories (of recognition): theories based on the hypothesis that recollection and familiarity can both support recognition that a stimulus was previously encountered.

dual-task coordination: the process of simultaneously performing two distinct tasks, each of which typically involves storage of information in working memory.

dual-task interference: interference in performance on one task while performing a second at the same time, compared with when the first task is performed alone.

dynamic inconsistency: in decision making, the observed tendency for preferences between outcomes to reverse depending on immediate availability versus a future payoff.

dynamic representation: refers to the ability of the cognitive system to construct, and to call on as necessary, many different representations of a category, each emphasizing the knowledge currently most relevant.

elaboration: the act of processing a stimulus by considering its meaning and relating it to other information stored in memory.

elimination by aspects: a choice strategy whereby a decision maker sets a cutoff for a particular aspect of the alternatives and eliminates all options that do not make the cutoff; then another aspect is selected, a cutoff set, and more alternatives eliminated until only one alternative remains.

Ellsberg paradox: a decision maker's choice of certainty over ambiguity even when the result is an inconsistent pattern of choice.

emotion: a relatively brief episode of synchronized responses (which can include bodily responses, facial expression, and subjective evaluation) that indicates the evaluation of an internal or external event as significant.

emotional classical conditioning: a means by which neutral stimuli can acquire emotional properties by simple association in time between the experience of the neutral event and an emotional event, so that the neutral event is perceived to predict the emotional event.

emotional learning: learning that results in objects and people being associated with an emotion.

encoding: the processes by which information or perceived events are transformed into a memory representation.

encoding specificity principle: our ability to remember a stimulus depends on the similarity between the way the stimulus is processed at encoding and at retrieval.

encoding variability: the encoding of different aspects of a stimulus as different features are selected for encoding in subsequent encounters.

endogenous attention: a form of attention in which top-down information drives the selection of information in the input.

endowment effect: the tendency for an item to acquire extra value by virtue of our possessing it; the effect has been used to explain why sellers often put a higher price on items than buyers do.

episodic buffer: a third storage buffer, recently added to the Baddeley-Hitch model, which may serve as a storage site in which complex, multimodal information (such as temporally extended events or episodes) can be stored and integrated.

episodic memory: memory of individual events that is associated with a particular spatial and temporal context.

event-related brain potentials (ERPs): electrical activity in the brain linked to a particular stimulus (or response).

executive attention: the type of attention that acts on the contents of working memory and directs subsequent processing.

executive processes: processes that modulate the operation of other processes and that are responsible for the coordination of mental activity.

exemplar variation: the differences among many possible examples of objects in a category.

exemplars: individual category members.

exogenous attention: a form of attention in which information in the input captures attention and is selected in a bottom-up fashion.

expected utility: the value or worth of a particular outcome weighted by the likelihood of that outcome's occurring.

expected utility model: a theory of decision making that assumes rational behavior on the part of the decision maker in evaluating the likelihood of alternatives, assessing the consequences, assigning utilities, and choosing the option with the highest utility.

experienced utility: the value or worth placed on a particular outcome at the time the outcome occurs.

explicit memory tests: memory tasks that make direct (that is, explicit) reference to memory for the past, such as recall and recognition.

extinction: the decrease in a learned response that occurs when a previously neutral stimulus, which has acquired properties through classical conditioning, is presented enough times without the occurrence of the unconditioned stimulus that the participant learns that this conditioned neutral stimulus no longer predicts the occurrence of the unconditioned stimulus.

face superiority effect: the finding that people are better able to discriminate between two features of a face (e.g., a wide nose and a narrow nose) when they are shown within the context of the rest of a face, than when the parts are presented alone.

fast-and-frugal strategy: a choice strategy whereby a decision maker chooses on the basis of specific aspects of each option.

feature (in perception): a meaningful sensory aspect of a perceived stimulus.

flashbulb memories: a term used to refer to memories for shocking or otherwise emotionally charged events, which are often described as recollected with a high level of confidence and apparent detail, like a picture taken with a flashbulb.

fluent aphasia (Wernicke's aphasia): a form of aphasia characterized by fluent but often meaningless speech, many made-up words or other speech errors, and poor comprehension.

focused attention: focusing on one source of input (e.g., a phone call) to the exclusion of others (e.g., watching a television program).

forgetting: the inability to recall or recognize previously encoded information.

form errors: errors in deductive reasoning that result from the structural form or format of the premise–conclusion relationship.

format (of a representation): the form of the code being used by a representation; the means by which it serves to convey information.

forward search: in solving a problem, moving from the initial state to the goal state.

fovea: the central part of the retina, which has the greatest visual acuity.

frame: a structure that specifies a set of relations that links objects in the environment. See also **semantic network**.

framing effects: the influence of the various ways a problem may be put, which can alter a decision maker's choice.

Freudian slip: a speech error in which the speaker chooses a word that means the opposite of what was intended.

frontal executive hypothesis: the proposal that every executive process is primarily mediated by the prefrontal cortex.

function morpheme: a morpheme that conveys syntactical information, such as the -s plural morpheme.

function words: words that convey information about the syntactical structure of a sentence, for example articles, auxiliary verbs, and conjunctions.

garden path sentence: an ambiguous sentence that initially seems to have one meaning but then is disambiguated with a different meaning.

generate and test (random search): attempting to solve a problem by a process of trial and error.

generation effect: the phenomenon that information that is retrieved or generated from memory is more likely to be remembered than information that is presented externally.

generative capacity (in language): the uniquely human ability to recombine morphemes, words, and sentences to convey an infinite number of thoughts.

geons: a set of 24 relatively simple geometrical three-dimensional shapes that can be combined to represent many common objects.

goal state: the solution to a problem.

goal-maintenance model: a theoretical account of working memory in which the prefrontal cortex actively maintains goal-related information so that this information can serve as a top-down influence that coordinates perception, attention, and actions necessary to attain the goal.

grammar: the implicit knowledge that one has of the structure of a language.

grammatical encoding: the second level in a model of the speech production process; at this level the speaker (or writer) chooses words to convey meaning and the syntactic structure of the sentence to be uttered.

grouping principles: conditions, such as proximity and similarity, that lead the visual system to produce perceptual units.

hemispatial neglect: an attention deficit in which the impairment leads the patient to ignore information appearing on the side of space opposite the damaged side of the brain.

heuristics: simple, efficient, quick rules of thumb that usually, but not always, give the correct answer to a problem and are used to make decisions and judgments; the rules work well in most circumstances, but in certain cases can lead to systematic biases.

hill climbing: a heuristic for solving a problem by choosing successive moves one at a time that most closely resemble the goal state.

ill-defined problems: problems in which the initial state and the goal state are not clearly known at the outset.

illusory conjunctions: incorrect combinations of features; for example, in a visual search task, reporting that the target was a shaded circle when the display contained shaded squares and unshaded circles.

imitation: the ability to understand the intent of an observed action and then to reproduce it.

immediacy: in language the principle that we interpret words as we encounter them.

implicit memory tests: memory tasks that make indirect (that is, implicit) reference to memory; the memory is revealed implicitly through a change in behavior rather than through recall or recognition of the contents of memory.

incidental learning: learning that occurs not as a result of a purposeful attempt to learn, but as a by-product of performing a particular task.

inductive reasoning: any thought process that uses knowledge of specific instances to draw further inferences (which are not necessarily correct).

information processing: the ways in which information is stored, manipulated, and transformed.

initial state (start state): the state of a problem when it is first faced by the problem solver.

insight problem: a problem to which the solution comes suddenly.

instrumental conditioning (operant conditioning): a means of learning in which a behavior or response increases or decreases in frequency depending on the outcome of that behavior—on whether it yields a reward or a punishment.

intentional learning: learning that occurs as a result of a purposeful attempt to learn.

intentions: mental plans designed to achieve a goal through action.

interference theories (of forgetting): theories based on the hypothesis that memories compete during retrieval, and forgetting occurs because other associates of a cue interfere with retrieval of the desired memory.

intonation: the "melody" of speech that results from the rise and fall of pitch and variations in stress.

introspection: the process of internal perception, that is, looking within oneself to assess one's mental events.

kinematic pattern: the pattern of motion associated with a specific action or set of movements.

knowledge: in the inclusive sense used in cognitive psychology, information in memory about the world, ranging from the everyday to the formal; often further defined as information about the world that is likely to be true and that one has justification for believing.

levels of analysis: the various degrees of abstraction we can use to describe an object or event.

levels-of-processing theory: theory based on the hypothesis that processing different aspects of a stimulus—perceptual, phonological, semantic—corresponds to increasingly deeper processing and increasingly more effective encoding.

lexical accessibility: the ease with which a word can be retrieved.

lexicon: one's collective mental representations of known words.

long-term memory: information that is acquired in the course of an experience and that persists so that it can be retrieved even long after the experience is past.

loss aversion: decision behavior to avoid a loss, even if the result is a less than optimal choice.

massed practice: repeatedly studying the same information without interleaving other information between study trials.

matching bias: in reasoning the tendency to accept a conclusion as valid if it contains the syntactic structure of the premises.

meaningful entity: an object or event that plays an important role in an organism's survival and pursuit of its goals.

means–ends analysis: a problem-solving strategy that breaks the problem into subproblems; if a subproblem at the first stage of analysis is not solvable, then the problem is further broken into subproblems until a soluble subproblem is found.

memory: the set of representations and processes by which information is encoded, consolidated, and retrieved.

mental activity (cognition): the internal interpretation or transformation of stored information.

mere exposure: the acquisition of a preference or attitude through familiarity alone.

message level: the first level in a model of the speech production process; at this level the speaker (or writer) formulates a nonlinguistic message to be conveyed.

mimicry: the tendency to adopt the behaviors, postures, or mannerisms of others without awareness or intent.

mirror neurons: cells in the premotor cortex that discharge both during the execution of a given action as well as during the observation of the same action performed by another individual.

misattribution: ascribing recollected information to an incorrect time, place, person, or source.

misinformation effect: misremembering of an original event in line with false information subsequently introduced.

modal model (Atkinson-Shiffrin model): a model of memory based on information processing, first developed in the 1960s, that emphasizes the role of short-term memory as an entryway for information to pass through before entering long-term memory.

modality switching: a process in which one shifts attention from one modality to another, for instance, from vision to audition.

monitoring: assessing one's performance on a task while the task is being performed.

mood: a low-intensity, diffuse, and long-lasting affective state.

mood-congruent memory effect: the tendency of mood to influence the type of information that is retrieved so that it is congruent with the present affective state; negative information is more likely to be retrieved during negative moods and positive information is more likely to be retrieved during positive moods.

morpheme: the smallest unit of meaning in a language; *cats* has two morphemes, *cat* and *–s*.

motivation: the propensity to action.

motor anticipation: the phenomenon by which a motor response is tuned prior to producing the response.

motor cognition: mental processing in which the motor system draws on stored information to contribute to the preparation and production of our own actions, as well as to anticipate, predict, and interpret the actions of others.

motor imagery: imagining making an intended action without actually producing it.

motor priming: the effect whereby watching an action automatically facilitates a similar action by oneself.

motor program: the representation of a sequence of movements that is planned in advance of actual performance.

movement: a voluntary displacement of a body part in physical space.

N-back task: a task used to study the effects of increases in working memory load by requiring participants to judge for each presented item whether it matches an item presented N items back in the series.

neighborhood density: the number of words in a given language with similar sounds and articulations.

neural-network models: models that rely on sets of interconnected units, each of which is intended to correspond to a neuron or a small group of neurons.

nondeclarative memory (implicit memory): nonconscious forms of long-term memory that are expressed as a change in behavior rather than as conscious recollection.

nonfluent aphasia (Broca's aphasia): a form of aphasia characterized by nonfluent speech, often with fairly good comprehension but deficits in processing complex sentences.

normative theories (prescriptive theories): in decision making, theories that describe how we *should* decide in order to make rational choices.

ontological types: categories for the general kinds of things in the world.

output interference: interference, leading to forgetting, during the act of retrieval because initially retrieved memories are strengthened and, thus, block retrieval of other memories.

pattern completion: a retrieval process in which a cue that is part of a stored memory serves to reactivate other aspects of the stored memory, resulting in retrieval of other information present during encoding of the event.

perception–action cycle: the transformation of perceived patterns into coordinated patterns of movements; the mutual functional interdependence between perception and action in the outside world.

perception-to-action transfer: the effect that watching an action facilitates the later ability to perform that action.

perceptual priming: facilitated processing of perceptual aspects of a stimulus due to processing a prior stimulus (priming is a form of nondeclarative memory).

phoneme: the minimal unit of sound that distinguishes words in a given language.

phoneme restoration effect: a perceptual phenomenon in which a missing or distorted phoneme is supplied by the listener.

phonetic alphabet: an alphabet of symbols in which the speech sounds of all languages can be represented.

phonological encoding: the third level in a model of the speech production process; at this level, prior to articulation, the phonological representation of the utterance is developed.

phonological loop: the storage buffer component of the Baddeley-Hitch working memory model that is responsible for maintaining verbal information.

phonological similarity effect: the reduction in working memory performance that occurs when simultaneously stored verbal items that have similar sounds must be serially recalled.

phonological store: the subcomponent of the phonological loop responsible for short-term storage of verbal information in the form of a sound-based (phonological) code.

phrase structure tree: a diagram of a sentence that illustrates its hierarchical syntactic structure.

potentiated eyeblink startle: eyeblink startle is potentiated, or increased, in the presence of a negative stimulus and is decreased in the presence of a positive stimulus.

prescriptive theories (normative theories): in decision making, theories that describe how we *should* decide in order to make rational choices.

primary memory: the term used by William James to describe a separate memory system that provides a storage site that enables information to remain accessible to consciousness.

primary reinforcer: an emotionally evocative stimulus that is inherently positive or negative, such as food or shock; for these stimuli the reinforcing properties occur naturally and do not need to be learned. See also **secondary reinforcer.**

priming: the facilitation of processing a stimulus or task by a preceding stimulus or task.

proactive interference: the case in which previous learning results in difficulty remembering newly learned information.

problem solving: the act of using a set of cognitive processes to reach a goal when the path to that goal is not obvious.

problem space: the set of states, or possible choices, that faces the problem solver at each step in moving from an initial state to a goal state.

procedural invariance: in decision making, the principle that a consistent preference should be expressed between options, even when they are presented in different form.

process: a transformation of information that obeys well-defined principles to produce a specific output when given a specific input.

process models: models that specify a sequence of processes that convert an input to an output; each process typically is treated as a "black box."

process-based organization: the idea that different working memory processes (storage and executive control) are carried out in different regions of the prefrontal cortex.

processing system: a set of processes that work together to accomplish a task, using and producing representations as appropriate.

property list: a list of the characteristics of the entities belonging to a category.

propositions: assertions that can be expressed in clauses in sentences.

prospect theory: a modern descriptive theory of decision behavior that updates the standard economic model of expected utility theory by assuming that we experience losses more keenly than gains of the same magnitude, that we are risk averse for gains and risk seeking for losses, that we use decision weights instead of objective probabilities, and that our decisions are often made from the perspective of a reference point.

prototype: the collection of properties most likely to be true of members of a category.

psycholinguistics: the study of the comprehension, production, and acquisition of language.

psychophysiology: the study of the relationship between mental states, typically affective states, and physiological responses.

random search (generate and test): attempting to solve a problem by the process of trial and error.

reasoning: the cognitive procedures we use to make inferences from knowledge.

recapitulation: the reinstatement during retrieval of the pattern of activation that was present during encoding.

receptive field (of a cell): the region of the visual field in which a stimulus will affect the activity of the cell.

reciprocal imitation: taking turns in imitation, as a mother and baby engaging in communicative exchanges.

recognition: the process of matching organized sensory input to stored representations in memory.

reconstructive memory: memory that is a reconstruction of the past rather than a reproduction of it (and is thus is susceptible to bias).

recursion: the successive embedding of grammatical phrases within sentences, leading to the infinite creativity of human language.

reference point: the psychological position from which we view the consequences of a decision.

repetition blindness: the failure to detect the subsequent appearance of a stimulus when stimuli are presented in a rapid sequence.

repetition suppression: the phenomenon observed in nonhuman primates and rats that the firing rate of neurons is less in subsequent encounters with a stimulus than in the initial encounter.

representation: a physical state that was created to convey information, specifying an object, event, or category or its characteristics or relations.

response bottleneck: a stage of processing in which a response (e.g., a button press) to a stimulus is selected in competition with other possible responses (e.g., a foot pedal response) for execution.

response inhibition: the suppression of a partially prepared response.

retention interval: the time between encoding and retrieval of an event.

retrieval-induced forgetting: forgetting that occurs when a memory is suppressed during the retrieval of another memory.

retroactive interference: the case in which new learning impairs the ability to remember previously learned information.

retrograde amnesia: the forgetting of events that occurred *before* brain damage.

reverberatory loop: a hypothesis about short-term storage in working memory in which a circuit of connected neurons recirculates activity among themselves, with each neuron both sending and receiving signals regarding the information being stored.

risk averse: describes the preference for receiving a small, certain gain to the chance of getting a larger, but uncertain, gain.

risk seeking: describes the preference for receiving a larger, but uncertain, gain to the chance of getting a small, certain gain.

rule: in categorization, a precise definition of the criteria for a category.

saccade: a quick eye movement during reading.

satisficing: a choice strategy whereby a decision maker finds not necessarily the best possible option, but rather one that is "good enough" on a number of dimensions; a common strategy in consumer choice.

schema: a structured representation that captures the information typically true for a situation or event.

secondary reinforcer: an emotionally evocative stimulus that is not inherently positive or negative, but rather acquires its reinforcing properties through learning (money is a prototypical example). See also **primary reinforcer**.

semantic memory: general knowledge about the world, including words and concepts, their properties and interrelations.

semantic network: a structure that diagrammatically specifies, by directional arrows, a set of relations that links objects or events. See also **frame**.

sense of agency: awareness of being the initiator or source of a movement, action, or thought.

sequencing: the ability to order information or actions to achieve a goal.

shared motor representations: representations that both control our own actions and specify actions made by other people; shared motor representations are critical in planning because they permit observational learning.

short-term memory: an alternative term for the storage component of working memory that emphasizes the limited duration of this storage system, which distinguishes it from the more permanent long-term memory.

simulation: in perception, the reactivation, in a statistical pattern, of image and feature information even after the original scene is no longer present; in reasoning and planning, the construction and "running" of a mental model of an object or situation, used to anticipate the consequences of an action or transformation.

skin conductance response: an indication of autonomic nervous system arousal assessed by passing a small electrical current through the skin and measuring changes in resistance to the current as a result of subtle changes in the sweat glands; often used as an indirect assessment of an emotional reaction.

sound exchange error: a speech error in which two sounds change places.

spaced practice: studying the same information but interleaving other information between study trials.

spacing effect: the phenomenon that memory for information is better when study trials are spaced rather than massed.

spatial rehearsal: the process of mentally refreshing spatial locations stored in the visuospatial component of working memory, possibly by covert movement of the eyes or body toward the stored locations.

spectrogram: the visual display produced on a spectrograph, an instrument used in acoustic phonetics for speech analysis; time is shown on one axis and the frequency of sound on the other.

start state (also known as initial state): the state of a problem when it is first faced by the problem solver.

state-dependent effect: the phenomenon that retrieval is typically better when aspects of our internal states at retrieval match those at encoding.

stimulus–response compatibility: a measure of the degree to which the assignment of correct responses to stimuli is consonant with the way people would act naturally. In a stimulus–response compatibility task, the "naturalness" of the assignment of stimuli to responses is varied.

stimulus–response habits: habits that emerge through the slow accumulation of knowledge about the predictive relationship between a stimulus and a response.

Stroop task: a test of attentional function in which color names are presented in different-colored ink; the participant's task is to name the color of the ink.

structural ambiguity: a linear string of words that is consistent with more than one syntactic structure and meaning.

subjective (or illusory) contour: a contour that is not physically present in the stimulus but is filled in by the visual system.

suppression: the active weakening of a memory.

switching attention: moving the focus of attention from one entity to another.

switching cost: the additional time taken when it is necessary to switch attention from one task or attribute to another, as opposed to keeping the attention focused on the same task or attribute.

syllogism: an argument in deductive reasoning that consists of two statements (the major premise and minor premise) and a conclusion.

syntax: the relationship between the types of words (such as nouns and verbs) in a sentence; this structure specifies the roles of the entities named by words (e.g., subject, object).

taxonomy: a set of nested categories that vary in abstraction, with each nested category a subset of its higher order category.

template: a pattern that can be used to compare individual items to a standard.

temporal discounting: the tendency to discount or devalue outcomes, both gains and losses, pleasant and unpleasant, that occur further in the future.

thinking: the process of mentally representing information and transforming these representations so that new representations, useful to our goals, are generated.

tilt aftereffect: a bias in perceiving orientation that results when right-tilting or left-tilting neurons are fatigued.

transfer appropriate processing: the principle that processing at encoding is effective to the extent that it overlaps with the processing to be performed at retrieval.

transitivity: in decision making, the principle that if object A is preferred to object B, and object B is preferred to object C, then object A must be preferred to object C.

triangle model: a theory of the lexicon, used to describe word representation, with three major components: spelling (orthography), sound (phonology), and meaning.

valence: the subjective quality, positive or negative, of the emotional reaction to a specific object or event.

ventral pathway: a visual pathway from the occipital lobes to the bottom parts of the temporal lobes that processes information that leads to the recognition of objects.

verbal protocol analysis: a procedure in which the thought process of a problem solver in the course of working on a problem is spoken aloud, recorded, and analyzed.

viewpoint dependence: sensitivity to the appearance of an object as viewed from a particular position.

visual field: the portion of the world that is visible at the present moment.

visuospatial scratchpad: the storage buffer component of the Baddeley-Hitch working memory model that is responsible for maintaining visuospatial information.

vocal tract: the set of anatomical structures that participate in speech production, principally the larynx (which includes the vocal cords), mouth, and nose.

weight-based memory: a form of memory storage that occurs by strengthening (or weakening) the connections, or weights, between neural populations.

well-defined problems: problems in which the initial state and the goal state are clearly defined and the possible moves (and the constraining rules) are known.

Wernicke's aphasia (fluent aphasia): a form of aphasia characterized by fluent but often meaningless speech, many made-up words or other speech errors, and poor comprehension.

word superiority effect: the phenomenon in which a letter is seen better in the context of a word than alone; surrounding letters may suggest a word, and thus influence the perception of the central letters.

word-exchange error: a speech error in which two words change places.

word-length effect: the reduction in working memory performance that occurs when storing items that take a long time to say out loud.

working memory: the system that enables the short-term storage and mental manipulation of information.

working memory capacity (working memory span): a measure that describes the maximum amount of information an individual can store in working memory.

References

Abbot, V., Black, J., & Smith, E. E. (1985). The representation of scripts in memory. *Journal of Memory and Language, 24*, 179–199.

Adolphs, R., Tranel, D., Hamann, S., Young, A. W., Calder, A. J., Phelps, E. A., et al. (1999). Recognition of facial emotion in nine individuals with bilateral amygdala damage. *Neuropsychologia, 37,* 1111–1117.

Ahn, W., & Luhmann, C. C. (2005). Demystifying theory-based categorization. In L. Gershkoff-Stowe & D. H. Rakison (Eds). *Building object categories in developmental time.* (pp. 277–300). Mahwah, NJ, US: Lawrence Erlbaum Associates, Publishers.

Allais, M. (1953/1979). Le comportement de l'homme rationnel devant le risqué: Critique des postulate et axioms de l'école américaine. *Econometrica, 21,* 503–546. [In M. Allais & O. Hagen (Eds. and Trans.). (1979). *Expected utility hypotheses and the Allais paradox.* Hingham, MA: Reidel.]

Allen, S. W., & Brooks, L. R. (1991). Specializing the operation of an explicit rule. *Journal of Experimental Psychology: General, 120,* 3–19.

Allison, T., Puce, A., & McCarty, G. (2000). Social perception from visual cues: Role of the STS region. *Trends Cognitive Science, 4,* 267–278.

Allopena, P. D., Magnuson, J. S., & Tanenhaus, M. K. (1998). Tracking the time course of spoken word recognition using eye movements: Evidence for continuous mapping models. *Journal of Memory and Language, 38,* 419–439.

Allport, A., Styles, E., & Hsieh, S. (1994). Shifting attentional set: Exploring the dynamic control of tasks. In C. Umilta & M. Moscovitch (Eds.), *Attention and performance XV* (pp. 421–452). Cambridge, MA: The MIT Press.

Altmann, G. T. M. (Ed.). (1990). *Cognitive models of speech processing.* Cambridge, MA: The MIT Press.

Amaral, D. G., Price, J. L., Pitkanen, A., & Carmichael, S. T. (1992). Anatomical organization of the primate amygdaloid complex. In J. P. Aggleton (Ed.) *The amygdala: Neurobiological aspects of emotion, memory and mental dysfunction* (pp. 1–65). New York: Wiley-Liss.

Anderson, A. K. (2004). *Pay attention! Psychological and neural explorations of emotion and attention.* Paper presented at 16th Annual Meeting of the American Psychological Society, Chicago, IL.

Anderson, A. K. (2005). Affective influences on the attentional dynamics supporting awareness. *Journal of Experimental Psychology: General, 134,* 258–281.

Anderson, A. K., Christoff, K., Stappen, I., Panitz, D., Ghahremani, D. G., Glover, G., et al. (2003). Dissociated neural representations of intensity and valence in human olfaction. *Nature Neuroscience, 6,* 196–202.

Anderson, A. K., & Phelps, E. A. (2001). The human amygdala supports affective modulatory influences on visual awareness. *Nature, 411,* 305–309.

Anderson, J. A., Silverstein, J. W., Ritz, S. A., & Jones, R. S. (1977). Distinctive features, categorical perception, and probability learning: Some applications of a neural model. *Psychological Review, 84,* 413–451.

Anderson, J. R. (1976). *Language, memory, and thought.* Hillsdale, NJ: Erlbaum.

Anderson, J. R. (1978). Arguments concerning representations for mental imagery. *Psychological Review, 85,* 249–277.

Anderson, J. R. (1983). *The architecture of cognition*. Cambridge, MA: Harvard University Press.

Anderson, J. R. (1990). *The adaptive character of thought*. Hillsdale, NJ: Erlbaum.

Anderson, J. R., Bothell, D., Byrne M. D., & Lebiere, C. (2005). An integrated theory of the mind. *Psychological Review, 111*, 1036–1060.

Anderson, M. C., & Green, C. (2001). Suppressing unwanted memories by executive control. *Nature, 410*, 366–369.

Anderson, M. C., & Spellman, B. A. (1995). On the status of inhibitory mechanisms in cognition: Memory retrieval as a model case. *Psychological Review, 102*, 68–100.

Andrews, T. J., Sengpiel, F., & Blakemore, C. (2005). From contour to object-face rivalry: Multiple neural mechanisms resolve perceptual ambiguity. In D. Alais & R. Blake (Eds). *Binocular rivalry*. (pp. 187–211). Cambridge, MA, US: MIT Press.

Armstrong, S. L., Gleitman, L. R., & Gleitman, H. (1983). On what some concepts might not be. *Cognition, 13*, 263–308.

Arocha, J. F., & Patel, V. L. (1995). Novice diagnostic reasoning in medicine: Accounting for clinical evidence. *Journal of the Learning Sciences, 4*, 355–384.

Ashbridge, E., Walsh, V., & Cowey, A. (1997). Temporal aspects of visual search studies by transcranial magnetic stimulation. *Neuropsychologia, 35*, 1121–1131.

Ashby, F. G., & Ell, S. W. (2001). The neurobiology of human category learning. *Trends in Cognitive Sciences, 5*, 204–210.

Ashby, F. G., & Maddox, W. T. (1992). Complex decision rules in categorization: Contrasting novice and experienced performance. *Journal of Experimental Psychology: Human Perception and Performance, 18*, 50–71.

Atkinson, R. C., & Shiffrin, R. M. (1968). Human memory: A proposed system and its control processes. In K. W. Spence (Ed.), *The psychology of learning and motivation: Advances in research and theory* (pp. 89–195). New York: Academic Press.

Atwood, M. E., & Polson, P. G. (1976). A process model for water jug problems. *Cognitive Psychology, 8*, 191–216.

Au, T. K. F., Knightly, L. M., Jun, S. A., & Oh, J. S. (2002). Overhearing a language during childhood. *Psychological Science, 13*, 238–243.

Awh, E., & Jonides, J. (2001). Overlapping mechanisms of attention and spatial working memory. *Trends in Cognitive Sciences, 5*, 119–126.

Awh, E., Jonides, J., & Reuter-Lorenz, P. A. (1998). Rehearsal in spatial working memory. *Journal of Experimental Psychology: Human Perception and Performance, 24*, 780–790.

Baars, B. J., Motley M. T., & MacKay, D. G. (1975). Output editing for lexical status in artificially elicited slips of the tongue. *Journal of Verbal Learning and Verbal Behavior, 14*, 382–391.

Baddeley, A. (1986). *Working memory*. New York: Clarendon Press/Oxford University Press.

Baddeley, A. D. (2000). The episodic buffer: A new component of working memory? *Trends in Cognitive Sciences, 4*, 417–423.

Baddeley, A. D. (2003). Working memory: Looking back and looking forward. *Nature Reviews Neuroscience, 4*, 829–839.

Baddeley, A. D., Bressi, S., Della Sala, S., Logie, R., & Spinnler, H. (1991). The decline of working memory in Alzheimer's disease. *Brain, 114*, 2521–2542.

Baddeley, A. D., Gathercole, S., & Papagno, C. (1998). The phonological loop as a language learning device. *Psychological Review, 105*, 158–173.

Baddeley, A. D., Grant, S., Wight, E., & Thomson, N. (1973). Imagery and visual working memory. In P. M. A. Rabbitt & S. Dornic (Eds.), *Attention and performance* (Vol. 5, pp. 205–217). London: Academic Press.

Baddeley, A. D., & Hitch, G. J. (1974). Working memory. In G. Bower (Ed.), *The psychology of learning and motivation*, (Vol. 8, pp. 47–89). New York: Academic Press.

Baddeley, A. D., Lewis, V. J., & Vallar, G. (1984). Exploring the articulatory loop. *Quarterly Journal of Experimental Psychology, 36*, 233–252.

Baddeley, A. D., & Lieberman, K. (1980). Spatial working memory. In R. S. Nickerson (Ed.), *Attention and performance* (Vol. 8, pp. 521–539). Hillsdale, NJ: Lawrence Erlbaum Associates.

Baddeley, A. D., Papagno, C., & Vallar, G. (1988). When long–term learning depends on short-term storage. *Journal of Memory and Language, 27*, 586–595.

Baddeley, A. D., Thomson, N., & Buchanan, M. (1975). Word length and the structure of short-term memory. *Journal of Verbal Learning and Verbal Behavior, 14*, 575–589.

Baddeley, A. D., & Warrington, E. K. (1970). Amnesia and the distinction between long- and short-term memory. *Journal of Verbal Learning and Verbal Behaviour, 9*, 176–189.

Baeyens, F., Elen, P., Vand Den Bergh, O., & Crombez, G. (1990). Flavor-flavor and color-flavor conditioning in humans. *Learning and Motivation, 21*, 434–455.

Baird, J. A., & Baldwin, D. A. (2001). Making sense of human behavior: action parsing and intentional inferences. In B. F. Malle, L. J. Moses, & D. A. Baldwin (Eds.), *Intentions and intentionality* (pp. 193–206). Cambridge, MA: The MIT Press.

Bakin, J. S., Nakayama, K., & Gilbert, C. D. (2000). Visual responses in monkey areas V1 and V2 to three-dimensional surface configurations. *Journal of Neuroscience, 20*, 8188–8198.

Baldwin, D. A., Baird, J. A., Saylor, M. M., & Clark, M. A. (2001). Infants parse dynamic action. *Child Development, 72*, 708–717.

Baldwin, J. M. (1897). *Social and ethical interpretations in mental development: A study in social psychology.* New York: Macmillan.

Banich, M. T. (1997). *Neuropsychology: The neural bases of mental function.* Boston: Houghton Mifflin.

Barclay, J. R., Bransford, J. D., Franks, J. J., McCarrell, N. S., & Nitsch, K. E. (1974). Comprehension and semantic flexibility. *Journal of Verbal Learning and Verbal Behavior, 13*, 471–481.

Barnes, J. M., & Underwood, B. J. (1959). "Fate" of first-list associations in transfer theory. *Journal of Experimental Psychology, 58*, 97–105.

Barr, R., Dowden, A., & Hayne, H. (1996). Developmental changes in deferred imitation by 6- to 24-month-old infants. *Infant Behavior & Development, 19*, 159–170.

Barr, R. F., & McConaghy, N. (1972). A general factor of conditionability: A study of Galvanic skin responses and penile responses. *Behaviour Research and Therapy, 10*, 215–227.

Barrett, L. F., & Russell, J. A. (1999). Structure of current affect. *Current Directions in Psychological Science, 8*, 10–14.

Barsalou, L. W. (1983). Ad hoc categories. *Memory & Cognition, 11*, 211–227.

Barsalou, L. W. (1985). Ideals, central tendency, and frequency of instantiation as determinants of graded structure in categories. *Journal of Experimental Psychology: Learning, Memory, and Cognition, 11*, 629–654.

Barsalou, L. W. (1987). The instability of graded structure: Implications for the nature of concepts. In U. Neisser (Ed.), *Concepts and conceptual development: Ecological and intellectual factors in categorization* (pp. 101–140). Cambridge, UK: Cambridge University Press.

Barsalou, L. W. (1989). Intraconcept similarity and its implications for interconcept similarity. In S. Vosniadou & A. Ortony (Eds.), *Similarity and analogical reasoning* (pp. 76–121). Cambridge, UK: Cambridge University Press.

Barsalou, L. W. (1990). On the indistinguishability of exemplar memory and abstraction in category representation. In T. K. Srull & R. S. Wyer (Eds.), *Advances in social cognition, Volume III: Content and process specificity in the effects of prior experiences* (pp. 61–88). Hillsdale, NJ: Lawrence Erlbaum Associates.

Barsalou, L. W. (1992). Frames, concepts, and conceptual fields. In E. Kittay & A. Lehrer (Eds.), *Frames, fields, and contrasts: New essays in semantic and lexical organization* (pp. 21–74). Hillsdale, NJ: Lawrence Erlbaum Associates.

Barsalou, L. W. (1999). Perceptual symbol systems. *Behavioral and Brain Sciences, 22*, 577–609.

Barsalou, L. W. (2003a). Abstraction in perceptual symbol systems. *Philosophical Transactions of the Royal Society of London: Biological Sciences, 358*, 1177–1187.

Barsalou, L. W. (2003b). Situated simulation in the human conceptual system. *Language and Cognitive Processes, 18*, 513–562.

Barsalou, L. W., & Hale, C. R. (1993). Components of conceptual representation: From feature lists to recursive frames. In I. Van Mechelen, J. Hampton, R. Michalski, & P. Theuns (Eds.), *Categories and concepts: Theoretical views and inductive data analysis* (pp. 97–144). San Diego: Academic Press.

Barsalou, L. W., Niedenthal, P. M., Barbey, A., & Ruppert, J. (2003). Social embodiment. In B. Ross (Ed.), *The psychology of learning and motivation* (Vol. 43, pp. 43–92). San Diego: Academic Press.

Bartlett, F. C. (1932). *Remembering: A study in experimental and social psychology.* Cambridge, UK: Cambridge University Press.

Bartolomeo, P., & Chokron, S. (2001). Levels of impairment in unilateral neglect. In F. Boller & J. Grafman (Eds.), *Handbook of neuropsychology* (Vol. 4, pp. 67–98). North-Holland: Elsevier Science.

Basso, A., Spinnler, H., Vallar, G., & Zanobio, M. E. (1982). Left hemisphere damage and selective impairment of auditory-verbal short-term memory: A case study. *Neuropsychologia, 20,* 263–274.

Bateson, M., & Kacelnik, A. (1998). Risk-sensitive foraging: Decision making in variable environments. In R. Dukas (Ed.), *Cognitive ecology: The evolutionary ecology of information processing and decision making* (pp. 297–341). Chicago: University of Chicago Press.

Bauer, R. H., & Fuster, J. M. (1976). Delayed-matching and delayed-response deficit from cooling dorsolateral prefrontal cortex in monkeys. *Journal of Comparative and Physiological Psychology, 90,* 293–302.

Bear, M. F., Connors, B. W., & Paradiso, M. A. (2002). *Neuroscience: Exploring the brain* (2nd ed.). Baltimore: Lippincott Williams & Wilkins.

Bechara, A., & Damasio, A. R. (2005). The somatic marker hypothesis: A neural theory of economic behavior. *Games and Economic Behavior, 52,* 336–372.

Bechara, A., Damasio, A. R., Damasio, H., & Anderson, S. W. (1994). Insensitivity to future consequences following damage to human prefrontal cortex. *Cognition, 50,* 7–15.

Bechara, A., Damasio, H., & Damasio, A. R. (2000a). Emotion, decision making and the orbitofrontal cortex. *Cerebral Cortex, 10,* 295–307.

Bechara, A., Tranel, D., & Damasio, H. (2000b). Characterization of the decision-making deficit of patients with ventromedial prefrontal cortex lesions. *Brain, 123,* 2189–2202.

Bechara, A., Tranel, D., Damasio, H., Adolphs, R., Rockland, C., & Damasio, A. R. (1995). Double dissociation of conditioning and declarative knowledge relative to the amygdala and hippocampus in human. *Science, 269,* 1115–1118.

Bechtel, W., & Abrahamsen, A. (2001). *Connectionism and the mind: Parallel processing, dynamics and evolution in networks.* Cambridge, MA: Blackwell.

Beckers, G., & Homberg, V. (1992). Cerebral visual motion blindness: transitory akinetopsia induced by transcranial magnetic stimulation of human area V5. *Proceedings of the Royal Society London B: Biological Science, 249,* 173–178.

Beckers, G., & Zeki, S. (1995). The consequences of inactivating areas V1 and V5 on visual motion perception. *Brain, 118*(Pt 1), 49–60.

Begley, S. (2002, September 13). Are your memories of September 11 really true? *Wall Street Journal.*

Behn, R. D., & Vaupel, J. W. (1982). *Quick analysis for busy decision makers.* New York: Basic Books.

Behrmann, M. (2000). The mind's eye mapped onto the brain's matter. *Current Directions in Psychological Science, 9,* 50–54.

Behrmann, M., Ebert, P., & Black, S. E. (2003). Hemispatial neglect and visual search: A large scale analysis from the Sunnybrook Stroke Study. *Cortex, 40,* 247–263.

Behrmann, M., & Tipper, S. P. (1994). Object-based visual attention: Evidence from unilateral neglect. In C. Umilta & M. Moscovitch (Eds.), *Attention and performance XV: Conscious and nonconscious processing and cognitive functions* (pp. 351–375). Cambridge, MA: The MIT Press.

Bekkering, H., & Wohlschlager, A. (2002). Action perception and imitation: A tutorial. In W. Prinz & B. Hommel (Eds.), *Attention and performance XIX: Common mechanisms in perception and action* (pp. 294–314). Oxford: Oxford University Press.

Bell, D. E. (1982). Regret in decision making under uncertainty. *Operations Research, 30,* 961–981.

Bell, D. E. (1985). Disappointment in decision making under uncertainty. *Operations Research, 33,* 1–27.

Benartzi, S., & Thaler, R. H. (1995). Myopic loss aversion and the equity premium puzzle. *Quarterly Journal of Economics, 110,* 73–92.

Berg, J., Dickhaut, J., & O'Brien, J. (1985). Preference reversal and arbitrage. In V. Smith (Ed.), *Research in experimental economics* (Vol. 3, pp. 31–72). Greenwich, CT: JAI Press.

Berlin, B., Breedlove, D. E., & Raven, P. H. (1973). General principles of classification and nomenclature in folk biology. *American Anthropologist, 75,* 214–242.

Bertenthal, B. I. (1993). Perception of biomechanical motion in infants: Intrinsic image and knowledge-based constraints. In C. Granrud (Ed.), *Carnegie symposium on cognition: Visual perception and cognition in infancy* (pp. 175–214). Hillsdale, NJ: Lawrence Erlbaum Associates.

Bertenthal, B. I., Proffit, D. R., & Cutting, J. E. (1984). Infant sensitivity to figural coherence in biomechanical motions. *Journal of Experimental Child Psychology, 37*, 213–230.

Beyer, L., Weiss, T., Hansen, E., Wolf, A., & Seidel, A. (1990). Dynamics of central nervous activation during motor imagination. *International Journal of Psychophysiology, 9*, 75–80.

Bialystok, E., Craik, F. I. M., & Klein, R. (2004). Bilingualism, aging, and cognitive control: Evidence from the Simon task. *Psychology & Aging, 19*, 290–303.

Bialystok, E., & Martin, M. M. (2004). Attention and inhibition in bilingual children: Evidence from the dimensional change card sort task. *Developmental Science, 7*, 325–339.

Biederman, I. (1981). On the semantics of a glance at a scene. In M. Kubovy & J. R. Pomerantz (Eds.), *Perceptual Organization* (pp. 213–253). Hillsdale, NJ: Lawrence Erlbaum Associates.

Biederman, I. (1987). Recognition-by-components: A theory of human image understanding. *Psychological Review, 94*, 115–147.

Biederman, I. (1995). Visual object recognition. In S. M. Kosslyn & D. N. Osherson (Eds.), *An invitation to cognitive science: Vol. 2, Visual cognition* (pp. 41–72). Cambridge, MA: The MIT Press.

Biederman, I., Mezzanotte, R. J., & Rabinowitz, J. C. (1982). Scene perception: Detecting and judging objects undergoing relational violations. *Cognitive Psychology, 14*, 143–177.

Binkofski, F., Buccino, G., Posse, S., Seitz, R. J., Rizzolatti, G., & Freund, H. (1999). A fronto-parietal circuit for object manipulation in man: Evidence from an fMRI study. *European Journal of Neuroscience, 11*, 3276–3286.

Bird, H., Lambon-Ralph, M. A., Seidenberg, M. S., McClelland, J. L., & Patterson, K. (2003). Deficits in phonology and past-tense morphology: What's the connection? *Journal of Memory and Language, 48*, 502–526.

Bisiach, E., & Luzzatti, C. (1978). Unilateral neglect of representational space. *Cortex, 14*, 129–133.

Bjork, R. A. (1989). Retrieval inhibition as an adaptive mechanism in human memory. In H. L. Roediger & F. I. M. Craik (Eds.), *Varieties of memory and consciousness: Essays in honour of Endel Tulving* (pp. 309–330). Hillsdale, NJ: Lawrence Erlbaum Associates.

Black, J. B., & Bower, G. H. (1980). Story understanding as problem solving. *Poetics, 9*, 223–250.

Blakemore, C., & Tobin, E. A. (1972). Lateral inhibition between orientation detectors in the cat's visual cortex. *Experimental Brain Research, 15*, 439–440.

Blakemore, S.-J., & Decety, J. (2001). From the perception of action to the understanding of intention. *Nature Reviews Neuroscience, 2*, 561–567.

Blakemore, S.-J., Rees, G., & Frith, C. D. (1998). How do we predict the consequences of our actions? A functional imaging study. *Neuropsychologia, 36*, 521–529.

Blakemore, S.-J., Wolpert, D. M., & Frith, D. D. (2002). Abnormalities in the awareness of action. *Trends in Cognitive Sciences, 6*, 237–242.

Blanchette, I., & Dunbar, K. (2002). Representational change and analogy: How analogical inferences alter target representations. *Journal of Experimental Psychology: Learning, Memory, and Cognition, 28*, 672–685.

Block, N., Flanagan, O., & Güzeldere, G. (Eds.). (1997). *The nature of consciousness: Philosophical debates*. Cambridge, MA: The MIT Press.

Blok, S., Newman, G., & Rips, L. J. (2005). Individuals and their concepts. In W-K Ahn, R. L. Goldstone, B. C. Love, A. B. Markman, & P. Wolff (Eds). *Categorization inside and outside the laboratory: Essays in honor of Douglas L. Medin*. (pp. 127–149). Washington, DC, US: American Psychological Association.

Bock, J. K. (1982). Toward a cognitive psychology of syntax: Information processing contributions to sentence formulation. *Psychological Review, 89*, 1–47.

Boltz, M. (1992). Temporal accent structure and the remembering of filmed narratives. *Perception and Psychophysics, 57*, 1080–1096.

Bonda, E., Petrides, M., Ostry, D., & Evans, A. (1996). Specific involvement of human parietal systems and the amygdala in the perception of biological motion. *Journal of Neuroscience, 16*, 3737–3744.

Bonnet, M., & Requin, J. (1982). Long loop and spinal reflexes in man during preparation for intended directional hand movements. *Journal of Neuroscience, 2*, 90–96.

Booth, J. R., Burman, D. D., Meyes, J. R., Gitelman, D. R., Parish, T. B., & Mesulam, M. M. (2002). Modality independence of word comprehension. *Human Brain Mapping, 6*, 251–261.

Boring, E. G. (1964). Size constancy in a picture. *American Journal of Psychology, 77*, 494–498.

Bornhovd, K., Quante, M., Glauche, V., Bromm, B., Weiller, C., & Buchel, C. (2002). Painful stimuli evoke different stimulus-response functions in the amygdala, prefrontal, insula, and somatosensory cortex: A single-trial fMRI study. *Brain, 125*, 1326–1336.

Bornstein, R. F. (1992). Subliminal mere exposure effects. In R. F. Bornstein & T. S. Pittman (Eds.), *Perception without awareness: Cognitive, clinical and social perspectives.* New York: Guilford Press.

Bottini, G., Corcoran, R., Sterzi, R., Paulesu, E., Schenone, P., Scarpa, P., et al. (1994). The role of the right hemisphere in the interpretation of figurative aspects of language. A positron emission tomography activation study. *Brain, 117*, 1241–1253.

Botvinick, M. M., Braver, T. S., Barch, D. M., Carter, C. S., & Cohen, J. D. (2001). Conflict monitoring and cognitive control. *Psychological Review, 108*, 624–652.

Bower, G. H. (1981). Mood and memory. *American Psychologist, 36*, 129–148.

Bower, G. H., & Cohen, P. R. (1982). Emotional influences in memory and thinking: Data and theory. In M. S. Clark & S. T. Fiske (Eds.), *Affect and cognition* (pp. 291–332). Hillsdale, NJ: Lawrence Erlbaum Associates.

Brainard, D. H., & Freeman, W. T. (1997). Baysian color constancy. *Journal of the Optical Society of America A, 14*, 1393–1411.

Braine, M. D. S., & O'Brien, D. P. (1991). A theory of if: A lexical entry, reasoning program, and pragmatic principles. *Psychological Review, 98*, 182–203.

Brase, G. L., Cosmides, L., & Tooby, J. (1998). Individuation, counting, and statistical inference: The role of frequency and whole-object representations in judgment under uncertainty. *Journal of Experimental Psychology: General, 127*, 3–21.

Brass, M., Bekkering, H., Wohlschlager, A., & Prinz, W. (2000). Compatibility between observed and executed finger movements: Comparing symbolic, spatial and imitative cues. *Brain and Cognition, 44*, 124–143.

Brass, M., Zysset, S., & von Cramon, D. Y. (2001, March). *The inhibition of imitative response tendencies: A functional MRI study.* Poster presented at the annual meeting of the Cognitive Neuroscience Society, New York.

Braver, T. S., & Cohen, J. D. (2000). On the control of control: The role of dopamine in regulating prefrontal function and working memory. In S. Monsell & J. Driver (Eds.), *Attention and performance XVIII* (pp. 713–738). Cambridge, MA: The MIT Press.

Braver, T. S., Cohen, J. D., & Barch, D. M. (2002). The role of the prefrontal cortex in normal and disordered cognitive control: A cognitive neuroscience perspective. In D. T. Stuss & R. T. Knight (Eds.), *Principles of frontal lobe function* (pp. 428–448). Oxford: Oxford University Press.

Braver, T. S., Cohen, J. D., Nystrom, L. E., Jonides, J., Smith, E. E., & Noll, D. C. (1997). A parametric study of prefrontal cortex involvement in human working memory. *Neuroimage, 5*, 49–62.

Brefczynski, J. A., & DeYoe, E. A. (1999). A physiological correlate of the "spotlight" of visual attention. *Nature Reviews Neuroscience, 2*, 370–374.

Bregman, A. S. (1981). Asking the "what for" question in auditory perception. In M. Kubovy & J. R. Pomerantz (Eds.), *Perceptual organization* (pp. 99–118). Hillsdale, NJ: Lawrence Erlbaum Associates.

Breiter, H. C., Aharon, I., Kahneman, D., Dale, A., & Shizgal, P. (2001). Functional imaging of neural responses to expectancy and experience of monetary gains and losses. *Neuron, 30*, 619–639.

Breiter, H. C., Gollub, R. L., Weisskoff, R. M., Kennedy, D. N., Makris, N., Berke, J. D., et al. (1997). Acute effects of cocaine on human brain activity and emotion. *Neuron, 19*, 591–611.

Bremner, J. D. (2002). Neuroimaging studies of post-traumatic stress disorder. *Current Psychiatry Reports, 4*, 254–263.

Brewer, J. B., Zhao, Z., Desmond, J. E., Glover, G. H., & Gabrieli, J. D. (1998). Making memories: Brain activity that predicts how well visual experience will be remembered. *Science, 281*, 1185–1187.

Brewer, W. F., & Treyens, J. C. (1981). Role of schemata in memory for places. *Cognitive Psychology, 13*, 207–230.

Broadbent, D. E. (1958). *Perception and communication.* London: Pergamon Press.

Brooks, L. R. (1968). Spatial and verbal components of the act of recall. *Canadian Journal of Psychology, 22*, 349–368.

Brooks, L. R. (1978). Nonanalytic concept formation and memory for instances. In E. Rosch & B. B. Lloyd (Eds.), *Cognition and categorization* (pp. 169–211). Hillsdale, NJ: Lawrence Erlbaum Associates.

Brown, J. (1958). Some tests of the decay theory of immediate memory. *Quarterly Journal of Experimental Psychology, 10,* 12–21.

Brown, M. W., & Aggleton, J. P. (2001). Recognition memory: What are the roles of the perirhinal cortex and hippocampus? *Nature Reviews Neuroscience, 2,* 51–61.

Brown, M. W., Wilson, F. A., & Riches, I. P. (1987). Neuronal evidence that inferomedial temporal cortex is more important than hippocampus in certain processes underlying recognition memory. *Brain Research, 409,* 158–162.

Brown, R., & Kulik, J. (1977). Flashbulb memories. *Cognition, 5,* 73–79.

Brugger, P., Kollias, S. S., Müri, R. M., Crelier, G., Hepp-Reymond, M. C., & Regard, M. (2000). Beyond re-membering: Phantom sensations of congenitally absent limbs. *Proceedings of the National Academy of Sciences USA, 97,* 6167–6172.

Brunel, N., & Wang, X.-J. (2001). Effects of neuromodulation in a cortical network model of object working memory dominated by recurrent inhibition. *Journal of Computational Neuroscience, 11,* 63–85.

Bruner, J. S. (1957). Going beyond the information given. In J. S. Bruner, E. Brunswik, L. Festinger, F. Heider, K. F. Muenzinger, C. E. Osgood, & D. Rapaport (Eds.), *Contemporary approaches to cognition* (pp. 41–69). Cambridge, MA: Harvard University Press.

Bruner, J. (1990). *Acts of meaning.* Cambridge, MA: Harvard University Press.

Bruner, J. S., Goodnow, J. J., & Austin, G. A. (1956). *A study of thinking.* New York: New York Science Editions.

Buccino, G., Binkofski, F., Fink, G. R., Fadiga, L., Fogassi, L., Gallese, V., et al. (2001). Action observation activated premotor and parietal areas in a somatotopic manner: An fMRI study. *European Journal of Neuroscience, 13,* 400–404.

Buchanan, T., Lutz, K., Mirzazade, S., Specht, K., Shah, N., Zilles, K., & Jancke, L. (2000). Recognition of emotional prosody and verbal components of spoken language: An fMRI study. *Cognitive Brain Research, 9,* 227–238.

Buckner, R. L., & Schacter, D. L. (2005). Neural correlates of memory's successes and sins. In M. S. Gazzaniga (Ed.), *The cognitive neuroscience III* (pp. 739–752). Cambridge, MA: MIT Press.

Buckner, R. L., & Wheeler, M. E. (2001). The cognitive neuroscience of remembering. *Nature Reviews Neuroscience, 2,* 624–634.

Burgess, A. E. (1985). Visual signal detection. III. On Bayesian use of prior knowledge and cross correlation. *Journal of the Optical Society of America A, 2,* 1498–1507.

Burgess, N., & Hitch, G. J. (1999). Memory for serial order: A network model of the phonological loop and its timing. *Psychological Review, 106,* 551–581.

Butterworth, G. (1999). Neonatal imitation: Existence, mechanisms and motives. In J. Nadel & G. Butterworth (Eds.), *Imitation in infancy* (pp. 63–67). Cambridge, MA: Cambridge University Press.

Cabeza, R., Rao, S. M., Wagner, A. D., Mayer, A. R., & Schacter, D. L. (2001). Can medial temporal lobe regions distinguish true from false? An event-related functional MRI study of veridical and illusory recognition memory. *Proceedings of the National Academy of Sciences USA, 8,* 4805–4810.

Cahill, L., Babinsky, R., Markowitsch, H. J., & McGaugh, J. L. (1995). The amygdala and emotional memory. *Science, 377,* 295–296.

Cahill, L., Haier, R. J., Fallon, J., Alkire, M. T., Tang, C., Keator, D., Wu, J., & McGaugh, J. L. (1996). Amygdala activity at encoding correlated with long-term, free recall of emotional information. *Proceedings of the National Academy of Sciences USA, 93,* 8016–8021.

Cahill, L., Prins, B., Weber, M., & McGaugh, J. L. (1994). β-Adrenergic activation and memory for emotional events. *Nature, 371,* 702–704.

Calder, A. J., Keane, J., & Lawrence, A. D. (2003). Impaired recognition of human signals of anger following damage to the striatum. Abstract presented at the 10th Annual Meeting of the Cognitive Neuroscience Society, San Francisco, CA.

Calder, A. J., Lawrence, A. D., & Young, A. W. (2001). Neuropsychology of fear and loathing. *Neuroscience, 2,* 352–363.

Capitani, E., Laiacona, M., Mahon, B., & Caramazza, A. (2003). What are the facts of semantic category-specific deficits? A critical review of the clinical evidence. *Cognitive Neuropsychology, 20,* 213–261.

Caramazza, A. (1984). The logic of neuropsychological research and the problem of patient classification in aphasia. *Brain and Language, 21,* 9–20.

Caramazza, A. (1986). On drawing inferences about the structure of normal cognitive systems from the analysis of patterns of impaired performance: The case for single-patient studies. *Brain and Cognition, 5,* 41–66.

Caramazza, A., & Shelton, J. R. (1998). Domain-specific knowledge systems in the brain: The animate-inanimate distinction. *Journal of Cognitive Neuroscience, 10,* 1–34.

Carlson-Radvansky, L. A., Covey, E. S., & Lattanzi, K. M. (1999). "What" effects on "where": Functional influences on spatial relations. *Psychological Science, 10,* 516–521.

Carrasco, M. (2004). Covert transient attention increases contrast sensitivity and spatial resolution: Support for signal enhancement. In L. Itti, G. Rees, & J. Tsotsos (Eds.), *Neurobiology of attention* (pp. 442–447). San Diego, CA: Elsevier.

Carruthers, P. (1992). *Human knowledge and human nature.* Oxford: Oxford University Press.

Carter, C. S., Braver, T. S., Barch, D. M., Botvinick, M. M., Noll, D., & Cohen, J. D. (1998). Anterior cingulate cortex, error detection, and the online monitoring of performance. *Science, 280,* 747–749.

Casey, B. J., Trainor, R. J., Orendi, J. L., Schubert, A. B., Nystrom, L. E., Giedd, J. N., et al. (1997). A developmental functional MRI study of prefrontal activation during performance of a go-no-go task. *Journal of Cognitive Neuroscience, 9,* 835–847.

Castelli, F., Happé, F., Frith, U., & Frith, C. D. (2000). Movement in mind: A functional imaging study of perception and interpretation of complex intentional movement patterns. *Neuroimage, 12,* 314–325.

Castiello, U., Lusher, D., Mari, M., Edwards, M., & Humphreys, G. W. (2002). Observing a human or a robotic hand grasping an object: Differential motor priming effects. In W. Prinz & B. Hommel (Eds.), *Common mechanisms in perception and action* (pp. 315–333). New York: Oxford University Press.

Cate, A., & Behrmann, M. (2002). Spatial and temporal influences on extinction in parietal patients. *Neuropsychologia, 40,* 2206–2225.

Cavanaugh, J. P. (1976). Holographic and trace-strength models of rehearsal effects in the item-recognition task. *Memory and Cognition, 4,* 186–199.

Cave, C. B., & Kosslyn, S. M. (1993). The role of parts and spatial relations in object identification. *Perception, 22,* 229–248.

Chambers, D., & Reisberg, D. (1992). What an image depicts depends on what an image means. *Cognitive Psychology, 24,* 145–174.

Chaminade, T., & Decety, J. (2002). Leader or follower? Involvement of the inferior parietal lobule in agency. *NeuroReport, 13,* 1975–1978.

Chaminade, T., Meary, D., Orliaguet, J. P., & Decety, J. (2001). Is perceptual anticipation a motor simulation? *NeuroReport, 12,* 3669–3674.

Chaminade, T., Meltzoff, A. N., & Decety, J. (2002). Does the end justify the means? A PET exploration of the mechanisms involved in human imitation. *Neuroimage, 12,* 318–328.

Chao, L. L., Haxby, J. V., & Martin, A. (1999). Attribute-based neural substrates in temporal cortex for perceiving and knowing about objects. *Nature Neuroscience, 2,* 913–919.

Chao, L. L., & Martin, A. (2000). Representation of manipulable man-made objects in the dorsal stream. *Neuroimage, 12,* 478–484.

Chao, L. L., Weisberg, J., & Martin, A. (2002). Experience-dependent modulation of category-related cortical activity. *Cerebral Cortex, 12,* 545–551.

Charness, N., & Campbell, J. I. (1988). Acquiring skill at mental calculation in adulthood: A task decomposition. *Journal of Experimental Psychology: General, 117,* 115–129.

Chartrand, T. L., & Bargh, J. A. (1999). The chameleon effect: The perception-behavior link and social interaction. *Journal of Personality and Social Psychology, 76,* 893–910.

Chase, W., & Simon, H. (1973). Perception in chess. *Cognitive Psychology, 4,* 55–81.

Chater, N., Oaksford, M., Nakisa, R., & Redington, M. (2003). Fast, frugal, and rational: How rational norms explain behavior. *Organizational Behavior and Human Decision Processes, 90,* 63–86.

Chein, J. M., & Fiez, J. A. (2001). Dissociation of verbal working memory system components using a delayed serial recall task. *Cerebral Cortex, 11,* 1003–1014.

Chen, K., & Wang, D. (2002). A dynamically coupled neural oscillator network for image segmentation. *Neural Networks, 15,* 423–439.

Chen, Y., Zhang, W., & Shen, Z. (2002). Shape predominant effect in pattern recognition of geometric figures of rhesus monkey. *Vision Research, 42,* 865–871.

Cheng, P. W., & Holyoak, K. J. (1985). Pragmatic reasoning schemas. *Cognitive Psychology, 17,* 391–416.

Cherry, E. C. (1953). Some experiments on the recognition of speech, with one and two ears. *Journal of the Acoustical Society of America, 25,* 975–979.

Chi, M. T. H., Feltovitch, P. J., & Glaser, R. (1981). Categorization of physics problems by experts and novices. *Cognitive Science, 5,* 121–152.

Chiodo, L., & Berger, T. (1986). Interactions between dopamine and amino-acid induced excitation and inhibition in the striatum. *Brain Research, 375,* 198–203.

Chochon, F., Cohen, L., van de Moortele, P. F., & Dehaene, S. (1999). Differential contributions of the left and right inferior parietal lobules to number processing. *Journal of Cognitive Neuroscience, 11,* 617–630.

Chomsky, N. (1957). *Syntactic structures.* Mouton: The Hague.

Chomsky, N. (1959). A review of B. F. Skinner's "Verbal Behavior." *Language, 35,* 26–58.

Chomsky N. (1967). *Current issues in linguistic theory.* The Hague: Mouton.

Christianson, S. A. (1989). Flashbulb memories: Special, but not so special. *Memory and Cognition, 17,* 443.

Christianson, S. A. (1992). *The handbook of emotion and memory: Research and theory.* Hillsdale, NJ: Lawrence Erlbaum Associates.

Chun, M. M., & Potter, M. C. (1995). A two-stage model for multiple target detection in rapid serial visual presentation. *Journal of Experimental Psychology: Human Perception and Performance, 21,* 109–127.

Clemen, E. T., & Reilly, T. (2001). *Making hard decisions.* Pacific Grove, CA: Duxbury Press.

Clement, C. A., & Gentner, D. (1991). Systematicity as a selection constraint in analogical mapping. *Cognitive Science, 15,* 89–132.

Cochin, S. Barthelemy, C., Roux, S., & Martineau, J. (1999). Observation and execution of movement: Similarities demonstrated by quantified electroencephalography. *European Journal of Neuroscience, 11,* 1839–1842.

Cohen, J. D., Braver, T. S., & O'Reilly, R. (1996). A computational approach to prefrontal cortex, cognitive control and schizophrenia: Recent developments and current challenges. *Philosophical Transactions of the Royal Society of London, B351,* 1515–1527.

Cohen, J. D., Dunbar, K., & McClelland, J. L. (1990). On the control of automatic processes: A parallel distributed processing account of the Stroop effect. *Psychological Review, 97,* 332–361.

Cohen, J. D., Perstein, W. M., Braver, T. S., Nystrom, L. E., Noll, D. C., Jonides, J., & Smith, E. E. (1997). Temporal dynamics of brain activation during a working memory task. *Nature, 386,* 604–608.

Cohen, N. J., & Eichenbaum, H. E. (1993). *Memory, amnesia, and the hippocampal system.* Cambridge, MA: The MIT Press.

Collette, F., Salmon, E., Van der Linden, M., Chicherio, C., Belleville, S., Degueldre, C., et al. (1999). Regional brain activity during tasks devoted to the central executive of working memory. *Cognitive Brain Research, 7,* 411–417.

Collins, A. M., & Quillian, M. R. (1969). Retrieval time from semantic memory. *Journal of Verbal Learning and Verbal Behavior, 8,* 240–247.

Coltheart, M., Inglis, L., Cupples, L., Michie, P., Bates, A., & Budd, B. (1998). A semantic subsystem of visual attributes. *Neurocase, 4,* 353–370.

Coltheart, V. (Ed.). (1999). *Fleeting memories: Cognition of brief visual stimuli.* Cambridge, MA: The MIT Press.

Colvin, M. K., Dunbar, K., & Grafman, J. (2001). The effects of frontal lobe lesions on goal achievement in the water jug task. *Journal of Cognitive Neuroscience, 13,* 1129–1147.

Condillac, E. (1754a/1947). Traitè des sensations. In G. LeRoy (Ed.), *Oeuvres phiosophiques de Condillac, Volume 1.* Paris: Presses Universitaires.

Condillac, E. (1754b/1948). La Logique. In G. LeRoy (Ed.), *Oeuvres philosophiques de Condillac, Volume II.* Paris: Presses Universitaires.

Conrad, R., & Hull, A. J. (1964). Information, acoustic confusion, and memory span. *British Journal of Psychology, 55,* 429–432.

Constantinidis, C., & Steinmetz, M. A. (1996). Neuronal activity in posterior parietal area 7a during the delay periods of a spatial memory task. *Journal of Neurophysiology, 76,* 1352–1355.

Conway, A. R. A., Kane, M. J., Bunting, M. F., Hambrick, D. Z., Wilhelm, O., & Engle. R. W. (2005). Working memory span tasks: A methodological review and user's guide. *Psychonomic Bulletin and Review, 12,* 769–786.

Conway, M. A., Anderson, S. J., Larsen, S. F., Donnelly, C. M., McDaniel, M. S., & McClelland, A. G. R. (1994). The formation of flashbulb memories. *Memory and Cognition, 22,* 326–343.

Corbetta, M. (1998). Frontoparietal cortical networks for directing attention and the eye to visual locations: Identical, independent, or overlapping neural systems? *Proceedings of National Academy of Science, USA, 95,* 831–838.

Corbetta, M., Miezin, F. M., Dobmeyer, S., Shulman, G. L., & Petersen, S. E. (1990). Attentional modulation of neural processing of shape, color and velocity in humans. *Science, 248,* 1556–1559.

Corbetta, M., Miezin, F. M., Shulman, G. L., & Petersen, S. E. (1993). A PET study of visuospatial attention. *Journal of Neuroscience, 13,* 1202–1226.

Corbetta, M., & Shulman, G. L. (2002). Control of goal-directed and stimulus-driven attention in the brain. *Nature Reviews Neuroscience, 3,* 201–215.

Coren, S., & Enns, J. T. (1993). Size contrast as a function of conceptual similarity between test and inducers. *Perception and Psychophysics, 54,* 579–588.

Corkin, S. (1984). Lasting consequences of bilateral medial temporal lobectomy: Clinical course and experimental findings in H. M. *Seminars in Neurology, 4,* 24–259.

Corkin, S., Amaral, D. G., González, R. G., Johnson, K. A., & Hyman, B. T. (1997). H. M.'s medial temporal lobe lesion: Findings from magnetic resonance imaging. *Journal of Neuroscience, 17,* 3964–3979.

Cornsweet, T. N. (1970). *Visual perception.* New York: Academic Press.

Cosmides, L., & Tooby, J. (1992). Cognitive adaptations for social exchange. In J. Barkow, L. Cosmides, & J. Tooby (Eds.), *The adapted mind: Evolutionary psychology and the generation of culture* (pp. 163–228). New York: Oxford University Press.

Cosmides, L., & Tooby, J. (1996). Are humans good intuitive statisticians after all? Rethinking some conclusions from the literature on judgment under uncertainty. *Cognition, 58,* 1–73.

Coull, J. T., Frith, C. D., Buechel, C., & Nobre, A. C. (2000). Orienting attention in time: Behavioral and neuroanatomical distinction between exogenous and endogenous shifts. *Neuropsychologia, 38,* 808–819.

Courtney, S. M., Ungerleider, L. G., Keil, K., & Haxby, J. V. (1996). Object and spatial visual working memory activate separate neural systems in human cortex. *Cerebral Cortex, 6,* 39–49.

Courtney, S. M., Ungerleider, L. G., Keil, K., & Haxby, J. V. (1997). Transient and sustained activity in a distributed neural system for human working memory. *Nature, 386,* 608–612.

Cowan, N. (1995). *Attention and memory.* Oxford: Oxford University Press.

Cowan, N. (2001). The magical number 4 in short-term memory: A reconsideration of mental storage capacity. *Behavioral and Brain Sciences, 24,* 87–185.

Cowan, N., Day, L., Saults, J. S., Keller, T. A., Johnson, T., & Flores, L. (1992). The role of verbal output time in the effects of word length on immediate memory. *Journal of Memory and Language, 31,* 1–17.

Cowey, A., & Walsh, V. (2000). Magnetically induced phosphenes in sighted, blind and blindsighted observers. *NeuroReport, 11,* 3269–3273.

Craik, F. I. M., & Lockhart, R. S. (1972). Levels of processing: A framework for memory research. *Journal of Verbal Learning and Verbal Behavior, 11,* 671–684.

Craik, F. I., & Tulving, E. (1975). Depth of processing and the retention of words in episodic memory. *Journal of Experimental Psychology: General, 104,* 268–294.

Craik, F. I., Govoni, R., Naveh-Benjamin, M., & Anderson, N. D. (1996). The effects of divided attention on encoding and retrieval processes in human memory. *Journal of Experimental Psychology: General, 125,* 159–180.

Craik, K. J. W. (1940). Visual adaptation. Unpublished doctoral thesis, Cambridge University, Cambridge, UK.

Cree, G. S, & McRae, K. (2003). Analyzing the factors underlying the structure and computation of the meaning of chipmunk, cherry, chisel, cheese, and cello (and many other such concrete nouns). *Journal of Experimental Psychology: General, 132,* 163–201.

Crick, F., & Koch, C. (1995). Are we aware of neural activity in primary visual cortex? *Nature, 375,* 121–123.

Crist, R. E., Li, W., & Gilbert, C. D. (2001). Learning to see: Experience and attention in primary visual cortex. *Nature Neuroscience, 4,* 519–525.

Crozier, S., Sirigu, A., Lehericy, S., van de Moortele, P. F., Pillon, B., & Grafman, J. (1999). Distinct prefrontal activations in processing sequence at the sentence and script level: An fMRI study. *Neuropsychologia, 37,* 1469–1476.

Cruse, D. A. (1977). The pragmatics of lexical specificity. *Journal of Linguistics, 13*, 153–164.

Curtis, C. E. (2005). Prefrontal and parietal contributions to spatial working memory. *Neuroscience,* Dec. 2.

Cutting, J. E., & Kozlowski, L. T. (1977). Recognising friends by their walk: Gait perception without familiarity cues. *Bulletin of the Psychonomic Society, 9*, 353–356.

Cynader, M. (1979). Competitive interactions in the development of the kitten's visual system. In R. D. Freeman (Ed.), *Developmental neurobiology of vision* (pp. 109–120). New York: Plenum Press.

Damasio, A. R. (1989). Time-locked multiregional retroactivation: A systems-level proposal for the neural substrates of recall and recognition. *Cognition, 33*, 25–62.

Damasio, A. R. (1994). *Descartes' error: Emotion, reason, and the human brain.* New York: Grosset/Putnam.

Damasio, A. R., & Damasio, H. (1994). Cortical systems for retrieval of concrete knowledge: The convergence zone framework. In C. Koch & J. L. Davis (Eds.), *Large-scale neuronal theories of the brain: Computational neuroscience* (pp. 61–74). Cambridge, MA: The MIT Press.

Damasio, H., Grabowski, T., Frank, R., Galaburda, A. M., & Damasio, A. R. (1994). The return of Phineas Gage: Clues about the brain from the skull of a famous patient. *Science, 264*, 1102–1105.

Daneman, M., & Carpenter, P. A. (1980). Individual differences in working memory and reading. *Journal of Verbal Learning and Verbal Behavior, 19*, 450–466.

Daugman, J. (1993). High confidence visual recognition of persons by a test of statistical independence. *IEEE Transactions on Pattern Analysis and Machine Intelligence, 15*, 1148–1161.

Davachi, L., Mitchell, J., & Wagner, A. D. (2003). Multiple routes to memory: Distinct medial temporal lobe processes build item and source memories. *Proceedings of the National Academy of Sciences USA, 100*, 2157–2162.

Davidson, R. J. (1998). Affective style and affective disorders: Perspectives from affective neuroscience. *Cognition and Emotion, 12*, 307–330.

Davidson, R. J. (2000). The neuroscience of affective style. In R. D. Lane & L. Nadel (Eds.), *Cognitive neuroscience of emotion* (pp. 371–388). New York: Oxford.

Davidson, R. J. (2002). Anxiety and affective style: Role of prefrontal cortex and amygdala. *Biological Psychiatry, 51*, 68–80.

Davidson, R. J., Ekman, P., Saron, C., Senulis, J., & Friesen, W. V. (1990). Approach/withdrawal and cerebral asymmetry: Emotional expression and brain physiology. *Journal of Personality & Social Psychology, 38*, 330–341.

Davidson, R. J., Jackson, D. C., & Kalin, N. H. (2000). Emotion, plasticity, context, and regulation: Perspectives from affective neuroscience. *Psychological Bulletin, 126*, 890–909.

Davis, M., & Whalen, P. J. (2001). The amygdala: vigilance and emotion. *Molecular Psychiatry, 6*, 13–34.

De Gelder, B., Vroomen, J., Pourtois, G., & Weiskrantz, L. (1999). Non-conscious recognition of affect in the absence of striate cortex. *NeuroReport, 10*, 3759–3763.

De Houwer, J., Thomas S., & Baeyens, F. (2001). Associative learning of likes and dislikes: A review of 25 years of research on human evaluative conditioning. *Psychological Bulletin, 127*, 853–869.

de Jong, R., Coles, M. G. H., & Logan, G. D. (1995). Strategies and mechanisms in nonselective and selective inhibitory motor control. *Journal of Experimental Psychology: Human Perception and Performance, 21*, 498–511.

De Renzi, E., & Nichelli, P. (1975). Verbal and nonverbal short term memory impairment following hemispheric damage. *Cortex, 11*, 341–353.

Decety, J. (1996). Do executed and imagined movements share the same central structures? *Cognitive Brain Research, 3*, 87–93.

Decety, J. (2002). Neurophysiological evidence for simulation of action. In J. Dokic & J. Proust, (Eds.), *Simulation and knowledge of action* (pp. 53–72). Philadelphia: Benjamins Publishing Company.

Decety, J., Chaminade, T., Grèzes, J., & Meltzoff, A. N. (2002). A PET exploration of the neural mechanisms involved in reciprocal imitation. *Neuroimage, 15*, 265–272.

Decety, J., & Grèzes, J. (1999). Neural mechanisms subserving the perception of human actions. *Trends in Cognitive Sciences, 3*, 172–178.

Decety, J., Grèzes, J., Costes, N., Perani, D., Jeannerod, M., Procyk, E., et al. (1997). Brain activity during observation of action: Influence of action content and subject's strategy. *Brain, 120*, 1763–1777.

Decety, J., Jeannerod, M., Germain, M., & Pastène, J. (1991). Vegetative response during imagined movement is proportional to mental effort. *Behavioral Brain Research, 42,* 1–5.

Decety, J., Kawashima, R., Gulyas B., & Roland, P. (1992). Preparation for reaching: A PET study of the participating structures in the human brain. *NeuroReport, 3,* 761–764.

Decety, J., Perani, D., Jeannerod, M., Bettinardi, V., Woods, R., Maziotta, J. C., et al. (1994). Mapping motor representations with positron emission tomography. *Nature, 371,* 600–602.

Decety, J., & Sommerville, J. A. (2003). Shared representations between self and others: A social cognitive neuroscience view. *Trends in Cognitive Science, 7,* 527–533.

Deese, J. (1959). On the prediction of occurrence of particular verbal intrusions in immediate recall. *Journal of Experimental Psychology, 58,* 17–22.

Dehaene, S., Spelke, E., Pinel, P., Stanescu, R., & Tsivkin, S. (1999). Sources of mathematical thinking: Behavioral and brain-imaging evidence. *Science, 284,* 970–974.

Delgado, M. R., Nystrom, L. E., Fissell, K., Noll, D. C., & Fiez, J. A. (2000). Tracking the hemodynamic responses for reward and punishment in the striatum. *Journal of Neurophysiology, 84,* 3072–3077.

Dell, G. S., & Reich, P. A. (1981). Stages in sentence production: An analysis of speech error data. *Journal of Verbal Learning and Verbal Behavior, 20,* 611–629.

Denis, M., & Kosslyn, S. M. (1999). Scanning visual images: A window on the mind. *Cahiers de Psychologie Cognitive/Current Psychology of Cognition, 18,* 409–465.

Descartes, René. (1641/1985). *The philosophical writings of Descartes* (Vols. 1 and 2), translated by J. Cottingham. Cambridge, UK: Cambridge University Press.

Desimone, R. (1996). Neural mechanisms for visual memory and their role in attention. *Proceedings of the National Academy of Sciences USA, 93,* 13494–13499.

Desimone, R., Albright, T. D., Gross, C. G., & Bruce, C. (1984). Stimulus-selective properties of inferior temporal neurons in the macaque. *Journal of Neuroscience, 4,* 2051–2062.

Desimone, R., & Duncan, J. (1995). Neural mechanisms of selective visual attention. *Annual Review of Neuroscience, 18,* 193–222.

D'Esposito, M., Aguirre, G. K., Zarahn, E., Ballard, D., Shin, R. K., & Lease, J. (1998). Functional MRI studies of spatial and nonspatial working memory. *Cognitive Brain Research, 7,* 1–13.

D'Esposito, M., Postle, B. R., Ballard, D., & Lease, J. (1999). Maintenance versus manipulation of information held in working memory: An event-related fMRI study. *Brain and Cognition, 41,* 66–86.

DeSousa, R. (1987). *The rationality of emotions.* Cambridge, MA: The MIT Press.

Di Lollo, V., Enns, J. T., Rensink, R. A. (2000). Competition for consciousness among visual events: The psychophysics of reentrant visual processes. *Journal of Experimental Psychology: General, 129,* 481–507.

Diamond, A. (1985). Development of the ability to use recall to guide action, as indicated by infants' performance on A-not-B. *Child Development, 56,* 868–883.

Diamond, A. (2002). Normal development of prefrontal cortex from birth to young adulthood: Cognitive functions, anatomy, and biochemistry. In D. T. Stuss & R. T. Knight (Eds.), *Principles of frontal lobe function* (pp. 466–503). New York: Oxford University Press.

Diamond, R., & Carey, S. (1986). Why faces are and are not special: An effect of expertise. *Journal of Experimental Psychology: General, 115,* 107–117.

Dietrich, E., & Markman, A. (Eds.) (2000). *Cognitive dynamics: Conceptual change in humans and machines.* Cambridge, MA: The MIT Press.

Dittrich, W. H. (1993). Action categories and the perception of biological motion. *Perception, 22,* 15–22.

Dobbins, I. G., Foley, H., Schacter, D. L., & Wagner, A. D. (2002). Executive control during episodic retrieval: Multiple prefrontal processes subserve source memory. *Neuron, 35,* 989–996.

Dodson, C. S., & Johnson, M. K. (1996). Some problems with the process-dissociation approach to memory. *Journal of Experimental Psychology: General, 125,* 181–194.

Dolan, R. (2002). Emotion, cognition, and behavior. *Science, 298,* 1191–1194.

Dominey, P., Decety, J., Broussolle, E., Chazot, G., & Jeannerod, M. (1995). Motor imagery of a lateralized sequential task is asymmetrically slowed in hemi-Parkinson's patients. *Neuropsychologia, 33,* 727–741.

Dowling, J. E. (1992). *Neurons and networks: An introduction to neuroscience.* Cambridge, MA: The Belknap Press of Harvard University Press.

Dowling, J. E. (2000). *Creating mind: How the brain works.* New York: W. W. Norton.

Dretske, F. (1995). *Naturalizing the mind*. Cambridge, MA: The MIT Press.

Driver, J., & Spence, C. (1998). Crossmodal attention. *Current Opinions in Neurobiology, 8*, 245–253.

Dubner, R., & Zeki, S. M. (1971). Response properties and receptive fields of cells in an anatomically defined region of the superior temporal sulcus in the monkey. *Brain Research, 35*, 528–532.

Dunbar, K. (1993). Concept discovery in a scientific domain. *Cognitive Science, 17*, 397–434.

Dunbar, K. (1997). "On-line" inductive reasoning in scientific laboratories: What it reveals about the nature of induction and scientific discovery. In *Proceedings of the Nineteenth Annual Meeting of the Cognitive Science Society* (pp. 191–192). Mahwah, NJ: Lawrence Erlbaum Associates.

Dunbar, K. (1999). The scientist *in vivo:* How scientists think and reason in the laboratory. In L. Magnani, N. Nersessian, & P. Thagard (Eds.), *Model-based reasoning in scientific discovery* (pp. 89–98). New York: Plenum Press.

Dunbar, K. (2000). How scientists think in the real world: Implications for science education. *Journal of Applied Developmental Psychology, 21*, 49–58.

Dunbar, K. (2002). Science as category: Implications of *in vivo* science for theories of cognitive development, scientific discovery, and the nature of science. In P. Caruthers, S. Stich, & M. Siegel (Eds.), *Cognitive models of science* (pp. 154–170). Cambridge, UK: Cambridge University Press.

Dunbar, K., & Blanchette, I. (2001). The *in vivo/in vitro* approach to cognition: The case of analogy. *Trends in Cognitive Sciences, 5*, 334–339.

Dunbar, K., & Sussman, D. (1995). Toward a cognitive account of frontal lobe function: Simulating frontal lobe deficits in normal subjects. *Annals of the New York Academy of Sciences, 769*, 289–304.

Duncan, J. (1984). Selective attention and the organization of visual information. *Journal of Experimental Psychology: General, 113*, 501–517.

Duncan, J., & Humphreys, G. W. (1989). Visual search and stimulus similarity. *Psychological Review, 96*, 433–458.

Duncan, J., Humphreys, G. W., & Ward, R. (1997). Competitive brain activity in visual attention. *Current Opinion in Neurobiology, 7*, 255–261.

Duncan, J., Seitz, R. J., Kolodny, J., Bor, D., Herzog, H. Ahmed, A., et al. (2000). A neural basis for general intelligence. *Science, 289*, 457–460.

Durstewitz, D., Kelc, M., & Gunturkun, O. (1999). A neurocomputational theory of the dopaminergic modulation of working memory functions. *Journal of Neuroscience, 19*, 2807–2822.

Durstewitz, D., Seamans, J. K., & Sejnowski, T. J. (2000). Neurocomputational models of working memory. *Nature Neuroscience, 3*, 1184–1191.

Ebbinghaus, H. (1885/1964). *Memory: A contribution to experimental psychology*. New York: Dover.

Edwards, W. (1954). Theory of decision making. *Psychological Bulletin, 51*, 380–417.

Eich, J. E., Weingartner, H., Stillman, R. C., & Gillin, J. C. (1975). State-dependent accessibility of retrieval cues in the retention of a categorized list. *Journal of Verbal Learning and Verbal Behavior, 14*, 408–417.

Eigsti, I., Zayas, V., Mischel, W., Shoda, Y., Ayduk, O., Dadlani, M. B., Davidson, M. C., Aber, J. L., & Casey, B. J. (in press). Predictive cognitive control from preschool to late adolescence and young adulthood. *Psychological Science*.

Eimer, M., & Driver, J. (2001). Crossmodal links in endogenous and exogenous spatial attention: Evidence from event-related brain potential studies. *Neuroscience and Biobehavioral Reviews, 25*, 497–511.

Eimer, M., van Velzen, J., & Driver, J. (2002). Cross-modal interactions between audition, touch, and vision in endogenous spatial attention: ERP evidence on preparatory states and sensory modulations. *Journal of Cognitive Neuroscience, 14*, 254–271.

Einstein, A. (1945). A testimonial from Professor Einstein (Appendix II). In J. Hadamard (Ed.), *An essay on the psychology of invention in the mathematical field* (pp. 142–143). Princeton, NJ: Princeton University Press.

Ekman, P., & Friesen, W. (1971). Constants across cultures in the face and emotion. *Journal of Personality & Social Psychology, 17*, 124–129.

Eldridge, L. L., Knowlton, B. J., Furmanski, C. S., Bookheimer, S. Y., & Engel, S. A. (2000). Remembering episodes: A selective role for the hippocampus during retrieval. *Nature Neuroscience, 3*, 1149–1152.

Ellis, N. C., & Hennelly, R. C. (1980). A bilingual word length effect: Implications for intelligence testing and the relative ease of mental calculations in Welsh and English. *British Journal of Psychology, 71,* 43–52.

Ellsberg, D. (1961). Risk, ambiguity, and the Savage axioms. *Quarterly Journal of Economics, 75,* 643–669.

Engle, R. W. (2002). Working memory capacity as executive attention. *Current Directions in Psychological Science, 11,* 19–23.

Engle, R. W., Tuholski, S. W., Laughlin, J. E., & Conway, A. R. A. (1999). Working memory, short-term memory, and general fluid intelligence: A latent-variable approach. *Journal of Experimental Psychology: General, 128,* 309–331.

Enns, J. T., & Prinzmetal, W. (1984). The role of redundancy in the object-line effect. *Perception and Psychophysics, 35,* 22–32.

Epstein, R., & Kanwisher, N. (1998). A cortical representation of the local visual environment. *Nature, 392,* 598–601.

Ericsson, K. A., & Simon, H. A. (1984). *Protocol analysis: Verbal reports as data.* Cambridge, MA: The MIT Press.

Estes, W. K. (1972). An associative basis for coding and organization in memory. In A. W. Melton & E. Martin (Eds.), *Coding processes in human memory* (pp. 161–190). New York: Halstead Press.

Evans, J. St. B. T. (1989). *Bias in human reasoning.* Hillsdale, NJ: Lawrence Erlbaum Associates.

Evans, J. St. B. T., Barston, J. L., & Pollard, P. (1983). On the conflict between logic and belief in syllogistic reasoning. *Memory and Cognition, 11,* 295–306.

Fadiga, L., Craighero, L., Buccino, G., & Rizzolatti, G. (2002). Speech listening specifically modulates the excitability of tongue muscles: A TMS study. *European Journal of Neuroscience, 15,* 399–402.

Fadiga, L., Craighero, L., & Olivier, E. (2005). Human motor cortex excitability during the perception of others' action. *Current Opinion in Neurobiology, 15,* 213–218.

Fadiga, L., Fogassi, L., Pavesi, G., & Rizzolatti, G. (1995). Motor facilitation during action observation: A magnetic stimulation study. *Journal of Neurophysiology, 73,* 2608–2611.

Falkenhainer, B., Forbus, K. D., & Gentner, D. (1989). The structure-mapping engine: Algorithm and examples. *Artificial Intelligence, 41,* 1–63.

Farah, M. J. (2000). The neural bases of mental imagery. In M. S. Gazzaniga (Ed.), *The cognitive neurosciences* (2nd ed., pp. 965–974). Cambridge, MA: The MIT Press.

Farah, M. J., Hammond, K. M., Levine, D. L., & Calvanio, R. (1988). Visual and spatial imagery: Dissociable systems of representation. *Cognitive Psychology, 20,* 439–462.

Farah, M. J., & McClelland, J. L. (1991). A computational model of semantic memory impairment: Modality specificity and emergent category specificity. *Journal of Experimental Psychology: General, 120,* 339–357.

Farah, M. J., Soso, M. J., & Dasheiff, R. M. (1992). Visual angle of the mind's eye before and after unilateral occipital lobectomy. *Journal of Experimental Psychology: Human Performance and Perception, 18,* 241–246.

Farah, M. J., Wilson, K. D., Drain, H. M., & Tanaka, J. R. (1995). The inverted face inversion effect in prosopagnosia: Evidence for mandatory, face-specific perceptual mechanisms. *Vision Research, 35,* 2089–2093.

Farah, M. J., Wilson, K. D., Drain, M., & Tanaka, J. N. (1998). What is "special" about face perception? *Psychological Review, 105,* 482–498.

Farrer, C., Franck, N., Georgieff, N., Frith, C. D., Decety, J., & Jeannerod, M. (2003). Modulating agency: A PET study. *Neuroimage, 18,* 324–333.

Farrer, C., & Frith, C. D. (2002). Experiencing oneself vs. another person as being the cause of an action: The neural correlates of the experience of agency. *Neuroimage, 15,* 596–603.

Felleman, D. J., & Van Essen, D. C. (1991). Distributed hierarchical processing in the primate cerebral cortex. *Cerebral Cortex, 1,* 1–47.

Fellows, L. K., & Farah, M. J. (2003). Ventromedial frontal cortex mediates affective shifting in humans: Evidence from a reversal learning paradigm. *Brain, 126,* 1830–1837.

Fellows, L. K., Heberlein, A. S., Morales, D. A., Shivde, G., Waller, S., & Wu, D. H. (2005). Method matters: An empirical study of impact in cognitive meuroscience. *Journal of Cognitive Neuroscience, 17,* 850–858.

Feltz, D. L., & Landers, D. M. (1983). The effects of mental practice on motor skill learning and performance: A meta-analysis. *Journal of Sport Psychology, 5*, 25–57.

Ferster, D., & Miller, K. D. (2000). Neural mechanisms of orientation selectivity in the visual cortex. *Annual Review of Neuroscience, 23*, 441–471.

Ferstl, E. C., & von Cramon, D. Y. (2002). What does the frontomedian cortex contribute to language processing: Coherence of theory of mind? *Neuroimage, 17*, 1599–1612.

Field, T. M., Woodson, R. W., Greenberg, R., & Cohen, C. (1982). Discrimination and imitation of facial expressions by neonates. *Science, 218*, 179–181.

Fiedler, K., Nickel, S., Muehlfriedel, T., & Unkelbach, C. (2001). Is mood congruency an effect of genuine memory or response bias? *Journal of Experimental Social Psychology, 37*, 201–214.

Fincham, J. M., Carter, C. S., van Veen, V., Stenger, V. A., & Anderson, J. R. (2002). Neural mechanisms of planning: A computational analysis using event-related fMRI. *Proceedings of the National Academy of Science, USA, 99*, 3346–3351.

Fink, G. R., Marshall, J. C., Halligan, P. W., Frith, C. D., Driver, J., Frackowiak, R. S. J., et al. (1999). The neural consequences of conflict between intention and the senses. *Brain, 122*, 497–512.

Finke, R. A. (1989). *Principles of mental imagery.* Cambridge, MA: The MIT Press.

Finke, R. A., & Pinker, S. (1982). Spontaneous mental image scanning in mental extrapolation. *Journal of Experimental Psychology: Learning, Memory, and Cognition, 8*, 142–147.

Finke, R. A., & Pinker, S. (1983). Directional scanning of remembered visual patterns. *Journal of Experimental Psychology: Learning, Memory, and Cognition, 9*, 398–410.

Finkenauer, C., Luminet, O., Gisle, L., El-Ahmadi, A., Van Der Linden, M., & Philippot, P. (1998). Flashbulb memories and the underlying mechanisms of their formation: Toward an emotional-integrative model. *Memory and Cognition, 26*, 516–531.

Fiorillo, D. D., Tobler, P. N., & Schultz, W. (2003). Discrete coding of reward probability and uncertainty by dopamine neurons. *Science, 299*, 1898–1902.

Fiske, S. T., & Taylor, S. E. (1991). *Social cognition* (2nd ed.). New York: McGraw-Hill.

Fitts, P. M., & Deininger, R. L. (1954). S-R compatibility: Correspondence among paired elements within stimulus and response codes. *Journal of Experimental Psychology, 48*, 483–492.

Fitts, P. M., & Posner, M. I. (1967). *Human performance.* Oxford, UK: Brooks/Cole.

Flanagan, J. R., & Johansson, R. S. (2003). Action plans used in action observation. *Nature, 424*, 769–770.

Flege, J. E., Yeni-Komshian, G. H., & Liu, S. (1999). Age constraints on second-language acquisition. *Journal of Memory and Language, 41*, 78–104.

Fleming, K., Bigelow, L. E., Weinberger, D. R., & Goldberg, T. E. (1995). Neurophysiological effects of amphetamine may correlate with personality characteristics. *Psychopharmacology Bulletin, 31*, 357–362.

Fletcher, P. C., & Henson, R. N. (2001). Frontal lobes and human memory: Insights from functional neuroimaging. *Brain, 124*, 849–881.

Fodor, J. (1983). *Modularity of mind.* Cambridge, MA: The MIT Press.

Forster, K. I. (1970). Visual perception of rapidly presented word sequences of varying complexity. *Perception and Psychophysics, 8*, 215–221.

Fox, C. R. (1999). Strength of evidence, judged probability, and choice under uncertainty. *Cognitive Psychology, 38*, 167–189.

Fox, C. R., & Tversky, A. (1995). Ambiguity, aversion and comparative ignorance. *Quarterly Journal of Economics, 110*, 585–603.

Fox, C. R., & Tversky, A. (1998). A belief-based account of decision under uncertainty. *Management Science, 44*, 879–895.

Fox, E., Russo, R., Bowles, R., & Dutton, K. (2001). Do threatening stimuli draw or hold attention in visual attention in subclinical anxiety? *Journal of Experimental Psychology: General, 130*, 681–700.

Francis, G., & Grossberg, S. (1996). Cortical dynamics of form and motion integration: Persistence, apparent motion, and illusory contours. *Vision Research, 36*, 149–173.

Frank, R. H. (1988). *Passions within reason: The strategic role of the emotions.* New York: Norton.

Franklin, B. (1772/1956). Letter to Joseph Priestly (originally written on September 19, 1772). Reprinted in W. B. Willcox (Ed.), *The papers of Benjamin Franklin* (Vol. 19, pp. 299–300). New Haven, CT: Yale University Press.

Frazier, L. (1987). Sentence processing: A tutorial review. In *Attention and performance XII: The psychology of reading* (pp. 559–586). Hillsdale, NJ: Lawrence Erlbaum Associates.

Freedman, D. J., Riesenhuber, M., Poggio, T., & Miller, E. K. (2001). Categorical representation of visual stimuli in the primate prefrontal cortex. *Science, 291*, 312–316.

Freedman, D. J., Riesenhuber, M., Poggio, T., & Miller, E. K. (2002). Visual categorization and the primate prefrontal cortex: Neurophysiology and behavior. *Journal of Neurophysiology, 88*, 929–941.

Frith, C. D. (1992). *The cognitive neuropsychology of schizophrenia.* Hillsdale, NJ: Lawrence Erlbaum Associates.

Frith, C. D., Blakemore, S.-J., & Wolpert, M. M. (2000). Abnormalities in the awareness and control of action. *Philosophical Transactions of the Royal Society of London: Biological Sciences, 355*, 1771–1788.

Fromkin, V. (1971). The non-anomalous nature of anomalous utterances. *Language, 47*, 27–52.

Frye, D. (1991). The origins of intention in infancy. In D. Frye & C. Moore (Eds.), *Children's theories of mind: Mental states and social understanding* (pp. 15–38). Hillsdale, NJ: Lawrence Erlbaum Associates.

Fugelsang, J., & Dunbar, K. (2005). Brain-based mechanisms underlying complex causal thinking. *Neuropsychologia, 48*, 1204–1213.

Funahashi, S., Bruce, C. J., & Goldman-Rakic, P. S. (1989). Mnemonic coding of visual space in the monkey's dorsolateral prefrontal cortex. *Journal of Neurophysiology, 61*, 331–349.

Funahashi, S., Bruce, C. J., & Goldman-Rakic, P. S. (1993). Dorsolateral prefrontal lesions and oculomotor delayed-response performance: Evidence for mnemonic "scotomas." *Journal of Neuroscience, 13*, 1479–1497.

Funayama, E. S., Grillon, C. G., Davis, M., & Phelps, E. A. (2001). A double dissociation in the affective modulation of startle in humans: Effects of unilateral temporal lobectomy. *Journal of Cognitive Neuroscience, 13*, 721–729.

Fuster, J. M. (1989). *The prefrontal cortex* (2nd ed.). New York: Raven Press.

Fuster, J. M. (1995). *Memory in the cerebral cortex.* Cambridge, MA: The MIT Press.

Gabrieli, J. D., Cohen, N. J., & Corkin, S. (1988). The impaired learning of semantic knowledge following bilateral medial temporal-lobe resection. *Brain and Cognition, 7*, 157–177.

Gabrieli, J. D. E., Desmond, J. E., Demb, J. B., Wagner, A. D., Stone, M. V., Vaidya, C. J., et al. (1996). Functional magnetic resonance imaging of semantic memory processes in the frontal lobes. *Psychological Science, 7*, 278–283.

Gabrieli, J. D. E., Fleischman, D. A., Keane, M. A., Reminger, S. L., & Morrell, F. (1995). Double dissociation between memory systems underlying explicit and implicit memory in the human brain. *Psychological Science, 6*, 76–82.

Gainotti, G., Silveri, M. C., Daniele, A., & Giustolisi, L. (1995). Neuroanatomical correlates of category-specific semantic disorders: A critical survey. *Memory, 3*, 247–264.

Gallese, V., & Goldman, A. (1998). Mirror neurons and the simulation theory of mind-reading. *Trends in Cognitive Sciences, 2*, 493–501.

Gandhi, S. P., Heeger, D. J., & Boynton, G. M. (1999). Spatial attention affects brain activity in human primary visual cortex. *Proceedings of the National Academy of Sciences USA, 96*, 3314–3319.

Ganis, G., Thompson, W. L., & Kosslyn, S. M. (2004). Brain areas underlying visual imagery and visual perception: An fMRI study. *Cognitive Brain Research, 20*, 226–241.

Garavan, H. (1998). Serial attention within working memory. *Memory and Cognition, 26*, 263–276.

Gardener, R. A., & Gardener, B. T. (1969). Teaching sign language to an ape. *Science, 165*, 664–672.

Gardner, H. (1985). *The mind's new science: A history of the cognitive revolution.* New York: Basic Books.

Garrett, M. F. (1975). The analysis of sentence production. In G. H. Bower (Ed.), *Psychology of learning and motivation* (Vol. 9, pp. 133–177). New York: Academic Press.

Gathercole, S. E., & Baddeley, A. D. (1989). Evaluation of the role of phonological STM in the development of vocabulary in children: A longitudinal study. *Journal of Memory and Language, 28*, 200–213.

Gauthier, I., Skudlarski, P., Gore, J. C., & Anderson, A. W. (2000). Expertise for cars and birds recruits brain areas involved in face recognition. *Nature Neuroscience, 3*, 191–197.

Gauthier, I., Tarr, M. J., Anderson, A. W., Skudlarski, P., & Gore, J. C. (1999). Activation of the middle fusiform "face area" increases with expertise in recognizing novel objects. *Nature Neuroscience, 2*, 568–573.

Gazzaniga, M. S., Ivry, R. B., & Mangun, G. R. (1998). *Cognitive neuroscience: The biology of the mind*. New York: W. W. Norton & Company.

Gehring, W. J., Goss, B., Coles, M. G. H., Meyer, D. E., & Donchin, E. (1993). A neural system for error detection and compensation. *Psychological Science, 4*, 385–390.

Gehring, W. J., & Willoughby, A. R. (1999). The medial frontal cortex and the rapid processing of monetary gains and losses. *Science, 295*, 2279–2282.

Gennari, S. P., Sloman, S., Malt, B., & Fitch, T. (2002). Motion events in language and cognition. *Cognition, 83*, 49–79.

Gentner, D. (1983). Structure-mapping: A theoretical framework for analogy. *Cognitive Science, 7*, 155–170.

Gentner, D., & Markman, A. B. (1997). Structure mapping in analogy and similarity. *American Psychologist, 52*, 45–56.

Gentner, D., Rattermann, M. J., & Forbus, K. D. (1993). The roles of similarity in transfer: Separating retrievability from inferential soundness. *Cognitive Psychology, 25*, 524–575.

Gergely, G., Bekkering, H., & Kilary, I. (2002). Rational imitation in preverbal infants. *Nature, 415,* 755.

Gerlach, C., Marstrand, L., Habekost, T., & Gade, A. (2005). A case of impaired shape integration: Implications for models of visual object processing. *Visual Cognition, 12*, 1409–1443.

Gibbs, R. W. (1994). Figurative thought and language. In M. A. Gernsbacher (Ed.), *The handbook of psycholinguistics* (pp. 447–477). San Diego, CA: Academic Press.

Gibson, J. J. (1966). *The senses considered as perceptual systems*. Boston: Houghton Mifflin.

Gick, M. L., & Holyoak, K. J. (1980). Analogical problem solving. *Cognitive Psychology, 12*, 306–355.

Gigerenzer, G. (1994). Why the distinction between single-event probabilities and frequencies is important for psychology (and vice versa). In G. Wright & P. Ayton (Eds.), *Subjective probability* (pp. 129–161). New York: Wiley.

Gigerenzer, G., Todd, P. M., & the ABC Research Group. (1999). *Simple heuristics that make us smart*. New York: Oxford University Press.

Gilbert, D. T., & Wilson, T. D. (2000). Miswanting: Some problems in the forecasting of human affective states. In J. Forgas (Ed.), *Feeling and thinking: The role of affect in social cognition* (pp. 178–198). New York: Cambridge University Press.

Gilovich, T., Griffin, D., & Kahneman, D. (2002). *Heuristics and biases: The psychology of intuitive judgment*. New York: Cambridge University Press.

Gladwell, M. (2002, August 5). The naked face. *The New Yorker*, pp. 38–49.

Glenberg, A. M. (1997). What memory is for. *Behavioral and Brain Sciences, 20*, 1–55.

Glenberg, A. M., & Kaschak, M. P. (2002). Grounding language in action. *Psychonomic Bulletin & Review, 9*, 558–569.

Glimcher, P. W. (2003). *Decisions, uncertainty, and the brain: The science of neuroeconomics*. Cambridge, MA: The MIT Press.

Godden, D., & Baddeley, A. D. (1975). Context-dependent memory in two natural environments: On land and under water. *British Journal of Psychology, 66*, 325–331.

Goel, V., & Dolan, R. (2000). Anatomical segregation of component processes in an inductive inference task. *Journal of Cognitive Neuroscience, 12*, 110–119.

Goel, V., Gold, B., Kapur, S., & Houle, S. (1998). Neuroanatomical correlates of human reasoning. *Journal of Cognitive Neuroscience, 10*, 293–302.

Goel, V., & Grafman, J. (1995). Are the frontal lobes implicated in "planning" functions? Interpreting data from the Tower of Hanoi. *Neuropsychologia, 33*, 623–642.

Goldenberg, G., & Hagmann, S. (1997). The meaning of meaningless gestures: A study of visuo-motor apraxia. *Neuropsychologia, 35*, 333–341.

Goldenberg, G., Mullbacher, W., & Nowak, A. (1995). Imagery without perception—a case study of anosognosia for cortical blindness. *Neuropsychologia, 33*, 1373–1382.

Golding, E. (1981). The effect of unilateral brain lesion on reasoning. *Cortex, 17*, 3–40.

Goldman, A. I. (2002). Simulation theory and mental concepts. In J. Dokic & J. Proust (Eds.), *Simulation and knowledge of action* (pp. 2–19). Philadelphia: Benjamins Publishing Company.

Goldman-Rakic, P. S. (1987). Circuitry of primate prefrontal cortex and regulation of behavior by representational memory. In F. Plum & V. Mountcastle (Eds.), *Handbook of physiology: The nervous system* (Vol. 5, pp. 373–417). Bethesda, MD: American Physiological Society.

Gollan, T. H., & Acenas, L. R. (2004). What is a TOT? Cognate and translation effects on tip-of-the-tongue states in Spanish–English and Tagalog–English bilinguals. *Journal of Experimental Psychology: Learning, Memory, & Cognition, 30*, 246–269.

Gonsalves, B., & Paller, K. A. (2000). Neural events that underlie remembering something that never happened. *Nature Neuroscience, 3*, 1316–1321.

Gonzalez, R., & Wu, G. (1999). On the shape of the probability weighting function. *Cognitive Psychology, 38*, 129–166.

Goodale, M. A., & Humphrey, G. K. (1998). The objects of action and perception. *Cognition, 67*, 181–207.

Goodale, M. A., & Milner, A. D. (1992). Separate visual pathways for perception and action. *Trends in Neuroscience, 15*, 20–25.

Goodale, M. A., Milner, A. D., Jakobson, L. S., & Carey, D. P. (1990). Kinematic analysis of limb movements in neuropsychological research: Subtle deficits and recovery of function. *Canadian Journal of Psychology, 44*, 180–195.

Goodale, M. A., Milner, A. D., Jakobson, L. S., & Carey, D. P. (1991). A neurological dissociation between perceiving objects and grasping them. *Nature, 349*, 154–156.

Goodglass, H., & Geschwind, N. (1976). Language disorders (aphasia). In E. C. Catarette & M. P. Friedman (Eds.), *Handbook of perception (Vol. 7, pp. 389–428): Language.* New York: Academic Press.

Goodman, N. (1955). *Fact, fiction, and forecast.* Cambridge, MA: Harvard University Press.

Goodman, N. (1976). *Languages of art.* Indianapolis, IN: Hackett.

Goolkasian, P. (1987). Ambiguous figures: Role of context and critical features. *Journal of General Psychology, 114*, 217–228.

Gordon, R. M. (1986). Folk psychology as simulation. *Mind and Language, 1*, 158–171.

Gorman, M. E. (1989). Error, falsification and scientific inference: An experimental investigation. *Quarterly Journal of Experimental Psychology: Human Experimental Psychology, 41A*, 385–412.

Gorman, M. E., Stafford, A., & Gorman, M. E. (1987). Disconfirmation and dual hypotheses on a more difficult version of Wason's 2–4–6 task. *Quarterly Journal of Experimental Psychology, 39A*, 1–28.

Gould, S. J. (1991). *Bully for brontosaurus: Reflections in natural history.* New York: Norton.

Graf, P., Squire, L. R., & Mandler, G. (1984). The information that amnesic patients do not forget. *Journal of Experimental Psychology: Learning, Memory, and Cognition, 10*, 164–178.

Grafen, A. (2002). A state-free optimization model for sequences of behaviour. *Animal Behaviour, 63*, 183–191.

Grafton, S. T., Arbib, M. A., Fadiga, L., & Rizzolatti, G. (1996). Localization of grasp representations in humans by positron emission tomography. *Experimental Brain Research, 112*, 103–111.

Grafton, S. T., Hazeltine, E., & Ivry, R. (1995). Functional mapping of sequence learning in normal humans. *Journal of Cognitive Neuroscience, 7*, 497–510.

Gratton, G., & Fabiani, M. (2001a). The event-related optical signal: A new tool for studying brain function. *International Journal of Psychophysiology, 42*, 109–121.

Gratton, G., & Fabiani, M. (2001b). Shedding light on brain function: The event-related optical signal. *Trends in Cognitive Sciences, 5*, 357–363.

Gray, J. R., Chabris, C. F., & Braver, T. S. (2003). Neural mechanisms of general fluid intelligence. *Nature Neuroscience, 6*, 316–322.

Greene, J. D., Sommerville, R. B., Nystrom, L. E., Darley, J. M., & Cohen, J. D. (2001). An fMRI investigation of emotional engagement in moral judgment. *Science, 293*, 2105–2108.

Greeno, J. G. (1978). Natures of problem-solving abilities. In W. K. Estes (Ed.), *Handbook of learning and cognitive processes: Vol. V: Human information* (pp. 239–270). Oxford, UK: Lawrence Erlbaum Associates.

Greenspan, S. L. (1986). Semantic flexibility and referential specificity of concrete nouns. *Journal of Memory and Language, 25*, 539–557.

Greenwald, A. G. (1970). Sensory feedback mechanisms in performance control: With special reference to the ideo-motor mechanism. *Psychological Review, 77*, 73–99.

Gregory, R. L. (1961). The brain as an engineering problem. In W. H. Thorpe & O. L. Zangwill (Eds.), *Current problems in animal behaviour* (pp. 547–565). Cambridge, UK: Cambridge University Press.

Grether, D. M., & Plott, C. R. (1979). Economic theory of choice and the preference reversal phenomenon. *American Economic Review, 69*, 623–638.

Grèzes, J., Costes, N., & Decety, J. (1998). Top-down effect of the perception of human biological motion: A PET investigation. *Cognitive Neuropsychology, 15*, 553–582.

Grèzes, J., Costes, N., & Decety, J. (1999). The effect of learning and intention on the neural network involved in the perception of meaningless actions. *Brain, 122*, 1875–1887.

Grèzes, J., & Decety, J. (2001). Functional anatomy of execution, mental simulation, observation, and verb generation of actions: A meta-analysis. *Human Brain Mapping, 12*, 1–19.

Grèzes, J., Fonlupt, P., Bertenthal, B., Delon, C., Segebarth, C., & Decety, J. (2001). Does perception of biological motion rely on specific brain regions? *Neuroimage, 13*, 775–785.

Grèzes, J., Frith, C. D., & Passingham, R. E. (2004). Inferring false beliefs from the actions of oneself and others: An fMRI study. *Neuroimage, 21*, 744–750.

Griggs, R. A., & Cox, J. R. (1982). The elusive thematic-materials effect in Wasonís selection task. *British Journal of Psychology, 73*, 407–420.

Grosjean, F. (1985). The recognition of words after their acoustic offset: Evidence and implications. *Perception and Psychophysics, 38*, 299–310.

Grosof, D. H., Shapley, R. M., & Hawken, M. J. (1993). Macaque V1 neurons can signal "illusory" contours. *Nature, 365*, 550–552.

Gross, J. J. (1998). Antecedent and response focused emotion regulation: Divergent consequences for experience, expression and physiology. *Journal of Personality and Social Psychology, 74*, 224–237.

Gross, J. J. (2002). Emotion regulation: Affective, cognitive, and social consequences. *Psychophysiology, 39*, 281–291.

Grossberg, S. (1980). How does the brain build a cognitive code? *Psychological Review, 87*, 1–51.

Grossberg, S., & Gutowski, W. E. (1987). Neural dynamics of decision making under risk: Affective balance and cognitive-emotional interactions. *Psychological Review, 94*, 300–318.

Grossman, E. E., & Blake, R. (2001). Brain activity evoked by inverted and imagined biological motion. *Vision Research, 41*, 1475–1482.

Grossman, M., Smith, E. E., Koenig, P., Glosser, G., DeVita, L., Moore, P., et al. (2002). The neural basis for categorization in semantic memory. *Neuroimage, 17*, 1549–1561.

Grossman, M., Smith, E. E., Koenig, P., Glosser, G., Rhee, J., & Dennis, K. (2003). Categorization of object descriptions in Alzheimer's disease and frontotemporal dementia: Limitation in rule-based processing. *Cognitive, Affective, & Behavioral Neuroscience, 3*, 120–132.

Guajardo, J. J., & Woodward, A. L. (2004). Is agency skin-deep? Surface attributes influence infants' sensitivity to goal-directed action. *Infancy, 6*, 361–384.

Guildford, J. P., & Dallenbach, K. M. (1925). The determination of memory span by the method of constant stimuli. *Journal of Psychology, 36*, 621–628.

Gyllensten, L., Malmfors, T., & Norrlin, M. L. (1966). Growth alteration in the auditory cortex of visually deprived mice. *Journal of Comparative Neurology, 126*, 463–469.

Haggard, P. (2005). Conscious intention and motor cognition. *Trends in Cognitive Sciences, 9*, 290–295.

Hall, J., Parkinson, J. A., Connor, T. M., Dickinson, A., & Everitt, B. J. (2001). Involvement of the central nucleus of the amygdala and nucleus accumbens core in mediating Pavlovian influences on instrumental behaviour. *European Journal of Neuroscience, 13*, 1984–1992.

Halpern, A. R. (2001). Cerebral substrates of musical imagery. *Annals of the New York Academy of Sciences, 930*, 179–192.

Hamann, S. B., Ely, T. D., Grafton, S. T., & Kilts, C. D. (1999). Amygdala activity related to enhanced memory for pleasant and aversive stimuli. *Nature Neuroscience, 2*, 289–293.

Hamm, A. O., Weike, A. I., Schupp, H. T., Trieg, T., Dressel, A., & Kessler, C. (2003). Affective blindsight: Intact fear conditioning to a visual cue in a cortically blind patient. *Brain, 126*, 267–275.

Hammond, K. R. (1996). *Human judgment and social policy: Irreducible uncertainty, inevitable error, unavoidable injustice.* New York: Oxford University Press.

Hampton, J. A. (1979). Polymorphous concepts in semantic memory. *Journal of Verbal Learning and Verbal Behavior, 18*, 441–461.

Hanley, J. R., Young, A. W., & Pearson, N. A. (1991). Impairment of the visuo-spatial sketch pad. *Quarterly Journal of Experimental Psychology, 43A*, 101–125.

Hansen, C. H., & Hansen, R. D. (1988). Finding the face in the crowd: An anger superiority effect. *Journal of Personality and Social Psychology, 54*, 917–924.

Hari, R., Forss, N., Avikainen, S., Kirveskari, E., Salenius, S., & Rizzolatti, G. (1998). Activation of human primary motor cortex during action observation: A neuromagnetic study. *Proceedings National Academy of Science, USA, 95*, 15061–15065.

Harman, G. (1996). Rationality. In E. E. Smith & D. N. Osherson (Eds.), *An invitation to cognitive science: Thinking* (Vol. 3, pp. 175–211). Cambridge, MA: The MIT Press.

Harnad, S. (1990). The symbol grounding problem. *Physica D, 42*, 335–346.

Harris, P. L. (1989). *Children and emotion*. Oxford: Blackwell Publishers.

Hasher, L., & Zacks, R. T. (1979). Automatic and effortful processes in memory. *Journal of Experimental Psychology: General, 108*, 356–388.

Hastie, R., & Pennington, N. (2000). Explanation-based decision making. In T. Connolly, H. R. Arkes, & K. R. Hammond (Eds.), *Judgment and decision making: An interdisciplinary reader* (pp. 212–228). New York: Cambridge University Press.

Haugeland, J. (1991). Representational genera. In W. Ramsey, S. P. Stitch, & D. E. Rumelhart (Eds.), *Philosophy and connectionist theory* (pp. 61–89). Hillsdale, NJ: Lawrence Erlbaum Associates.

Hauser, M. D. (1996). *The evolution of communication*. Cambridge, MA: The MIT Press.

Hauser, M. D., Chomsky, N., & Fitch, W. T. (2002). The faculty of language: What is it, who has it, and how did it evolve? *Science, 298*, 1569–1579.

Haxby, J. V., Gobbini, M. I., Furey, M. L., Ishai, A., Schouten, J. L., & Pietrini P. (2001). Distributed and overlapping representations of faces and objects in ventral temporal cortex. *Science, 293*, 2425–2430.

Heal, J. (1998). Co-cognition and off-line simulation: Two ways of understanding the simulation approach. *Mind and Language, 13*, 477–498.

Hebb, D. O. (1949). *The organization of behavior*. New York: Wiley.

Hebb, D. O., & Pennfield, W. (1940). Human behavior after extensive bilateral removals from the frontal lobes. *Archives of Neurology and Psychiatry, 4*, 421–438.

Hecht, H., Vogt, S., & Prinz, W. (2001). Motor learning enhances perceptual judgement: A case for action-perception transfer. *Psychological Research, 65*, 3–14.

Heider, F., & Simmel, M. (1944). An experimental study of apparent behavior. *American Journal of Psychology, 57*, 243–259.

Heit, E. (2000). Properties of inductive reasoning. *Psychonomic Bulletin & Review, 7*, 569–592.

Hellige, J. B. (1993). *Hemispheric asymmetry: What's right and what's left*. Cambridge, MA: Harvard University Press.

Henderson, J. M., & Hollingworth, A. (2003). Eye movements and visual memory: Detecting changes to saccade targets in scenes. *Perception and Psychophysics, 65*, 58–71.

Hernandez-Garcia, L., Wager, T. D., & Jonides, J. (2003). Functional brain imaging. In J. Wixted & H. Pashler (Eds.), *Stevens handbook of experimental psychology, Vol. 4: Methodology in experimental psychology* (3rd ed., pp. 175–221). New York: Wiley.

Herrnstein, R. J. (1990). Behavior, reinforcement and utility. *Psychological Science, 1*, 217–224.

Hesse, M. B. (1963). *Models and analogies in science*. London: Sheed and Ward.

Hesslow, G. (2002). Conscious thought as simulation of behaviour and perception. *Trends in Cognitive Sciences, 6*, 242–247.

Heuer, F., & Reisberg, D. (1992). Emotion, arousal, and memory for detail. In S. Christianson (Ed.), *The handbook of emotion and memory* (pp. 151–164). Hillsdale, NJ: Lawrence Erlbaum Associates.

Higuchi, S. I., & Miyashita, Y. (1996). Formation of mnemonic neuronal responses to visual paired associates in inferotemporal cortex is impaired by perirhinal and entorhinal lesions. *Proceedings of the National Academy of Sciences USA, 93*, 739–743.

Hilgetag, C. C., Thâeoret, H., & Pascual-Leone, A. (2001). Enhanced visual spatial attention ipsilateral to rTMS-induced "virtual lesions" of human parietal cortex. *Nature Neuroscience, 4*, 953–957.

Hinson, J. M., Jameson, T. L., & Whitney, P. (2002). Somatic markers, working memory, and decision making. *Cognitive, Affective, & Behavioral Neuroscience, 2*, 341–353.

Hintzman, D. L. (1986). "Schema abstraction" in a multiple-trace memory model. *Psychological Review, 93*, 411–428.

Hintzman, D. L., & Curran, T. (1994). Retrieval dynamics of recognition and frequency judgments: Evidence for separate processes of familiarity and recall. *Journal of Memory and Language, 33*, 1–18.

Hobson, R. P. (1989). On sharing experiences. *Development and Psychopathology, 1*, 197–203.

Hobson, R. P., & Lee, A. (1999). Imitation and identification in autism. *Journal of Child Psychology and Psychiatry, 10*, 649–659.

Hochberg, J. (1998). Gestalt theory and its legacy: Organization in eye and brain, in attention and mental representation. In J. Hochberg (Ed.), *Perception and cognition at century's end: Handbook of perception and cognition* (2nd ed., pp. 253–306). San Diego, CA: Academic Press.

Hockett, C. F. (1959). Animal "languages" and human language. *Human Biology, 31*, 32–39.

Hockett, C. F. (1960). The origin of speech. *Scientific American, 203*, 88–96.

Hockett, C. F. (1966). The problem of universals in language. In J. H. Greenberg (Ed.), *Universals of language* (2nd ed., pp. 1–29). Cambridge, MA: The MIT Press.

Hoffman, J. E., & Nelson, B. (1981). Spatial selectivity in visual search. *Perception and Psychophysics, 30*, 283–290.

Hoffman, J., & Subramaniam, B. (1995). The role of visual attention in saccadic eye movements. *Perception and Psychophysics, 57*, 787–795.

Holdstock, J. S., Mayes, A. R., Roberts, N., Cezayirli, E., Isaac, C. L., O'Reilly, R. C., et al. (2002). Under what conditions is recognition spared relative to recall after selective hippocampal damage in humans? *Hippocampus, 12*, 341–351.

Hollingworth, A., & Henderson, J. M. (1998). Does consistent scene context facilitate object perception? *Journal of Experimental Psychology: General, 127*, 398–415.

Holyoak, K. J., & Thagard, P. (1989). Analogical mapping by constraint satisfaction. *Cognitive Science, 13*, 295–355.

Holyoak, K. J., & Thagard, P. (1995). *Mental leaps*. Cambridge, MA: The MIT Press.

Howard, R. J. (1996). A direct demonstration of functional specialization within motion-related visual and auditory cortex of the human brain. *Current Biology, 6*, 1015–1019.

Hubel, D. H., & Wiesel, T. N. (1959). Receptive fields of single neurons in the cat's striate cortex. *Journal of Physiology, 148*, 574–591.

Hugdahl, K., & Ohman, A. (1977). Effects of instruction on the acquisition and extinction of electrodermal responses to fear-relevant stimuli. *Journal of Experimental Psychology: Human Learning and Memory, 3*, 608–618.

Hume, D. (1739). *A treatise of human nature* (L. A. Selby-Bigge, Ed.). Oxford: Clarendon Press.

Hummel, J. E., & Biederman, I. (1992). Dynamic binding in a neural network for shape recognition. *Psychological Review, 99*, 480–517.

Hummel, J. E., & Holyoak, K. J. (1997). Distributed representations of structure: A theory of analogical access and mapping. *Psychological Review, 104*, 427–466.

Hummel, J. E., & Holyoak, K. J. (2003). A symbolic-connectionist theory of relational inference and generalization. *Psychological Review, 110*, 220–264.

Humphreys, G. W., & Forde, E. M. E. (2001). Hierarchies, similarity, and interactivity in object recognition: "Category-specific" neuropsychological deficits. *Behavioral & Brain Sciences, 24*, 453–509.

Humphreys, G. W., & Riddoch, M. J. (1987). *To see but not to see: A case study of visual agnosia*. London: Lawrence Erlbaum Associates.

Humphreys, G. W., & Riddoch, M. J. (1993). Interactions between space and object systems revealed through neuropsychology. In D. Meyer & S. Kornblum (Eds.), *Attention and performance XIV* (pp. 143–162). Cambridge, MA: The MIT Press.

Husain, M., Shapiro, K., Martin, J., & Kennard, C. (1997). Abnormal temporal dynamics of visual attention in spatial neglect patients. *Nature, 385*, 154–156.

Huttenlocher, P. R. (1990). Morphometric study of human cerebral cortex development. *Neuropsychologia, 28*, 517–527.

Huttenlocher, P. R. (1993). Morphometric study of human cerebral cortex development. In M. H. Johnson (Ed.), *Brain development and cognition* (pp. 112–124). Oxford: Basil Blackwell Ltd.

Huttenlocher, P. R. (2002). *Neural plasticity: The effects of environment on the development of the cerebral cortex*. Cambridge, MA: Harvard University Press.

Hyde, T. S., & Jenkins, J. J. (1969). Differential effects of incidental tasks on the organization of recall of a list of highly associated words. *Journal of Experimental Psychology, 82,* 472–481.

Hyman, I. E., Husband, T. H., & Billings, F. J. (1995). False memories of childhood experiences. *Applied Cognitive Psychology, 9,* 181–197.

Hyman, I. E., Jr., & Pentland, J. (1996). The role of mental imagery in the creation of false childhood memories. *Journal of Memory and Language, 35,* 101–117.

Intraub, H. (1980). Presentation rate and the representation of briefly glimpsed pictures in memory. *Journal of Experimental Psychology: Human Learning and Memory, 6,* 1–12.

Irwin, D. (1993). Perceiving an integrated visual world. In D. E. Meyer & S. Kornblum (Eds.), *Attention and performance XIV.* Cambridge, MA: The MIT Press.

Iversen, S. D., & Mishkin, M. (1970). Perseverative inference in monkeys following selective lesions of the inferior prefrontal convexity. *Experimental Brain Research, 11,* 376–386.

Jackson, P. L., Lafleur, M. F., Malouin, F., Richards, C., & Doyon, J. (2001). Potential role of mental practice using motor imagery in neurological rehabilitation. *Archives of Physical Medicine and Rehabilitation, 82,* 1133–1141.

Jacob, P., & Jeannerod, M. (2005). The motor theory of social cognition: A critique. *Trends in Cognitive Sciences, 9,* 21–25.

Jacobs, R. A. (1999). Computational studies of the development of functionally specialized neural modules. *Trends in Cognitive Sciences, 3,* 31–38.

Jacoby, L. L., & Dallas, M. (1981). On the relationship between autobiographical memory and perceptual learning. *Journal of Experimental Psychology: General, 110,* 306–340.

Jacoby, L. L., & Kelley, C. M. (1991). Unconscious influences of memory: Dissociations and automaticity. In D. Milner & M. Rugg (Eds.), *Consciousness and cognition: Neuropsychological perspectives* (pp. 201–234). New York: Academic Press.

James, W. (1890). *Principles of psychology.* New York: Holt, Rinehart and Winston.

Janowsky, J. S., Shimamura, A. P., & Squire, L. R. (1989). Source memory impairment in patients with frontal lobe lesions. *Neuropsychologia, 27,* 1043–1056.

Jared, D., & Seidenberg, M. S. (1991). Does word identification proceed from spelling to sound to meaning? *Journal of Experimental Psychology: General, 120,* 358–394.

Jarmasz, J., Herdman, C. M., & Johannsdottir, K. R. (2005). Object-based attention and cognitive tunneling. *Journal of Experimental Psychology: Applied, 11,* 3–12.

Jeannerod, M. (1995). Mental imagery in the motor context. *Neuropsychologia, 33,* 1419–1432.

Jeannerod, M. (1997). *The cognitive neuroscience of action.* Cambridge, MA: Blackwell Press.

Jenkins, W. M., Merzenich, M. M., Ochs, M. T., Allard, T. T., & Guic-Robles, E. (1990). Functional reorganization of primary somatosensory cortex in adult owl monkeys after behaviorally controlled tactile stimulation. *Journal of Neurophysiology, 63,* 82–104.

Jha, A. P., & McCarthy, G. (2000). The influence of memory load on delay-interval in a working-memory task: An event-related functional MRI study. *Journal of Cognitive Neuroscience, 12,* 90–105.

Jiang, Y., Haxby, J. V., Martin, A., Ungerleider, L. G., & Parasuraman, R. (2000). Complementary neural mechanisms for tracking items in human working memory. *Science, 287,* 643–646.

Johansson, G. (1973). Visual perception of biological motion and a model for its analysis *Perception and Psychophysics, 14,* 201–211.

Johansson, G. (1975). Visual motion perception. *Scientific American, 232,* 76–88.

Johnson, J., & Newport, E. (1989). Critical period effects in second language learning: The influence of maturational state on the acquisition of English as a second language. *Cognitive Psychology, 21,* 60–99.

Johnson, K. E., & Mervis, C. B. (1997). Effects of varying levels of expertise on the basic level of categorization. *Journal of Experimental Psychology: General, 126,* 248–277.

Johnson, M. K., Kim, J. K., & Risse, G. (1985). Do alcoholic Korsakoff's syndrome patients acquire affective reactions? *Journal of Experimental Psychology: Learning, Memory, and Cognition, 11,* 22–36.

Johnson, M. K., Kounios, J., & Nolde, S. F. (1997). Electrophysiological brain activity and memory source monitoring. *NeuroReport, 8,* 1317–1320.

Johnson-Laird, P. N. (1983). *Mental models: Towards a cognitive science of language, inference, and consciousness.* Cambridge, UK: Cambridge University Press.

Johnson-Laird, P. N., & Byrne, R. M. J. (1991). *Deduction*. Hillsdale, NJ: Lawrence Erlbaum Associates.

Johnson-Laird, P. N., Legrenzi, P., Girotto, V., Legrenzi, M. S., & Caverni, J.-P. (1999). Naive probability: A mental model theory of extensional reasoning. *Psychological Review, 106*, 62–88.

Johnson-Laird, P. N., Legrenzi, P., & Legrenzi, M. S. (1972). Reasoning and a sense of reality. *British Journal of Psychology, 63*, 395–400.

Johnson-Laird, P. N., & Steedman, M. (1978). The psychology of syllogisms. *Cognitive Psychology, 10*, 64–99.

Jolicoeur, P., Gluck, M., & Kosslyn, S. M. (1984). Pictures and names: Making the connection. *Cognitive Psychology, 16*, 243–275.

Jonides, J., Badre, D., Curtis, C., Thompson-Schill, S. L., & Smith, E. E. (2002). Mechanisms of conflict resolution in prefrontal cortex. In D. T. Stuss & R. T. Knight (Eds.), *The frontal lobes*. Oxford: Oxford University Press.

Just, M. A., & Carpenter, P. A. (1980). A theory of reading: From eye fixations to comprehension. *Psychological Review, 87*, 329–354.

Just, M. A., & Carpenter, P. A. (1987). *The psychology of reading and language comprehension*. Boston: Allyn & Bacon.

Kahneman, D., Knetsch, J. L., & Thaler, R. H. (1991). The endowment effect, loss aversion, and the status quo bias: Anomalies. *Journal of Economic Perspectives, 5*, 193–206.

Kahneman, D., Slovic, P., & Tversky, A. (1982). *Judgment under uncertainty: Heuristics and biases*. New York: Cambridge University Press.

Kahneman, D., & Tversky, A. (1979). Prospect theory: An analysis of decision under risk. *Econometrica, 47*, 263–291.

Kahneman, D., & Tversky, A. (1982). The psychology of preferences. *Scientific American, 246*, 160–173.

Kandel, S., Orliaguet, J. P., & Boe, L. J. (2000). Detecting anticipatory events in handwriting movements. *Perception, 29*, 953–964.

Kane, M. J., & Engle, R. W. (2002). The role of prefrontal cortex in working-memory capacity, executive attention and general fluid intelligence: An individual-differences perspective. *Psychonomic Bulletin and Review, 9*, 637–671.

Kanizsa, G. (1979). *Organization of vision*. New York: Praeger.

Kanwisher, N. (1987). Repetition blindness: Type recognition without token individuation. *Cognition, 27*, 117–143.

Kanwisher, N. (1991). Repetition blindness and illusory conjunctions: Errors in binding visual types with visual tokens. *Journal of Experimental Psychology: Human Perception and Performance, 17*, 404–421.

Kanwisher, N., McDermott, J., & Chun, M. M. (1997). The fusiform face area: A module in human extrastriate cortex specialized for face perception. *Journal of Neuroscience, 17*, 4302–4311.

Kanwisher, N., Yin., C., & Wojciulik, E. (1997). Repetition blindness for pictures: Evidence for the rapid computation of abstract visual descriptions. In V. Coltheart (Ed.), *Cognition of brief visual stimuli* (pp. 119–150). Cambridge, MA: The MIT Press.

Kapadia, M. K., Westheimer, G., & Gilbert, C. D. (2000). Spatial distribution of contextual interactions in primary visual cortex and in visual perception. *Journal of Neurophysiology, 84*, 2048–2062.

Kapp, B. S., Supple, W. F., & Whalen, P. J. (1994). Stimulation of the amygdaloid central nucleus produces EEG arousal. *Behavioral Neuroscience, 108*, 81–93.

Kapp, B. S., Wilson, A., Pascoe, J. P., Supple, W., & Whalen, P. J. (1990). A neuroanatomical systems analysis of conditioned bradycardia in the rabbit. In M. Gabriel & J. Moore (Eds.), *Learning and computational neuroscience: Foundations of adaptive networks* (pp. 53–90). Cambridge, MA: The MIT Press.

Kapur, S., Craik, F. I. M., Tulving, E., Wilson, A. A., Houle, S., & Brown, G. M. (1994). Neuroanatomical correlates of encoding in episodic memory: Levels of processing effect. *Proceedings of the National Academy of Sciences USA, 91*, 2008–2011.

Kastner, S., De Weerd, P., Desimone, R., & Ungerleider, L. G. (1998). Mechanisms of directed attention in the human extrastriate cortex as revealed by functional MRI. *Science, 282*, 108–111.

Kawamoto, A. H. (1993). Nonlinear dynamics in the resolution of lexical ambiguity: A parallel distributed processing account. *Journal of Memory and Language, 32*, 474–516.

Kay, J., & Ellis, A. (1987). A cognitive neuropsychological case study of anomia. Implications for psychological models of word retrieval. *Brain, 110*, 613–629.

Keane, M. (1987). On retrieving analogues when solving problems. *Quarterly Journal of Experimental Psychology: Human Experimental Psychology, 39A*, 29–41.

Keenan, J. P., Wheeler, M. A., Gallup, G. G., & Pascual-Leone, A. (2000). Self-recognition and the right prefrontal cortex. *Trends in Cognitive Science, 4*, 338–344.

Keil, F. C. (1979). *Semantic and conceptual development: An ontological perspective.* Cambridge, MA: Harvard University Press.

Kellenbach, M. L., Brett, M., & Patterson, K. (2001). Large, colorful, and noisy? Attribute- and modality-specific activations during retrieval of perceptual attribute knowledge. *Cognitive, Affective, & Behavioral Neuroscience, 1*, 207–221.

Kelley, W. M., Miezin, F. M., McDermott, K. B., Buckner, R. L., Raichle, M. E., Cohen, N. J., et al. (1998). Hemispheric specialization in human dorsal frontal cortex and medial temporal lobe for verbal and nonverbal memory encoding. *Neuron, 20*, 927–936.

Kellman, P. J., & Shipley, T. F. (1991). A theory of visual interpolation in object perception. *Cognitive Psychology, 23*, 141–221.

Kennett, S., Spence, C., & Driver, J. (2002). Visuo-tactile links in covert exogenous spatial attention remap across changes in unseen hand posture. *Perception and Psychophysics, 64*, 1083–1094.

Kenny, A. (1988). *The self.* Milwaukee, WI: Marquette University Press.

Kerzel, D., Bekkering, H., Wohlschlager, A., & Prinz, W. (2000). Launching the effect: Representations of causal movements are influenced by what they lead to. *Quarterly Journal of Experimental Psychology: Human Psychology, 53*, 1163–1185.

Kim, J.-M., & Shadlen, M. N. (1999). Neural correlates of a decision in the dorsolateral prefrontal cortex of the macaque. *Nature Neuroscience, 12*, 176–185.

Kim, K. S., Relkin, N. R., Lee, K. M., & Hirsch, J. (1997). Distinct cortical areas associated with native and second languages. *Nature, 388*, 171–174.

Kimberg, D. Y., D'Esposito, M., & Farah, M. J. (1997). Effects of bromocriptine on human subjects depend on working memory capacity. *NeuroReport, 8*, 381–385.

King, R., Barchas, J. D., & Huberman, B. A. (1984). Chaotic behavior in dopamine neurodynamics. *Proceedings of the National Academy of Science, USA, 81*, 1244–1247.

Kintsch, W. (1998). *Comprehension: A paradigm for cognition.* New York: Cambridge University Press.

Kirkpatrick, L. A., & Hazan, C. (1994). Attachment styles and close relationships: A four year prospective study. *Personal Relationships, 1*, 123–142.

Kirwan, C. B., & Stark, C. E. (2004). Medial temporal lobe activation during encoding and retrieval of novel face-name pairs *Hippocampus, 14*, 919–930.

Klahr, D. (2000). *Exploring science: The cognition and development of discovery processes.* Cambridge, MA: The MIT Press.

Klauer, K., Musch, J., & Naumer, B. (2000). On belief bias in syllogistic reasoning. *Psychological Review, 107*, 852–884.

Klayman, J., & Ha, Y. (1987). Confirmation, disconfirmation, and information in hypothesis testing. *Psychological Review, 94*, 211–228.

Klein, G. S. (1964). Semantic power measured through the interference of words with color-naming. *American Journal of Psychology, 77*, 576–588.

Klein, I., Dubois, J., Mangin, J., Kherif, F., Flandin, G., Poline, J., Denis, M., Kosslyn, S. M., & Le Bihan, D. (2004). Retinotopic organization of visual mental images as revealed by functional magnetic resonance imaging. *Cognitive Brain Research, 22*, 26–31.

Kleinschmidt, A., Buchel, C., Zeki, S., & Frackowiak, R. S. (1998). Human brain activity during spontaneously reversing perception of ambiguous figures. *Proceedings of the Royal Society of London B: Biological Science, 265*, 2427–2433.

Kleinsmith, L. J., & Kaplan, S. (1963). Paired-associate learning as a function of arousal and interpolated interval. *Journal of Experimental Psychology, 65*, 190–193.

Kleist, K. C., & Furedy, J. J. (1969). Appetitive classical autonomic conditioning with subject-selected cool-puff UCS. *Journal of Experimental Psychology, 81*, 598–600.

Kling, A. S., & Brothers, L. A. (1992). The amygdala and social behavior. In J. P. Aggleton (Ed.), *The amygdala: Neurobiological aspects of emotion, memory, and mental dysfunction* (pp. 353–377). New York: Wiley-Liss.

Knez, M., & Smith, V. L. (1987). Hypothetical valuations and preference reversals in the context of asset trading. In A. Roth (Ed.), *Laboratory experimentation in economics: Six points of view* (pp. 131–154). Cambridge, UK: Cambridge University Press.

Knill, D. C., & Richards, W. (1996). *Perception as Bayesian inference*. Cambridge, UK: Cambridge University Press.

Knowlton, B. J., Mangels, J. A., & Squire, L. R. (1996). A neostriatal habit learning system in humans. *Science, 273*, 1399–1402.

Knowlton, B. J., Squire, L. R., & Gluck, M. A. (1994). Probabilistic category learning in amnesia. *Learning and Memory, 1*, 106–120.

Knutson, B., Adams, C. M., Fong, G. W., & Hommer, D. (2001). Anticipation of increasing monetary reward selectively recruits nucleus accumbens. *Journal of Neuroscience, 21*, RC159.

Knutson, B., Westdorp, A., Kaiser, E., & Hommer, D. (2000). fMRI visualization of brain activity during a monetary incentive delay task. *Neuroimage, 12*, 20–27.

Kornblum, S., Hasbroucq, T., & Osman, A. (1990). Dimensional overlap: Cognitive basis for stimulus-response compatibility—a model and taxonomy. *Psychological Review, 97*, 253–270.

Kornblum, S., & Lee, J. W. (1995). Stimulus–response compatibility with relevant and irrelevant stimulus dimensions that do and do not overlap with the response. *Journal of Experimental Psychology, 21*, 855–875.

Koski, L., Iacoboni, M., & Mazziotta, J. C. (2002). Deconstructing apraxia: Understanding disorders of intentional movement after stroke. *Current Opinion in Neurology, 15*, 71–77.

Kosslyn, S. M. (1975). Information representation in visual images. *Cognitive Psychology, 7*, 341–370.

Kosslyn, S. M. (1978). Measuring the visual angle of the mind's eye. *Cognitive Psychology, 10*, 356–389.

Kosslyn, S. M. (1980). *Image and mind*. Cambridge, MA: Harvard University Press.

Kosslyn, S. M. (1994). *Image and brain: The resolution of the imagery debate*. Cambridge, MA: The MIT Press.

Kosslyn, S. M., & Chabris, C. F. (1990). Naming pictures. *Journal of Visual Languages and Computing, 1*, 77–96.

Kosslyn, S. M., Pascual-Leone, A., Felician, O., Camposano, S., Keenan, J. P., Thompson, W. L., et al. (1999). The role of area 17 in visual imagery: Convergent evidence from PET and rTMS. *Science, 284*, 167–170.

Kosslyn, S. M., & Pomerantz, J. R. (1977). Imagery, propositions, and the form of internal representations. *Cognitive Psychology, 9*, 52–76.

Kosslyn, S. M., Shin, L. M., Thompson, W. L., McNally, P. J., Rauch, S. L., Pitman, R. K., et al. (1996). Neural effects of visualizing and perceiving aversive stimuli: A PET investigation. *NeuroReport, 7*, 1569–1576.

Kosslyn, S. M., & Thompson, W. L. (2003). When does visual mental imagery activate early visual cortex? *Psychological Bulletin, 129*, 723–746.

Kosslyn, S. M., Thompson, W. L., & Alpert, N. M. (1997). Neural systems shared by visual imagery and visual perception: A positron emission tomography study. *NeuroImage, 6*, 320–324.

Kosslyn, S. M., Thompson, W. L., & Ganis, G. (2006). *The case for mental imagery*. New York: Oxford University Press.

Kosslyn, S. M., Thompson, W. L., Kim, I. J., & Alpert, N. M. (1995). Topographical representations of mental images in primary visual cortex. *Nature, 378*, 496–498.

Kosslyn, S. M., Thompson, W. L., Wraga, M., & Alpert, N. M. (2001). Imagining rotation by endogenous versus exogenous forces: Distinct neural mechanisms. *NeuroReport, 12*, 2519–2525.

Koutstaal, W., Schacter, D. L., Galluccio, L., & Stofer, K. A. (1999). Reducing gist-based false recognition in older adults: Encoding and retrieval manipulations. *Psychology and Aging, 14*, 220–237.

Koutstaal, W., Vertaellie, M., & Schacter, D. L. (2001). Recognizing identical versus similar categorically related common objects: Further evidence for degraded gist representations in amnesia. *Neuropsychology, 15*, 268–289.

Kozlowski, L. T., & Cutting, J. E. (1977). Recognizing the sex of a walker from point-lights display. *Perception and Psychophysics, 21*, 575–580.

Krakauer, J., & Ghez, C. (2000). Voluntary movement. In E. Kandel, J. H. Schwartz, & T. M. Jessel (Eds.), *Principles of neural science* (pp. 756–781). New York: McGraw-Hill.

Krauss, R. M., & Fussell, S. R. (1991). Perspective-taking in communication: Representations of others' knowledge in reference. *Social Cognition, 9*, 2–24.

Krawczyk, D. C. (2002). Contributions of the prefrontal cortex to the neural basis of human decision making. *Neuroscience and Biobehavioral Reviews, 26*, 631–664.

Krebs, J. R., & Davies, N. B. (1997). *Behavioural ecology: An evolutionary approach*. Malden, MA: Blackwell Science.

Krebs, J. R., & Kacelnik, A. (1991). Decision making. In J. R. Krebs & N. B. Davies (Eds.), *Behavioral ecology: An evolutionary approach* (pp. 105–136). Oxford: Blackwell Scientific Press.

Kroger, J. K., Sabb, F. W., Fales, C. L., Bookheimer, S. Y., Cohen, M. S., & Holyoak, K. J. (2002). Recruitment of anterior dorsolateral prefrontal cortex in human reasoning: A parametric study of relational complexity. *Cerebral Cortex, 12*, 477–485.

Kubovy, M., Holcombe, A. O., & Wagemans, J. (1998). On the lawfulness of grouping by proximity. *Cognitive Psychology, 35*, 71–98.

Kubovy, M., & Wagemans, J. (1995). Grouping by proximity and multistability in dot lattices: A quantitative gestalt theory. *Psychological Science, 6*, 225–234.

Kulkarni, D., & Simon, H. A. (1988). The processes of scientific discovery: The strategy of experimentation. *Cognitive Science, 12*, 139–176.

Külpe, O. (1895). *Outlines of psychology* (trans. by E. B. Titchener). New York: Macmillan and Company.

Kyllonen, P. C., & Christal, R. E. (1990). Reasoning ability is (little more than) working memory capacity? *Intelligence, 14*, 389–433.

Labar, K. S., Ledoux, J. E., Spencer, D. D., & Phelps, E. A. (1995). Impaired fear conditioning following unilateral temporal lobectomy in humans. *Journal of Neuroscience, 15*, 6846–6855.

LaBar, K. S., & Phelps, E. A. (1998). Role of the human amygdala in arousal mediated memory consolidation. *Psychological Science, 9*, 490–493.

Laeng, B., Chabris, C. F., & Kosslyn, S. M. (2002). Asymmetries in encoding spatial relations. In R. J. Davidson & K. Hugdahl (Eds.), *Brain asymmetry* (2nd edition). Cambridge, MA: The MIT Press.

Laeng, B., Shah, J., & Kosslyn, S. M. (1999). Identifying objects in conventional and contorted poses: Contributions of hemisphere-specific mechanisms. *Cognition, 70*, 53–85.

Lakoff, G. (1987). *Women, fire, and dangerous things: What categories reveal about the mind*. Chicago: University of Chicago Press.

Lamberts, K. (1998). The time course of categorization. *Journal of Experimental Psychology: Learning, Memory, and Cognition, 24*, 695–711.

Land, E. H., & McCann, J. J. (1971). Lightness and retinex theory. *Journal of the Optical Society of America, 61*, 1–11.

Lang, P. J., Bradley, M. M., & Cuthbert, B. N. (1990). Emotion, attention and the startle reflex. *Psychological Review, 97*, 377–395.

Lang, P. J., Bradley, M. M., & Cuthbert, B. N. (1992). A motivational analysis of emotion: Reflex-cortex connections. *Psychological Science, 3*, 44–49.

Lang, P. J., Bradley, M. M., & Cuthbert, B. N. (2005). International affective picture system (IAPS): Digitized photographs, instruction manual and affective ratings (Technical Report A-6). Gainesville: University of Florida.

Lang, W., Petit, L., Höllinger, P., Pietrzyk, U., Tzourio, N., Mazoyer, B., & Berthoz, A. (1994). A positron emission tomography study of oculomotor imagery. *NeuroReport, 5*, 921–924.

Lavenex, P., & Amaral, D. G. (2000). Hippocampal–neocortical interaction: A hierarchy of associativity. *Hippocampus, 10*, 420–430.

Lavie, N. (1995). Perceptual load as a necessary condition for selective attention. *Journal of Experimental Psychology: Human Perception and Performance, 21*, 451–468.

Lawrence, A. D., Clader, A. J., McGowan, S. W., & Grasby, M. (2002). Selective disruption of the recognition of facial expressions of anger. *NeuroReport, 13*, 881–884.

Lazarus, R. S. (1981). A cognitivist's reply to Zajonc on emotion and cognition. *American Psychologist, 36*, 222–223.

Lazarus, R. S. (1984). On the primacy of cognition. *American Psychologist, 39*, 124–129.

Lazarus, R. S. (1966). *Psychological stress and the coping process*. New York: McGraw-Hill.

Le, T. H., Pardo, J. V., & Hu, X. (1998). 4T-fMRI study of nonspatial shifting of selecting attention: cerebellar and parietal contributions. *Journal of Physiology, 79*, 1525–1548.

LeVay, S., Wiesel, T. N., & Hubel, D. H. (1980). The development of ocular dominance columns in normal and visually deprived monkeys. *Journal of Comparative Neurology, 191*, 1–51.

Ledoux, J. E. (1991). Emotion and the limbic system concept. *Concepts in Neuroscience 2*, 169–199.

Ledoux, J. E. (1992). Emotion and the amygdala. In J. P. Aggleton (Ed.), *The amygdala: Neurobiological aspects of emotion, memory, and mental dysfunction* (pp. 339–351). New York: Wiley-Liss.

LeDoux, J. E., Iwata, J., Chicchetti, P., & Reis, D. J. (1988). Different projections of the central amygdaloid nucleus mediate autonomic and behavioral correlates of conditioned fear. *Journal of Neuroscience, 8*, 2517–2529.

Legerstee, M. (1991). The role of person and object in eliciting early imitation. *Journal of Experimental Child Psychology, 51*, 423–433.

Lehrer, K. (1990). *Theory of knowledge.* Boulder, CO: Westview.

Leland, J. W., & Grafman, J. (2005). Experimental tests of the Somatic Marker Hypothesis. *Games and Economic Behavior, 52*, 386–409.

Leopold, D. A., & Logothetis, N. K. (1996). Activity changes in early visual cortex reflect monkeys' percepts during binocular rivalry. *Nature, 379*, 549–553.

Leopold, D. A., O'Toole, A. J., Vetter, T., & Blanz, V. (2001). Prototype-referenced shape encoding revealed by high-level aftereffects. *Nature Neuroscience, 4*, 89–94.

Lettvin, J. Y., Maturana, H. R., McCulloch, W. S., & Pitts, W. H. (1959). What the frog's eye tells the frog's brain. *Proceedings of the Institute of Radio Engineers, 47*, 1940–1951.

Levelt, W. J. M. (1965). *On binocular rivalry.* PhD thesis. Soesterberg, The Netherlands: Institute for Perception RVO-TNO.

Levelt, W. J. M. (1989). *Speaking: From intention to articulation.* Cambridge, MA: The MIT Press.

Leven, S. J., & Levine, D. S. (1996). Multiattribute decision making in context: A dynamic neural network methodology. *Cognitive Science, 20*, 271–299.

Lewandowsky, S., Duncan, M., & Brown, G. D. (2004). Time does not cause forgetting in short-term serial recall. *Psychon Bull Rev, 11*, 771–790.

Lezak, M. D. (1983). *Neuropsychological assessment* (2nd ed.). New York: Oxford University Press.

Lichtenstein, S., & Slovic, P. (1971). Reversals of preference between bids and choices in gambling decisions. *Journal of Experimental Psychology, 89*, 46–55.

Lichtenstein, S., & Slovic, P. (1973). Response-induced reversals of preference in gambling: An extended replication in Las Vegas. *Journal of Experimental Psychology, 101*, 16–20.

Lichtenstein, S., Slovic, P., Fischhoff, B., Layman, M., & Combs, B. (1978). Judged frequency of lethal events. *Journal of Experimental Psychology: Human Learning and Memory, 4*, 551–578.

Lickliter, R. (2000). The role of sensory stimulation in perinatal development: Insights from comparative research for care of the high-risk infant. *Journal of Developmental & Behavioral Pediatrics, 21*, 437–447.

Lieberman, M. D., Ochsner, K. N., Gilbert, D. T., & Schacter, D. L. (2001). Do amnesiacs exhibit cognitive dissonance reduction? The role explicit memory and attention in attitude change. *Psychological Science, 80*, 294–310.

Lindsay, D. S. (1990). Misleading suggestions can impair eyewitnesses' ability to remember event details. *Journal of Experimental Psychology: Learning, Memory, and Cognition, 16*, 1077–1083.

Lindsay, P. H., & Norman, D. A. (1977). *Human information processing: An introduction to psychology* (2nd ed.). New York: Academic Press.

Lisman, J. E., & Idiart, M. A. P. (1995). Storage of 7+2 short-term memories in oscillatory subcycles. *Science, 267*, 1512–1515.

Liu, T., Slotnick, S. D., Serences, J. T., & Yantis, S. (2003). Cortical mechanisms of feature-based attentional control. *Cerebral Cortex, 13*, 1334–1343.

Livingstone, M. S., & Hubel, D. H. (1984). Anatomy and physiology of a color system in the primate visual cortex. *Journal of Neuroscience, 4*, 309–356.

Loewenstein, G. (1996). Out of control: Visceral influences on behavior. *Organizational Behavior and Human Decision Processes, 65*, 272–292.

Loewenstein, G., & Lerner, J. S. (2003). The role of affect in decision making. In R. J. Davidson, K. R. Scherer, & H. H. Goldsmith (Eds.), *Handbook of affective sciences* (pp. 619–642). New York: Oxford University Press.

Loftus, E. F. (2005) A 30-year investigation of the malleability of memory. *Learning and Memory 12*, 361–366.

Loftus, E. F. & Bernstein, D. M. (2005). Rich False Memories. In A. F. Healy (Ed.) Experimental Cognitive Psychology and its Applications. Washington DC: *Amer Psych Assn Press*, 101–113.

Loftus, E. F., Miller, D. G., & Burns, H. J. (1978). Semantic integration of verbal information into a visual memory. *Journal of Experimental Psychology: Human Learning and Memory, 4*, 19–31.

Logan, G. D. (1983). On the ability to inhibit simple thoughts and actions: I. Stop-signal studies of decision and memory. *Journal of Experimental Psychology: Learning, Memory, and Cognition, 9*, 585–606.

Logie, R. H. (1995). *Visuo-spatial working memory*. Hove, UK: Lawrence Erlbaum Associates.

Logothetis, N. K., Pauls, J., & Poggio, T. (1995). Shape representation in the inferior temporal cortex of monkeys. *Current Biology, 5*, 552–563.

Longoni, A. M., Richardson, J. T. E., & Aiello, A. (1993). Articulatory rehearsal and phonological storage in working memory. *Memory and Cognition, 21*, 11–22.

Loomes, G., & Sugden, R. (1982). Regret theory: An alternative theory of rational choice under uncertainty. *Economic Journal, 92*, 805–824.

Luce, P. A., & Pisoni, D. B. (1998). Recognizing spoken words: The neighborhood activation model. *Ear and Hearing, 19*, 1–36.

Luce, R. D. (1986). *Response times: Their role in inferring elementary mental organization*. New York: Oxford University Press.

Luciana, M., Collins, P. F., & Depue, R. A. (1998). Opposing roles for dopamine and serotonin in the modulation of human spatial working memory functions. *Cerebral Cortex, 8*, 218–226.

Luck, S. J., & Hillyard, S. A. (2000). The operation of selective attention at multiple stages of processing: Evidence from human and monkey electrophysiology. In M. S. Gazzaniga (Ed.), *The new cognitive neurosciences* (2nd ed., pp. 687–700). Cambridge, MA: The MIT Press.

Luria, A. R. (1966). *Higher cortical functions in man*. New York: Basic Books.

MacDonald, A. W., Cohen, J. D., Stenger, V. A., & Carter, C. S. (2000). Dissociating the role of the dorsolateral prefrontal and anterior cingulate cortex in cognitive control. *Science, 288*, 1835–1838.

MacDonald, M. C., Pearlmutter, N. J., & Seidenberg, M. S. (1994). The lexical nature of syntactic ambiguity resolution. *Psychological Review, 89*, 483–506.

Mach, E. (1865). Über die Wirkung der raumlichen Vertheilung des Lichtreizes auf die Netzhaut. *I. S.-B. Akad. Wiss. Wein. math.-nat. Kl., 54*, 303–322 (trans. by Ratliff, 1965).

Mack, A., & Rock, I. (1998). *Inattentional blindness*. Cambridge, MA: The MIT Press.

Maia, T. V., & McClelland, J. L. (2004). A reexamination of evidence for the somatic marker hypothesis: What participants really know in the Iowa gambling task. *Proceedings of the National Academy of Sciences USA, 101*, 16075–16080.

Malle, B. F. (1999). How people explain behavior: A new empirical framework. *Personality and Social Psychology Review, 3*, 23–48.

Malloy, P., Bihrle, A., Duffy, J., & Cimino, C. (1993). The orbital frontal syndrome. *Archives of Clinical Neuropsychology, 8*, 185–201.

Malt, B. C. (1995). Category coherence in cross-cultural perspective. *Cognitive Psychology, 29*, 85–148.

Mandler, J. M., & McDonough, L. (1998). Studies in inductive inference in infancy. *Cognitive Psychology, 37*, 60–96.

Mandler, J. M., & McDonough, L. (2000). Advancing downward to the basic level. *Journal of Cognition and Development, 1*, 379–403.

Mangun, G. R., & Hillyard, S. A. (1991). Modulations of sensory-evoked brain potentials indicate changes in perceptual processing during visual-spatial priming. *Journal of Experimental Psychology: Human Perception & Performance, 17*, 1057–1074.

Manns, J. R., Hopkins, R. O., Reed, J. M., Kitchener, E. G., & Squire, L. R. (2003a). Recognition memory and the human hippocampus. *Neuron, 37*, 171–180.

Manns, J. R., Hopkins, R. O., & Squire, L. R. (2003b). Semantic memory and the human hippocampus. *Neuron, 38*, 127–133.

Markman, A. B., & Gentner, D. (2001). Thinking. *Annual Review of Psychology, 52*, 223–247.

Markman, A. B., & Medin, D. L. (1995). Similarity and alignment in choice. *Organizational Behavior & Human Decision Processes, 63*, 117–130.

Markovits, H., & Nantel, G. (1989). The belief–bias effect in the production and evaluation of logical conclusions. *Memory & Cognition, 17*, 11–17.

Markus, G. B. (1986). Stability and change in political attitudes: Observed, recalled, and "explained." *Political Behavior, 8*, 21–44.

Marr, D. (1982). *Vision: A computational investigation into the human representation and processing of visual information.* New York: Freeman.

Marshuetz, C., Smith, E. E., Jonides, J., DeGutis, J., & Chenevert, T. L. (2000). Order information in working memory: fMRI evidence for parietal and prefrontal mechanisms. *Journal of Cognitive Neuroscience, 12*, 130–144.

Marslen-Wilson, W. D. (1984a). Function and process in spoken word-recognition. In H. Bouma & D. Bouwhuis (Eds.), *Attention and performance X: Control of language processes.* Hillsdale, NJ: Lawrence Erlbaum Associates.

Marslen-Wilson, W. D. (1984b). Perceiving speech and perceiving words. In M. P. R. van de Broecke & A. Cohen (Eds.), *Proceedings of the Tenth International Congress of the Phonetic Sciences.* Dordrecht, Holland: Foris.

Marslen-Wilson, W. D., & Warren, P. (1994). Levels of perceptual representation and process in lexical access: Words, phonemes, and features. *Psychological Review, 101*, 653– 675.

Martin, A. (2001). Functional neuroimaging of semantic memory. In R. Cabeza & A. Kingstone (Eds.), *Handbook of functional neuroimaging of cognition* (pp. 153–186). Cambridge, MA: The MIT Press.

Martin, A., & Chao, L. L. (2001). Semantic memory and the brain: Structure and process. *Current Opinion in Neurobiology, 11*, 194–201.

Martin, A., Haxby, J. V., Lalonde, F. M., Wiggs, C. L., & Ungerleider, L. G. (1995). Discrete cortical regions associated with knowledge of color and knowledge of action. *Science, 270*, 102–105.

Martin, A., Ungerleider, L. G., & Haxby, J. V. (2000). Category-specificity and the brain: The sensory-motor model of semantic representations of objects. In M. S. Gazzaniga (Ed.), *The new cognitive neurosciences* (2nd ed., 1023–1036). Cambridge, MA: The MIT Press.

Martin, A., Wiggs, C. L., Ungerleider, L. G., & Haxby, J. V. (1996). Nerual correlates of category-specific knowledge. *Nature, 379*, 649–652.

Martineau, J., & Cochin, S. (2003). Visual perception in children: Human, animal and virtual movement activates different cortical areas. *International Journal of Psychophysiology, 51*, 37–44.

Massaro, D. W., & Stork, D. G. (1998). Sensory integration and speechreading by humans and machines. *American Scientist, 86*, 236–244.

Mattay, V. S., Goldberg, T. E., Fera, F., Hariri, A. R., Tessitore, A., Egan, M. F., et al. (2003). COMT genotype and individual variation in the brain response to amphetamine. *Proceedings of the National Academy of Sciences USA, 100*, 6186–6191.

McCarthy, G., Puce, A., Gore, J. C., & Allison, T. (1997). Face-specific processing in the human fusiform gyrus. *Journal of Cognitive Neuroscience, 9*, 605–610.

McClelland, J. L., McNaughton, B. L., & O'Reilly, R. C. (1995). Why there are complementary learning systems in the hippocampus and neocortex: Insights from the successes and failures of connectionist models of learning and memory. *Psychological Review, 102*, 419–457.

McClelland, J. L., & Rumelhart, D. E. (1981). An interactive activation model of context effects in letter perception: Part 1. An account of basic findings. *Psychological Review, 88*, 375–407.

McClelland, J. L., Rumelhart, D. E., & the PDP Research Group. (1986). *Parallel distributed processing: Explorations in the microstructure of cognition: Vol. 2. Psychological and biological models.* Cambridge, MA: The MIT Press.

McCloskey, M., & Zaragoza, M. (1985). Misleading postevent information and memory for events: Arguments and evidence against memory impairment hypothesis. *Journal of Experimental Psychology: General, 114*, 1–16.

McClure, S. M., Laibson, D. I., Loewenstein, G., & Cohen, J. D. (2005a). Separate neural systems value immediate and delayed monetary rewards. *Science, 306,* 503–507.

McClure, S. M., Li, J., Tomlin, D., Cypert, K. S., Montague, L. M., & Montague, P. R. (2005b). Neural correlates of behavioral preference for culturally familiar drinks. *Neuron, 44,* 379–387.

McElree, B., & Dosher, B. A. (1989). Serial position and set size in short-term memory: The time course of recognition. *Journal of Experimental Psychology: General, 118,* 346–373.

McEwen, B. S., & Sapolsky, R. M. (1995). Stress and cognitive function. *Current Opinion in Neurobiology, 5,* 205–216.

McFarland, C., & Ross, M. (1987). The relation between current impressions and memories of self and dating partners. *Personality and Social Psychology Bulletin, 13,* 228– 238.

McGaugh, J. L. (2000). Memory—A century of consolidation. *Science, 287,* 248–251.

McGaugh, J. L., Introini-Collision, I. B., Cahill, L., Munsoo, K., & Liang, K. C. (1992). Involvement of the amygdala in neuromodulatory influences on memory storage. In J. P. Aggleton (Ed.), *The amygdala: Neurobiological aspects of emotion, memory, and mental dysfunction* (pp. 431–451). New York: Wiley-Liss.

McGeogh, J. A. (1942). *The psychology of human learning.* New York: Longmans, Green.

McGeogh, J. A., & McDonald, W. T. (1931). Meaningful relation and retroactive inhibition. *American Journal of Psychology, 43,* 579–588.

McGurk, H., & MacDonald, J. (1976). Hearing lips and seeing voices. *Nature, 264,* 746–748.

McNeil, B. J., Pauker, S. G., Sox, H. C., & Tversky, A. (1982). On the elicitation of preferences for alternative therapies. *New England Journal of Medicine, 306,* 1259–1262.

McQueen, J. M. (1998). Segmentation of continuous speech using phonotactics. *Journal of Memory and Language, 39,* 21–46.

Meadows, J. C. (1974). The anatomical basis of prosopagnosia. *Journal of Neurology, Neurosurgery and Psychiatry, 37,* 489–501.

Medin, D. L., & Schaffer, M. (1978). A context theory of classification learning. *Psychological Review, 85,* 207–238.

Mehra, R., & Prescott, E. C. (1985). The equity premium: A puzzle. *Journal of Monetary Economics, 15,* 145–161.

Mellers, B. A. (2000). Choice and the relative pleasure of consequences. *Psychological Bulletin, 126,* 910–924.

Melton, A. W., & Irwin, J. M. (1940). The influence of degree of interpolated learning on retroactive inhibition and the overt transfer of specific responses. *American Journal of Psychology, 53,* 173–203.

Meltzoff, A. N. (1995). Understanding the intentions of others: Re-enactment of intended acts by 18-month-old children. *Developmental Psychology, 31,* 838–850.

Meltzoff, A. N., & Gopnik, A. (1993). The role of imitation in understanding persons and developing a theory of mind. In S. Baron-Cohen, H. Tage-Flushberg, & D. J. Cohen (Eds.), *Understanding other minds* (pp. 9–35). Cambridge, UK: Cambridge University Press.

Meltzoff, A. N., & Moore, M. K. (1977). Imitation of facial and manual gestures by human neonates. *Science, 198,* 75–78.

Meltzoff, A. N., & Moore, M. K. (1995). Infants' understanding of people and things: From body imitation to folk psychology. In J. Bermúdez, A. J. Marcel, & N. Eilan (Eds.), *Body and the self* (pp. 43–69). Cambridge, MA: The MIT Press.

Mervis, C. B., & Pani, J. R. (1980). Acquisition of basic object categories. *Cognitive Psychology, 12,* 496–522.

Merzenich, M. M., & Kaas, J. H. (1982). Reorganization of mammalian somatosensory cortex following peripheral nerve injury. *Trends in Neurosciences, 5,* 434–436.

Mesulam, M. M. (1998). From sensation to cognition. *Brain, 121*(Pt 6), 1013–1052.

Metcalfe, J., & Shimamura, A. P. (1994). *Metacognition: Knowing about knowing.* Cambridge, MA: The MIT Press.

Meyer, D. E., Evans, J. E., Lauber, E. J., Rubinstein, J., Gmeindl, L., Junck, L., et al. (1998). *The role of dorsolateral prefrontal cortex for executive cognitive processes in task switching.* Paper presented at the Cognitive Neuroscience Society, San Francisco.

Meyer, D. E., & Kieras, D. E. (1997a). A computational theory of executive cognitive processes and multiple-task performance: Part 1. Basic mechanisms. *Psychological Review, 104*, 3–65.

Meyer, D. E., & Kieras, D. E. (1997b). A computational theory of executive cognitive processes and multiple-task performance: Part 2. Accounts of psychological refractory-period phenomena. *Psychological Review, 104*, 749–791.

Milham, M. P., Banich, M. T., Webb, A., Barad, V., Cohen, N. J., Wszalek, T., et al. (2001). The relative involvement of anterior cingulate and prefrontal cortex in attentional control depends on nature of conflict. *Cognitive Brain Research, 12*, 467–473.

Miller, E. K. (2000). The prefrontal cortex and cognitive control. *Nature Reviews Neuroscience, 1*, 59–65.

Miller, E. K., & Cohen, J. D. (2001). An integrative theory of prefrontal cortex function. *Annual Review of Neuroscience, 21*, 167–202.

Miller, E. K., & Desimone, R. (1994). Parallel neuronal mechanisms for short-term memory. *Science, 263*, 520–522.

Miller, E. K., Erickson, C. A., & Desimone, R. (1996). Neural mechanisms of visual working memory in prefrontal cortex of the macaque. *Journal of Neuroscience, 16*, 5154–5167.

Miller, E. K., Freedman, D. J., & Wallis, J. D. (2002). The prefrontal cortex: Categories, concepts and cognition. *Philosophical Transactions of the Royal Society of London: Biological Sciences, 357*, 1123–1136.

Miller, G. A. (1956). The magical number seven, plus or minus two: Some limits on our capacity for processing information. *Psychological Review, 63*, 81–97.

Mills, B., & Levine, D. S. (2002). A neural theory of choice in the Iowa gambling task. Unpublished paper, University of Texas, Arlington.

Milner, A. D., Perrett, D. I., Johnston, R. S., Benson, P. J., Jordan, T. R., Heeley, D. W., et al. (1991). Perception and action in "visual form agnosia." *Brain, 114*(Pt 1B), 405–428.

Milner, B. (1962). Les troubles de la mémoire accompagnant des lésions hippocampiques bilatérales. In P. Passouant (Ed.), *Physiologie de l'hippocampe* (pp. 257–272). Paris: Centre de la Recherche Scientifique.

Milner, B. (1964). Some effects of frontal lobectomy on man. In J. M. Warren & K. Akerts (Eds.), *The frontal granular cortex and behaviour* (pp. 313–334). New York: McGraw-Hill.

Milner, B. (1966). Amnesia following operation on the temporal lobes. In C. W. M. Whitty & O. L. Zangwill (Eds.), *Amnesia* (pp. 109–133). London: Butterworths.

Milner, B. (1971). Interhemispheric differences in the localization of psychological processes in man. *British Medical Bulletin, 27*, 272–277.

Milner, B. (1972). Disorders of learning and memory after temporal lobe lesions in man. *Clinical Neurosurgery, 19*, 421–446.

Milner, B., Corsi, P., & Leonard, G. (1991). Frontal lobe contribution to recency judgments. *Neuropsychologia, 29*, 601–618.

Mineka, S., Davidson, M., Cook, M., & Keir, R. (1984). Observational conditioning of snake fear in rhesus monkeys. *Journal of Abnormal Psychology, 93*, 355–372.

Minsky, M. (1986). *The society of mind.* New York: Simon and Schuster.

Minsky, M., & Pappert, S. (1969). *Perceptrons.* Cambridge, MA: The MIT Press.

Miyake, A., & Shah, P. (Eds.). (1999). *Models of working memory: Mechanisms of active maintenance and executive control.* New York: Cambridge University Press.

Miyake, A., Friedman, N. P., Emerson, M. J., Witzki, A. H., Howerter, A., & Wager, T. D. (2000). Fractionating the central executive: Evidence for separability of executive functions. *Cognitive Psychology, 41*, 49–100.

Monchi, O., Petrides, M., Petre, V., Worsley, K., & Dagher, A. (2001). Wisconsin card sorting revisited: Distinct neural circuits participating in different stages of the task identified by event-related functional magnetic resonance imaging. *Journal of Neuroscience, 21*, 7733–7741.

Monsell, S. (1978). Recency, immediate recognition memory, and reaction time. *Cognitive Psychology, 10*, 465–501.

Montague, P. R., & Berns, G. S. (2002). Neural economics and biological substrates of valuation. *Neuron, 36*, 265–284.

Moran, J., & Desimone, R. (1985). Selective attention gates visual processing in the extrastriate cortex. *Science, 229*, 782–784.

Moray, N. (1959). Attention in dichotic listening: Affective cues and the influence of instructions. *Quarterly Journal of Experimental Psychology, 11*, 56–60.

Moray, N. (1970). Attention: Selective processes in vision and audition. New York: Academic Press.

Morris, C. D., Bransford, J. D., & Franks, J. J. (1977). Levels of processing versus transfer appropriate processing. *Journal of Verbal Learning and Verbal Behavior, 16*, 519–533.

Morris, J. S., Buchel, C., & Dolan, R. J. (2001a). Parallel neural responses in amygdala subregions and sensory cortex during implicit fear conditioning. *Neuroimage, 13*, 1044–1052.

Morris, J. S., Degelder, B., Weiskrantz, L., & Dolan, R. J. (2001b). Differential extrageniculostriate and amygdala responses to presentation of emotional faces in a cortically blind field. *Brain, 124*, 1241–1252.

Morris, J. S., Friston, K. J., Buchel, C., Frith, C. D., Young, A. W., Calder, A. J., et al. (1998). A neuro-modulatory role for the human amygdala in processing emotional facial expressions. *Brain, 121*(Pt. 1), 47–57.

Moscovitch, M., & Craik, F. I. M. (1976). Depth of processing, retrieval cues, and uniqueness of encoding as factors in recall. *Journal of Verbal Learning and Verbal Behavior, 15*, 447–458.

Moscovitch, M., Winocur, G., & Behrmann, M. (1997). What is special about face recognition? Nineteen experiments on a person with visual object agnosia and dyslexia but normal face recognition. *Journal of Cognitive Neuroscience, 9*, 555–604.

Motter, B. C. (1993). Focal attention produces spatially selective processing in visual cortical areas V1, V2, and V4 in the presence of competing stimuli. *Journal of Neurophysiology 70*, 909–919.

Mountcastle, V. B., Motter, B. C., Steinmetz, M. A., & Sestokas, A. K. (1987). Common and differential effects of attentive fixation on the excitability of parietal and prestriate (V4) cortical visual neurons in the macaque monkey. *Neuroscience, 7*, 2239–2255.

Muller, M. M., & Hillyard, S. (2000). Concurrent recording of steady-state and transient event-related potentials as indices of visual-spatial selective attention. *Clinical Neurophysiology, 111*, 1544–1552.

Muller, N., & Hulk, A. (2001). Crosslinguistic influence in bilingual language acquisition: Italian and French as recipient languages. *Bilingualism: Language and Cognition, 4*, 1–53.

Münte, T. F., Altenmüller, E., & Jäncke, L. (2002). The musician's brain as a model of neuroplasticity. *Nature Reviews Neuroscience, 3*, 473–478.

Murphy, G. L. (2000). Explanatory concepts. In F. C. Keil & R. A. Wilson (Eds.), *Explanation and cognition* (pp. 361–392). Cambridge, MA: The MIT Press.

Murphy, G. L. (2002). *The big book of concepts.* Cambridge, MA: The MIT Press.

Murphy, G. L., & Brownell, H. H. (1985). Category differentiation in object recognition: Typicality constraints on the basic category advantage. *Journal of Experimental Psychology: Learning, Memory, and Cognition, 11*, 70–84.

Murphy, G. L., & Lassaline, M. E. (1997). Hierarchical structure in concepts and the basic level of categorization. In K. Lamberts & D. R. Shanks (Eds.), *Knowledge, concepts and categories.* (pp. 93–131). Cambridge, MA: The MIT Press.

Murphy, G. L., & Medin, D. L. (1985). The role of theories in conceptual coherence. *Psychological Review, 92*, 289–316.

Murray, E. A., & Mishkin, M. (1986). Visual recognition in monkeys following rhinal cortical ablations combined with either amygdalectomy or hippocampectomy. *Journal of Neuroscience, 6*, 1991–2003.

Mushiake, H., Inase, M., & Tanji, J. (1991). Neuronal activity in the primate premotor, supplementary and precentral motor cortex during visually guided and internally determined sequential movements. *Journal of Neurophysiology, 66*, 705–718.

Müssler, J., & Hommel, B. (1997). Blindness to response-compatible stimuli. *Journal of Experimental Psychology: Human Perception and Performance, 23*, 861–872.

Nadel, J., & Butterworth, G. (1999). *Imitation in infancy.* Cambridge, UK: Cambridge University Press.

Nadel, J., Guérini, C., Pezé, A., & Rivet, A. (1999). The evolving nature of imitation as a format for communication. In J. Nadel & G. Butterworth (Eds.), *Imitation in infancy* (pp. 209–234). Cambridge, UK: Cambridge University Press.

Nadel-Brufert, J., & Baudonnière, P. M. (1982). The social function of reciprocal imitation in 2-year-old peers. *International Journal of Behavioral Development, 5,* 95–109.

Nairne, J. S. (2002). Remembering over the short-term: The case against the standard model. *Annual Review of Psychology, 53,* 53–81.

Naito, E., Roland, P. E., & Ehrsson, H. H. (2000). I feel my hand moving: A new role of the primary motor cortex in somatic perception of limb movement. *Neuron, 36,* 979–988.

Nakayama, K., & Silverman, G. H. (1986). Serial and parallel processing of visual feature conjunctions. *Nature, 320,* 264–265.

Nakazawa, K., Quirk, M. C., Chitwood, R. A., Watanabe, M., Yeckel, M. F., Sun, L. D., et al. (2002). Requirement for hippocampal CA3 NMDA receptors in associative memory recall. *Science, 297,* 211–218.

Nasrallah, H., Coffman, J., & Olsen, S. (1989). Structural brain-imaging findings in affective disorders: An overview. *Journal of Neuropsychiatry and Clinical Neuroscience, 1,* 21–32.

Naya, Y., Yoshida, M., & Miyashita, Y. (2001). Backward spreading of memory-retrieval signals in the primate temporal cortex. *Science, 291,* 661–664.

Neisser, U. (1967). *Cognitive psychology.* New York: Appleton-Century-Crofts.

Neisser, U., & Becklen, R. (1975). Selective looking: Attending to visually specified events. *Cognitive Psychology, 7,* 480–494.

Neisser, U., & Harsch, N. (1992). Phantom flashbulbs: False recollections of hearing news about the *Challenger.* In E. Winograd & U. Neisser (Eds.), *Affect and accuracy in recall: Studies of "flashbulb" memories* (pp. 9–31). Cambridge, UK: Cambridge University Press.

Neisser, U., Winograd, E., Bergman, E. T., Schreiber, C. A., Palmer, S. E., & Weldon, M. S. (1996). Remembering the earthquake: Direct experience vs. hearing the news. *Memory, 4,* 337–357.

Neri, P., Morrone, M. C., & Burr, D. C. (1998). Seeing biological motion. *Nature, 395,* 894–896.

Neville, H. J., & Bavelier, D. (1998). Neural organization and plasticity of language. *Current Opinion in Neurobiology, 8,* 254–258.

Newcomer, J. S., Craft, S., Hershey, T., Askins, K., & Bardgett, M. E. (1994). Glucocorticoid-induced impairment in declarative memory performance in adult humans. *Journal of Neuroscience, 14,* 2047–2053.

Newell, A. (1990). *Unified theories of cognition.* Cambridge, MA: Harvard University Press.

Newell, A., & Simon, H. A. (1972). *Human problem solving.* Upper Saddle River, NJ: Prentice Hall.

Newman, E. A., & Zahs, K. R. (1998). Modulation of neuronal activity by glial cells in the retina. *Journal of Neuroscience, 18,* 4022–4028.

Newsome, W. T. (1997). Deciding about motion: Linking perception to action. *Journal of Comparative Physiology, Series A, 181,* 5–12.

Newton, N. (1996). *Foundations of understanding.* Philadelphia: John Benjamins.

Newtson, D. (1976). Foundations of attribution: The perception of ongoing behavior. In J. Harvey, W. J. Ickes, & R. F. Kidd (Eds.), *New directions in attribution research* (pp. 223–247). Hillsdale, NJ: Lawrence Erlbaum Associates.

Nisbett, R. E., Kratnz, D. H., Jepson, D., & Kunda, Z. (1983). The use of statistical heuristics in everyday inductive reasoning. *Psychological Review, 90,* 339–363.

Noesselt, T., Hillyard, S. A., Woldorff, M. G., Schoenfeld, A., Hagner, T., et al. (2002). Delayed striate cortical activation during spatial attention. *Neuron, 35,* 575–587.

Nolde, S. F., Johnson, M. K., & D'Esposito, M. (1998). Left prefrontal activation during episodic remembering: An event-related fMRI study. *NeuroReport, 9,* 3509–3514.

Norman, D. A., & Shallice, T. (1986). Attention to action: Willed and automatic control of behavior. In R. J. Davidson, G. E. Schwartz, & D. Shapiro (Eds.), *Consciousness and self-regulation: Advances in research and theory* (Vol. 4, pp. 1–18). New York: Plenum Press.

Nosofsky, R. M. (1984). Choice, similarity, and the context theory of classification. *Journal of Experimental Psychology: Learning, Memory, and Cognition, 10,* 104–114.

Nosofsky, R. M., Palmeri, T. J., & McKinley, S. C. (1994). Rule-plus-exception model of classification learning. *Psychological Review, 101,* 53–79.

Nyberg, L., Cabeza, R., & Tulving, E. (1996). PET studies of encoding and retrieval: The HERA model. *Psychonomic Bulletin & Review, 3,* 135–148.

Nyberg, L., Habib, R., & McIntosh, A. R. (2000). Reactivation of encoding-related brain activity during memory retrieval. *Proceedings of the National Academy of Sciences USA, 97,* 11120–11124.

Nystrom, L. E., Braver, T. S., Sabb, F. W., Delgado, M. R., Noll, D. C., & Cohen, J. D. (2000). Working memory for letters, shapes, and locations: fMRI evidence against stimulus-based regional organization of human prefrontal cortex. *NeuroImage, 11,* 424–446.

O'Brien, V. (1958). Contour perception, illusion and reality. *Journal of the Optical Society of America, 48,* 112–119.

Obrig, H., & Villringer, A. (2003). Beyond the visible—imaging the human brain with light. *Journal of Cerebral Blood Flow and Metabolism, 23,* 1–18.

Ochsner, K. N., Bunge, S. A., Gross, J. J., & Gabrieli, J. D. E. (2002). Rethinking feelings: An fMRI study of the cognitive regulation of emotion. *Journal of Cognitive Neuroscience, 14,* 1215–1229.

O'Connor, D. H., Fukui, M. M., Pinsk, M. A., & Kastner, S. (2002). Attention modulates responses in the human lateral geniculate nucleus. *Nature Neuroscience, 5,* 1203–1209.

O'Craven, K. M., Downing, P. E., & Kanwisher, N. (1999). fMRI evidence for objects as the units of attentional selection. *Nature, 401,* 584–587.

O'Doherty, J., Kringelbach, M. L., Rolls, E. T., Hornak, J., & Andrews, C. (2001). Abstract reward and punishment representations in the human orbitofrontal cortex. *Nature Neuroscience, 4,* 95–102.

Oh, J. S., Jun, S. A., Knightly, L. M., & Au, T. K. F. (2003). Holding on to childhood language memory. *Cognition, 86,* B53–B54.

Ohman, A., Flykt, A., & Esteves, F. (2001a). Emotion drives attention: Detecting the snake in the grass. *Journal of Experimental Psychology: General, 130,* 466–478.

Ohman, A., Lundqvist, D., & Esteves, F. (2001b). The face in the crowd revisited: A threat advantage with schematic stimuli. *Journal of Personality and Social Psychology, 80,* 381–396.

Ohman, A., & Mineka, S. (2001). Fear, phobias, and preparedness: Toward an evolved module of fear and fear learning. *Psychological Review, 108,* 483–522.

Ohman, A., & Soares, J. J. F. (1998). Emotional conditioning to masked stimuli: Expectancies for aversive outcomes following nonrecognized fear-relevant stimuli. *Journal of Experimental Psychology: General, 127,* 69–82.

O'Kane, G., Kensinger, E. A., & Corkin, S. (2004). Evidence for semantic learning in profound amnesia. An investigation with patient H. M. *Hippocampus, 14,* 417–425.

Olsson, A., Nearing, K., Zheng, J., & Phelps, E. A. (2004). *Learning by observing: Neural correlates of fear learning through social observation.* Paper presented at 34th Annual Meeting of the Society for Neuroscience, San Diego, CA.

Oram, M., & Perrett, D. (1994). Response of the anterior superior polysensory (STPa) neurons to "biological motion" stimuli. *Journal of Cognitive Neuroscience, 6,* 99–116.

O'Reilly, R. C., Braver, T. S., & Cohen, J. D. (1999). A biologically based computational model of working memory. In A. Miyake & P. Shah (Eds.), *Models of working memory: Mechanisms of active maintenance and executive control* (pp. 375–411). New York: Cambridge University Press.

O'Reilly, R. C., & Munakata, Y. (2000). *Computational explorations in cognitive neuroscience.* Cambridge, MA: The MIT Press.

O'Reilly, R. C., Noelle, D. C., Braver, T. S., & Cohen, J. D. (2002). Prefrontal cortex and dynamic categorization tasks: Representational organization and neuromodulatory control. *Cerebral Cortex, 12,* 246–257.

Osherson, D. N., Perani, D., Cappa, S., Schnur, T., Grassi, F., & Fazio, F. (1998). Distinct brain loci in deductive versus probabilistic reasoning. *Neuropsychologia, 36,* 369–376.

Osherson, D. N., Smith, E. E., Wilkie, O., Lopez, A., & Shafir, E. (1990). Category-based induction. *Psychological Review, 97,* 185–200.

Owen, A. M. (1997). The functional organization of working memory processes within human lateral frontal cortex: The contribution of functional neuroimaging. *European Journal of Neuroscience, 9,* 1329–1339.

Packard, M. G., & Teather, L. A. (1998). Amygdala modulation of multiple memory systems: Hippocampus and caudate-putamen. *Neurobiology of Learning and Memory, 69,* 163–203.

Pagnoni, G., Zink, C. F., Montague, P. R., & Berns, G. S. (2002). Activity in human ventral striatum locked to errors of reward prediction. *Nature Neuroscience, 5,* 97–98.

Paller, K. A., & Wagner, A. D. (2002). Observing the transformation of experience into memory. *Trends in Cognitive Science, 6,* 93–102.

Pallier, C., Dehaene, S., Poline, J.-B., LeBihan, D., Argenti, A.-M., Dupoux, E., et al. (2003). Brain imaging of language plasticity in adopted adults: Can a second language replace the first? *Cerebral Cortex, 13,* 155–161.

Palmer, S. E. (1975). The effects of contextual scenes on the identification of objects. *Memory & Cognition, 3,* 519–526.

Palmer, S. E. (1978). Fundamental aspects of cognitive representation. In E. Rosch & B. B. Lloyd (Eds.), *Cognition and categorization* (pp. 259–303). Hillsdale, NJ: Lawrence Erlbaum Associates.

Palmer, S. E. (1999). *Vision science: Photons to phenomenology.* Cambridge, MA: The MIT Press.

Papafragou, A., Massey, C., & Gleitman, L. (2006). When English proposes what Greek presupposes: The cross-linguistic encoding of motion events. *Cognition, 98,* B75–B87.

Parsons, L. M. (1994). Temporal and kinematic properties of motor behavior reflected in mentally simulated action. *Journal of Experimental Psychology: Human Perception and Performance, 20,* 709–730.

Parsons, L. M., & Fox, P. T. (1998). The neural basis of implicit movement used in recognizing hand shape. *Cognitive Neuropsychology, 15,* 583–615.

Parsons, L. M., & Osherson, D. N. (2001). New evidence for distinct right and left brain systems for deductive versus probabilistic reasoning. *Cerebral Cortex, 11,* 954–965.

Pascual-Leone, A., & Walsh, V. (2001). Fast backprojections from the motion to the primary visual area necessary for visual awareness. *Science, 292,* 510–512.

Pashler, H. E. (1998). *The psychology of attention.* Cambridge, MA: The MIT Press.

Pashler, H., & Johnston, J. C. (1998). Attentional limitations in dual-task performance. In H. Pashler (Ed.), *Attention* (pp. 155–190). Hove, East Sussex, UK: Psychology Press.

Pasley, B. N., Mayes, L. C., & Schultz, R. T. (2004). Subcortical discrimination of unperceived objects during binocular rivalry. *Neuron, 42,* 163–172.

Passingham, R. E. (1993). *The frontal lobes and voluntary action.* New York: Oxford University Press.

Patalano, A. L., Smith, E. E., Jonides, J., & Koeppe, R. A. (2001). PET evidence for multiple strategies of categorization. *Cognitive, Affective & Behavioral Neuroscience, 1,* 360–370.

Patel, V. L., Arocha, J. F., & Kaufman, D. R. (1994). Diagnostic reasoning and medical expertise. In D. Medin (Ed.), *The psychology of learning and motivation: Advances in research and theory* (Vol. 31, pp. 187–252). San Diego, CA: Academic Press.

Paulesu, E., Frith, C. D., & Frackowiak, R. S. J. (1993). The neural correlates of the verbal component of working memory. *Nature, 362,* 342–345.

Pavlova, M., Staudt, M., Sokolov, A., Birbaumer, N., & Krägeloh-Mann, I. (2003). Perception and production of biological movement in patients with early periventricular brain lesions. *Brain, 126,* 692–701.

Payne, J. W., Bettman, J. R., & Johnson, E. J. (1993). *The adaptive decision maker.* New York: Cambridge University Press.

Pearson, B. Z., Fernandez, S. C., Lewedeg, V., & Oller, D. K. (1997). The relation of input factors to lexical learning by bilingual infants. *Applied Psycholinguistics, 18,* 41–58.

Pearson, B. Z., Fernandez, S. C., & Oller, D. K. (1993). Cross-language synonyms in the lexicons of bilingual infants: One language or two? *Journal of Child Language, 22,* 345–368.

Pecher, D., Zeelenberg, R., & Barsalou, L. W. (2003). Verifying properties from different modalities for concepts produces switching costs. *Psychological Science, 14,* 119–124.

Pegna, A. J., Khateb, A., Lazeyas, F., & Seghier, M. L. (2005). Discriminating emotional faces without primary visual cortices involves the right amygdala. *Nature Neuroscience, 8,* 24–25.

Penev, P. S., & Atick, J. J. (1996). Local feature analysis: A general statistical theory for object representation. *Network: Computation in Neural Systems, 7,* 477–500.

Perani, D., Fazio, F., Borghese, N. A., Tettamanti, M., Ferrari, S., Decety, J., et al. (2001). Different brain correlates for watching real and virtual hand actions. *NeuroImage, 14,* 749–758.

Perrett, D. I., Harries, M. H., Bevan, R., Thomas, S., Benson, P. J., et al. (1989). Frameworks of analysis for the neural representation of animate objects and action. *Journal of Experimental Biology, 146,* 87–114.

Perrett, D. I., Oram, M. W., Harries, M. H., Bevan, R., Hietanen, J. K., Benson, P. J., et al. (1991). Viewer-centred and object-centred coding of heads in the macaque temporal cortex. *Experimental Brain Research, 86,* 159–173.

Perrett, D. I., Rolls, E. T., & Caan, W. (1982). Visual neurones responsive to faces in the monkey temporal cortex. *Experimental Brain Research, 47*, 329–342.

Pessoa, L., McKenna, M., Gutierrez, E., & Ungerleider, L. G. (2002). Neural processing of emotional faces requires attention. *Proceedings of the National Academy of Sciences USA, 99*, 11458–11463.

Pessoa, L., & Ungerleider, L. G. (2004). Neuroimaging studies of attention and the processing of emotion-laden stimuli. *Progress in Brain Research, 144*, 171–182.

Petersen, S. E., Fox, P. T., Posner, M. I., Mintun, M., & Raichle, M. E. (1988). Positron emission tomography studies of the cortical anatomy of single-word processing. *Nature, 331*, 585–589.

Peterson, L. R., & Peterson, M. J. (1959). Short-term retention of individual items. *Journal of Experimental Psychology, 61*, 12–21.

Petrides, M. (1986). The effect of periarcuate lesions in the monkey on the performance of symmetrically and asymmetrically reinforced visual and auditory go, no-go tasks. *Journal of Neuroscience, 6*, 2054–2063.

Petrides, M. E., Alivisatos, B., Evans, A. C., & Meyer, E. (1993a). Dissociation of human mid-dorsolateral from posterior dorsolateral frontal cortex in memory processing. *Proceedings of the National Academy of Sciences USA, 90*, 873–877.

Petrides, M. E., Alivisatos, B., Meyer, E., & Evans, A. C. (1993b). Functional activation of the human frontal cortex during the performance of verbal working memory tasks. *Proceedings of the National Academy of Sciences USA, 90*, 878–882.

Petrides, M. E., & Milner, B. (1982). Deficits on subject-ordered tasks after frontal- and temporal-lobe lesions in man. *Neuropsychologia, 20*, 249–269.

Pezdek, K. (2003). Event memory and autobiographical memory for the events of September 11, 2001. *Applied Cognitive Psychology, 17*, 1033–1045.

Phelps, E. A. (2002). Emotions. In M. S. Gazzaniga, R. B. Ivry, & G. R. Mangun (Eds.), *Cognitive neuroscience: The biology of mind* (2nd ed., pp. 537–576). New York: W. W. Norton & Company.

Phelps, E. A., Ling S., & Carrasco, M. (in press). Emotion facilitates perception and potentiates the perceptual benefit of attention. *Psychological Science*.

Phelps, E. A., O'Connor, K. J., Gatenby, J. C., Gores, J. C., Grillon, C., & Davis, M. (2001). Activation of the left amygdala to a cognitive representation of fear. *Nature Neuroscience, 4*, 437–441.

Piaget, J. (1953). *The origins of intelligence in the child*. London: Routledge.

Piaget, J. (1954/1936). *The construction of reality in the child* (trans. by M. Cook). New York: Basic Books.

Pillemer, D. B. (1984). Flashbulb memories of the assassination attempt on President Reagan. *Cognition, 16*, 63–80.

Pinker, S. (1997). *How the mind works*. New York: Norton.

Pinker, S. (2002). *The blank slate: The modern denial of human nature*. New York: Viking Penguin.

Platt, M. L. (2002). Neural correlates of decisions. *Current Opinion in Neuroscience, 12*, 141–148.

Platt, M. L., & Glimcher, P. W. (1999). Neural correlates of decision variables in parietal cortex. *Nature, 400*, 233–238.

Plaut, D. C., McClelland, J. L., Seidenberg, M. S., & Patterson, K. E. (1996). Understanding normal and impaired word reading: Computational principles in quasi-regular domains. *Psychological Review, 103*, 56–115.

Pochon, J. B., Levy, R., Poline, J. B., Crozier, S., Lehericy, S., Pillon, B., et al. (2001). The role of dorsolateral prefrontal cortex in the preparation of forthcoming actions: An fMRI study. *Cerebral Cortex, 11*, 260–266.

Poldrack, R. A., Clark, J., Paré-Blagoev, E. J., Shohamy, D., Moyano, J. C., Myers, C., et al. (2001). Interactive memory systems in the human brain. *Nature, 414*, 546–550.

Poldrack, R. A., Prabakharan, V., Seger, C., & Gabrieli, J. D. E. (1999). Striatal activation during cognitive skill learning. *Neuropsychology, 13*, 564–574.

Polk, T. A., Simen, P., Lewis, R., & Freedman, E. (2002). A computational approach to control in complex cognition. *Cognitive Brain Research, 15*, 71–83.

Pollio, H. R., Barlow, J. M., Fine, H. J., & Pollio, M. R. (1977). *Psychology and the poetics of growth: Figurative language in psychology, psychotherapy and education*. New York: Lawrence Erlbaum Associates.

Polonsky, A., Blake, R., Braun, J., & Heeger, D. J. (2000). Neuronal activity in human primary visual cortex correlates with perception during binocular rivalry. *Nature Neuroscience, 3*, 1153–1159.

Posner, M. I. (1980). Orienting of attention. *Quarterly Journal of Experimental Psychology, 32,* 3–25.

Posner, M. I. (1990). Hierarchical distributed networks in the neuropsychology of selective attention. In A. Caramazza (Ed.), *Cognitive neuropsychology and neurolinguistics* (pp. 187–210). Hillsdale, NJ: Lawrence Erlbaum Associates.

Posner, M. I., & Boies, S. J. (1971). Components of attention. *Psychological Review, 78,* 391–408.

Posner, M. I., Choate, L. S., Rafal, R. D., & Vaughn, J. (1985). Inhibition of return: Neural mechanisms and function. *Cognitive Neuropsychology, 2,* 211–228.

Posner, M. I., & Cohen, Y. (1984). Components of performance. In H. Bouma & D. Bouwhuis (Eds.), *Attention and performance X* (pp. 531–556). Hillsdale, NJ: Lawrence Erlbaum Associates.

Posner, M. I., Cohen, Y., & Rafal, R. D. (1982). Neural systems control of spatial orienting. *Proceedings of the Royal Society of London, Series B, 298,* 187–198.

Posner, M. I., & Keele, S. W. (1968). On the genesis of abstract ideas. *Journal of Experimental Psychology, 77,* 353–363.

Posner, M. I., & Snyder, C. R. R. (1974). Attention and cognitive control. In R. L. Solso (Ed.), *Information processing and cognition: The Loyola Symposium* (pp. 55–85). Hillsdale, NJ: Lawrence Erlbaum Associates.

Posner, M. I., Snyder, C. R. R., & Davidson, B. J. (1980). Attention and the detection of signals. *Journal of Experimental Psychology: General, 109,* 160–174.

Posner, M. I., Walker, J. A., Friedrich, F. J., & Rafal, R. D. (1984). Effects of parietal injury on covert orienting of visual attention. *Journal of Neuroscience, 4,* 1863–1874.

Posner, M. I., Walker, J. A., Friedrich, F. J., & Rafal, R. D. (1987). How do the parietal lobes direct covert attention? *Neuropsychologia, 25*(1A), 135–145.

Postle, B. R., Awh, E., Jonides, J., Smith, E. E., & D'Esposito, M. (2004). The where and how of attention-based rehearsal in spatial working memory. *Cognitive Brain Research, 20,* 194–205.

Postle, B. R., & D'Esposito, M. (2000). Evaluating models of the topographical organization of working memory function in frontal cortex with event-related fMRI. *Psychobiology, 28,* 132–145.

Potter, M. C., & Levy, E. I. (1969). Recognition memory for a rapid sequence of pictures. *Journal of Experimental Psychology, 81,* 10–15.

Powell, H. W., Koepp, M. I., Symms, M. R., Boulby, P. A., Salek-Haddadi, A., Thompson, P. J., Duncan, J. S., & Richardson, M. P. (2005). Material-specific lateralization of memory encoding in the medial temporal lobe: blocked versus event-related design. *Neuroimage, 27,* 231–239.

Pratto, F., & John, O. P. (1991). Automatic vigilance: The attention grabbing power of negative social information. *Journal of Personality and Social Psychology, 61,* 380–391.

Prinz, W. (1997). Perception and action planning. *European Journal of Cognitive Psychology, 9,* 129–154.

Prusiner, S. B. (2002). Historical essay: Discovering the cause of AIDS. *Science, 298,* 1726.

Pugh, K. R., Mencl, W. E., Jenner, A. R., Lee, J. R., Katz, L., Frost, S. J., et al. (2001). Neurobiological studies of reading and reading disability. *Journal of Communication Disorders, 34,* 479–492.

Pulvermüller, F. (1999). Words in the brain's language. *Behavioral and Brain Sciences, 22,* 253–336.

Pylyshyn, Z. W. (1973). What the mind's eye tells the mind's brain: A critique of mental imagery. *Psychological Bulletin, 80,* 1–24.

Pylyshyn, Z. W. (1981). The imagery debate: Analogue media versus tacit knowledge. *Psychological Review, 87,* 16–45.

Pylyshyn, Z. W. (2002). Mental imagery: In search of a theory. *Behavioral & Brain Sciences, 25,* 157–238.

Pylyshyn, Z. (2003). Return of the mental image: Are there pictures in the brain? *Trends in Cognitive Sciences, 7,* 113–118.

Quinn, P. C. (2002). Early categorization: A new synthesis. In U. Goswami (Ed.), *Blackwell handbook of childhood cognitive development* (pp. 84–101). Oxford, UK: Blackwell Publishers.

Rabbitt, P. (1998). *Methodology of frontal and executive function.* Hove: Psychology Press.

Rachlin, H. (1989). *Judgment, decision, and choice: A cognitive/behavioral synthesis.* New York: Freeman.

Rafal, R. (2001). Bálint's syndrome. In F. Boller & J. Grafman (Eds.), *Handbook of Neuropsychology* (pp. 121–142). Amsterdam: Elsevier Science.

Rafal, R. D., & Posner, M. I. (1987). Deficits in visual spatial attention following thalamic lesions. *Proceedings of the National Academy of Sciences USA, 84,* 7349–7353.

Ranganath, C., Yonelinas, A. P., Cohen, M. X., Dy, C. J., Tom, S. M., & D'Esposito, M. (2004). Dissociable correlates of recollection and familiarity within the medial temporal lobes. *Neuropsychologia, 42,* 2–13.

Ratliff, F. (1965). *Mach bands*. San Francisco: Holden-Day Publishers.

Raymond, J. E. (2003). New objects, not new features, trigger the attentional blink. *Psychological Science, 14,* 54–59.

Rayner, K. (1975). Parafoveal identification during a fixation in reading. *Acta Psychologica, 39,* 271–281.

Rayner, K., Foorman, B. R., Perfetti, E., Pesetsky, D., & Seidenberg, M. S. (2001). How psychological science informs the teaching of reading. *Psychological Science in the Public Interest Monograph, 2,* 31–74.

Rayner, K., & Pollatsek, A. (1989). *The psychology of reading.* Hillsdale, NJ: Lawrence Erlbaum Associates.

Read, D. E. (1981). Solving deductive-reasoning problems after unilateral temporal lobectomy. *Brain and Language, 12,* 116–127.

Redelmeier, D. A., & Tibshirani, R. J. (1997). Association between cellular-telephone calls and motor vehicle collisions. *New England Journal of Medicine, 336,* 453–458.

Reicher, G. M. (1969). Perceptual recognition as a function of the meaningfulness of stimulus material. *Journal of Experimental Psychology, 81,* 275–281.

Reingold, E. M., & Jolicoeur, P. (1993). Perceptual versus postperceptual mediation of visual context effects: Evidence from the letter-superiority effect. *Perception & Psychophysics, 53,* 166–178.

Rensink, R., O'Regan, K., & Clark, J. J. (1997). To see or not to see: The need for attention to perceive changes in scenes. *Psychological Science, 8,* 368–373.

Reynolds, J. H., Chelazzi, L., & Desimone, R. (1999). Competitive mechanisms subserve attention in macaque areas V2 and V4. *Journal of Neuroscience, 9,* 1736–1753.

Rhodes, G., Brennan, S., & Carey, S. (1987). Identification and ratings of caricatures: Implications for mental representations of faces. *Cognitive Psychology, 19,* 473–497.

Riehle A., & Requin, J. (1989). Monkey primary motor and premotor cortex: Single-cell activity related to prior information about direction and extent of an intended movement. *Journal of Neurophysiology, 61,* 534–549.

Rips, L. J. (1975). Inductive judgments about natural categories. *Journal of Verbal Learning & Verbal Behavior, 14,* 665–681.

Rips, L. J. (1989). Similarity, typicality, and categorization. In S. Vosniadou & A. Ortony (Eds.), *Similarity and analogical reasoning.* Cambridge, UK: Cambridge University Press.

Rips, L. J. (1994). *The psychology of proof: Deductive reasoning in human thinking.* Cambridge, MA: The MIT Press.

Rips, L. J. (1995). Deduction and cognition. In E. E. Smith & D. N. Osherson (Eds.), *Thinking: An invitation to cognitive science* (Vol. 3, 2nd ed.). (pp. 297–344). Cambridge, MA: The MIT Press.

Rizzolati, G., Fadiga, L., Gallese, V., & Fogassi, L. (1996). Premotor cortex and the recognition of motor actions. *Cognitive Brain Research, 3,* 131–141.

Rizzolatti, G., Fadiga, L., Fogassi, L., & Gallese, V. (2002). From mirror neurons to imitation: Facts and speculations. In A. N. Meltzoff & W. Prinz (Eds.), *The imitative mind: Development, evolution, and brain bases.* (pp. 247–266). New York: Cambridge University Press.

Robertson, L. C., & Rafal, R. (2000). Disorders of visual attention. In M. S. Gazzaniga (Ed.), *The new cognitive neurosciences* (2nd ed., pp. 633–650). Cambridge, MA: The MIT Press.

Robinson, J. (1999). *The psychology of visual illusions.* New York: Dover Publications. Republication of the work published by Hutchinson & Co., London, 1972.

Rochat, P. (1999). *Early social cognition: Understanding others in the first months of life.* Mahawah, NJ: Lawrence Erlbaum Associates.

Rochat, P., & Hespos, S. J. (1997). Differential rooting response by neonates: Evidence for an early sense of self. *Early Development and Parenting, 6,* 105–112.

Rockland, K. S. (2002). Visual cortical organization at the single axon level: A beginning. *Neuroscience Research, 42,* 155–166.

Roediger, H. L. (1973). Inhibition in recall from cueing with recall targets. *Journal of Verbal Learning and Verbal Behavior, 12,* 644–657.

Roediger, H. L., & McDermott, K. (1993). Implicit memory in normal human subjects. In F. Boller & J. Grafman (Eds.), *Handbook of neuropsychology* (Vol. 8, pp. 63–131). New York: Elsevier.

Roediger, H. L., & McDermott, K. B. (1995). Creating false memories: Remembering words not presented in lists. *Journal of Experimental Psychology: Learning, Memory, and Cognition, 21,* 803–814.

Rogers, R. D., Everitt, B. J., Baldacchino, A., Blackshaw, A. J., Swainson, R., Wynne, K., et al. (1999a). Dissociable deficits in the decision-making cognition of chronic amphetamine abusers, opiate abusers, patients with focal damage to prefrontal cortex, and tryptophan-depleted normal volunteers: Evidence for monoaminergic mechanisms. *Neuropsychopharmacology, 20,* 322–339.

Rogers, R. D., Owen, A. M., Middleton, H. C., Pickard, J. D., Sahakian, B. J., & Robbins, T. W. (1999b). Choosing between small and likely reward and large and unlikely rewards activates inferior and orbital prefrontal cortex. *Journal of Neuroscience, 20,* 9029–9038.

Rogers, R. D., & Monsell, S. (1995). Costs of a predictable switch between simple cognitive tasks. *Journal of Experimental Psychology: General, 124,* 207–231.

Rogers, S. J. (1999). An examination of the imitation deficit in autism. In J. Nadel & G. Butterworth (Eds.)., *Imitation in infancy* (pp. 254–283). Cambridge, UK: Cambridge University Press.

Rolls, E. T. (2000). The orbitofrontal cortex and reward. *Cerebral Cortex, 10,* 284–294.

Rolls, E. T., Burton, M. J., & Mora, F. (1980). Neurophysiological analysis of brain stimulation reward in the monkey. *Brain Research, 194,* 339–357.

Romanski, L. M., & Ledoux, J. E. (1993). Information cascade from auditory cortex to the amygdala: Corticocortical and corticoamygdaloid projections of the temporal cortex in rat. *Cerebral Cortex, 3,* 515–532.

Rosch, E. (1973). On the internal structure of perceptual and semantic categories. In T. Moore (Ed.), *Cognitive development and the acquisition of language* (pp. 111–144). San Diego, CA: Academic Press.

Rosch, E. (1975). Cognitive representations of semantic categories. *Journal of Experimental Psychology: General, 104,* 192–233.

Rosch, E., & Mervis, C. B. (1975). Family resemblances: Studies in the internal structure of categories. *Cognitive Psychology, 7,* 573–605.

Rosch, E., Mervis, C. B., Gray, W. D., Johnson, D. M., & Boyes-Braem, P. (1976). Basic objects in natural categories. *Cognitive Psychology, 8,* 382–439.

Rosenbaum, D. A. (1983). The movement precuing technique: Assumptions, applications and extensions. In R. A. Magill (Ed.), *Memory and control in motor behavior* (pp. 231–274). Amsterdam: North-Holland.

Ross, B. H. (1996). Category learning as problem solving. In D. L. Medin (Ed.), *The psychology of learning and motivation: Advances in research and theory, 35,* 165–192.

Ross, M. (1989). Relation of implicit theories to the construction of personal histories. *Psychological Review, 96,* 341–357.

Roth, M., Decety, J., Raybaudi, M., Massarelli, R., Delon, C., Segebarth, C., et al. (1996). Possible involvement of primary motor cortex in mentally simulated movement: An fMRI study. *NeuroReport, 7,* 1280–1284.

Rothi, L. J. G., Ochipa, C., & Heilman, K. M. (1991). A cognitive neuropsychological model of limb praxis. *Cognitive Neuropsychology, 8,* 443–458.

Rottenstreich, Y., & Hsee, C. K. (2001). Money, kisses, and electric shocks: On the affective psychology of risk. *Psychological Science, 12,* 185–190.

Rottenstreich, Y., & Shu, S. (2004). The connections between affect and decision making: Nine resulting phenomena. In D. J. Koehler & N. Harvey (Eds.), *Blackwell handbook of judgment and decision* (pp. 444–463). Malden, MA: Blackwell.

Rottenstreich, Y., & Tversky, A. (1997). Unpacking, repacking, and anchoring: Advances in support theory. *Psychological Review, 104,* 406–415.

Rougier, N. P., Noelle, D. C., Braver, T. S., Cohen, J. D., & O'Reilly, R. C. (2005). Prefrontal cortex and flexible cognitive control: Rules without symbols. *Proceedings of the National Academy of Sciences, 102,* 7338–7343.

Rubinstein, J. S., Meyer, D. E., & Evans, J. E. (2001). Executive control of cognitive processes in task switching. *Journal of Experimental Psychology: Human Perception & Performance, 27,* 763–97.

Ruby, P., & Decety, J. (2001). Effect of subjective perspective taking during simulation of action: A PET investigation of agency. *Nature Neuroscience, 4,* 546–550.

Ruby, P., & Decety, J. (2003). What do you believe versus what do you think they believe? A neuroimaging study of perspective taking at the conceptual level. *European Journal of Neuroscience, 17,* 2475–2480.

Ruby, P., Sirigu, A., & Decety, J. (2002). Distinct areas in parietal cortex involved in long-term and short-term action planning. A PET investigation. *Cortex, 38,* 321–339.

Rueckl, J. G., Cave, K. R., & Kosslyn, S. M. (1989). Why are "what" and "where" processed by separate cortical visual systems? A computational investigation. *Journal of Cognitive Neuroscience, 1,* 171–186.

Rugg, M. D., & Wilding, E. L. (2000). Retrieval processes and episodic memory. *Trends in Cognitive Science, 4,* 108–115.

Rumelhart, D. E., McClelland, J. L., & the PDP Research Group (1986). *Parallel distributed processing: Explorations in the microstructure of cognition: Vol. 1. Foundations.* Cambridge, MA: The MIT Press.

Rumelhart, D. E., & Norman, D. A. (1988). Representation in memory. In R. C. Atkinson, R. J. Herrnstein, G. Lindzey, & R. D. Luce (Eds.), *Stevens' handbook of experimental psychology: Vol. 2. Learning and cognition* (pp. 511–587). New York: Wiley.

Rumiati, R. I., & Tessari, A. (2002). Imitation of novel and well-known actions. *Experimental Brain Research, 142,* 425–433.

Russell, J. A. (1980). A circumplex model of affect. *Journal of Personality and Social Psychology, 39,* 1161–1178.

Russell, J. A., & Barrett, L. F. (1999). Core affect, prototypical emotional episodes, and other things called emotion: Dissecting the elephant. *Journal of Personality and Social Psychology, 76,* 805–819.

Rypma, B., & D'Esposito, M. (1999). The roles of prefrontal brain regions in components of working memory: Effects of memory load and individual differences. *Proceedings of the National Academy of Sciences USA, 96,* 6558–6563.

Sakurai, S., & Sugimoto, S. (1985). Effect of lesions of prefrontal cortex and dorsomedial thalamus on delayed go/no-go alternation in rats. *Behavioral Brain Research, 17,* 295–301.

Salin, P. A., & Bullier, J. (1995). Corticocortical connections in the visual system: structure and function. *Physiological Review, 75,* 107–154.

Salzman, C. D., Britten, K. H., & Newsome, W. T. (1990). Cortical microstimulation influences perceptual judgments of motion direction. *Nature, 346,* 174–177.

Sanfey, A. G., Hastie, R., Colvin, M. K., & Grafman, J. (2003a). Phineas gauged: Decision making and the human prefrontal cortex. *Neuropsychologica, 41,* 1218–1229.

Sanfey, A. G., Rilling, J. K., Aronson, J. A., Nystrom, L. E., & Cohen, J. D. (2003b). The neural basis of economic decision making in the ultimatum game. *Science, 300,* 1755–1758.

Savage, L. J. (1954). *The foundations of statistics.* New York: Wiley.

Savage-Rumbaugh, E. S., McDonald, K., Sevcik, R. A., Hopkins, W. D., & Rupert, E. (1986). Spontaneous symbol acquisition and communicative use by pygmy chimpanzees (*Pan paniscus*). *Journal of Experimental Psychology: General, 115,* 211–235.

Sawaguchi, T. (2001). The effects of dopamine and its agonists on directional delay period activity of prefrontal neurons in monkeys during an oculomotor delayed-response task. *Neuroscience Research, 41,* 115–128.

Sawaguchi, T., & Goldman-Rakic, P. S. (1994). The role of D1-dopamine receptor in working memory: Local injections of dopamine antagonists into the prefrontal cortex of rhesus monkeys performing an oculomotor delayed-response task. *Journal of Neurophysiology, 71,* 515–528.

Schachter, S., & Singer, J. (1962). Cognitive, social and physiological determinants of emotional state. *Psychological Review, 69,* 379–399.

Schacter, D. L. (1987). Implicit memory: History and current status. *Journal of Experimental Psychology: Learning, Memory, and Cognition, 13,* 501–518.

Schacter, D. L. (2001). *The seven sins of memory: How the mind forgets and remembers.* Boston: Houghton Mifflin.

Schacter, D. L., Dobbins, I. G., & Schnyer, D. M. (2004). Specificity of priming a cognitive neuroscience perspective. *Nat Rev Neurosci, 5,* 853–862.

Schacter, D. L., Harbluk, J. L., & McLachlan, D. R. (1984). Retrieval without recollection: An experimental analysis of source amnesia. *Journal of Verbal Learning and Verbal Behavior, 23,* 593–611.

Schall, J. D. (2001). Neural basis of deciding, choosing and acting. *Nature Neuroscience, 2*, 33–42.

Schank, R. C., & Abelson, R. P. (1977). *Scripts, plans, goals and understanding: An inquiry into human knowledge structures.* Hillsdale, NJ: Lawrence Erlbaum Associates.

Schenk, T., & Zihl, J. (1997). Visual motion perception after brain damage: II. Deficits in form-from-motion perception. *Neuropsychologia, 35*, 1299–1310.

Scherer, K. R. (2000). Psychological models of emotion. In J. C. Borod (Ed.), *The neuropsychology of emotion* (pp. 137–162). New York: Oxford University Press.

Schmidtke, V., & Heuer, H. (1997). Task integration as a factor in secondary-task effects on sequence learning. *Psychological Research, 60*, 53–71.

Schmolck, H., Buffalo, E. A., & Squire, L. R. (2000). Memory for distortions develop over time: Recollections of the O. J. Simpson trial verdict after 15 and 32 months. *Psychological Science, 11*, 39–45.

Schmolesky, M. T., Wang, Y., Hanes, D. P., Thompson, K. G., Leutgeb, S., Schall, J. D., & Leventhal, A. G. (1998). Signal timing across the macaque visual system. *Journal of Neurophysiology, 79*, 3272–3278.

Schneider, W., & Shiffrin, R. M. (1977). Controlled and automatic human information processing: I. Detection, search, and attention. *Psychological Review, 84*, 1–66.

Schooler, J. W., Fiore, S. M., & Brandimonte, M. A. (1997). At a loss from words: Verbal overshadowing of perceptual memories. *The Psychology of Learning and Motivation, 37*, 291–340.

Schooler, J. W., Ohlsson, S., & Brooks, K. (1993). Thoughts beyond words: When language overshadows insight. *Journal of Experimental Psychology: General, 122*, 166–183.

Schultz, W. (2002). Getting formal with dopamine and reward. *Neuron, 36*, 241–263.

Schwarz, N., & Ciore, G. L. (1988). How do I feel about it? The informative function of affective states. In K. Fiedler & J. P. Forgas (Eds.), *Affect, cognition and social behavior* (pp. 44–62). Toronto: Hogrefe.

Scoville, W. B., & Milner, B. (1957). Loss of recent memory after bilateral hippocampal lesions. *Journal of Neurological and Neurosurgical Psychiatry, 20*, 11–21.

Searcy, J. H., & Bartlett, J. C. (1996). Inversion and processing of component and spatial-relational information in faces. *Journal of Experimental Psychology: Human Perception and Performance, 22*, 904–915.

Searle, J. R. (1980). Minds, brains, and programs. *Behavioral and Brain Sciences, 3*, 417–424.

Sebanz, N., Knoblich, G., & Prinz, W. (2003). Representing others' actions: Just like one's own? *Cognition, 88*, B11–B21.

Seger, C., Poldrack, R., Prabhakaran, V., Zhao, M., Glover, G., & Gabrieli, J. (2000). Hemispheric asymmetries and individual differences in visual concept learning as measured by functional MRI. *Neuropsychologia, 38*, 1316–1324.

Seidenberg, M. S., & McClelland, J. L. (1989). A distributed, developmental model of word recognition and naming. *Psychological Review, 96*, 523–568.

Seidenberg, M. S., & Petitto, L. A. (1987). Communication, symbolic communication, and language. *Journal of Experimental Psychology: General, 116*, 279–287.

Selfridge, O. (1955). Pattern recognition and modern computers. In *Proceedings of the Western Joint Computer Conference*, Los Angeles, CA (pp. 91–93). New York: Institute of Electrical and Electronics Engineers.

Selfridge, O. (1959). Pandemonium: A paradigm for learning. In *Symposium on the mechanisation of thought processes* (pp. 513–526). London: H. M. Stationery Office.

Sereno, M. I., Dale, A. M., Reppas, J. B., & Kwong, K. K. (1995). Borders of multiple visual areas in humans revealed by functional magnetic resonance imaging. *Science, 268*, 889–893.

Servan-Schreiber, D., Printz, H., & Cohen, J. D. (1990). A network model of catecholamine effects: Gain, signal-to-noise ratio, and behavior. *Science, 249*, 892–895.

Shadlen, M. N., Britten, K. H., Newsome, W. T., & Movshon, J. A. (1996). A computational analysis of the relationship between neuronal and behavioral responses to visual motion. *Journal of Neuroscience, 16*, 1486–1510.

Shallice, T. (1982). Specific impairments of planning. *Philosophical Transactions of the Royal Society of London, B298*, 199–209.

Shallice, T. (1988). *From neuropsychology to mental structure* (2nd ed.). Cambridge, UK: Cambridge University Press.

Shallice, T., Fletcher, P., Frith, C. D., Grasby, P., Frackowiak, R. S., & Dolan, R. J. (1994). Brain regions associated with acquisition and retrieval of verbal episodic memory. *Nature, 368*, 633–635.

Shallice, T., & Warrington, E. K. (1970). Independent functioning of verbal memory stores: A neuropsychological study. *Quarterly Journal of Experimental Psychology, 22*, 261–273.

Shanteau, J. (1975). An information-integration analysis of risky decision making. In M. F. Kaplan & S. Schwartz (Eds.), *Human judgment and decision processes* (pp. 109–137). New York: Academic Press.

Shanteau, J., & Nagy, G. F. (1976). Decisions made about other people: A human judgment analysis of dating choice. In J. S. Carroll & J. W. Payne (Eds.), *Cognition and social behavior* (pp. 128–141). New York: Academic Press.

Shanteau, J., & Nagy, G. F. (1979). Probability of acceptance in dating choice. *Journal of Personality and Social Psychology, 37*, 522–533.

Shapiro, K. L., Raymond, J. E., & Arnell, K. M. (1984). Attention to visual pattern information produces the attentional blink in rapid serial visual presentation. *Journal of Experimental Psychology: Human Perception and Performance, 20*, 357–371.

Shepard, R. N. (1984). Ecological constraints on internal representation: Resonant kinematics of perceiving, imagining, thinking, and dreaming. *Psychological Review, 91*, 417–447.

Shepard, R. N., & Cooper, L. A. (1982). *Mental images and their transformations.* New York: Cambridge University Press.

Shepard, R. N., & Metzler, J. (1971). Mental rotation of three-dimensional objects. *Science, 171*, 701–703.

Shiffrar, M., & Freyd, J. J. (1990). Apparent motion of the human body. *Psychological Science, 1*, 257–264.

Shiffrar, M., & Pinto, J. (2002). The visual analysis of bodily motion. In W. Prinz & B. Hommel (Eds.), *Common mechanisms in perception and action* (pp. 381–399). New York: Oxford University Press.

Shiffrin, R. M., & Schneider, W. (1977). Controlled and automatic human information processing: II. Perceptual learning, automatic attending, and a general theory. *Psychological Review, 84*, 127–190.

Shillcock, R. (1990). Lexical hypotheses in continuous speech. In G. T. M. Altmann (Ed.), *Cognitive models of speech processing* (pp. 24–49). Cambridge, MA: The MIT Press.

Shimamura, A. P. (1995). Memory and frontal lobe function. In M. S. Gazzaniga (Ed.), *The cognitive neurosciences* (pp. 803–813). Cambridge, MA: The MIT Press.

Shimojo, S., Silverman, G. H., & Nakayama, K. (1988). An occlusion-related mechanism of depth perception based on motion and interocular sequence. *Nature, 333*, 265–268.

Shulman, G. L. (1992). Attentional modulation of size contrast. *Quarterly Journal of Experimental Psychology A, 45*, 529–546.

Shwarz, N., & Clore, G. L. (1988). How do I feel about it? The informative function of affective states. In K. Fiedler & J. P. Forgas (Eds.), *Affect, cognition and social behavior* (pp. 44–62). Toronto: Hogrefe.

Simmons, W. K., & Barsalou, L. W. (2003). The similarity-in-topography principle: Reconciling theories of conceptual deficits. *Cognitive Neuropsychology, 20*, 451–486.

Simmons, W. K., Martin, A., & Barsalou, L. W. (2005). Pictures of appetizing foods activate gustatory cortices for taste and reward. *Cerebral Cortex, 15*, 1602–1608.

Simon, H. A. (1955). A behavioral model of rational choice. *Quarterly Journal of Economics, 69*, 99–118.

Simon, H. A. (1981). *Sciences of the artificial.* Cambridge, MA: The MIT Press.

Simon, J. R. (1990). The effect of an irrelevant directional cue on human information processing. In R. W. Proctor & T. G. Reeve (Eds.), *Stimulus–response compatibility: An integrated perspective* (pp. 31–86). Amsterdam: North Holland.

Simons, D. J., & Levin, D. T. (1998). Failure to detect changes to people during a real-world interaction. *Psychonomic Bulletin & Review, 5*, 644–649.

Simons, D. J., & Rensink, R. A. (2005). Change blindness: Past, present, and future. *Trends in Cognitive Sciences, 9*, 16–20.

Singer, Y., Seymour, B., O'Doherty, J., Kaube, H., Dolan, R. J., & Frith C. D. (2004). Empathy for pain involves the affective but not sensory components of pain. *Science, 303,* 1157–1162.

Sirigu, A., Zalla, T., Pillon, B., Grafman, J., Dubois, B., & Agid, Y. (1995). Planning and script analysis following prefrontal lobe lesions. *Annals of the New York Academy of Sciences, 769,* 277–288.

Slackman, E. A., Hudson, J. A., & Fivush, R. (1986). Actions, actors, link and goals: The structure of children's event representations. In K. Nelson (Ed.), *Event knowledge: Structure and function in development* (pp. 47–69). Hillsdale, NJ: Lawrence Erlbaum Associates.

Slamecka, N. J., & Graf, P. (1978). The generation effect: Delineation of a phenomenon. *Journal of Experimental Psychology: Learning, Memory, and Cognition, 4,* 592–604.

Stotnick, S. D., & Schacter, D. L. (2004). A sensory signature that distinguishes true from false memories. *Nat Neurosci, 7,* 664–672.

Slovic, P., Finucane, M., Peters, E., & MacGregor, D. G. (2002). Rational actors or rational fools: Implications of the affect heuristic for behavioral economics. *Journal of Socio-Economics, 31,* 329–342.

Slovic, P., Fischhoff, B., & Lichtenstein, S. (1979). Rating the risks. *Environment, 21,* 14–20.

Slovic, P., & Lichtenstein, S. (1983). Preference reversals: A broader perspective. *American Economic Review, 73,* 596–605.

Slovic, P., & Tversky, A. (1974). Who accepts Savage's axiom? *Behavioral Science, 19,* 368–373.

Smith, E. E. (2000). Neural bases of human working memory. *Current Directions in Psychological Science, 9,* 45–49.

Smith, E. E., & Jonides, J. (1999). Storage and executive processes in the frontal lobes. *Science, 283,* 1657–1661.

Smith, E. E., Jonides, J., & Koeppe, R. A. (1996). Dissociating verbal and spatial working memory using PET. *Cerebral Cortex, 6,* 11–20.

Smith, E. E., Jonides, J., Koeppe, R. A., Awh, E., Schumacher, E. H., & Minoshima, S. (1995). Spatial vs. object working memory: PET investigations. *Journal of Cognitive Neuroscience, 7,* 337–356.

Smith, E. E., Marshuetz, C., & Geva, A. (2002). Working memory: Findings from neuroimaging and patient studies. In F. Boller & J. Grafman (Eds.), *Handbook of neuropsychology* (2nd ed., Vol. 7, pp. 55–72). New York: Elsevier.

Smith, E. E., & Medin, D. L. (1981). *Categories and concepts.* Cambridge, MA: Harvard University Press.

Smith, E. E., Patalano, A. L., & Jonides, J. (1998). Alternative strategies for categorization. *Cognition, 65,* 167–196.

Smith, E. E., Shoben, E. J., & Rips, L. J. (1974). Structure and process in semantic memory: A featural model for semantic decisions. *Psychological Review, 81,* 214–241.

Smith, E. E., & Sloman, S. A. (1994). Similarity- versus rule-based categorization. *Memory and Cognition, 22,* 377–386.

Smith, I. M., & Bryson, S. E. (1994). Imitation and action in autism: A critical review. *Psychological Bulletin, 116,* 259–273.

Smith, J. D., & Minda, J. P. (2002). Distinguishing prototype-based and exemplar-based processes in dot-pattern category learning. *Journal of Experimental Psychology: Learning, Memory, and Cognition, 28,* 800–811.

Smith, K., Dickhaut, J., McCabe, K., & Pardo, J. V. (2002). Neuronal substrates for choice under ambiguity, risk, gains, and losses. *Management Science, 48,* 711–718.

Smith, L. B., & Samuelson, L. K. (1997). Perceiving and remembering: Category stability, variability and development. In K. Lamberts & D. R. Shanks (Eds.), *Knowledge, concepts and categories.* (pp. 161–195). Cambridge, MA: The MIT Press.

Smith, M. L., & Milner, B. (1984). Differential effects of frontal-lobe lesions on cognitive estimation and spatial memory. *Neuropsychologica, 22,* 697–705.

Smith, M. L., & Milner, B. (1988). Estimation of frequency of occurrence of abstract designs after frontal or temporal lobectomy. *Neuropsychologica, 26,* 297–306.

Smolensky, P. (1988). On the proper treatment of connectionism. *The Behavioral and Brain Sciences, 11,* 1–74.

Sobotka, S., & Ringo, J. L. (1993). Investigations of long-term recognition and association memory in unit responses from inferotemporal cortex. *Experimental Brain Research, 96,* 28–38.

Solomon, K. O., & Barsalou, L. W. (2001). Representing properties locally. *Cognitive Psychology, 43,* 129–169.

Solomon, K. O., & Barsalou, L. W. (2004). Perceptual simulation in property verification. *Memory & Cognition, 32,* 244–259.

Solomon, P. R., Stowe, G. T., & Pendlbeury, W. W. (1989). Disrupted eyelid conditioning in a patient with damage to cerebellar afferents. *Behavioral Neuroscience, 103,* 898–902.

Somers, D. C., Dale, A. M., Seiffert, A. E., & Tootell, R. B. H. (1999). Functional MRI reveals spatially specific attentional modulation in human primary visual cortex. *Proceedings of the National Academy of Sciences USA, 96,* 1663–1668.

Sommers, F. (1963). Types and ontology. *Philosophical Review, 72,* 327–363.

Sommerville, J. A., & Woodward, A. L. (2005). Pulling out the structure of intentional action: The relation between action processing and action production in infancy. *Cognition, 95,* 1–30.

Sommerville, J. A., Woodward, A. L., & Needham, A. (2005). Action experience alters 3-month-old infants' perception of others' actions. *Cognition, 96,* B1–B11.

Spector, A., & Biederman, I. (1976). Mental set and mental shift revisited. *American Journal of Psychology, 89,* 669–679.

Spelke, E. S. (1998). Nativism, empiricism, and the origins of knowledge. *Infant Behavior and Development, 21,* 181–200.

Spelke, E., Hirst, W., & Neisser, U. (1976). Skills of divided attention. *Cognition, 4,* 215–230.

Spellman, B. A., & Holyoak, K. J. (1992). If Saddam is Hitler then who is George Bush? Analogical mapping between systems of social roles. *Journal of Personality and Social Psychology, 62,* 913–933.

Spellman, B. A., & Holyoak, K. J. (1996). Pragmatics in analogical mapping. *Cognitive Psychology, 31,* 307–346.

Spence, C., Nicholls, M. E. R., & Driver, J. (2000). The cost of expecting events in the wrong sensory modality. *Perception & Psychophysics, 63,* 330–336.

Sperling, G. (1960). The information available in brief visual presentations. *Psychological Monographs, 74,* 1–29.

Sperling, G., & Weichselgartner, E. (1995). Episodic theory of the dynamics of spatial attention. *Psychological Review, 102,* 503–532.

Sperry, R. W. (1952). Neurology and the mind–body problem. *American Scientist, 40,* 291–312.

Spitzer, H., Desimone, R., & Moran, J. (1988). Increased attention enhances both behavioral and neuronal performance. *Science, 240,* 338–340.

Spivey, M., Tyler, M., Richardson, D., & Young, E. (2000). Eye movements during comprehension of spoken scene descriptions. *Proceedings of the 22nd Annual Conference of the Cognitive Science Society* (pp. 487–492). Mahwah, NJ: Lawrence Erlbaum Associates.

Squire, L. R. (1992). Memory and the hippocampus: A synthesis from findings with rats, monkeys, and humans. *Psychological Review, 99,* 195–231.

Squire, L. R., Stark, C. E., & Clark, R. E. (2004). The medial temporal lobe. *Annual Review of Neuroscience, 27,* 279–306.

Stanfield, R. A., & Zwaan, R. A. (2001). The effect of implied orientation derived from verbal context on picture recognition. *Psychological Science, 12,* 153–156.

Stellar, J. R., & Stellar, E. (1984). *The neurobiology of motivation and reward.* New York: Springer-Verlag.

Stephan, K. M., Fink, G. R., Passingham, R. E., Silbersweig, D., Ceballos-Baumann, O., Frith, C. D., et al. (1995). Functional anatomy of the mental representation of upper extremity movements in healthy subjects. *Journal of Neurophysiology, 73,* 373–386.

Sternberg, S. (1966). High-speed scanning in human memory. *Science, 153,* 652–654.

Sternberg, S. (1967). Retrieval of contextual information from memory. *Psychonomic Science, 8,* 55–56.

Sternberg, S. (1969a). The discovery of processing stages: Extensions of Donders' method. In W. G. Koster (Ed.), *Attention and performance II* (pp. 276–315). Amsterdam: North-Holland.

Sternberg, S. (1969b). Memory-scanning: Mental processes revealed by reaction-time experiments. *American Scientist, 57,* 421–457.

Sternberg, S. (2003). Process decomposition from double dissociation of subprocesses. *Cortex, 39,* 180–182.

Stevens, J. A. (2005). Interference effects demonstrate distinct roles for visual and motor imagery during the mental representation of human action. *Cognition, 95,* 329–350.

Stevens, J. A., Fonlupt, P., Shiffrar, M. A., & Decety, J. (2000). New aspects of motion perception: Selective neural encoding of apparent human movements. *NeuroReport, 11*, 109–115.

Stone, V. E., Cosmides, L., Tooby, J., Kroll, N., & Knight, R. T. (2002). Selective impairment of reasoning about social exchange in a patient with bilateral limbic system damage. *Proceedings of the National Academy of Sciences USA, 99*, 11531–11536.

Strayer, D. L., & Johnston, W. A. (2001). Driven to distraction: Dual-task studies of simulated driving and conversing on a cellular telephone. *Psychological Science, 12*, 462–466.

Strayer, D. L., Drews, F. A., & Johnston, W. A. (2003). Cell-phone induced failures of visual attention during simulated driving. *Journal of Experimental Psychology: Applied, 9*, 23–32.

Stroop, J. R. (1935). Studies of interference in serial verbal reactions. *Journal of Experimental Psychology, 18*, 643–662.

Strotz, R. H. (1956). Myopia and inconsistency in dynamic utility maximization. *Review of Economic Studies, 23*, 165–180.

Sturmer, B., Aschersleben, G., & Prinz, W. (2000). Correspondence effects with manual gestures and postures: A study of imitation. *Journal of Experimental Psychology: Human Perception and Performance, 26*, 1746–1759.

Stuss, D. T., & Benson, D. F. (1986). *The frontal lobes*. New York: Raven Press.

Stuss, D. T., & Knight, R. T. (Eds.). (2002). *Principles of frontal lobe function*. New York: Oxford University Press.

Sugita, Y. (1999). Grouping of image fragments in primary visual cortex. *Nature, 401*, 269–272.

Sulin, R. A., & Dooling, D. J. (1974). Intrusion of a thematic idea in the retention of prose. *Journal of Experimental Psychology, 103*, 255–262.

Suzuki, W. A., & Amaral, D. G. (1994). Perirhinal and parahippocampal cortices of the macaque monkey: Cortical afferents. *Journal of Comparative Neurology, 350*, 497–533.

Swinney, D. A. (1979). Lexical access during sentence comprehension: (Re)consideration of context effects. *Journal of Verbal Learning and Verbal Behavior, 18*, 645–659.

Sylvester, C. Y., Wager, T. D., Lacey, S. C., Hernandez, L., Nichols, T. E., Smith, E. E., et al. (2003). Switching attention and resolving interference: fMRI measures of executive functions. *Neuropsychologia, 41*, 357–370.

Tabossi, P. (1988). Effects of context on the immediate interpretation of unambiguous nouns. *Journal of Experimental Psychology: Learning, Memory, and Cognition, 14*, 153–162.

Tai, Y. F., Scherfler, C., Brooks, D. J., Sawamoto, N., & Castiello, U. (2004). The human premotor cortex is "mirror" only for biological actions. *Current Biology, 14*, 117–120.

Talaricho, J. M., & Rubin, D. C. (2003). Confidence, not consistency, characterizes flashbulb memories. *Psychological Science, 14*, 455–461.

Tanaka, J. W., & Curran, T. (2001). A neural basis for expert object recognition. *Psychological Science, 12*, 43–47.

Tanaka, J. W., & Farah, M. J. (1993). Parts and wholes in face recognition. *Quarterly Journal of Experimental Psychology, 46*, 225–245.

Tanaka, J. W., & Gauthier, I. (1997). Expertise in object and face recognition. In R. L. Goldstone, P. G. Schyns, & D. L. Medin (Eds.), *Psychology of learning and motivation series, special volume: Perceptual mechanisms of learning* (Vol. 36, pp. 83–125). San Diego, CA: Academic Press.

Tanaka, J. W., & Sengco, J. A. (1997). Features and their configuration in face recognition. *Memory and Cognition, 25*, 583–592.

Tanaka, K. (1997). Inferotemporal cortex and object recognition. In J. W. Donahoe & V. P. Dorsel (Eds.), *Neural-network models of cognition: Biobehavioral foundations* (Vol. 121, pp. 160–188). Amsterdam: North-Holland/Elsevier Science Publishers.

Tanaka, K., Saito, H., Fukada, Y., & Moriya, M. (1991). Coding visual images of objects in the inferotemporal cortex of the macaque monkey. *Journal of Neurophysiology, 66*, 170–189.

Tanenhaus, M. K., Leiman, J. M., & Seidenberg, M. S. (1979). Evidence for multiple stages in the processing of ambiguous words in syntactic contexts. *Journal of Verbal Learning and Verbal Behavior, 18*, 427–440.

Tanji, J. (1994). The supplementary motor area in the cerebral cortex. *Neuroscience Research, 19*, 251–268.

Terrace, H. S. (1979). *Nim: A chimpanzee who learned sign language.* New York: Knopf.

Thaler, R. H., & Shefrin, H. M. 1981. An economic theory of self-control. *Journal of Political Economy, 89,* 392–406.

Thaler, R. H., Tversky, A., Kahneman, D., & Schwartz, A. (1997). The effect of myopia and loss aversion on risk taking: An experimental test. *Quarterly Journal of Economics, 112,* 647–661.

Thioux, M., Pillon, A., Samson, D., de Partz, M. P., & Noël, M. P. (1998). The isolation of numerals at the semantic level. *Neurocase, 4,* 371–389.

Thompson, P. (1980). Margaret Thatcher: A new illusion. *Perception, 9,* 483–484.

Thompson, R., Emmorey, K. & Gollan, T. H. (2005). "Tip of the fingers" experiences by Deaf signers: Insights into the organization of a sign-based lexicon, *Psychological Science, 16,* 856–860.

Thompson, R. F., & Kim, J. J. (1996). Memory systems in the brain and localization of a memory. *Proceedings of the National Academy of Sciences USA, 93,* 13438–13444.

Thompson, W. L., & Kosslyn, S. M. (2000). Neural systems activated during visual mental imagery: A review and meta-analysis. In A. W. Toga & J. C. Mazziotta (Eds.), *Brain mapping: The systems* (pp. 535–560). San Diego, CA: Academic Press.

Tipper, S. P., & Behrmann, M. (1996). Object-centred not scene-based visual neglect. *Journal of Experimental Psychology: Human Perception and Performance, 22,* 1261–1278.

Tomarken, A. J., Davidson, R. J., Wheeler, R. E., & Doss, R. C. (1992). Individual differences in anterior brain asymmetry and fundamental dimensions of emotion. *Journal of Personality and Social Psychology, 62,* 676–682.

Tomasello, M. (1999). *The cultural origins of human cognition.* Cambridge, MA: Harvard University Press.

Tomb, I., Hauser, M., Deldin, P., & Caramazza, A. (2002). Do somatic markers mediate decisions on the gambling task? *Nature Neuroscience, 5,* 1103–1104.

Tomita, H., Ohbayashi, M., Nakahara, K., Hasegawa, I., & Miyashita, Y. (1999). Top-down signal from prefrontal cortex in executive control of memory retrieval. *Nature, 401,* 699–703.

Tong, F., & Engel, S. A. (2001). Interocular rivalry revealed in the human cortical blind-spot representation. *Nature, 411,* 195–199.

Tong, F., Nakayama, K., Moscovitch, M., Weinrib, O., & Kanwisher, N. (2000). Response properties of the human fusiform face area. *Cognitive Neuropsychology, 17,* 257–279.

Tong, F., Nakayama, K., Vaughan, J. T., & Kanwisher, N. (1998). Binocular rivalry and visual awareness in human extrastriate cortex. *Neuron, 21,* 753–759.

Tootell, R. B. H., Silverman, M. S., Switkes, E., & DeValois, R. L. (1982). Deoxyglucose analysis of retinotopic organization in primates. *Science, 218,* 902–904.

Tourangeau, R., Rips, L. J., & Rasinski, K. R. (2000). *The psychology of survey response.* New York: Cambridge University Press.

Townsend, J. T. (1990). Serial vs parallel processing: Sometimes they look like tweedledum and tweedledee but they can (and should) be distinguished. *Psychological Science, 1,* 46–54.

Townsend, J. T., & Ashby, F. G. (1983). *The stochastic modeling of elementary psychological processes.* Cambridge, UK: Cambridge University Press.

Travis, L. L. (1997). Goal-based organization of event memory in toddlers. In P. W. van den Broek, P. J. Bauer, & T. Bovig (Eds.), *Developmental spans in event comprehension and representation: Bridging fictional and actual events* (pp. 111–138). Mahwah, NJ: Lawrence Erlbaum Associates.

Treisman, A. M. (1960). Contextual cues in selective listening. *Quarterly Journal of Experimental Psychology, 12,* 242–248.

Treisman, A. (1969). Strategies and models of selective attention. *Psychological Review, 76,* 282–299.

Treisman, A. (1990). Variations on the theme of feature integration: Reply to Navon. *Psychological Review, 97,* 460–463.

Treisman, A. (1996). The binding problem. *Current Opinion in Neurobiology, 6,* 171–178.

Treisman, A., & Gelade, G. (1980). A feature-integration theory of attention. *Cognitive Psychology, 12,* 97–136.

Treisman, A., & Sato, S. (1990). Conjunction search revisited. *Journal of Experimental Psychology: Human Perception and Performance, 16,* 459–478.

Treisman, A., & Schmidt, H. (1982). Illusory conjunctions in the perception of objects. *Cognitive Psychology, 14,* 107–141.

Treisman, A., & Souther, J. (1985). Search asymmetry: A diagnostic for preattentive processing of separable features. *Journal of Experimental Psychology: General, 114*, 285–310.

Treue, S., & Martinez Trujillo, J. C. (1999). Feature-based attention influences motion processing gain in macaque visual cortex. *Nature, 399*, 575–579.

Treue, S., & Maunsell, J. H. (1996). Attentional modulation of visual motion processing in cortical areas MT and MST. *Nature, 382*, 539–541.

Trueswell, J. C., & Tanenhaus, M. K. (1994). Toward a lexicalist framework for constraint-based syntactic ambiguity resolution. In C. Clifton, L. Frazier, & K. Rayner (Eds.), *Perspectives in sentence processing* (pp. 155–179). Hillsdale, NJ: Lawrence Erlbaum Associates.

Tulving, E. (1972). Episodic and semantic memory. In E. Tulving & W. Donaldson (Eds.), *Organization of memory* (pp. 382–403). New York: Academic Press.

Tulving, E. (1983). *Elements of episodic memory*. Cambridge, UK: Cambridge University Press.

Tulving, E. (1985). Memory and consciousness. *Canadian Psychologist, 26*, 1–12.

Tulving, E., & Markowitsch, H. J. (1998). Episodic and declarative memory: Role of the hippocampus. *Hippocampus, 8*, 198–204.

Tulving, E., & Schacter, D. L. (1990). Priming and human memory systems. *Science, 247*, 301–306.

Tulving, E., & Thompson, D. M. (1973). Encoding specificity and retrieval processes in episodic memory. *Psychological Review, 80*, 359–380.

Tversky, A. (1967). Utility theory and additivity analysis of risky choices. *Journal of Experimental Psychology, 75*, 27–36.

Tversky, A. (1969). Intransitivity of preferences. *Psychological Review, 76*, 31–48.

Tversky, A. (1972). Elimination by aspects: A theory of choice. *Psychological Review, 79*, 281–299.

Tversky, A., & Fox, C. R. (1995). Weighing risk and uncertainty. *Psychological Review, 102*, 269–283.

Tversky, A., & Kahneman, D. (1974). Judgment under uncertainty: Heuristics and biases. *Science, 185*, 1124–1131.

Tversky, A., & Kahneman, D. (1981). The framing of decisions and the psychology of choice. *Science, 211*, 453–458.

Tversky, A., & Kahneman, D. (1984). Extensional versus intuitive reasoning: The conjunction fallacy in probability judgment. *Psychological Review, 91*, 293–315.

Tversky, A., & Kahneman, D. (1992). Advances in prospect theory: Cumulative representation of uncertainty. *Journal of Risk and Uncertainty, 5*, 297–323.

Tversky, A., & Koehler, D. J. (1994). Support theory: A nonextensional representation of subjective probability. *Psychological Review, 101*, 547–567.

Tversky, B., & Hemenway, K. (1985). Objects, parts, and categories. *Journal of Experimental Psychology: General, 113*, 169–193.

Tweney, R. D., Doherty, M. E., & Mynatt, C. R. (1981). *On scientific thinking*. New York: Columbia University Press.

Tyler, L. K., & Moss, H. E. (1997). Imageability and category-specificity. *Cognitive Neuropsychology, 14*, 293–318.

Tyler, L. K., & Moss, H. E. (2001). Towards a distributed account of conceptual knowledge. *Trends in Cognitive Sciences, 5*, 244–252.

Tzschentke, T. M., & Schmidt, W. J. (2000). Functional relationship among medial prefrontal cortex, nucleus accumbens, and ventral tegmental area in locomotion and reward. *Critical Reviews in Neurobiology, 14*, 131–142.

Ullian, E. M., Sapperstein, S. K., Christopherson, K. S., & Barres, B. A. (2001). Control of synapse number by glia. *Science, 291*, 657–661.

Ulmità, M. A., Kohler, E., Gallese, V., Fogassi, L., Fadiga, L., Keysers, C., et al. (2001). I know what you are doing: A neurophysiological study. *Neuron, 31*, 155–165.

Uncapher, M. R., & Rugg, M. D. (2005). Effects of divided attention on fMRI correlates of memory encoding. *J Cogn Neurosci, 17*, 1923–1935.

Underwood, B. J. (1957). Interference and forgetting. *Psychological Review, 64*, 49–60.

Ungerleider, L. G., & Haxby, J. V. (1994). What and where in the human brain. *Current Opinion in Neurobiology, 4*, 157–165.

Ungerleider, L. G., & Mishkin, M. (1982). Two cortical visual systems. In D. J. Ingle, M. A. Goodale, & R. J. W. Mansfield (Eds.), *Analysis of visual behavior* (pp. 549–586). Cambridge, MA: The MIT Press.

Usher, M., & Cohen, J. D. (1999). Short term memory and selection processes in a frontal-lobe model. In D. Heinke, G. W. Humphries, & A. Olsen (Eds.), *Connectionist models in cognitive neuroscience.* Brighton, UK: Psychology Press.

Vaidya, C. J., Gabrieli, J. D. E., Keane, M. M., Monti, L. A., Gutierrez-Rivas, H., & Zarella, M. M. (1997). Evidence for multiple mechanisms of conceptual priming on implicit memory tests. *Journal of Experimental Psychology: Learning, Memory, and Cognition, 23,* 1324–1343.

Vaina, L. M., LeMay, M., Bienefang, D., Choi, A. Y., & Nakayama, K. (1990). Intact biological motion and structure from motion perception in a patient with impaired motion measurements. *Visual Neuroscience, 6,* 353–369.

Vakil, E., Galek, S., Soroker, N., Ring, H., & Gross, Y. (1991). Differential effect of right and left hemispheric lesions on two memory tasks: Free recall and frequency judgment. *Neuropsychologica, 29,* 981–992.

Vallar, G., & Baddeley, A. D. (1984). Fractionation of working memory: Neuropsychological evidence for a phonological short-term store. *Journal of Verbal Learning and Verbal Behavior, 23,* 151–161.

Vallar, G., & Papagno, C. (1986). Phonological short-term store and the nature of the recency effect: Evidence from neuropsychology. *Brain and Cognition, 5,* 428–432.

Vallar, G., & Papagno, C. (1995). Neuropsychological impairments of short-term memory. In A. D. Baddeley & B. A. Wilson (Eds.), *Handbook of memory disorders* (Vol. XVI, pp. 135–165). Oxford: Wiley.

Van Orden, G. C. (1987). A ROWS is a ROSE: Spelling, sound, and reading. *Memory and Cognition, 15,* 181–198.

Vandenberghe, R., Gitelman, D. R., Parrish, T. B., & Mesulam, M. M. (2001). Functional specificity of superior parietal mediation of spatial shifting. *NeuroImage, 14,* 661–673.

Veltman, D. J., Rombouts, S. A., & Dolan, R. J. (2003). Maintenance versus manipulation in verbal working memory revisited: An fMRI study. *NeuroImage, 18,* 247–256.

Vingerhoets, G., de Lange, F. P., Vandemaele, P., Deblaere, K., & Achten, E. (2002). Motor imagery in mental rotation: An fMRI study. *NeuroImage, 17,* 1623–1633.

Vitevitch, M. S. (2003). Change deafness: The inability to detect changes between two voices. *Journal of Experimental Psychology: Human Perception and Performance, 29,* 333–342.

Viviani, P. (2002). Motor competence in the perception of dynamic events: A tutorial. In W. Prinz & B. Hommel (Eds.), *Common mechanisms in perception and action, attention and performance XIX* (pp. 406–442). New York: Oxford University Press.

Vogels, R., Biederman, I., Bar, M., & Lorincz, A. (2001). Inferior temporal neurons show greater sensitivity to nonaccidental than to metric shape differences. *Journal of Cognitive Neuroscience, 13,* 444–453.

Vogels, T. P., Rajan, K., & Abbott, L. E. (2005). Neural network dynamics. *Annual Review of Neuroscience, 28,* 357–376.

Vuilleumier, P., Armony, J. L., Driver, J., & Dolan, R. J. (2001). Effects of attention and emotion on face processing in the human brain: An event-related fMRI study. *Neuron, 30,* 829–841.

Vuilleumier, P., Armony, J. L., Driver, J., & Dolan, R. J. (2003). Distinct spatial frequency sensitivities for processing faces and emotional expressions. *Nature Neuroscience, 6,* 624–631.

Vuilleumier, P., Richardson, M. P., Armony, J. L., Driver, J., & Dolam, R. J. (2004). Distant influences of amygdala lesion on visual cortical activation during emotional face processing. *Nature Neuroscience, 7,* 1271–1278.

Vuilleumier, P., & Schwartz, S. (2001). Beware and be aware: Capture of spatial attention by fear-related stimuli in neglect. *NeuroReport, 12,* 1119–1122.

Wade, N. J. (1998). *A natural history of vision.* Cambridge, MA: The MIT Press.

Wager, T. D., Jonides, J., & Smith, E. E. (in press). Individual differences in multiple types of shifting attention. *Memory & Cognition.*

Wager. T. D., Reading, S., & Jonides, J. (2004). Neuroimaging studies of shifting attention: A meta-analysis. *Neuroimage, 22,* 1679–1693.

Wagner, A. D. (2002). Cognitive control and episodic memory: Contributions from prefrontal cortex. In L. R. Squire & D. L. Schacter (Eds.), *Neuropsychology of memory* (3rd ed., pp. 174–192). New York: Guilford Press.

Wagner, A. D., Bunge, S. A., & Badre, D. (2005). Cognitive control, semantic memory, and priming: Contributions from prefrontal cortex. In M. S. Gazzaniga (Ed.), *The cognitive neurosciences III* (pp. 709–725). Cambridge, MA: MIT Press.

Wagner, A. D., & Koutstaal, W. (2002). Priming. In *Encyclopedia of the human brain* (Vol. 4, pp. 27–46). New York: Elsevier Science.

Wagner, A. D., Koutstaal, W., Maril, A., Schacter, D. L., & Buckner, R. L. (2000). Process-specific repetition priming in left inferior prefrontal cortex. *Cerebral Cortex, 10,* 1176–1184.

Wagner, A. D., Paré-Blagoev, E. J., Clark, J., & Poldrack, R. A. (2001). Recovering meaning: Left prefrontal cortex guides controlled semantic retrieval. *Neuron, 31,* 329–338.

Wagner, A. D., Schacter, D. L., Rotte, M., Koutstaal, W., Maril, A., Dale, A. M., et al. (1998). Building memories: Remembering and forgetting of verbal experiences as predicted by brain activity. *Science, 281,* 1188–1191.

Walsh, V., Ashbridge, E., & Cowey, A. (1998). Cortical plasticity in perceptual learning demonstrated by transcranial magnetic stimulation. *Neuropsychologia, 36,* 363–367.

Walsh, V., & Pascual-Leone, A. (2003). *Transcranial magnetic stimulation: A neurochronometrics of mind.* Cambridge, MA: The MIT Press.

Warren, R. M. (1970). Perceptual restoration of missing speech sounds. *Science, 167,* 392–393.

Warrington, E. K., & McCarthy, R. A. (1983). Category specific access dysphasia. *Brain, 106,* 859–878.

Warrington, E. K., & McCarthy, R. A. (1987). Categories of knowledge: Further fractionations and an attempted integration. *Brain, 110,* 1273–1296.

Warrington, E. K., & Shallice, T. (1984). Category specific semantic impairments. *Brain, 107,* 829–854.

Warrington, E. K., & Weiskrantz, L. (1968). A new method of testing long-term retention with special reference to amnesic patients. *Nature, 217,* 972–974.

Warrington, E. K., & Weiskrantz, L. (1974). The effect of prior learning on subsequent retention in amnesic patients. *Neuropsychologia, 12,* 419–428.

Wason, P. C. (1966). Reasoning. In B. Foss (Ed.), *New horizons in psychology* (pp. 135–151). Harmondsworth, UK: Penguin.

Webster, M. A., & MacLin, O. H. (1999). Figural aftereffects in the perception of faces. *Psychonomic Bulletin and Review, 6,* 647–653.

Webster, M. A., Kaping, D., Mizokami, Y., & Duhamel, P. (2004). Adaptation to natural face categories. *Nature, 428,* 557–561.

Weinberger, M. R. (1995). Retuning the brain by fear conditioning. In M. S. Gazzaniga (Ed.), *The cognitive neurosciences* (pp. 1071–1090). Cambridge, MA: The MIT Press.

Weisberg, R. W. (1993). *Creativity: Beyond the myth of genius.* New York: W. H. Freeman.

Weiss, Y., & Adelson, E. H. (1998). Slow and smooth: A Bayesian theory for the combination of local motion signals in human vision (CBCL Paper #158/AI Memo 1624). Cambridge, MA: Massachusetts Institute of Technology.

Weisstein, N., & Harris, C. S. (1974). Visual detection of line segments: An object-superiority effect. *Science, 186,* 752–755.

Werker, J. F., & Tees, R. C. (1984). Cross-language speech perception: Evidence for perceptual reorganization during the first year of life. *Infant Behavior and Development, 7,* 49–63.

Wertheimer, M. (1945). *Productive thinking.* New York: Harper.

Whalen, P. J. (1998). Fear, vigilance, and ambiguity: Initial neuroimaging studies of the human amygdala. *Current Directions in Psychological Science, 7,* 177–188.

Whalen, P. J., Rauch, S. L., Etcoff, N. L., McInerney, S. C., Lee, M. B., & Jenike, M. A. (1998). Masked presentations of emotional facial expressions modulate amygdala activity without explicit knowledge. *Journal of Neuroscience, 18,* 411–418.

Wharton, C. M., & Grafman, J. (1998). Deductive reasoning and the brain. *Trends in Neuroscience, 2,* 54–59.

Wharton, C. M., Grafman, J., Flitman, S. S., Hansen, E. K., Brauner, J., Marks, A., et al. (2000). Toward neuroanatomical models of analogy: A positron emission tomography study of analogical mapping. *Cognitive Psychology, 40,* 173–197.

Wheeler, D. D. (1970). Processes in word recognition. *Cognitive Psychology, 1,* 59–85.

Wheeler, M. E., Petersen, S. E., & Buckner, R. L. (2000). Memory's echo: Vivid remembering reactivates sensory-specific cortex. *Proceedings of the National Academy of Sciences USA, 97,* 11125–11129.

Whorf, B. (1956). *Language, thought & reality.* Cambridge, MA: The MIT Press.

Wickens, D. D., Dalezman, R. E., & Eggemeier, F. T. (1976). Multiple encoding of word attributes in memory. *Memory and Cognition, 4,* 307–310.

Wiesel, T. N., & Hubel, D. H. (1963). Single-cell responses in striate cortex of kittens deprived of vision in one eye. *Journal of Neurophysiology, 26,* 1003–1017.

Wiesel, T. N., & Hubel, D. H. (1965). Comparison of the effects of unilateral and bilateral eye closure on cortical unit responses in kittens. *Journal of Neurophysiology, 28,* 1029–1040.

Wiggs, C. L., & Martin, A. (1998). Properties and mechanisms of perceptual priming. *Current Opinion in Neurobiology, 8,* 227–233.

Wikman, A. S., Nieminen, T., & Summala, H. (1998). Driving experience and time-sharing during in-car tasks on roads of different widths. *Ergonomics, 41,* 358–372.

Williams, A., & Weisstein, N. (1978). Line segments are perceived better in a coherent context than alone: An object-line effect in visual perception. *Memory and Cognition, 6,* 85–90.

Williams, J. M. G., Matthews, A., & Macleod, C. (1996). The emotional Stroop task and psychopathology. *Psychological Bulletin, 120,* 3–24.

Williams, M. A., Morris, A. P., McGlone, F., Abbott, D. F., & Mattingly, J. B. (2004). Amygdala responses to fearful and happy facial expressions under conditions of binocular suppression. *Journal of Neuroscience, 24,* 2898–2904.

Wilson, F. A. W., Scalaidhe, S. P. O., & Goldman-Rakic, P. S. (1993). Dissociation of object and spatial processing domains in primate prefrontal cortex. *Science, 260,* 1955–1957.

Wilson, M. A., & McNaughton, B. L. (1994). Reactivation of hippocampal ensemble memories during sleep. *Science, 265,* 676–679.

Wilson, W. R. (1979). Feeling more than we can know: Exposure effects without learning. *Journal of Personality and Social Psychology, 37,* 811–821.

Wise, R. A., & Rompre, P. P. (1989). Brain dopamine and reward. *Annual Review of Psychology, 40,* 191–225.

Witelson, S. F., Kigar, D. L., & Harvey, T. (1999). The exceptional brain of Albert Einstein. *Lancet, 353,* 2149–2153.

Witkin, H. A., Oltman, P. K., Raskin, E., & Karp, S. A. (1971). *A manual for the Embedded Figures Test.* Palo Alto, CA: Consulting Psychologists Press.

Wixted, J. T., & Ebbesen, E. B. (1991). On the form of forgetting. *Psychological Science, 2,* 409–415.

Wixted, J. T., & Squire, L. R. (2004). Recall and recognition are equally impaired in patients with selective hippocampal damage. *Cognitive, Affective, & Behavioral Neuroscience, 4,* 58–66.

Wojciulik, E., & Kanwisher, N. (1999). The generality of parietal involvement in visual attention. *Neuron, 23,* 747–764.

Wolfe, J. M. (1999). Inattentional amnesia. In V. Coltheart (Ed.), *Fleeting memories: Cognition of brief visual stimuli* (pp. 71–94). Cambridge, MA: The MIT Press.

Wolfe, J. M. (2003). Moving towards solutions to some enduring controversies in visual search. *Trends in Cognitive Science, 7,* 70–76.

Wolfe, J. M., Cave, K. R., & Franzel, S. L. (1989). Guided search: An alternative to the modified feature integration model for visual search. *Journal of Experimental Psychology: Human Perception and Performance, 15,* 419–433.

Wolfe, J. M., Yu, K. P., Stewart, M. I., Shorter, A. D., Friedman-Hill, S. R., & Cave, K. R. (1990). Limitations on the parallel guidance of visual search: Color x color and orientation x orientation conjunctions. *Journal of Experimental Psychology: Human Perception and Performance, 16,* 879–892.

Wolff, P., Medin, D. L., & Pankratz, C. (1999). Evolution and devolution of folkbiological knowledge. *Cognition, 73,* 177–204.

Wood, N., & Cowan, N. (1995). The cocktail party phenomenon revisited: How frequent are attention shifts to one's name in an irrelevant auditory channel. *Journal of Experimental Psychology: Learning, Memory and Cognition, 21,* 255–260.

Woodward, A. L. (1998). Infants selectively encode the goal object of an actor's reach. *Cognition, 69,* 1–34.

Woodward, A. L. (2003). Infants' developing understanding of the link between looker and object. *Developmental Science, 6*, 297–311.

Woodward, A. L., & Guajardo, J. J. (2002). Infants' understanding of the point gesture as an object-directed action. *Cognitive Development, 83*, 1–24.

Woodworth, R. S., & Sells, S. B. (1935). An atmosphere effect in formal syllogistic reasoning. *Journal of Experimental Psychology, 18*, 451–460.

Wright, D. B. (1993). Recall of the Hillsborough disaster over time: Systematic biases of "flashbulb" memories. *Applied Cognitive Psychology, 7*, 129–138.

Wu, L., & Barsalou, L. W. (2004). Perceptual simulation in property generation. Manuscript under review.

Wundt, W. M. (1907). *Outlines of psychology.* Leipzig, Germany: Wilhelm Engelmann.

Yeh, W., & Barsalou, L. W. (2004). The situated character of concepts. Manuscript under review.

Yin, R. K. (1969). Looking at upside-down faces. *Journal of Experimental Psychology, 81*, 141–145.

Yonelinas, A. P. (2002). The nature of recollection and familiarity: A review of 30 years of research. *Journal of Memory and Language, 46*, 441–517.

Yonelinas, A. P., & Jacoby, L. L. (1994). Dissociations of processes in recognition memory: Effects of interference and of response speed. *Canadian Journal of Experimental Psychology, 48*, 516–534.

Yonelinas, A. P., Kroll, N. E., Quamme, J. R., Lazzara, M. M., Sauve, M. J., Widaman, K. F., et al. (2002). Effects of extensive temporal lobe damage or mild hypoxia on recollection and familiarity. *Nature Neuroscience, 5*, 1236–1241.

Yonelinas, A. P., Otten, L. J., Shaw, K. N., & Rugg, M. D. (2005). Separating the brain regions involved in recollection and familiarity in recognition memory. *Journal of Neuroscience, 25*, 3002–3008.

Young, A. W., Hellawell, D., & Hay, D. C. (1987). Configural information in face perception. *Perception, 16*, 747–759.

Young, M. P., & Yamane, S. (1992). Sparse population coding of faces in the inferotemporal cortex. *Science, 256*, 1327–1331.

Yue, G., & Cole, K. J. (1992). Strength increases from the motor program: Comparison of training with maximal voluntary and imagined muscle contractions. *Journal of Neurophysiology, 67*, 1114–1123.

Zacks, J., Braver, T. S., Sheridan, M. A., Donaldson, D. I., Snyder, A. Z., Ollinger, J. M., et al. (2001). Human brain activity time-locked to perceptual event boundaries. *Nature Neuroscience, 4*, 651–655.

Zacks, J. M., & Tversky, B. (2001). Event structure in perception and conception. *Psychological Bulletin, 127*, 3–21.

Zacks, J. M., Tversky B., & Iyer, G. (2001). Perceiving, remembering, and communicating structure in events. *Journal of Experimental Psychology General, 130*, 29–58.

Zajonc, R. B. (1980). Feeling and thinking: Preferences need no inferences. *American Psychologist, 35*, 151–175.

Zajonc, R. B. (1984). On the primacy of affect. *American Psychologist, 39*, 117–123.

Zeki, S. (1990). A century of cerebral achromatopsia. *Brain, 113*(Pt. 6), 1721–1777.

Zeki, S. (1993). *A vision of the brain.* Cambridge, MA: Blackwell.

Zhang, H., Zhang, J., & Kornblum, S. (1999). A parallel distributed processing model of stimulus–stimulus and stimulus–response compatibility. *Cognitive Psychology, 38*, 386–432.

Zhao, L., & Chubb, C. (2001). The size-tuning of the face-distortion after-effect. *Vision Research, 41*, 2979–2994.

Zihl, J., von Cramon, D., & Mai, N. (1983). Selective disturbance of movement vision after bilateral brain damage. *Brain, 106*(Pt. 2), 313–340.

Zipf, G. K. (1935). *The psycho-biology of language.* Boston: Houghton Mifflin.

Zola-Morgan, S., Squire, L. R., Amaral, D. G., & Suzuki, W. A. (1989). Lesions of perirhinal and parahippocampal cortex that spare the amygdala and hippocampal formation produce severe memory impairment. *Journal of Neuroscience, 9*, 4355–4370.

Zola-Morgan, S., Squire, L. R., Avarez-Royo, P., & Clower, R. P. (1991). Independence of memory functions and emotional behavior: Separate contributions of the hippocampal formation and the amygdala. *Hippocampus, 1*, 207–220.

Zwaan, R. A., Stanfield, R. A., & Yaxley, R. H. (2002). Language comprehenders mentally represent the shapes of objects, *Psychological Science, 13*, 168–171.

Subject Index

Name Index